LAW AND REVOLUTION, II

LAW and REVOLUTION, II

The Impact of the Protestant Reformations
on the Western Legal Tradition

Harold J. Berman

THE BELKNAP PRESS *of*
HARVARD UNIVERSITY PRESS
CAMBRIDGE, MASSACHUSETTS · LONDON, ENGLAND
2003

Printed in the United States of America

First Harvard University Press paperback edition, 2006

Library of Congress Cataloging-in-Publication Data

Berman, Harold Joseph, 1918–
Law and Revolution, II: the impact of the Protestant Reformations on the western legal tradition / Harold J. Berman.
p. cm.
Includes bibliographical references and index.
ISBN-13 978-0-674-01195-3 (cloth)
ISBN-10 0-674-01195-3 (cloth)
ISBN-13 978-0-674-02230-0 (pbk.)
ISBN-10 0-674-02230-0 (pbk.)
1. Law—Europe—History. 2. Reformation—Influence.
3. Christianity and the law—History. I. Title
KJ147.B47 2003
349.4/09 2004301872

To Ruth—always, all ways

CONTENTS

PREFACE

Despite its formidable subtitle and its massive notes, this book is written primarily for the general reader. It is, to be sure, about a technical subject: law. But law is too important to be left to the technicians. Indeed, law today is on the minds of most thinking people. The policies and actions of lawmakers, the regulations and procedures of governmental and nongovernmental bodies, the decisions of judges are prominently featured in all the major media of information, whether the story is about international relations or political campaigns or the economy or crime or race or gender or even sports.

This book is also about history and about religion, and these, as well, are matters too important to be left to the specialists. Moreover, specialists tend to stick to their individual specialties. Very few have put law together with both history and religion, although the three intersect with one another in remarkable ways. Indeed, nowadays prominent legal scholars who put law together with something else tend to put it together only with politics. And that is troubling to those of us who believe that in the Western tradition the life of the law is linked inextricably not only with a society's politics but also with its moral values and with its historical experience.

Most people who have read the earlier volume of *Law and Revolution,* including even professional legal scholars and historians, may have been surprised to learn from it that the Western legal tradition was formed in the twelfth and thirteenth centuries under the impact of the Papal Revolution, which liberated the hierarchy of the Roman Catholic Church from control by emperors, kings, and feudal lords, and resulted in the creation of the first modern Western legal system, the Roman Catholic canon law. Partly in response, secular systems of royal law, feudal law, urban law, and mercantile law were gradually created throughout Europe. The dualism of spiritual and secular jurisdictions and the pluralism of secular jurisdictions within the same polity were at the heart of the formation of the Western legal tradition. Judging from the existing body of legal and historical literature, one may safely predict that most people who read the present volume, including specialists, will also be surprised to learn that German Lutheranism and English Calvinism exerted enormous influence on the transformation of the Western legal tradition from the early sixteenth to the early eighteenth centuries. Protestantism transferred spiritual authority and spiritual responsibilities to the secular lawmakers of the various principalities and nation-states, whose supreme authorities now embraced all the jurisdictions that had previously been autonomous. Secular law may thus be said to have been spiritualized at the same time that it became nationalized. These important historical facts were well known to earlier generations of scholars but were forgotten in the twentieth century, as secularism itself became secularized and the common legal heritage of the West dissolved into intense nationalisms.

Why is it important to remember the influence of Roman Catholic and Protestant Christianity on the Western legal tradition in past centuries? First because we are the heirs of that tradition and our law is a product of those influences. We cannot understand what our legal institutions are if we do not know how they came to be what they are, just as we cannot know who we ourselves are if we do not know how we came to be who we are. Our history is our group memory, without which we as a group are lost. If we live only in the present we suffer from memory impairment, a kind of social amnesia, not knowing whence we came or whither we are going.

Second, without a knowledge of the past there can be no authentic commitment to the future. As Edmund Burke taught more than two centuries ago, a people that does not look backward to its ancestry will not look forward to its posterity. In the contemporary words of Teilhard de Chardin, it is the past that reveals to us how the future is built.

Third, it is important for us to be aware that our legal heritage is rooted historically in different forms of Christian faith precisely because in recent generations that fact has been forgotten, and partly as a consequence we no longer seek to identify the fundamental beliefs that now underlie our prevailing legal institutions. As recently as 1952, a Justice of the Supreme Court of the United States could state in a judicial opinion that Americans "are a religious people whose institutions presuppose a Supreme Being."* Today that may still be said by politicians and by some sections of the population, but it would no longer be said by a court. Legally, religion has become the private affair of individuals; it has largely dropped out of legal discourse. And today it is not evident what new fundamental beliefs have replaced orthodox religious beliefs as a foundation on which our legal institutions rest. Consequently, our legal discourse, our network of legal values, lacks the power and vitality that it once had.

Fourth, it is important to recover an awareness of the religious dimension of our legal tradition, including its roots in various forms of Christian belief, in order to respond creatively to the new age of world history into which we have entered in the twentieth and twenty-first centuries. in which the West is in continual interaction with other civilizations and cultures. Especially in the second millennium of the Christian era, gradually, century by century,

* Opinion of Justice William O. Douglas in *Zorach v. Clauson,* 343 U.S. 306, 313 (1952).

the peoples of the world were brought into contact with one another. Western Christendom, through its missionaries, its merchants, and its military, gradually made a world around itself. Now the West is no longer the center of that world. All humanity is joined together in a common destiny through global communications, global science and technology, and global markets, on the one hand, and, on the other hand, through global challenges of environmental destruction, disease, poverty, oppression, and devastating war. Although most people still think of law primarily in national terms, as the law made by nation-states, in fact there is emerging a whole new body of world law made by transnational nongovernmental and intergovernmental associations. In a new era of global integration, world law must draw on the material and spiritual resources not only of the West but also of other cultures, and not only of Christianity but also of other world religious and nonreligious belief systems. It is from the perspective of a new era of world law that the memory of the historical sources of the Western legal tradition must be revived.

Finally, the Western legal tradition can contribute to world society a unique time sense, a sense of the normative significance of gradual, ongoing institutional evolution over generations and centuries. In the West this was once linked with the concept that the God of history challenges mankind to seek salvation through reformation of the world. Indeed, each of the Great Revolutions that have periodically punctuated the evolution of law in the West has been based on a belief in a violent apocalyptic transformation of society that would inaugurate a new era of human brotherhood; and each has eventually shed its apocalyptic program and reconciled its new vision with the prerevolutionary past. If the Western legal tradition is now to make a positive contribution to the development of a multicultural world law, it will be not through an apocalyptic vision that leads to violent revolution but through a postrevolutionary belief in the capacity of law to evolve, that is, to maintain continuity while adapting itself to changing social needs and values.

It is, in fact, its evolutionary character, its capacity for gradual growth, its self-conscious adaptation to new circumstances that is one of the chief virtues of the Western legal tradition. Contemporary legal thought in both the United States and Europe has been dominated by a debate between legal positivists, who view law as primarily a political instrument consisting of rules promulgated by political authority and enforced by state sanctions, and adherents of a theory of natural law, who view law as primarily a moral instrument, in which legal rules are valid only if they conform to fundamental principles of justice. In the nineteenth century a third school of legal philosophy, the historical school, arose in opposition to both positivist and natural law theories. The historical school, which today is largely discredited among legal theorists, partly because of its identification with what is thought to be a romantic nationalism, found the origin of law and the source of its validity in the historical experience and the historical values of the society whose law it is. In Germany, emphasis was placed on the *Volksgeist,* "the spirit of the people"; in the United States, emphasis was placed on the beliefs of the Founding Fathers and the successive interpretations of those beliefs. The present work returns to a pre-Enlightenment jurisprudence which combines all three dimensions of law—the political, the moral, and the historical. Such an integrative jurisprudence defines law as a process of balancing order and justice in the light of experience. It returns to an earlier meaning of the Latin words *integrare,* "to heal," and *integratio,* "renewal."

Thus the impact on the Western legal tradition of the Protestant Reformations of the sixteenth and seventeenth centuries is to be viewed not just as an episode of the past but as a living memory that influences our present and future. There is, of course, no going back to the past. Nor would we want to go back to a past in which Lutheran and Calvinist belief systems were not only, as is emphasized here, important sources of renewal of legal order and legal justice but also sources of monarchical and aristocratic class domination, devastating religious wars, repression of dissent and apostasy, discrimination against Jews, persecution of persons charged with witchcraft, and other evils.

But is there not a possibility and a need to go back to what was good in it? And was not the belief in the religious foundations of law an important part of what was good in it? Would it not be a good thing for the world today if all people believed, as the Europeans of the sixteenth and seventeenth centuries believed, following their Judaic heritage, that Law—with a capital *L*—is founded on the divine commandment to love God and to love one's neighbor, and, more particularly, to honor authority, not to murder, not to steal, not to violate moral standards of marital relations, not to "bear false witness," and not to seek to deprive others of their legal rights. Anthropologists have shown that the last six of the Ten Commandments have counterparts in every known culture.

This book is written, then, in the belief that the rediscovery and revival of the historical connections between the Western legal tradition and the Western religious tradition will not only strengthen both but also facilitate dialogue and cooperation among adherents of the major cultures of the world in the development of universal legal standards and common legal institutions.

LAW AND REVOLUTION, II

INTRODUCTION

This book tells the story of two successive transformations of the Western legal tradition under the impact of two Great Revolutions—the sixteenth-century German Revolution, of which the Lutheran Reformation was a critical part, and the seventeenth-century English Revolution, of which the Calvinist Reformation was a critical part. It was, of course, not just the legal tradition that was affected by these revolutions; also involved were new forms of nationhood, new forms of government, new economic institutions, new class relations, new concepts of history, new concepts of truth. These were two total political and social upheavals, reflecting two new belief systems, whose repercussions were felt throughout Europe.

One cannot properly tell the story of what happened to the Western legal tradition in these two successive periods of history without also sketching its background in the revolutionary changes as a whole: what happened in Germany—and in Europe—after October 31, 1517, when Martin Luther posted his Ninety-five Theses on the door of his prince's church in Wittenberg, declaring, in effect, the abolition of the Roman Catholic priesthood, and rulers of German principalities raised armies to defend the Lutheran cause against the forces of the German emperor and the papacy; and what happened in England, and in Europe, after November 1640, when, following eleven years of personal rule by Charles I, a Puritan-dominated Parliament, elected by the English landed gentry, voted to establish the Presbyterian Church in Scotland, causing Charles to bring four hundred troops into the House of Commons for the purpose of arresting leading members, after which Parliament raised an army of its own to bring down royal supremacy. The main focus of the book, however, is not on the course of the two revolutions but rather on what happened eventually, in their wake, to the systems of law in the two countries, viewed in the context of the larger legal tradition of which the two national legal systems were a part.

An earlier volume told the story of the formation of the Western legal tradition. Under the impact of the Papal Revolution of the late eleventh and early twelfth centuries, there were created in the twelfth and thirteenth centuries the first modern legal system, the "new" canon law of the Roman Catholic Church (*jus novum,* as it was called), and, more gradually, coexisting secular legal systems—royal, feudal, urban, and mercantile.[1] Indeed, the canon law served in important respects as a model for the development of secular legal systems. Later transformations of the Western legal tradition took place under the impact of the eighteenth-century French and American Revolutions, the twentieth-century Russian Revolution, and the crisis of the Western legal tradition in the twentieth and early twenty-first centuries.

The principal purpose of this introduction is to recapitulate, in relatively brief compass, the main themes of the entire work, in order to place the sixteenth- and seventeenth-century transformations of German and English law, respectively, in the context of the Western legal tradition as a whole, from its origins in the late eleventh century, through its successive major transformations, to its precarious situation in the twentieth and early twenty-first centuries. It is ultimately from the perspective of the present crisis of the nine hundred–year-old Western legal tradition that the story of its formation and subsequent transformations is to be told.

It may be helpful at the outset to indicate briefly what is meant here by the words "Western," "legal,"and "tradition," especially when they are brought together in a single concept, and also by the word "Revolution"—henceforth with a capital *R*—when applied to the great political and social upheavals that have erupted periodically in the history of the West.

By "the West" I mean the historically developing culture of the peoples of Europe who, from the early twelfth to the early sixteenth centuries, shared a common political and legal subordination, as well as a common religious subordination, to the papal hierarchy of the Roman Catholic Church, and who from the sixteenth to the twentieth century experienced a series of great national Revolutions, each of which was directed partly against Roman Catholicism and each of which had repercussions throughout Europe. Included as Western are also non-European nations such as the United States that have been brought within the historically developing Western culture by colonization or, as in the case of Russia, by cultural and political affinity and interaction.

By "legal" I mean the systems of law—including constitutional law, legal philosophy, and legal science, as well as principles and rules of criminal and civil law and procedure—that have developed in the nations of the West since the twelfth century. Despite their diversity in time and space, these legal systems share common historical foundations and common concepts and methods. Also included is what may be called spiritual law, or social law—that is, law regulating ecclesiastical affairs, marriage and the family, moral offenses, education, and poor relief. Prior to the sixteenth century, these were in the competence of the Roman Catholic Church; the Protestant Reformations brought them within the competence of the secular authorities.

By "tradition" I mean the sense of an ongoing historical continuity between past and future, and in law, the organic development of legal institutions over generations and centuries, with each generation consciously building on the work of its predecessors. The historian Jaroslav Pelikan has contrasted such allegiance to tradition with traditional*ism:* traditionalism, he has written, is the dead faith of the living, tradition is the living faith of the dead.[2] Similarly, one may contrast *historicism,* adherence to the past for its own sake, with *historicity,* drawing on the past in building a new future. The sociologist Edward Shils called tradition "not the dead hand of the past but rather the hand of the gardener, which nourishes and elicits tendencies of judgment which would otherwise not be strong enough to emerge on their own."[3] Characteristically Western is the concept of a "body" of law that consciously develops in time, that "grows" over generations and centuries. It is presupposed, in the Western legal tradition, that legal change does not occur at random but proceeds by conscious reinterpretation of the past to meet present and future needs. The law evolves, is ongoing, it has a history, it tells a story. Yet the evolution of law in the West began with a Great Revolution and has been interrupted periodically in the past five centuries by a series of Great Revolutions. Every nation of the West traces its law back to such a Revolution. The interaction of long-term evolution and periodic Great Revolutions is an essential part of the story.

By "Revolution" is meant here a fundamental change, a rapid change, a violent change, a lasting change, in the political and social system of a society, involving a fundamental change in the people themselves—in their attitudes, in their character, in their belief system. This meaning of the word is often dated from the outbreak of the French Revolution of 1789, when the duke of Liancourt brought the news of the storming of the Bastille to King Louis XVI at Versailles. "But that is a revolt," exclaimed the king. "No, Sire," said Liancourt, "it is a Revolution."[4] The same word had been applied to the American War of Independence of 1776–1783, and was subsequently applied to the Russian Revolutions of 1905 and 1917.[5] It may properly be applied also to the English Revolution of 1640, which, however, was called the Glorious Revolution only when it was brought to a conclusion in 1689; to the German Revolution, which was called at the time the Lutheran Reformation; and to the Papal Revolution of 1075–1122, which was called at the time the Gregorian Reformation, after Pope Gregory VII, who initiated it. In each of these six Great Revolutions there was a violent upheaval, a civil war, fought for great ideals. Each required more than one generation to take root. Each sought legitimacy in a fundamental law and an apocalyptic vision. Each eventually produced a new body of law that reflected some of the major purposes of the Revolution. Each of the Great Revolutions transformed the Western legal tradition but ultimately remained within it.

Thus the tradition itself looks not only to the past but also to the future. A slogan of each of the Great Revolutions was "the reformation of the world." The first three—the Papal, the German, and the English—invoked the biblical vision of "a new heaven and a new earth." The American and the French Revolutions adopted Deist versions of the same—the supremacy of God-given reason, God-given inalienable rights and liberties. The Russian Revolution proclaimed the messianic mission of the atheist Communist Party to prepare the way for a classless society in which all would be brothers and sisters and each would receive according to his needs. The belief systems that accompanied these apocalyptic visions were reflected not only in radical political, economic, and social changes but also in new concepts and new institutions of public and private law.

Thus the story told here of the transformations of the Western legal tradition that took place under the impact of the Lutheran and Calvinist Reformations of the sixteenth and seventeenth centuries must be seen as part of a still larger story, in a millennial perspective.

The Origin of the Western Legal Tradition in the Papal Revolution

The larger story begins with the separation of the ecclesiastical and secular jurisdictions, accomplished by a revolutionary movement to free the Church of Rome from subservience to emperors, kings, and feudal lords, and to establish an independent hierarchy of the priesthood, under the papacy, including a hierarchy of professional ecclesiastical courts to resolve disputes and to enforce papal legislation. Led initially by Pope Gregory VII, the Gregorian Reformation, as it was called at the time, or the Investiture Contest, as it was also called, or the Papal Revolution, as it came to be called in the twentieth century, was marked by civil wars throughout Europe during a period of almost fifty years, from 1075 to 1122.[6] The pan-European Church of Rome became the first modern state. It established a body of law that was systematized in Gratian's great treatise of 1140, characteristically titled *A Concordance of Discordant Canons.* This was the first modern systematic treatise on an entire body of law, and it was accepted—and still is—as an authoritative statement of the canon law. It was followed in the thirteenth century by authoritative treatises on English, German, French, and other systems of territorial secular law.

The secular law covered chiefly matters of royal jurisdiction over questions involving landed property and violent crimes, feudal and manorial jurisdiction over lord-vassal and lord-peasant relations, urban jurisdiction over civil matters that arose in the thousands of new cities and towns founded in the twelfth and thirteenth centuries, and mercantile jurisdiction over commercial transactions in markets and fairs. The canon law was much broader in scope than the various systems of secular law, covering not only all matters directly involving the clergy but also many involving the laity. Indeed, laymen often chose to litigate contract disputes in the ecclesiastical courts, especially because secular contract law was much less highly developed. There were many overlapping matters giving rise to the concurrent jurisdiction of ecclesiastical and secular courts, as there was also concurrent jurisdiction among royal, feudal, urban, and mercantile courts within the secular sphere.

The coexistence and competition of diverse autonomous legal systems and diverse autonomous jurisdictions within a given political community helped to make possible the supremacy of law within that community. The supremacy of law both within the church and within each of the kingdoms was supported also by the rise in the twelfth century of a professionally trained class of people who engaged in legal activities as a more or less full-time occupation—professional lawyers, judges, and legal scholars, both ecclesiastical and secular. The texts of Roman law compiled in the sixth century under the Byzantine emperor Justinian, rediscovered in the West five centuries later, not accidentally, at the height of the Papal Revolution, were now analyzed and synthesized by a new method, later called scholasticism, of reconciling contradictions in authoritative texts and deriving general concepts from the disparate rules and cases set forth in those texts.

Finally, the concept of law as a coherent body or system of rules and principles was given vitality by the accompanying belief in its ongoing character, its capacity for continuous growth over generations and centuries—a belief that is uniquely Western. The law, like the Gothic cathedrals, was intended to be built and rebuilt over centuries. It was accepted that the body of law contains a built-in mechanism for organic change and, further, that the growth of the law, its changes over time, have an internal logic, are part of a pattern of changes. The law, it was thought, develops by reinterpretation of past rules and decisions to meet present and future needs.

The historicity of law, as it came to be understood in the West in the twelfth century and thereafter, was linked with the concept of its autonomy and of its supremacy over political rulers. The supreme political authority—the king, the pope himself—may make law, it was said, but he may not make it arbitrarily, and until he has remade it—lawfully—he is bound by it. In Bracton's famous words, written in the early thirteenth century, "The king must not be under man but under God and under the law, because law makes the king."[7] And in the words of Bracton's German counterpart Eike von Repgau, "God is law and therefore law is dear to him."[8]

The First Protestant Revolution: Lutheran Germany

The vision of the Papal Revolution was a vision of the dialectical reconciliation of opposites: of the spiritual and the secular, the papal and the royal, the clergy and the laity—and, within the secular, the royal and the feudal, the feudal and the urban. The realization of this vision depended on the faithfulness of the priesthood in wielding the powerful "spiritual sword," as well as on the responsibility of the royal and feudal and urban powers in wielding the "secular sword." In the course of time, however, the "two swords" vision of the Papal Revolution underwent substantial impairment.

In the late fourteenth and fifteenth centuries, the West experienced a widespread clamor for additional so-called reformations, both of the spiritual and of the secular regimes. Religious revolts, however, and humanist calls for more just, more humane ecclesiastical policies met with only a weak response from the papal hierarchy, which by the end of the fifteenth century had sunk into the deepest corruption. The demand for reformation extended also to the secular realm, but again, little came of it. In hindsight one can see that things were building up to an explosion. This was also recognized by many at the time. None of the changes that were made in order to forestall such an explosion, however, prior to the rise of Lutheranism in the early sixteenth century, addressed the crucial problem of the time, namely, in the historian Myron Gilmore's words, that "the Gregorian Revolution had finally failed." Indeed, "the idea that secular government was directed ultimately to the attainment of grace or justice," goals set for it by the Roman Catholic Church, Gilmore wrote, "[was] no longer taken seriously."[9]

In 1517 Martin Luther and his followers broke the evolutionary process by proclaiming, in effect, the abolition of the ecclesiastical jurisdiction. The church, Luther said, is not a lawmaking institution; the church is the invisible community of the faithful, in which all believers are priests, serving one another, each is a "private person" in his relation to God, and each is to respond individually to the Bible as the Word of God. The secular political authority, the prince and his councilors, the high magistracy, the *Obrigkeit,* must undertake the lawmaking responsibilities that previously were within the jurisdiction of the Roman Catholic Church.

Lutherans replaced the "two swords" theory of the Papal Revolution with a new "two kingdoms" theory: the invisible church, the priesthood of all believers, they taught, belongs to the heavenly kingdom, which is governed by the Gospel; the earthly kingdom, the kingdom of "this world," including the visible institutional church, is governed by law, which is in the exclusive competence of the Christian prince and his councilors.

Because they taught that the salvation of souls in the heavenly kingdom comes only by the grace of God to those who have faith, and is not earned by "works of the law," it is often supposed that Luther and his colleagues did not have a positive legal philosophy and a program of law reform. That is quite untrue. They taught that in the earthly kingdom, in which God is present, though hidden, law—including both the moral law of the Ten Commandments, the Decalogue, and the positive law of the secular ruler based on it—is needed: first, by its moral principles to make sinners conscious of their sinfulness and thus to help to bring them to repentance; second, by its threat of sanctions to deter sinners from antisocial conduct; and third, by its principles and procedures to educate and guide righteous people in the paths of justice and the common weal.

To accomplish these three "uses of the law," as they were called, Lutheran rulers of German principalities enacted comprehensive statutes, called *Ordnungen,* "ordinances," regulating matters that previously had been within the competence of the Roman Catholic hierarchy: these were called church ordinances, governing the structure and functions of the Lutheran Church within the principality; marriage ordinances, governing marriage and family relations; disciplinary ordinances, governing moral offenses; school ordinances, governing public education of children; and poor ordinances, governing relief of the poor, the sick, widows and orphans, the homeless, the unemployed.[10] Most of these princely ordinances were drafted by Lutheran law-trained theologians, including in some instances Luther himself and his younger friend and close colleague Philip Melanchthon.

In contrast to the scholastic method of the earlier Roman Catholic legal science, Lutheran jurists emphasized the unity of the entire body of law and its division into branches, first, of public and private law, and second, within private law, of property and obligations, and then, within obligations, of contract, tort, and unjust enrichment. This classification was based on Melanchthon's topical method, which, in contrast to the earlier scholastic method, proceeded first from general topics, or truths, applicable to all science, and then from special topics applicable to individual branches of science, of which legal science was one, and subdivided each topic into genera and species. Melanchthon's topical method was applied by scholars throughout Europe in treatises on what was conceived as a pan-European common law, a new *jus commune,* that embraced principles and doctrines and rules derived from the two earlier pan-European systems of common law—Roman law and canon law—and from the common features of the various systems of royal law, feudal law, mercantile law, and urban law.

This was a professorial legal science, adapted to the teaching of law in the universities, including, in Germany, the legal education of future councilors of princes as well as future professional judges who would preside over secular tribunals of laymen. It was also well adapted to the introduction of a new system of decision of cases by the professors themselves. This was the famous system of "the sending of the file"—*Aktenversendung*—of difficult cases by German courts to university law faculties for final decision, an institution that lasted in Germany until 1878.

This was also biblical law. As Roman Catholic jurists had systematized the canon law on the basis of the seven sacraments, so Lutheran jurists used Melanchthon's topical method in basing the various branches of the law on the

Ten Commandments. Thus, Johann Oldendorp, whose principal treatise three centuries later was in the library of United States Supreme Court Justice Joseph Story, followed Melanchthon in founding criminal law on the commandment "Thou shalt not kill," property law on the commandment "Thou shalt not steal," family law on the commandment "Thou shalt not commit adultery," the law of contract and delict on the commandments "Thou shalt not bear false witness" and "Thou shalt not covet." These were "topics" not only in the sense of categories or headings but also in the sense of general principles—theologically based moral principles in light of which subordinate species of legal rules were to be interpreted. This was a new method of legal synthesis which transcended the earlier divisions among coexisting legal systems within the same polity. A new hermeneutics, which treated the texts of the Old and New Testaments as an integrated whole, was applied also to law. It found expression in the systematic codification of German criminal law—the first comprehensive modern code of a branch of the law.

Lutheran jurists also developed a new legal philosophy that combined a positivist theory of law as a body of formal rules expressing the will of the lawmaker with a natural law theory of the application of rules by resort to the divinely guided conscience of the Lutheran judge.

Repercussions of the German Lutheran Revolution were felt everywhere in Europe. Where Protestantism triumphed, as in England, a state church, headed by the monarch, was introduced, to which all persons in the kingdom were required by law to belong. Also in countries that remained Roman Catholic, such as France, Spain, and Austria, royal powers over the church within the kingdom greatly increased. National legal systems, covering the entire spectrum of jurisdictions within each country, began to be created.

The Second Protestant Revolution: Calvinist England

In both Protestant and Roman Catholic countries, problems that came in the wake of the German Revolution became acute in succeeding generations. A *religious* crisis arose from the division of Protestantism into various denominations, including especially those consisting of followers of the sixteenth-century French theologian and jurist John Calvin. The threat to Lutheranism of Calvinists from the left and the continued antagonism of Roman Catholic rulers from the right led eventually to the so-called Thirty Years' War that raged intermittently on the European continent from 1618 to 1648. A closely related *political* crisis arose from the emergence in Europe of repressive "absolute" monarchs who, as supreme legislators, supreme judges, and supreme executors of the laws, were themselves "absolved" from subjection to such laws. Henry VIII, in inaugurating the sixteenth-century English Reformation, expressly claimed such absolute power, as did his contemporary the Roman Catholic French monarch

Francis I. Jean Bodin's treatise expounding the doctrine of absolute monarchy, written in the latter part of the sixteenth century, became widely accepted as authoritative among the ruling circles of most countries of Europe.[11]

In the seventeenth century, however, the concept of royal supremacy came increasingly under attack, first by international Calvinism, which taught an aristocratic, as opposed to a monarchical, principle of government; and second by members of the landed gentry as well as by other classes that suffered from real or imagined oppression at the hands of royal households and their bureaucracies. In the mid-seventeenth century, various countries of Europe experienced anti-monarchical revolts roughly parallel, though on a smaller scale, to the massive English Revolution that broke out in 1640, with its Civil War of 1642–1649 and its subsequent periods of Puritan Commonwealth from 1649 to 1660, Restoration from 1660 to 1688, and finally the so-called Glorious Revolution of 1688–89.

The English Revolution of 1640–1689 established the supremacy of Parliament over the Crown. This is not to be confused with democracy: only some 2 or 3 percent of the adult male population were eligible to vote. It was, in effect, the rule of an aristocracy made up principally of some eight or ten thousand landed gentry and some hundreds of leading merchants, who together replaced the approximately 120 titled nobility as the ruling class.[12] In Parliament, the House of Commons now for the first time assumed greater power than the House of Lords.

England remained Protestant Christian. The Church of England, however, now under the control of Parliament, was reduced from a state church, to which all Christian subjects were required to adhere, to an established church, that is, a privileged church supported by the state but coexisting, under the 1689 Act of Toleration, with Calvinist denominations that had initiated the Revolution in 1640. In fact, Anglicanism, as it came to be called, absorbed much of the Calvinist belief system that had motivated the Puritans, in the first phase of the Revolution, to rise up against the Anglican state church.

The Revolution also produced a fundamental and lasting transformation of the English legal system. Judges were no longer to serve at the will of the monarch but were given independence and life tenure. The so-called prerogative courts established by the Tudor monarchs, of which the High Court of Star Chamber and the Court of High Commission were the most notorious, were abolished, and the common law courts were made supreme over the courts of Chancery and Admiralty. Jury trial was transformed: the jury could no longer be dominated by the judge, and witness proof and rules of evidence were introduced. The ancient forms of action were preserved but were now used to help modernize the English law of property, contract, and tort. The doctrine of precedent—the hallmark of the English common law—was given its modern meaning by the introduction of the distinction between the rule of law that is necessarily implicit in the decision of a given case, called "the holding" of the case, and reasons stated by the court in its opinion that are not necessary to the decision, called "dicta." As the German emphasis on the consistency of legal principles was related to the emergence of the monarchical civil service state, the prince and his councilors, so the English emphasis on the historical continuity of the law was related to the emergence of the aristocratic parliamentary state, with its party system of Whigs and Tories and its guilds of judges and barristers. The conceptualism of the former had led to a legal science in which every question was to be "placed" within a system of genus and species. The empiricism of the latter led to a legal science in which the principles, being drawn from cases, were subject to argument in an adversary procedure.

These seventeenth- and early-eighteenth-century innovations in English law were rooted partly in Calvinist concepts. The English Puritans, despite strong differences of belief among different branches, different sects, and indeed different congregations, shared the belief that human history is wholly within the providence of God, that it is primarily a spiritual story of the unfolding of God's own purposes. This strong belief in divine providence led them to view England as God's elect nation, destined to reveal and embody God's mission for mankind. They believed, further, that God willed and commanded what they called "the reformation of the world," and they emphasized the role of law as a means of such reformation. An additional element in the Puritan belief system that strongly affected the development of English political and legal institutions was its emphasis on the corporate character of Christian communities. Anglo-Calvinist Puritanism was essentially a communitarian religion. It emphasized the existence of a divine covenant, under which the congregation of the faithful was to be "a light to all the nations of the world," "a city on a hill." This, in turn, led to an emphasis not only on the virtues of hard work, austerity, frugality, discipline, self-improvement, and other features of what has come to be called the Puritan work ethic, but also on the sanctity of human covenants of public responsibility, community service, corporate enterprise, mutual trust, and other qualities associated with the concept of public spirit.

The belief that England is God's elect nation supported the movement to embark on a new Reformation—what the great Puritan poet-philosopher John Milton in the 1650s called "a reformation of the reformation"—based partly on the traditions of the pre-Tudor English past. Anglo-Norman history was invoked—Magna Carta and the early common law—to support revolutionary political change. Anglo-Calvinist thought contributed to a new historical jurisprudence, which was added to the diverse natural law and positivist theories of Roman Catholic and Lutheran legal philosophy.

The French Revolution: Deist Rationalism

As the sixteenth-century German Revolution produced a body of law that reflected a Lutheran belief system, and the seventeenth-century English Revolution produced a body of law that reflected a Calvinist belief system, so the

French Revolution of 1789–1830 produced a body of law that reflected a Deist belief system.

Deism is a Western belief system that was widely shared in the eighteenth century by people who did not believe in the divinity of Christ, and who were, indeed, in many instances avowed anti-Christians, but who did believe that the universe was originally created by God, that God had appointed a purpose for everything in it, and that human beings were given by God certain faculties—above all, reason—to enable them to secure their own welfare. Eighteenth-century French *philosophes* such as Voltaire, Diderot, Rousseau, and other famous "lights" *(lumières)*, as they were called, were Deists who taught that human beings are born free and equal, with the capacity to achieve, by use of reason, both knowledge and happiness. The "Enlightenment," as this philosophy came to be called in the early nineteenth century, first in Germany and then elsewhere,[13] originally had a religious dimension. The Deist faith in the purity and power of reason and in the promise of science challenged Christian beliefs in the inherent sinfulness of man and in the providential character of human history, beliefs emphasized by both Lutherans and Calvinists, as well as Christian beliefs in ecclesiastical traditions and in the corporate character of faith, beliefs emphasized by Roman Catholicism. Yet Deism was certainly a product of both Roman Catholicism and Protestantism; it shared their common belief in a God who created man and gave him reason, their common moral values, and their confidence in law as a means of reforming the world.

The Deism of the eighteenth-century French *philosophes*, including especially its essential rationalism, was reflected in fundamental changes in public and private law introduced in the wake of the French Revolution. In contrast to the emphasis of the German Revolution on monarchy and royal prerogatives, and of the English Revolution on aristocracy and aristocratic privileges, the emphasis of the partisans of the French Revolution was on democracy and on civil rights and liberties—in the words of the 1789 French Declaration of the Rights of Man and of Citizen, "the natural and imprescriptible rights of man." Indeed, the French Revolution was fought, in the first instance, to abolish the oppressive and irrational system of customary privileges of the French aristocracy, and only in the second instance to abolish the oppressive and irrational exercise of autocratic powers by the monarchy. Supreme power was given to a democratically elected legislature charged with carrying out policies reflecting the public opinion of the propertied middle class that elected it. A series of written constitutions introduced a system of strict separation of powers, by virtue of which the executive was only to execute, and the judiciary was only to apply in individual cases, the law that the legislature alone had power to create.

In addition to establishing a new constitutional system, the French Revolution introduced a new legal science and a new legal philosophy. As the Germans emphasized the professorial "placing" of legal principles in a topical system of genus and species, and the English emphasized the judicial "debating" of legal questions in the context of historical precedents, so the French now came to emphasize the "clarification" of legal doctrine through enactment of comprehensive legislation. Professorial principles and judicial precedents were subordinated, in France, to doctrines and rules laid down by the legislature in comprehensive codes. At the same time, the natural law theory that had predominated in the sixteenth and early seventeenth centuries, and the historical jurisprudence that had been placed alongside it in the seventeenth and early eighteenth centuries, yielded to a positivist theory of law, which became increasingly accepted in the nineteenth century and virtually dominated Western legal philosophy in the twentieth century.

Both the new legal science and the new legal theory were closely connected with important changes in substantive law. In civil law, the famous *Code civil* of 1804, in whose drafting Napoleon himself played a part, and which was intended to express the spirit of the Revolution, gave especially strong protection to rights or private property and contract. In tort law ("delict"), the principle was established that, as a general rule, liability should be based on fault: the doer of harm should not be civilly liable to the victim unless he intended to cause the harm or else caused it negligently. In family law, marriage was viewed like any other civil contract, and divorce was obtainable by mutual consent, for cause, or for proven incompatibility. The husband's disciplinary power over his wife and his children was restricted. Wives were accorded greater property rights and greater civil rights generally.[14]

Striking law reforms were also introduced in the field of criminal law. New criminal codes prohibited retroactive criminal laws, declared a presumption of innocence, and imposed like punishments on like offenses regardless of the rank of the offender. All crimes were to be defined by statute. At the same time, Napoleon's 1810 Criminal Code placed strong emphasis on deterrence of criminal conduct by threat of penalties rather than on retribution. This reflected the utilitarian philosophy that had prevailed among the great reformers of the late eighteenth century. "Reason" taught that criminal acts were to be punished not, as in Lutheran Germany, primarily because they were morally wrong and deserved retribution, and not, as in Anglo-Calvinist England, primarily because they violated traditional community standards that needed to be reaffirmed, but primarily because they were harmful to society and the punishment of the offender would serve to deter others, as well as himself, from committing them in the future.

The philosophy of rationalism, individualism, and utilitarianism that underlay the new French legal science was closely connected with the rejection of orthodox Christian doctrines, on the one hand, and, on the other hand, the strong belief in a Creator God who endowed humanity with the gift of reason and the power to use that gift by exercising freedom of will, freedom of expression, equality of opportunity, and other "natural rights" that were embodied in the new French constitutions and codes.

The American Revolution: Part "English," Part "French"

The American Revolution, from one perspective, appears as a War of Independence, fought by the colonists to secure for themselves the same rights that their English cousins enjoyed in the mother country. It was this aspect of the Revolution that was emphasized in the Declaration of Rights of the First Continental Congress of 1774, which demanded for the colonists "all the rights, liberties, and immunities of free and natural-born subjects within the realm of England."[15] Many of these "rights, liberties, and immunities" had been denied to them; under British imperial law, the American colonists were not entitled to the English common law as a matter of right, but only to those parts of it which the Privy Council considered to be applicable to their condition. They were not entitled as a matter of right to the benefit of such common law statutes as Magna Carta, the Petition of Right, the Habeas Corpus Act, the Bill of Rights of 1689, or any other statutes that were enacted before their particular colony was settled, nor were they entitled to the benefit of post-settlement statutes unless the colony was specifically named in them. They were not entitled to trial by jury. Moreover, their governors were appointed by the Crown, and their judges were subject to removal by the Crown. In short, they were under royal prerogative powers which Parliament had successfully fought to abolish at home in the period from 1640 to 1689 but which Parliament had allowed to be exercised in the overseas colonies. Perhaps most important of all, the colonists were not represented in Parliament. From their perspective, they fought the War of Independence to secure for themselves the political and legal institutions which had been forged in the fires of the English Revolution. This was the "English" face of the American Revolution.

From another perspective, however, the American Revolution appears not as a movement to assert the rights of colonists to English forms of government and English law, but rather as a movement to establish a new kind of government and law that would be essentially different from English law.[16] Thomas Jefferson, who was an exponent of the latter view, wrote some years after the Revolution: "I deride . . . the ordinary doctrine, that we brought with us from England the common law rights. This *narrow notion* was a *favorite* in the first moment of rallying to our rights against Great Britain. But it was that of men who felt their rights, before they had thought of their explanation. The truth is, that we brought with us the rights of men, of expatriated men."[17]

Jefferson's philosophy of the natural and equal rights of all men, and of the right of the majority of the community to overthrow a government which does not protect such rights—vividly expressed by him in the Virginia Bill of Rights of June 12, 1776, and in the first paragraph of the Declaration of Independence—links the American Revolution not to the earlier English Revolution, whose ideology was essentially traditionalist and whose political structure was essentially aristocratic and corporate, but rather to the subsequent French Revolution, whose ideology was essentially rationalist and whose political structure was essentially democratic and individualistic.

It is a striking fact that Edmund Burke and Thomas Paine, from completely opposite ideological standpoints, could both support the American cause. Burke, in his *Reflections on the French Revolution* (1790), defending the English Revolution of the previous century, glorified tradition and the corporate evolution of the English people. A nation, he wrote in a famous passage, is indeed formed by a social contract, but it is a contract of partnership of past, present, and future generations, not to be confused with a contract for the sale of goods.[18] Burke looked for the source of liberty not in the will of transitory majorities but in the public spirit of the leaders of the nation in the legislature and on the bench. Responding to Burke's book, Paine, in his *Rights of Man* (1791), defending the French Revolution, glorified reason—that is, the rationality of each person—and saw the nation as a voluntary association of individuals. He looked for the source of liberty in the public opinion of a given society at a given moment. Thus, Burke could support the colonists in what he saw as a legitimate secession from the mother country, a War of Independence. Paine could support them in what he saw as a Revolutionary War.

It would be a grave mistake, however, to suppose that each American colonist who supported the American cause fell on one side of this ideological division or the other. On the contrary, many if not most of them, and certainly many of their greatest leaders—men such as John Adams, James Wilson, and James Madison—accommodated the tension between the two perspectives. These three—Adams, Wilson, Madison—each of whom played a major role in shaping American constitutional law at its formation, were men of strong Protestant Christian convictions. None of them accepted the dogmatic rationalism and individualism that was characteristic of the Deistic thought of such men as Franklin, Paine, and Jefferson.[19] Nevertheless, they enthusiastically supported democratic political institutions and the natural rights and liberties of the individual against aristocratic privilege and monarchical prerogative, although they also supported substantial constitutional restraints on the will of the majority. Finally, all three believed firmly in the English common law with its strong element of historicity, of continuity between past and future. In sum, they combined and reconciled, albeit each in his own way, liberal ideas that were preached by the French philosophes and their English and American sympathizers and that ultimately found reflection in the law of the first French Republic, on the one hand, and, on the other hand, conservative ideas—in the progressive Burkean sense—which had been preached by supporters of the seventeenth-century English Revolution such as John Milton and Matthew Hale and which had found reflection in the development of English law in the late seventeenth and eighteenth centuries.[20]

The dialectical tension between aristocratic and conservative ideals associated with the earlier English Revolution and democratic and liberal ideals associated with the contemporaneously brewing French Revolution was reflected both in the constitutional law and in the civil and criminal law of the new American republic. In constitutional law, the members of the U.S. Senate, elected for long terms and, at first, by the state legislatures, were supposed, like the members of the English House of Commons, to represent the nation as a whole, while the members of the House of Representatives, like the members of the French Estates General, were supposed to represent their particular constituencies. The nine justices of the Supreme Court, appointed for life, were a kind of House of Lords, whose Law Lords to this day constitute the supreme judicial body in England. Likewise, the president of the United States, who, like the senators, was at first elected by the state legislatures, was to be, in foreign policy at least, a kind of monarch, albeit not a hereditary monarch.

Yet the same persons who carried over and adapted English traditions to the new republic—men such as Wilson and Madison—also introduced into the United States Constitution, in modified form, democratic and liberal ideas associated with the eighteenth-century European reform movement whose underlying belief system was most effectively articulated by the French *philosophes* and which culminated in the French Revolution. These included not only the very idea of a written constitution, a modified doctrine of separation of powers, and the theory of a government directly responsible to the opinion of the electorate, but also, and even more striking, guarantees of freedom of religion, speech, press, and assembly. Indeed, the entire Constitution gives political and legal expression to the eighteenth-century concept that all persons, by virtue of their human nature, possess certain universal and equal rights of life, liberty, and property, which it is the obligation of government, if not always to protect, at least never to repress.

In civil law as well—including the law of property, contract, tort, and other civil obligations, and the law of business and other associations—there existed in the several states a tension between the more conservative English legal tradition that had prevailed in the colonial period and the more liberal legal science and philosophy reflected in the French Civil Code. State courts struggled with the question whether English common law precedents should be "received." A movement to codify the civil law emerged, and civil codes were adopted in several states. Similarly, in criminal law there was a strong tendency to restrain judges from applying common law doctrines to new types of situations, and the United States Supreme Court early adopted the democratic principle that Congress alone can make the federal criminal law—that all federal criminal law is statutory.

It is, to be sure, a unique feature of American law, brought about by the American Revolution, that its federal and state constitutions and its systems of federal and state civil and criminal law effectively combine the two conflicting belief systems—Puritanism, traditionalism, and communitarianism versus Deism, rationalism, and individualism—as well as the two conflicting political systems associated with those belief systems: aristocracy based on public spirit versus democracy based on public opinion. What was radically new in American law, however, was not restricted to the synthesis of these opposites. The new American republic also introduced three constitutional principles which were neither "English" nor "French" nor a combination of the two, and, indeed, which had never existed before in the West in anything like the same form. One of these was American federalism.[21] Closely related to it was a principle that might be called continentalism—the implicit provision for an expanding polity of continental scope, with virtually unlimited mobility of persons and goods and virtually unlimited absorption of immigrants. A third principle was the institution of judicial review of the constitutionality of legislation. The full impact of these three principles on the development of the Western legal tradition has only been apparent since the end of the Second World War.

The Russian Revolution: Atheist State Socialism

If one takes a stance in 1914, at the outbreak of the First World War, one can look back on the evolution of an eight hundred–year-old legal tradition in the West, which, on the one hand, was interrupted in the course of centuries by violent national revolutions, each directed against the existing legal system in the name of a new vision of a transcendent justice, but which, on the other hand, survived those revolutions and was reformed and ultimately renewed by them.

Surviving from those origins, in the early twentieth century, was the concept of the coexistence of integrated legal systems, "bodies" of law; surviving also was the technique, later called "scholastic," of reconciling contradictions in authoritative texts and deriving general concepts from the legal rules and cases presented in those texts; surviving also was a belief in the ongoing character of law in time, its capacity for growth over generations, its historicity; surviving also was a belief in the capacity of law to resolve conflicts between competing political authorities within a territory and its ultimate supremacy over political authorities.

These fundamental characteristics of the Western legal tradition were founded on Christian belief, first in its Roman Catholic form, later in its Lutheran and Calvinist forms. Deism, the religious faith of the so-called Enlightenment, substituted for the Christian belief in divine law a belief in God-given reason and the supremacy of public opinion. Nevertheless, in 1914 it continued to be widely believed in the West that the ultimate sources of authentic positive law are divine law, especially the Ten Commandments, natural law discovered by reason and conscience, and historical tradition expressed in sources such as Magna Carta and constitutional requirements of due process and equal protection of the laws.

The widespread belief in these sources of law underlay the belief in its historical evolution as well as the acceptance of the historical necessity that had arisen periodically in the past to replace the existing legal system by violence, because of its abject failure to realize its transcendent goals. Every nation of the West traced its legal system back to such a Revolution. The slogans of each of the Great Revolutions were derived from Jesus' reproach to the Pharisees: "Woe unto you, lawyers, for you tithe mint and dill and cummin"—you stick with the technicalities and formalities—"and neglect the weightier matters of the law, which are justice and mercy and good faith."

As of 1914, different forms of legal systems and different forms of legal science coexisted in the West within a common tradition. The Roman Catholic version of separation of church and state coexisted with Lutheran, Calvinist, and Deist versions. Constitutional monarchy coexisted with aristocracy and democracy. The prerogatives of the German Kaiser coexisted with the privileges of the ruling classes represented in the British Parliament and the rights of the citizen represented in the French Estates General and the American House of Representatives. Moreover, within each country of the West, and not only among them, there coexisted, in different proportions, the Aristotelian concepts of the rule of the one, the rule of the few, and the rule of the many.

In legal science the scholasticism of the First Modern Age—miscalled the High Middle Ages—coexisted in 1914, again in various proportions in different countries, with German conceptualism, English empiricism, and French doctrinalism. Everywhere in the West, code law coexisted with case law—again, in various proportions. A Western *jus commune* still existed underneath the surface of national legal systems.

That was in 1914, at the end of the long nineteenth century.

It may be more difficult today than it was in the past to identify and keep in memory important events and important characteristics of the millennial history of the West. Nine centuries, or five, or even three, seem like a very long time. In the light of the entire history of world civilizations, however, even a millennium is only a fraction of the cosmic time frame in which humanity now finds itself, as the entire human race, for the first time in its recorded history, has come together in a world economy, the beginnings of a world society, and the gradual creation of a body of world law.

It is easier to identify and keep in our memory the main events and the main characteristics of the long twentieth century—the century that began in 1914 and appears to be coming to an end in the first decades of the 2000s.

It was—it still is—a century of terrible wars, starting with the civil war among the European states that eventually became the first of two World Wars. It was—and still is—a century of inter-ethnic wars and genocide. At the same time, it was—it still is—a century of both the clash of ethnic and territorial cultures and their gradual coming together. It is a century of global technological communication, global economic intercourse, and global environmental interdependence among members of disparate cultures that lack a common belief system.

The long nineteenth century ended with World War I. The long twentieth century began with the Russian Revolution.

Some would not agree that Russia is part of the West, or that Russian history is part of Western history, or that the Russian Revolution belongs in the same series of Great Revolutions as the German, the English, the American, and the French. Historically, Eastern Orthodox Russia strongly opposed the Western Papal Revolution of the late eleventh and early twelfth centuries and its creation of an independent church-state and an autonomous system of canon law. Nor did Russia experience, at the time they happened, the Lutheran and Calvinist and Deist Revolutions and the successive formations of a monarchical high magistracy, an aristocratic Parliament, and a democratic separation of powers. Until its demise in 1917, the Russian tsardom proclaimed itself to be an autocracy, with supreme spiritual as well as supreme secular authority. Moreover, Russia first came into close contact with the West only in the eighteenth century, when its ruling classes came under the influence of the French Enlightenment. Its first university was founded in Moscow in 1756, almost seven hundred years after the founding of the first Western university in Bologna. And only in the nineteenth century, after the Napoleonic Wars, did there emerge in Russia legal institutions similar to those that had existed in the West for seven centuries: a class of learned jurists, the systematization of the laws, a body of legal literature, and finally, in the 1860s, a hierarchy of courts with a professional judiciary and a professional class of lawyers.

Nevertheless, Russia was, indeed, gradually "Westernized" in the eighteenth, nineteenth, and early twentieth centuries, and the Marxian socialist belief system of the leaders of the 1917 Russian Bolshevik Revolution was itself a Western belief system. Soviet Marxist atheism was a Christian heresy. Even the utopian Marxist-Leninist vision of a future classless society that would have no need for a state or for a body of law was a utopian Western vision, paralleling the antinomianism of the earliest radical phases of the German, English, and French Revolutions. There was much, indeed, that was purely Russian in twentieth-century Russian socialism, just as there was much that was purely national in the earlier German, English, American, and French national revolutions, but there was also much that had been foreshadowed in nineteenth-century Western socialist movements, and much that later spread to other countries in the West, including the United States.

We usually draw very sharp contrasts between Western legal systems and Soviet Russian law as it existed prior to the collapse of the Soviet Union in December 1991. We stress the absence in Soviet Russia of the concept of a law that is higher than the state and that binds the top leadership of the state; the absence of private ownership of land and of the means of production; the repression of freedom of speech and press and religion and other basic civil liberties; the dictatorship of the Communist Party and, within the Party, of the General Secretary and the Politburo. But if we study carefully the Soviet legal system as it developed in the course of seventy-five years, and especially in the post-Stalin decades, culminating in the seven years under Mikhail Gorbachev, and if we look critically at the development of our own European and American legal systems since the Great Depression of the late 1920s and 1930s, we can see many parallels.

The post-Stalin Soviet civil and criminal codes and judicial system had much in common with contemporary Western civil and criminal codes and judicial systems. Not rule *of* law but nevertheless rule *by* law came to play an increasingly important role in the Soviet Union from the late 1950s to the 1980s. There were over 250,000 university-trained lawyers in the Soviet Union when it dissolved in December 1991. Until the end, however, two essential differences—even apart from Communist Party domination—remained between Soviet law and the law of Western countries: first, the far greater extent to which law, and especially administrative regulation, was used by the Soviet state to operate and control economic and social activities, and second, the far greater extent to which the Soviet state used law to guide and train and discipline the beliefs and attitudes of the Soviet people. This was what the Soviets called "the educational role of law," or, more precisely, "the nurturing role of law."[22] In the 1930s and 1940s Karl Llewellyn called it "parental law," and added that our own law "moves in a parental direction."[23]

These two—state planning, through law, of the economy and state nurturing, through law, of the beliefs and attitudes of the entire population—mark the chief contributions of the Russian Revolution, for good and for ill, to the Western legal tradition in the long twentieth century. The Soviet total state distorted the ideals of social democracy that were an essential part of the original vision of the Revolution. Many of those ideals were nevertheless written into Soviet law and, after Stalin's death, increasingly implemented in practice. Soviet law early established the right to work, the right to old age pensions, free medical care, and free higher education. Discrimination on the basis of race or gender as well as anti-racial actions or statements and sexual harassment by superiors in employment were made violations of criminal law.

At the foundation of Soviet law was an atheist vision that postulated the fundamental goodness of human nature, the inherent ability of humankind to build a society in which each person would now receive income according to his work and eventually according to his needs, and the willingness of a people, when freed from economic class exploitation and hence from addiction to the "opiate" of religious beliefs, to respond positively to the will of a dedicated leadership.[24]

It was the loss of faith in this utopian vision, more than any other factor, that eventually caused the collapse of the Soviet Union. Soviet efforts to instill and enforce by law the altruism necessary to make socialism work exceeded the limits of effective legal action. Despite many experiments in balancing state planning with state enterprise autonomy, and collective goals of workers with incentives for individual initiative, the planned economy eventually broke down. Similarly, strenuous efforts of Party and State failed to strengthen—on the contrary, ultimately weakened—the inner cohesion and sense of social responsibility of the family, the neighborhood, the school, the workplace, and other associations that constitute civil society.

That the vision that motivated the Russian Revolution collapsed in Russia in the 1990s reminds one of the fact that much of the vision that motivated the French Revolution eventually suffered defeat in France in the 1870s in the reign of Emperor Napoleon III, much of the vision that motivated the English Revolution eventually suffered defeat in the early 1800s, and much of the vision that motivated the German Revolution eventually suffered defeat a century later in Germany in the Thirty Years' War. Yet the twin legal innovations introduced by the Russian Revolution—the enormous enhancement of the social and economic role of the state and the parallel enhancement of the parental role of law—have survived and have had repercussions throughout the West and throughout the world.

In virtually all countries of the West, governmental bureaucracies in the twentieth and twenty-first centuries have come to control, directly and actively, the economy, communications, education, health care, conditions of work, and other aspects of economic and social life. To a large extent these are governed by administrative regulations. By no means entirely, but nevertheless to a considerable extent, administrative regulation as a major source of law has invaded the civil code in France, common law precedents in England, and professorial concepts and principles in Germany. In the United States as well, though not to the same extent, both legislatures and courts have yielded to governmental agencies much of their control over large parts of economic and social life. At the same time, American courts have themselves become to a certain extent agencies of active control of economic and social life, as so-called judicial activism has increasingly become openly accepted.

The use of law to implement direct state regulation of economic and social activities has been linked in our time with the use of law directly to influence people's beliefs and attitudes, to educate people to be socially responsible, and to treat one another equally, regardless of differences in race or gender or age or class. More and more we have seen the socializing functions of the family, the school, the church, the factory, the commercial enterprise, and other local associations subjected to direct legislative, administrative, and judicial controls. Not just in Russia but throughout the West, the law of the state has come to play the role of parent or teacher in nurturing attitudes officially considered to be socially desirable. As the Polish-American poet and prophet Czeslaw Milosz said of the twentieth century, "the state has eaten up all the substance of society."[25]

Millennial Historiography

It is because we are at the end of an era that we are able to discern its entire course; and it is because we are at the beginning of a new era of transnational and transcultural interaction that we must search our past in order to find what from its beginning gave it its vitality and what in it can help us meet the challenges of the future.

It is not accidental that in the last decades of the twentieth century, the nationalist legal historiography that predominated in the West prior to the two World Wars began to give way to the study of a transnational European legal history.[26] The study of European legal history, however, taken as a whole, requires a different periodization from that which has been applied to the study of individual national legal systems taken separately. Western history, including Western legal history, has moved in long time spans, with recurrent motifs. It is thus the task of the historian of Western law to establish the right periodization.

Among Western academic historians generally, periodization has often been taken for granted and, indeed, often ignored, as historical researches have tended to become narrower and narrower. In the words of a great—and greatly neglected—twentieth-century scholar, Eugen Rosenstock-Huessy, "scientific" or "objective" historiography of the nineteenth and twentieth centuries, which placed the historian outside of history, led to the continual breaking down of the past into smaller parts and the eventual loss of any sense of direction. The historian, he wrote, should count not only days and years but also, and above all, generations and centuries if he is to "avoid the Scylla of disordered detail and the Charybdis of meaningless generalities."[27] Rosenstock-Huessy's method of periodizing the history of the West was to stress the recurrence of Great Revolutions from the eleventh to the twentieth century, each ultimately building on the experience of its predecessors. I have applied this method to the study of the history of Western law.

Paradoxically, those scholars who, by concentrating on bits and pieces of history, have thought to avoid the necessity of larger periodizations have had imposed on them by academic convention a *wrong* periodization—namely, the sixteenth-century division of the past into "ancient," "medieval," and "modern" segments. No matter how specialized their fields, historians are in fact identified as working within one or more of these three traditional categories. They have to a certain extent rebelled against such identification by dividing "medieval" into the "Early Middle Ages" of the fifth to the eleventh century and "High Middle Ages" of the twelfth to the fifteenth century, and dividing "modern" into "early modern history" of the sixteenth and seventeenth centuries and "modern history" of the eighteenth century to the World Wars. It seems to have been forgotten that it was the sixteenth-century Lutherans who first popularized the terms "Middle Age" *(medium aevum, Mittelalter)* and "medieval" in order to characterize the period between early Christianity and themselves. The term was also congenial to humanists of that time, who used it to characterize the period between classical antiquity and themselves.[28] Today, however, it is wholly unclear what "the Middle Ages" are in the middle *of.*

Especially in speaking about the Western legal tradition, it is important to avoid the use of the anachronistic terms "Middle Ages" and "medieval" to refer to the pre-Protestant period of European history. The partisans of the Papal Revolution in fact referred to their own time as "modern,"[29] and it was their separation of the ecclesiastical and secular jurisdictions that resulted in the creation of the first modern legal systems. Also to be avoided is the eighteenth-century term "feudalism": there had, indeed, been feudal law, governing feudal military relations and feudal land tenure, but these had largely ceased to exist more than two centuries before the French Estates General declared in 1789 that "the feudal regime is abolished."[30] The oppressive aristocratic privileges against which the French bourgeoisie rebelled were, to be sure, survivals of a much earlier time when lord-vassal relations did exist. But even in that earlier time, "feudalism" had not prevailed in the thousands of European cities founded from the twelfth to the fourteenth century, nor did "feudalism" exist in the regime of the "medieval" church or in the flourishing world of "medieval" commerce.

Similarly, the term "Renaissance," or Rebirth, invented in the mid-nineteenth century to refer primarily to Italian literary, artistic, and scholarly movements of the late fifteenth and sixteenth centuries, is wholly misleading as a designation of the beginning of "modern" times. Both the great fourteenth-century artist Giotto and his contemporary the great writer Dante are now considered to be part of "the Renaissance." Indeed, books are now written on "the Renaissance of the twelfth century."[31]

The conventional periodizations reflect the view that the "modern" history of the West began with the transition from Roman Catholicism to Protestantism, from feudalism to capitalism, from scholasticism to humanism, and from a common culture to the diverse cultures of national states. Such a view cuts off "modern" Western history—and certainly the history of Western law—from its roots.

A new millennial history of the West, which traces the development of Western institutions from the eleventh to the twenty-first century, has in fact emerged in recent decades, inspired in part, as the present study is inspired, by the participation of Western civilization with other civilizations in the early stages of the development of a world economy and a multicultural world society. Economic historians in particular have written books to explain "the rise of the West" as a great economic power in the world, and have traced that rise partly to the commercial revolution in the eleventh and twelfth centuries and to subsequent revolutionary periods of rapid economic growth, and partly to the development of systems of law that facilitated such growth.[32]

Now that leading economic historians, taking a millennial view, have recognized that changes in legal institutions have played a key role in the economic development of the West, it remains for legal historians to show that changes in the belief system have played a key role in the development of those legal institutions. The context of such an inquiry is the emerging world society and an emerging world law. The West may export its technology to other cultures; may it similarly export its law? Can its legal tradition be received effectively in other cultures without the belief system on which that tradition is based? What changes in its legal tradition, and in its belief system, are needed to facilitate its participation in the formation, with other cultural traditions, of a new tradition of world law?

The present volume is intended not to give answers to those questions but rather to provide a necessary background for understanding the nature of the legal tradition that is to be, or not to be, shared, and the nature of the belief system on which it is based.

Early Protestant Belief Systems and the "Rise" of the West

Sixteenth- and seventeenth-century Protestant belief systems have had a mixed reception in the twentieth- and twenty-first-century scholarly literature of European history. On the one hand, they have been credited—or debited—with having facilitated the rise of (militant) nationalism, (rugged) individualism, (acquisitive) capitalism, and (rational) secularism. Both the political and economic "rise" of the West in the sixteenth and seventeenth centuries and its spiritual and moral "decline" in the twentieth and twenty-first centuries have been attributed to nationalist, individualist, capitalist, and secularist forces whose historical origins have been linked with Lutheran and Calvinist Protestantism. On the other hand, the positive contributions of Protestantism to the development of legal thought and legal institutions have been largely ignored.

A study of the impact of early Protestant Christianity on German and English law, respectively, and, more generally, on the Western legal tradition, can help to correct the fallacy implicit in attributing to its founders and early adherents the consequences of later modifications of their beliefs. Such a study will show that it was not the *-isms*—not national*ism,* individual*ism,* capital*ism,* secular*ism*—that were fostered by the Protestant vision of justice and order but rather national interests, individual responsibilities and opportunities, a market economy, and public spirit. And it was not the rise of Protestant Christianity in the sixteenth and seventeenth centuries but rather the decline of Protestant (as well as Roman Catholic) Christianity in the nineteenth and early twentieth centuries that led to the substitution of new *-isms,* new overriding faiths in the nation, the individual, the private accumulation of wealth, and the supremacy of rational calculation.

The thesis that early Protestantism, especially in its Calvinist form, had a decisive influence on the emergence of capitalism in the West was set forth most powerfully by Max Weber, the patron saint of twentieth-century social theory, who also forecast the demise of capitalism in the twentieth century and its replacement by a political and legal order committed to social welfare. Weber's book *The Protestant Ethic and the Spirit of Capitalism* has had a powerful influence on leading historians, sociologists, theologians, economists, political scientists, and jurists.[33] Literally hundreds of books and thousands of articles have been devoted to discussion of its argument. Despite widespread criticism of particular points, its main thesis is presented with approval in recent works on "the rise of the West."

It is appropriate to address Weber's thesis at the outset of this study, first because it sets forth conceptions both of early Protestant Christianity and of the spirit of early capitalist enterprise that are widely accepted but—as will be shown—are essentially false; and second, because those false conceptions can be exposed and corrected by analysis of values that were implicit in sixteenth- and seventeenth-century legal institutions—institutions that were virtually ignored, or else minimized, in Weber's analysis. Thus a rebuttal of Weber's thesis can serve as an introduction to some of the principal themes of this book.

Weber's argument, as one of its most knowledgeable critics observed, has been "widely misunderstood by friends and enemies alike." It is, indeed, very complex and very subtle. Weber did *not* say that "Protestantism" was a "cause" of "capitalism." He said, rather, that one form of Protestantism, namely, Calvinism, as found especially among seventeenth-century English Puritans, was congruent with, and supportive of, "the spirit"—a word which, in the original title of his book, he put in quotation marks for emphasis—of the bourgeois industrial capitalism that *later* emerged in Europe. Moreover, Weber's view of English Calvinism's congruence with, and support of, the capitalist spirit was itself complex and subtle, for he defined the spirit of capitalism as consisting of an overriding desire on the part of individual capitalist entrepreneurs to acquire great wealth, while at the same time he acknowledged that English Calvinists denounced such a desire as sinful worship of Mammon. This paradox was resolved, he argued, by the Calvinist doctrine of predestination, according to which, first, God has chosen only a small proportion of the human race to receive eternal salvation, and second, God's decision to send an individual person to ultimate damnation or ultimate salvation is wholly beyond the ability of humanity either to comprehend or to influence. The Calvinist believer was thus placed, Weber wrote, in a state of terrifying uncertainty as to whether he was chosen to be one of the damned or one of the elect. In that situation, his only hope consisted in the fact that if he conscientiously carried out the vocation to which (as he believed) God had called him, then God might grant him great success in that calling, and if God did so bless him with great success, then that would be some evidence, a sign, though no more than a sign, that God had placed him among the elect. It was this belief, Weber contended, that motivated the Calvinist entrepreneur, called to undertake business enterprise, to seek to acquire great wealth. Whereas Roman Catholicism, in Weber's view, disparaged such a worldly desire and sought salvation, above all, in "otherworldly asceticism" ("ausserweltliche Askese"), and Lutheranism, in Weber's view, also sought salvation, above all, through otherworldly faith, Calvinism alone, in his view, prized what he called "this-worldly asceticism" ("innerweltliche Askese"), which was the dedication of the individual to his secular calling. In the case of the capitalist entrepreneur, that calling was "the earning of more and more money, combined with the strict avoidance of all spontaneous enjoyment of life,"[34] in the hope that the inscrutable will of God would bless and reward him with worldly success, and in the belief that such blessing and reward would be a sign that he was one of God's elect, one of the chosen few.

Weber's argument is further complicated by his view that it was not the mid-seventeenth-century English Puritan Calvinists who preached the pursuit of wealth but rather the eighteenth-century rationalist proponents of free enterprise; indeed, it was certain sayings of the eighteenth-century American Deist Benjamin Franklin—hardly a Calvinist—advocating parsimony for the sake of material aggrandizement that Weber quoted early in his essay to illustrate "the spirit of capitalism."[35] Moreover, it was only in the nineteenthcentury, in Weber's view, that the capitalism of which he spoke, namely, "bourgeois industrial capitalism," came into being—motivated by the eighteenth-century "spirit" which was in turn founded on the seventeenth-century "Protestant ethic." Indeed, in the light of Weber's view that the eighteenth-century Enlightenment, the French Revolution, and British utilitarianism were immediate ideological progenitors of nineteenth-century bourgeois industrial capitalism, his essay should perhaps have been titled "*The Decline* of the Protestant Ethic and the Spirit of Capitalism."

One may nevertheless agree that Calvinism did in fact contribute to the capitalist spirit without accepting Weber's problematic theory of the effect of the doctrine of predestination on the motivation of capitalist entrepreneurs. One may also agree that the effort on the part of entrepreneurs to maximize profits is indeed an important aspect of the capitalist spirit without accepting

Weber's premise that such effort is primarily motivated by the overwhelming desire of individuals to acquire great wealth.

It was not, in fact, Calvinist doctrines of salvation that fostered the spirit of entrepreneurial activity in the seventeenth and eighteenth centuries but rather Calvinist doctrines of the nature of the Christian community—in technical theological terms, not Calvinist soteriology but Calvinist ecclesiology. The Calvinist—and Lutheran—belief in the unity and fellowship of the congregation of believers supported the formation of close-knit covenanted God-centered communities. In fact, both Lutheranism and Calvinism, contrary to the conventional view of contemporary social theorists, were strongly communitarian. The individual, Luther wrote, is a "private person" in his relation to God but a social person in relation to "the three estates"—the family, the church, and the ruling high magistracy *(Obrigkeit)*. Both the Lutheran congregation, headed by the pastor, and the Calvinist congregation, led by its elders, were close-knit, self-governing "covenanted" fellowships. The Christian doctrine of divine covenants—solemn agreements—between God and God's people, on the one hand, and, on the other hand, among members of the Christian community in their various callings was shared by both Lutherans and Calvinists, but was stressed particularly by Calvinists. Similarly, sixteenth- and seventeenth-century economic enterprise—not yet "bourgeois" and not yet "industrial"—was basically communitarian, not individualistic, and certainly not "ascetic."[36]

A striking example of seventeenth-century capitalist communitarianism is the invention of the joint-stock company as a means of bringing investors together to engage in a common cause, often of political as well as economic significance. Thus a 1692 act of Parliament granting a corporate charter to a Company of Merchants of London to carry on trade with Greenland recited the great importance of such trade, how it had fallen into the hands of other nations, and the need to regain it by the joint efforts of many persons.[37] Similar recitals of a public purpose marked the corporate charters of other joint-stock companies. These were, to be sure, entrepreneurial activities intended to be profitable to the shareholders. At the same time, the enterprise depended on the close cooperation of many like-minded people, who were motivated partly by a desire to participate with others in a joint venture serving a public cause. Nothing is more symbolic of the "spirit of capitalism" in England in the late seventeenth century than the creation of the joint-stock company called the Bank of England, which was founded by act of Parliament in 1694 principally in order to finance the government's war against France. Under the act, commissioners were appointed by the Crown to receive subscriptions, and the Crown was empowered to incorporate "subscribers and contributors, their heirs, successors, or assigns, to be one body politick and corporate."[38] Shareholders were required to identify their collective interests with the welfare of the English economy. Subscribers included many members of Parliament. Of the first twenty-six members of the Court of Directors, six subsequently became Lord Mayors of London. The bylaws of the bank required the Court of Directors to meet every week and the General Court of the shareholders to meet twice a year "for considering the general state and condition of this Corporation and for the making of dividends . . . according to their several shares."[39]

The late seventeenth century also witnessed the creation of another important legal institution that served communitarian as well as individual purposes, namely, the modern English (and American) law of trusts. Like the joint-stock company, the trust device, whereby the use of investments by owners of capital is controlled by trustees committed to carrying out equitably the purposes for which the investments were made, facilitated the formation of both business and charitable associations embracing numerous members in common endeavors.

These examples should suffice to establish that had Weber considered legal developments in seventeenth-century England, his thesis would have had to be quite different. When one looks at the lawyers and the institutions they were creating, one does not see ascetic individualists trembling before the prospect of ultimate damnation or salvation. Rather, one sees community-minded men creating communitarian legal institutions such as joint-stock companies, bank credits, and the trust device. They understood that the success of a market economy rests on trust, on credit, on common enterprise, not, as many later came to believe, on personal greed. This communitarianism, involving large-scale cooperation among landed gentry and merchant elites, itself had deep Calvinist roots. The spirit of Weber's capitalism in the seventeenth and early eighteenth centuries was the product not, as he thought, of "secular asceticism" but of what was called at the time public spirit, which, in turn, reflected not the individualist doctrines of predestination and calling but the collectivist Calvinist doctrines of covenant and covenanted communities.

Weber's failure—in his analysis of both Protestantism and capitalism—to consider legal values such as those implicit in corporate structures, in the trust device, in the rules for establishing and regulating charitable organizations, or, indeed, in the constitutional law governing both religious and commercial associations, was due in part to the sharp distinction that he made in all his works between facts and values, coupled with his relegation of law to the realm of facts. In his copious writings on the sociology of law, Weber defined law as rules and procedures laid down and enforced by the state in order to bring about compliance with its will. He repeatedly traced the derivation of legal institutions to political domination. The different "ideal types" of legal systems that he detected in various cultures and various historical periods were conceived by him as sources of legitimation of political authority whereby coercion could be more effectively exerted. He classified the English common law of the seventeenth and eighteenth centuries, with its emphasis on judicial precedents, as a type of "traditionalist" law, as contrasted with the "formal-rational" type of law characteristic of nineteenth-century France and Germany, with its emphasis on codification; yet he classified Calvinism of the same period as "anti-traditionalist" and congenial to, and supportive of, the rationalism that he associated with the spirit of capitalism, without taking into account that the English Calvinist Puritans fought a civil war partly to establish the supremacy of the "traditionalist" common law.

Despite Weber's genius in classifying "ideal types" of political and legal systems, and despite his enormous erudition, his misunderstanding of religion (indeed, his wife said of him that he was "religiously unmusical"),[40] and especially of sixteenth- and seventeenth-century Lutheran and Calvinist Protestantism in Germany and England, respectively, was coupled with a misunderstanding of the legal developments that took place in those countries during those centuries, and in both cases this was due to the fallacy of his sharp separation of fact from value and of his strict positivist view of law as fact alone and as primarily an instrument of political coercion.

Subsequent chapters will present in more detail the changes in law that facilitated the economic changes that were part of the German and English Revolutions, including the relationship of those economic and legal changes to the change from Roman Catholic to Protestant Christianity. In contrast to Weberian social theory, a more positive view is taken here of the ultimate impact of the two Great Revolutions on the systems of order and justice that emerged from them. Each Revolution, to be sure, was marked by violence, destruction, bigotry, persecution, oppression, and gross injustices. Yet each eventually ended, after two generations, with a settlement that reconciled some of the utopian visions of the original revolutionists with some of the traditions against which they had originally revolted. Each transformed the Western legal tradition, but each eventually remained within it.

I

THE GERMAN REVOLUTION AND THE TRANSFORMATION OF GERMAN LAW IN THE SIXTEENTH CENTURY

CHAPTER 1

The Reformation of the Church and of the State, 1517–1555

Viewed as a political event, and in its simplest formulation, the German Revolution was the successful fight of territorial princes of Germany against the pope and the German emperor for the right to establish the Lutheran faith and to be the supreme rulers in their principalities.

What made this a Great Revolution was, of course, much more than that. Not only territorial princes together with their councilors and other high officials—the *Obrigkeit,* or "high magistracy," as they were collectively called—but also mayors and councilors and other officials of free cities within the territories led the violent struggle against papal and imperial power and authority. The Revolution not only outlawed the Roman Catholic Church in Protestant principalities, with massive expropriation of church property, but also established therein unitary secular states with integrated legal systems. Both the clergy and the nobility were subordinated to a new type of monarchy. Also in principalities that remained Roman Catholic, the power and the jurisdiction of the princes was measurably increased.

Moreover, the political reformation, or reformation of the state, even when viewed in such broad terms, was only one aspect of the German Revolution. At least equally important was the religious reformation, the reformation of the church. In Germany these two types of radical change coalesced. The revolt of princely and urban authorities against papal and imperial power became wholly intertwined with Luther's prior call for reformation of the church from within. The two reformations became two sides of the same coin.

Yet even the combined reformations of church and state do not exhaust the full dimensions of the Revolution. Not just the high magistracy, and not just the religious leaders, but the whole population was involved, directly or indirectly, in civil war: the city merchants and artisans, the peasants, the mine workers, various ranks of the nobility, various ranks of the clergy, the lawyers, the intellectuals, and others. There was a social-economic reformation, a cultural and intellectual reformation, and a reformation of the entire legal order.

Finally, both the reformation of the church and the reformation of the state were not only German events. The German Revolution was also a European Revolution. Prior to its outbreak, the cry for reformation both of the church and of the state had been heard throughout Europe for over a century. While reforming efforts of the German territorial princes had been largely frustrated, in Spain the ecclesiastical hierarchy itself, under the control and with the support of powerful royal rulers, had been able to introduce substantial reforms, some of which anticipated changes later adopted by the German Lutherans. And after the outbreak of the Revolution in Germany, Protestantism and monarchical hegemony, together or separately, spread to other European countries. Moreover, the Roman Catholic Church, outlawed in Protestant principalities, itself underwent its own Reformation, later sometimes called the Counter-Reformation.

Thus when one speaks of the German Revolution, one must have in mind a total upheaval, a "turning around" of a whole people and a whole culture. The Revolution constituted a lasting transformation of the very nature of the German people, both collectively and individually, and not only of the German people but also eventually of Western society as a whole.

Yet in telling the story it is useful to start with the simplest formulation, and to ask, Who and what were the princes? What was Germany? Who and what was the emperor? Who and what was the pope? Who was Luther and what was Lutheranism?

Germany: Empire (*Reich*) and Territories (*Länder*)

Germany in 1500 was the largest country in Europe, both in area and in population, with approximately 12 million souls.[1] It consisted of several hundred secular and ecclesiastical territories, called "lands," and some dozens of free cities, within a very loose imperial structure that in the twelfth century had for the first time been called "the Roman Empire," in the thirteenth century "the Holy Roman Empire," and in the fifteenth century the "Holy Roman Empire of the German Nation." The reference to the "German Nation" was added in order to designate the German part of a larger, loosely knit imperial domain which at various times also included northern Italy (Lombardy), the Netherlands, Burgundy (Franche-Comté), and Spain and Portugal.

When it was founded by Charlemagne—prior to his coronation by the bishop of Rome in 800—the empire was not called Roman at all but sometimes the Empire of the Franks and sometimes the Christian Empire. After the division of the empire among Charlemagne's three grandsons, the title of emperor descended to the ruler of the eastern Franks, who were eventually called *teutonici*, or *deutsche*. The English call them "Germans." The French call them "Alemans." The Russians call them "Nemtsy," meaning "not us." The Italians call them—properly—"Tedeschi," the Italian word for "Deutsche."[2]

In the early eleventh century the practice was instituted of giving to the heir selected to be the future emperor the title "King of the Romans" (instead of "King of the Franks"), and after the emperor's death that son would normally proceed to Rome to be crowned by the pope as "Emperor of the Romans." This practice symbolized, above all, the Frankish emperor's claim to the theocratic authority of the Roman emperor Constantine and his successors, as vicar of Christ and head of the church. After papal supremacy was established in the late eleventh and early twelfth centuries, and the pope assumed for the first time the title of vicar of Christ,[3] the word "Roman" in the titles "King of the Romans" and "Roman Empire" no longer symbolized the emperor's theocratic claims but rather his authority in the secular sphere. Yet even more than other European monarchs, the Holy Roman Emperor also continued to assert religious authority as supreme protector of the church within his realm.

The empire had no capital city and no permanent officials. Until 1495 it had no professional court of law. The emperor had no power to tax his subjects but had to raise his revenues from his own estates, which were scattered throughout the empire. Although he was overlord of the rulers of the various constituent territories of the empire, he became, in the late eleventh and twelfth centuries, dependent on the dukes and other leading princes for his election. By the end of the twelfth century, it was established that emperors were to be chosen by an electoral college of ecclesiastical and secular princes, in which the archbishops of Mainz, Cologne, and Trier and the Count Palatine of the Rhineland had preferred places. To these four "prince-electors" were eventually added three others, the duke of Saxony, the king of Bohemia, and the margrave of Brandenburg.

In the course of the early twelfth to early sixteenth centuries, the empire developed new political and legal institutions and went through several phases of comparatively greater strength and weakness. As supreme judge of the empire, the emperor on his travels heard appeals against judgments of courts of princes and noblemen as well as of city courts. He also had the right to summon the great princes, both secular and ecclesiastical, as well as the leading knights, and representatives of the imperial cities, to participate in deliberative assemblies, called "imperial days" or "diets" (from the Latin *dies,* "day"; in German, *Tag, Reichstag*), which became regularized in the thirteenth century. The periodic assemblies of notables symbolized a political structure in which power was divided among various estates *(Stände):* higher clergy and lesser clergy, higher nobility and lesser nobility, leading merchants and other urban notables ("burghers"). Especially in the twelfth and thirteenth centuries, the emperors, through imperial diets, promulgated new laws, often under the title of a "land peace" *(pax terrae, Landfriede).* Despite weak enforcement machinery, these imperial laws had validity and often penetrated the territorial law of the duchies and other principalities as well as the law of the cities.[4]

Both imperial power and imperial law gradually declined in the thirteenth, fourteenth, and early fifteenth centuries, while the power and law of the German principalities continued to grow increasingly strong. This did not mean that there was no Germany. There were, in the first place, the elements of a common German customary language, though the various German tribal groups, or "stems" *(Stämme),* spoke different dialects of that language. There was a common vernacular literature, especially of epic and lyric poetry.[5] There was, moreover, a common German law. That law was represented, in part, in the *Sachsenspiegel* (Mirror of the Saxons), a book written in about 1220 by a Saxon lawyer named Eike von Repgau (ca. 1180–ca. 1235), who first wrote the book in Latin and then translated it into German. It was a systematic collection of concisely stated legal principles and legal rules, which in a modern edition takes up approximately 240 pages. The subject matter was chiefly the customary local and feudal law of Saxony and the royal law of the German emperor. It concerned property and inheritance law, criminal law, the judicial system, constitutional law, and lord-vassal relations. Very early the *Sachsenspiegel* came to have a quasi-official validity throughout the German-speaking territories. It was glossed by learned jurists. The *Frankenspiegel* (Mirror of the Franks), *Schwabenspiegel* (Mirror of the Swabians), and other authoritative "mirrors" of the law were written in imitation of it.[6]

Germany was also held together by a common law of the German cities. In the eleventh to fifteenth centuries, many hundreds of new cities were founded in Germany, and certain ones among them became famous quite early for their legal institutions and their written collections of laws. New cities would adopt the laws of the older cities. Thus the laws of Magdeburg, dating from the twelfth century, were received in over eighty new cities, the laws of Lübeck were received in forty-three cities, those of Frankfurt in forty-nine, of Freiburg in nineteen, of Munich in thirteen. Typically, the newly founded "daughter city" would send for the laws of the "mother city," whose leading judicial officers would prepare a new edition of them. Also the courts of the daughter city would often submit individual cases to the judges of the mother city in order to obtain declarations of the rules applicable to the particular fact situations. In this sense, although each city had its own laws, one may speak of a pan-German urban type of law, which, although portions of it were written, was (like the law contained in the *Sachsenspiegel*) largely customary law.[7] Of course, the customs of one city differed from the customs of another, and these differences tended to increase over generations and centuries, as did the differences in the largely customary law systems of the principalities and other polities. Yet there remained important common features and, at the very least, a common political and legal culture.

Thus Germany—Deutschland—in the year 1500 constituted a nation, a people, though not a nation-state. It was held together not only by bonds of language and literature and customary law but also by ethnic bonds as well as by many common cultural characteristics. It shared a common historical consciousness of its past and a sense of a common future. Though not politically, yet culturally, ethnically, and legally, it was surely no less united in the year 1500 than only slightly less populous France or Italy.

In addition to being governed by imperial law, territorial law, and urban law, Germany, like the rest of Western Christendom, was also governed by the canon law of the Roman Catholic Church. The sources of the canon law were the body of judicial decisions, learned legal writings, and legislation of the Church of Rome, including papal court decisions (called decretals), Gratian's authoritative treatise (the *Decretum*) and other treatises and collections, and canons of church councils and popes. The canon law was applied in bishops' courts throughout the West; everywhere it was called *jus commune*—"common law"—although occasional local variations of the canon law were sometimes called *lex terrae,* "law of the [particular] land," or *lex propria,* "particular law." The jurisdiction claimed by the Roman Catholic Church—not always successfully—extended to all matters affecting the clergy and church property as well as to many matters directly affecting the laity, such as schooling, poor relief and other forms of charity, marriage and support of family members, spiritual crimes such as heresy, witchcraft, sex offenses, and immoral lifestyle generally, as well as contracts and other arrangements in which the parties pledged their faith. Canon law covered all these and other matters. Laymen would often voluntarily submit their contract, property, and tort disputes to ecclesiastical courts to be settled according to canon law.[8] In the fourteenth and fifteenth centuries the church courts in Germany probably had a wider jurisdiction and played a more important role than in any other country of Europe with the possible exception of England.

A good deal of the terminology and some of the rules of canon law were derived from the Roman law texts of the sixth-century Eastern Roman emperor Justinian, as glossed and commented on and systematized by European scholars from the late eleventh century on. The learned Roman law had also come to be called "common law," *jus commune,* applicable throughout the West. In contrast to canon law, however, Roman law was largely an academic discipline taught in the universities; it could be drawn on to fill gaps in the prevailing law, and some of its principles were adopted in legislation and judicial decisions, but—with a few exceptions—it was subsidiary to the enacted and customary law of both the ecclesiastical and secular polities.

Though united by imperial law, by a common customary law, and by the canon law of the church, as well as by a common religious faith and the elements of a common popular language and literature, Germany was divided politically into a very large number of individual territorial units, ranging from large and powerful principalities, some of them comparable in size and population to the Netherlands, down to small counties (*Grafschaften,* "count-doms") sometimes comprising only a few hundred people. There were also numerous ecclesiastical polities of diverse sizes, as well as many free cities. Thus in the year 1521, the Holy Roman Empire of the German Nation consisted, in hierarchical order, of the emperor, the seven prince-electors, 50 archbishops and bishops, 83 ecclesiastical prelates (chiefly abbots and abbesses), 31 secular princes, 138 counts and lords, and representatives of 85 imperial free cities—almost 400 political jurisdictions in all.[9]

In the twelfth to fifteenth centuries, many of the individual German territorial principalities, both secular and ecclesiastical, had developed quite sophisticated political and legal institutions, comparable to the royal law of England, France, or the Norman kingdom of Sicily.[10] They had established professional central judicial tribunals as well as central chanceries and treasuries, with permanent staffs of officials. A modern system of criminal and civil law, with a trial procedure based on so-called rational proofs, as contrasted with earlier so-called formal proofs by ordeals and oath-helping, had been introduced alongside customary legal institutions adapted from Germanic tribal institutions. Like the canon law of the church, the developing law of the German territories during the fourteenth and fifteenth centuries drew increasingly on the terminology and concepts of the scholarly Roman law, especially as German jurists returned from studying at Italian and French universities and as Roman law, like canon law, came to be taught in universities newly established in Germany itself.[11]

In broadest outline, the political-legal structure of Germany in the year 1500 was essentially similar to that which had emerged throughout Europe after the Papal Revolution. It was based on the dualism of ecclesiastical and secular jurisdictions and on the pluralism of jurisdictions within the secular sphere. It was based also on hierarchy within each type of polity. This political-legal model had survived for four centuries. There were, to be sure, severe tensions within it. One was the increasing competition between the ecclesiastical and the secular powers—aggravated in Germany by the dual role of the emperor as overlord of all his imperial subjects, on the one hand, and spiritual ally of the pope, on the other. Another was the increasing competition between royalty and feudal nobility—aggravated in Germany, again, by the competition between the emperor and the princes. With the election of Emperor Maximilian I in 1493, there was an expansion of imperial power and jurisdiction that threatened to reduce further the autonomy of various princely rulers in the hierarchy of which the emperor was the head. A diet called by Maximilian in 1495 issued a *Landfriede* declaring for the first time that the Roman law was to be the official positive secular law of the empire—though not of the separate territorial principalities and non-imperial cities within the empire—and establishing for the first time an imperial court to apply that law and to hear appeals from princely courts and from courts of imperial cities in the limited number of cases governed by imperial law.[12]

Portents of Change

Maximilian's empire was so large and diverse, and the military and political challenges to his ambitions were so great, that it was impossible for him to maintain more than a weak central control over the German principalities. He had inherited from his father the Hapsburg possessions in Austria, and in addition he had acquired through marriage the duchy of Burgundy, which at that time included Flanders and Holland. Much of his reign was spent in external wars defending Burgundian interests in the Netherlands and Hapsburg interests in Italy against attack by kings of France. These wars were not popular with the German territorial princes, who were continually solicited for funds to support Maximilian's military campaigns.

The imperial realm of influence became even more enlarged after Maximilian's death in 1519, when his grandson Charles was elected emperor. The nineteen-year-old Charles V inherited not only Maximilian's lands but also, through his mother, Spain and southern Italy. Charles set out to reestablish the concept of the Christian unity of Europe under papal and imperial leadership—a concept that had been in almost continual decline since the mid-fourteenth century. Yet he, too, was deeply involved in military engagements—again, chiefly against France. The fact that he had been brought up in the Burgundian court and spoke German with a foreign accent only aggravated the political and economic tensions between the imperial and the princely authorities within the German part of the empire.

Another and even greater source of tension within the empire was the increasing competition between the Roman Catholic hierarchy and the secular princes. This was especially acute because the territorial jurisdiction of an archbishop or bishop normally included portions of more than one secular territory. Indeed, in the duchy of the prince-elector of Saxony, at least six different bishops exercised jurisdiction both over portions of the duchy and over portions of other territories. In other words, each bishop, while directly subordinate to the pope in certain matters and to the emperor in others, at the same time exercised a concurrent jurisdiction with the various secular rulers whose territories his bishopric overlapped.[13] Moreover the church, which owned something like one-third of the land of Germany, was exempt from secular taxation. Thus the princes had cause to dislike both ecclesiastical power and ecclesiastical wealth. At the same time, the lay population was subjected to onerous financial exactions by the church. Indeed, resentment against ecclesiastical abuses was easily transferable to the imperial authority, which was closely identified with the Roman Catholic hierarchy, since the Holy Roman Emperor, despite his defeat in the Papal Revolution of the late eleventh and early twelfth centuries, had retained a sacred mission within the Roman Catholic Church.

A similar tension prevailed in the German cities and towns, which typically were governed by a mayor and a city council drawn from among the leading citizens. The patrician rulers were generally not disposed to welcome radical change. At the same time, they were not unsympathetic, nor were the merchants and artisans and the urban poor, to efforts to reduce economic and political pressures imposed by papal power, although they also often looked to emperors and popes for protection against princely expansion.

Tensions between the secular and the ecclesiastical authorities were greatly aggravated by campaigns of the papacy to raise money through the sale of so-called indulgences. The pope claimed the power to intercede with God on behalf of sinners in order to remit punishments that otherwise would be inflicted upon them in purgatory after death, and, since 1476, not only upon them but also upon their deceased loved ones.[14] Indulgences had been granted in special circumstances ever since the First Crusade at the end of the eleventh century, but in the fourteenth and fifteenth centuries they became a crude form of taxation imposed not by physical but by spiritual coercion. The money was considered "a good work of almsgiving" to be credited against the church's "treasury of merits."[15] Although the sale of indulgences was also carried on in the other countries of Europe, Germany was considered an especially fertile soil for it. As Martin Luther asked, in denouncing papal "robberies and extortions," "Why do we Germans let them make such fools and apes of us?"[16]

Thus in the year 1500 tensions between the supreme ruler and his subordinate nobility, as well as between the ecclesiastical and the secular authorities, were more acute in Germany than in France, England, Spain, the Netherlands, and other parts of the West. Everywhere in Europe, however, royal power over the feudal nobility was increasing, secular authority was asserting itself against ecclesiastical authority, and territorial loyalties were intensifying. Everywhere in Europe strong voices were advocating reduction of ecclesiastical power and reformation of both church and state. Everywhere the cities were seeking greater autonomy.

Indeed, for at least three generations the entire West had lived in a prerevolutionary state. In the early part of the sixteenth century, the religious revolts of the Lollards, still active in England for over a century after the death in 1384 of their original leader, John Wyclif, were ruthlessly repressed,[17] as were those of the Hussites, who continued to fight in Bohemia for more than two generations after the execution of Jan Hus in 1415.[18] Paradoxically, it was by order of the Council of Constance of 1415, the first of a series of church councils that sought to decentralize power and authority within the church and to relax the rigidities of Roman Catholic dogma, that Hus was burned at the stake. Subsequent church councils, in which German princes, among others, expressed grievances against ecclesiastical policy, were also unsuccessful. In the latter decades of the fifteenth century and first years of the sixteenth, the Spanish Inquisition constituted a virtual reign of terror among professed Christian converts from Judaism and Islam, and the campaign by northern humanists—Erasmus was the most famous among them—for more humane and more liberal ecclesiastical policies encountered sharp resistance from a notoriously corrupt papacy.[19]

In Germany demands for reformation came not only from prophets and humanists but also from secular rulers. As early as 1438, a widely circulated pamphlet purporting to represent reform plans of the emperor Sigismund, titled "The Reformation of Sigismund," proposed thoroughgoing changes, both secular and ecclesiastical.[20] Although it was revised and republished many times in the fifteenth century, little came of it. To be sure, many cities adopted far-reaching legal reforms, called "reformations," which had the effect, in part, of rationalizing the law of commerce and also expanding secular authority against ecclesiastical.[21] These reforms did not, however, meet the real grievances of most classes of the people. Peasants in various regions revolted sporadically without success. Vagabonds, beggars, and robbers roamed the highways, and crime was rampant. Urban commercial interests exerted a certain economic and social pressure on the depressed knightly class, which itself eventually rose up in revolt—again, without success. Everywhere the church was increasingly on the defensive. But everywhere it resisted fundamental reform.

In hindsight one can see that things were building for an explosion. This was also recognized by many at the time. None of the advocates of reform, however, prior to Luther, addressed the crucial problem of the time, namely, in Myron Gilmore's words, "the secular world could no longer derive its ultimate meaning from the tasks set for it by the Church of Rome."[22]

This, indeed, was the revolutionary situation: that the apocalyptic vision of the Papal Revolution had failed, and that the political and legal order, whose inner tensions had produced an overwhelming pressure for fundamental reform, was inherently incapable of accomplishing that reform. That was especially true in Germany, where the tensions between the secular and the ecclesiastical authorities were greater than in other parts of Europe.

Luther and the Pope: The Reformation of the Church

The spark that ignited the German Revolution was struck in 1517 by a thirty-four-year-old theology professor at the University of Wittenberg, the Augustinian monk Martin Luther. Very soon, many outstanding persons joined him and in some instances rivaled him. Nevertheless, until his death in 1546, Luther remained the chief spiritual and intellectual leader of both the reformation of the church and the reformation of the state in Germany. The extraordinary role played by Luther himself in the revolutionary movement may be explained partly in terms of the doctrines he taught and partly in terms of the ways in which he represented those doctrines in his own life.

Lutheranism

The attack on clerical abuses, including the sale of indulgences, constituted only the surface of the Lutheran Reformation. Indeed, such abuses had been widely condemned for over a century. The earlier condemnation, however, was intended to move the existing authorities to effectuate the required changes. After the suppression of the Hussites and the Wycliffites, the persistent calls for reformations were largely calls for moral, legal, and administrative reforms within the church and within the secular realm—within, that is, the operation of the "two swords" theory of the Roman Catholic Church as it had been proclaimed by Pope Gregory VII. A few other voices, such as that of Marsilius of Padua (1275–1342), had called for the subordination of the Church of Rome to the secular power.[23] Luther, on the contrary, called not merely for the reform of the Roman Catholic hierarchy, or for additional limitations on its authority, but for its abolition.

Luther addressed the question of ecclesiastical authority directly and in the most radical terms by demanding an end to the entire ecclesiastical jurisdiction, its entire legislative, judicial, and administrative power. That was the underlying significance of the Ninety-five Theses which in 1517 he sent to the archbishop of Mainz and also posted on the door of the prince-elector of Saxony's castle church in Wittenberg: they not only attacked indulgences and other abuses of papal authority but also denied the necessity of any third person to administer penance. No priest, Luther wrote, is authorized to come between God and the individual human soul that seeks forgiveness for sins.[24] The implication was there, and was soon articulated by Luther and others, that the mediation of a priesthood is not necessary to administer other sacraments as well. Indeed, no priest, Luther later wrote, is authorized to promulgate the laws by which Christians should live. The true church is not a lawmaking institution. It is, rather, the invisible community of all believers, in which all are priests, serving one another, and each is a "private person" in his relation to God. Each responds directly to the Bible as the Word of God.[25]

Luther replaced the Gregorian two swords theory—that the spiritual and secular powers, church and state, interact with each other—with a new "two kingdoms" theory. The church, he taught, belongs to the heavenly kingdom of grace and faith; it is governed by the Gospel. The earthly kingdom, the kingdom of "this world," is the kingdom of sin and death; it is governed by the Law. Luther considered this doctrine to be revolutionary. "Of this difference between Law and Gospel," he wrote, "there is nothing to be found in the books of the ancient fathers. Augustine did somewhat understand this difference and showed it. Jerome and others knew it not."[26]

Thus Luther's doctrine withdrew from the church its character as a sword-wielding entity—a visible, corporate, hierarchical, political and legal community. Instead, the church was to be a purely spiritual community, part of the heavenly realm of peace, joy, grace, salvation, and glory. This concept of the church was based on the pivotal doctrine of "justification"—that is, becoming "just," or "righteous," in the sight of God—by faith alone, and thereby qualifying for God's free gift of salvation. Luther denied that a person could work his way, so to speak, into the heavenly kingdom. Nothing that a person *does* can "save" him, that is, can make him acceptable to God. Man's fallen nature, his essential selfishness, penetrates everything he does—indeed, everything he thinks (his reason) and everything he wants (his will). His "depravity" is "total." Therefore salvation—in this life as in the next—is only by grace, which is bestowed only on those who have faith. For this, no mediation by a priesthood is needed, or possible. Just as salvation is by faith alone, so the church is a community of faith, without legal powers. And faith itself, in Lutheran theology, is a "passive" virtue, freely given by the grace of God to those he has chosen, his "elect."

The paradox of salvation by the grace of God for those who, by reason of their inherent sinfulness, are unworthy of salvation is at the heart of Luther's theology. Roman Catholic doctrine of the twelfth through the fifteenth centuries had taught a fundamentally optimistic view of human will and human reason: despite man's sinfulness, his will and reason were thought to remain capable of obtaining a "natural"—though not a "supernatural"—perfectibility. Further, Roman Catholicism taught that through Christian baptism, humanity's "original sin"—that is, Adam's rebelliousness against God, transmitted to succeeding generations—is forgiven, and although individuals remain responsible for the "actual sins" committed in the exercise of their free will, nevertheless they can, by faith *and* good works, and by the sacrament of penance, attain some measure at least of divine forgiveness. In that sacrament, the priest is invested with divine authority to prescribe penitential works through which the baptized Christian can be purged of his actual sins and thus be spared eternal damnation. Luther and his associates, by contrast, taught that baptism, although it brought faithful people, whether adults or infants, into the church and thus made them ready for salvation, cannot automatically cancel their inherent depravity. Forgiveness of sins can be granted only through a direct confrontation between the repentant sinner and God, by divine grace, without rules and procedures.

Indeed, humankind, in Luther's view, is wholly incapable of lifting itself out of its fallen state. This part of Lutheran theology, which is perhaps the hardest for post-Enlightenment Western society to accept, was in fact what appealed most to early-sixteenth-century European Christendom, with its daily experience of oppression, corruption, and wretchedness, coupled with a moral doctrine that had come to appear unrealistically optimistic.

Superficially understood, Luther's doctrine seems to take an entirely negative view of the earthly kingdom. It is a realm of sin and death, and there is no way out of it by exercise of will or reason. Politics and law are not a path to grace and faith. But are not grace and faith a path to the right politics and the right law? Here Luther was torn between his belief in man's essential wickedness and his belief that that wickedness itself, and the earthly realm which embodies it, are ordained by God. It was an essential tenet of the Lutheran doctrine of creation that sinful man is a creature of God and that God is present, though hidden, in the earthly realm. The Lutheran reformers taught that it is the duty of Christians "to work the work of God in the world," and to use their will and reason—however defective—to do as much good and to attain as much understanding as possible. The doctrine of the presence of a hidden God even in the sinfulness of humanity is an essential part of what might otherwise be considered the moral pessimism of Lutheran thought. "God himself ordained and established this temporal realm and its distinctions," Luther wrote, "[and] we must remain and work in them so long as we are on earth."[27]

Closely connected with the Lutheran doctrine of the two kingdoms were the twin doctrines of the priesthood of all believers and of universal Christian callings. Having abolished the special priestly jurisdiction and the traditional Roman Catholic distinction between a higher clergy and a lower laity, the Lutheran Reformers transferred to each individual believer the responsibility to minister to others—to pray for them, to instruct them, to serve them. In that sense, all believers were said to be priests. Likewise, the Lutheran Reformers replaced the Roman Catholic doctrine of calling, or vocation, which attached that term to the "spiritually perfect," primarily the monastic and priestly professions, with the doctrine that every occupation in which a Christian engages should be treated as a calling *(Beruf, vocatio)* of God. Both the carpenter and the prince, the housewife and the judge, should accept the Christian responsibility to perform their tasks conscientiously and in the service of others. Public officials, in particular, were said to have a special calling to serve the community. This calling might require them to adopt a Christian social ethic that differed from a Christian personal ethic. A Christian's duty in his direct relationship with God, "as a private person, a person for himself alone," is to love his enemy and to suffer injustice and abuse from his neighbor without resistance and without revenge. As a "public person," serving in such offices as the military, the judiciary, or the legal profession, a Christian may be required to resist his neighbor and to avenge injustice even to the point of violence and bloodshed.[28]

Luther and his followers applied this doctrine, above all, in their theory of the Christian prince: the Christian prince should be inspired to govern in a decent and godly way, promoting the well-being of his subjects.[29] This was interpreted to mean that as a ruler in the earthly kingdom, he had to recognize that "there should be no tolerance shown toward any injustice, but rather a defense against wrong and a punishment of it, and an effort to defend and maintain the right, according to what each one's office or station may require."[30]

The Lutheran concept of the prince, rooted in the theological doctrine of vocation and office, was essentially different from that of Luther's famous contemporary, Niccolò Machiavelli (1469–1527). Machiavelli also believed in the secular state, removed from divine law; in that respect he too can be said to have had a "two kingdoms" theory. But Machiavelli's prince was to act solely from considerations of power politics, whereas Luther's prince was to strive also to do justice. Machiavelli's prince was to foster religion as a means of keeping his people satisfied, united, and loyal. Luther's prince was to be guided by religion in regulating relationships between him and his subjects as well as their relationships to one another. The German Lutherans of the sixteenth century did not accept the Machiavellian view that makes selfishness and the struggle for power the basic principle of political action. They were unwilling to abandon the earthly kingdom to its own Satanic devices.[31] In this respect they continued the older Roman Catholic tradition, though from a different theological and philosophical perspective.

The Lutheran concept of the prince was also essentially different from the one later presented by the French jurist Jean Bodin (1530–1596), who was among the first to develop a theory of the absolute authority and power of the monarch. Bodin's prince, like Machiavelli's, was to strive to do justice and to follow divine law. He was, however, the sole representative of God in the political life of his principality, an "absolute" monarch, that is, one who is "absolved" from subjection to any earthly authority and institutionally free to violate even his own laws.[32] Luther's prince, on the contrary, though ordained by God to rule, and though politically supreme in his territory, was subject to institutional checks on his power. He ruled not alone but with his entire "house"—his household officers and his counselors—as well as his entire "high magistracy." Indeed, Bodin's *souveraineté,* which was exercised by the monarch alone, was rendered in the first German translation of Bodin as *Oberkeit,* "superiority," a word interchangeable with *Obrigkeit,* which is translated here as "high magistracy" and which was used normally to refer not to the prince alone but to his entire entourage, the whole corps of "superior" ruling persons to whom he turned for counsel and for administration of his domains. Indeed, his university professors, on whom he drew for counsel, were free in theory to oppose him and in practice to depart to a post in another territory. Moreover, the Lutheran prince, in contrast to Bodin's, was considered to be no nearer to God than any of his subjects, who were all under divine injunction not to obey any laws or commands which contravened fundamental biblical precepts.

The support which Luther and his followers eventually gave to the authority of the prince was also based on biblical authority. The Fourth Commandment of the Decalogue, "Honor thy father and thy mother," according to the Lutheran Reformers, requires each citizen to render the same obedience to the prince that the child owes to a father, the wife to a husband, or the individual to God.[33] The application of the Fourth Commandment to the political ruler was the foundation of the Lutheran conception of civil obedience. At the same time, the Fourth Commandment "called" the prince to be just and to rule in the spirit of love and service to his subjects. As *Landesvater*, "father of his country," he was to show everyone by his example how to be a good manager of his household and his property as well as an upright person. Lutherans feared and denounced the tendency toward tyranny that is inherent in monarchical rule; yet civil disobedience to tyrannical violations of divine law was to stop short of popular rebellion, which was itself a violation of divine law.

Thus the connection between law and religion was preserved in Lutheran theology. Politics and law were not paths to grace and faith, but grace and faith remained paths to right politics and right law. The Christian was supposed to be law-abiding, and the law of a Christian prince was supposed to achieve both order and justice. Law was supposed to induce people to avoid evil, to cooperate, and to serve the community. The Christian was not to think that by doing good he could earn credits in heaven; nevertheless, he was to use his will and reason—with full consciousness of their defective nature—to do as much good as God has made possible.

It is apparent even from this brief account of some basic features of Luther's religious thought that it sharply challenged not only certain fundamental doctrines of Roman Catholicism but also the very legitimacy of the Roman Catholic hierarchy. Yet Lutheran religious thought could not in itself have brought about the violent upheaval that resulted in the downfall of the Roman Catholic Church in most of Germany as well as in much of the rest of Europe. If the institutional Roman Catholic Church was to be abolished, what was to keep order in the fellowship of Christian believers? Who was to replace the archbishops, bishops, and other ecclesiastics in the governing bodies of principalities and cities? Who was to regulate worship, baptism, marriage, ordination, morals, or doctrine? Who would assume jurisdiction over education, poor relief, and church property? Indeed, who was to succeed to the vast wealth of the Roman Catholic Church, which included approximately one-third of the land of Germany and at least one-fourth of the land of the rest of Europe?

The answers to such questions as these were not given at all in the doctrine of salvation and were only foreshadowed in the most general way in the doctrines of the two kingdoms and of Christian callings. Lutheran theology could be invoked to support various political developments at various times. Taken by itself, however, it did not purport to offer solutions to the critical political problems in whose creation it played such a crucial part.

Nevertheless, Lutheran theology did have a decisive influence on the character of the new political order that was introduced in Germany during the decades after 1517. For that influence to be felt, it was necessary that Lutheran religious thought be acted upon. It was by the actions of Luther himself and of his many colleagues, and eventually of large sections of the population, led in part by the princes and councilors of most of the German territories, in part by the mayors and councilors of most of the German cities, and in part by leaders of popular movements, that the Revolution became a reality—first in the church and then in the state. And it was not only the actions of Luther and his supporters that were decisive, but also the reactions of those who opposed them, for the character of a total revolution is ultimately determined not only by the thoughts and actions of those who support it but also by the responses of all who are affected by it.

Luther the Person

The character and personality of Luther himself played a significant part both in winning support for his doctrines and in causing his enemies to react in ways that were ultimately detrimental to themselves.

Born in Saxony in 1483 of a mining family that had become moderately prosperous, he matriculated in 1501 at the University of Erfurt, where in 1505, having taken preparatory courses in philosophy, theology, and canon law, he completed his master's examination in the liberal arts. He then enrolled in the doctorate program in civil law, but soon thereafter, having nearly been killed by lightning, he underwent a religious experience that led him to enter a monastery of Augustinian brothers in Erfurt, where he continued his study of canon law and church government. In 1507 he was ordained a priest, and in 1510 he represented the Erfurt chapter before the papal Curia in Rome in a legal dispute within the Augustinian order. In 1511 Luther left the monastery—though not the order—to take up the study of theology at the University of Wittenberg, which had been founded in 1502 by Frederick the Wise, prince-elector of Saxony. Upon receiving his doctorate in theology, he began teaching at the University of Wittenberg. His 1516 lectures on the Psalms and on Saint Paul's Epistle to the Romans gave the first indications of a radical new theology. In 1517 Professor Luther startled the whole of Western Christendom by his public denunciation of indulgences as an example of the usurpation by the priesthood of an authority that belongs only to God.

Written first in Latin and translated almost immediately into German, the Ninety-five Theses circulated in printed form rapidly throughout Germany and into neighboring countries.[34] They aroused enormous support and enormous controversy. In October 1518 Luther was required to defend them against a papal legate, and throughout 1518 and 1519 he defended them against many other accusers and elaborated them in response to many questioners. Finally, in June 1520, the pope issued a bull giving Luther sixty days to recant and ordering that his writings be publicly burned. In December 1520 Luther responded by leading a large delegation of teachers and students of the University of Wittenberg to a place just outside the city, where the books of canon law on which papal power was predicated were thrown into a huge bonfire. "One after the other the various tomes were consigned to the flames. Finally, Luther unexpectedly drew a copy of the [papal] bull from his gown and threw it into the flames with the remark: 'Because thou hast destroyed the truth of God, may the Lord consume thee in these flames.'"[35]

In January 1521 the pope issued a second bull, excommunicating Luther as a heretic, and he referred the excommunication to the emperor for action. Accordingly, Emperor Charles V summoned Luther to the imperial diet held at Worms (pronounced "Vawrms") in 1521 to answer whether he was the author of the books condemned by the pope and whether he recanted. There Luther acknowledged his authorship and defended his views, reportedly uttering the famous words, "Here I stand. I can do no other."[36] The emperor then signed the document known as the Edict of Worms, which branded Luther a "devil in the habit of a monk," declared him a heretic, and commanded that

> all princes, estates and subjects shall not . . . offer to the aforesaid Martin Luther either shelter, food or drink nor help him in any way with words or deeds secretly or openly. On the contrary wherever you should get possession of him you shall at once put him into prison and send him over to me, or at any rate inform me thereof without any delay. . . . Likewise you ought in virtue of the holy constitution and of our and the empire's ban to deal in the following manner with all his allies, accomplices, abettors, collaborators, patrons, and followers. You shall subdue them and confiscate their estates to your own profit unless the said persons can prove that they have mended their ways and asked for papal absolution. Furthermore we command . . . that nobody shall buy, sell, read, keep, copy or print all writings in Latin or German or other language by the aforesaid Martin Luther or in his behalf which have been condemned by our holy father the Pope. . . . And likewise we command all persons of every estate and nature, and especially those who are high magistrates [*Oberkeit*] or judges, to have the aforesaid writings, books and pictures . . . collected all through our Holy Roman Empire and our patrimonial principalities and territories and have them torn to pieces and publicly burned.[37]

Many of the territorial princes, however, would not enforce the imperial edict. Luther's own prince, Frederick the Wise, safeguarded him from arrest in Wartburg Castle, where he devoted almost a year of seclusion to translating the New Testament from Greek into German. This translation, together with his later translation of the Old Testament, played an important part in establishing the modern German language, just as the dozens of hymns he wrote became a primary source of German choral music.

In the next years Luther continued to teach theology at Wittenberg and traveled widely in the German territories—avoiding imperial diets but otherwise ignoring the fact that he was nominally an outlaw. He carried on a massive and impassioned correspondence with pastors, theologians, jurists, and scholars of many kinds, as well as with political leaders on many levels, and at the same time published a series of pathbreaking theological pamphlets and sermons. As the movement spread, he became involved politically in many aspects of it, though always behind the scenes.

In 1525 Luther broke his monastic vows and married the nun Catherine von Bora. Their marriage and their family life expressed his revolt against the concept of a priesthood set apart, whether by celibacy or otherwise, as a calling higher than that of the laity. At the same time they served as a model of the close-knit independent German household, free from tribal or clan relationships, and of the dominant role of the benevolent husband and father. Luther's domestic paternalism matched his paternalist philosophy of the state.[38]

Thus Luther in his own life and work represented with integrity the doctrines which he preached. Although he remained until his death under the imperial ban, and hence always in some danger of arrest and execution, he was able through both his writings and his personal contacts to help guide the spread of the Reformation to cities and territories throughout Germany. At first the names "Lutheranism" and "Lutheran" were attached to his teachings by his enemies. He himself rejected such characterizations and spoke instead of the "evangelical" faith and the "evangelical" church—from the Latin and German words for Gospel *(Evangelium, evangelisch).* Eventually his supporters also accepted "Lutheran" and "Lutheranism" as alternatives.

Luther was seen in his own time as the long-awaited divinely ordained prophet, a new Moses or Elijah or Daniel or John the Baptist, sent by God to save the German people. Contemporary portraits showed him with the dove of the Holy Spirit above his head, and even a halo.[39] His fame and influence were due in part to his intellectual powers; he was perhaps the most brilliant and certainly the most original theologian of his time.[40] They were due also to his personal power as a speaker, both in conversation and in the pulpit, and as a writer and composer and singer of popular hymns.[41] Finally, they were due to the intense passion with which he was driven by forces that seemed—both to him and to others—to be outside himself. This passion, it must be added, led him to vitriolic denunciations of those with whom he strongly disagreed. In such denunciations he did not hesitate to resort to scatological language. His bigoted verbal assaults on Jews who refused to convert to Christianity, written in his later years,[42] are matched by his similar assaults on papists, Anabaptists, Turks, and others.[43] In some ways he was like the historical figure he most despised, the monk Hildebrand, who in 1073 became Pope Gregory VII, initiator of the Papal Revolution, who was once called by his friend and co-worker Peter Damian "a Holy Satan."[44]

The Spread of the Reform Movement

The comparison with Pope Gregory VII must be qualified by the fact that Luther occupied no political position either in the church or in the state. He was a university professor—a scholar and a teacher. Who, then, was to execute his revolutionary message?

At first he hoped that the Roman Catholic hierarchy itself would accept his new teaching. His first appeal was, in effect, to the pope himself.[45] When he found no support from Rome, he turned to the emperor and to the imperial nobility for help.[46] In this, too, he was unsuccessful. When the emperor outlawed him, his own prince protected him but did not endorse his views.[47] Not until 1524 did another prince, the twenty-year-old Philip of Hesse, become a convert.[48] In the meantime, his main support came at first from a substantial number of his university colleagues and soon thereafter from scores of outside scholars, including theologians, philosophers, and jurists, who fell under the spell of his personality, his sermons, and his writings. The word spread rapidly to thousands of individual members of the priesthood and hundreds of thousands of people in the congregations which they led. It also spread to many leaders of city and town governments, and sharp struggles ensued concerning the liturgy and doctrine authorized by those governments to be used in their churches.

Outstanding religious leaders allied themselves with Luther. Some of them, like Philip Melanchthon (1497–1560), Johann Bugenhagen (1485–1551), and Martin Bucer (1491–1551), were almost his equal in stature, and it is hard to imagine how the reform movement would have survived without them. At least half a dozen other religious leaders who came under Luther's direct personal influence were also instrumental in converting one or more cities to the new faith. Still other religious leaders, though strongly influenced by Luther, went their separate ways, and some ultimately clashed with him.[49]

In the early 1520s a number of cities in Switzerland and southern Germany officially adopted one or another form of the evangelical faith—among them Zürich, Basel, Strasbourg, Nuremberg, Augsburg, and Constance.[50] The new faith also spread among the imperial knights, and when, in 1522, a substantial number of them, with their mercenaries, rose up in military revolt against imperial and ecclesiastical authorities (the Knights' War), two of their most prominent leaders, Franz von Sickingen and Ulrich von Hutten, justified their cause in Lutheran terms.[51] The reform movement also spread among the peasants, the mine workers, and the urban artisans, whose armed uprising in 1524 and 1525 (the Peasants' War) was also justified by resort partly to Lutheran theology. In short, the German Revolution, sparked by Luther's attack on the Roman Catholic priesthood in the name of biblical faith, became in its early stages a mass movement which was supported at various times by substantial numbers from virtually all classes of the German nation.

Like the other great revolutionary movements of European history, the German Revolution in its early stages sprouted "wings": a left wing of Zwinglians and Calvinists, a still more radical left wing of Anabaptists and Spiritualists, a moderate right wing of humanists, and, at the far right, proponents of radical reform within the Roman Catholic Church itself. Luther himself denounced both those who were to the left of him and those who were to the right. He strongly opposed the reliance on force by the knights and the peasants. He attacked the Anabaptists and the Spiritualists for preaching doctrines that threatened both organized religion and the state itself. He assailed Erasmus and other humanists who, in his view, exalted human reason and human will at the expense of personal faith.[52] His theological differences with Zwingli and Calvin were minor, but his ecclesiological differences were fundamental.[53]

Luther and the Princes: The Reformation of the State

In the first years after 1517, the Lutheran Reformation was a spontaneous popular movement which seemed to spread to various cities by its own force, without an organized political center. The Peasants' War, however, coupled with the emergence of radical Anabaptist and Spiritualist sects, brought matters to a head. To many it now seemed necessary, if anarchy was to be avoided, either to return to the Roman Catholic imperial regime that had existed before 1517 or else to bring the religious reform under the control of the territorial princes. Ultimately, it was the alliance of Lutherans with territorial princes, and of those princes with one another, which—more than any other single factor—secured the victory of Lutheranism in the territories inhabited by a majority of the German people.

Not all the princes who at first supported Luther were drawn to his cause; some were only defending their own powers and rights against the emperor and the pope. Indeed, the grievances of the princes coincided in many respects with Luther's grievances. Lower Saxony's prince-elector Frederick the Wise, Luther's protector, who remained a Roman Catholic and who met Luther only once (at the Diet of Worms in 1521), was nevertheless eager to protect, against both pope and emperor, the freedom of "his" university professor to post theological statements on the door of "his" princely chapel. The territorial princes who in 1521 refused to enforce the imperial ban against Luther included the archbishop of Mainz, who was chancellor of the empire and an arch-foe of Lutheran theology.

The political situation changed radically in the mid-1520s. An alliance of Catholic princes was organized in 1525 for the purpose of crushing the evangelical movement; it included the duke of (upper) Saxony, the archbishop of Mainz, and the elector of Brandenburg. Other princes—Philip of Hesse; John, the successor to Frederick as prince-elector of (lower) Saxony; and the rulers of Mecklenburg, Anhalt, and Brunswick-Lüneberg—banded together in alliance to defend the Lutheran cause. In 1529, at an imperial diet held at Speyer, the Catholic majority endorsed an imperial resolution to end all religious innovations and to restore bishops to their jurisdictions. In response, the rulers of five Lutheran territories and of fourteen Lutheran cities issued a "protestation," stating that "in matters concerning God's honor and the soul's salvation, each must stand before God and answer for himself."[54] The name "Protestant" was given to those who issued the Speyer Protestation and eventually to the many millions who followed in their footsteps.

Emperor Charles V returned to Germany in 1530, after an absence, to preside over the Diet of Augsburg, where a group of Catholic theologians presented a document listing 404 errors contained in Lutheran, Zwinglian, and Anabaptist writings. Luther's supporters read to the emperor another document, which became known as the Augsburg Confession, prepared chiefly by Melanchthon and approved by Luther, setting forth the fundamental doctrines of the Protestant faith. It was signed by the same princes who had issued the Speyer Protestation as well as by representatives of several cities. The Protestant princes left before the end of the diet. In their absence, the Catholic representatives adopted a resolution which forbade heretical innovations, demanded the restoration of secularized ecclesiastical properties, and established a censorship of both printing and preaching. In response, the signatories of the Augsburg Confession held meetings and, in 1531, formed the Schmalkaldic League for the defense of the Protestant faith. They were soon joined by other cities and other principalities from both northern and southern Germany. Faced with the continual threat of Turkish invasion from the east, the emperor for many years took no action to suppress the Schmalkaldic League, which became the political and military backbone of the rapidly growing Protestant movement within the empire.[55]

His vision of a united Roman Catholic empire having been frustrated by the spread of Protestantism, Charles V finally launched a war against the Schmalkaldic League in 1546–47 and defeated the Protestant forces. In 1552, however, the Protestant princes allied themselves with Henry II of France and defeated the emperor. In 1555 another imperial diet at Augsburg enacted the Peace of Augsburg, which finally brought an end to the German civil wars by permitting the prince of each territory to determine the religion of that territory. Thus the support of the Lutheran cause by German territorial princes was a crucial factor in bringing to fruition the German Revolution.

The Peace of Augsburg established basic principles for resolving the intense religious conflicts that had raged for thirty-five years within and among the estates that constituted the German portion of the Holy Roman Empire.[56] The effect of its provisions was that the ruler of each principality of the empire was to determine whether the Lutheran or Roman Catholic religion was to be the sole religion in that principality and consequently whether he and those who shared his high magistracy were to exercise supreme legislative, administrative, and judicial powers over the affairs of the territorial church. Subsequently the Latin phrase *cuius regio eius religio* ("whose realm—his religion") was applied to that principle. It should be stressed, however, that the choice was to be limited either to "the Augsburg Confession," that is, Lutheranism, or to "the old religion," that is, Roman Catholicism. Anabaptists, Calvinists, and adherents of other religious denominations were excluded.[57]

Certain exceptions were made to the power of each prince to determine which of the two faiths was to be imposed. In those imperial free cities where the two religions were concurrently practiced, both Lutheranism and Roman Catholicism were to be tolerated (Article 14). Also the free imperial knights were not required to be subject to the religious jurisdiction of their territorial rulers (Article 13). Article 11 also provided for the freedom of religious minorities to emigrate to another territory *(jus emigrandi),* provided that they paid any arrears in taxes and—more significantly—provided that they were not legally obligated, as serfs, to remain where they were. In an oral agreement that supplemented the written treaty, the Protestant estates wrested from the emperor the commitment that knights, cities, and communes subject to ecclesiastical rulers who had previously converted to Protestantism would not be brought back to the old faith.[58]

The Peace of Augsburg granted what the Lutheran princes wanted most: the *jus reformandi,* "the right of reforming," that is, the right to establish in their respective territories the Lutheran religion as a state church. Yet it also represented substantial compromises in favor of "the old religion." Not only could Lutherans be banned in secular principalities that remained Roman Catholic, and not only were Roman Catholic knights protected in Lutheran territories and Roman Catholic citizens in free imperial cities that were Protestant, but also certain restrictions were placed on the right of Protestant princes to appropriate property belonging to the Roman Catholic Church in their territories. Article 5 of the Peace of Augsburg provided that if any bishop or prelate abandoned the Roman Catholic faith in the future, his or her office and income attached thereto would revert to the Roman Catholic Church. The Protestant estates of the Diet of Augsburg refused their assent to this "ecclesiastical reservation," and their refusal was duly noted in Article 5 itself. Moreover, Article 6 recognized the validity of the secularization of church property already carried out by Protestant estates prior to the 1552 Peace of Passau.

It has been argued by some historians that the Peace of Augsburg was only "a confirmation of the status quo" and that it "did not point a way to the future" but only led to the catastrophic religious conflicts that culminated two generations later in the outbreak of the so-called Thirty Years' War (1618–1648).[59] Religious conflicts continued within the principalities. Also a different form of Protestantism, namely, Calvinism, eventually found increasing numbers of adherents in Germany. Frederick III, elector of the Palatinate, a leading principality of the empire, became a convert to Calvinism in 1563 and established that religion in his territories. The count of Nassau did likewise in 1577, and the cities of Bremen and Anhalt followed suit in the 1580s.[60] At the same time, Catholicism was restored in the bishopric of Würzburg in the 1570s and in the lands of the abbey of Fulda in the early 1600s. The electorate of Cologne survived a Protestant challenge in the 1580s. Catholicism aggressively reasserted itself in Hapsburg Austria and in Bavaria. Thus residents of both Protestant and Catholic territories were faced with the threat of forced conversion. Yet the Thirty Years' War itself culminated in the Peace of Westphalia (1648), which essentially reaffirmed the basic principles of the Peace of Augsburg, enlarging them by bringing Calvinism into the fold of acceptable faiths and by requiring that a prince forfeit his lands if he changed his religion.

One might argue that nothing in history is ever new and nothing is ever final; yet it is undeniable that the hegemony of the Roman Catholic Church over the German principalities was finally broken by the Peace of Augsburg, which finally established the new principle that within the community of states that made up the German nation, the religion of each territorial ruler—Roman Catholicism or Lutheranism—was to be the sole religion of his territory. After 1555, Charles V's dream of restoring a unified, centralized Roman Catholic empire could never be realized. Charles himself acknowledged this in 1556 by abdicating the imperial throne and becoming a monk. Indeed, there were times when it seemed possible that a Lutheran prince might be elected emperor.[61]

Moreover, the recognition of the power of the prince to establish the Lutheran—and eventually the Calvinist—religion in his principality also contributed substantially to the power of those princes who remained Roman Catholic, since it was now by their decision, and not by decision of the papal hierarchy, that their principalities continued in "the old religion."

Despite its ambiguities, and possibly because of them, the Peace of Augsburg may be said to have brought to a close the series of political events which constituted the German Revolution. Luther's initial apocalyptic vision had proved incapable of full realization. Compromises had had to be made with opposing forces, including those that represented the ancien régime. Yet a lasting transformation had taken place which affected not just Germany but the whole of Europe.[62]

The Role of the Cities

Thus far, the story of the German Revolution has been presented here largely in its traditional version, as a story of "Luther and the princes" against "papacy and empire." In recent decades, however, this version of the story has been severely challenged by leading historians because of its "magisterial" bias. They have stressed that it was not only, and not primarily, the combination of religious prophets and a secular high magistracy that was responsible for the great transformation of church and state but rather the actions of large segments of the German people as a whole, and especially of the merchant and artisan classes within the German cities. Thus one of the exponents of the newer view has written: "I reject the traditional course of the narrative, which concentrates on Luther's theology and then moves through the Knights' and Peasants' Wars to the princely Reformation. I see the creative and irrevocable events largely in terms of the urban Reformation, a movement effectually springing from the new dynamic added by the preachers, pamphleteers and printers to the old turmoil of city politics."[63] In oft-quoted words of the same writer, "the German Reformation was an urban event."[64]

A related theory, which also stresses the "grassroots" character of the Reformation, attributes the main impetus for reform to the peasantry and urban poor, whose massive revolt of 1524–1526 was crushed by the high magistracy.

It is not necessary here to try to sort out what is more true and what is less true in these interpretations. As is so often the case in scholarly debates, the dilemma may be resolved by seizing both of its horns. The princes, the burghers, the peasantry and urban poor, the preachers and other clergy, the jurists, the humanists, and others—all played crucial parts. As Steven Ozment has said, depending on the point at which one examines the process it is possible to identify the Reformation as a preacher's, a people's, or a magistrate's reform."[65]

Indeed, if we see the Reformation in Germany as part of a total revolution, a total transformation, in which the whole German people was involved, then we may say that it was "caused" by all those who participated in it, on whatever side. No single class or group or set of classes or groups simply imposed its will on others; ultimately the German Revolution was made by the vanquished as well as the victors.[66] Power was reciprocal: the will of the stronger was deeply affected by the responses of the weaker. As is often the case in civil war, the outcome was not simply the victory of one side but a new kind of interaction among all the opposing sides. Moreover, if one places the Reformation within the context of a total revolution of both church and state, then one must focus not only on the replacement of Roman Catholicism—in most German territories—by Lutheranism and by Calvinism, but also on the entire political, economic, and social transformation of the German people. Finally, if one abandons the search for a "first cause uncaused" of the German Revolution and instead seeks to tell the story of what happened, and how it happened, and with what results, then it is entirely proper to *begin* with Luther and the princes, and to *follow* with an account of the role played by other major groups of the population, including those who gave the Revolution its lasting institutional and legal forms.

With respect to developments within the cities of Germany, however, as contrasted with the countryside, the grassroots elements cannot easily be distinguished from the magisterial element, since the sentiments and interests of the urban population found expression, to a considerable extent, in actions taken by the urban magistracy. In cities where the mayor and city councilors were opposed by a substantial majority of the population, intense struggles ensued, and in many instances a new elite replaced the old elite. Moreover, internal urban strife was often strongly affected by the political will of the princely magistracy of the territory in which a particular city was located.

Cities and towns contained a relatively small percentage of the total population of Germany in 1500—in most territories less than 10 percent, in Saxony and possibly some others up to 20 percent. Moreover, of the roughly 3,000 German cities and towns, approximately 2,800 had populations of under a thousand. Luther's hometown of Wittenberg contained approximately 2,500 souls. Cologne with 45,000 souls and Nuremberg with 38,000 were the largest of the twelve German cities whose population exceeded 15,000. These urban population figures are roughly comparable with those that prevailed generally in western Europe, although Germany had no cities to compare in size with Paris, Naples, Milan, Venice, Prague, and Granada.[67]

Intellectually, the cities and towns were receptive to Lutheranism. In Steven Ozment's words, "The Protestant Reformation presupposed for its success a literate urban culture and seems particularly to have attracted rising urban groups who had either experienced or were determined to come into a new political and economic importance."[68] It is by no means clear, however, that the factors which induced the high magistracy of many cities and towns to establish the Lutheran faith were substantially different from the factors that induced the territorial high magistracy—the princes and their councilors—to do the same in their principalities. Some of those factors were economic and political in the narrow sense of those terms, namely, the economic interest in confiscating Roman Catholic Church property and the political interest in acquiring Roman Catholic political and legal jurisdiction. A broader political factor—the interest in yielding to religious and intellectual pressures from below, especially from the parish congregations themselves—was more evident in the cities than in the larger territories. It must be noted, however, that except in the free imperial cities, which were entitled to make their own decision within the terms of the Peace of Augsburg, the establishment of one faith or the other depended ultimately not on city authorities but on the prince of the territory in which the city was situated.

Eventually, more than half of the approximately sixty-five or more imperial cities became and remained Protestant during the sixteenth century. In others, a Protestant congregation and a Roman Catholic congregation existed side by side. Still others adopted Protestantism but later renounced it. At least a dozen imperial cities gave no recognition to the Reformation.[69] These figures justify calling the Reformation an "urban event," reflecting "communal values," but only to the same extent that it may be called a "territorial event," or a "princely event," reflecting "official values." Also both the cities and the territories played a significant role in giving the Reformation institutional and legal form through elaborate legislative enactments regulating political, economic, social, and religious conduct.

The Peasants' War: "The Revolution of the Common Man"

Starting in June 1524 and continuing into 1525, widespread revolts broke out in the south of Germany, eventually involving very large numbers—some hundreds of thousands—of armed peasants, supported often by urban artisans and mine workers as well as by prominent preachers and other spiritual and intellectual leaders. These revolts were met by armed resistance on the part of some of the princes, who had earlier united in a coalition called the Swabian League. By early 1526, the rebellion was crushed. Heavy physical and financial sanctions were imposed on its leaders and on the villages that had participated in it. Contemporaries reported 100,000 dead on the battlefields and on the gallows.[70]

Although it was initiated by peasant leaders and was later called the Peasants' War, the revolt was in fact a mass movement whose partisans were drawn from the poorer classes of the cities and towns as well as the countryside, and it was fought not only in the name of the peasants as such but also in the name of the "common man" against oppression by "the spiritual and temporal powers."[71] It was based expressly on the new biblical faith proclaimed by Luther, Zwingli, Thomas Müntzer, and other Reformers, which was interpreted to signify the social, economic, and political equality of all classes. As the German historian Peter Blickle has shown, the movement had many of the qualities of a revolution in the classical sense of that much-abused word. Contrary to Blickle's interpretation, however, it should be seen not as "the" (failed) German Revolution of 1525 but rather as a single part of the larger, more complex (successful) German Revolution of 1517–1555.

Early in 1525 the leaders of the peasant revolt issued a manifesto, called the Twelve Articles, addressed to "the Christian reader" and citing extensive scriptural authority for all of its provisions. The preamble stated that the Gospel teaches "nothing but love, peace, patience, and unity," and that the demands of the peasants were based on these virtues, but that the devil had driven foes of the Gospel to resist and reject those demands.[72] The first article then asked that individual parishes be given the right to appoint their own pastors. The second article asked that the tithe on grain be collected by the church wardens, appointed by the parishes, and that it be used only to pay the pastor and (with what remained) to distribute to the poor and (with whatever remained after that) for military defense, "so that no general territorial tax will be laid upon the poor folk." The tax on livestock was to be abolished all together. Article 3 denounced "the custom for the lords to own us as their property," although it added that "we should willingly obey our chosen and rightful ruler, set over us by God, in all proper and Christian matters." Articles 4 to 11 demanded the removal of restrictions on hunting and fishing, the return to the village of its woods and forests so that building timber and firewood could be collected by the peasants, the reduction of labor services, observance by lords of the terms of the leases to which they had previously agreed, the adjustment of rents to conform to the land's yield, a reduction of the level of criminal penalties "according to the ancient written law and the circumstances of the case and not according to the judge's bias," the return of communal meadows and fields by people who had seized them, and the total abolition of death taxes. Article 12 declared that "if any one or more of these articles are not in agreement with God's word (which we doubt), then this should be proved to us from Holy Writ. We will abandon it, when this is proved by the Bible."

It should be noted that most of the peasants' economic grievances were directed against specific practices that had only been introduced in the late fifteenth and early sixteenth centuries, as the economic situation of landed noblemen deteriorated and many of them resorted to measures that violated long-established peasant rights. Underlying the uprising, however, was a new revolutionary vision of social equality based on Christian brotherhood. One of the most prominent leaders of the revolt, the Anabaptist Thomas Müntzer, anticipating Karl Marx by three centuries, declared that "everyone should properly receive according to his need. Any prince, count, or lord who refuses to do this even when seriously warned should be hanged or have his head chopped off." The egalitarian vision of Christian brotherhood found an institutional framework in the widespread formation of so-called Christian Associations in various parts of southern Germany, and eventually of a League of Christian Associations, and in the adoption of what has been called a republican constitutional model. In that model, the rural and urban commune formed the basis of a territorial political structure in which all political offices were to be based ultimately on communal elections. In larger territories a territorial assembly *(Landschaft)* was established to represent the various communes.[73] The foundation of the new political order was to be the law of God. "The common good," prescribed by divine law, was understood to require economic relief of the poor. Christian brotherly love was understood to require equal justice for all. The autonomy of the Christian community was understood to require communal elections of both spiritual and temporal powers. Thus the revolutionary movement had a religious as well as an economic and a political dimension.

The "revolution of the common man" challenged Lutheranism from the left. Luther himself denounced both sides—the peasants for their resort to violence, the princes for their unwillingness to yield to just economic and social demands.

His repudiation of the peasants, coupled with the ruthlessness of the penalties which they suffered in defeat, undoubtedly contributed to the defection of large numbers of the German peasantry from the Lutheran cause and ultimately to their adherence to Roman Catholicism. Yet the endorsement, if only for a time, of Anabaptist ideas by large segments of the German people substantially influenced the course of the German Revolution not only negatively but also positively. Negatively, it helped to delay the progress of both the Lutheran religious cause and the princely political cause against the papal and the imperial power. Positively, it contributed to the subsequent alleviation of many of the peasants' grievances and to the eventual peaceful participation of the peasantry in the economic, social, and religious life of princely territories.

In the imperial diet held at Speyer in 1526, the so-called Large Committee, responding to the emperor's instruction, gave special consideration to peasants' grievances. The committee's "Memorial Concerning the Abuses and Burdens of Subjects" implicitly took as its point of departure the Twelve Articles. It recommended the abolition of various taxes payable to Rome since they were paid largely by the common man and gave "cause for rebellion and other forms of disobedience." It also recommended certain limitations on the payment of the tax on livestock, the abolition or reduction of death taxes, and certain restrictions on labor services exacted by lords from peasants. The "Memorial" did not endorse the demand of the Twelve Articles that serfdom as such be abolished, but it did recommend that other restrictions on freedom of movement be abolished, that fishing waters and land which rulers had appropriated be restored to the villages, that local and village courts not be bypassed, and that criminal punishments be reduced.[74] Although these recommendations did not find their way into imperial law, they nevertheless constituted a recognition of the legitimacy of many of the peasants' grievances. Various German cities also granted substantial concessions to the peasants, both during and after the civil war, and even many of the territorial rulers who had participated in the Swabian League yielded to various demands of the Twelve Articles once they had won the victory.[75]

Again, as Steven Ozment has said, although it is a mistake to identify the Reformation with the Peasants' War, and an even greater mistake to conclude that therefore the Reformation was a failure, it is also erroneous to discount the revolt of the peasants as having "left behind no important and lasting changes in Germany's political and social landscape."[76] Their uprising was brutally repressed, but many of their grievances were ultimately heard and met.

European Repercussions of the German Revolution

The German Revolution was a European Revolution. It had been prepared throughout Europe for over a century by strong movements to reform the church as well as by the substantial increase, almost everywhere, in royal power over both ecclesiastical and feudal institutions. Its outbreak in Germany in 1517 and its subsequent course of development there had profound repercussions, both positive and negative, in all countries of the West, from Poland to England and from Denmark and Sweden to Italy and Spain. Indeed, Lutheranism took hold in the Scandinavian countries more rapidly and in a more extreme form than in Germany itself. In the early 1520s Denmark (and eventually Norway and Iceland, which were under Danish control) and Sweden (and eventually Finland, which was under Swedish control) adopted a rigid state-mandated Lutheranism, with severe criminal penalties for open adherence to a non-Lutheran faith.[77]

In Poland, which in the sixteenth century was part of a Lithuanian polity that included also parts of the Ukraine and Belarus, significant numbers of the nobility became Lutherans in the 1520s and 1530s, and in the 1540s and 1550s about half the gentry became Calvinists. While Protestantism ultimately almost disappeared in Poland, Lutheranism from an early time established a permanent presence in the Baltic countries of Latvia, Estonia, and East Prussia, all three of which were governed by the Teutonic Knights, a Roman Catholic monastic military order. Indeed, in East Prussia the Grand Master of the Teutonic Knights himself became a Lutheran in 1525 and dissolved the order there.[78]

While Lutheranism spread from German territories mainly to central and eastern Europe, Calvinism, its close relative, spread mainly to France, Holland, Scotland, and England. French by birth and education, John (Jean) Calvin early became a partisan of Lutheran doctrines, and in 1535, at the age of twenty-six, fled from France to Switzerland to avoid royal persecution. An outstanding theologian and jurist, he published the first version of his famous *Institutes of the Christian Religion* in 1536. He eventually settled in Geneva, where he led a Protestant community which, on the one hand, adhered to doctrines of salvation and of the sacraments that differed only in part from those of Luther's followers, but which, on the other hand, adhered also to doctrines of ecclesiastical organization and authority and rituals of worship that differed fundamentally from Lutheranism. Perhaps the most important difference between Lutheranism and Calvinism as they were practiced in the sixteenth century was the Calvinist belief in the ultimate authority in ecclesiastical matters of the elders of the local congregation of the faithful, as contrasted with the Lutheran belief in the ultimate authority in ecclesiastical matters of the territorial prince.

Calvinism, like Lutheranism, came to have different versions in different countries. In France, Calvinist evangelicals, the Huguenots,[79] in 1534 posted placards attacking the Mass on the doors of Roman Catholic churches in Paris and some other cities (the "Affair of the Placards"), which led to the first serious religious persecutions. Repression of Calvinism burst into civil war in

1562, and over the next thirty-six years a total of eight successive civil wars, known collectively as the Wars of Religion, were fought by royal Roman Catholic forces to put down urban Huguenot uprisings. In 1572 and thereafter, large-scale massacres of Huguenots, called collectively the Saint Barthole-mew's Day Massacre, were carried out in many parts of France. Finally, in 1598, the violence was ended—for almost a century—by Henry IV's Edict of Nantes, which granted Huguenots liberty of conscience, albeit with some severe restrictions.[80]

The Wars of Religion in France had a parallel in the bloody repression of Protestants in the Netherlands, where Lutheranism and other evangelical movements attracted large followings from the early 1520s and Calvinism spread rapidly in the 1540s and 1550s. Prior to his abdication in 1555, Emperor Charles V had used the legal procedure of the Inquisition to bring about the execution of many thousands of Dutch Protestants.[81] Thereafter, his son, King Philip of Spain, used Spanish troops to occupy and ravage the northern (Dutch) provinces of the Netherlands. In 1581, after over two decades of intermittent warfare, the United Provinces of the Netherlands, formed under the leadership of the Calvinist Prince William of Orange, formally declared their independence, which they succeeded in maintaining, partly with the help of the Protestant English queen, Elizabeth.

England itself, starting in the 1520s and 1530s, was torn by conflict between various forms of Protestantism, on the one hand, and a new non-Roman Anglicanism, on the other, while Anglicanism itself was torn between its original Roman Catholic theology and later Protestant theological and political influences. Also Roman Catholicism, though outlawed in 1534 by Henry VIII and again by his son, Edward VI, restored in 1553 by Henry's elder daughter, Queen Mary, and outlawed again by his younger daughter, Queen Elizabeth, in 1558, remained a strong underground movement. The Anglican Book of Common Prayer, which contains much that was derived from the Roman Catholic missal, was also, however, strongly influenced by Lutheran theology and liturgy. Lutheran monarchism was also congenial to Anglicanism. Although Lutheranism itself made little headway in England, Calvinism, its more radical counterpart, made inroads in the latter half of the sixteenth century, and in the seventeenth century played a major role in establishing parliamentary supremacy.

Even in countries which throughout the sixteenth and seventeenth centuries remained militantly Roman Catholic, such as Italy and Spain, Protestantism had profound repercussions. These were, in the first instance, negative; that is, a ruthless Inquisition was used to execute, drive out, or otherwise repress the small numbers of Protestants in those countries who dared to raise their voices against Rome. Although it was the church that conducted the heresy trials, it was the secular authority that dominated the proceedings and imposed the death sentences, and in Spain, as later in the Netherlands, the

Inquisition was primarily a political instrument of royal and imperial power. At the same time, the papacy, in response to the Reformation, asserted greatly heightened powers over the internal operations of the church. The movement to strengthen papal authority was reinforced by the emergence of the Society of Jesus, founded by Ignatius of Loyola in the 1530s and given papal recognition in 1540. Living dispersed in the secular community, the Jesuits were active missionaries of Roman Catholicism, stressing the importance of obedient submission to papal and episcopal authority.

Theologically, however, the Roman Catholic Counter-Reformation, as it was later called, was in part a positive response to the challenge of Protestantism. Its theological character was shaped, above all, by the Council of Trent, which met first in 1545–1547, again in 1551–52, and finally in 1562–63. Early sessions of the council reaffirmed traditional Roman Catholic theological doctrines that had been challenged by Protestantism, denouncing the Protestant doctrine of salvation by faith alone, the assault on the legitimacy and effectiveness of traditional sacraments, and the acceptance of any interpretation of the Bible that differed from that of the Roman Catholic church. The council also took steps, however, to correct some of the principal abuses which the Protestants attacked. It decreed, among other reforms, that the education and discipline of the priesthood were to be improved, that the Bible was to be read regularly in churches and in schools and was to have equal validity with tradition, and that henceforth Roman Catholic marriages were to take place before a priest and two witnesses, a response to the Lutheran criticism that the acceptance by the church of informal or clandestine marriages was a subversion of parental authority. Also the Jesuits emulated the Protestant emphasis on education of the laity, founding a great many schools throughout Europe; so effective was their method of teaching that even Protestants sometimes sent their children to them.

These and related developments in Spain and other Roman Catholic countries were, however, not only a Counter-Reformation but also part of an independent movement within Catholicism, an autonomous Catholic Reformation.[82] In Spain, Archbishop and later Cardinal Francisco Ximenes de Cisneros (1437–1517) led a movement that emphasized the importance of returning to Scripture and oversaw the production in 1517 of the first critical edition of the Bible, published in parallel columns in Greek, Hebrew, and a new Latin translation.[83] In 1506 Cardinal Ximenes also founded a university in order to train a more liberally educated clergy. There he gathered around himself an important circle of scholars, including the great theologian and jurist Francisco de Vitoria (1482?–1546), whose treatises "On Law" *(De Lege)* and "On the Law of War" *(De Jure Belli)* were a foundation on which later Protestant jurists built.[84] Vitoria and other jurists of the Catholic Reformation in Spain returned to the writings of Saint Thomas Aquinas but gave Thomism new interpretations, later called "neo-Thomist" or "neo-scholastic," which in some ways were similar to contemporaneous Protestant developments in legal philosophy and legal science.[85]

The religious repercussions of the Lutheran reformation of the church were closely linked with political repercussions across Europe of the accompanying German reformation of the state. There took place what has been called the "confessionalization" of Europe.[86] Each of the confessions became identified with the territories whose rulers proclaimed it. The Roman Catholic Church itself, though led by the papacy, became in some respects a federation of territorial churches—the Italian, the Spanish, the Portuguese, the French, the Bavarian, the Austrian, and others. It preserved, to be sure, through the Council of Trent, its doctrinal integrity, but its temporal jurisdiction was greatly restricted as it came under the political domination of various monarchs. Thus Western Christendom was transformed from a society of plural secular polities within a single ecclesiastical state into a society of plural Christian confessions, each identified politically with one or more particular secular states.

It was, in fact, the confessionalization of Europe, that is, the virtual unification of church and state within each of the various European polities, that led to the first Great European War, the Thirty Years' War of 1618–1648. The Peace of Augsburg of 1555 had successfully resolved the German civil war of Protestant principalities against the Roman Catholic empire. But after two generations, and after large parts of Europe had become Protestant, the Austrian Hapsburg emperor, Ferdinand II, who had succeeded to the much weakened imperial throne, mobilized the remaining Roman Catholic princes to launch a war against Protestant territories and cities in Germany in order to recover all ecclesiastical power and property that had been surrendered to Protestant rulers since the Peace of Augsburg. For over three decades, chiefly on German soil, mercenary armies of the Austrian emperor intermittently fought mercenary armies of Protestant kings of Denmark and Sweden, with the periodic military involvement of France, Spain, England, the Netherlands, and other countries.[87] Eventually religious motives were subordinated to greed and power as Catholic France fought Catholic Spain and generals changed their religious affiliations to suit their royal employers. The various armies plundered the German countryside and besieged and ravaged German cities. Thousands of German villages were entirely wiped out. The population of the city of Augsburg was reduced from 80,000 to 16,000 and of Germany as a whole from 12 million to 8 million. It took almost a century and a half for Germany to recover from the impoverishment and exhaustion that had been inflicted upon it.

The Thirty Years' War ended with a multilateral treaty, the Peace of Westphalia, which applied to all the major European powers certain basic terms of the German religious settlement that had been reached at Augsburg over ninety years earlier. As before, the religion of the ruler was to be the established religion of the territory. Within each territory, however, the non-established religious confessions, whether Protestant or Roman Catholic, were given the right to assemble and worship as well as the right to educate their children in their own faith. Thus a principle of religious toleration was established between Lutherans, Calvinists, and Roman Catholics. Roman Catholic clerics, however, were divested of any remaining privileges and immunities in the civil courts of Protestant territories.[88]

From the point of view of the constitutional law of the countries that participated in the Peace of Westphalia, the principle of royal supremacy over both church and state, first established by the German Revolution, was reaffirmed, but with certain limitations for the benefit of non-established churches. At the same time, the new constitutional principle of limited religious toleration became a foundation of a new concept of international law based on state sovereignty. The treaty recognized the sovereignty not only of each of the German principalities but also of the other European states, including Spain, the United Provinces of the Netherlands, Switzerland, and Austria, all of which had formerly been part of the Holy Roman Empire. The empire itself continued to exist in name but was in fact a phantom; it could not enact laws or raise taxes or mount armies or otherwise function as a state. At the same time, each of the German principalities, whether Protestant or Catholic, was recognized in international law as an independent sovereign state capable of entering into treaty relations with all other states.

Thus the principle of sovereignty, vested in princes and their councilors and high officials (the *Obrigkeit*), which was finally established within Germany in the Peace of Augsburg of 1555, was extended, after much bloodshed, to all the European nations in their relations with one another under international law. The emergence of the modern system of sovereign European states, all viewed as equal from a legal point of view, and of the modern system of international law, based on the coincidence of the wills of such states, is usually dated from the 1648 Peace of Westphalia, but its foundation was laid in the 1555 Peace of Augsburg, which in effect established within the German Empire the principle of state sovereignty by making the prince, the monarch, the supreme source of law, both secular and ecclesiastical, within his principality, his kingdom.

The Reformation of Law

Although the story told thus far has been the subject of a vast literature and much of it is generally familiar to well-educated persons, little has been written in the past century and a half on the relationship of the Lutheran Reformation—or of the German Revolution as a whole—to the accompanying transformation of law. Rarely mentioned in contemporary scholarly literature is the fact that fundamental changes were made in law in the sixteenth century, in Germany and elsewhere, by persons whose ideas and interests, both religious and political, were under the strong influence of Protestant beliefs.

Indeed, the impression is usually left that any connection between law and religion that may have existed in the "Middle Ages" quickly evaporated in the sixteenth century not only in Germany but in other Protestant countries of Europe as well. In addition, little has been written of the enormous effect on German law of the striking increase in the political and religious authority of the Protestant territorial princes. The failure of *general* historians to take sufficient account of the reformation of German law in the sixteenth century, and the failure of *legal* historians sufficiently to connect changes that took place in German law in the sixteenth century to parallel changes in religion and politics, have led to serious misunderstandings of each of these aspects of the German Revolution and hence to a misunderstanding of the nature of the upheaval as a whole and of its significance for the future.

At the outset of the Lutheran Reformation, many of its leaders launched a bitter attack not only on the old law but on law altogether. This was the apocalyptic phase of the Revolution, when Luther and other Reformers sometimes seemed to want to replace the visible, legal, hierarchical Roman Catholic Church with an invisible egalitarian fellowship of believers who would live by faith alone. Frequently at first, and occasionally later, Luther coupled his theological doctrine of a heavenly kingdom, in which law is replaced by grace, with a broadside attack on the prevailing legal order in the German principalities and in the empire, as well as on jurists generally. "Truth and law are always enemies," he wrote at one time. "Show me the jurist who studies to discover truth. . . . No, they study law only for the profit it brings them."[89] The Anabaptists, left wing of the Reformation, carried the antinomian tendencies of Protestantism much farther, advocating the establishment of communities which would be governed only by the teachings of the Gospel. Thus not only the canon law of the Roman Catholic Church came under attack but also the secular law, including the greatly modified and modernized scholarly Roman law that had increasingly penetrated the law of the cities, the principalities, and, after 1495, the empire.

As the Reformation gained momentum, however, it became apparent that the attack on the old law, coupled with an attack on all law, would lead to anarchy. Indeed, Thomas Müntzer and other leaders of the massive revolt of large sections of the peasantry in 1524 and 1525 expressly expounded a radical antinomianism that bordered on anarchism.[90] It was at this point that Luther's doctrine that the earthly kingdom, governed by law, is ordained by God, although it is a kingdom of sin and God is only hidden in it, assumed political importance as a basis for assigning positive value to legal institutions and legal principles. Eventually the alliance of Lutheran theology with the civil authority of princes and city councilors resulted in the elaboration of both a new legal philosophy and a new legal "method" or "science," that is, a new mode of systematization of law, as well as in the introduction of substantial changes in the various branches of positive law itself.

Later chapters will examine these developments in some detail. Suffice it here to summarize briefly some of the principal legal changes that took place, in order to show that the ultimate success of the German Revolution of 1517–1555, and indeed its very nature as one of the Great Revolutions of Western history, is to be measured in part by the extent to which its foundational ideals and ideas, on the one hand, and its political and social objectives, on the other, became embodied in a new and enduring type of legal order.

The intimate connection between Lutheran theology and princely authority found legal expression, in the first instance, in new principles of constitutional law affecting both the religious and the secular spheres. In Protestant principalities, as well as in free imperial cities that opted for Protestantism, princes and city magistrates enacted ordinances in the 1530s and 1540s closing Roman Catholic places of worship and ending or severely limiting traditional Roman Catholic practices such as fasting, penance, veneration of saints, indulgences, masses for the dead, the giving of alms to mendicant friars, and numerous festivals and holidays. As Steven Ozment has noted, "so literally and piously do these ordinances enshrine the doctrinal teachings of Protestants in law that an unobservant reader might think that he had stumbled upon evangelical sermons and pamphlets from the 1520s."[91]

In addition to succeeding to the jurisdiction of the papal hierarchy over ecclesiastical affairs, the Protestant prince—and in Protestant cities the urban high magistracy—also succeeded to its jurisdiction over the laity in marital and family relations, moral offenses, education, poor relief, and other fields. Divorce on grounds of adultery or desertion was introduced. Heresy, blasphemy, and sex offenses were made crimes under secular law. Secular laws were enacted on vagrancy, begging, respectability, sumptuousness of dress, and the like. The Reformation also introduced secular control of education: public schools and libraries were instituted to replace cathedral schools, and universities were placed under princely authority. Indeed, it was part of the Protestant ruler's Christian calling to provide for the widest possible elementary education of both boys and girls, so that all persons, not only clerics, would have the ability to read the Bible. In addition, protection of widows and orphans, hospitals for the ill and aged, and other forms of charitable works, which had previously been in large part the responsibility of monastic and other ecclesiastical foundations acting under the canon law, were now left to secular authorities acting under secular law.

A whole body of ordinances on these matters poured forth from princely and urban legislative bodies in the wake of the Reformation. Although they also introduced revolutionary reforms, many of their provisions were drawn from the older canon law of the Roman Catholic Church, except that they were now to be carried out by secular authorities and enforced in secular courts. What has traditionally been called a process of secularization of the spiritual law of the church must thus also be viewed as a process of spiritualization of the secular law of the state.

The ascendancy of the prince and his high magistracy also marked a final stage in the transition from what is called in German the *Ständestaat,* rule by estates, to the *Fürstenstaat,* rule by princes, or sometimes *Hofstaat,* rule by the palace. The three ruling estates had consisted of ecclesiastical prelates, nobles, and a third estate of gentry, merchants, and other leading burghers; peasants, artisans, and household servants also constituted estates, but they were without a voice in political bodies and hardly could be said to have "ruled." In the fifteenth century in Germany, as throughout the West, the territorial rulers, the monarchs, the princes or dukes or counts, had gradually acquired more and more power vis-à-vis the estates; yet they had remained dependent on the estates for revenues, and the estates—especially the ecclesiastical prelates—were also a chief source of their counselors. Periodic assemblies of representatives of the estates were called by the ruler to levy taxes and enact laws. A turning point came with the German Revolution, when important functions previously performed by representatives of the higher estates, as well as much of their power, were vested in the new high magistracy, a civil service, many of whose members were recruited from persons educated in the universities who were of humbler origin. Also, the Protestant princes, in addition to being greatly enriched by the confiscation of Roman Catholic wealth, began to exercise an independent power of taxation. Assemblies of representatives of the estates continued to be called, and their support was sometimes required for action by the prince, but their deliberations often consisted in the listing of their grievances against alleged abuses by the high magistracy—grievances that were increasingly left unsatisfied. The palace council *(Hofrat)* and the palace court *(Hofgericht)* replaced in importance the assembly of notables and their patrimonial courts.[92]

In emphasizing the calling of the prince as father of his country, Luther not only made him the ultimate source of law but also imposed limits on the subject's right and duty of civil disobedience when the ruler commanded him to act in ways that were evil or ungodly. On the one hand, the subject had a moral obligation to disobey such a command since it would be a perversion of the authority which God had granted to princes. On the other hand, the ruler was not to be actively resisted, since it is a biblical precept that tyranny is not to be resisted but endured. Luther's own views on this subject changed as the fortunes of the Reformation ebbed and flowed. He was always for resistance to evil and ungodly laws of Roman Catholic authorities. He often insisted, however, on absolute non-resistance to the commands of the true Christian—that is, Protestant—prince. His followers differed widely on this point among themselves and at various times.

Apart from the thorny question of civil disobedience, important limitations were placed on the competence, jurisdiction, and power of the secular ruler both by Lutheran theory and by the political realities within which that theory was applicable. The first such limitation was the fact that the prince ruled not alone but through his civil servants, who constituted, together with him, the *Obrigkeit,* or high magistracy. Like the prince, they too were bound by their Christian calling to serve the public interest. At the same time, their higher degree of public responsibility also gave civil servants a higher degree of independence than that of the ordinary citizen. Moreover, now that each of the Protestant German principalities was in effect a sovereign state, civil servants could, and sometimes did, leave the employ of one territorial ruler to enter into that of another. Similarly, university professors, who were also part of the *Obrigkeit,* had an obligation to truth higher than their obligation to their prince, and, moreover, they too had the practical possibility of leaving their university to accept a call from another university in another German principality.

As oppressive as these various types of officials might be to the population generally, they also served as a limitation on the arbitrary exercise of the prince's powers, in part through their freedom to respond to calls to enter the service of princes of other territories. Indeed, the power of a German prince was limited generally by the existence of the de facto confederation of the separate German principalities, with a high degree of similarity in their individual political-legal structures. Before 1517, all the various rulers of the Holy Roman Empire formed a hierarchy, with the emperor at the top and, under him, ranked in descending order of authority, the princes, dukes, counts, and other rulers, the clergy, the nobility, and the burghers. Within the various subordinate territorial, ecclesiastical, noble, and urban polities there were concurrent imperial, territorial, ecclesiastical, and noble jurisdictions. After 1555, however, each territorial ruler was equal to every other in his authority vis-à-vis his own subjects. They were not equals, of course, in power or in wealth, but each was supreme in his territory. In the Lutheran territories, each prince had the duty and right to make his own independent decisions in matters of religion. Each governed by his own law—the territorial law *(Landesrecht)* of the principality. Each selected his own officials and advisers free of outside imperial or papal pressures. At the same time, the exclusive jurisdiction of each ruler over his own territory was to be respected by every other. Each principality became a sovereign state in its foreign relations. Indeed, each received its character as a state in part from the recognition of it as such by other states within the de facto confederation.

Moreover, the Revolution crystallized a new concept of territory *(Land)* in the geographical sense. Before 1500, the contours of princely rule were set by dynastic factors: a "kingdom" or "princedom" was defined by the jurisdiction of the royal or princely household, which jurisdiction, in turn, was defined more by office, including feudal rights, than by territory. It was only in the sixteenth century that patronage began to yield to territorial sovereignty.[93] Such sovereignty was limited, however, by the interstate or federal character of the German principalities, considered in relation to one another.

A further limitation on arbitrary exercise of the prince's powers was imposed by the concept of the republic, the commonwealth, the state—the three terms came to be used interchangeably—as a polity that rules by law, a "law state" *(Rechtsstaat)*. It was presupposed that the rulers of the state would effectuate their policies by law, that is, by legislative and judicial and administrative actions, and further that they would themselves be morally bound to observe the laws of which they themselves were the authors. Moreover, their duty to govern by law was reinforced by a distinctive Lutheran philosophy both of revealed biblical law, expressed particularly in the Ten Commandments, and of natural law, corresponding to the Ten Commandments, whose principles God has planted in the conscience of every person.

Thus the supreme political authority of the Protestant prince was tempered, first, by the coexistence of his sovereign territory with the sovereign territories of other rulers within a common German framework, together with the freedom of members of the high magistracy to move from the service of one Protestant prince to that of another; and second, by the belief that the prince's law was to be based ultimately on the Ten Commandments, together with the belief that he and his *Obrigkeit,* though they had the legal power to change the law, were bound by the law in conscience until they lawfully changed it. These principles made the German prince, in theory at least, a constitutional monarch rather than an absolute monarch.

Apart from its effect on German constitutional law, the abolition of the Roman Catholic jurisdiction in Protestant principalities also left substantial gaps in German criminal law, civil law, and other related branches of the legal system, as well as in legal philosophy and legal science. It needs only to be said in this chapter that tendencies toward secularization and systematization of all branches of law received an enormous impetus from the reformation of the state, on the one hand, and of the church, on the other. In criminal law and procedure, systematic and comprehensive territorial codes were enacted—the first such codifications of a single branch of law in the history of the West and possibly in the history of mankind. In the law as a whole, including civil law, unification was achieved not through formal codification but through systematic scholarly treatises on the entire body of law applicable in a given territory, ecclesiastical as well as secular, royal and urban as well as feudal and customary—again, the first such treatises in the history of the West and possibly in the history of mankind. Like the codes of criminal law and procedure, the treatises purported to constitute an entire body of principles and rules to be applied by learned jurists and professional courts—a kind of legislation, not in the contemporary sense of a statute enacted by a legislative body but rather in the sense of a system of written rules contained in authoritative texts. Thus scholarly treatises took a place alongside statute and custom as a principal source of law in the new German *Rechtsstaat.*

Lutheran legal thought also played a significant part in the new systematizations of criminal and civil law. It emphasized the importance of relatively precise legal rules as the essential form which law takes. This tenet of legal positivism was related to the Lutheran doctrine of the wickedness of man and the consequent utility of coercive sanctions as a deterrent to misconduct. Because of the excessive generality of natural law, Luther wrote, written laws are necessary not only to deter ordinary lawbreakers but also to restrain officials, including judges, from their natural inclination to wield their powers arbitrarily. At the same time, Lutheran emphasis on general legal principles as the starting point for analysis of legal texts and cases led to the concept that the primary task of a court is to *apply* the law, that is, to bring the text or case before it under the appropriate given general principle or rule by a process of logical deduction from that kind of rule, rather than to *find* the law (as in the earlier scholastic analysis) through glosses and commentaries that inductively draw general principles from concrete results in specific texts and cases.

The emphasis on systematization through deduction from general principles to specific rules and cases led to an exaltation of the role of the professor. There developed in the sixteenth century the widespread practice of submitting the most difficult cases to university law faculties for decision. Courts of territories and of cities as well as the Imperial High Court itself, when faced with a particularly difficult application of the law, were supposed to send the entire file of the case to a law faculty, and the law professors would study and discuss the case and render a reasoned judgment binding upon the court. Called *Aktenversendung*, "the sending of the file," this institution, which lasted in Germany until 1878, had an enormous influence on the substance as well as on the style of German law. It was also highly time-consuming—and lucrative—for the professors. The widespread adoption of the professorial *Aktenversendung* procedure was part of the more general tendency to systematize the law through comprehensive treatises and, in the case of criminal law and procedure, through comprehensive codification.

Not only constitutional law, and not only philosophy and the method of law, but also basic principles of criminal law, civil law, and what may be called social law, changed substantially under the impact of the German Revolution. It is left to subsequent chapters to recount those changes.

Matters Omitted

A historical jurisprudence is especially helpful in determining what to report in telling the story of the impact of the German and English Revolutions on the Western legal tradition. In Europe in the early 1500s, and again in the mid-1600s, the time had come for certain radical legal changes which will be discussed in the chapters that follow, but not for others, which will be mentioned but not analyzed.

One such change whose time had not yet come was the emancipation of the Jews. In the sixteenth-century Lutheran Protestant lands, as in Roman Catholic principalities and kingdoms, Jews who did not convert to Christianity were required to live in ghettos and to wear a badge of identification and were restricted to certain vocations. Engaging in financial transactions was one such permitted vocation, and Jews who succeeded greatly in finance, and were therefore useful to princes and others in high places, were sometimes accepted by them socially as well. Others, however, were virtually ostracized and sometimes ruthlessly persecuted. A century later, Calvinist England was much more hospitable to Jews, inviting them to return after five centuries of expulsion, although there, too, they were segregated and deprived of civil rights.

Another change whose time had not yet come was the abolition of the crime of witchcraft. In this, too, Roman Catholics and Protestants shared responsibility. Indeed, it was Pope Innocent VIII who, in a papal bull of 1490, first defined witchcraft as a heretical departure from the Christian faith on the part of persons who have abandoned themselves to devils. Thus persons accused of practicing magic were for the first time to be prosecuted as heretics. There were few major differences among the laws against witchcraft enacted in the sixteenth and seventeenth centuries in Roman Catholic and Protestant lands, and here Calvinist English legal practice was even more severe than Lutheran German or Roman Catholic.

Most important of all, the time had not yet come to reduce the number and the cruelty of wars in Europe. Even the existence for four centuries of a common Roman Catholic faith among the rulers and peoples of all the countries of the West had not prevented the continual recurrence of wars between Roman Catholic principalities. In the fifteenth century, Roman Catholic France and Roman Catholic England were at war with each other periodically for almost a hundred years. With the emergence of Protestantism, wars of religion were fought recurrently between Protestant and Catholic principalities and kingdoms. The Peace of Augsburg of 1555 inaugurated two generations of religious peace between nations, though not, as in France, within them. Thereafter there came thirty years of almost continuous war between alliances of Roman Catholic and Protestant countries, respectively, decimating populations on both sides. It was only the Peace of Westphalia in 1648 that brought about a religious settlement that ended international religious wars and at the same time established a body of international law that served to place a limitation, however feeble, on international wars generally.

Omitted also from this volume—with less justification—is an extensive analysis of legal developments in countries that remained Roman Catholic, such as Spain, which in the sixteenth century underwent important changes in law and in legal thought. In the late fifteenth and early sixteenth centuries, before Luther's call for radical change, there was a Catholic Reformation in Spain in which the Spanish monarchy wrested from the papacy almost full control of the Spanish church. During the long joint reign of Ferdinand and Isabella—notorious for their ruthless conduct of the Spanish Inquisition—there emerged a class of distinguished legal scholars which in the course of the sixteenth century created a new "neo-Thomist" legal philosophy and legal science that paralleled in some ways the new legal philosophy and legal science of the Protestant German jurists. Under the threat of Protestantism, the Spanish Reformation, led by the newly founded Jesuit order, increasingly took on the character of an anti-Protestant Counter-Reformation. Nevertheless, the legal writings of the great sixteenth-century Spanish jurists show a similarity in some important respects to those of contemporary Protestant jurists, and occasionally the Spanish and the German jurists refer favorably to each other's works. A book remains to be written on the similarities and differences between the legal writings of the Spanish "late scholastics," as they are sometimes called, and those of the German "early Biblicists," if one may call them that.

CHAPTER 2

Lutheran Legal Philosophy

Conventional accounts of the history of Western legal thought have obscured the important contribution made by Lutheran legal philosophers of the sixteenth century. Most writers have treated the sixteenth century as a mere transition period between what they call the scholastic Middle Ages and the seventeenth-century inauguration of modern times. "The jurists of the sixteenth century," it is argued, "were doorkeepers to the modern age of legal philosophy," who "were largely incapable of entering ideas of their own."[1] At best, they are said to have served as middle links between the "medieval" legal philosophies of Aquinas and Ockham, on the one hand, and the "modern" legal philosophy of Hobbes and Locke, on the other. Indeed, when sixteenth-century legal thought has been taken more seriously, it has usually been connected not with the Lutheran Reformation but with the Italian and French "Renaissance" jurisprudence, which sought to restore the original meaning of the Roman texts and to organize them in terms of general underlying principles, or else with "neo-Thomism," sometimes called "neo-scholasticism," which revived and renewed the earlier scholastic thought and method of Thomas Aquinas.[2] The novelty and significance of the Lutheran legal reformers' philosophical teachings have thus been lost on most contemporary interpreters.[3] Lutheran legal philosophy, in particular, has remained largely in the shadows of legal humanism.

Lutheran legal philosophy has also been obscured by the narrow perspective in which Lutheran thought in general has been treated. Many legal scholars have confined their analysis to the writings of Martin Luther alone and have found therein only the rudiments of a legal philosophy haphazardly arranged. They have failed to consider the systematic exposition of Lutheran teachings in the many confessions, catechisms, and creeds of sixteenth-century Germany, in the voluminous writings of Philip Melanchthon and other important Lutheran theologians and ethicists, and in the legal treatises of Johann

Apel, Konrad Lagus, Johann Oldendorp, and other outstanding Lutheran jurists.

One major reason for the neglect of Lutheran jurisprudence has been an assumption that the Reformation was confined to matters of religion. The fact that Luther and his colleagues consigned law to a secular realm under civil authority has misled many scholars to suppose that they had made law and religion mutually irrelevant, and further, that their new beliefs and doctrines were applicable only to religion. This thesis was argued forcefully by the prominent German historian and theologian Ernst Troeltsch (1865–1923), who stated that Protestantism produced no substantial change in "legal theory . . . or in legal forms; in essentials it continued the medieval conditions."[4] If one starts from that assumption, it is easy to conclude that whatever contributions Lutheran writers did make to legal philosophy remained unoriginal, eclectic, and superficial, comprising little more than Ciceronian, patristic, and Roman Catholic commonplaces. In fact, just the opposite is true. Lutheran conceptions of the relationship of the earthly to the heavenly realms, of law to faith, was the source not only of a new theology but also of a new political science and a new jurisprudence.

Finally, some writers have stopped with the question whether Lutheran legal philosophy belongs to the natural law school or to the positivist school of jurisprudence. They have sought answers in those terms to analytical questions that are currently in vogue—concerning the nature of legal rules, the sources of legal rights, the definition of a legal system, the relation of law to politics, and the like. These categories and questions of contemporary jurisprudence leave large portions of Lutheran legal philosophy untouched.

The Lutheran Reformers did, in fact, have a distinctive legal philosophy, rooted in their basic theological and political beliefs, and this legal philosophy had a great influence not only in Germany but also in other countries of Europe and eventually in America and elsewhere.

The basic structure of Western legal philosophy had been established during and after the revolutionary upheaval of the late eleventh and early twelfth centuries.[5] Then, for the first time, great scholars of the new system of canon law and of the newly revived and resystematized Roman law had undertaken to formulate a coherent set of principles concerning the nature and purposes of law, the sources of law, the various kinds of law, and the relationship of law to justice and to order. They drew, to be sure, on the works of Plato and Aristotle and of the Greek and Roman Stoics as well as on the writings of the Church Fathers and of later theologians. Nevertheless, none of their predecessors had treated legal philosophy—as they did—as a separate comprehensive body of thought, distinct from, though related to, both moral philosophy and theology.

Not only the basic structure but also some of the basic postulates of Western legal philosophy were first articulated in the twelfth and thirteenth centuries. The jurists of that time taught that human law, including both customary and statutory law, derives its legitimacy from natural law, which is in turn, they said, a reflection of divine law. Natural law was thought to be immediately accessible to human reason. Divine law was revealed to human reason in sacred texts and in the traditions of the church. At the same time, they recognized that human selfishness, pride, and the drive for power are sources of unjust laws, which are contrary both to natural law and to divine law. Thus human law, though a response to divine will, was seen to be also a product of a defective human will which could be, and needed to be, corrected by human reason. Human reason, it was said, coincided with natural law and divine law in postulating that crimes should be punished, that contracts should be enforced, that relationships of trust and confidence should be protected, that accused persons should be heard in their own defense, and, in sum, that legal rules and procedures should conform to standards of justice.

Stated broadly, these and other postulates of Western legal philosophy, first articulated by twelfth- and thirteenth-century Roman Catholic jurists and theologians, survived in the writings of the Lutheran Reformers. Lutheran legal philosophy must, therefore, be understood in the first instance in terms of its continuity with Roman Catholic teachings. The Lutheran assault on scholastic legal philosophy came from within a tradition which the earlier so-called scholastic jurists had first established.

Nevertheless, the Lutheran Reformers introduced revolutionary changes in that tradition. In analyzing those changes, I draw on the writings of the two persons who may be said to have founded Lutheran legal philosophy—Luther himself and his cohort Philip Melanchthon—and one person, Johann Oldendorp, who developed it more fully. All three were trained in theology, philosophy, and law, though Luther was more the theologian, Melanchthon was more the philosopher, and Oldendorp was more the jurist. Despite differences among them, they all shared the same basic theological, philosophical, and legal outlook. This summary will stress what they had in common.

Luther's Legal Philosophy

Throughout his career, Luther maintained an active interest in questions of legal and political philosophy, although he did not write systematically on these subjects. After he matriculated at the University of Erfurt in 1501, his father presented him with a book of Roman law and urged him to pursue legal studies. Accordingly, Luther took preparatory courses in philosophy, theology, and canon law, and after receiving the master's degree in 1505, he enrolled in the doctorate program in civil law. Although he left the university two months later, he continued his study of canon law at the Augustinian monastery at Erfurt. In 1510 he journeyed to the papal Curia in Rome to represent the Erfurt chapter in a legal dispute within the Augustinian order.

After joining the theology faculty of the newly founded University of Wittenberg in 1511, he counted among his closest friends two of his colleagues on the law faculty, Hieronymous Schuerpf and Johann Apel, who were among the outstanding German jurists of the time.[6]

In the course of his revolt against Rome from 1517 to 1522, Luther drew on his new theological insights as well as on his extensive knowledge of the canon law. Both in his Ninety-five Theses of 1517 and in his subsequent debates and polemics, he cited a litany of abuses and injustices not only in the confessional practices of the church but also in the canon laws. He exposed, too, what he considered to be the "fallacious legal foundation" of papal authority and the "myriad" inconsistencies between "the divine precepts and practices" of Scripture and the "human laws and traditions" of the Roman Catholic Church.[7]

In the course of the next two decades, Luther prepared a number of learned commentaries and sermons on the Old Testament and devoted a large portion of his famous catechisms to exegesis of the Ten Commandments. He embellished even his densest exegetical writings on other biblical passages with citations to, and quotations from, Roman law and canon law texts. He gave public lectures and published learned tracts on various legal and moral questions of marriage, crime, usury, property, commerce, and social welfare. He drafted comprehensive laws on poor relief and on public schools. He endorsed enthusiastically the efforts of legal humanists to reconstruct the ancient texts of Roman law and to reform legal education in the German universities. He corresponded regularly with jurists throughout Europe.[8]

From his theology Luther drew the implication that it is the duty of Christians to accept the Ten Commandments as a divine law to be applied not only directly in their personal lives but also indirectly, through laws of civil authorities derived from it, in their political lives. The civil ruler, Luther argued, holds his authority of God and serves as God's vice-regent in the earthly kingdom. His law should therefore respect and reflect God's law. The civil ruler is thus not free to rule arbitrarily. Luther found those principles of justice expressed most perfectly in the Ten Commandments, which he believed to be a summary of the natural law and thus accessible to pagans as well as to Christians.[9] He found justice also expressed, though less perfectly, in Roman law, which, in his view, was an embodiment of human reason—a reason implanted by God but corrupted by human sinfulness.[10]

"The polity and the economy," Luther wrote, "are subject to reason. Reason there has first place, and there one finds civil laws and civil justice."[11] Such reason is to be found not only in Christian texts. "The heathen books," he wrote, "teach virtue, law, and wisdom for temporal life, just as the Scriptures teach faith and good works for eternal life in heaven." Homer, Plato, Demosthenes, Virgil, Cicero, and Ulpian, he wrote, are "apostles, prophets, theologians, and preachers for worldly government."[12]

Luther's understanding of law differed, however, from that of his Roman Catholic predecessors in its philosophical and theological foundations. The prevailing Roman Catholic doctrine had made conscience a handmaiden of reason. It had distinguished between a faculty of apprehension, which was called *synderesis,* and a faculty of application, which was called *conscientia.* A rational person, it was said, uses his synderesis to apprehend and elucidate the principles and precepts of natural law; he uses his conscience to apply those principles and precepts to concrete practical circumstances. Thus, for example, through the exercise of synderesis a person apprehends and understands the principle of loving his neighbor; through the exercise of conscience he connects this principle with the practice of aiding the poor and helpless and of keeping his promises. For the scholastics, reason was considered a superior cognitive or intellectual faculty, conscience an inferior practical or applicative skill.[13] Luther, by contrast, subordinated reason to conscience. Conscience, he taught, is not merely the skill of applying rational principles of natural law and knowledge. Conscience is the "bearer of man's relationship with God," the "religious root of man" that shapes and governs all the activities of his life, including both his rational apprehension and his application of the natural law.[14] "Where a man's conscience remains fallen," Luther wrote, "his reason will also inevitably be darkened, distorted, and deficient." Where his conscience is redeemed, "his rational apprehension will also be enhanced."[15] Luther did not deny that all people possess the rational faculty of distinguishing between good and evil; he differed from Roman Catholic scholastics, however, in their assertion that this faculty is independent of, and even superior to, conscience. Conscience, in Lutheran theology, is derived directly from faith; it not only applies principles of divine and natural law to concrete situations but also is a source and an embodiment of our understanding of those principles.

Neither the understanding nor the application of those principles, however, brings us nearer to salvation. Theologically, Luther's conception of law differed from that of the Roman Catholic scholastics in that he considered not only civil law but also natural law and divine law to be ordained by God only for the earthly and not for the heavenly realm. Luther did not consider law to be an integral part of the objective reality of God himself, nor did he consider that law was ordained by God as a way of leading people to union with him. Such union depended solely on faith *(sola fide),* the content of which was revealed solely in the Bible *(sola scriptura).* In Luther's theology all law, including the Ten Commandments, was ordained by God for sinful man, fallen man, as a means of helping him to fulfill his calling. Obedience to it did not rescue man from his sinfulness, nor did it make him acceptable to God.[16]

The Uses of the Law

Once it is granted that salvation does not depend on "the works of the law," the question arises: Then why does God ordain the law? What are, from God's point of view, its "uses?"[17] This is an essentially different question from that put by earlier Roman Catholic theologians, who placed obedience to the moral law, together with faith, in the realm of divine justification. For the scholastic theologian, to speak of "the uses" of the law would be like speaking of "the uses" of faith—or, indeed, the uses of God.

Luther set forth two "uses of the law" *(usus legis)* and endorsed a third. One such use is to restrain people from misconduct by threat of penalties. He called this the "civil" or "political" use of the law. God, Luther argued, wants even sinners to observe the moral law—to honor their parents, to avoid killing and stealing, to respect marriage vows, to testify truthfully, and the like—so that "some measure of earthly order, concourse, and concord may be preserved."[18] Fallen man, not naturally inclined to observe these commandments, may nevertheless be induced to do so by fear of punishment—divine punishment as well as human punishment. This "first use" of the law applies both to the Ten Commandments and to the civil laws derived therefrom.[19]

Luther's civil use of the law helped to lay the foundation for modern theories of legal positivism. Luther wrote, "Stern, hard civil rule is necessary in the world, lest the world be destroyed, peace vanish, and commerce and common interest be destroyed."[20] He emphasized that to maintain order it is important that there be precise legal rules, not only to deter lawbreakers but also to restrain officials, including judges, from their natural inclination to wield their powers arbitrarily. Especially in wicked times, he wrote, written laws are needed because of the excessive generality of natural law.[21] Thus Lutheran jurisprudence was an important source of the modern legal positivist's definition of law as the will of the state expressed in rules and enforced by coercive sanctions.

In contrast to nineteenth-century legal positivism, however, Lutheran jurisprudence postulated that the state, its will, its rules, and its sanctions are ordained by God, and that they have, in addition to their civil use, a second and even more important "theological use." Divine and natural law, as well as civil laws derived therefrom, serve to make people conscious of their duty to give themselves completely to God and their neighbors and, at the same time, of their utter inability—without divine help—to fulfill that duty. Through the law man is thus driven to seek God. Here Luther relied on Saint Paul's explanation of the significance of the Ten Commandments for Christians: to make them conscious of their inherent sinfulness and to bring them to repentance.[22]

Luther also acknowledged a third use of the law, called its "pedagogical use," namely, to educate the faithful—those who are already penitent and do not need to be coerced to obey—in what God wants of them and thus to guide them to virtue. Luther himself never expounded this third use,[23] although he endorsed without qualification confessions and treatises in which it was set forth.[24] It was his colleague and close friend Philip Melanchthon who systematically developed the doctrine of the threefold use of the law in both theological and jurisprudential terms.

The Legal Philosophy of Philip Melanchthon

It has been said that whereas Luther taught the justice of God, Melanchthon taught the justice of society, and that his teaching on social justice "deserves to be viewed alongside the teachings of an Aristotle, a Thomas Aquinas, a Leibniz, and alongside the teachings of the German school of jurisprudence of the nineteenth century."[25] Wilhelm Dilthey calls him "the ethicist of the Reformation" and the "greatest didactic genius of the [sixteenth] century, [who] liberated the philosophical sciences from the casuistry of scholastic thought. . . . A new breath of life went out from him."[26] Indeed, in his own time Melanchthon was called "the teacher of Germany" *(praeceptor Germaniae)*.[27] His teachings on social justice and on ethics were combined with a new theory of natural and positive law which came to replace Thomistic and other Roman Catholic theories in those parts of Europe where Lutheranism triumphed.

Born in 1497 and orphaned by the age of ten, Philip Melanchthon was a child prodigy. He received his bachelor's degree at the University of Heidelberg at fourteen and his master's degree at the University of Tübingen at seventeen. Thereafter, from 1514 to 1518, he worked as an editor at a publishing house and prepared both his own translations of Greek verse and an important book of classical grammar, *Rudiments of the Greek Language.*

In 1518, at the age of twenty-one, Melanchthon was called to the University of Wittenberg to serve as its first professor of Greek. In his brilliant inaugural address, "The Improvement of Education," he urged his colleagues to abandon the "arid, barbaric fulminations of the scholastics" and to return to the study of classical and Christian sources.[28] Melanchthon's iconoclastic manifesto won the accolade of Luther, who was in the audience. The thirty-five-year-old Luther defended his young colleague against detractors and ultimately became one of his staunchest friends and supporters.

Under Luther's inspiration, Melanchthon joined the cause of the German Protestant Reformation. In his first year at Wittenberg, he studied theology while he taught Greek and rhetoric, and early in 1519 he received the bachelor's degree in theology. He soon became a gifted professor of theology: as many as six hundred students attended his lectures. He also became an eloquent exponent of Lutheran theology. In 1519 and 1520 he wrote several learned defenses of Luther against his Roman Catholic opponents and a number of short popular theological pamphlets. In 1521 he published his famous *Loci Commu-*

nes Rerum Theologicarum, "The Common Topics of Theological Matters," the first systematic treatise on Protestant theology.[29]

During the 1520s and 1530s, Melanchthon played a leading role in the debates between the Lutheran Reformers and their Roman Catholic and radical Protestant opponents. He drafted the chief declaration of Lutheran theology, the Augsburg Confession (1530) and its Apology (1531), and participated in the drafting of the Schmalkaldic Articles (1537), another important Lutheran creed. He prepared a number of Lutheran catechisms and instruction books and published more than a dozen commentaries on biblical books and ancient Christian creeds as well as several revised and expanded editions of his *Loci Communes* (1535, 1543, 1555, 1559).

Although Melanchthon's theological writings were less acrimonious than Luther's and more systematic and logical in form, they differed little in substance.[30] Despite variations in emphasis which eventually led their successors to split into two rival camps, at no time did Luther and Melanchthon ever oppose each other on any major point either of theology or of moral, political, or legal philosophy.[31] Although Melanchthon drew freely on the entire tradition of Western legal philosophy, particularly on Graeco-Roman sources, he restated and revised that tradition in a new way, reconciling it with, and subordinating it to, the cardinal Lutheran doctrines of the two kingdoms, total depravity, justification by faith alone, Scripture as the sole source of divine revelation, the Christian calling, and the priesthood of all believers.[32]

Melanchthon wrote much on legal philosophy, chiefly in the context of moral and political philosophy. He taught university courses in Roman law and wrote widely on the theological and philosophical foundations of legal institutions. He also participated in the drafting of a number of urban and territorial statutes and was frequently consulted on cases that raised intricate legal, political, and moral questions. He developed on Lutheran foundations a systematic philosophy of law. It may be summarized under three headings: (1) the relationship of natural law to divine law (the Ten Commandments); (2) the uses of natural law in civil society; and (3) the relationship of natural law to positive law.[33]

The Relationship of Natural Law to Divine Law

Melanchthon departed in only minor respects from the traditional Roman Catholic doctrine that there are certain moral principles inscribed in the hearts of all people by which they should be governed in their relations with one another, and that these are accessible to human reason. Like his Roman Catholic predecessors and contemporaries, he called these moral principles the law of nature *(lex naturae),* or natural law *(jus naturale).* He postulated, as did they, that reason was given to man by God partly in order to discern and apply this natural law.

Melanchthon offered, however, a radically new theory of the ontology of natural law, that is, its origin in the essential nature of man.[34] Building on the two kingdoms theory, he taught that God has implanted in all persons certain "elements of knowledge" *(notitiae),* which are a light from above, a "natural light," without which we could not find our way in the earthly kingdom.[35] These *notitiae* include not only certain logical concepts, such as that the whole is bigger than any one of its parts, and that a thing either exists or does not, but also certain moral concepts, such as that God is good, that offenses which harm society are to be punished, and that promises should be kept.[36]

These inborn moral concepts, Melanchthon argued, are "facts of [human] nature," which form the premises, not the objects, of rational inquiry.[37] They are thus beyond the power of human reason either to prove or to disprove. This was a marked departure from the Roman Catholic scholastic tradition, which taught that human reason can prove moral propositions that are consistent with divine revelation.[38] Melanchthon also rejected the related scholastic doctrine that the universal acceptance of a given principle of justice is proof of its rationality; thus he did not include the universal law of nations *(jus gentium)* automatically within the category of natural law.[39]

Human reason, according to Melanchthon, being corrupted by original sin, is incapable not only of proving the existence of certain fundamental inborn moral concepts but also of apprehending and applying them without distortion.[40] The scholastics, too, had recognized that human reason can be distorted by self-interest, but they had argued that it need not be. For Melanchthon, however, as for Luther, human reason not only can be but is inevitably corrupted by man's innate inclination to greed and power.[41]

Melanchthon's strong emphasis on the limitations of human reason rendered his doctrine of natural law paradoxical. On the one hand, he argued that "the law of nature is the law of God concerning those virtues which the reason understands."[42] On the other hand, he argued that "in this enfeebled state of nature" human reason is "darkened," and thus "the law of nature is distorted . . . and invariably misunderstood."[43] His resolution of this paradox was to subordinate the natural law that is both discernible to, and distorted by, human reason to the biblical law that is revealed to faith.[44] The biblical law (which Melanchthon also called the divine law) reiterates and illuminates the natural law.[45] This biblical law is summarized in the Ten Commandments, whose two "tables" Melanchthon divided (as did Saint Augustine, the scholastics, and the other early Lutherans) into the first three commandments and the remaining seven.[46] The first three commandments—to acknowledge one God and make no graven images, to utter no blasphemy, and to keep the Sabbath holy—correspond to the human need for union with God. The remaining seven—to honor authority, to preserve life, to protect the family, to respect property, to maintain truth, to avoid envy, and to avoid greed—correspond to the human need for community of persons with one another.

Thus Melanchthon, following Luther's lead, transformed traditional Western moral and legal philosophy by making not reason but the Bible, and more particularly the Ten Commandments, the basic source and summary of natural law. Earlier Roman Catholic writers—particularly in the fifteenth century—had, to be sure, also discussed and interpreted the Ten Commandments at some length. They had also argued that "the Old Law [i.e., the Ten Commandments] clearly set forth the obligations of the natural law."[47] Most Roman Catholic writers, however, had relied on the Ten Commandments not to develop a natural law for the outer civil life but to develop a moral law for the inner spiritual life. Accordingly, most of the discussion of the Ten Commandments in the Roman Catholic tradition occurred in confessional books and in treatments of the internal forum and the sacrament of penance, and not in books on law.[48] For Melanchthon, by contrast, the Ten Commandments were both the ultimate source and summary of the natural law and hence a model for the positive law enacted by the earthly rulers.

This represented a new way of reconciling faith and reason. In contrast to traditional Roman Catholic thought, Melanchthon asserted that human reason can discern divine and natural law only if it is guided by faith. At the same time he conflated divine and natural law, identifying both with the Ten Commandments. By so doing, he restructured the traditional learning about natural law in such a way as to bring it entirely within the Bible, and he reinterpreted the Bible in such a way as to embrace the traditional learning about natural law.

Basic to Melanchthon's theory of the Ten Commandments was the theory of the two kingdoms. The first three (or, by later count, four) commandments, in Melanchthon's conception, relate to a person's direct relationship with God, that is, the heavenly kingdom; the last seven (or, by later count, six) relate to civil society, the human community, that is, the earthly kingdom. Only if people accepted by faith the first table of the Decalogue could they, by reason, establish an ethic, and hence a law, based on the second table.[49]

The Uses of Natural Law in Civil Society

Like Luther, Melanchthon believed that in "the drama" of faith and grace, that is, in the heavenly kingdom, law "plays no useful role."[50] "So one may ask," he wrote, "for what, then, is the law useful?"[51] By "law," in this context, he meant both the natural law embodied in the second table of the Ten Commandments and positive law reflecting it. His answer, like Luther's, was that both natural law and positive law have important uses within the earthly kingdom—for Christians and non-Christians alike.

Melanchthon elaborated systematically the "civil" and "theological" uses of the law which Luther had adumbrated. The first use is to coerce people, by fear of punishment, to avoid evil and do good.[52] Although such "external morality . . . does not justify a person before God," Melanchthon wrote, "it is pleasing to God,"[53] since it allows persons of all faiths to live peaceably together within the earthly kingdom that God has created,[54] it enables persons who are Christians to fulfill the vocations to which God has called them, and it allows "God continually to gather to himself a Church among men."[55]

The second use of the law, for Melanchthon as for Luther, was to make people conscious of their inability, by their own will and reason, without coercion, to avoid evil and do good.[56] Such consciousness, Melanchthon argued, is a precondition to both their search for God's help and their faith in God's grace.[57]

Melanchthon added a third "pedagogical" or "educational" use of the law, namely, to educate the faithful themselves, the righteous, "those saints who now are believers, who have been born again through God's word and the Holy Spirit." They, too, Melanchthon said, need the law so they may "know the works that please God."[58] Though not articulated by Luther, Melanchthon's third use of the law built on Luther's teaching that the Christian believer, though saved, is not yet perfect. He is at once saint and sinner, citizen of both the heavenly kingdom and the earthly kingdom.[59] Thus even the greatest saints, Melanchthon insisted, need the instruction of the natural law, "for they carry with them . . . weakness and sin," although their sin "is not counted against them," and they "are still partly ignorant of God's will and desire for their lives."[60]

Melanchthon's emphasis on the educational use of the law brought the heavenly kingdom into a close relationship, though not a complete interdependence, with the earthly kingdom. The law which, on the one hand, was revealed on Mount Sinai and, on the other, is implanted by God in every human heart guides all persons, whether Christians or non-Christians, in ways that are pleasing to God.[61] It imbues in them a respect for authority, a concern for society, a love for justice and fairness, a desire for right living. Melanchthon called this a form of "civic" or "political righteousness," which, though "it must be sharply distinguished from religion or evangelical righteousness," is, nonetheless, a "useful benefit" that the law provides.[62]

The Relationship of Natural Law to Positive Law

Melanchthon's concept of the educational role of natural law in guiding saints and sinners alike in their understanding of "political righteousness" is an important link between his theory of the uses of natural law in civil society and his theory of the relationship of natural law to positive law. His theory of that relationship, put briefly, was that even as God sets guidelines for civil society through natural law, so civil society, especially through the state, has the task of transforming the general principles of natural law into detailed rules of positive law. That is what natural law "educates" the state to do. At the same time, the state—and here Melanchthon used the word "state" in its modern sense[63]—is to exercise, through its laws, an educational function with respect to its subjects parallel to the educational function which God, through natural law, exercises with respect to the state.

For Melanchthon, as for Luther, political rulers were called to be God's "mediators" and "ministers," and their subjects were under a duty to render to them the same obedience that they rendered to God.[64] Melanchthon went beyond Luther, however, in articulating the divinely imposed task of political authorities to promulgate "rational positive laws" for the governance of both the church and the state in the earthly kingdom.[65] To be rational, and therefore legitimate, Melanchthon stated, positive laws have to be based on the general principles of natural law. Those principles themselves, however, taken as a whole, require that positive laws be based also on practical considerations of social utility and the common good. Thus Melanchthon added to the first criterion of the rationality of positive laws, namely, their correspondence to natural law, viewed as a system of general principles, a second criterion, namely, their correspondence to political, economic, and social needs in given times and places.

In elaborating the first criterion, Melanchthon started from the position that it is the office of political rulers to be the "custodians or guardians of both the first table and the second table of the Decalogue."[66] As such, they were responsible for defining and enforcing by positive laws the right relationship between man and God, as reflected in the first three commandments, and the right relationships among men, as reflected in the last seven commandments.

As guardians of the first table, political rulers were not only to proscribe and punish all idolatry, blasphemy, and violations of the Sabbath.[67] They were also to "establish pure doctrine" and right liturgy, "to prohibit all wrong doctrine," "to punish the obstinate," and to root out the heathen and the heterodox.[68] Thus Melanchthon laid a theoretical basis for the welter of new religious laws that were promulgated in Lutheran territories and cities, many of which contained comprehensive compendia of orthodox confessions and doctrines, hymns and prayers, liturgies and rites. The principle of *cuius regio eius religio,* which was adopted (though not in those terms) in the Religious Peace of Augsburg (1555) and again (expressly) in the religion clauses of the Peace of Westphalia (1648), rested ultimately on Melanchthon's theory of the role of positive law in defining and enforcing the first table of the Decalogue.

As guardians of the second table of the Decalogue, political rulers were responsible for governing "the multiple relationships by which God has bound men together."[69] Thus, on the basis of the Fifth Commandment as we now count them ("Honor thy father and thy mother"), officials were obligated to prohibit and punish disobedience, disrespect, or disdain of authorities such as parents, political rulers, teachers, employers, and others; on the basis of the Sixth Commandment ("Thou shalt not murder"), unlawful killing, violence, assault, battery, wrath, hatred, mercilessness, and other offenses against one's neighbor; on the basis of the Seventh Commandment ("Thou shalt not commit adultery"), unchastity, incontinence, prostitution, pornography, obscenity, and other sexual offenses; on the basis of the Eighth Commandment ("Thou shalt not steal"), theft, burglary, embezzlement, and similar offenses against another's property, as well as waste or noxious use or sumptuous use of one's own property; on the basis of the Ninth Commandment ("Thou shalt not bear false witness"), all forms of dishonesty, fraud, defamation, slander, calumny, sophistry, false pretenses, deception, and other violations; and, finally, on the basis of the Tenth Commandment ("Thou shalt not covet"), all attempts to perform these or other offensive acts against others.

Many of these aspects of social intercourse had traditionally been governed by the Roman Catholic Church both through the confessional laws of the internal forum and through the canon laws of the external forum. Melanchthon's legal philosophy provided a rationale for political officials to bring these subjects within the province of the state. Thus in elaborating his second criterion for the rationality of positive laws, namely, their correspondence to practical considerations of social utility and the common good,[70] Melanchthon drew from the Ten Commandments as a whole, in the context of Scripture as a whole, a general duty, imposed on the state by divine will, "to maintain discipline, judgment, and peace in accordance with the divine commandments and the rational laws of the land."[71] Neither the divine commandments, however, nor the rational laws of the land based on them contained a systematic statement of the nature of the legal order required for maintaining "discipline, judgment, and peace." In laying foundations for such a systematic statement, Melanchthon developed general theories of both criminal and civil law.

In criminal law, Melanchthon listed "four very important reasons" for punishing crime:

> (1) God is a wise and righteous being, who out of his goodness created rational creatures to be like him. Therefore, if they strive against the One who is the order of righteousness, he blots them out. The first reason for punishment, therefore, is the order of righteousness in God. (2) The need to curb some men. If murderers, adulterers, robbers, and thieves remained in our midst, nobody would be safe. (3) [To set an] example. If some are punished, others will be reminded to consider God's wrath and to fear his punishment. And thus the source of punishment will be lessened. (4) The importance of divine judgment and eternal punishment, which men will not escape if they are not converted to God. God's punishment now shows that he upholds a standard of virtue. He is a righteous Judge, and thus reminds us that after this life all sinners who are not converted to God will be punished.[72]

Thus for Melanchthon criminal punishment serves as a form of divine retribution, special deterrence, general deterrence, and education.

In explaining the source of civil law, as contrasted with criminal law, Melanchthon postulated the duty of the ruler to facilitate and regulate the formation and functioning of various types of voluntary social relationships. He focused on three in particular: contractual relationships, family relationships, and relationships involving the visible church. Each of these relationships, too, had traditionally been subject, at least in part, to the jurisdiction of the Roman Catholic Church. The canon law had governed all contracts supported by the parties' oaths or pledges of faith as well as most aspects of marriage and family life and of church polity and property. In the jurisprudence of Melanchthon, these social relationships were brought within the jurisdiction of the Protestant state and regulated by an elaborate system of civil law.

God has ordained contracts of various kinds, Melanchthon wrote, to facilitate the sale, lease, or exchange of property, the procurement of labor and employment, and the lending of money and extension of credit.[73] God has called his political officials to promulgate general contract laws that prescribe "fair, equal, and equitable" agreements, that invalidate contracts based on fraud, duress, mistake, or coercion, and that proscribe contracts that are unconscionable, immoral, or offensive to the public good. Melanchthon was content, for the most part, to state these general principles of contract law in categorical form. Occasionally he applied these general principles to specific cases. He condemned with particular vehemence loan contracts that obligated debtors to pay excessive rates of interest or entitled creditors to secure the loan with property whose value far exceeded the amount of the loan, unilateral labor and employment contracts that conditioned a master's obligation to pay on full performance from the servant, and contracts of purchase and sale that were based on inequality of the exchange.

Officials were also to promulgate rules to govern family relations. Civil laws were to prescribe monogamous heterosexual marriages between two fit parties and to proscribe homosexual, polygamous, bigamous, and other "unnatural" relations. They were to ensure that each marriage was formed by voluntary consent of both parties and to undo relationships based on fraud, mistake, coercion, or duress. They were to promote the created marital functions of propagation and child rearing and to prohibit all forms of contraception, abortion, and infanticide. They were to protect the authority of the paterfamilias over his wife and children but to punish severely all forms of adultery, desertion, incest, and wife or child abuse.[74]

The church, too, in Melanchthon's view, was to be regulated by laws promulgated by the political ruler, not only with respect to doctrine and liturgy, according to the first table of the Decalogue, but also with respect to its internal organization and administration and its external property relations. "The prince is God's chief bishop [*summus episcopus*] in the church," Melanchthon wrote.[75] It is his responsibility to define the episcopal hierarchy within the church—from local congregations to urban ecclesiastical circuits to the territorial council or synod; to decide the responsibilities and procedures of congregational consistories, of circuit councils, and of the territorial synod; to appoint ecclesiastical officials, to pay them, to supervise them, and, if necessary, to admonish and discipline them; to ensure that the local universities and schools produce the pastors, teachers, and administrators needed to operate the church; and to furnish the land, the supplies, and the services necessary to erect and maintain each church building. He is also to oversee the acquisition, use, and alienation of church property.[76]

Thus Melanchthon, in the style of modern legal positivism, described the political rulers as the makers and enforcers of positive law. Yet he also insisted that the validity of positive law was limited by the natural law revealed in Scripture and written in the hearts of men. It was natural law that gave the ruler authority to make positive laws, but only such positive laws as are consistent with natural law. Moreover, since the ultimate source of positive law was natural law, the ruler was himself bound by the positive laws which he had made.

Melanchthon described the duties and rights not only of political officials but also of those subject to their authority and law. Early in his career, Melanchthon, like Luther, taught that all subjects have the duty to obey and no right to resist political authority and positive law—even where such authority and such law have become arbitrary and abusive. If "the magistrate commands anything with tyrannical caprice," he wrote in 1521, "we must bear with this magistrate because of love, since nothing can be changed without a public uprising or sedition, although those subject to such tyranny should escape if they can do so without turmult."[77] Melanchthon based this theory of absolute obedience on the political texts of Saint Paul: that "the powers that be are ordained by God," that unswerving obedience to them is "mandated by conscience," and that to defy them is to defy God and to incur his wrath.[78]

As the power of German princes continued to grow, however, Melanchthon became more deeply concerned to safeguard subjects from abuse and to restrain princes from tyranny. At least by 1555 he had joined those who recognized a right of resistance against tyrants, based on natural law. "Deliberate disobedience against legitimate temporal authority, and against true and rational laws," he still maintained, "is deadly sin, sin which God punishes with eternal damnation if we obstinately continue in it."[79] But if the positive law promulgated by the political official contradicts natural law, particularly the Ten Commandments, it is not binding in conscience. That positive law cannot bind in conscience if it contradicts the fixed standards of natural law is, of course, consistent with Roman Catholic jurisprudence. The principle, however, had radically different implications in a unitary Protestant state in which there were no longer concurrent ecclesiastical and secular jurisdictions to challenge each other's legislation on the ground of violation of natural law. It was now left to the people—acting either individually or else collectively through territorial and imperial diets—

to resist officials who had strayed beyond the authority of their office and to disobey laws that had defied the precepts of natural law.

In addition, Melanchthon emphasized from an early time the importance of published written law as a restraint on arbitrary power.[80] All the great legal civilizations of the past, including the Israelite, Cretan, Greek, and Roman, Melanchthon argued, have met this requirement. Written and published laws are more secure, more predictable, and more permanent. They protect citizens against groundless violations of their person and property by officials. They also protect authorities against unjustified rebellions and groundless charges of arbitrariness or capriciousness. Written positive laws provide "an iron wall against the ruthlessness of the crowd" and a common bond between ruler and people for the defense of order and peace.[81]

Melanchthon also considered Roman law to be a restraint on arbitrary authority. Roman law, he argued, was positive law, imposed by the ruler; in that connection he stressed both its written and its detailed character. Yet he also, like the Roman Catholic jurists, considered it to be *ratio scripta,* "written reason," implementing natural law. He countered the argument that the Roman laws were of pagan, not Christian, origin by stating that they "are pleasing to God, although they were promulgated by a heathen ruler," and that they "stem not from human cleverness [but] rather they are beams of divine wisdom," and "a visible appearance of the Holy Spirit" to the heathen.[82] Thus the Roman law bound the *Obrigkeit.* It was *their* law, positive law imposed *by* them; yet since it stemmed from their predecessors, and since it was in the form of glosses and commentaries on ancient texts, it was to a certain extent beyond their reach. It had a certain objectivity and exercised a certain restraint over them.[83]

Melanchthon's effusive praise of Roman law was not based on ignorance of its content. He studied it intensively and knew its development from the texts of Justinian through the glosses of Irnerius, the commentaries of Bartolus, and the revisions of his contemporaries.[84] Colleagues and friends with whom he discussed Roman law included some of the foremost legal scholars of the age.[85] At one time he taught a course in Roman law. He found in Roman law a source of political order which protects against "seizure of power by the crowd," on the one hand, and a restraint on abuse of authority which "guards us against tyranny," on the other.[86] Thus Melanchthon set forth the idea, made popular in the nineteenth century by Rudolf von Jhering, that "Roman law . . . is in a certain sense a philosophy."[87]

Melanchthon helped to shape the content and character of German legal philosophy until well into the seventeenth century. A whole generation of Germany's leading jurists in the sixteenth century—Johann Oldendorp (ca. 1486–1567), Hieronymous Schuerpf (1481–1554), Johann Apel (1486–1536), Konrad Lagus (ca. 1499–1546), Basilius Monner (ca. 1501–1566), Melchior Kling (1504–1571), Johannes Schneidewin (1519–1568), Nicolas Vigelius (1529–1600), and many others—came under his direct influence as students, colleagues, and correspondents.[88] Generations of students thereafter studied his legal, political, and moral writings, many of which were still being published in the late seventeenth century and used as textbooks in the universities. His basic jurisprudential insights dominated German legal scholarship at least until the late seventeenth century.

The Legal Philosophy of Johann Oldendorp

Melanchthon's legal philosophy was neither the only nor the most comprehensive Lutheran legal philosophy developed in the sixteenth century. Although sixteenth-century Lutheran jurists and moralists accepted Melanchthon's basic insights, they sometimes criticized the formulation and focus of these insights, and they systematized and supplemented them in their own way. Perhaps the most significant such critical systematization of Lutheran legal philosophy was that of Johann Oldendorp.

Oldendorp was "one of the strongest legal figures of his epoch,"[89] "surpassing all others," in Roderich von Stintzing's words, "in the power of his personality . . . and in his significance as a writer and as a teacher."[90] Born in Hamburg in the 1480s,[91] he studied law from 1504 to 1508 at the University of Rostock and from 1508 to 1515 at Bologna, then a leading center of humanist thought. In 1516 he became a professor of Roman law and civil procedure at the University of Greifswald. In these early years, Oldendorp was steeped in the new humanism. He became a close student of the classics—Plato, Aristotle, and Cicero—and of Roman law.

In the early 1520s, Oldendorp resolved to dedicate his life to the cause of the Lutheran Reformation. Accordingly, in 1526 he left Greifswald to become a leading city official *(Stadtsyndikus)* of Rostock and leader of the city's Reformation party. Eventually he was influential in inducing the Rostock city council to adhere to the Reformation, and he himself played an important part in supervising church activities there and in establishing a public school for the education of the young. Roman Catholic opposition, however, led him in 1534 to leave Rostock in order to accept the post of city counsel *(Stadtsyndikus)* in Lübeck, one of Germany's chief commercial centers. There, too, he worked to bring Protestantism to the city, but, again, opposition eventually forced him out. In 1536 he accepted a teaching position in Frankfurt an der Oder, where he had also taught for a short time in 1520–21. In 1539 he was invited to Cologne, both to teach at the university and to serve the city government. The Roman Catholic archbishop of Cologne, Cardinal Hermann von Wied, was himself drawn to Protestantism and befriended Oldendorp. Oldendorp also came in personal contact there with Melanchthon and the Strassburg reformer Martin Bucer. Once again, however, facing opposition, Oldendorp left Cologne in 1541. Following a brief term as professor at the University of Marburg, he returned to Cologne at the urging of Cardinal Hermann, but in 1543 he was finally expelled from the city by the Roman Catholic authorities. He returned to Marburg, where Protestantism was firmly established, and taught in the law faculty there for twenty-four years until his death in 1567.

Oldendorp accepted the call to Marburg on condition that he be freed from the usual requirement of lecturing on the texts of the Corpus Juris Civilis in the order and manner imposed by the post-glossators—the famous *mos italicus* that had dominated European legal education and legal scholarship for some two centuries. He would come, he insisted, only if he could "teach the laws with special attention to their just consequences and in their relationship to God's word, which, above all, must be pursued and taught."[92] Eventually Oldendorp was authorized by the royal founder of the university, Landherr Philip the Magnanimous, to introduce a basic reform of legal education at Marburg, whereby the entire body of law was considered philosophically and historically in its relationship to the word of God.[93]

Oldendorp's copious legal writings present a complex legal philosophy, in which classical Greek, Stoic, Roman, scholastic, humanist, and other elements are recombined in an original way and are subordinated to biblical faith and the Christian conscience.[94] Thus one may say that Oldendorp, like Melanchthon, was both a humanist and a Lutheran.

Oldendorp's legal philosophy may be divided into three parts: (1) his theory of the interrelationships of divine law, natural law, and positive law; (2) his theory of equity; and (3) his theory of politics and the state.

Divine Law, Natural Law, and Positive Law

Oldendorp's jurisprudence starts with a deceptively simple definition of law *(Recht, ius)* as the totality of legal norms. Legal norms, in turn, are defined as general rules, issued by certain authorities, which command, prohibit, permit, or punish conduct. Thus, Law with a capital *L (Recht, ius)* is identified with particular laws with a small *l (Gesetze, leges)*, in the style of modern positivism.[95]

Laws issued by civil authorities *(leges rei publicae)* are, however, subordinate, in Oldendorp's theory, to the laws which are implanted by God in the human heart and which are discerned by conscience; these Oldendorp calls *lex in hominibus*, "law inside people," and also natural law *(lex naturalis, ius naturae)*, and are considered by him to be directly binding on the civil authorities. Laws promulgated by God in the Bible *(leges Bibliae)* are themselves to be discerned, in Oldendorp's view, by the conscience of each believer.[96]

Thus in Oldendorp's theory, as in the traditional Roman Catholic scholastic jurisprudence first enunciated systematically by the great twelfth-century canonist Gratian, there are three states, or levels, of law, which form a hierarchy:

divine law, natural law, and human law. In contrast, however, to Gratian, Thomas Aquinas, and other Roman Catholic theorists, Oldendorp restricted *lex divina* to the *leges* set forth in the Bible, which in effect meant chiefly the Ten Commandments. In that, he followed both Luther and Melanchthon, who early declared that of the many rules laid down in the Old Testament, only the Ten Commandments are binding on Christians. Also, like Luther and Melanchthon, and unlike Gratian and Aquinas, Oldendorp did not speak of a *lex aeterna* transcending the Bible.

Oldendorp also departed from Roman Catholic teaching in deriving *lex in hominibus,* or natural law, not from human reason as such, that is, the reason that originates in man's mind, but, once again, from the Bible. Natural law, Oldendorp writes, is derived from those parts of the Bible, especially the Ten Commandments and portions of the New Testament, which establish general moral principles of love and truthfulness—especially love of one's fellowman as a community, love of one's individual neighbors, the Golden Rule, and the duty to be truthful in one's relations with others.[97] This is a God-given, biblical natural law; through his God-given conscience each person has the capacity to discern it and to observe it. Conscience is, for Oldendorp, indeed a form of reason; it is not, however, ordinary human reason, or civil reason *(ratio civilis),* but a divine reason implanted in man, which Oldendorp calls natural reason *(ratio naturalis).* For nature, in Oldendorp's concept, is the creative power of God; indeed, "nature is God the creator of all things."[98] The natural law implanted by God in man's conscience "does not depend on the power of the person. . . . God has written it into your mind."[99] "Conscience," he wrote, "is an infallible guide."[100]

"Civil reason," *ratio civilis,* which does depend on the power of the person, operates primarily in the sphere of the law of the civil polity. That law, too, however, is derived ultimately from Holy Scripture. Like Luther and Melanchthon, Oldendorp traced all laws for ordering the earthly kingdom (*weltliches Regiment,* "the secular regime") to what later came to be numbered as the Fifth Commandment ("Honor thy father and thy mother"—the prince being the parent). More clearly than Melanchthon, he traced all penal laws to the Sixth Commandment ("Thou shalt not kill"), the law of private property to the Eighth Commandment ("Thou shalt not steal"), and the law of procedure to the Ninth Commandment ("Thou shalt not bear false witness"). He also (unlike Melanchthon) traced family law to the Tenth Commandment ("Thou shalt not covet . . . thy neighbor's wife") and the law of taxation to the general commandment "Thou shalt love thy neighbor as thyself."[101]

Oldendorp placed special emphasis on the Eighth Commandment ("Thou shalt not steal"), in which he saw the source not only of private property but also of contract law. Here, as elsewhere in his writings, he applied the four Aristotelian "causes" to his analysis. The "efficient cause" of contract law, what "effectuates" it, he contended, is "natural or divine law," which he identified also with the *jus gentium,* the law common to all nations. Contract law, he wrote, comes into being as a result of the fact that God has created all of us to be brothers and has therefore given us, through our natural reason, the opportunity to enter into contracts with one another for our mutual benefit, honestly and fairly, "without any oppression of others" *(sine ullo gravamine).* The "material cause" of contract law, its subject matter, Oldendorp stated, is its method of bringing the enormous variety of human affairs into a common order. The "formal cause," that is, the forms through which contract law operates, include, in Oldendorp's analysis, purchase and sale, leases, donations, and other devices for the mutual sharing of wealth. Here again, he emphasized forms of (Aristotelian) liberality and inveighed against the use of contracts to take advantage of the indigent. And last, but most important, the "final cause" of contract law, that is, its "end" *(finis),* its purpose, is the exercise of responsibilities of mutual sharing through preserving the commutative equality of the contracting parties, that is, equality of their burdens and benefits, thereby avoiding oppression of the indigent and helping to maintain constancy in commercial affairs.[102]

Thus Oldendorp viewed the laws by which Germany was governed in his time *(leges rei publicae)* as ordained by God. Yet he also subjected those laws to the tests of natural law *(lex in hominibus)* and divine law *(leges Bibliae),* and he said that in the exceptional instances in which they were found wanting, it is the duty of the Christian conscience to disavow and disobey them. "For the civil law," he wrote, "as Philip [Melanchthon] says, can prescribe nothing that is contrary to natural law. If it totally departs from natural reason it is not binding."[103] He did in fact find a number of such instances. He condemned as directly contrary to *leges Bibliae* human laws permitting the sale of church benefices, divorce, and usury, and as contrary to *lex in hominibus* human laws permitting bad faith possession of property, disinheritance of family members, delay of justice, interest of a judge in the outcome of proceedings before him, privileges granted by a ruler against natural law, conduct of war on the basis of a mere advance declaration, strict forms of servitude such as slavery, and some others.[104] More generally, he argued that natural law requires an owner to use his property for social ends and not, for example, to exclude others from use of it in instances where such use does him no harm.[105] As we shall see, he also argued that natural law imposes substantial duties on the state.

Thus the positivist character of Oldendorp's definition of law ("law is the totality of legal norms") was corrected, to a certain extent, by his invocation of divine legal norms revealed in the Bible and, through biblical faith, in the individual conscience.

Equity

There remained, for Oldendorp, another equally crucial question which neither Luther nor Melanchthon had adequately addressed, namely, by what criteria legal norms, whether biblical, natural, or civil, are to be applied in individual cases. The very generality of a legal norm or rule, Oldendorp wrote, presupposes that it is applicable in a wide variety of situations, each with its own unique circumstances; yet the rule itself contains no indication of how the multiplicity of differences are to be taken into account. Two centuries after Oldendorp, Immanuel Kant expressed this point succinctly in his dictum that "there is no rule for applying a rule."[106]

Melanchthon had addressed the problem in the manner of the scholastic jurists. Rulers were required, he wrote, to "tailor the general principles of natural law to fit . . . the circumstances."[107] General principles, he said, anticipating a famous twentieth-century American jurist, do not decide concrete cases.[108] If a "generally just law works injustice in a particular case," Melanchthon wrote, it is the responsibility of a judge to apply the law "equitably and benevolently," if he can, so as to remove the injustice.[109] Nevertheless, a "generally just law" must be maintained even if in a particular case it results in injustice, since "pious persons may not be left in uncertainty" about the requirements of the law.[110]

Oldendorp filled the gap between rule and application with a different concept of equity *(Billigkeit, aequitas).* Equity, in his view, is that which requires careful examination of the concrete circumstances of the particular case and which enables the judge properly to apply the general rule, the abstract norm, to those circumstances.[111] Here Oldendorp built on, and went beyond, Aristotle's conception (largely repeated by Melanchthon) that equity corrects the defect in a rule whose excessive generality would work an injustice if the rule were applied in a particular case which literally falls within it but which it was not actually meant to include.[112] The Aristotelian contrast is between equity and *strict* law, not between equity and *all* law: equity is for the exceptional case that the rule is not intended to cover. The scholastic jurists had built on this Aristotelian concept of equity, but had filled it with new content: equity, they said, protects the poor and helpless, enforces relations of trust and confidence, and otherwise departs from particular laws that work hardship in particular types of cases.[113] For Oldendorp, however, all law is strict law, since all law is general and abstract.[114] Therefore, every application of the law needs to be governed by equity. Thus law and equity, *Recht und Billigkeit, ius et aequitas,* stand opposite each other and complete each other, becoming a single thing.[115]

Oldendorp concluded that equity has a threefold function: first, to suspend legal norms that conflict with conscience; second, to improve legal norms (for example, by favoring widows, orphans, the aged, the sick); and, third, to interpret legal norms in every case to which such norms are to be applied.[116] The first and second of these functions reflect traditional Roman Catholic views of equity, and identify it, as Oldendorp identified it, with natural law. The third, to which Oldendorp subordinated the other two, reflects his own distinctive jurisprudence, in which natural law is merged with human law as it is merged with divine law.[117]

Equity is, in fact, for Oldendorp, the law of conscience. It is natural (that is, God-given) law *(lex naturalis, ius naturae)*, the law inside people *(lex in hominibus)*. It is not the product of human will, or of the kind of reason which depends on human will and which Oldendorp called civil reason.[118] Equity, or natural law, is instilled by God in the conscience of the individual person, that is, in that faculty "which enables us to distinguish good from evil, just from unjust, and to give judgment."[119]

Oldendorp thus drew on an earlier scholastic conception of conscience, insofar as he defined it as an aspect of practical reason through which general moral principles are applied to concrete circumstances. Thomas Aquinas had developed the conception of conscience as an act of applying knowledge of good and evil to a particular case.[120] Aquinas, however, had not translated—as Oldendorp did—this moral concept into a legal concept. Moreover, Oldendorp, in contrast to Aquinas, followed the Lutheran conception of conscience as pertaining to the whole person of man, that is, his faith, and not simply his intellectual and moral qualities. Thus for Oldendorp, as for Luther, the conscience of sinful man can be redeemed by faith, through God's grace.[121]

One must ask: How is the individual person, faced with the difficult question of applying legal norms to concrete cases, to retrieve equity from his conscience? How is he to determine what it is that conscience tells him and to know whether it is his conscience speaking or merely his civil reason or his will? Oldendorp's answer may not satisfy the non-Lutheran reader. A "conscience-decision" *(Gewissensentscheidung)*, he wrote, is a personal spiritual judgment, a judgment of the soul *(iudicium animae)*. In the first instance, it is based, as is any legal decision *(Rechtsentscheidung)*, on civil reason, that is, on human, legally trained reason, by which the relevant legal authorities are carefully studied, analyzed, and systematized. But it is also based on natural reason, that is, on God-given reason, which is instilled into the soul of each person who subjects himself to the laws of Holy Scripture. "A judgment cannot be made in conscience," Oldendorp wrote, "without some formula of law which indicates in the heart of man that that which he does is just or unjust. Therefore law [i.e., the law of Holy Scripture] is in the person."[122] The answer, in short, is that in order to discern what is equitable, the individual jurist, having exercised his civil reason to the maximum degree, must study the Bible, pray to God, and search his conscience.

Thus Oldendorp built on Luther's belief in the Christian conscience as the ultimate source of moral decisions. Luther had justified his own breach of his monastic vows and his defiance of Emperor Charles V at Worms as acts "for God and in my conscience."[123] He denounced laws that conflict with conscience. Oldendorp developed the Lutheran emphasis on conscience into a constituent element of a systematic legal philosophy.

Politics and the State

Emphasis on the supremacy of the natural law of conscience over the positive laws of the civil polity did not, however, lead Oldendorp to a broad doctrine of civil disobedience. On the contrary, Oldendorp, like Luther and Melanchthon, emphasized that the civil polity—which he variously called *civitas, weltliches Regiment* (the secular regime), *politien Regiment* (the political regime), *res publica, ordo civilis,* the *Obrigkeit,* and *universitas civium* (corporation of citizens)—is ordained by God and commands the unconditional obedience of its subjects.[124] Yet Oldendorp was willing—in contrast to Luther and in elaboration of Melanchthon—to give a substantial list of exceptional instances in which the citizen's conscience may require him to disobey the civil authorities. Moreover, Oldendorp went beyond both Luther and Melanchthon in providing a systematic conception of the responsibility of the civil authorities to adhere to the laws of the Bible, to the *lex in hominibus,* and to the civil laws, including, in addition to its own civil laws, the law of nations. "It is an old question," he wrote, "whether the magistrates are superior to the law or whether the law binds the magistrates." His answer was, "The magistrates are ministers [i.e., servants] of the laws."[125] Therefore "it is false and simplistic," he wrote, "to assert that the prince has power to go against the law. For it is proper to such great majesty . . . to serve the laws."[126]

In addition to placing limitations on state power, Oldendorp developed a consistent theory of the tasks of the civil polity, one which built on, but also went beyond, that of Melanchthon. As servant of the law of nature and of the laws of the Bible, he wrote, the state has the legislative task of enacting laws that conform to God's will. In doing so, the civil authorities should compare the laws of other states, present and past.[127] Administratively, it is the task of the civil polity to support the true faith by seeing to it (among other things) that there are enough preachers, that they are well qualified, and that they are well enough paid, so that they may combat unbelief—not by force but only by God's word; to punish acts of greed, idleness, sumptuousness of dress, and other immoral conduct; and to institute and support good schools and universities, since only thereby can capable, conscientious people be trained who will enable the civil polity to achieve its God-given objectives.[128]

It is also the task of each civil polity to maintain peace with other civil polities. The people of all republics, he said, form a *corpus Christianum,* and should live, as Nature (that is, God) requires, "next to one another, not against one another."[129] War is justified only for defense against an unjust attack. Even when attacked, Oldendorp wrote, a civil polity should seek to settle the conflict peaceably, and even when that is impossible should leave three days before defending itself in order to give the imminent attacker a chance to change his mind. Moreover, defense should be limited to that which is necessary, since its only purpose is to restore peace.[130]

Oldendorp emphasized the legal personality of the civil polity. The state, like a single person, has rights and duties. It is bound internationally by the customary laws of international relations and by the principle that international treaties and agreements must be kept *(pacta sunt servanda).* It is also bound by similar legal principles to its own people. Oldendorp carried his idea of state responsibility to the point of requiring the civil polity, as a legal person, to compensate for harm done to its people by its illegal acts, citing the great fourteenth-century jurist Bartolus in support of the view that a court (he did not say which court) should have jurisdiction to impose both criminal and civil liability on a *res publica* which has failed to perform its legal duties or has otherwise failed in legislating, judging, or administering.[131]

Peter Macke states that Oldendorp was closer to Erasmus than to Luther in his concern to Christianize public life through law.[132] Oldendorp's concern, however, was based directly on Lutheran principles. "The purpose of law," Oldendorp wrote, "is that we may peacefully pass through this shadowy life and be led to Christ and to eternal life."[133] He emphasized "the third use" of the law—its pedagogical, or educational, function. Oldendorp called law *paedagogus noster ad Christum,* our teacher in the path to Christ.[134] This involved a certain confidence in human reason; while emphasizing the depravity of man, Oldendorp wrote that despite the Fall, an *igniculum,* a spark, of human reason had been retained.[135] To be sure, he built a huge fire out of that spark by uniting it with conscience and by uniting conscience, as Melanchthon did not do, with Holy Scripture.

By their theology, and especially by their twin doctrines of salvation by faith alone and the priesthood of all believers, the Lutheran Reformers undermined the canon law and the sacramental system, and therewith the entire jurisdiction, of the Roman Catholic Church. This gave to civil rulers the ultimate prerogative of legislation, administration, and adjudication within their respective territories. By the same token, however, laws enacted by civil rulers now lacked the sanctity which they had formerly had by virtue of ecclesiastical endorsement under the two swords theory, with its division of powers between the universal church organized under the papacy and the plurality of secular kingdoms, feudal lordships, and urban polities.[136]

Moreover, Lutheran theology attacked the Roman Catholic belief that reason, standing alone, is compatible with faith and is capable of proving independently what is revealed by faith. It was this belief in the synthesis of reason and revelation that underlay the Roman Catholic doctrine of natural law.[137] Lutherans, however, taught that not only the will but also reason itself is corrupted by innate pride, greed, and other forms of egoism. They did not doubt that there were transcendent moral principles by which human conduct and human laws were to be judged, but they did not believe that such principles could be derived ultimately from reason.

Absent the endorsement of an independent ecclesiastical hierarchy, absent a positive role in procuring the salvation of souls, and absent a foundation in objective and disinterested human reason, what was to justify civil laws, other than mere expediency? Why should anyone obey them unless he were compelled to do so? What made them laws and not mere commands?

The theological answer to these fundamental jurisprudential questions was rooted in the Lutheran two kingdoms theory, with its postulate that God is present, though hidden, in the earthly kingdom. Despite their corruption, Christians living in the earthly kingdom are called to carry out God's work there. They are called to maintain order and to do justice, however defective such order and justice will inevitably be. Order and justice are not paths to salvation, but they are forms in which God's presence in the earthly kingdom is concealed. They are ordained by God partly to make human life livable, and partly to point the way—though they themselves are not the way—to faith.

Although these theological beliefs do not in themselves constitute a legal philosophy, they nevertheless negate the conventional view that Lutheran theology is concerned solely with the spiritual life of the individual and is indifferent to politics and law. In addition, they provide a theological basis for distinguishing between the duties which the individual person owes to God and the duties he owes to his neighbors.

Both sets of duties, according to Lutheran theology, are set forth in the Bible, and especially in the Ten Commandments. Not only for Lutheran theology but for legal philosophy as well, the Ten Commandments replaced ecclesiastical tradition and the canon law as the transcendent source of divine, natural, and human law. With respect to that part of law that regulates civil relationships, the last six commandments were interpreted as an authoritative statement of fundamental principles of public and private law, including respect for authority, for human life, for family relationships, for property rights, for procedural justice, and for the rights of others.

Lutheran legal philosophy was not content, however, to rest the ultimate test of the validity of law on the Bible alone, although early in his career Luther was tempted to do so.[138] The Bible speaks to the faithful, but not all people subject to civil authority are believers. God ordains civil authority and civil law for pagans as well as for Christians. Indeed, it is because of the fallen state of humankind that law in any form is needed—primarily to show sinful man what is required of him and how helpless he is to fulfill those requirements. Therefore, outside the Bible, and independently of it, God has implanted in the conscience of every man certain moral insights which, in fact, correspond to the principles revealed to faith in the Ten Commandments. These universal moral insights Melanchthon classified among the "elements of knowledge" which themselves shape reason and hence cannot be proved by reason. Nevertheless, if reason is guided by faith, it can understand and accept, even though it cannot prove, that which is revealed directly to conscience. Thus reason can be rescued, so to speak, by faith. In Oldendorp's terms, conscience is a higher form of reason—not ordinary reason but divine reason.

As the Lutheran theory of conscience brought faith into contact with reason, so the Lutheran theory of civic, or political, righteousness brought the heavenly kingdom into contact with the earthly kingdom. Here the "third use" of the law, emphasized by both Melanchthon and Oldendorp, plays a major role. Natural law—the moral legal principles known to conscience and confirmed in the Decalogue—serves as a guide to faithful people, especially those in high places, in the ways of justice, fairness, altruism, and peace.

The concept of the educational role of law was carried over in Lutheran legal philosophy from natural law to positive law. As it is an important function of natural law to educate the civil authorities, Melanchthon and Oldendorp wrote, so it is an important function of the positive law of the civil authorities to nurture the moral attitudes and sentiments of those who are subject to such laws. Here Melanchthon and Oldendorp spelled out in detail the ways in which various branches of positive law, including criminal law, civil law, ecclesiastical law, and constitutional law, contribute not only to social order and social welfare but also to the moral improvement of society.

Of special significance for the development of Western legal philosophy was Oldendorp's insight that the generality and objectivity inherent in legal rules is both their great virtue and their great vice. Equally important was his further insight that the vice of generality and objectivity in legal rules can be cured, and the virtue preserved, through their conscientious application in specific circumstances. Melanchthon the philosopher sought to reconcile legal norms with reason and conscience in the general sense of those terms. Oldendorp the jurist explored at length and in depth particular applications of rules and principles, and showed the paradoxes that arise when general rules and principles are invoked in concrete cases. Oldendorp concluded that not only in exceptional cases but in all cases it is necessary to go beyond the letter of the law to its spirit—necessary not only from the point of view of fairness in the particular case but also from the point of view of the ultimate consistency of the rules themselves. He found that ultimate consistency not exclusively in logical synthesis but also, and primarily, in the purposes which the rules were intended to serve in their application. Thus Oldendorp made conscience the master key to the unity and integrity of the legal system in action. This was perhaps the most important specific contribution made by Lutheran legal thought to Western jurisprudence. Oldendorp's theory of equity as a higher reason that is brought into play in the conscientious application of general rules to concrete cases is reflected in many modern Western legal institutions. Among the most striking of these are the Anglo-American concepts of judicial discretion and jury equity.[139]

The Lutheran emphasis on the role of individual conscience as a source of justice must be balanced against its equal emphasis on the role of civil authority in defining and enforcing justice and, more generally, in guarding religious worship, morality, and social welfare ("the common weal"). Luther himself considered that his conception of the dignity and mission of the state—the *Obrigkeit*—was one of his most important contributions to the religious and political thought of his time.[140] Indeed, the Lutheran Reformation created the modern secular state by allocating to the occupiers of state offices ultimate responsibility for the exercise of functions that had previously been in the jurisdiction of occupiers of ecclesiastical offices. Thus state officials in Lutheran territories assumed jurisdiction over the clergy, church property, education, poor relief, medical care, moral and religious crimes, marriage and family relations, wills, and many other matters which in Roman Catholic territories were regulated by ecclesiastical officials operating under canon law. The very concept of secular state sovereignty was closely associated with the expanded role of the secular *Obrigkeit,* a German word which is cognate with the Latin word *superanitas,* "overness," "superness," and which was translated into French as *souveraineté* and into English as "sovereignty."

The elimination of the checks on secular authority traditionally exercised by the Roman Catholic hierarchy increased substantially the danger that the prince would assert absolute power, that is, a power above the law. Moreover, Lutheran theology emphasized that the prince ruled by divine right and that his subjects were bound to honor and obey him as the father of his country. Nevertheless, Lutheran legal philosophy, like Roman Catholic legal philosophy, contained important counterbalances to tyranny. First, the concept of the prince as a father to his people itself implied a responsibility on his part inconsistent with tyranny. Second, Lutheran legal philosophy emphasized the importance of written published laws, whose function was, in part, to restrain wicked rulers. Third, it declared the authority of Roman law as the written embodiment of reason; although each territorial prince was thought to have succeeded to Roman imperial authority, nevertheless Roman law was also seen as a transnational *jus commune,* whose interpretation was entrusted to learned jurists who glossed and commented on and synthesized the ancient texts. Finally, the Lutheran jurists found both in Scripture and in conscience a general right of resistance to tyrannical rule. Conscience was the seat of both civil obedience and civil disobedience. When positive law contradicts natural law, the conscientious Lutheran Christian is torn between his duty to obey the divinely ordained "powers that be" and his duty to obey his own divinely ordained sense of justice.

A contemporary American legal philosopher may be frustrated by the inability of Lutheran legal philosophy to resolve the tension between law and morals by rational means. Yet it is important to recognize that Lutheran legal philosophy is a primary source, in the philosophical as well as the historical sense, both of contemporary legal positivism and of contemporary natural law theory. Viewed as a positivist theory, Lutheran legal philosophy defines the law of civil society as the will of the lawmaker expressed in a system of rules, backed by coercive sanctions, whose primary function is to preserve social order. Melanchthon wrote that "politics"—which he also called "the state," and sometimes "the *Obrigkeit*"—is the method of "creating legitimate order within the community" and of creating laws "to govern property, contracts, succession, and other matters."[141] This was the first statement of the German concept of the *Rechtsstaat,* "the law state."[142] To be fully effective, such laws, Melanchthon and Oldendorp stressed, must be promulgated, predictable, generally applicable, and binding on both political authorities and their subjects. The claim of a legal system, or of a given law or legal decision, to be an expression of reason and justice cannot be verified, according to Lutheran legal philosophy, from within the legal system itself but only on the basis of moral standards derived from outside the legal system. Thus Lutheran legal philosophy accepted the basic premise of contemporary legal positivism, namely, that law and morals are to be sharply distinguished from each other, and that the law that *is* should not be confused with what the law *ought to be.* To identify law with morality is to foster uncertainty and instability in the law, and hence disorder; it is also to make the civil law the source rather than the object of moral criticism, and thus to foster injustice.

Thus Lutheran legal philosophy rejects the definition of law propounded by Thomas Aquinas: that law is an ordinance of reason for the common good, made by one having the care of the community.[143] Such a definition, according to Lutheran thought, gives an unwarranted sanctity to both law and reason. It rests on an overoptimistic conception of human nature and consequently on an overoptimistic conception of the role of the state as an instrument of justice. A lawfully promulgated decree of a sovereign is law, in Lutheran legal philosophy, even though it is arbitrary in its purpose and effect.

Viewed, however, as a natural law theory, Lutheran legal philosophy postulates that every person has within himself or herself certain moral sentiments relating to legal justice, including a respect for civil authority, for human life, for property, for family responsibilities, for fair procedures, and, in general, for the rights of oneself and of others. These moral sentiments, or insights, or inclinations, reside partly in reason and will but primarily in conscience. The conscience of every person is thus the source of a natural law, that is, of a principle of thought and action which is inherent in human nature. Lutheran, in contrast to Roman Catholic, natural law theory is essentially a moral theory, not a legal theory. It rests primarily on an innate sense of justice, to which reason is subordinate. Reason, from a Lutheran standpoint, is too weak, too biased by egoism, fully to sustain such a sense of justice. Thus there are bound to be rational disagreements among people concerning the meanings of the various principles of the moral law and concerning their application to concrete cases. In the event of rational disagreement, each person must turn to his or her own conscience in making such application.

To the extent that the Lutheran theory of natural law is essentially a moral rather than a legal theory, it is reconcilable with contemporary legal positivism. It goes beyond the parameters of legal positivism, however, by invoking conscience for the application of legal rules to specific circumstances. In the legal process of judging or administering, injustices that would flow from a purely rational application of broad rules to concrete cases can be corrected only by sensitivity to the particular circumstances of the case, including the character of the parties, their motivation, the consequences of alternative decisions, and various other such factors. Similarly, in the legal process of legislating, legislators should be concerned not only with policy in the general sense but also with the specific circumstances which give rise to the need for the law in question and the specific consequences entailed in its application. Thus, as we shall see in the next chapter, Lutheran legal philosophy is congenial to—and in fact in sixteenth-century Germany led to—a new legal science consisting of the massive classification and systematization of the rules of public and private law, coupled with a flexibility in their application based on conscience and called equity.

Stated in this condensed and abstract form, Lutheran legal philosophy has something to offer to contemporary jurisprudential thought. Above all, it suggests a mode of reconciling differences between, on the one hand, what may be called the "higher law" school of legal thought, which would treat values such as equality and privacy as transcendent rights that are beyond the jurisdiction of the political community to infringe, and, on the other hand, what may be called the "political realities" school, which would deny the character of law to principles that have not been formally accepted as such by the duly constituted lawmaking authorities. Lutheranism claims that the conflict between these two schools cannot be resolved by the exercise of reason. It claims further that it can be resolved, in practice, by the exercise of conscience. It offers no guide, however, to the exercise of conscience except a theological one. Those who cannot accept a theological guide are thus left with a hard but nevertheless interesting and even valuable lesson.[144]

CHAPTER 3

The Transformation of German Legal Science

THE political and religious upheaval in sixteenth-century Germany was accompanied and reinforced by a transformation of the "method," as it was called at the time—or "science," as it was also sometimes called—by which law was analyzed and systematized, including the method by which legal decisions and rules were related to legal principles, concepts, and theories. To understand the scope and significance of these changes, it is necessary to recognize that they constituted a transformation, but again, as in the case of Lutheran legal philosophy, by no means a repudiation, of the Western tradition of legal science that originated in the late eleventh and twelfth centuries. In the first European universities, founded in that earlier period, law was treated as a distinct and systematized body of knowledge, in which individual legal decisions, rules, and enactments were studied objectively and were explained in terms of general principles, concepts, and theories basic to the system as a whole.[1] This was, in fact, Europe's first modern science—different, to be sure, from the natural sciences that emerged later but also different from the literary, aesthetic, philosophical, and theological studies that had been pursued previously in the cathedral schools and in other centers of learning. The systematic character of legal science was preserved by sixteenth-century German jurists, but the earlier "scholastic" method, as it was then called, was transformed by a new "topical" method.

Eleventh- and twelfth-century Western legal science differed also from the intensely casuistic legal scholarship that had prevailed in the Roman Empire from the first to the sixth centuries. Yet it was primarily to the casuistic sixth-century Roman law texts of Justinian, conveniently discovered in an Italian library at the height of the Papal Revolution, that a principled and systematic Western legal science was first applied in the late eleventh and twelfth centuries, and it was partly to those texts that sixteenth-century legal scholars applied their new topical method. Indeed, Roman law played an even more important role in the legal reforms of the sixteenth century than it had played earlier.

The term "Roman law" has, of course, many different meanings, some of which, such as the archaic Roman law of the Twelve Tables and the post-Justinian Roman law of the Eastern Roman Empire, are only remotely related to the Western legal tradition. Moreover, even those parts of Roman law that have substantially contributed to Western legal systems, especially the copious texts collected under Emperor Justinian's auspices, have undergone radical changes of interpretation in the course of making their contributions. The Western Romanist jurists of the eleventh through fifteenth centuries concentrated largely on Justinian's Digest, at first glossing its thousands of scattered legal rules and decisions and later writing commentaries on the glosses.[2] Jurists of the sixteenth to the early eighteenth centuries, by contrast, focused their attention chiefly on Justinian's Institutes, and at the same time combined their study of Roman law concepts, principles, and rules with those of the various legal systems that constituted the positive law of the various polities of Europe—the canon law of the church, imperial and royal and princely law, urban law, mercantile law, and feudal law.

Thus Roman law must be seen as an evolving element in an evolving legal tradition. What many legal historians continue to call the "practical reception" of Roman law in the late fifteenth and sixteenth centuries, as contrasted with the "theoretical reception" of Roman law in the late eleventh through fifteenth centuries, should be seen as parts of a much longer historical process in which both practical and theoretical elements were always present. In fact, from the twelfth to the nineteenth century Roman law was continually "received" in Europe, in the same sense that Greek philosophy and Hebrew theology were continually received. Each was assimilated, transformed, and given a new life, a new history, and each was repeatedly replenished by new approaches to its principal classical texts—the Bible, Plato and Aristotle, and the law books of Justinian.

The misconception that in the so-called High Middle Ages Roman law was received theoretically, and that its practical reception came only in the late fifteenth and early sixteenth centuries, neglects the fact that all the various "practical" legal systems that emerged in the twelfth and thirteenth centuries, such as the canon law applicable in the ecclesiastical courts and the royal law applicable in royal courts of various European kingdoms, "received" and put into practice various Roman law concepts, principles, and rules.[3] Except as incorporated in other legislation, the legal rules and principles contained in the texts of Justinian were not, as such, positive law; except in Pisa and perhaps a few other Italian cities, they were not officially adopted. In a broader sense, however, Roman law was a *source* of law, to be drawn on to fill gaps and resolve ambiguities both in the canon law and in the various secular legal systems. Only in 1495 did Emperor Maximilian, in establishing the first and only court of the so-called Holy Roman Empire of the German Nation, require that it apply Roman law, by which was understood the Justinian texts as glossed and commented on by Western legal scholars and as interpreted by the university professors appointed to be judges on the new court.[4] In other courts in Germany and elsewhere in the West, Roman law was considered to be an ideal law, "written reason," *ratio scripta;* its principles and rules, as interpreted, served as a screen through which the prevailing law could be interpreted and supplemented.

The legal science that was first developed in the late eleventh, twelfth, and thirteenth centuries came under attack in the fifteenth and early sixteenth centuries, principally at the hands of scholars who adhered to what was called at the time "humanism," and sometimes "the new humanism." The humanists attacked, in the first instance, the earlier jurists' understanding of the ancient texts of Justinian, and, in the second instance, their techniques of glossing and commenting on those texts. Behind the attack lay new conceptions of language, of history, of philosophy, and of law itself—conceptions which ultimately played a considerable part in undermining the worldview that had prevailed in the West for four centuries. The attack on the so-called scholasticism of the earlier jurists came in three stages, the first of which, often called philological and historical, may also be called "skeptical," the second of which may be called "principled," and the third of which may be called "systematic." In all three stages the attack was made in the name of humanism.[5] It was the third, "systematic" stage that embodied the spirit of the German Revolution.

The Skeptical Stage of Humanist Legal Science

As early as the mid-fourteenth century, great pioneers of Italian humanism such as Francesco Petrarch (1304–1374) and Giovanni Boccaccio (1313–1375) had attacked contemporary jurists for their ignorance of ancient Rome and of the origins of Roman law, for their prolix discussions of trivial questions, for their barbaric and inelegant style, for their lack of a true science, and for their general lack of culture.[6] In the fifteenth century these allegations were taken up by the humanist philologist Lorenzo Valla (1407–1457).[7] A master of grammar and rhetoric, and famous for his writings on classical Latin usage, Valla was a champion of concreteness against abstraction, and of clarity against ambiguity. As Donald Kelley has put it, "For Valla as for most humanists, . . . [u]nderstanding proceeded from literal meaning and not from any figurative construction; and so with his usual uncompromising logic he insisted that there be an unequivocal relation between words and things. Properly speaking, words were signs, and meaning was essentially signification."[8] Signification, in turn, was to be derived from the meanings accepted by those learned in language. Thus, in order to understand the meaning of words handed down from the past, it was essential to know what those words meant to the learned writers who first used them. Consequently, in order to understand the Roman law of Justinian, it was necessary to know what the words contained in the Justinian texts meant—not only at the time they were collected and edited by Justinian's compiler of the texts, Tribonian (d. 545), but also, and primarily, at the time they were written, centuries earlier, by the jurists whom Tribonian was quoting. Tribonian himself, Valla showed, abused the original texts that he compiled.[9]

Valla railed both at the barbaric language of the glossators and commentators and at their distortions of the meaning of the ancient texts they were interpreting. The scholastic jurists, he complained, "turned his stomach." They had introduced "Gothic" terms into Latin. They had combined Roman law with corrupt language drawn from the later canon law. "What is more"—to quote Kelley again—"they had inflicted upon [Roman] law the same kind of atrocities which their Aristotelian brethren had inflicted upon philosophy. With their quibblings and their quiddities, they had detached Roman law from common sense as well as from historical context; they had dehumanized a 'human science.' For this flock of philistines, who preferred the company of such 'geese' as Bartolus and Accursius to the 'swans' of ancient jurisprudence, Valla had nothing but scorn."[10]

The *Glossa Ordinaria* or *Magna Glossa,* the "Great Gloss" of Accursius, completed in about 1250, was a massive concordance of the glosses that had been written on the Digest of Justinian since the time of the first great Western Romanist, Irnerius (ca. 1060–1125). It had an enormous success throughout Europe, and to a considerable extent its authority replaced that of the Digest itself. Thus from Valla's standpoint it was a dark screen hiding the purity of the original texts. The post-glossators, or commentators, of whom one of the greatest was Bartolus of Sassoferrato (1314–1357), had built on the Great Gloss. They speculated about the premises underlying the divergent opinions of the earlier glossators. They were less interested in the literal meaning of the original Roman texts than in their nature, their concepts, and their possible applications to various cases.[11] This offended Valla even more. Valla called Bartolus an "ass," an "idiot," and a "madman" who completely distorted the Roman law.[12] Eventually, Valla's low opinion of Bartolus—which today seems wholly unjustified—came to be shared by other humanists, including many humanist jurists. This was a fifteenth-century parallel to the radical attack against traditional legal scholarship by "realist" and "critical" movements in American jurisprudence of the twentieth century.

The philological-historical approach to Roman law, initiated by Valla, had a strong negative effect on scholastic jurisprudence, helping to undermine its scientific character in two principal ways. First, it deprived the original legal sources of their sanctity. Second, it thereby also deprived the secondary legal sources of their authority. The earlier legal science had assumed the sacred,

God-given character—in that sense, the objectivity—of the ancient Roman texts. It is true that those texts had been accepted only selectively; many individual rules and phrases were simply ignored, while whole portions of them (for example, the religious portions, which occupied a prominent place in the original sources) were for the most part treated as irrelevant. Nevertheless, taken as a whole, the texts had been considered to constitute a human reflection of divine law.[13] Not only justice, virtue, legality, and other abstract qualities but also general principles of procedural fairness, contractual responsibility, liability based on fault, and the like were seen as a sacred meta-law embodied in the texts themselves. Valla and his successors, however, treated the texts simply as a literary invention of the sixth century, historically relative, eclectic, and self-contradictory. In doing so, they inevitably challenged the authority of the interpretations of the texts given centuries later by successive generations of glossators and commentators. Once the texts themselves were reduced to mere literature, the traditional glosses and comments upon them, which had assumed their sanctity, came to be seen as a distortion of their original meaning.

Insofar as legal humanism remained purely philological and historical, its achievements remained, from the legal point of view, largely negative. It exposed many distortions of the original Roman, Greek, Germanic, and canon law texts, including some significant forgeries.[14] In time its adherents succeeded in reconstructing a substantial portion of the ancient texts. French, Italian, German, Swiss, Dutch, Spanish, and English legal scholars of the late fifteenth and sixteenth centuries searched out and restored and annotated hundreds of ancient manuscripts of Roman law.[15] They rid the texts of the accumulation of medieval accretions and they rid legal language of much of its jargon. But in this first stage of its development, legal humanism could not bring constructive solutions to contemporary legal problems. For that, a second stage was needed, which would build on, but go beyond, the philological-historical method of textual criticism.

The Principled Stage of Humanist Legal Science

The second stage of humanist legal science was introduced in the first decades of the 1500s by a new generation of humanist jurists. Like the humanists of the first stage, representatives of the new school advocated and practiced a philological approach to the study of law, criticizing much—though not all—of the earlier jurisprudence for its alleged crudity and its looseness in the interpretation of the texts of Justinian. They also emphasized the historical relativity of those texts and their consequent lack of relevance, in some cases, to sixteenth-century problems. Legal humanists of the second stage went beyond their predecessors, however, in two respects: first, they simplified the law by omitting large areas of traditional analysis, and second, they arranged and interpreted the specific rules of law according to broader principles and concepts. Thus the more skeptical philological-historical approach was gradually superseded by a more positive synthesizing method, through which particular areas of law and particular legal questions were viewed more comprehensively, in terms of general principles.

The new principled style of legal thought, which came gradually to the fore (though the earlier philological-historical style continued to be prominent and in some places continued to prevail), went beyond the clarification of texts. Not texts, and not glosses on texts, but legal principles and legal concepts became the starting points of legal analysis. At the same time, and by the same token, emphasis on Justinian's Digest, with its thousands of scattered opinions of jurists concerning the application of particular legal rules to particular cases, gave way to a new emphasis on Justinian's Institutes, which, being a short introductory textbook for students, contained statements of general principles, albeit loosely defined and arranged in a loose manner.

In this second stage of the revolt against scholastic jurisprudence, humanist jurists developed a new style of teaching law, called the *mos juris docendi gallicus,* the "Gallic" (i.e., French) style of law teaching, which was contrasted with the pre-existing ("Bartolist") *mos juris docendi italicus,* the Italian style of law teaching. (In fact, the "Gallic" style was introduced in many Italian universities and the "Italian" style continued to be used in many French universities.)[16] The *mos gallicus* tended to exclude the glosses from the curriculum, thereby shortening it substantially. It also placed emphasis—as had been done in the first stage of legal humanism—on philological and historical aspects of the Justinian texts and on the aesthetic use of language. Its most important feature, however, was that the teacher would start with principles and concepts, and would show how they gave rise to specific applications. In contrast to scholastic jurisprudence, the humanists' principles and concepts, whether drawn from the Institutes or elsewhere, were treated as external to the text and as of self-evident validity. Thus the *mos gallicus,* and legal humanism generally in its second stage, represented a new type of legal logic, more deductive in nature, whereby specific legal rules appeared as necessary inferences from self-evident principles and concepts.[17] At the same time, the jurists of the second stage, in opposing the humanist scholars of the first stage, were somewhat more respectful of the scholastic jurists; they attacked their method, but they did not hesitate to accept many of their solutions to specific problems. Moreover, many if not most of the principles and concepts that appeared to the humanist mind to be of self-evident validity were the same as those which the scholastic jurists had found to be implicit in the sacred texts.

The main characteristics of the second stage of humanist legal science are well illustrated in the work of the German jurist Uldaricus Zasius (in German, Ulrich Zäsi) (1461–1535) and the Italian jurist Andreas Alciatus (in Italian,

Andrea Alciato) (1492–1550). These two, together with the Frenchman Guillelmus Budaeus (in French, Guillaume Budé) (1468–1540), were called by Erasmus (1466–1536) the "great triumvirate" of the Roman law.[18] The writings of Budaeus, however, belong to the first stage of legal humanism; unlike Zasius and Alciatus, he was concerned not with interpreting the Roman legal texts in the light of their underlying principles but rather with using philological and historical methods to uncover their original meaning and to show their anomalies. Indeed, Budaeus, like Valla before him, was not primarily a jurist but a classicist.[19]

Zasius—despite Erasmus—attacked both Valla and Budaeus mercilessly: their ignorance and impudence in "robbing" the great works of the Roman jurisconsults can "in no way ever be expiated," Zasius wrote in 1518, "either by sulphur or by the torch." Their crime is worse than Adam's, he wrote, for they "not only tampered with the fruit of the tree of knowledge of good and evil, as Adam did, but tore up the entire tree by the roots."[20]

Zasius shared with Valla and Budaeus the belief in a "return to the sources," their antipathy to the replacement of analysis of the original texts by analysis of the glosses, and their revulsion against the "corruption" of the Latin language by the scholastic jurists. But Zasius was too much a lawyer to insist, as the earlier humanists had insisted, on simplicity in the original texts, and he was not inclined, as they were, to expand textual ambiguities into self-contradictions. To demand that legal wisdom be expounded in such a way as to be clear to all readers, Zasius wrote, is to treat the texts "like a prostitute who stands around in the street, available to anyone who approaches or (I might say) bursts in."[21] The legal writings of the Roman jurisconsults, he wrote, are necessarily complex and difficult; to decipher them requires the learning of trained jurists.

Zasius was, however, much more than just a trained jurist. At the University of Freiburg he taught, at first, not only law but also rhetoric and poetry. His brilliant lectures and writings earned him a wide audience. He carried on a voluminous correspondence with leading figures throughout Europe. He was a friend of Erasmus. He served in important posts in the government of the imperial city of Freiburg. He was also a renowned practitioner of the law, and his legal opinions in concrete cases were published and circulated in many countries. Perhaps his greatest practical achievement was the drafting of a comprehensive codification of laws for the city of Freiburg; adopted in 1520, Zasius's Freiburger Stadtrecht served as a model for other German cities as well.[22]

Zasius's place in legal scholarship is marked by a series of writings, commencing in 1508, on specific legal themes as well as by several comprehensive treatises on particular branches of law.[23] In contrast to the scholastic jurists, Zasius usually started his analysis from principle, not from authority, and the issues which he addressed included not only those that arose from specific legal texts but also general questions that transcended the texts and for which the texts served as illustrations rather than as sources. In contrast to the philological-historical school, Zasius was concerned not only, and not primarily, to criticize the texts but also, and primarily, to elaborate general legal concepts and principles and to show their implications for the resolution of the specific legal problems which the texts exemplified. "Legal truth [*Rechtswahrheit*]," Zasius wrote, "is created only out of the text itself and out of reason, not out of the authorities of the doctors."[24] And again, "All doctrines which contradict the texts or legal reason [*Rechtsvernunft*] we unashamedly call what they are: a sin against truth."[25] Zasius's emphasis on the interpretation of legal texts by reference to their source in basic legal principles—in "legal truth" and "legal reason"—helped to rescue legal humanism from the negativism and skepticism of its first stage.

A similar role in introducing the second stage of legal humanism was played by Andreas Alciatus, a younger contemporary whom Zasius greatly admired. A native of Milan, Alciatus studied law in Pavia and Bologna. In 1518, after having practiced law in Milan for several years, he was appointed professor, at the young age of twenty-six, at the University of Avignon in France. Four years later he returned to Milan to practice law. He taught civil law from 1518 to 1522 and again from 1527 to 1529 at the University of Avignon, practiced law from 1522 to 1527 in Milan, and taught again in France from 1529 to 1533 at the University of Bourges, before returning permanently to Italy, where he taught principally at the universities of Pavia and Bologna and practiced law and wrote legal essays until his death in 1550. Students flocked from all over Europe to hear his lectures, and notables, including even the French king Francis I, visited his classes. His prolific writings went through many editions.[26]

Alciatus's gifts as a philologist and historian were enormous, and in part he used them—like Budaeus and other philological-historical humanists—to expose the anomalies of traditional European legal scholarship and of the Justinian texts themselves. From an early time in his career, however, he found himself in sympathy with the northern humanists, especially Erasmus, and this led him, as it led Zasius, to go beyond the philological-historical method in order to interpret many of the ancient legal texts in the light of what he conceived to be their underlying logic and spirit and thus to adapt them to contemporary needs. He sought not only to expose but also to resolve legal anomalies, and in doing so he often defended Justinian's Digest against jurists of the first stage of legal humanism such as Valla and Budaeus.

Like Zasius, Alciatus was a leading scholar and teacher of the law as well as a leading legal practitioner. His writings, like those of Zasius, were directed primarily toward the training of lawyers and the solution of legal problems. Like Zasius, he gave many hundreds of legal opinions—*consilia* and *responsa*—in concrete cases involving municipal law, canon law, feudal law, criminal law, wills, contracts, and other types of legal questions.[27] Despite a difference of thirty-one years in age, the two men shared a common outlook, and corresponded with each other enthusiastically. Indeed, Alciatus joined Zasius in attacking Budaeus and Valla for their excessive emphasis on philology and their excessive historicism in the interpreting of texts.

Among the important contributions of these two men to legal scholarship were their treatises on various aspects of Roman law, in which they set out a detailed analysis of the multitude of rules, concepts, and principles constituting each part. Their main concern in these treatises was to present the legal subject under consideration in a principled way—coherently, comprehensively, and systematically. The various books on obligations arising from words *(De Verborum Obligationibus)* written by Alciatus, Zasius, and some of their contemporaries constituted comprehensive treatments of general contract law. Zasius's treatise runs to 742 pages, Alciatus's to 1,020 pages.

Zasius and Alciatus were hailed in their own time as great reformers of legal science, and this characterization has been kept alive by legal historians of subsequent centuries. A careful study of their writings, however, reveals them as transitional figures rather than as founders of a new method. On the one hand, they helped to save European legal thought from the ravages of the first, skeptical phase of humanist legal science—the ravages of Boccaccio and of Valla and of their sixteenth-century successors, especially in France. They introduced important pedagogical reforms and wrote the first comprehensive treatises on discrete branches of law. They substantially reduced the prolixity and the casuistry of scholastic legal analysis. Like their humanist predecessors, they accepted the historical relativity of the texts, but they nevertheless found a way of synthesizing rules by deduction from principles and concepts which they took to be self-evident but which, in fact, corresponded to those that their scholastic predecessors had found to be implicit in the texts.

On the other hand, neither Zasius nor Alciatus introduced substantial innovations in legal science. They did not attempt to systematize the whole of the law or to formulate its underlying themes and purposes. Their contributions constituted "technological reforms, improvement in the techniques of teaching and learning and transmitting legal knowledge,"[28] but not any fundamental changes in legal analysis or the conceptualization of legal doctrine.[29] Both their strength and their weakness lay in their preservation of the basic elements of the so-called scholastic legal science without its scholastic philosophical and theological underpinnings.

The Systematic Stage of Legal Science: *Usus modernus protestantorum*

A third stage in the transformation of Western legal science was needed to bring to fruition and to surpass the "skeptical" first stage and the "principled" second stage of humanist legal science. In the third, "systematic" stage, beginning in the late 1520s and 1530s, leading jurists, chiefly German and chiefly Protestant, undertook to derive from basic principles and concepts not simply individual aspects or parts of law but the entire body of law. This completed the shift—both the technical shift and the logical shift—to a new legal science.

The scholastic legal science that originated in the late eleventh and twelfth centuries (1) classified and analyzed legal rules (2) derived primarily from authoritative texts and from authoritative interpretations of those texts, (3) inferring from them interrelated concepts and principles corresponding to conventional standards of reason. Underlying scholastic legal science was the belief that the authoritative legal texts both of canon law and of Roman law embodied a universal truth and a universal justice, and therefore they could be taken as starting points for apodictic reasoning which would establish new insights into truth and justice. At the same time, however, they contained gaps, ambiguities, and contradictions and therefore had to be analyzed dialectically as well; that is, problems *(quaestiones)* had to be put, classifications and definitions made, opposing opinions stated, and conflicts reconciled. Ultimately, legal maxims (maximum propositions) could be formulated, embodying universal legal principles. Thus the sanctity of the texts, known by faith, could be proved by reason. In Saint Anselm's famous formula, "Credo ut intelligam," "I believe and so I may know"—*ut* in its "result" sense, not (as is often thought) in its "purpose" sense. Humanist legal scholars such as Zasius and Alciatus refined but did not fundamentally change this method. They started from the rules found in the texts and proceeded to the concepts and principles implicit in them.

In contrast, the new Protestant school of legal science of the second, third, and fourth quarters of the sixteenth century (1) classified and analyzed legal concepts and principles (2) derived from inborn reason and conscience, (3) illustrating them by interrelated legal rules (4) found in a wide variety of legal sources. The new method of analysis and synthesis built on the first two stages of legal humanism—the skeptical and the principled—but went beyond them. It was linked with an effort to bring the entire body of legal rules within a common framework of concepts and principles.

In its second stage (which, like the first stage, continued to be prominent and in some places to prevail), humanist jurisprudence had indeed often emphasized basic legal concepts and principles as a starting point of legal reasoning and as an explanation of legal rules and solutions to specific legal problems. Such synthesis, however, was only partial; only individual legal topics or branches, and not the law as a whole, were synthesized. Important treatises were written on consensual obligations, on interpretation of rules, and on other particular legal subjects. Indeed, some humanist jurists of the second stage themselves expressed the desire for a systematization of the entire body of law.[30] Others, including Zasius himself, said there was no need for it.[31] In fact, humanism alone provided no basis for such a systematization.

It was in connection with fundamental changes in religious thought that the new systematic legal science emerged in the 1520s, 1530s, and 1540s to replace the systematic legal science of the scholastic jurists. The third stage was founded on the marriage of the newer legal humanism with Protestantism.

Despite important tensions between them, the Protestant Reformation went hand in hand with humanism and ultimately transformed it. The prime example is that of the great humanist Lutheran Reformer Philip Melanchthon (1497–1560), whose influence on the new legal science was enormous. In addition, the new legal science drew in part on the older scholasticism itself. The German jurists who played a decisive part in creating the new legal science—Johann Apel (1486–1536), Konrad Lagus (ca. 1499–1546), Johann Oldendorp (ca. 1488–1567), Nicolas Vigelius (1529–1600), and Johannes Althusius (1557–1638), among many others—acknowledged their debt not only to Luther and Melanchthon but also to the great scholastic jurists of earlier times. Without a return to some of the basic achievements of scholastic legal science, there could not have been a lasting transformation of it by a new legal science.

Protestant faith, especially in its Lutheran form, added to legal humanism a belief—shared by the scholastic theologians and jurists whom the humanists had attacked—in the objectivity of human law as an integral part of God's creation. In Lutheran theology, God ordains human law, as he ordains everything in the earthly kingdom, and commands that it be made to conform as nearly as possible to the divine law of the Decalogue. At the same time, Protestants denied both the sanctity of the Roman law and canon law texts and the authority of the tradition of interpretation of those texts; in that, they differed from the earlier Roman Catholic scholastics and were at one with the earlier humanists. They differed from both, however, in their belief that the principles by which human law ought to be guided were to be found, in the first instance, in the reason and conscience of Christians, that is, in the knowledge implanted in them by God. In other words, God was not revealed in the legal texts but hidden in them; to find their hidden meaning, it was necessary to bring to the texts truths from outside them—concepts and principles implanted in the reason and conscience of the faithful jurist. The purpose was not (as the scholastics had taught) to achieve maximum legal propositions implicit in legal rules found in authoritative texts, or to prove by reason what is known by faith, but rather to establish the validity of legal rules by showing their derivation from principles known to the Christian conscience to be just.

This was not only a question of legal theory, that is, theory of the sources of law; it was also a question of legal authority, legal legitimacy, itself. In defying both the pope and eventually the emperor, Luther rejected the two ultimate guarantors of legal authority in the political world in which he lived. It was this defiance which turned many of the leading humanist jurists against him—including the three whom Erasmus had called "the great triumvirate," Zasius, Alciatus, and Budaeus, all of whom, like Erasmus himself, and many other humanists, had initially been attracted to Luther's cause. When they saw, however, that Luther's theology led not to reforming the church of Rome but to abolishing it, and with it the political authority of the Holy Roman Emperor, they turned against Luther, if only because he seemed to them to be attacking the very foundations of legality, leaving no basis for fidelity to law on the part of either rulers or subjects.

Luther, however, was by no means an antinomian. He attacked the existing legal order both in the church and in the secular realm, but he sought to lay the foundations of a new legal order which would correspond to scriptural requirements. It was therefore no accident that a large number of sixteenth-century Protestant jurists, many of them closely associated with Luther himself,[32] were deeply concerned to explore the nature of law and to find clues to its unity and integrity—and more than that, to establish its "method," by which they meant the scientific explication and systematization of the basic legal concepts and principles which give rise to specific legal rules. This was not only a matter of jurisprudential concern but also a matter of political concern in the highest sense: to find a new objective basis for the legitimacy, the authority, of legal regulation.

Melanchthon's Topical Method

It was also no accident that the new systematic legal science grew in the first instance out of the spiritual and intellectual ferment at the University of Wittenberg following the arrival there of the young Philip Melanchthon in 1518.[33]

As noted in the previous chapter, Melanchthon's earliest major work, *Loci Communes Rerum Theologicarum* (Common Topics of Theological Matters), first published in 1521,[34] laid the foundations of a new systematic theology—one which fully reflected the basic theological doctrines espoused by Luther but which added to Luther's theology a new "topical" method of analysis applicable also to other branches of knowledge, including not only the philosophy of law but also the method or science of law.

To construct any science, Melanchthon taught, the topics common to all sciences (*loci communes*) should be applied to the subject matter being investigated, in the form of a series of questions: (1) What is the definition of the thing under investigation? (2) What is its division into genus and species? (3) What are its various causes? (4) What are its various effects? (5) What things are adjacent to it? (6) What things are cognate to it? (7) What things are repugnant to it?[35] Moreover, every particular subject matter, every "art," he wrote, requires its own "method" *(methodus)* which presents concisely and in an ordered way its own "special topics" *(praecipui loci)*.[36] Just as the special topics of theology provide the basic for a concise and systematic statement of the fundamental doctrines of theology, so the special topics of law, in Melanchthon's view, provide the basis for a systematic legal science.

Similar common topics, which were originally derived from Aristotle, had been given new meaning by the scholastics; their meaning had been revised again by the humanists of the fifteenth century, especially Rudolph Agricola (1443–1485), whose *De Inventione Dialectica* of 1479 strongly influenced Melanchthon. Before Melanchthon, however, the common topics had been viewed merely as a classificatory index (frequently arranged alphabetically) of the materials under examination. Moreover, neither the common topics nor special topics had been applied systematically to the "arts" of theology and law.[37]

The scholastics had considered *loci* as a branch of rhetoric, and hence primarily as a guide to debate. The humanists of the late fifteenth and early sixteenth centuries removed the *loci* from rhetoric to dialectic, which they defined as the science or art of exposition and proof. Nevertheless, in practice the humanists—before Melanchthon—confined the use of *loci* to the "exposition" side of dialectic, which they called *inventio,* or "finding," as contrasted with the "proof" side, which they called *iudicium,* or "judgment." That is, the *loci,* the topics, were a way of organizing the materials, a way of exploring, or "finding," the structure of the subject under investigation; and it was that "finding" of the structure of the subject that constituted, for the earlier humanists, the *methodus,* the scientific method. In 1520 Melanchthon wrote, "The dialecticians have adopted this word *methodus* for the most correct order of explication." He himself went beyond that.

Some historians of philosophy have said that it was Peter Ramus (1515–1572), the famous French grammarian and logician, who transformed the *loci* method of explication *(inventio)* into a method also of proving truth *(iudicium).*[38] In fact, although Ramus did assert that his *loci* method was a method of proof as well as of explication, it remained in his hands almost entirely the latter.[39] It was, in fact, Melanchthon, not Ramus, who first showed how "the most correct order of explication" could be at the same time a method of determining the validity or invalidity of propositions and arguments. He did this by drawing on the general part of the method, the *loci communes,* to take specific items of knowledge out of their particular branches and to define their essential nature. For Melanchthon, the *loci communes* (genus and species, causes, and the like) were basic axioms applicable not only to language and philosophy but also to theology and law. By combining them with the *praecipui loci* of specific branches of knowledge, and thus to ask, in theology, such questions as, What is the genus "sin"? What are its species? What are their causes? What is grace? and so on was not only to facilitate explication but also to arrive at truth, in this case the true distinction between Law and Gospel. The specific *loci* of theology were drawn from the Bible; more particularly, Melanchthon derived the specific *loci* of sin, grace, and law expressly from

Saint Paul.[40] In law, as was shown in the previous chapter, Melanchthon derived from the second table of the Decalogue the basic topics of constitutional law, family law, criminal law, moral offenses, property law, fraud, and others.

Melanchthon's disciples adopted his method of classification of law based on the Decalogue and, going beyond that, read into the Roman law texts pairs of *loci* such as rule and equity, substance and procedure, ownership and obligation, contract and delict. By applying the *loci communes*—the general or "common" *loci*—to these specifically legal categories, they not only explicated the legal materials concisely and systematically but also, in so doing, derived new insights from those materials and gave them new meaning and new applications. They believed, with Melanchthon, that if knowledge is "located"—we might say today "packaged"—by the right "method," then its underlying principles will be validated.

Johann Apel

Among the first jurists to respond to Melanchthon's call for "method" was his Wittenberg colleague Johann Apel (1486–1536). Apel was two years younger than Luther and twelve years older than Melanchthon.[41] Born in Nuremberg, he entered the newly founded University of Wittenberg at the age of sixteen. Later he also studied at Erfurt and at Leipzig. After concentrating in the arts, he eventually received his doctorate in law. It is not known where he first lectured. He entered the ecclesiastical hierarchy, though not as a priest, and became a canon and a councilor of Bishop Konrad of Würzburg. In 1523, although he had previously taken vows of celibacy, he secretly married a nun of noble birth. In a tract titled *Defensio pro Suo Coniugio,* he argued that a marriage such as his, entered into in the sight of God, from love and not from lust, is legitimate and may not be challenged either by the imperial or by the ecclesiastical authority. Whether because of the marriage or the tract or both, Bishop Konrad caused Apel and his wife to be arrested and imprisoned. After three months, however, the case having become a cause célèbre, they were released. The following year Apel became a professor of law at Wittenberg. He became a close friend and disciple of both Luther and Melanchthon. Indeed, he attended Luther's own notorious marriage ceremony in 1525.

In 1524 Apel was appointed rector of the University of Wittenberg for one year. Thereafter he became a councilor to the elector of Saxony. In 1529 he was appointed to the Saxon supreme court *(Hofgericht).* During this time he lectured at Wittenberg on both Roman law and canon law. In 1530 he left Wittenberg to become chancellor to Duke Albrecht of Prussia, in Königsberg. Four years later he returned to his native Nuremberg as city councilor and advocate. He died in 1536.

Although Apel, like many leading jurists of his time, thus combined an academic career with an active practice as judge and as councilor to territorial and city authorities, he nevertheless also produced two important scholarly works which grew directly out of his teaching. These two books may be said to have founded modern German legal science. The first, whose Latin title, which starts with the word *Methodica,* may be rendered in translation *The Method of Dialectical Reason Applied to Legal Knowledge,* was an attempt to organize and systematize the entire body of law.[42] The second, titled in translation *Isagoge: A Dialogue on the Study of Law Properly Instituted,* was a treatise on legal education in which the pedagogical need for such a systematization of the entire body of law was set forth.[43]

The *Methodica,* which was first published in 1535, was based on Apel's course of lectures at the University of Wittenberg during several years immediately prior to his departure in 1530. It starts by directing attention to Justinian's Institutes. It does not, however, recapitulate, paraphrase, or elucidate the text of the Institutes but instead draws on it for a multitude of examples of legal rules, which it classifies and analyzes in terms of the Melanchthonian *loci*—both *loci communes* and *praecipui loci.* Thus Apel systematized legal rules by using them to answer the questions: What is law? What are its genera and species? What is its efficient cause? What are its effects? What concepts and things are related to it? What are contrary to it? What circumstances alter the answers to the above question?[44] Each of these questions ("topics") forms the heading of a chapter, in which charts and examples are used to elucidate the analysis. The answers to the questions resulted in a new synthesis, in which concepts and principles are stated which are not to be found as such in the original text but which nevertheless are reflected in its various passages. It is perhaps for that reason that the great nineteenth-century German legal historian Roderich Stintzing states, "Of the jurists of that time whose efforts were directed to the systematic method, Apel is the most original."[45]

Apel's *Isagoge* is in the form of a conversation between an ordinary jurist (Alberich), a neophyte law student (Sempronius), and a third person, Sulpitius, who represents the author himself. All three complain bitterly about the teaching of law through glosses on the text of the Digest—"the absinthe of Accursius" (in Ulrich von Hutten's phrase), which dulls and poisons the mind. In the lectures he must attend, Sempronius complains, "I hear individual words but I no more understand them than I would if they were in Russian." He dreads the thought of spending five years on such drudgery. Sulpitius advises him to attend no lectures except those on the Institutes, which, he says, can be taught in a single year. "This little work," he states, "contains the essence of jurisprudence."

Up to that point the book is humanist both in style and in content. Eventually, however, the dialogue moves beyond what I have called the second stage of humanist legal science. Sulpitius attributes to the Institutes a systematic derivation of legal rules from the idea of law itself, embedded in reason. He states that basic legal principles and concepts underlying such rules may be traced to the (Melanchthonian) "elements of knowledge that are inborn in human nature."[46] Apel does not stop, however, with "inborn ideas" but goes on to apply the rest of Melanchthon's dialectical "method." He proposes, in effect, a complete reordering of the Institutes, based, on the one hand, on the requirements of legal education—that is, on the need to simplify and systematize the enormous mass of technical legal rules so that students may grasp them—and, on the other hand, on the desire to derive the rules from a rational and comprehensive set of principles. Apel then introduces into the *Isagoge* a recapitulation and expansion of much of the analysis which he had presented in his earlier work, the *Methodica.*

Franz Wieacker has charged Apel with a certain duplicity in his use of the Roman law. Apel and his circle, Wieacker writes, resorted to the Institutes only in order to satisfy the antiquarian need for a pure source, an authoritative precedent, but in fact they distorted its meaning, presenting it in fundamentally new terms.[47] There is, however, another way of judging Apel's work. He went "back to the sources" *not,* to be sure, according to the philological-historical method advocated by humanist critics since the time of Valla, but rather according to the hermeneutical method used by Luther, Melanchthon, and other Protestant theologians in interpreting the Bible. Sixteenth-century Protestant hermeneutics sought to disclose the hidden meaning of Scripture for the contemporary reader. It started not from an antiquarian motive but from a concern to understand the message of the Bible for the present and the future. In addition, Scripture was to be interpreted according to its spirit, not according to its letter. That involved the interpretation of individual parts by reference to Scripture as a whole. The motto of Lutheran hermeneutics was "Scriptura sui ipsius interpretes" (Scripture is its own interpreter).[48] This meant also that tradition—that is, the traditional interpretation accepted in previous centuries—lost its authority. Each reader who had faith and learning was free to give meaning to the text. Thus Protestant theology was able to systematize biblical principles and concepts in a form quite different from the form in which those principles and concepts appear in the text of the Bible itself and also quite different from the form established by previous authorities.

Apel was perhaps the first jurist to apply Protestant hermeneutics to law and thereby to present it as an integrated set of principles and concepts from which the various legal rules are logically derived. He set out to do in law what his colleagues had done in theology: to synthesize the principles and concepts in a form quite different from that in which they appeared in the original texts and also quite different from that established by previous authoritative writings.

One of Apel's main contributions was to criticize and reinterpret the division of law, as declared in Justinian's Institutes, into "persons," "actions," and "things." The author of the Institutes did not define these three terms in a satisfactory way and did not in fact organize his exposition around them. Apel contended, first, that the category "persons" is incidental to "things." He then went on to divide "things" *(res)* into "right *in* a thing" *(jus in re),* to which he applied the term "ownership" *(dominium),* and "right *to* a thing" *(jus ad rem),* to which he applied the term "obligation" *(obligatio),* under which he also subsumed "actions." The concept *jus ad rem,* not to be found in the Institutes, had been invented by the scholastic jurists of the twelfth century and had become an integral and fundamental concept of European law.[49] Apel's division of civil law into ownership (direct and beneficial) and obligations (contractual and quasi-contractual, delictual and quasi-delictual)[50] established basic terms of modern Western legal science as it has existed into the twenty-first century. To the two fundamental genera of ownership and obligation everything else in the civil law was said by Apel to be related as (1) species, (2) effective cause, (3) effect, (4) affine, (5) contrary, or (6) circumstance. Thus "persons" were to be treated as "circumstances" of ownership and obligation and "actions" as the "effects" of ownership and obligation. It is characteristic of Apel that he expanded the method of diagramming, or charting, law, which had been used previously to explicate individual topics, into a method for comprehending the entire civil law (as he conceived that term). (See Figure 1.)

Apel was among the first Western jurists to use the term "civil law" to refer primarily to the law of property, contract, delict, and other branches of law chiefly governing relations among private persons. The Roman *jus civile* was originally understood to be the whole law governing Roman citizens, including not only what came in the sixteenth century to be called "private law" but also constitutional law, administrative law, criminal law, church law, and other branches of "public law."[51] After the Papal Revolution, some branches of law such as marriage law and criminal law came to be seen as separate subsystems within the two main systems of canon law and Roman law; a sharp division between public law and private law, however, and the treatment of *jus civile* chiefly (though not exclusively) as private law, became characteristic of Western legal thought only in the sixteenth and succeeding centuries.[52] In many German territories and cities in the sixteenth century, separate codes of criminal law and separate legislation governing public administration *(Polizeiordnungen)* were enacted. Starting with Apel's, the great sixteenth-century German treatises summarizing "civil law" often dealt only briefly with public law, typically under "the law of persons" (especially the person of the king), and also often neglected criminal law, concentrating primarily (though, once again, not exclusively) on ownership and civil obligations, together with inheritance, family law, and other related fields of private law. At the same time, substantive civil law was analytically separated from civil procedure.

The emphasis on definition, and the elaborate classification of legal principles

Figure 1. Apel's chart.

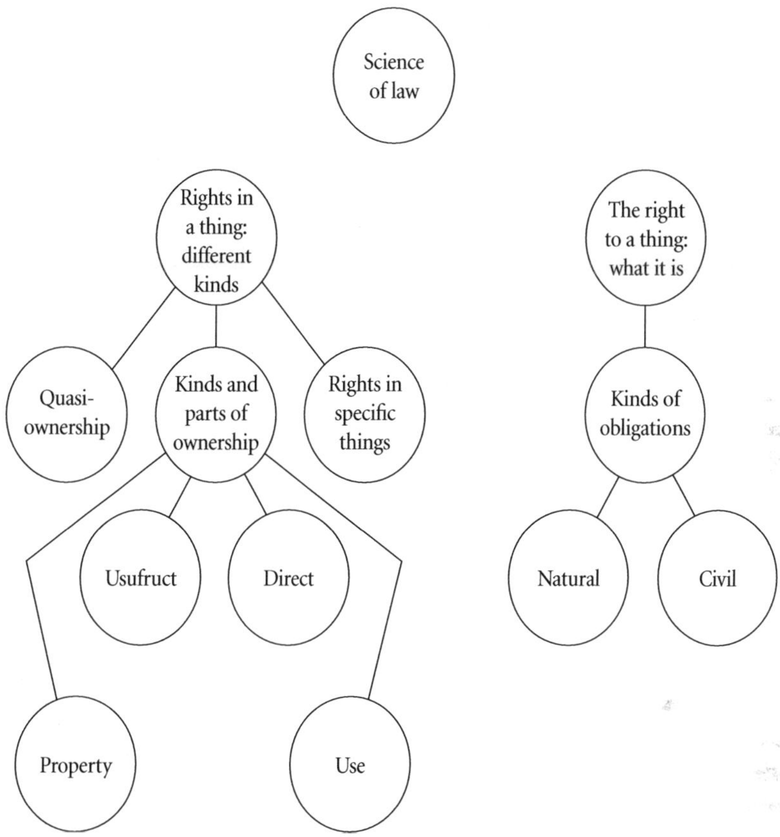

From Johan Apel, *Methodica Dialectices Radio ad Jurisprudentiam Adcommodata* (The Dialectical Method Accommodated to the Science of Law) (Lyon, 1549).

into genus and species, led to sharp conceptual distinctions within the body of civil law itself. One such division was the separation of contract from acquisition of ownership. Contract, according to Apel, gives rise to a "cause" of obligation, which in turn is a right "to," not a right "in," property. Ownership, which is a right "in" property, may be acquired in a variety of ways, including not only occupation and inheritance but also contract; nevertheless, a contract which results in acquisition of ownership, such as a contract of sale, may not be said to be a "proximate cause" of ownership, but only a "remote cause." The contract of sale is a "proximate cause" of a personal action, that is, an obligation; thus it may give rise to a right to delivery of the thing sold. It is the actual (even though symbolic) delivery, however, and not the right to delivery, that is the proximate cause—the mode of acquisition—of ownership.[53]

This analysis remained orthodox until the nineteenth century—not just in Germany but throughout the West. It has not been totally abandoned, even in the United States. A distinction is still made between the buyer's right of property in goods which have been delivered by the seller (for example, to a carrier) and his contractual right to the delivery of goods which have remained in the possession of the seller; in the former case they are the buyer's goods and he may recover them from a third person, whereas in the latter case he normally may only recover damages for nondelivery. With regard to land, as contrasted with goods, differences between contractual rights and property rights remain even sharper. A contract to transfer ownership of land is different from a conveyance of the land.

A key to Apel's legal science was his concept of the logical unity of the civil law. As Wieacker has put it, Apel and his circle recognized that "the deconstruction of the authorities would not in itself lead to a new basis for finding the law." Having discarded "the scrupulous subdivision of the *mos italicus,*" they saw the possibility of "deriving [specific rules and] decisions from the larger integration [*Zusammenhang*]."[54]

Apel's *Methodica* seems to have been the first of a long series of works, similarly titled, in which sixteenth-century jurists—most of whom were German[55] and almost of all whom were Protestant[56]—set out not merely to propose, but actually to present, a synthesis of the entire law. In the course of the century these syntheses became increasingly comprehensive and increasingly detailed.

Konrad Lagus

Apel's work was considerably less comprehensive and detailed than the *Methodica*—published eight years later—of his younger colleague Konrad Lagus (ca. 1499–1546), who taught at Wittenberg from 1522 to 1540.[57] Like Apel, Lagus came to law while teaching in the faculty of arts. Having received the master of arts degree in 1529, Lagus only received the doctor of laws degree in 1540, although he had previously lectured and written on both philosophical and technical legal subjects as well as on dialectics and on theology. Lagus was also active in government, participating in the Zwickau city reformation in 1539 and finally leaving Wittenberg in 1540 to become a syndic of the Protestant city of Danzig. Like Apel, Lagus ardently shared the beliefs of Luther and Melanchthon, and strove to structure legal science, as Melanchthon had structured theology, according to its basic themes or concepts, its *praecipui loci.* Lagus wrote that "the natural order requires that we arrive through the understanding of genera to the elements of knowledge of species."[58] Also as in the case of Melanchthon, of Apel, and of the humanist jurists generally, the search for general legal principles and concepts led Lagus to the Institutes, which, he said, provided "the structure of the legal order."[59] Nevertheless, Lagus, like Apel, did not attempt to follow the "structure" of the Institutes but only used its legal rules and concepts as building blocks for his own *Methodica,* which was written between 1536 and 1540 and first published in 1543. It was a book of 830 pages—some six times the length of Apel's *Methodica*—devoted to a presentation of basic principles of law drawn from both Roman law and canon law.[60] In it he attempted to set forth in a systematic way the "principal parts of which the science and art of law consist."[61] The publisher stated in the advertisement of the book that no one in the previous four centuries had ever written a "compendium" (a word often used in those times interchangeably with *methodica*) of the entire learned law.[62] Lagus himself made a similar claim, referring favorably to the thirteenth-century canon law and Roman law *summae* of Hostiensis and Azo, respectively, but pointing out that they dealt with the materials according to the order in which they appeared in the authoritative texts rather than according to the basic principles which pervaded the texts.[63] His own aim, Lagus stated, was to present to students a picture of the whole law, so that from its genera their thoughts could be reflected onto its species and they could thus rightly perceive the particular legal rules and decisions that are deduced from them.[64]

Lagus did not mention his colleague Apel, although he followed Apel's conception of the unity of the civil law and its division into ownership and obligations. Nor did he mention his colleague Melanchthon, though (like Apel) he adopted Melanchthon's concept of innate knowledge of fundamental truths as well as Melanchthon's topical method.[65]

Although Lagus's legal science was similar in many respects to Apel's, it nevertheless marked a major advance. It was not only much longer and much more comprehensive but also philosophically much richer. In his *Methodica* Apel had set forth the principles of dialectical reasoning (the method of *loci*) and had used them as a basis for systematizing legal principles, starting with the general and proceeding to their particular species. But Apel did not, in his *Methodica,* systematically address philosophical questions regarding the purposes of law. He was concerned to systematize legal principles and rules independently of the equity which motivates their application to concrete cases. Lagus, by contrast, separated his treatise into two parts, one of which he called philosophical and the other historical. The philosophical part, which occupies only fifty-eight pages of the 1544 edition, deals with the general nature of law and sets forth the method of the book. The historical part, which occupies the bulk of the book—766 of its 830 pages—is a detailed analysis of the entire legal structure.

Of special interest is Lagus's systematization of the law, in the philosophical part, in accordance with the Aristotelian analysis of four kinds of "causes": "efficient causes," "material causes," "formal causes," and "final causes." This analysis had been familiar to scholastic theologians, jurists, and philosophers, but it had not been used as a basis for systematizing the branches of knowledge that they explicated. Apel also, following Melanchthon, used the Aristotelian causes as one set of devices, though not the principal basis, for systematizing law.[66] Lagus carried Apel's "causal" analysis of law much farther. He classified law, first, according to its efficient causes, that is, according to the particular source or maker of each particular type of legal order. Thus he divided natural law, whose source is "the sense of nature or the judgment of reason," from civil law, whose source is "the consent of the people" as reflected in statute or custom; he further subdivided statutory and customary law into laws made by the empire, laws made by the church, laws made by individual municipalities, laws issued by specific legislators (such as praetorian laws, Caesarian laws, etc.), and others.

Lagus's second classification of law was according to its material causes, that is, the subject matter of which particular types of law are composed. These he divided first into divine law, which concerns sacred things (such as temples and tombs), the priesthood, and the like, and human law, which concerns civil affairs *(negotia civilia).* By virtue of its material cause, human law consists of military law, feudal law, and religious rites and traditions (which Lagus distinguished from divine law), as well as civil law, which in turn is divided into public and private law, each with its own branches.

Lagus's third classification of law was according to its formal causes, that is, the forms which it takes, and these he divided into strict law and equity, subdividing equity, in turn, into written and unwritten (or natural) equity.

Lagus's fourth classification was according to final causes, that is, the ends which law serves, and under this heading he divided laws into those which chiefly concern public matters *(res publicae)* and those which chiefly concern private matters such as contracts and injuries. Thus the division between public and private law was made basic to the purpose of law, although Lagus added that the protection of public interests serves the utility of individuals *(utilitatem singulorum)* and the protection of individuals ultimately serves the public welfare. "The highest end of all laws," Lagus wrote, "is the public welfare [*salus publica*]."

Lagus concludes his introduction to the "causal" analysis of law by saying, "And these"—that is, public welfare and private utility—"are the final causes of each of the individual laws, by which they are brought into being, so that if these causes should cease then the binding force [*obligatio*] of these laws is also taken away."

Lagus's application to law of Aristotelian and Melanchthonian categories of causation had important philosophical implications. One can see in it elements both of legal positivism (especially in the idea that the efficient cause is the lawmaker) and of natural law theory (especially in the idea that a law loses its binding force if it ceases to serve the common good). At least equally important, however, are its technical implications for the systematization of the law. The entire historical part of his treatise is organized around classifications derived from the four Aristotelian causes. This is apparent from the chart which Lagus included (see Figure 2). This chart dealt only with the

Figure 2. Lagu's chart.

What kind of matters pertain to

- Divine law, namely, those which are
  - Sacred, religious, holy — such as — Temples, household tombs, city walls. And these may not be alienated nor may they come into the power of individuals, with the exception of those cases mentioned in the law
- Human law, and these are
  - Public, and these are
    - Common — which means that — They belong to no one in particular
    - Corporate *(universitatis)* — which means that — They are common by use, not by ownership
  - Private, and these are
    - Corporeal, namely, — Land *(fundus),* clothing, gold, silver
    - Incorporeal, namely, — Rights of use and enjoyment and obligation
  - These are acquired
    - According to the law of nations, by — Occupation, capture, finding, birth, allurium, specificiation, accession, mingling, construction, planting, sowing, cultivation, delivery
    - According to civil law, by — Usucaption, prescription, donation, testament, legacy, trust *(fidei commissium),* succession, arrogation, annexation *(adiectio)*

From Conrad Lagus, *Methodica* (Method) (Lyon, 1544), pp. 137–138.

subject matter of which law is composed (the "material causes"). Lagus's successors expanded his method of charting to include "the whole law" *(universum),* including its sources, its forms, and its purposes as well as its subject matter.

The historical part of Lagus's treatise is divided into (1) the law of persons, (2) modes of acquiring, alienating, and losing property, (3) agreements and obligations, (4) actions and pleadings, (5) judgments, and (6) privileges and legal grants (benefices). The theory of law and the "causes" of law set forth in the philosophical part are embedded in the historical part in an analysis of the entire body of legal principles and concepts and of their breakdown into specific rules. Of his sixfold division Lagus wrote, "I deem these headings to be capable of embracing every form of law."[67]

In each of the six chapters of the second part, the general topic is broken down into its species, and each species, each form of law, is treated in one or more titles. The first chapter, "On the Law of Persons," deals with certain aspects of family law (rights and duties of family members) and of constitutional law (powers and responsibilities of emperor, princes, and public officials). The second chapter, "On Modes of Acquiring, Transferring, and Losing Property [*Res*]," deals with property law, the law of succession, and marital property. The third chapter, "On Agreements and Obligations," deals with contractual, delictual, and other forms of civil liability as well as criminal law. Marriage and divorce are also included in this chapter. The fourth chapter, "On Actions and Pleadings," covers civil and criminal procedure. The fifth chapter, "On Judgments," deals with the composition of courts. The sixth chapter, "On Privileges and Grants," deals partly with constitutional law and partly with the law of obligations. The breaking down of genera into species is carried out systematically down to the smallest details. As Gerhard Theuerkauf states, "Lagus's course of thinking is determined by a firm plan, down to the individual details, and this plan is held to."[68]

Lagus's "plan" brought to fruition Apel's conception of a systematic organization of the entire body of rules contained in the law. This involved two new methodological principles. First, Lagus organized the subject matter of law, on Melanchthonian principles, around general topics common to all sciences *(loci communes),* including the Aristotelian four causes; previously, legal scholars using a topical method had organized the subject matter of law around the topics and in the order set forth in the authoritative legal texts themselves, called the *loci ordinaria,* "the usual topics," with the result that the same general topic was discussed in a variety of places and sometimes inconsistently.

Second, Lagus combined Roman law sources and canon law sources; previously these had been analyzed separately, the Roman law texts being read in courses in Roman law and written about by Romanists and the canon law texts being read in courses in canon law (which, to be sure, drew on Roman law concepts and rules) and written about by canonists.[69] Lagus was one of the first jurists who undertook to present a compendium of concepts and rules of law drawn from both systems.[70] (Apel had restricted his treatise largely to a synthesis of Roman law.) Under each general topic discussed in his *Methodica,* Lagus would list the chief Roman law sources and the chief canon law sources on which the discussion was based.[71]

Lagus was conscious of the novelty of his method and was concerned about opposition to it on the part of the traditionalists. He forbade his students to circulate their notes of his lectures without his permission and refused to allow publication of his *Methodica* on the ground that it was unfinished. Indeed, in 1538, while he was still only a "lecturer" *(Privatdozent)* and not yet a "professor," he was the object of a rescript issued by the elector of Saxony censuring those insufficiently trained lecturers on law who dispensed with the traditional exegesis of legal texts. It is not known precisely why he left Wittenberg in 1540, at the age of forty-one, but three years later, when his *Methodica* was printed in Frankfurt am Main without his authorization, he protested vigorously and even published a *Protestatio* setting forth his objections to its premature publication and attempting to clarify its purposes and its method.

In fact, Lagus's *Compendium of Civil Law* (as the Frankfurt publisher retitled it) was highly successful. At least eight editions of it were published between 1543 and 1592, in addition to numerous reprintings. The 1571 Basel edition, reprinted in 1581, bore on the title page the words "not only for lawyers but also for others desirous of wisdom." As Theuerkauf has pointed out, it was only after a series of other similar systematic presentations of law were published in the late 1580s and 1590s that Lagus's *Compendium* went out of print.[72] By that time the systematic method initiated by Apel and perfected by Lagus had become firmly established as the dominant legal science of Germany.

Once the "topical" method of systematization of law was introduced, it was inevitable that not only Roman law and canon law but also various other types of law, such as territorial law *(Landrecht),* urban law *(Stadtrecht),* and imperial law *(Reichsrecht),* would be brought into a common focus. Here Lagus, once again, was a pioneer. In addition to his compendium of civil law, which is devoted primarily but by no means exclusively to Roman law and canon law, he wrote a compendium of Saxon law, in which he analyzed systematically the law of Saxony, principally as it was set forth in two great texts, namely, the *Sachsenspiegel* and the Magdeburg Law. The *Sachsenspiegel* (Mirror of the Saxons), written in about 1220, was the first major law book in the German language; it was chiefly concerned with, first, the customary law of Saxony and second, the royal law (both customary and statutory) of the German emperor applicable in Saxony and elsewhere. In it, a body of rules and principles was presented in detail but with little conceptual analysis and with few concrete illustrations. Though privately written by a Saxon jurist, Eike von Repgau, the *Sachsenspiegel* was generally treated as authoritative, was glossed by learned jurists, and for centuries was considered to be a subsidiary law which could be used to supplement the prevailing urban, territorial, or imperial law throughout Germay. In 1534, the Supreme Court of Saxony recommended to the elector that the *Sachsenspiegel,* being in many parts obsolete, should be revised. Lagus's compendium, which was written in about 1540, may have been intended to serve as a theoretical basis for such a revision.

Lagus divided his compendium of Saxon law, as he had divided his compendium of Roman and canon law, into two main parts, the philosophical part and the historical part. Within each part he followed more or less the same topical breakdown as in the civil law compendium: the philosophical part dealt consecutively with the sources of law, the divisions of law, the applicability of law, and the interpretation of law, while the historical part, which occupied the bulk of the book, dealt consecutively with the law of persons, property, obligations, actions and pleadings, and judgment.

In both his compendium of civil law and his compendium of Saxon law, Lagus based his classification, in the first instance, on the threefold source of all human law in God-given reason, the will of the public authority, and custom. These concepts were made much more specific, however, when used with reference to the unitary law of a distinct historical community, the people of Saxony, than when used with reference to the texts of Justinian and the decretals of the popes. In the first place, Lagus treated both Roman law and canon law as subsidiary law in Saxony, applicable only for filling gaps in the territorial law. The territorial law was supreme, and was not to yield, in cases of conflict, to the imperial law; even imperial statutes *(Reichspolizeiordnungen)* were not necessarily binding in Saxony. In the second place, Lagus viewed territorial law as the law promulgated by the *Obrigkeit,* the high magistracy, of the territory. Even the customary law summarized in the *Sachsenspiegel* was considered by him to owe its validity to the tacit consent of the *Obrigkeit,* and it was to yield to the written law in case of conflict.[73] Likewise, the Magdeburg Law, though it was in form the law of the city of Magdeburg and its numerous daughter cities, was treated by Lagus as applicable thoughout Saxony, but it, too, was to yield to territorial law in case of conflict. In short, Saxon territorial law, the law of the principality as such, the *Landrecht,* was now superior in Saxony to all other kinds of human law. It would yield only to divine law (the Decalogue) and natural law, which were treated as one and were identified with inborn reason planted by God in every person. Thus in rationalizing Saxon law, Lagus also nationalized it.

The Subsequent Development of Legal Systematization

The "method" of legal systematization initiated at Wittenberg by Apel and Lagus in the late 1520s and 1530s, and the new legal science which it reflected, were developed further in various directions chiefly in Germany but also in other European countries throughout the sixteenth century and into the seventeenth. Among the most prominent German legal "methodists" of the latter part of the sixteenth century were Nicolas Vigelius and Johann Althusius. Vigelius was a pupil of Oldendorp at Marburg and taught there from 1560 to 1594.[74] In his *Methodus Universi Iuris Civilis* (Method of the Entire Civil Law), published in 1561, he classified the "kinds" *(genera)* of law into public law and private law—a distinction which, as noted earlier, only became basic to legal analysis in the sixteenth century. Public law is treated in the first three of the twenty-five "books" that make up Vigelius's work; private law and modes of acquiring private rights occupy the next twenty-one books; and the final book deals with a miscellaneous group of topics which do not fit into the other categories.[75]

In terms of legal science generally, Vigelius, like Lagus, freed himself entirely from the agenda imposed by the Roman law texts. "The entire civil law" was not *Roman* law as such but *the* law as such, that is, the entire law that prevailed in the empire and the principalities and municipalities of Germany. Vigelius used concepts and principles which the scholastic jurists had developed out of the Roman texts, but like the jurists of the first stage of legal humanism, he examined the texts much more critically than the scholastic jurists had done. In addition, like the jurists of the second stage of legal humanism, Vigelius emphasized the importance of basic principles (such as those set forth in the Institutes) in the systematization of individual branches of law. What is most striking and most significant in Vigelius's work, however, as in Apel's and Lagus's, was his effort to organize the whole of the law, proceeding from general to specific—dividing it first into public and private law, subdividing public law into legislative, executive, and judicial activities, and subdividing private law into the law of persons (including family law, master and servant, and guardianship), the law of property, the law of inheritance and trusts and gifts, and the law of obligations arising from contracts, torts, and unjust enrichment, with systematization of the specific rules of each branch. These remain to this day the basic "topics" of Western legal science.

Like Lagus, Vigelius presented a chart in which the structure of his *Methodus* was depicted visually. Vigelius's chart, which in the 1581 edition occupies an insert equal to eight printed pages, is different in some important respects from Lagus's. It omits divine law and natural law, focusing solely on positive law. It classifies contract, tort, and unjust enrichment as modes of acquiring (private) rights rather than as the private law of obligations, parallel to the private law of ownership, and it is more comprehensive in its treatment of private rights. Vigelius's chart is a visual table of contents for his entire treatise, whereas Lagus diagrams only one section of his book. Yet the two methods of systematization are essentially similar. Vigelius's systematization has more sophistication and breadth; Lagus's has more originality and power.

The systematic analysis of "the entire law" and its graphic representation through charts reached a climax in the writings of Johann Althusius (1557–1638), a German Calvinist who became famous both as a legal scholar and as a political theorist.[76] Althusius received his doctorate in laws at Basel in 1586 and in the same year published his first major work, *Jurisprudentia Romana*, a massive synthesis of law. This book was later substantially revised and published in 1603 under the title *Dicaelogica* (The Logic of Law). These works, which were republished many times in the seventeenth and eighteenth centuries, were in the tradition of Lagus and Vigelius; like them, Althusius divided all law into public law and private law, subdivided private law into ownership and obligation, subdivided obligation into contract, tort, and unjust enrichment, and sought to deduce from general concepts and general principles the detailed rules applicable to individual transactions.[77]

The new legal science pioneered in the works of Apel, Lagus, Vigelius, and other sixteenth-century German Protestant jurists was cultivated and developed over the next two centuries by jurists throughout Europe, both Catholic and Protestant. It differed from the earlier legal sciences, both scholastic and humanist, in its use of the topical method to analyze and synthesize law as a whole as well as to analyze and synthesize common features of the various systems of law that prevailed throughout Europe—especially Roman law and canon law, but also common features of the various systems of royal, urban, feudal, and mercantile law. It was this legal science, above all, that constituted the basis of the new European *jus commune* of the sixteenth to eighteenth centuries. The legal scholars who developed it formed a pan-European estate of jurists, a *Juristenstand,* who wrote not only for their respective countrymen but also, and sometimes primarily, for one another. (Some of the prominent among them are listed in note 78).[78]

The new *jus commune* differed from the first European *jus commune,* the canon law of the Roman Catholic Church, in that it was not the official law of a corporate pan-European polity. It differed also, however, from the second European *jus commune,* the Roman law of Justinian as parsed and summarized and elaborated by the Romanist glossators and commentators, in that it was not confined to scholarly analysis and synthesis of the Roman texts. Nor was it a fusion of these two kinds of law. Although even some of the most outstanding twentieth-century legal historians consistently write of "the reception of Roman-canon law," in fact there was never a body of law called "Roman-canon." The new structure of legal concepts, principles, and rules that was built on the basis of the new legal science did, to be sure, take much both from the older canon law and from the Roman law, each of which had previously been called a *jus commune* and which together were called *utrumque jus,* "each law."[79] It also took something from royal law, feudal law, mercantile law, and urban law. But it always distinguished these legal systems from one another.[80] One of the genres of early European legal literature consists of books on the differences among the various legal systems by which a given polity was governed.[81] Yet the Roman law and the canon law occupied a special position as transcendent sources of legal principles—a new *jus naturale.*[82]

Political and Philosophical Implications of the New Legal Science

The need for a new kind of systematization of law arose, in the first instance, from a loss of confidence in the sanctity of the ancient Roman legal texts and the authority of the traditional glosses and commentaries on them. This in itself, however, could only produce the first two stages of legal humanism—the skeptical stage of Valla and Budaeus and the principled stage of Zasius and Alciatus. The principled stage rescued the older scholastic legal science by adding to it some of the philological and historical insights of the skeptical stage; there was a return not to the sanctity of the ancient texts, to be sure, but to their authority, and not to the authority of the traditional glosses and commentaries but to their respectability. This second stage was not enough, however, to restore to legal science the degree and kind of objectivity that was required to meet either the political or the philosophical needs of a Germany transformed by Protestantism and territorialism.

The new legal science developed by sixteenth-century Lutheran jurists served the cause of the Protestant princes by giving both legitimacy and efficiency to the legal order within their principalities. The earlier scholastic legal science had given legitimacy and efficiency to the legal order of a Christendom ruled jointly by a single unified ecclesiastical hierarchy and a multiplicity of secular polities. By the same token, the earlier legal science could not adequately have served the cause of Protestantism viewed as a political movement. Even as modified by the new humanism, pre-Reformation legal science presupposed the diversity of ecclesiastical and secular jurisdictions, each with its own authoritative legal texts. The purpose of the scholastic method was to construct principles out of the specific rules and decisions found in the texts. Thus, for example, canon law recognized the binding force of an informal agreement *(nudum pactum),* while Roman law did not; feudal law recognized serfdom, while urban law did not; mercantile law enforced bills of exchange independently of the underlying contract that called for their use, while royal law did not. These contradictions, and many others like them, could be tolerated in a "federal" Christendom, in which competing jurisdictions relied on diverse legal texts. It could not, however, be so easily tolerated in a unified princely or royal legal order governing both church and state within each territory, such as was introduced by the Reformation.

One of the most striking differences between the new legal science and the old was the bringing together of Roman and canon law—and more than that, of urban and feudal and mercantile law with them. What historians have miscalled the Reception of Roman Law in sixteenth-century Germany was in fact a movement to unify all the various kinds of law, including Roman law, within each polity.

From a purely political point of view, the unification of all jurisdictions, secular and ecclesiastical, under the prince and his councilors, the *Obrigkeit,* was much better served by a legal science which started by attempting to identify and systematize the principles that underlie the entire legal order than by a legal science which started by attempting to identify and systematize the rules and decisions contained in the authoritative legal texts of diverse jurisdictions. Thus the new legal science served the princely political cause.

Likewise the Lutheran jurists' analysis of law—*all* law—in terms of the distinction between the efficient cause (who makes the law?) and the final cause (what purposes does the law serve?) had important political implications. It emphasized the legislative character of law, its source in the will of the lawmaker. It went together with the distinction between rules and application of rules: the rules made by the political authority were given an abstract existence separate from, although intended to serve and be corrected by, reason and equity revealed to conscience.

Together with these rather obvious links between the new legal science and the new political order in Protestant principalities, there existed a more subtle link: the exaltation of the political role of the legal scholar. In pre-Reformation Europe as well, legal scholars had played an important role as advisers to popes, emperors, and kings. Also they had sometimes been asked by judges to decide cases. Never before, however, had legal scholars been recruited as councilors and judges so systematically and on such a large scale as in the sixteenth-century German Protestant principalities. This was due in part, of course, to purely political factors; but it was also due in part to the character of the new legal science, which was so intellectually complex and intricate as to require professorial expertise to articulate and elucidate it.

The political implications of the new German legal science are closely linked with its philosophical implications. The prince, to be sure, was now the supreme lawmaker. Nevertheless, the law that he made had its own built-in requirements. It served a cause higher than the prince. That higher cause was embodied in the legal science itself, which divided all law into divine law (the Ten Commandments) and human law, human law into natural law (reason and conscience implanted in the human heart by God) and positive law, and positive law into public law and private law. The prince, to be sure, was an "efficient cause" of public law, but divine law, natural law, and—*in practice*—large areas of private law were beyond his competence. Moreover, *all* law was to be *applied* equitably, that is, according to God-given conscience. The legal science of the Lutheran jurists could hardly be termed Machiavellian, nor would it support the kind of absolute monarchy advocated by Bodin.

Of special importance are the implications of the new German legal science for that branch of philosophy called dialectics, and especially for that branch of dialectics which is concerned with scientific methods of proof. Here the key figure is Melanchthon, who taught the jurists that every branch of knowledge should be arranged according to its own topics (*praecipui loci,* "special places"), and that by the use of certain general topics common to all the different branches of knowledge (*loci communes,* "common places") it is possible to take items of knowledge out of their specific branches and to define their essential nature. This was a giant step forward in the development in the natural sciences of a method based not only on "Aristotelian" empiricism but also on "Platonic," and eventually mathematical, conceptualism.

Apel, Lagus, and Vigelius were among the first of a large number of German Protestant legal scholars who helped to create a new legal science in the universities of Germany in the sixteenth century. A parallel movement, though not nearly as pronounced, took place later in other countries of Europe, in which Roman Catholic as well as Protestant jurists participated. This was a European phenomenon, then, although it was pioneered in Germany, and nowhere else in Europe did the law professors play such an important practical role in developing the law.

The French experience sheds an oblique light on the German. Following Budaeus (Budé), distinguished French jurists—Cujacius (Cujas), Hotmannus (Hotman), and others—continued to emphasize philology and history at the expense of legal analysis.[83] In searching out ancient Roman texts in order to purge from the law the later interpretations and glosses, they were led to the ultimate rejection of those texts as a living law and to the return to "Gallic" legal institutions. Eventually, a number of French law faculties, or at least many of the most famous French law professors, became alienated from law altogether and devoted themselves to history and theology—subjects which were at that time in France closely connected with national politics. Other leading French jurists, such as Corasius and Bodin, turned away from an initial interest in encyclopedias of law and instead developed political theories of absolute monarchy, according to which the ruler was the "efficient cause" of law and was therefore absolved from bondage to it. It is a striking fact that three of the most outstanding French jurists of the sixteenth century, Duarenus (Duaren), Donellus (Doneau), and Du Moulin, did indeed organize and analyze the enormous mass of rules of law found in the texts of Justinian by use of Melanchthon's topical method, and that one of them, Duarenus, was sympathetic to Protestantism, and the other two, Donellus and Du Moulin, were converts to Protestantism who fled to Lutheran universities in Germany to write and teach.

To understand what was at stake in the transition of sixteenth-century European legal thought from a skeptical to a principled to a systematic legal science, it may be useful to compare it with developments in American legal thought in the twentieth and early twenty-first centuries. "Legal realism," which came to the fore in American law schools in the late 1920s, 1930s, and 1940s, like late-fifteenth- and early-sixteenth-century humanism, attacked the validity of the prevailing body of legal rules partly from a philological and partly from a historical standpoint. The texts of legal rules were dissected to show the distortions that they underwent in the decisions of those who applied them. From the late 1950s through the 1970s, a new school of jurisprudence in the United

States, emphasizing "the legal process," built on some of the insights of the legal realist school but sought to rescue the formal aspects of law by placing them within the context of general principles relating to specific types of problems requiring legal solution. As in the case of the second "principled" stage of legal humanism, represented by Zasius and Alciatus, American advocates of the concept of "law as a process" succeeded for a time in restoring a qualified respect for rules and in synthesizing individual branches of law. They could not, however, by their method give the same sense of the integrity of the legal system as a whole, and of its rootedness in an objective reality, which had existed before the nihilistic attack of the realists. As of the beginning of the twenty-first century, there seemed to be no objective basis for systematizing American law as a whole; that is, there seemed to be no generally shared belief in inborn elements of knowledge constituting fundamental principles from which all legal institutions can be rationally derived. Likewise, there seemed to be, at least among legal scholars, no generally shared belief in, or at least no analysis of, the capacity of the individual conscience to reach just results in actual cases on the basis of reasoned compassion. An awareness of this experience can enhance our appreciation of the magnitude of the achievement of German Protestantism in overcoming the insufficiencies of preexisting legal humanism and in inspiring the creation of a new systematic legal science.

CHAPTER 4

The German Revolution and the Reform of Criminal Law

GERMAN criminal law, in both its procedural and its substantive aspects, underwent a substantial transformation during the sixteenth century.[1] One cause of this transformation was the need to control the widespread violence that characterized the German social order in the late fifteenth and early sixteenth centuries. Huge numbers of wanderers—vagabonds, lawbreakers, Gypsies, unruly pilgrims, fugitive monks and nuns, ex-students, beggars, and others—populated the highways, constituting both a source of criminals and a source of victims. Armed bands led by robber knights attacked travelers and plundered the countryside.[2] The preexisting system of criminal law, based as it was on the presupposition of stable local communal institutions, was not adequate to deal effectively with widespread and mobile crime of a quasi-professional and professional character. Moreover, the ecclesiastical courts, which had had a very broad criminal (as well as civil) jurisdiction, were losing substantial parts of that jurisdiction to princely and urban courts, whose procedures were, once again, not well suited to deal with the increased number and variety of cases. Similar problems, though not as acute, existed in England, France, and other countries of Europe.

Still, it is not easy to transform a whole system of criminal law, and the fact that there was a need for change is hardly a sufficient explanation of why change occurred. The need had existed for decades and generations before substantial changes even began to take place. Moreover, dissatisfaction with the old system does not explain why certain kinds of change occurred and not others.

For several centuries there had existed in Germany, at the village, city, and territorial levels, a system of adjudication, in both criminal and civil cases, by tribunals composed of prominent laymen, called *Schoeffen* (assessors), usually seven to twelve in number, who sat with an official called a *Richter* (director). The German word *Richter* now means "judge," but prior to the sixteenth century, the *Schoeffen* were the judges, the *Urteiler* (i.e., they gave judgment,

Urteil). The *Richter* presided over and directed the proceedings. This system was fundamental to the development of German secular law, whether local or urban or territorial or imperial, in the twelfth to fifteenth centuries. A chief source of that law was custom, and the *Schoeffen*, being responsible, intelligent, educated (though not university-trained) leaders in the local community, the city, or the territory, knew the custom or else were capable of finding it out. The fact that a substantial part of the customary law came to be expressed—and modified—in written treatises, such as the *Sachsenspiegel*, or in written collections of city laws, or in occasional princely ordinances, changed its character somewhat, but not entirely; it was presupposed in the written texts themselves that the law contained therein remained integrated with customary law, to be interpreted partly in the light of custom by benches of amateur, part-time *Schoeffen* sitting under the direction of an official *Richter*.[3]

The procedure applicable in criminal cases in the *Schoeffen* courts prior to the sixteenth century retained some features of one of the more ancient pre-twelfth-century tribal modes of criminal procedure, in which criminal cases were initiated on accusation by the victim or a relative or friend of the victim, and the accused was to be acquitted or convicted on the basis of oaths sworn by him or his accusers and supported by others. He was to be acquitted if he was able, in a religious procedure, to swear a solemn oath purging himself of the charges against him and if his oath was supported by so-called oath-helpers ("compurgators"). If convicted, he was required to pay compensation, a "composition," to the victim or the victim's relatives. The pre-twelfth-century tribunal was not a professional court but a local assembly. This older system of compurgation and composition—like other older modes of trial by ordeal and trial by duel ("battle")—rested on a conception of the trial as an appeal to divine judgment and as a part of the process of reconciliation of feuding kinship groups, with few significant distinctions being made between criminal and civil cases.[4]

In the twelfth century, in the wake of the Papal Revolution, the tribal system was transformed in Germany, as in the rest of Europe. Serious crime (felony) became clearly distinguished from less serious (misdemeanor, delict), and punishment for serious crime, namely, death or mutilation, imposed by a court, replaced settlement by negotiation of the parties or their relatives. Although oath procedure survived, other modes of proof invoking divine judgment, such as trial by ordeal and by duel or battle, were denounced by the church and were virtually eliminated. Moreover, oath procedure was itself transformed from a magical-mechanical mode of proof, in which the test was the swearing of oaths "without slip or trip," to a more rational mode, in which the *Schoeffen* decided which of the parties was to offer proof by oath and whether the proof was sufficient. Purgative oaths were barred if adequate witness proof was presented.

In addition, in the twelfth and thirteenth centuries princely and urban authorities began to take the initiative in prosecuting persons charged with the most serious offenses, and in such cases legal officials interrogated suspects in advance of trial. In many German principalities, cities, and towns, official prosecutors were appointed to bring charges against notorious criminal offenders. Some elements of the system of interrogation of the parties and of witnesses that was first developed in the ecclesiastical courts, which modern scholars have erroneously called "Romano-canonical," or "Roman-canon" (although it was entirely different from the criminal procedure described in the books of classical and post-classical Roman law), gradually infiltrated the secular courts as well.[5] Elements of the earlier Germanic "accusatorial" model of criminal procedure, in which the trial was a contest between accuser and accused and the outcome was considered to be a judgment of God, were combined with elements of the post-eleventh-century canonist "inquisitorial" model, in which the trial was an interrogation of the accused and witnesses by the court and the outcome was considered to be a human judgment based on reason and conscience. In the course of the fifteenth century the accusatory elements came to be subjected to official control to a far greater extent than they had been previously. At the same time, the inquisitorial elements were considerably less sophisticated and less systematized than they became in the sixteenth century under the impact of the German Revolution. Moreover, throughout the period prior to the sixteenth century a modified accusatorial procedure preserved much of its vitality in cases of non-capital crimes.[6]

An important element of the inquisitorial procedure was the resort to torture—in some types of cases—to induce a confession from the accused. Historians have explained the introduction of torture as a consequence of the abolition of ordeals by the Fourth Lateran Council in 1215. It is said that to replace the ordeals a method of proof was needed that would achieve a degree of certainty comparable to that of divine judgment. Such certainty was to be found in what was called "full proof," that is, proof either by two unimpeachable eyewitnesses to the essential elements of the crime or by voluntary confession at trial in open court.[7] If full proof was not available, but only so-called half proof—for example, if there was strong circumstantial evidence but only one eyewitness—then a confession was needed to achieve the desired certainty. It was thought that to permit a conviction to be based solely on circumstantial evidence would leave discretion in the judge to decide on the basis of his subjective evaluation of the weight to be accorded the various circumstantial factors.

This explanation, although widely accepted,[8] leaves many questions open. In the first place, full proof was not required in cases of non-capital offenses, such as assault and battery, forgery, petty stealing, usury, brawling, drunkenness, or blasphemy. If, for example, a person was charged with stealing a relatively small amount of money, for which the penalty might be a fine or the pillory or ducking in water or flogging or banishment, he could be convicted on the basis of possession of the stolen money, presence of a motive for stealing it, absence of an alibi, furtive behavior, and other circumstantial evidence, as well as testimony of witnesses concerning his subsequent statements and other direct evidence short of two eyewitnesses. The question then arises, if without full proof by two eyewitnesses or confession the court could achieve substantial certainty in non-capital cases (misdemeanors), why was such proof required in capital cases (felonies)?

In the second place, although confession was called "the queen of proofs," there was always a great suspicion about the validity of a confession induced by torture. Partly for that reason it was required that the confession be repeated voluntarily at trial. But even the confession reiterated at trial was subject to doubt in view of the fact that the accused who repudiated his confession at trial was to be remanded to a renewed investigation and renewed torture and again asked to repeat the confession in court. The question then arises, if an extorted confession was recognized to be of dubious probative value, why was it insisted upon?

In the third place, certain privileged classes were exempted from examination under torture, except in cases of treason or heresy. These included aristocrats, higher officials, clergy, physicians, and doctors of law, as well as children under twelve or fourteen, pregnant women, and infirm persons for whom torture would create a risk of death.[9] If confession was the "queen of proofs," why was it not insisted on in prosecutions of medical doctors and law professors?

In the fourth place, even a confession corroborated by other circumstances—one, for example, which led to the capture of accomplices—was in itself no better evidence of the guilt of the accused than were the corroborating circumstances. The repetition of the confession at trial would add little to its probative value. The question then arises, why was it not sufficient to present evidence of the previous confession and of the resulting corroboration?

Thus the statement of a leading American scholar that the "Roman-canon" system was "unworkable" without torture must be limited to cases of capital crimes committed by certain classes of people.[10] And even then the requirement of a confession (absent two eyewitnesses) cannot be explained solely on the basis of the need for certainty.

Here again it is important to distinguish between Roman law and canon law and, with respect to Roman law, between the Roman law contained in the books of the Eastern Roman emperor Justinian and the *Romanist* law taught and written about (under the name of "Roman law") by Romanist legal scholars in the West in the eleventh through fifteenth centuries, and, still further, between that Romanist law and the positive law of some secular rulers and secular courts which sometimes drew on Romanist legal science and which was also sometimes called "Roman law." With respect to the two-witness rule, confession, and torture, there were, indeed, some scattered notions to be found in Justinian's texts, none of which, however, meant in Justinian's time (or earlier) what the Romanist legal scholars of western Europe interpreted them to mean, since the western European law of criminal procedure which developed after 1100 was quite different from the earlier Roman law. Moreover, in Italy, where Romanist legal scholarship was highly developed, many of the city-states from the thirteenth to the fifteenth century enacted their own rules of criminal procedure, including, in particular, rules concerning full proof and torture. Such municipal statutes often authorized the annually elected mayor *(podestà)* of the city to dispense with the requirements of full proof even in capital cases and gave him discretion to replace those requirements with half proofs.[11] Quoting and building on such statutes, authors of leading Romanist treatises on criminal law written in those centuries stated that judges were to apply their personal judgment (*arbitrium,* "will") to set aside the two-witness rule and to convict or acquit on the basis of the totality of the evidence. The great fourteenth-century Italian legal scholar Bartolus of Sassoferrato wrote that full proof did not necessarily require a confession or two eyewitnesses but "occurs when the judge, on the basis of the evidence produced before him, is led to faith and credit concerning that which is litigated," and that he can thereby acquire certitude through direct sensory experience, as witnesses do, or through reasoning and demonstration.[12]

The canonists of that period, by contrast, gave somewhat less leeway to judicial discretion, and retained a rigid rule of full proof (two witnesses or confession, and hence the possibility of torture) for certain types of cases, namely, cases of serious crime known only to a few people (*pene occultum,* "almost secret").[13] Of these, of course, heresy was the most obvious, and in cases of heresy a confession seemed most desirable.

It may be that insistence on a confession in some types of capital cases arose not primarily from the desire for certainty but from the desire to induce the repentance of the accused prior to his execution so that he would be rescued from eternal damnation. This view is supported by the fact that the requirement of a confession, to be extorted by force if necessary, originated in the thirteenth century in the ecclesiastical courts in cases of persons charged with being heretics. In the first place, one can hardly prove the state of mind of the accused heretic at the time of judgment except by his own testimony, since he may always change his mind before judgment and cease to be a heretic. In the second place, it was considered necessary for the soul of the heretic that he disavow the devil and return to the fold of the church. The fact that he ceased to be a heretic prior to conviction did not, of course, absolve him from capital punishment as expiation for the crime of having previously uttered heretical statements and/or performed heretical acts. But in order to be convinced of that crime, the court did not necessarily need a confession. Indeed, it was precisely because the court was convinced by other evidence that the accused had committed heresy that it wanted him to confess and repent.

There nevertheless remains the anomaly that if there were two eyewitnesses, a confession was not required.

In the German territories in the fourteenth and fifteenth centuries, many features of the ecclesiastical inquisitorial procedure, including the requirement of full proof in certain types of cases, were transferred to the German secular courts in cases of secular crimes punishable by death. Typical of these were treason, various forms of homicide, rape, arson, robbery, riot, counterfeiting, forgery, blasphemy, and unnatural sexual behavior. Motivated not only by the same desire to rescue the soul of the accused from eternal damnation but also, and more powerfully, by the felt need for ruthless repression of criminal elements, the secular *Richter,* like the ecclesiastical judges, resorted to the barbaric practice of physical torture as a means of extracting confessions, which were then presented to the *Schoeffen* together with the other evidence.

This practice became especially widespread in the late fifteenth century as the problem of crime in the highways became increasingly acute. So-called plunderers of the countryside, *(Landschaedliche)* were put to trial on the basis of their "ill repute" *(Leumund)* and then induced by torture to confess. The procedure for prosecuting open and notorious criminals had originated with the rule of the older Germanic law that a person caught in the act of committing a violent crime could be killed by his captor, who could then obtain compensation for the victim of the crime and his relatives by raising, with the assistance of oath-helpers, a "complaint against the dead man" enforceable against members of his family. Legislation of the twelfth century and thereafter extended to the *Landschaedliche,* on the ground of *Leumund,* the law applicable to criminals caught in the act, and a procedure developed for subjecting such persons to prosecution on the basis of oaths of accusers. In effect, all that had to be proved was that the accused person was socially dangerous. Needless to say, this procedure, even without the use of torture to extract confessions, was subject to serious abuse. An increasing number of innocent people were convicted and executed. At the same time, the alternative method of proof by oaths of one kind or another tended to result in the acquittal of the guilty.

There were grave defects not only in the law of criminal procedure but also in the substantive law applicable to capital crimes in the secular courts—in Germany as well as in other parts of Europe. The types of offenses that gave rise to liability were not clearly defined. Different degrees of murder were not clearly distinguished, and there was no clearly delineated gradation of punishability in light of mitigating and aggravating circumstances. At the same time, an unsuccessful attempt to commit a crime was not itself, as a general matter, considered to be a crime. Also complicity in the commission of a crime carried out by another was generally not punishable.

With the increase in violent crime in the fifteenth century, territorial and urban authorities reacted by imposing harsher measures of law enforcement. Yet because of the inadequacies of both procedural and substantive criminal law, these measures were often ineffective either in convicting the guilty or in acquitting the innocent. In 1497–98 the Imperial Diet of Freiburg resolved: "Because complaints have been brought to [the imperial] court against princes, imperial cities, and other authorities, that they have allowed innocent people to be condemned to death and executed unlawfully and without sufficient cause . . . it is therefore necessary to undertake in the Empire a general reformation and ordering of the mode of proceeding in criminal matters."[14]

In light of the great increase in violent crime in many countries of the West in the last decades of the twentieth century and the beginning of the twenty-first, one can appreciate the poignancy of the conflict that raged in Germany at the end of the fifteenth and the beginning of the sixteenth centuries between adherents of the "crime control model" and the "due process model" of criminal procedure.[15]

The necessary reforms could not occur without a fundamental change both in legal philosophy and in legal science. In legal philosophy, new moral motifs were needed to bring together justice and utility, tradition and innovation, popular legal consciousness and professional legal scholarship. In legal science, a new method of systematization and rationalization of the criminal law was required to supersede the older method of piecemeal changes in the preexisting mix of secular and ecclesiastical legal concepts. In short, a fundamental change in German criminal law depended on fundamental changes in legal philosophy and legal science such as those analyzed in the preceding chapters.

Needed as well were people who not only shared that philosophy and that science but also had sufficient dedication, imagination, knowledge, and practical ability to translate justice and utility, tradition and innovation, popular legal consciousness and professional legal scholarship, into an effective system of criminal law.

Schwarzenberg and the Bambergensis and the Carolina

One person who had the requisite qualities was Johann von Schwarzenberg, who has been called "the greatest German legislator of the Reformation era" and "one of the great legal thinkers of the [German] nation."[16]

Schwarzenberg was born in 1463 or 1465. His father was a knight who served in the government of the episcopal principality of Brandenburg and who for a time also served in the Brandenburg princely high court *(Hofgericht).* The son was educated in the military arts, and after serving as a knight in the entourage of Emperor Maximilian, he entered into the civil service of the rulers first of the imperial city of Würzburg, then of the duchy of Saxony, and eventually of the episcopal principality of Bamberg. In Bamberg in the early 1500s he was the chief officer *(Hofmeister)* of the prince-bishop, and also the chief justice *(erster Justizbeamter)* of the Bamberg and later of the Brandenburg princely high court. In addition, he served as a judge of local courts of domains which he inherited from his father. He was a delegate to the 1521 Imperial Parliament *(Reichstag)* at Worms and played a leading role in the Imperial Governing Council *(Reichsregiment)* from 1522 to 1524.

There is nothing that is known of Schwarzenberg's upbringing and early career to indicate that he was to become the principal author of the first modern code of criminal law. He lacked a formal legal or other higher education; indeed, he did not even know the Latin language. Only from his later achievements is it apparent that he was nevertheless very well educated, that he read Cicero and other ancient classics in German translation, that he had a superb command of the German language, and that he was a person of great intelligence and dedication, a deeply religious person, and a man of substantial poetic gifts, as well as a first-rate judge, legal scholar, and legislator. He became an ardent follower of Luther, with whom he was in close personal contact in the early 1520s.

In 1507, when Schwarzenberg was in his early forties, he produced for Bamberg—with, of course, the help of others[17]—a code of substantive law and procedure governing capital crimes that acquired almost instant fame throughout Germany. Called the Bamberg Capital Court Statute (Bambergische Halsgerichtsordnung, or Bambergensis) for short, it served as a model for almost identical legislation in Brandenburg in 1516 and later for similar legislation in various other German principalities. In 1521 the Imperial Diet *(Reichstag)* at Worms voted to adopt an imperial code governing capital crimes, and Emperor Charles V commissioned Schwarzenberg, who had been a participant in the *Reichstag,* to serve on a commission to rework his Bamberg code for that purpose.[18] Successive drafts were rejected by *Reichstag*s in 1523, 1524, 1529, and 1530. Finally in 1532, four years after Schwarzenberg's death, the imperial Constitutio Criminalis Carolina, or Carolina for short, modeled in large part word for word on the Bambergensis code,[19] was proclaimed.[20]

We shall return to the relationship between Schwarzenberg's personal qualities, including his deep religious convictions, on the one hand, and the reform of German criminal law which he initiated, on the other. But let us turn first to a discussion of the contents and significance of the Bambergensis and the Carolina.

Schwarzenberg's code, promulgated by the prince-bishop of Bamberg, was the first of its kind, certainly in the West, perhaps in world history, that is, the first systematic and comprehensive codification, in the full sense of that word, of a single branch of law, namely, the law of crimes punishable by death, twenty-six in all, ranging from blasphemy and perjury to robbery and murder. There had been, to be sure, in the previous three centuries, some systematic scholarly treatises on particular branches of law, including criminal law and procedure, written by learned Romanist and canonist jurists,[21] and one must assume that Schwarzenberg and his associates drew on concepts and definitions contained in such treatises, although they made no reference to them. Yet those treatises, though sometimes treated by courts as authoritative, were not legislation; they were not the same, either in style or effect, as a comprehensive statute promulgated by the legislative power of a sovereign authority. The nearest German analogues were a rather primitive treatise of the first quarter of the fifteenth century, the *Klagspiegel,* and several statutes on capital crimes promulgated by the emperor and by German territorial princes in the years preceding promulgation of the Bambergensis.[22] Also many of the northern Italian city-states that emerged in the thirteenth, fourteenth, and fifteenth centuries had enacted elaborate statutes *(statuti)* defining many types of crimes and stating the punishment applicable to each, and these also are generally assumed to have provided an important source of the Bambergensis and, later, the Carolina.[23] Never before the Bambergensis, however, had there been enacted a comprehensive statute purporting to set forth an entire branch of the law as a complete and integrated system of general principles and specific rules.

A word needs to be said about the difference in authority between the Bambergensis and the Carolina. The latter was to be applied by the Imperial Chamber Court *(Reichskammergericht),* the sole imperial court, whose criminal jurisdiction, however, was quite narrow in comparison with that of the territorial and other non-imperial courts. The Carolina was also to serve as a model for territorial legislation; it contained, however, a "savings clause" which expressly made it optional for the principalities, and in fact only a few principalities adopted it while others occasionally borrowed from it and some simply ignored it. Indeed, in the final clause of the Carolina, the emperor acknowledges the initiative of the electoral princes, other princes, and estates in seeking reform of the imperial law, and he states, in the first person, "We have not intended through this gracious recollection to take from them anything of their traditional, lawful, and equitable customs."[24] Thus the Carolina was, in effect, only a subsidiary law in those few principalities that adopted it. It nevertheless had considerable influence on the legislation and the judicial practice of all the German principalities. In particular, it was studied and applied by university law professors who came to play a significant role in the decision of criminal cases throughout Germany as well as in the drafting of laws. As various territories enacted their own comprehensive criminal statutes, partly in response to both the Bambergensis and the Carolina, there developed throughout Germany—as the German legal historian Reinhart Maurach has said—a "common German criminal law."[25] The Carolina remained the criminal law of the German imperial courts until 1870.

Both the Bambergensis and the Carolina were permeated with a spirit of reform, which was the spirit of the age. In this connection Schwarzenberg drew not only on a Bamberg court reform of 1503, of which he himself had been the chief author, but also on the reformations of city law in Nuremberg, in Worms, in Frankfurt, and elsewhere.[26] The guiding principles of the reform were summarized in the text of the Bambergensis itself as "justice and the common good"

("Gerechtigkeit und Gemeinnutz").[27] Justice had a transcendent moral dimension. The common good had a practical historical dimension.

The complementary character of these two goals was reflected in Schwarzenberg's combination of legal principles found in canon law and Romanist legal science, and to a lesser extent in Italian city laws, with customary German substantive criminal law and with a German procedure characterized by lay participation. The code was to govern the *Schoeffen;* therefore, it had to be understandable to them, and for that purpose Schwarzenberg wrote it in clear, strong German. Three hundred years later—in 1814—the great jurist Friedrich Karl von Savigny was to say that he knew of no German legislation of the eighteenth or early nineteenth century that could compare with the Carolina in force and power of expression.[28]

The purpose of codifying the criminal law was not to make the *Schoeffen* into learned jurists. Nor was the purpose to import a foreign law. The purpose was, rather, to reform the German secular law and, in that connection, to give it the benefit of the legal science that had developed—in Germany as elsewhere—first in the church courts and second in the scholarly literature of the university jurists.

The Bambergensis and later the Carolina were concerned with reforming—in order to serve "justice and the common good"—the procedural and substantive law applicable to capital crimes, that is, those crimes that brought into operation the inquisitorial procedure that had developed in the German secular courts in the fifteenth century. These included—in the order in which they were listed in the Carolina—blasphemy, perjury, violation of a sworn recognizance, sorcery, criminal libel, counterfeiting, falsification of legal documents, falsification of weights and measures, malicious disturbing of boundary signs, violation by attorneys of their duties to clients, unnatural sex acts, incest, kidnapping of women, rape, adultery, bigamy, selling of wives or children into sexual traffic, pimping, treason, arson, robbery, agitation of the populace, wickedly living outside the law, and feuding (to each of which one article of the code was devoted); and finally homicide (to which twenty-eight articles were devoted) and theft (to which twenty-five articles were devoted).

Schwarzenberg and his colleagues did not make up these crimes; most of them were offenses that had been identified, named, and punished—by death—under the customary law of the Germanic and other peoples of Europe as it had developed during previous centuries. Nor did Schwarzenberg and his colleagues invent the gruesome punishments that were applicable to persons convicted of these crimes: execution on the wheel, execution by the sword, death by hanging, death by being dragged, drawn, and quartered (for traitors), death by fire (for arsonists), death by drowning (for infanticide), and the like; and where there were mitigating circumstances or guilt of lesser offenses, mutilation by cutting off of hands, flogging, banishment, and others. These were the traditional criminal sanctions of a Western culture whose capacity for sadistic cruelty was much more transparent and personal in 1500 than it is today.[29]

It was the virtue of the Bambergensis and the Carolina that they substantially reduced the arbitrariness and uncertainty of the preexisting criminal law. In the realm of criminal procedure, they introduced a rational system of evaluation of evidence, placing restrictions on the use of torture and increasing substantially the probability that only the guilty would be convicted. In the realm of substantive criminal law, they established clear definitions of the elements of the various crimes, criteria of guilt based on intent or negligence, proportionality of punishment to the degree of guilt of the wrongdoer, and other basic principles of justice.

Some of the major changes embodied in both the Bambergensis and the Carolina were the following:

(1) Archaic survivals of private remedies, such as wergeld, were finally eliminated or, in the case of blood feud, severely restricted.

(2) Proof by oath-helping was finally eliminated.

(3) Although private criminal prosecution was authorized except in certain types of cases,[30] it was severely limited by the requirement that the private complainant provide surety for the costs of the proceedings and for the indignity and damage inflicted on the accused in the event that the case did not proceed to trial and to a finding of guilt.[31] If the private complainant was unable to provide such surety and nevertheless wished to prosecute, he was to be held in jail, along with the accused, pending trial and conviction.[32] These provisions had the practical effect of eliminating private prosecution in most cases of serious crimes.

(4) An official prosecutor was designated by the presiding judicial officer, the *Richter,* in most cases, to act as complainant *(Ankläger)* and to initiate and carry out the prosecution. At the same time, limits on the power of the complainant were set with care. The proceedings were to take the form of an inquest ("inquisition"), that is, an official investigation, with the judges inquiring and collecting evidence. The members of the court—*Richter* and *Schoeffen*—were to interrogate the accused and the witnesses.

(5) The extraordinary procedures against persons charged merely with being socially harmful ("of evil repute") were eliminated.

(6) High standards of proof were set. Persuasive evidence (*redliche Anzeigung,* "sufficient indication")[33] of each element of the crime was required. Only if such evidence existed could the accused, in a capital case, be subjected to torture in order to extract a confession. Before any examination under torture, the accused was to be given opportunity to refute inferences of guilt that might be drawn from the evidence offered against him.[34] It was expressly provided that "if sufficient indication of the crime which it is desired to investigate has not been produced and proven beforehand, then no one shall be examined; and should, nevertheless, the crime be confessed under

torture, it shall not be believed nor shall anyone be condemned upon that basis. If, notwithstanding, any of the *Obrigkeit* or judges proceed in this way, then they shall be bound to make appropriate compensation to the person who was tortured in this illegal way . . . for his injury, pain, costs, and damages."[35] Thus torture was permitted only to extract a confession from a person charged with a capital crime whose guilt was sufficiently indicated by other evidence. Moreover, the Carolina provides that if "after sufficient proof" *(nach genugsamer beweisung)* the accused will not confess—presumably in an examination under torture—"he shall nonetheless be condemned on account of the proven crime without any [further] examination under torture."[36] Thus "full proof" was desired but not required in capital cases under the reformed German criminal law.

In addition, wounded persons were not to be subjected to torture, and sick persons were not to be made worse by torture.[37]

(7) Particular kinds of proof required to prosecute were specified in detail for various types of crimes. For example, for clandestine murder it was required that the accused "be seen with bloody clothes or a weapon and acting in a suspicious manner; or that he took, sold, gave away, or still retained property of the murder victim; unless he can contradict such suspicion with credible indication or proof."[38] For secret poisoning it was required that "the suspect bought or otherwise dealt with poison, and the suspect had quarreled with the poisoned person or could have anticipated gain or advantage from his death or was otherwise a wanton person of whom the crime could be believed . . . unless he can produce credible indication that he used or wanted to use the said poison for other noncriminal ends."[39] For theft it was required that "the stolen property be found with the suspect, or . . . that it was in whole or in part possessed, sold, dispersed, or squandered by him, and he refuses to name his seller or supplier . . . so long as he does not establish that he brought the said property upon himself in an undeceitful noncriminal manner in good faith." Furthermore, "when a particularly large theft occurs and . . . [the suspect] is found to be more effusive with his spending than could be within his means apart from the crime, and he cannot show other good ground where he got the indicated suspicious wealth and he is a sort of person of whom the crime could be believed, then there is present against him legally sufficient indication of the crime."[40] For the crime of treason, however, it was sufficient, in addition to proof of the treasonable act, that "the suspect was seen behaving stealthily, unusually, and insidiously with those he is suspected of having betrayed, and when he pretends that he is afraid of them, and when he is such a person of whom such a crime can be believed."[41]

(8) Witness testimony was to be taken "according to law" and "diligently" by the *Richter* and two other persons capable of taking witness testimony, with the court scribe recording it, and the scribe was to "pay particular attention to whether the witness is found inconsistent and shifting in his testimony, and

shall transcribe such circumstances, and how he observes the demeanor of the witness in the proceeding." The accused had the right to proffer witness testimony to exculpate himself. Witnesses were to "testify from their own true knowledge, declaring the detailed grounds of their knowledge," and "hearsay" evidence was to be considered "inadequate."[42]

(9) In general, the accused was to be acquitted unless proved to be guilty. A special provision shifted to the accused the burden of proving self-defense or necessary defense of others.[43]

(10) The *Richter* and *Schoeffen* were instructed repeatedly, in various contexts, that in difficult cases they should "seek advice" of those who are "legally knowledgeable" *(rechtsverstendigen),* that is, persons in the universities or in cities or in the high courts elsewhere who know the law. Indeed, forty-two of the seventy-seven articles of the Carolina that define or identify specific substantive crimes contain such an instruction.[44] In addition, Article 105, which contains a general preface to the substantive law articles, states that in all "odd and incomprehensible cases" where guilt is apparent but the punishment to be imposed is not "understandable," the *Richter* and *Urteiler* "shall seek advice"; and Article 219, the final article of the code, provides even more generally that "since in many places previously in this . . . ordinance the seeking of advice has been spoken of, it is therefore required that all criminal courts, when they find themselves in doubt as to their criminal procedure, court practices, and sentences, be obliged to seek advice of their superior courts [or in the absence of such courts] of other [superior] authorities . . . [or] from the nearest universities, cities, free cities, or others legally knowledgeable."

Specific reference is made to Article 219 in such articles as Article 113, on falsification of weights and measures, which provides that in cases of repeated offenses the court should seek advice as to whether or not the death penalty should be applied, and Article 142, which gives a series of examples of when homicide committed without witnesses is or is not justified on the ground of reasonable self-defense, adding that difficult cases involving "highly subtle distinctions . . . which cannot be explained to the comprehension of the common man" should be referred to legal experts.[45]

These provisions reflect doubt that the lay *Schoeffen* would always understand or, if they understood, would always accept the new standards of criminal responsibility and proof.[46] They also reflect great confidence in the capacity of persons learned in the law—professors as well as judges of higher courts—to review decisions of trial courts on the basis of the written files of the cases. In Hesse, for example, a law of 1540 required local courts to send up to the high court the file of every case of capital crime. In Saxony in the early seventeenth century, the sending of the file in serious cases to a higher court or to the university law faculty was mandatory, and local criminal courts could impose only very minor punishments.[47]

To reform German criminal procedure it was necessary to introduce substantial changes in substantive criminal law as well. Previously, in the heyday of the more adversarial ("accusatory") trial procedure, justice could be served by reliance on popular legal consciousness as reflected in customary criminal law, largely (though not entirely) unwritten. The community "knew" what was criminal and what was not. In the fifteenth century, however, with the gradual introduction of an investigatory ("inquisitorial") official procedure, modeled partly on the criminal procedure of the ecclesiastical courts, the older, more communal customary law appeared confused and arbitrary and was subject to abuse by the secular officials charged with conducting criminal investigations and presenting indictments. More precise definitions of offenses and more clearly articulated principles for determining guilt or innocence were needed.

The Schwarzenberg codes met those needs in a brilliant way. Among their major contributions to substantive German criminal law were the following:

(1) The first 105 of the Carolina's 219 articles lay down rules and definitions applicable to crimes and punishments generally, constituting, in effect, a "general part" of the statute. For example, Article 19 gives a definition of the word "indication," and is followed by Article 20, "That no one shall be examined under torture without legally sufficient indication," and Article 21, "Concerning how the legally sufficient indication of a crime shall be proven."[48]

(2) The necessary elements of almost every one of the dozens of crimes listed in the codes are carefully defined[49]—in most instances for the first time in secular German law.[50] General concepts such as self-defense, complicity, and attempt are also defined. Emphasis is placed on requirements of intent and causation. Exculpating circumstances are indicated.

(3) Specific punishments, some mandatory and some discretionary, are provided for all the various specific crimes. Punishments differ in severity depending on the nature of the crime and the degree of guilt of the offender. In most cases, to be sure, the difference consists in the method of inflicting capital punishment—for example, execution by the wheel for intentional homicide *(Mord)*, execution by the sword for unintentional but otherwise culpable homicide *(Totschlag)*. Presumably the different degrees of cruelty in the diverse methods of execution reflected a primitive concept of proportionality of the punishment to the crime. In some other cases, however, where mitigating circumstances reduce the crime from a capital offense to a misdemeanor, punishment is limited to sanctions such as banishment or flogging or to what were called "civil penalties" such as fines, reflecting a more sophisticated concept of proportionality of the punishment to the crime and permitting a substantial reduction of the types of crimes to which torture is applicable.[51]

(4) The general principle is established that criminal responsibility is to be limited to prohibited acts committed either intentionally or, in some cases, negligently. There is to be no criminal responsibility without culpability (in

German, *Schuld*), in the sense of *mens rea*, "a guilty mind." Moreover, a distinction is drawn between intentional misconduct and impetuous acts provoked by justifiable anger. Article 150 of the Carolina states expressly that homicide committed in provoked anger is not punishable because of the absence of the necessary intent. Article 166 states that stealing food to satisfy acute hunger of the accused or his wife or children is to be excused.

(5) In sharp contrast to the earlier secular German law, but in conformity with the canon law applied in the ecclesiastical courts of Germany and other European countries, the Carolina (like the Bambergensis) imposes criminal responsibility for the attempt to commit a crime, regardless of the absence of harm to the victim, where the interruption of the criminal act occurred against the will of the actor (Article 178). This marked a sharp turning point in the transition both from the pre-twelfth-century Germanic concept of criminal punishment as compensation for harm, to be paid to the victim, and from the post-twelfth-century concept of secular criminal punishment as retribution for harm, to be paid to the king or lord or other civil authority. The Schwarzenberg codes adopt the ecclesiastical concept of criminal punishment as retribution not for harm as such but for misconduct, for sin. This was not, however, retribution in the sense of vengeance but rather retribution in the sense of exaction of a price proportionate to the sinful offense. If, indeed, the basis of criminal responsibility is to be blameworthiness, *Schuld*, then the *Schuld* of attempting to commit a crime should be punished—though not as severely—even if the fulfillment of the attempt is frustrated by external circumstances.

(6) Nevertheless, Schwarzenberg considered that certain offensive acts should not be criminal at all unless they caused harm. With respect to sorcery, for example, the causing of "injury or disadvantage" was declared to be a necessary element of the crime itself.[52] At a time when the attack on witchcraft was becoming rampant throughout Europe, the requirement of the Bambergensis and the Carolina that a person could not be convicted of witchcraft unless actual harm was proved was a remarkable concession to legality. Erik Wolf has attributed this provision to Schwarzenberg's experience as a judge, which "showed him that the danger of superstitious activities lies more in the poisoning of the soul than in rarely provable external harms; only if such were evident should the actor, as was traditional, suffer death by fire."[53]

(7) With respect to the capacity to commit a crime, both the Bambergensis and the Carolina provide that one who "on account of youth or other infirmity lacks understanding" shall be excused from criminal punishment, and further, that cases in which this defense is raised must be submitted to legally knowledgeable persons in universities or cities or to other legally knowledgeable persons, and the accused are to be "dealt with or punished according to the advice of those . . . persons."[54]

(8) Necessary defense of oneself or others is treated in the Bambergensis

and the Carolina as an excuse for homicide, and guidelines are established for it. The burden of proof that the act of defense was necessary falls on the person charged with the homicide. He is to prove that he could not "appropriately" *(füglich)* have escaped and that the homicide was necessary to protect his own life or limb. Moreover, it is provided that the person defending himself does not exceed the limits of justified self-defense merely because he strikes the first blow. As John Langbein has stated, Article 140 of the Carolina, "What genuine self-defense is," "ranks among the most precocious of the Carolina's generalizing, conceptualizing dispositions."[55]

The Relationship of Criminal Law Reform to the German Revolution

To focus attention on Schwarzenberg's great reform of German criminal law, first enacted in Bamberg ten years *before* Luther denounced the sacramental authority of the Roman Catholic priesthood, might seem at first to foreclose any argument that the great changes in German criminal law were connected with the Lutheran Reformation. Moreover, while the Carolina was enacted in 1532, fifteen years *after* Luther first took his stand, it was based entirely on Schwarzenberg's earlier work and, moreover, was promulgated by Emperor Charles V, an arch-foe of Lutheranism and of territorial independence. Presumably the Carolina could have been promulgated even if the Protestant Reformation had not occurred. In any event, the Bambergensis was in fact promulgated before the Protestant Reformation took place.

Schwarzenberg did, however, become an ardent and prominent Lutheran, who corresponded with Luther, who wrote tracts in defense of the new evangelical theology, and who had to leave Bamberg in 1524 when its prince-bishop cracked down on those who supported the Lutheran cause. Schwarzenberg simply moved to his estates in Protestant Brandenburg. In the same year he had to leave the Imperial Governing Council, together with other members of that body who were open supporters of the Lutheran cause. Indeed, while he was serving as director of the commission that drafted the Carolina, Schwarzenberg used his position to protect Luther and Lutherans from repression. In 1522 he helped to prevent the enforcement of the Edict of Worms against Frederick the Wise for harboring Luther in Wartburg Castle, and in 1523 he helped to protect Lutheran pastors from the edict so long as a council was not called to review it. He died in 1528 before the draft of the Carolina was finally adopted but was succeeded as director by another outstanding supporter of the Lutheran cause, Christian Baier, chancellor of the prince-elector of Saxony.[56]

Because the reformation of German criminal law began before the reformation of the church, and also because it was supported by many Catholics as well as by many Protestants, it is not wholly surprising that almost all modern historians have entirely ignored the relationships between the two reformations, the legal and the religious.[57] They have preferred—when they have given it any larger explanation at all—to connect Schwarzenberg's work with humanism and with the so-called reception of Roman law, both of which movements are usually presented as essentially antagonistic to Lutheranism. Indeed, the Bambergensis and the Carolina are generally treated as examples of a pan-European scholarly legal science—the *jus commune*—which happened, rather surprisingly, to produce a new body of criminal legislation in Germany in the early sixteenth century.

Yet the fact that Luther's religious revolt did not cause the enactment of the Bambergensis in some *post hoc ergo propter hoc* sense of causation does not mean that the two events may properly be viewed as independent of each other. The biography of Johann von Schwarzenberg strongly suggests otherwise. Also the later adoption of similar codes in some German Protestant principalities, and the writing by German Protestant jurists of important treatises on criminal law based on the Carolina, indicate that the criminal law reform initiated by Schwarzenberg was congenial, at least, to the new evangelical jurisprudence. One writer has called it "an achievement of the spirit of the Reformation."[58] The great nineteenth-century German legal historian Roderich von Stintzing wrote that "although it is difficult to find particular points where the Reformation influenced the Carolina, the Carolina was influenced by the general movement."[59] The outstanding twentieth-century German legal historian Erik Wolf has shown that Schwarzenberg's early religious beliefs anticipated Lutheran theology in important respects, and that they were broadly reflected in the Bambergensis (and hence in the Carolina), but Wolf, too, stops short of anything more than a connection with "the spirit of the time."[60]

In fact it can be shown, partly on the basis of Wolf's own analysis, that contrary to what he concludes, the Bambergensis contains important legal principles that reflect basic tenets of the theology later developed by Luther and his followers. In addition, the new criminal legislation was congenial to—indeed, it was integral with—two other aspects of the German Revolution which, as we have seen, were themselves linked with Lutheran theology, namely, the new Melanchthonian scientific method, which stressed the derivation of all knowledge from general principles or concepts ("topics"), and the new territorial politics, which stressed the supremacy of the territorial prince and his learned councilors over a unified system of ecclesiastical and secular law. The reform of criminal law embodied in Schwarzenberg's codifications was closely connected with each of these three aspects of the German Revolution: the religious, the scientific, and the political.

The Religious Aspect

The fact that Schwarzenberg was a Roman Catholic when he wrote the Bambergensis, that his reform was promulgated by the Roman Catholic emperor

Charles V, and that it also strongly influenced legislation in German principalities that remained Roman Catholic must be seen in the light of the fact that the Reformation itself was a product of Roman Catholicism. Martin Luther, too, like John Wyclif and Jan Hus before him, was, after all, a Roman Catholic, who initially intended his theology and his ecclesiology to be a reformation within the Roman Catholic Church. Similarly, Schwarzenberg's reform of German criminal law was intended to be a reformation within the legal tradition that had been established throughout Roman Catholic Europe during the previous four centuries. Yet it transformed that tradition, as Luther's religious reformation transformed Roman Catholic theology and ecclesiology, and as Melanchthon's new scientific method transformed the earlier scholasticism, and as the expanded role of the princes transformed the earlier system of plural sovereignties within a given territory.

The Bambergensis and the Carolina reflect the Lutheran belief that law—including both the moral law of the Bible and the civil law—is primarily an instrument of God's will for the earthly kingdom alone, and that, contrary to Roman Catholic doctrine, works of the law are not a path to salvation in the heavenly kingdom. Underlying Roman Catholic legal philosophy was the doctrine of purgatory: that sins not punished proportionally to their gravity in this world will be so punished in the next, but that good deeds compensate proportionally for sins and can serve to reduce punishment after death. Thus there was in Roman Catholic theology an important connection between the external forum of the church, in which ecclesiastical courts imposed criminal penalties for violations of the canon law of crimes, and its internal forum, in which priests in the confessional imposed works of penance for sins not judged as crimes. Lutheran theology, in contrast, rejected both the doctrine of purgatory and the sacramental character of penance. Salvation, Luther taught, that is, life in the heavenly kingdom, is by faith alone.

Schwarzenberg shared these views. In several theological writings he expressed a firm belief in salvation by faith alone, that is, by faith in Christ's redemptive act. Moral conduct, he wrote, is to be practiced for its own sake and not for salvation. Such moral conduct is to be governed, he wrote, by free exercise of one's God-given conscience. As Wolf notes, these are principles "to which a few years later Luther gave theological expression." Also in developing his ethical, as contrasted with theological, principles, Schwarzenberg relied heavily on the writings of Cicero—just as Lutheran scholars later did, in opposition to Aristotelian scholasticism.[61]

But if observance of moral and civil laws is not a path to salvation, what are its divine purposes? To this question Lutheran theology, as we have seen in Chapter 2, posed a threefold answer: the "uses of the law" are (1) to define and condemn sins—its theological use; (2) to restrain people from committing sins by threat of penalties—its civil use; and (3) to teach all people, including those who are already justified by faith, what God considers to be right conduct—its educational use. As has been noted earlier, the Schwarzenberg legislation stressed the first two uses of criminal law, which today are called its retributive and its deterrent funcitons. It also stressed—even more than Luther himself did—the third Lutheran use of the law, its educational function. The Bambergensis, its preamble states, is not only a law but also a textbook *(Lehrbuch)* that will teach the unlearned "a form and way of acting and of judging according to the laws and good custom of the empire." The preamble states further that "in order to help overcome misunderstanding," it is written in a popular and understandable form. In fact, Schwarzenberg scattered throughout the various sections of the code little poems—rhymed couplets—as well as many handsome woodcuts designed to dramatize the meaning of the rules and to make it easier to remember them as well as to show their religious basis. The frontispiece of the Bambergensis is a woodcut showing Christ as judge of the world, enthroned on a rainbow, with rhymed couplets warning that at the Last Judgment one will be dealt with as one has lived in the world ("Das Urteil dort wird dir gefällt/wie du gelebt hast in der Welt").

The religious connection is also apparent in the very secularism of the Schwarzenberg reform. Schwarzenberg accepted the limitations of what Luther called the earthly kingdom, in which God is only hidden. Schwarzenberg's mission was to reform the German customary criminal law, not to replace it with a new body of law. As noted earlier, the Bambergensis and the Carolina, though they substantially limited torture, did not abolish it. They eliminated death by burial alive as the penalty for infanticide but substituted death by drowning. They did not eliminate the crime of sorcery, though they required proof that the words or acts of the sorcerer caused actual harm to another person. They provided that when an accused person is to be jailed pending trial, "the jails should be erected and maintained for the custody of the prisoner and not intentionally to intensify his suffering."[62]

Other provisions required that the young (no particular age was specified), the mentally ill, and the feeble should be referred to knowledgeable persons to determine whether they should be tried or treated, and that persons who are sick should not be subjected to torture that would make their condition worse. As Erik Wolf writes, the tempering of justice with mercy in the Bambergensis "had its ethical basis less in the humanism of Erasmus than in Christian love of neighbor, which extended especially to care for the sick, the feeble, and the mentally ill."[63]

Moreover, the implicit retributive, deterrent, and educational "uses" of the Bambergensis and the Carolina reflected—as did the general Lutheran doctrine of the uses of the law—the developing concept of secular law as essentially a product of political will and not, as in Thomistic Roman Catholic thought, essentially an embodiment of natural reason. Indeed, the great emphasis in sixteenth-century Germany on statute law *(Ordnungen),* of which the Bambergensis and the Carolina are prime examples, like parallel sixteenth-century developments in England, France, the Spanish Netherlands, and elsewhere, was wholly consistent with Lutheran theological concepts of the separation of, and interrelationships between, the earthly and the heavenly kingdoms.

The Schwarzenberg legislation did, indeed, draw heavily on substantive canon law (for example, in its punishment of attempt and its requirement that an act, to be punishable, must reflect a guilty mind and, more precisely, that it must be performed with criminal intent or criminal negligence); it also drew on the canon law of criminal procedure (for example, in its restriction of hearsay evidence and in its requirement that the burden of proof of self-defense be on the defendant). It did not, however, seek, as the canonists did, to create a body of law that conformed wholly to moral standards but instead accepted as a starting point the customary German law, which it sought to make more conformable to the two ideals of justice and the common weal. Conflicts between these two ideals—between humaneness, on the one hand, and civil order, on the other—were to be resolved by the wisdom of the prince and his councilors, especially those "learned in the law." It was their will and their wisdom that was the source of all earthly law. This, too, was congenial to Lutheran legal theory, which associated the moral law, or natural law, with individual human conscience in the earthly realm rather than with the corporate conscience of the church reflected in authoritative texts.

Scientific Aspects

As much that was congenial to Lutheran theology was implicit in the Bambergensis and the Carolina, so was much that corresponded to the new scientific method represented later in the philosophical writings of Melanchthon and the legal writings of Lutheran jurists. The very concept of a codification—and therewith reformation—of a branch of the law was characteristic of the system of thought associated with the German Revolution. This was professors' law—written, to be sure, in simple language so that, like the Lutheran Bible, it could be read and understood by everyone, but also, again like the Lutheran Bible, often requiring sophisticated interpretation by scholars. It is characteristic of the Schwarzenberg legislation—and of the times—that, as noted previously, forty-two of the seventy-seven articles of the Carolina that define individual crimes provide that in difficult cases arising under those articles, courts "shall seek advice" from the "legally knowledgeable." This was statutory law, handed down from on high, written in a clear, concise language understandable to all, yet, like the Bible itself, requiring the knowledge and wisdom of learned men to interpret and apply it conscientiously to concrete cases.

Melanchthon's topical method was embodied in the Schwarzenberg legislation. Universally applicable categories of thought such as the interrelationship of genus and species—Melanchthon's *loci communes*—were implicit in the division of the codification into two parts, the first of which set forth general principles applicable to all capital crimes and the second of which set forth particular species of capital crimes in a manner that conformed to those principles. In later centuries such a division into a "general part" and a "special part" became characteristic of European criminal codes. The principles themselves constituted, in Melanchthonian terms, the special topics, *praecipui loci*, of legal science. In Stintzing's words, the Schwarzenberg legislation "put together for the first time and in a new way" fundamental legal categories such as attempt, necessary defense, and cumulation of penalties.[64] Indeed, the great sixteenth-century German Lutheran jurist Nicolaus Vigelius, who wrote a book applying the topical method to the whole of the civil law, later applied that method specifically to criminal law and procedure in a work expressly based on the Carolina. This work was one of the first systematic scholarly treatises devoted specifically to German criminal law and procedure.

Both the Bambergensis and the Carolina reflect the Melanchthonian method in combining a vigorous system of legal doctrines with rules and procedures permitting their flexible application in particular cases. This method also corresponded to the Lutheran concept of the role of conscience.

The Bambergensis and the Carolina also marked a new stage of development in conceptualization at the legislative level, and this, too, reflected Lutheran methodology. Doctrines that had previously been set forth in treatises of canon law and Roman law, and applied in the ecclesiastical courts, were now transposed into a comprehensive set of precise definitions and rules to be available to the public and to be applied by prosecutors and courts. As Langbein has said, "Virtually every offense definition in the Carolina marks an advance in conceptualization."[65] Also the general rules of criminal responsibility are for the most part set forth in a way that is at the same time systematic and precise. Thus Article 140 of the Carolina, "What is a lawful self-defense," provides as follows:

> If one challenges, attacks, or strikes another with a deadly weapon or arm, and the one imperiled cannot fittingly escape without danger or injury to his body, life, honor, and good repute, he may save his body and life through a lawful counterforce without any punishment. And if he thus kills his assailant, he is not liable for that, nor is he liable if he has failed to withhold his counterforce until he is struck, notwithstanding whether written laws and customs are to the contrary.

There is, of course, much to be said about this provision. Its limitation of self-help is a significant change in the German law, as the last clause suggests. It also needs, and in subsequent articles receives, some elaboration.[66] In terms of legal science, however, what is most significant is its quality as a statutory provision that is comprehensive, convincing, and clear.

As Erik Wolf has written concerning Schwarzenberg's method:

> We owe to him . . . the first . . . basic typing *(Typisierung)* of offenses. His precise descriptions of such offenses as secret and open stealing, counterfeiting, and infanticide and abortion are a significant contribution of indigenous legal understanding. . . . Still valid today are his list of circumstances essential to the definition of necessary defense, and his definition of punishable attempt contains all viewpoints that later became basic to the development of this controversial concept. Also his . . . description of the forms of criminal complicity shows a sure feeling for what is essential.[67]

Significant in this characterization is the implicit contrast between Schwarzenberg's method and both the traditional scholastic method and the early humanist method. Schwarzenberg applied to criminal law the topical method that Melanchthon later defined, expounded, and demonstrated in the fields of philosophy and theology.

It must be acknowledged that the emphasis placed here on the novelty—indeed, the revolutionary character—of the Bambergensis and the Carolina, from the point of view of method, or science, diverges sharply from conventional scholarship. Some scholars have contended that the Schwarzenberg legislation merely applied to German criminal law the learning and experience of the canon law that had accumulated in Germany, as elsewhere, in the fourteenth and fifteenth centuries. Others have stressed that the German legislation was essentially part of a general reception of the "Roman-canon" *jus commune* in Germany in the late fifteenth and early sixteenth centuries. The influence of Italian legal scholarship and of Italian city legislation on the Schwarzenberg legislation is also stressed. The fact that Schwarzenberg was not learned in these other "foreign" legal systems, and could not even read Latin, is treated as somewhat surprising, but it is simply assumed that he knew them from German translations and was advised about them by his more learned colleagues. These points have a certain validity. The new legislation did indeed reflect the strong influence of the canon law; it also did indeed draw some of its terminology and concepts from what was taught in the Roman law courses in the universities as well as in Italian legal treatises and, to a much lesser extent, in Italian city criminal statutes. What is generally neglected, however, in the emphasis on these influences, and what is examined here, is the unique character of the German legislation, namely, its character as the first attempt at a total legislative systematization, the first modern codification—and reformation—of a particular branch of the law. The explanation of such an epoch-making event cannot be exhausted by an examination of its various antecedents but must also include a consideration of related changes that were taking place simultaneously.

As has been shown in earlier chapters, neither Roman law nor canon law was any more "foreign" to Germans than to any other European peoples. Like

Christianity itself, both Roman law and canon law had been thoroughly Europeanized. Surely Schwarzenberg, a leading judicial officer of the episcopal principality of Bamberg, was entirely familiar with the work of its ecclesiastical courts. That he was able, as we have seen, to translate into secular law some of the principles of the canon law applied in those courts does not detract from, but on the contrary adds to, the originality of his contribution. As for sixteenth-century Roman law or, more accurately, Romanist legal science, it, too, was as German as it was Italian or Spanish or French (or, for that matter, English), since it was taught in all the European universities and was everywhere (including England) a subsidiary law not only in ecclesiastical courts but in some types of secular courts as well. To be sure, the texts of Justinian had almost nothing to contribute, other than some terminology, to the criminal law of any of the various legal systems of the West. In the words of Franz Wieacker, "No coherent, well-developed conceptual system [of criminal law] is to be found in the Roman sources; no general principles were formulated."[68] Nevertheless, leading Romanist scholars of the fourteenth and fifteenth centuries, such as the Italians Gandinus and Bartolus and Baldus, wrote important treatises on criminal law, using Roman law terminology but drawing most on the canon law, and many of their ideas were reflected in the Bambergensis and the Carolina.

Conventional scholarship has stressed the influence of Italian law, and especially the criminal statutes *(statuti)* of the Italian city-states, even more than the influence of canon law and Romanist legal science on the German criminal legislation of the sixteenth century. Each of these *statuti* purported to list and define many types of crimes prohibited by the city law and, for each type of crime, the applicable punishment. It may well be that Schwarzenberg and his colleagues were influenced by the example of the Italian *statuti* to do the same for German principalities. Also many scattered provisions in various *statuti* have parallels in the German legislation. The differences, however, between the Bambergensis and the Carolina, on the one hand, and the Italian *statuti,* on the other, are far more striking than the similarities. As a rule, the *statuti* contained a few introductory articles of a general character, usually dealing with procedure, but these were very skimpy and can hardly be called a general part.[69] Moreover, the crimes listed in the *statuti* are described only briefly; there is rarely if ever anything like a systematic presentation of the state of mind required to constitute a particular type of crime, the excuses or justifications that limited its applicability, or other circumstances that constituted what the Germans call the *Tatbestand,* the totality of elements, that composed it. One need only place the Bambergensis or Carolina alongside the Italian *statuti* to see the enormous differences between them in comprehensiveness and depth.[70]

Likewise, the German criminal law reform, as Langbein has shown, differed substantially from the statutory reforms of criminal law that took place not long afterward in France and in England. The 1539 French ordinance of Villers-

Cotterets did, indeed, introduce a substantial reform of French criminal law, eliminating many of its irrational features, but as Langbein shows, it was addressed to professionals and was largely remedial and interstitial, leaving much uncovered. Also the important English "bail statute" and "committal statute" enacted in 1554 lacked the character of a criminal code, being addressed principally to the correction of procedural defects in the investigation and prosecution of crimes.[71]

The Bambergensis and the Carolina are German law—not canon law or Roman law and not Italian city law. That the German lawmakers drew many of their ideas from legal currents circulating throughout the West, including Germany itself, is hardly surprising. What is interesting is that they did not "receive" those ideas, in some mechanical sense, but that they chose some of them and not others, and the ones they chose from abroad they combined with their own German ideas, transforming the whole, for the first time, into a modern criminal code.

Political Aspects

The reform of German criminal law in the early decades of the sixteenth century was strongly connected not only with contemporary religious changes introduced by the Lutheran Reformation of the church, on the one hand, and related changes in legal philosophy and legal method, on the other, but also with the political changes of the time—the reformation of the state.

As we saw earlier, many German princes had acquired, during the fifteenth and early sixteenth centuries, increased political power vis-à-vis the Church of Rome, the emperor, and one another, on the one hand, and vis-à-vis their subjects, on the other. Nevertheless, prior to 1517, the diversity of jurisdictions within each principality remained a predominant characteristic of political life in Germany as in the rest of Europe. In addition, however, to concurrent ecclesiastical, princely, feudal, urban, mercantile, and local jurisdictions, there was in Germany, as in some other countries, the jurisdiction of the Holy Roman Empire of the German Nation, which in the late fifteenth and early sixteenth centuries had come to be very closely allied to the papacy. Thus the Lutheran attack on the ecclesiastical jurisdiction of the papal hierarchy inevitably turned also—though with considerably less venom—against the imperial jurisdiction, thereby aiding the German princes in their struggle for territorial autonomy. The alliance of the German knights with the anti-Lutheran imperial cause further identified Lutheranism with princely authority over feudal jurisdictions. Finally, Lutheran theology, as we have seen, identified the territorial prince as the father of his country, to whom filial duty was owed under the Fifth Commandment of the Decalogue. All of these factors contributed to the concept and theory of the superiority of the prince's jurisdiction over all others within his territory.

The Bambergensis gave the prince and the high magistracy, the *Obrigkeit,* of the episcopal principality of Bamberg, one of the larger German polities at the time, jurisdiction over all capital crimes within its borders. Other German principalities enacted similar legislation. As shown earlier, the emperor's law, the Carolina, was directly applicable only in the very limited class of cases tried in the sole imperial court, the *Reichskammergericht.* The emperor was apparently emulating the princes: they had their codes of criminal law and he wanted his! As Friedrich Engels wrote more than a century and a half ago, "The Emperor was becoming more and more a prince like the others."[72]

CHAPTER 5

The Transformation of German Civil and Economic Law

As with constitutional law and criminal law, substantial changes took place in the sixteenth century in German civil and economic law, especially the law of contract, property, and credit transactions.[1] These changes were reflected partly in scholarly writings on civil law by sixteenth-century German legal scholars reinterpreting Roman law and canon law doctrines, and partly in sixteenth-century territorial and urban legislation elaborating and reforming the body of customary law governing economic relationships. It is necessary to consider the changes in both the scholarly civil law and the statutory and customary civil law in order to determine their relationship to the political, social-economic, and religious aspects of the German Revolution.

Contract

The Scholarly Law *(jus commune)*

A unified and systematized law of contract emerged in Europe for the first time in the writings of European jurists, including German jurists, in the sixteenth century. In previous centuries, to be sure, in Germany as elsewhere in Europe, many types of agreements were taken to be legally binding and were enforced in one or more of the various coexisting jurisdictions. There was a law of contracts, in the plural—indeed, several different kinds of law of contracts: royal, ecclesiastical, feudal, urban, mercantile. Even before the revival of the study of Roman law and the emergence of the modern canon law in the late eleventh and twelfth centuries, the laws of the Western tribal peoples and royal households had recognized the legally binding character of certain types of solemnly entered agreements in which oaths were sworn and ceremonial objects exchanged. Likewise in classical and post-classical Roman law, the various types of agreements that were recognized to be contracts acquired their binding force by being "clothed" in special forms and formulas. In the Roman law of Justinian a "naked agreement" *(nudum pactum)* was not actionable; it could not be a *contractus.* Roman law, moreover, named the types of formal contracts that were enforceable (contracts of loan, of pledge, of sale, of rent, of partnership, and several others), leaving room also for a class of unnamed ("innominate") contracts entered into by "stipulations" in which the parties exchanged precisely formulated promises to give certain things or to perform certain acts. A contract had to conform to one of these types in order to be enforceable. Both the nominate and the innominate contracts created duties arising from half-completed exchanges of land or goods or services. Generally speaking, under both Roman law and pre-twelfth-century Germanic customary law, a mere exchange of promises did not give rise to a contractual obligation until one of the parties had begun, at least, to perform his promise.

In sharp contrast both to Germanic customary law and to the rediscovered Roman law, the twelfth-century canonists asserted that the legally binding force of various types of agreements depended ultimately neither on their solemnity nor on their form, nor on part performance by one of the parties, but rather on the intention of the parties. It was the consent of the parties to enter into a contract that made it a contract. Their consent, moreover, did not need to be "clothed"; in canon law a *nudum pactum* might be enforceable. This principle rested on the theological premise, supported by many texts from both the Old and the New Testament, that failure to perform a promise is a sin. It was also supported by philosophical concepts of natural law drawn partly from writings of the Church Fathers as well as by principles of canonical equity. For the canonists, the validity of a contract depended ultimately on the good faith *(bona fides)* of the parties in entering into it, made firm by the inclusion of a so-called pledge of faith, and breach of such a contract was a breach of faith *(fidei laesio),* giving jurisdiction to the ecclesiastical court in case of dispute.

The principle of the canon law that the binding force of an agreement is based ultimately on the consent of the parties, that is, on their shared state of mind in making it, made it both necessary and possible to develop certain common principles applicable to all contracts. Offer and acceptance had to manifest mutual consent, a meeting of minds. The contract had to have a legitimate purpose *(causa).* A contract induced by fraud or duress or based on mistaken assumptions was void. A contract oppressive to one of the parties *(laesio enormis)* was also void. The canonists did not, however, attempt to bring these and other basic principles and rules into a separate comprehensive branch of contract law applicable to all types of agreements. Their short "treatises on agreements" *(tractatus de pactis)* were usually concerned chiefly with the application of principles of contract law to the law of marriage and other sacraments, to the authority of bishops to enter into transactions involving church property, and to other contractual matters governed by canon law.[2]

With the subordination of all the various preexisting ecclesiastical and secular jurisdictions to territorial princes, especially in Protestant principalities, the sixteenth-century German unifiers and systematizers of the civil law created a separate branch of contract law, theoretically applicable in all jurisdictions, which they classified, together with tort law (delict) and unjust enrichment (quasi-contract), as part of the law of obligations. They took as its foundation the canonist principle of contractual fidelity—in German, *Vertragstreue*—and with it, canonist doctrines of offer and acceptance, *causa, laesio enormis,* and nullity due to fraud, duress, or mistake. Other canon law doctrines that were introduced into the scholarly *jus commune* in the sixteenth century included the binding character of a promise to make a gift, the protection of third-party beneficiaries of contracts, the right to assign rights under a contract, the right of a representative to enter into a contract that would bind his principal, and the seller's warranty that goods sold are fit for the purpose for which they were sold.[3]

There was much also in the Roman law texts of Justinian that could be adduced to support the general concept of contract, although that concept itself was not articulated in those texts. For example, the fourfold classification of civil obligations into contract, delict, quasi-contract, and quasi-delict, set forth at the beginning of Justinian's *Institutes,* was invoked by the legal reformers, although in the older Roman law itself that terminology did not give rise to an analysis of separate fields of law but was only a convenient way of introducing diverse texts. Also the reformers drew on Roman rules of nominate and innominate contracts, but superimposed on them the body of general rules applicable to all contracts.

Most, though not all, of the leading learned sixteenth-century jurists who systematized the German law of contract, starting from the consensualist position of the canon law, were Lutherans.[4] That the new science of contract law expounded in Protestant German principalities drew far more heavily on the earlier canon law than on the "received" Roman law has been noted by some leading German legal historians, sometimes with surprise.[5] Virtually no attempt has been made by contemporary legal historians, however, to draw connections between the jurisprudence of the Protestant reformers of contract law and their religious convictions.

Statutory and Customary Law

Comprehensive territorial statutes, called "policy ordinances" *(Polizeiordnungen)* or "territorial ordinances" *(Landesordnungen),* had been enacted occasionally by German princes and city councils in the fifteenth century, but in the sixteenth century they came to be issued for the first time on a large scale.[6] In at least one German principality over 450 such statutes were issued between 1500 and 1600.[7] Such legislation systematized and modified the prevailing customary law that governed most aspects of the economic life of the German people.

The learned German jurists of the sixteenth century who wrote authoritative treatises on civil law are themselves partly responsible for the failure of contemporary legal historians to combine analysis of general principles of sixteenth-century civil law with analysis of the extensive territorial and urban statutory and customary regulation of contract, property, and other civil law relations. In the German city of Constance, for example, there were enacted in the early sixteenth century dozens of ordinances regulating trade and other economic activities; yet the great sixteenth-century jurist Ulrich Zasius, a native of Constance, who received his first practical legal training in the Constance municipal chancery, and who was himself chief author of the highly important Freiburg City Law of 1520, disdained to discuss such ordinances in his scholarly work. In the words of the editors of a twentieth-century collection of the titles of some two hundred laws enacted in Constance between 1510 and 1548, "In the systematics of the Roman law, the developed economic law . . . of a German city of the Middle Ages had no place, and a man like Zasius could therefore disdainfully consider it as not worthy of his scientific investigation."[8] There was, however, a sizable body of sixteenth-century German legal literature, written primarily for practitioners, listing hundreds of differences between the "learned laws" and the territorial law of a particular principality.

As subsidiary law, both Roman law and canon law—the "learned laws"—were drawn on by German courts to fill gaps and resolve ambiguities both in the statutory law of the various principalities and in local and regional customary law. Yet in the event of a contradiction between either statutory or customary law, on the one hand, and the *jus commune*, on the other, the former was to prevail. Absent a clear contradiction, the *jus commune* provided general principles by which both statutory law and customary law were interpreted by the learned jurists who came increasingly to sit in princely, urban, and local courts and in the university law faculties that decided cases referred to them by such courts. Also general principles of the *jus commune* often found their way into the burgeoning princely and urban legislation. Nevertheless, it was not the *jus commune* but innovations in the statutory and customary law that played the dominant role in transforming German civil law in the sixteenth century.

What chiefly distinguished the *jus commune*—especially in the fields of contracts, property, and other branches of civil law—was its scholarly, that is, its systematic character. Statutory law and customary law were less systematized, less expressed in general principles; they were more diffuse and more tied to practical economic and social conditions. In the writings on contract of the great sixteenth-century Protestant legal scholar Mattheus Wesenbeck, for example, one finds a discussion of the nature of contractual obligation, how a contract is formed, sources of the validity or invalidity of a contract, and similar general characteristics of contract law, as well as discussion of various types of contracts, but one finds little analysis of the abundant customary and statutory regulations governing particular contract practices in various types of trade. The same is true of major nineteenth- and twentieth-century historical works on German law in the sixteenth century.

Differences between the general law of contract set forth in treatises on the *jus commune,* on the one hand, and the law of particular types of contracts set forth in territorial and urban statutes and in customary law, on the other hand, are strikingly illustrated in the preservation, and indeed increase, of formal requirements in the statutory and customary law. In the *jus commune,* as Wesenbeck and others stated, a *nudum pactum* could constitute a binding contract. Yet according to comprehensive territorial statutes such as the Württemberg *Landesordnung* of 1555, contracts involving property transactions had to be recorded in the registry of the local court in the presence of both parties; until then they were said to be inoperative, and either party could withdraw at will.[9] Similarly, the customary law of promissory notes and bills of exchange, which came to play a decisive role in trade and finance in this period, was marked by a high degree of formalism.

The Württemberg statute, like other sixteenth-century German comprehensive territorial and urban statutes dealing with civil law, does, to be sure, follow the *jus commune* in setting forth some general rules concerning different types of contracts. Its second part, "On Contracts and Transactions," begins with the contract of loan *(Leihe),* defining it in Romanist terms as consisting of three types: (1) the loan of money or goods for consumption, the precise equivalent to be returned *(mutuum);* (2) loan of goods for use, to be returned in specie *(commodatum);* and (3) loan (that is, lease) of land *(locatio).* Subsequent sections of the statute deal with deposit, purchase and sale, rent of houses and other property, gifts, pledges of goods, and pledges of property as security for debts. Although there is no substantial difference between the general definitions of these types of transactions given in the Württemberg statute and the general definitions of contemporary Romanist and canonist jurists, there are important variations in the particulars; and in addition, virtually all the types of contracts set forth in the statute are made subject to certain formal restrictions, on the one hand, and to certain substantive restrictions, on the other. Moreover, all transactions affecting rights in land were to be approved by a court before being entered in the court registry *(Gerichtsbuch).* Thus, as indicated earlier, the canon law doctrine of the enforceability of "naked agreements" was inapplicable to various types of contracts. Similarly, the Roman law doctrine that contracts other than those specifically "named" in the Roman law (so-called innominate contracts) required certain defined steps ("stipulations") to be taken was inapplicable to the wide variety of new types of transactions that characterized sixteenth-century European commerce.

The law applicable to credit transactions illustrates vividly the relationship between the "learned laws," on the one hand, and sixteenth-century German customary and statutory law, on the other. The twelfth- to fifteenth-century Romanists had found in the texts of Justinian a variety of rules applicable to various forms of transfer of land, goods, and money, including rules of lease, pledge, and loans of money. Living, however, in a quite different economy and a quite different culture from that of Justinian, and applying to the Justinian texts a quite different method of legal reasoning, the European glossators and commentators gave new meanings to the classical and post-classical Roman texts. At the same time, Roman Catholic theologians introduced new moral considerations, of which two important ones were that credit should not be extended at an excessive rate of interest,[10] and that property should not be transferred at an unjust price.[11] These moral principles could be enforced in the internal forum of the church, the confessional, as well as in the external forum, the ecclesiastical courts. They were also occasionally invoked in secular courts in civil actions such as actions of debt as well as in criminal prosecution.[12]

The Roman Catholic moral and legal doctrines of just price and usury were inherited by sixteenth-century European moral philosophers and jurists, both Roman Catholic and Protestant; contrary to what is often supposed by twentieth-century historians and social theorists, Lutheran and Calvinist moral philosophy with respect to both doctrines did not differ substantially in its conclusions from that of leading fourteenth- and fifteenth-century Roman Catholic theologians, and the basic legal principles governing them propounded by secular Protestant jurists did not differ fundamentally from those that had been propounded by the canonists and enforced in the Roman Catholic ecclesiastical courts.

Moreover, neither in the sixteenth century nor in the preceding period—again, contrary to what is often supposed—were the twin doctrines of just price and usury anti-capitalist in their practical implications.[13] The doctrine of just price was generally understood in the sixteenth century, as in the twelfth to fifteenth centuries, to mean the price fairly agreed upon in the market, without fraud or deceit, though with one qualification, namely, that it was also required, in the case of food and other necessities, to be sufficiently low to permit the poor to afford them.[14] Similarly, usury was generally understood, both in the sixteenth century and in the preceding period, as it is generally understood today, to refer not to interest as such but rather to an excessive rate of interest, which was defined in law (though not always in theology and moral philosophy) as a rate that exceeds the return which a creditor can justifiably demand to cover his labor, his costs, and his risks.[15] Thus both doctrines constituted flexible rules against unconscionability and against unfair competition—basic principles of a successful market economy.

To be sure, a simple noncommercial loan of a specific sum of money was supposed to be repaid without interest; payment of any additional sum, or indeed any benefit over and above the amount of the loan, was denounced as usury. Also some theologians inveighed against any payment of interest on the loan of a specific sum of money, even in commercial transactions.[16] Canon lawyers, however, were virtually unanimous in distinguishing lawful interest charges from unlawful usury. Interest charged on a commercial loan was not called usury and was not considered unlawful if the terms were reasonable, and it was not defined by law. Church organizations themselves—including the papacy—paid interest on loans made to them and charged interest on loans which they made to others.[17] In the fourteenth century, long-term loans to commercial towns or municipal governments were made at rates ranging between 5 and 15 percent, while rates for loans to kings or princes, being riskier, might be as high as 40 or even 50 percent per annum. According to some studies, loans to consumers in the towns were also generally made at interest rates ranging from 15 to 50 percent per annum.[18] Many cities fixed maximums: in thirteenth-century Genoa, for example, the maximum was fixed at 15 percent, in Zürich at one time it was fixed at 43.3 percent, and in France at one time it was fixed at 20 percent for the entire realm.[19] The rate of interest often depended, of course, on the security given by the debtor. Moreover, payments of annual installments on a commercial obligation, payments under futures contracts for commodities, discounting of bills of exchange, and other forms of market transactions that became increasingly widespread in the fifteenth century were not subject at all to the law of usury, provided market rates were not blatantly violated.

Contrary to the widely accepted Weberian social theory, the Protestant ethic, both Lutheran and Calvinist, was essentially the same in these matters as the Roman Catholic.[20] Thus Luther's 1524 *Treatise on Trading and Usury,* while denouncing in the strongest terms excessive prices and rates of interest, carefully elaborated the conditions under which it is morally justified to profit from the sale of goods and from the extension of credit. Luther condemned greed, but at the same time he defended normal profit-making business activity, stating that "it is fair and right that a merchant take as much profit on his wares as will reimburse him for their cost and compensate him for his trouble and his labor and his risk." Goods, he wrote, should be "valued at the price for which they are bought and sold in the common market or in the land generally. . . . [A]ny profit made in this way I consider honest and proper."[21] Improper, however, Luther wrote, and to be prohibited by law, were monopolies and the accumulation of products for the purpose of driving up prices. Likewise, while denouncing usury, Luther defended a reasonable interest rate on a loan, which he said would normally be 5 percent, although it might go up to 6 or 7 percent in special cases. Once again, he based this not only on what he perceived to be the legitimate return on the labor of the lender but also on the loss of the use of the money during the period of the loan and the risk of non-repayment by the borrower. The creditor's risk, he asserted, is a form of work, for which he deserved—and the law should permit him to receive—a just profit. This did not differ substantially from the theory of leading Roman Catholic theologians and moral philosophers.[22] Nor did it differ in result from Calvinist theories.[23]

What did differ substantially—both in Germany and elsewhere in Europe—were, on the one hand, the economic conditions and, on the other hand, the political and legal conditions in which Luther and other sixteenth-century theologians and lawmakers found themselves as compared with earlier times.

Economically, credit transactions were increasing enormously in scope and in importance. Leases and purchases by peasants of parcels of land from large landowners were replacing feudal tenancies, and such leases and purchases were usually made partly on credit. Peasant proprietors also borrowed money to enable them to plant crops and to tide them over until the next harvest. These credits were usually secured by pledges of collateral. In addition, princes engaging in large-scale military operations in the sixteenth century were using mercenary armies, and this usually required huge outlays of cash, which the princes often obtained by secured loans from bankers at high rates of interest.

In addition, a large rise in prices, estimated at 50 percent in Germany in the first half of the sixteenth century,[24] coupled with a substantial increase in population, estimated at over 25 percent in Germany, roughly from 12 to 15 million between 1500 and 1600,[25] contributed to increased demand for credit as well as to increased risk of default in repayment.[26] Finally, importation of gold and silver as a result of the Spanish conquest of Mexico (1519–1521) and Peru (1532), as well as increased importation of high-priced silks and other foreign products, tended to drive up interest rates.

This was, indeed, a period of great expansion of commercial and financial activity, both local and long-distance, in all of Europe. To say, however, as many economic historians have done, and as has been widely accepted by social historians, that "capitalism" first emerged in the late fifteenth and sixteenth centuries is to neglect the fact that for over three centuries prior, there had existed a pan-European market for a host of products as well as the commercial institutions needed for their private production and distribution. Production for sale at a profit, price competition, private financing through credit transactions, concentrated capital accumulation, and other features usually listed in definitions of capitalism were all present in the twelfth, thirteenth, and fourteenth centuries. The mid-fourteenth century to the latter fifteenth was a period of depression, owing in part to a massive decline in population greatly accelerated by the Black Death and in part to devastating wars such as the so-called Hundred Years' War between England and France. This was followed, however, by a period of substantial economic growth, stimulated by new economic factors. In "the long sixteenth century" (as Fernand Braudel has properly called it) of the late 1400s to the early 1600s,[27] there was, indeed, what has been called a second commercial revolution, but it built on structures that had emerged during the earlier commercial revolution of the long twelfth century, from the late 1000s to the early 1200s.[28]

Politically and legally, the struggle against the twin sins of unjust price and usury, which in the earlier period the church had claimed to be its own responsibility, to be enforced chiefly through penitential sanctions, now became, especially in Protestant lands, the responsibility chiefly of the princes, enforced mainly through secular legislation and secular judicial and administrative sanctions. Thus Prince Philip of Hesse and his son William IV, both ardent Lutheran Reformers, enacted into law Luther's call not only for regulation of prices and of proper interest rates but also for public warehousing of grain in times of surpluses in order to protect against future shortages and for the listing in official registries of collateral for loans, item by item, in order to protect both creditors and debtors in event of default.[29] Prince Ulrich of Württemberg, also an ardent Lutheran, introduced similar laws in his territory.[30]

This was an age to which economic historians have attached the word "mercantilist," signifying, in part, extensive control by "the state," that is, political authorities, over economic activity.[31] Taxes were imposed on certain types of sales. Incentives were given for production of goods for export, in part, once again, to raise money through taxation. Restrictions were placed on the purchase of foreign goods. Market regulations were introduced to protect against monopolistic trade practices. Monopolies in grain and wool production were prohibited. Rules were enacted to protect peasants, weavers, and others against onerous credit arrangements. Above all, the drastic change in the character of warfare, with mercenary armies replacing the older feudal military service, encouraged the expansion of the public debt through the borrowing of large sums from large-scale banking enterprises.[32] Whereas secured credit transactions had formerly been linked primarily with the purchase and sale of goods, permitting future payments against present deliveries, large-scale financing reversed the relationship between money and goods: creditors' rights in the goods now served to secure the financier against default in repayment of his loan. Thus great banking houses acquired massive property holdings in mines and other resources from defaulting emperors and princes whose armies suffered defeat.[33] The "learned laws"—the *jus commune*—had little or nothing to say about either the legislation or the changing customary law through which these policies were effectuated.

German contract law was transformed in the sixteenth century not only by territorial legislation regulating prices of goods, interest rates, and other matters related to trade but also by changes in customary law, including customary law regulating financial transactions. Of particular importance was the development of new banking and mercantile practices connected, on the one hand, with the financing of the substantially expanded military and economic activities of territorial rulers and, on the other hand, with the substantial expansion of private transnational monetary transactions. The principal legal instruments used to effectuate the private financing of both governmental and commercial activities were bills of exchange. These had been known and had been in use on a much smaller scale ever since the dramatic expansion of commerce in the twelfth and thirteenth centuries, but they acquired a new significance with the second commercial revolution of the sixteenth century.

Promissory notes had first come into use chiefly to pay for goods in distant places. As traveling merchants became increasingly sedentary, operating through a network of correspondents and branches in different cities, they would, on behalf of their clients, accept from foreign buyers or send to foreign sellers written promises to pay a certain sum at a fixed time in the future. At least since the fourteenth century these promissory notes were occasionally addressed to the payee "or bearer," or to the payee "or order," permitting transfer by endorsement.[34] At what time "bearer" or "order" notes acquired modern attributes of negotiability, whereby the indorsee, as holder in due course, could take the instrument free of certain so-called personal defenses (such as that of fraud) available to the maker of the note against the original payee, is a matter of dispute among historians. Such commercial transactions were governed almost entirely by unwritten customary law. Moreover, they were dealt with only rarely in the writings of the learned jurists of the time. One can assume that with the dramatic expansion of international trade in Europe in the sixteenth century, and with the concomitant rationalization and systematization of the customary law of credit transactions, a distinction would have begun to be made between the rights of an assignee of a nonnegotiable promissory note, on the one hand, who takes it subject to personal defenses that were available to the maker against the original payee and to subsequent indorsees against indorsers, and, on the other hand, the rights of an indorsee of a negotiable promissory note, who takes it free of those defenses.

Promissory notes payable in a foreign country were called letters—"bills"—of exchange. The word "exchange" referred specifically to the exchange of different currencies. The English word "bill" is derived from the Latin *bulla,* meaning "letter." When merchants traveled from place to place throughout Europe to buy and sell their goods, or when they assembled at international fairs for that purpose, they could themselves or through money-changers exchange the multiplicity of metal currencies issued by rulers of principalities and cities—coins usually made of a combination of copper and silver or gold and valued, theoretically at least, according to their weight.[35] There was, of course, no official printed paper money, if only because there were no printing presses to produce it. In the fourteenth and fifteenth centuries, as merchants tended to become sedentary, payment in foreign exchange took place increasingly at a distance, and long-distance carriage of large quantities of metal coins became wholly impractical. The problem was solved through contracts of exchange between merchant bankers and their customers. Such contracts involved four parties: (1) a holder of local currency—typically the local agent of a foreign exporter who had sold the foreign product to a local importer—who would deliver the purchase price paid by the importer (minus a commission) to (2), a local banker, who would take the local currency and, in return, address a letter to (3), his correspondent banker in the exporter's place of business, instructing him to pay an equivalent amount (minus a commission) in the currency of that place to (4), the exporter.

What happened in the sixteenth century was that such letters, embodying exchange contracts connected with the sale of goods, were often transformed into transferable commercial paper and thus into a means not only of payment but also of credit. That is, whether or not there was an underlying sales transaction, one who desired foreign exchange might induce a local banker (the drawer) to draw such an instrument on a foreign bank (the drawee) in his own favor or that of his creditor (as payee). If the words "or bearer" or "or order" were added, and if the drawee wrote "accepted" on the face of the draft, the instrument would be transferable by indorsement, and an indorsee would have the right to be paid the amount of the draft by the payee or, if the payee defaulted, by the drawee or, if the drawee defaulted, by the drawer. The time when payment was due was stated on the face of the draft. Whereas in the earlier exchange contract the drawer (at that time called "taker") was paid in advance in local currency by the party (at that time called "deliverer") who wanted the currency to be exchanged, in the sixteenth-century bill of exchange, properly so called, the drawer became the ultimate debtor and the payee or last indorsee became the ultimate creditor, while the instrument itself could be circulated among intermediate parties. There being no official paper money anywhere in Europe, and most cross-border commercial obligations being expressed in "ghost money" of pounds, livres, guilders, et cetera that had no material counterparts,[36] it was the bill of exchange that became the international, interregional, and inter-city European money, while relatively small local payments were normally made in coins or barter.

This story, which is not recounted in the learned legal treatises of the time, has in the past century been left almost entirely to economic historians to tell;[37] yet it is critical also for legal history, since it reveals that a primary source of contract law in the sixteenth century was the customary law of merchants and bankers. Those few learned jurists of the time who deigned to discuss the emergence of bills of exchange found little or nothing in either Roman law or canon law to support their analysis.

Property

The Scholarly Law *(jus commune)*

As in the case of contract, a new general law of property emerged in the scholarly writings of German and other European jurists in the sixteenth century, when the various jurisdictions that had previously coexisted in each country—the ecclesiastical, the royal (imperial and princely), the feudal, the urban, the mercantile, the local—were in most principalities subordinated to the princely jurisdiction and to princely lawmaking power. Especially in Protestant principalities, where the ecclesiastical jurisdiction over various types of property rights was either abolished or, as in England, subordinated to royal control, new general concepts of ownership were created.

Although previously each of the various preexisting jurisdictions had had its own body of law relating to property rights, there was an overlapping of legal concepts among the different jurisdictions. In all of them, the Latin word *dominium* meant not only rights in land or in goods but also lordship, *Herrschaft,* over persons. In none of them, moreover, was the law of property clearly distinguished from the law of contractual and other obligations. Thus under feudal law land was not "owned," in the modern sense of that word, but "held" in some form of tenure, which meant that rights of possession, rights of use, and rights of disposal of the land were linked with the landholder's duties to superiors, and privileges over subordinates, in the feudal chain. Princes, to be sure, the supreme overlords, had supreme *dominium* with respect to certain land and goods that belonged to the royal household, but much of their property also consisted in feudal dues and services contributed by subordinate landholders as well as in taxes voted by assemblies of representatives of the several estates. Thus the personal property of the monarch was mingled with both his feudal property and his political property. Moreover, *dominium* of land and goods pertaining both to royal households and to feudal households was not unitary ownership in the modern sense, but was instead divided ownership, with various rights of possession, use, and disposal often being shared among different parties. A vassal or other tenant in the feudal chain could not alienate land without permission of the superior to whom services or other duties were owed.

The Roman Catholic Church, which prior to the Protestant Reformation held from one-fourth to one-third of the land in most of western Europe, including Germany, did often have an exclusive *dominium* of lands and goods used solely for ecclesiastical purposes. Nevertheless, even in those instances the various episcopal jurisdictions could exercise rights of possession, use, and disposal of their land and goods only within the carefully defined purposes and procedures established by the canon law, and such exercise was strictly controlled by the corporate hierarchy of the church. Rights of disposal, in particular, were severely limited.

Moreover, there were different types of ecclesiastical property rights. Under the rules of their order, for example, Franciscans could not have *dominium* over either land or goods; they were to "own" nothing. The land and goods which they required to fulfill their spiritual duties and their material needs were said to be held in trust for them by others. As beneficiaries, they were said to have a right *to* the land and goods *(jus ad rem)* but not a right *in* them *(jus in re).* Feudal rights of vassals in land "held" by them "of" superior lords were also said to be rights *to* the land as distinct from rights *in* the land. The absence of full rights of property among feudal tenants as well as among the Franciscans gave impetus to the creation in the thirteenth century of the legal concept of *dominium utile,* or "beneficial ownership," which gave a right of possession and use but not of disposal, as contrasted with "direct ownership," *dominium directum,* which included a right of disposal. The holder of a *dominium utile* had the rights of a beneficiary of the holder of the *dominium directum.*[38]

The canonists had also developed rules protecting one in possession of land or of goods against physical interference, even by one who had a superior right to possession. Even one lawfully entitled to possess a plot of land had no right to dispossess a tenant by force. This was essentially a rule against self-help; disputes over rights of possession were to be settled in court, by due process of law.[39] Moreover, possession was defined not as a factual condition, as in Roman law, but as a legal condition, a *right* to occupy; one could have a possessory right in land—in Latin *saisina,* in English "seisin," in German *Gewere*—even when away on pilgrimage or crusade. The absent tenant forcibly deprived of seisin was, on his return, to have a right to be reinstated and to recover damages if he could prove in a court of law that his seisin was violated.

These doctrines of canon law, first developed to help settle peacefully disputes between contenders for bishoprics, had found parallels in secular English and French land law.[40] They had not been clearly enunciated in German secular law, but they had been applied by German ecclesiastical courts. In the sixteenth century, however, German secular law applied the concept of seisin, *Gewere,* to possession not only of the right to occupy land or hold goods but also of the right to receive duties and taxes, the right to deliveries of goods, the right to services, the right to interest payments, and an increasingly wide variety of other rights.[41] Learned German Romanists set forth these possessory rights *(Besitzrechte)* as part of a newly systematized property law *(Sachenrecht).*[42] They usually traced their source, however, not to the canon law of the Roman Catholic Church but to remote analogies in the texts of Justinian. Thus as authority for the right not to be dispossesed except by judgment of a court they would cite the ancient Roman interdicts *Uti possidetis* and *Utrubi,* the first of which was in fact only an order by the praetor addressed to all parties in a case to leave unchanged the existing possessory situation with respect to immovable property until final disposition of the case, and the second of which was a similar order applicable to movables.[43]

Sixteenth-century German Romanists also gave new emphasis to the distinction between *dominium directum* and *dominium utile.* The concept of beneficial ownership became especially important in the sixteenth century as credit transactions became increasingly widespread. With the decline of feudal lord-vassal and lord-peasant relationships and the widespread substitution of lessor-lessee relations, rights in land as well as in goods came increasingly to be subject to what the Romanists called *emphyteusis* (lease), whereby the lessee undertook, for a price, to make annual deliveries of goods or services or payment of money in return for long-term occupation of the land, or *hypotheca* (pledge), whereby the purchaser of land pledged it as security for the undertaking to make such annual deliveries or payments.[44]

The economic and social changes that took place in Germany, as in other parts of Europe, in the late fifteenth and early sixteenth centuries eventually demanded a rethinking of both the philosophy and the science of the law of property—both its theory and its method. There was a need to harmonize the various concepts of property law that were reflected in the various legal systems—ecclesiastical, royal, feudal, urban, mercantile—that prevailed within each of the German and other European principalities and kingdoms. Also, as feudal relations and the manorial agricultural system declined, there was a need to redefine property rights and to make them more secure, and this in turn involved separating the concept of property from concepts of other types of legal relations—above all, to separate ownership from lordship and to interrelate, in certain types of cases, the owner's rights of possession, use, and disposal. This led, finally, to distinguishing property rights from rights arising from contractual and other obligations.

These fundamental changes in the theory and method of the law of property were first set forth systematically by the great Lutheran jurist Johann Apel in lectures at Wittenberg and Nuremberg in the late 1520s and early 1530s and were published in 1535 and 1540 in his two major works on legal science and legal education, respectively.[45] His revision of the law of property was further developed by his younger colleague and fellow Lutheran Konrad Lagus and by the great French Protestant jurist Hugo Donellus.

Apel overturned the earlier Romanist analysis of civil law, which, following the scheme set forth in Justinian's *Institutes,* distinguished between the law concerning things *(de rebus)* and concerning actions *(de actionibus).* The Roman legal term *res,* usually translated as "thing," had a very broad meaning; it included not only land and goods but also money debts and other assets. The Roman legal term *actio,* by contrast, had the restricted meaning of a procedural remedy. The word *obligatio* (obligation) was sometimes used to refer to a *res* and sometimes to an *actio.* These original Roman meanings were not systematically amplified by the classical and post-classical Roman jurists; it was only the glossators and post-glossators of the late eleventh to fifteenth centuries who defined them systematically and built theories around them. Their theories did not, however, clearly distinguish between a law of things, of which *dominium* was one part, and a law of obligations. Since, for example, under Roman law a debt could be sold, it was treated both as a *res* and as an *obligatio.*

Using his colleague Melanchthon's topical method, Apel fundamentally revised this terminology, creating out of it the basic division, which survives to this day, between the law of property and the law of obligations. He limited the law of property to rights in land and goods, ownership of which, he argued, should be distinguished from contractual and other obligations through which such ownership may be acquired. Obligations, he wrote, give rise to "personal" actions, especially claims to be compensated for losses, while ownership gives rise to "real" (from the word *res*) actions, claims of rights of possession, use, and disposal of land or goods. Ownership rights *in* a thing *(jus in re)* included, for Apel, not only full ownership *(dominium directum)* but also beneficial ownership *(dominium utile),* including the right to possess and enjoy the fruits of the land or goods of another. Such beneficial ownership had previously been classified as a right *to* a thing *(jus ad rem),* based on a contractual or other obligation, rather than an ownership right. On the basis of Apel's analysis, which was further developed by Lagus, *dominium directum* lost its connotation of *Herrschaft,* "lordship," and became synonymous with *proprietas,* in German *Eigentum,* "one's own." At the same time, proprietary rights less than full ownership, such as the rights of a lessee or a pledgee, came to be classified as property rights in land or goods of another *(jus in re aliena),* rather than as part of the law of obligations.[46]

Apel's division of civil law into the law of ownership and the law of obligations, controversial at the time, came to prevail in Germany and other countries.[47] Even today European civil codes distinguish sharply between ownership of land or goods and obligations arising from contract, from tort, or from unjust enrichment. Also the English common law, inherited in the United States and elsewhere, although it does not usually speak of a general law of obligations, nevertheless distinguishes the law of property from contract law, tort law, and unjust enrichment ("restitution"). Everywhere in the West today, as in Apel's scheme, a simple contractual obligation to sell land, for example, does not in itself, without some form of conveyance, normally give rise to a transfer of property rights in the land, valid against the whole world, but gives rise only to the right to a remedy against the seller for breach of contract. Similarly, the contractual obligations of a lessor and lessee vis-à-vis each other are distinguished from the property rights of the lessee and lessor against the world. English law and its offspring resisted the continental European concept of a "real," that is, a "property," contract, but it reached similar results through the law of trusts and the law of conveyancing.

Statutory and Customary Law

Concepts, principles, and rules of modern property law, first expounded by Apel and later by other sixteenth-century European jurists of the new *jus commune,* were a scholarly response to economic and social changes that were being legally effectuated by changes in customary law and in statutory regulations. As in the case of the law of contracts, so with the law of property, the writers of the *jus commune* helped to draft, and in drafting to systematize, the new legislation. But also in the law of property, as in the law of contracts, the positive law that was created both by changes in custom and by territorial and urban statutes differed in important ways from the law described and analyzed in scholarly literature. In particular, the scholarly law of ownership was reflected only very partially in the gradual replacement of feudal tenures by various forms of autonomous proprietorship. The Romanist concepts of *emphyteusis* (lease) and *hypotheca* (pledge) were unable fully to embrace the wide variety of customary tenures that emerged, and princely and urban legislation and administration were required to regulate them. Characteristically, Apel's younger contemporary Johann Oldendorp classified all the different kinds of customary lease or rental agreements as *emphyteusis*, which, he wrote, transfers from the owner to the tenant either the full right *(jus)* to the land or beneficial ownership *(dominium utile);* such transfers are typical among "our farmers" *(nostros rusticos)*, especially for putting new land under cultivation.[48] Similarly, legal scholars such as Apel and Oldendorp classified all the different kinds of customary secured credit transactions that accompanied transfers of land as forms of the Roman contract of *hypotheca*. In practice, however, the multiplicity of species of these genuses transcended their conceptual boundaries.

What is largely missing from sixteenth-century treatises on the *jus commune* is an analysis of the detailed regulation of changing civil law relations by customary law and by territorial legislation. This gap was partly filled by a different kind of sixteenth-century legal literature, written primarily for practitioners, listing and summarizing differences between the *jus commune* and the law of a particular territory; one such book lists and summarizes 343 such differences between the *jus commune* and the law of the electoral principality of Saxony, followed by brief summaries of 162 princely enactments in force in Saxony as of 1572.[49] The authors of these handbooks of "differences" emphasize that the law of the territory prevails over the *jus commune* where the two conflict. Modern legal historians have not systematically analyzed these differences but have focused their attention, for the most part, on the scholarly *jus commune*, with only passing references to customary law and legislation; conversely, modern economic and social historians have focused attention on economic and social changes in property relations, sometimes analyzing the customary law and legislation of a particular territory or city, with only passing references to the *jus commune*.

In property law, both the new *jus commune* and the territorial legislation were responses to the enormous changes that were taking place at that time in the customary interrelations of property holders, including landed nobility and peasants as well as producers and merchants. The response of the scholars, however, was quite different from the response of the legislators. The learned jurists applied to the new property relationships preexisting concepts, principles, and rules of Roman law and canon law. Their terminology was derived largely from the jurisprudence of an era when feudal (lord-vassal) and manorial (lord-peasant) relations predominated. In the late fifteenth and sixteenth centuries, however, feudal law and manorial law gradually receded in importance. The knightly class declined drastically both economically and politically, and peasants, being gradually freed from the more severe obligations of personal and economic service to superior lords, were able to acquire land in relatively autonomous proprietorship. Princely control of land use and princely taxation of landholders supplemented and often replaced control and taxation by the nobility. Money and credit came to play a more decisive role not only in industrial production and commerce but also in agricultural relations. The major legal developments through which such changes were effectuated were, on the one hand, developments in customary law, such as new types of contractual and property transactions, and, on the other hand, developments in territorial and urban legislation. The learned jurists translated these developments into Roman legal language and synthesized and "scientificized" them. To become effective, however, the new legal institution required new language—new terminology and new syntax—which came largely from usage and from statutes. In the words of a leading twentieth-century historian of German private law, the learned jurists of the sixteenth century did not change the legal situation which they found; instead, "their task was to lay hold of existing relationships by means of the learned laws and to integrate them into the *Ius Commune*."[50]

An example of both the virtues and the defects of such integration may be seen in the Württemberg statutory provisions on the contract of loan *(Leihe)*, to which reference has already been made. Here was a statute, drafted with the help of a distinguished scholar of the Roman law, which in its first paragraphs on contracts attempted to "lay hold of" and "integrate" the large variety of types of existing credit relationships which had developed in the customary law of Württemberg and which were subjected in subsequent articles of the statute to detailed regulation. Treatises would, of course, analyze the contracts of *mutuum, commodatum,* and *locatio* in sophisticated ways, and their analysis would serve as a subsidiary law to fill gaps and resolve ambiguities in custom and legislation, but it was the latter two sources of law that played the primary role in the legal transformation that was taking place. For example, one of the critical differences between the *jus commune* and the territorial law with respect to the contract of lease *(locatio)* was the freedom of certain types of leaseholders, under territorial law, to transfer their rights in the land without permission of the lessor. The *jus commune,* by contrast, preserved the feudal principle that one who held a fief of a superior lord could not transfer his rights in it without the lord's permission. Territorial law also provided, however, that in the case of transfer of a lease without the lessor's permission, the value of the property must not be adversely affected. Thus the *jus commune* could be drawn upon in defining the value of the property.

One of the most widely used legal devices for transfer of property rights in the sixteenth century, in Germany as in other parts of Europe, had no counterpart at all in classical and post-classical Roman law. It was called in German *Rentenkauf*, or *Zinskauf*, meaning, literally, "the purchase of a right to periodic payments" or "the purchase of an annuity"; the Latin term was *census*, from which the German word *Zins*, which eventually came to mean "interest," was derived; the French term was *rente*, the Italian *rendita* or *reddita*, the Spanish *cense*. This unique legal institution seems to have originated in the twelfth or thirteenth century, when it consisted typically of the grant to a church by a landholder of the right to annual deliveries of produce of the land, typically fruit or wine or crops but also, in time, animals and other chattels associated with the land. Such a right to annual deliveries, sometimes in perpetuity, committed not only the grantor but also future tenants of the land. It created in the grantee a property right in the land, and not just a personal obligation of the grantor. In case of default the grantee could take possession of the land to secure the obligation. At the same time, the grant escaped feudal restrictions, in that it did not require the consent of a superior lord in the feudal chain. Indeed, in its origin the *census* was chiefly applicable to city land, which was usually held in a tenure that gave the landholder much greater rights of disposal than did non-city tenures.

In the fifteenth and sixteenth centuries, the purchase of the right to annual deliveries became very widespread throughout Europe and often consisted of annual deliveries of money rather than goods. Moreover, it became common for the sale of such an annuity to be connected with the purchase of land; the buyer of the land would pay a substantial price, called in German a *Kapital*, as a down payment for the purchase of the land, the balance of the purchase price to be paid in the form of annual deliveries of money or of produce. Thus the *Rentenkauf*, or *census*, came to resemble a modern real estate mortgage, that is, a credit to be repaid in annual installments and secured by a property interest in land and buildings. Its form, however, as the sale of an annuity, had many legal consequences that distinguished it from an ordinary secured loan. The creditor was secured against default by retention of a property interest in the land; if the debtor failed to make an annual payment, the creditor had the right to obtain a judicial decree to conduct a judicial sale of the land in order to satisfy the debt.

Moreover, a great many different types of *census* came to be used. Thus for a down payment *(Kapital)*, land might be either (1) sold, or (2) leased, (3) subject to subsequent annual deliveries of produce of the land and/or (4) annual payments of money, (5) for a specified term of years or (6) for the life of the purchaser or lessee of the land or (7) in perpetuity, (8) with, or (9) without, the power of the annuitant to buy back the land in case of default in one or more annual deliveries or payments by the purchaser or lessee or their heirs, (10) by repaying the amounts previously paid to the annuitant, or (11) otherwise. Moreover, the purchaser or lessee (12) might, or (13) might not, have the right to sell, lease, or sublet the land, with transfer of the obligation to pay the annuity.

It was chiefly through such various forms of sale or lease of land in return for down payments plus annual "rents" that peasant feudal tenures were transformed into private landholdings in the sixteenth century in Germany, France, Italy, Spain, and other countries of Europe (though English law took a different tack).[51] Although the Romanist jurists gave special names to these various forms of *census,* they were entirely a product of European customary law as modified in the sixteenth century by territorial legislation. In Protestant territories of Germany, for example, legislation severely limited the number of years for which an annuity was payable and also severely limited the ratio between the annual *Zins* and the initial down payment of *Kapital.* These limitations were made partly in response to the strong attack by Martin Luther against oppressive terms of such annuities, including especially his attack against the annuitant's right to repossess the land upon default in annual payments.[52]

In various German territories a *Rentenkauf,* like every sale, exchange, or other transaction by which property rights in land or buildings were transferred, was required to be brought before a court, in the presence of both contracting parties, and if approved, the terms were registered under seal in the court book *(Gerichtsbuch)* or land book *(Grundbuch).*[53] Prior to registration the transaction was considered not to be consummated and either party could withdraw from it. Moreover, the court was to withhold approval if the transaction was oppressive to one of the parties or otherwise violated legal norms. Territorial statutes often provided that the annual payments were to be in money, not goods, and were generally to be limited in time (e.g., not more than ten years) and amount (e.g., 5 or 6 percent of the total to be paid). The creditor's right to levy execution on the land was often made subject to the debtor's right to repurchase the annuity *(Wiederkauf),* that is, the right to repay the remaining balance due and thus to free the land from its burden as security for the debt—what in the English law of mortgages came to be called an equity of redemption.

Business Associations

Although both production and commerce expanded dramatically throughout Europe in the sixteenth century, and changed in character, with concomitant changes in property law and contract law, the legal forms of business associations did not undergo comparable changes. Partnership remained the basic method of pooling financial and other resources, and the use of agents, often family members, continued to be the principal means of carrying on an enterprise's long-distance transactions. Banking, too, though it increased greatly in the volume and scope of its activities, remained largely in the form of family and other partnerships. Production continued to be carried on largely through craft guilds, whose sense of a godly work calling was supported by Lutheranism, although there was a great increase in "putting out," that is, advance payments by middlemen to craft and other workers to finance their initial production of goods. Especially in cross-border trade, traditional mercantile fairs were expanded into bourses, in which bankers played a leading role. These developments have been characterized by some economic historians as the birth of capitalism;[54] lacking, however, was the chief institutional mechanism of capitalist enterprise, namely, the joint-stock company, and lacking also was the free market.[55] This was not capitalism in the strict sense of that term but mercantilism, whose "essence," as Eli Hecksher has stated in his classic work on the subject, "is that the state stands at the center of all economic affairs."[56]

The increased power of the sixteenth-century "state"—that is, the prince and his high magistracy, the king and his nobility—was linked with the decline, and in Protestant countries the abolition, of the Roman Catholic Church. In Protestant countries especially, new religious beliefs had a strong influence on the development of civil and economic law, especially the law of property and contract, including credit transactions. The principal impact of Protestantism on the law of business associations, however, seems to have come first in the next century, in England.

CHAPTER 6

The Transformation of German Social Law

THE dialectical opposition and interaction of the secular and the spiritual realms of life has deep roots in Christian thought. Jesus enjoined his challengers to "render unto Caesar the things which are Caesar's and unto God the things that are God's" (Matthew 22:21); and to his disciples he said, "That which is born of the flesh is flesh, and that which is born of the Spirit is spirit" (John 3:6), and "Except a man be born of . . . the Spirit, he cannot enter the kingdom of God" (John 3:5). Saint Paul, in turn, contrasted "the inward man," who delights in "the law of God," with one who is "in the flesh," the law of whose "members" wars against "the law of the spirit" (Romans 7: 5–7, 22–23). "To be carnally minded," he wrote, "is death, but to be spiritually minded is life and peace" (Romans 8:6). He listed among the "spiritual gifts" implanted by God in followers of Christ the gifts of wisdom, of knowledge, of faith, of healing, of miracles, and of prophecy (1 Corinthians 12:1–7). The spiritually minded, inner-directed follower of Christ fights against the materialism of the unredeemed age, the time-bound world, into which he was born.

Four centuries later Saint Augustine applied this concept to the society in which he lived, drawing a sharp contrast between the sinful and, indeed, Satanic character of the temporal "earthly city" and the purity of the eternal "city of God." For Saint Augustine, both the church and the empire lived in an evil age, "in hoc maligno saeculo," in which the true Christian, whether priest or layman, was in effect an alien. In Peter Brown's words, "For Augustine, this *saeculum* is a profoundly sinister thing. It is a penal existence . . . it wobbles up and down without rhyme or reason."[1] In the City of God, by contrast, Christian spirituality, for Saint Augustine, was effectuated through the "vestiges" of the triune God implanted in human memory and imagination, human reason and understanding, and human desire and love.[2]

A quite different concept of the relationship of the secular to the spiritual was introduced in the Papal Revolution of the late eleventh and early twelfth centuries, when the Western church established its transnational and transterritorial corporate legal identity and its freedom from imperial, royal, and feudal domination. Now the spiritual realm came to be identified with the visible, hierarchical Roman Catholic Church; its priests were called for the first time "spirituals" (*spirituales,* in German *Geistliche*), and the newly unified Western ecclesiastical hierarchy, under the papacy, was said to wield the "spiritual sword," as contrasted with the tribal and feudal and urban laity, including emperor and kings, who wielded the "secular sword."[3] Pope Gregory VII maintained that "the kings and princes of the earth . . . prefer their own interests to the things of the spirit," whereas the priesthood "sets the things of God above the things of the flesh."[4] The papal hierarchy did not despair, however, as Augustine had done, of the possibility of spiritual progress in the secular city. On the contrary, the newly centralized, organized, independent church had great hope for the *saeculum,* so long as it would accept the tutelage of the "spirituals," who came to constitute not only the officials of the church but also a large part of the civil service of the secular rulers.

The Church of Rome, in creating the first modern Western legal system, the canon law, called it "spiritual law" *(jus spirituale, geistliches Recht),* as contrasted with the coexisting royal, feudal, urban, mercantile, and local laws, which were called, collectively, "temporal law" or "secular law" *(jus temporale, jus saeculare, weltliches Recht).* "Spiritual law," promulgated and administered by ecclesiastical authorities, included the law relating not only to purely ecclesiastical matters such as the administration of the sacraments, liturgy, the authoritative declaration of Christian doctrine, clerical discipline, ecclesiastical property, and papal and episcopal and priestly authority generally, but also to many matters involving the laity, such as marriage, education, certain types of crimes committed by laymen, and poor relief, as well as the numerous property, contract, and other civil disputes between laymen which the parties voluntarily submitted to ecclesiastical adjudication or arbitration.[5] Royal, feudal, urban, and local secular law, however, was considerably more restricted in scope as well as less systematized and more formalistic. The title "spiritual law" was justified by the canonists not only on the ground that canon law had its source in the legislative, administrative, and judicial powers of the church but also on the ground that it was "higher" than secular law, being more directly guided, they contended, by divine law and by natural law.[6]

In sixteenth-century Germany, under the impact of the Lutheran Reformation, the words "secular" and "spiritual" acquired still other meanings. The Lutheran "two kingdoms" doctrine placed the visible institutional church, *ecclesia manifesta,* within the secular kingdom. Similarly, the Lutheran "three estates" doctrine characterized the clergy as a secular estate, alongside the high magistracy, called the *Obrigkeit,* and the family, which Luther viewed as the basis of the economy and the polity.[7] What in Roman Catholic terminology were called "spirituals," *Geistliche,* now became, in Protestant terminology, ecclesiastical officers, *kirchliche Beamten,* part of the earthly kingdom of human frailty and sin. Only faithful members of the *invisible* church, the spiritual priesthood of all believers, lived in the heavenly kingdom of faith and grace.

The Lutheran secular kingdom, however, was quite different from Saint Augustine's earthly *civitas diaboli.* Like the Roman Catholicism against which it revolted but in which it was originally nurtured, Lutheran theology was far more optimistic about secular law than Augustinian theology. On the one hand, not only canon law but *all* law, including even the divine positive law of the Ten Commandments, was, for Luther, secular, *weltlich,* and of the flesh, *leiblich;* only divinely inspired faith and love and grace were to be called, in a special sense of the word "law," spiritual law, *geistliches Recht*—wholly different from other kinds of law since it is without rules and without coercive sanctions.[8] Even the moral law of the Decalogue was intended by God not as a means of salvation but only to punish, deter, and correct sinful human conduct. Though divinely instituted, it was not "of the spirit," it could not bring Christians into communion with God; and the Evangelical Church, whose whole purpose was to do just that, was not, in Luther's view, a legal entity and had no business creating or administering a system of law. To rule by law, and, indeed, to rule the church by law, was exclusively the task of the secular political authority, the prince and his *Obrigkeit.* Nevertheless, the Protestant prince, educated by Evangelical Christian teachers and inspired by the preaching of the Gospel, should and could assist the church in its mission by enacting and administering appropriate laws to regulate religious activities in the earthly kingdom. Such secular religious law, promulgated by the secular prince and enforced by the secular *Obrigkeit,* including the secular courts, was the work of the "powers that be," which, in Saint Paul's words, often quoted by Luther, were "ordained by God." For Luther and his followers, secular law, though not itself spiritual in his sense of that word, nevertheless had "spiritual uses";[9] just as other secular institutions, including the earthly visible church itself, had spiritual uses, so secular law was a manifestation of divine will and was to conform, to the maximum extent possible, to divine positive law of the Decalogue, making people conscious of their sinfulness and needful of redemption. Lutherans did not deny the morality and rationality of law but rather its spirituality, its sanctity, its *Geistlichkeit.*

The dialectical interaction of the spiritual and the secular in Lutheran Germany is graphically illustrated in the hundreds of new laws dealing with what will here be called—despite Luther, and despite contemporary German usage—"spiritual" responsibilities and rights, promulgated by German Lutheran princes and city councils in the sixteenth century. These were almost always called ordinances, *Ordnungen,* "orderings"; each of them was a comprehensive set of regulations giving *Ordnung,* "order," to a broad sphere of activities and relationships covering an entire branch of the law. The ordinances that are here called spiritual—though Lutherans at the time would not have called them *geistlich*—

transferred to the secular authorities jurisdiction over matters that had been governed by what had been called the spiritual law of the Church of Rome.

The new spiritual *Ordnungen,* promulgated by the secular authority, were called—as has been noted in earlier chapters—by a variety of names, including general church ordinances *(Kirchenordnungen),* often covering virtually all spiritual matters, as well as more specialized marriage ordinances *(Eheordnungen),* school ordinances *(Schulordnungen),* disciplinary ordinances *(Zuchtordnungen),* and poor people's ordinances, that is, poor laws *(Armenordnungen).*[10] They were usually drafted by leading Protestant theologians, including in some instances by Luther and his partner Philip Melanchthon themselves, as well as by Luther's close friend Johann Bugenhagen, who, like Luther and Melanchthon, was also trained in law. These ordinances combined theological and legal doctrines concerning matters that were considered to be most closely connected with Christian faith.

The various types of spiritual ordinances were revolutionary in four respects. First, they were promulgated not by the ecclesiastical hierarchy but by municipal councils and other representative assemblies of the *Obrigkeit* acting under the authority of the secular ruler, the prince, in his capacity as chief officer in the Evangelical Church. Second, violations were subject to administrative and criminal sanctions by the secular authorities and in the secular courts. Third, these ordinances contained and implemented Protestant theology, which differed in important respects from the earlier Roman Catholic theology. And fourth, they reflected the new legal science, which combined the previously coexisting separate systems of canon law and Roman law, drawing also on the previously coexisting separate systems of royal (princely), urban, and feudal law. They also reflected the new legal science in their comprehensive coverage of particular branches of the law.[11]

The Spiritualization of Secular Law

Five principal types of spiritual matters were regulated by ordinances promulgated by secular authority in Protestant German lands during the sixteenth century. These ordinances regulated (1) church liturgy, (2) marriage, (3) schooling, (4) moral discipline, and (5) poor relief. Each of these types of laws contained some elements of radical change as well as some elements of continuity with the preexisting Roman Catholic canon law.

Liturgy

Composed by leading Lutheran theologians,[12] church ordinances *(Kirchenordnungen)* promulgated in the sixteenth century by most of the secular rulers of the major Lutheran principalities and cities,[13] in addition to regulating institutional structures of the church, also regulated the liturgy, including the three remaining sacraments, namely, the eucharist (*Abendmahl*, "Lord's Supper"), baptism, and confession and absolution from sins, and also the worship service and sermons.[14] In all these aspects, the new Lutheran liturgy contained important innovations in the Roman Catholic liturgy which it replaced.[15]

A most important innovation was the replacement of Latin by the German vernacular. Luther himself translated into German the Ten Commandments, the Lord's Prayer, the Creed, the baptismal ceremony, and other parts of the worship service. Related innovations were the strong emphasis on congregational participation in the administration of the sacraments as well as in congregational prayers[16] and the singing of the great Lutheran hymns.

Lutheran emphasis on congregational participation in the administration of the Lord's Supper reflected both an ecclesiological and a theological change in the character of the sacrament and had, in addition, important social implications. The Roman Catholic practice was to distribute to the congregation only the bread, representing Christ's body, reserving the wine, representing Christ's blood, to the priest alone, and to give sacramental effect to the communion when the priest spoke the words, "This is my body" (in Latin, "Hoc est corpus meum," ridiculed by the Reformers as "hocus pocus"). Thus the Roman Catholic sacrament was consummated by the priest, who very often performed the ceremony alone, without the presence of a congregation. Indeed, the laity were only required to receive the eucharist annually, in Holy Week, after annual confession and assignment of penances. Lutherans, on the contrary, insisted that the sacrament was consummated when both the bread and the wine were consumed by the congregants, who were collectively to partake of the sacrament weekly. This change, embodied in princely laws, reflected the Lutheran doctrine of the priesthood of all believers. "The significance or effect of this sacrament," Luther wrote, "is fellowship of all the saints. . . . Hence it is that Christ and all the saints are one community and body, each citizen being a member of the other and of the entire city."[17] The person in need, Luther wrote, should "go joyfully to the sacrament of the altar and lay down his woe in the midst of the community . . . and seek help from the entire company."[18]

Thus in Lutheran thought the sacrament had a social aspect effectuating membership in the community. As Carter Lindberg has written, "the person in need" is enjoined by Luther's words to "seek help from the entire company," "just as a citizen would ask the authorities and fellow citizens for help."[19] Indeed, Luther based on this sacrament his theology of poor relief, including the responsibility of city authorities to feed the hungry and care for the sick and to "fight, work, pray" for the needy. "In times past," Luther wrote, referring to the early church, "this sacrament was so properly used, and the people were taught to understand this fellowship so well, that they even gathered food and material goods in the church and there . . . distributed [them] among those who were in need."[20]

With respect to the sacrament of baptism, the chief Lutheran change in the Roman Catholic ritual was its translation into German, which for Luther had a theological significance. Both Lutheran and Roman Catholic theology supported infant baptism, and both opposed re-baptism of persons who returned to the faith after leaving it. Both permitted solitary administration of the sacrament, in unusual circumstances, by a layman outside church premises. And in the usual case of infant baptism administered by a cleric in church, both Roman Catholic and Lutheran liturgy provided for congregational participation and congregational acceptance of responsibility for the Christian upbringing of the baptized infant. Lutheran infant baptism differed, however, in the emphasis it placed on such congregational responsibility. In an essay accompanying his translation of the baptismal rite, Luther stated that he put the prayers in the German vernacular because the entire corporate faith of the congregation is needed to protect the infant from the snares of the devil.[21] Indeed, in defending the baptismal rite of exorcism of the devil, carried over from Roman Catholicism, Luther wrote: "In all Christian earnestness, I would ask all those who administer baptism, who hold the children, or witness it, . . . to take sides against the devil and . . . to drive him away from the little child. . . . And I suspect," he added, "that people turn out so badly after baptism because our concern for them has been so cold and careless [and because] we at their baptism, interceded for them without zeal."[22]

Also connected with translation of the liturgy into the German vernacular was the introduction of a new form of congregational prayer, namely, hymnody. In sixteenth-century Roman Catholic services, few hymns were sung by the congregation, and those were chiefly Latin chants; written church music was designed for the most part to be sung solely by the cantor or pastor and by choirs, not by the congregation.[23] Indeed, few members of the congregation could read musical notes. Luther, however, was not only trained in both humanist and ecclesiastical musical traditions but also had a beautiful tenor voice, had sung in popular choruses, and was a devotee of the musical guild of Meistersingers. He believed that music was a gift of God and one of the highest expressions of faith; he referred to ears as "the organs of the Christian man," and said that "the miracles which present themselves to our eyes are much less than those which we apprehend with our ears."[24]

Starting in the early 1520s and continuing during the next decades, Luther wrote several dozen German hymns, usually with music adapted from contemporary folk melodies and with strong simple words, drawn often from biblical texts. He wrote the preface and contributed four of eight hymns contained in the first German hymnal, published in 1524.[25] He also wrote prefaces to other Protestant hymnals, almost one hundred of which were published in his lifetime.[26]

In his "German Mass and Order of Service" *(Deutsche Messe und Gottesdienst),* called a "Song Mass" *(Lied Messe),* published in 1525, Luther substituted congregational hymns for many parts of the Mass that in the Roman Catholic liturgy were recited or chanted by the priest or cantor alone or sung by a church choir. Moreover, whereas the Roman Catholic sung Mass was usually performed only annually, during Holy Week, the Lutheran Mass, with its congregational hymns, was celebrated every Sunday. Thus, in contrast to Roman Catholic practice, the Nicene Creed was not left to be recited or chanted weekly by the priest or cantor and sung annually by the choir but was sung weekly by the congregation; similarly, the sacrament of the eucharist, which in the Roman Catholic liturgy was normally celebrated by the congregation only once a year, was in the Lutheran Mass not only celebrated each week but was also preceded each week by a congregational hymn affirming the Lutheran theology of the Lord's Supper.[27]

Luther wrote to a friend in 1524 that he intended "to compose German songs for the German people so that God's word may resound in the singing of the people. . . . Let the words be as simple as possible but at the same time pure and suitable; and see that the meaning be clear and as close as possible to the Psalms."[28] He also stressed that the music should be melodic, so that the hymns would have "the widest circulation."[29] "Both text and music," he wrote, "[including] accent, melody, and gesture," must come from the mother tongue and voice, otherwise it is but an imitation like that of monkeys."[30] Indeed, Luther's hymns and those of his followers changed radically the sound and the rhythm of both the ecclesiastical and the popular music of their time. In contrast to the prevailing Roman Catholic church music, it stressed melody in a single voice rather than polyphony, and in contrast to the prevailing secular music it stressed an isometric rhythm, with all notes having equal measure, thereby emphasizing the character of the text as a proclamation of faith. In the words of a modern musicologist, in Luther's hymns "the melodic progression accentuates the main stresses of the text."[31]

There is an old German saying that "Luther sang many millions out of the Roman Catholic Church."[32] His best known hymn, "A Mighty Fortress Is Our God" ("Ein feste Burg ist unser Gott"), has been called "the battle cry of the German Protestant Movement." Another of his hymns, "Look Down, O Lord, from Heaven" ("Ach Gott vom Himmel Sieh Darein"), was once sung by four hundred persons standing in the palace courtyard of a prince, in protest against his refusal to reinstate a popular Lutheran pastor.[33]

From a political and legal point of view, the main significance of the new hymnody, as of other aspects of Protestant liturgical reform, was, first, that in Protestant principalities the regulation of ecclesiastical liturgy was transferred from the Roman Catholic Church, under the papacy, to the Protestant prince and his *Obrigkeit* acting under the inspiration of leading Protestant theologians; and second, that the new hymnody, like other liturgical reform, transferred to the congregations, "the German people," spiritual powers hitherto identified solely with the priesthood. In Roman Catholic canon law, the priests were "the spirituals" and the congregants, the laity, constituted the less exalted secular realm. In Roman Catholic church services, the congregants from the highest to the lowest estate played a relatively passive role, speaking infrequently in response to the clergy. The German Revolution spiritualized the congregation; it gave the laity a priestly role in the celebration of the liturgy. It transformed secular music into spiritual music. Above all, the congregational singing of the great Protestant hymns was an effective symbol of the Lutheran doctrine that every true believer is a priest.

Another fundamental Lutheran liturgical innovation was the increased significance of the pastor's sermon: his preaching of the Word was for the first time made a central part of the liturgy, and he was given a new freedom and a new responsibility to teach and inspire his hearers according to his own conscience, relatively free of hierarchically established dogmas and hierarchical controls.

Sermons were, of course, preached in the Roman Catholic liturgy, but they did not play a central role in the service, and they followed set patterns, usually based on allegorical interpretations of biblical texts. Lutheran sermons, by contrast, were intended to have a salvific effect, that is, to help bring the congregation to salvation through hearing the pastor's inspired preaching. In the words of a leading modern student of Lutheran theology, "the sermon was the best and most necessary part of the Mass. Luther invested it with an almost sacramental quality and made it the central focus of the liturgy. . . . Protestant worship centered around the pulpit and open Bible with the preacher facing the congregation. . . . So important was the preaching office that even those church members under the ban were not to be excluded from its benefits: 'The Word of God shall remain free, to be heard by everyone.'"[34]

Lutheran sermons were supposed to make biblical passages come alive for the congregation through interpretation of the meaning of the words in the context in which they were spoken. The preacher's task, Luther wrote, was to explain the Bible—"the Word"—in the language of the people. The content of the sermon was theological, but the preacher was to make that content understandable to all. "I do not preach to Drs. Pomeranus, Jonas, and Philip," Luther said, "but to my little Hans and Elizabeth."[35]

Implicit in Luther's doctrine of the role and character of the sermon was the principle of freedom of preaching—a principle which in 1525, at the time of the Peasants' War, he made explicit in defending the right of peasant communities to choose their pastors independently of princes and lords. Not only ought rulers not to interfere in such choice, Luther wrote, but also, "indeed, no ruler ought to prevent anyone from teaching or believing what he pleases, whether Gospel or lies. It is enough if he prevents the teaching of sedition and rebellion."[36] Although Luther later severely qualified this statement,[37] nevertheless, a considerable freedom of preaching remained a constitutional principle of the German Lutheran Church.[38]

Though promulgated by princes, the new church ordinances invoked theological authority for a law higher than the prince, namely, the authority of the Bible ("God's Word") and "the command of our Lord Jesus Christ."[39] Indeed, one of the more widely adopted church ordinances expressly stated that "freedom from the law [*vom Gesetz*] in subservience to Christ is the law [*Recht*] of the Christian."[40] The "divine law of grace," which operates without coercion, and which alone "justifies" the faithful in the sight of God, was stated to be the measure of whether positive human law can be adhered to.[41]

Marriage

The new Lutheran law of marriage was sometimes contained in the more general *Kirchenordnungen* and sometimes in special territorial marriage ordinances *(Eheordnungen),* in which the Lutheran theology of marriage was set forth together with a systematic statement of marriage law, including requirements of consent, rules of the wedding ceremony, impediments, spousal duties, divorce, and related matters.[42]

Like the Roman Catholic canon law of marriage, the Lutheran marriage ordinances declared that monogamous marriage was instituted by God and that it was intended to be a lifelong union of the spouses and the foundation of the family. Nevertheless, the Lutheran marriage was not a sacrament since, unlike baptism and the Lord's Supper, it was not intended to be an effective symbol of divine grace and of membership in the heavenly kingdom but was essentially, in Luther's words, "an outward, physical, and secular station."[43] If, owing to human sinfulness, one spouse betrayed his or her promise of fidelity by committing adultery or by desertion, the marriage—under Lutheran marriage law, and contrary to Roman Catholic marriage law—could be dissolved. At the same time, however, whereas the Roman Catholic concept of marriage placed it at a lower level of spirituality than priestly celibacy, the Lutheran concept raised it to the level of a sacred calling, instituted by God as the foundation of the family, which in turn was one of the three divinely instituted estates.

As John Witte has shown, the Lutheran theology of marriage and the family led to a new legal concept of marriage, involving not only, as before, a personal bond between the spouses but also a social bond, in which the parents of the spouses, the congregation, and the whole community was involved. Contrary to the earlier Roman Catholic canon law, a public ceremony and parental consent were required in order to enter into a valid marriage. Also two good and honorable witnesses were required to be present at the wedding, which had to be solemnized by a church ceremony and recorded in the church registry with signatures of the spouses, the witnesses, and others. At the wedding ceremony the pastor was to instruct the couple concerning their responsibilities, and if they violated their responsibilities they were to be disciplined and in extreme cases excommunicated. These provisions of the Lutheran marriage ordinances conflicted sharply with the preexisting Roman Catholic canon law, which recognized the validity of secret marriages as well as of informal marriages in which the couple cohabited as spouses without any marriage ceremony.

Luther's strong view of the "worldly" character of marriage led him to advocate not only the exclusive competence of secular political authorities to legislate the conditions of marriage but also the exclusive jurisdiction of secular courts to adjudicate marital causes. Other Lutheran reformers, including Melanchthon, advocated a less extreme position, leaving to Protestant ecclesiastical tribunals, called consistories, the adjudication of marital causes. Different principalities and different cities went in different directions in the matter. The differences were reduced by the fact that in some places pastors were co-opted to sit on secular courts in marital cases and in other places jurists and theologians were co-opted to sit on consistorial courts in such cases. In the course of the seventeenth and early eighteenth centuries, jurisdiction over marital disputes came to be viewed as mixed spiritual and secular causes, and jurisdiction over them came to be concentrated in the consistories, with both clerical and lay membership.[44]

School Laws

Like the church ordinances and the marriage ordinances, so the numerous school ordinances *(Schulordnungen)* promulgated by secular authorities in Lutheran territories and cities in the sixteenth century took the form, on the one hand, of theological proclamations and, on the other hand, of systematic statements of a particular branch of the law.[45] Also, like the church ordinances and the marriage ordinances, the Lutheran school ordinances drew partly on the preexisting canon law. They also drew on the experience of those lay schools which, in various parts of Europe, especially in Italy, from the fourteenth century to the early sixteenth, had broken the virtual monopoly of the Roman Catholic Church in matters of education.[46] Neither the earlier church schools nor the lay schools, however, had the same purposes that infused the new Lutheran system of universal public schooling.

Luther and his followers grounded their educational reforms on the doctrine of the two kingdoms and, more particularly, on the belief that in the propagation of knowledge of the Gospel and of the Christian faith, and hence in the fulfillment of the task of the earthly kingdom to prepare Christians to live also in the heavenly kingdom, education (as Luther put it) is "second only to the church in importance."[47] In addition, the Lutheran reformers considered education to be essential to the maintenance of the earthly kingdom itself. As Luther stated, "Were there neither soul, nor heaven, nor hell, it would still be necessary to have schools for the sake of things here below," and especially for producing "many able, learned, wise, honorable, and well-educated citizens."[48] And as Melanchthon wrote, "Better letters bring better morals, better morals bring better communities."[49]

Roman Catholics certainly shared the Lutheran belief in the importance of education as a preparation for living a spiritual life. Principal differences, however, lay in the Lutheran belief, first, that *all* persons should be educated, and second, that it is primarily the responsibility of the political authority, the *Obrigkeit,* and not of the ecclesiastical authorities, to secure universal public schooling. These two interrelated beliefs rested, in turn, on the Lutheran theological concept that not just the clerical calling but every calling is sacred; and further, that the partnership of the three divinely instituted secular estates—the family, the clergy, the political authorities—are responsible for preparing persons of faith to live in the heavenly kingdom.[50]

Luther and his partners—especially Melanchthon and Bugenhagen—constructed elaborate detailed curricula for public schools, which, together with statements of the theology embedded in them, were incorporated in many of the more than one hundred school ordinances that were adopted by various German cities and principalities between 1523 and 1600. Both Latin schools and vernacular schools were to be established. In those cities and territories that accepted the Luther-Melanchthon plan, children in the Latin schools, starting at the first level, were to be taught reading, Latin grammar, and various prayers; at the second level, they were to study more advanced grammar in various classical and humanist authors, religious instruction from the Psalms and the Gospels, the Lord's Prayer, the Ten Commandments, the Creed, verses of Terence, Plautus, and Erasmus, and Aesop's *Fables* (which Luther himself translated); at the third level, advanced students were to study the works of Ovid, Cicero, and Virgil, and to learn dialectics, rhetoric, and poetics. At all three levels music, mathematics, science, and history were to be taught, as time allowed. Later Lutheran humanists developed an even more refined Latin school curriculum, dividing lower school students into up to ten classes, each with its own combination of religious and humanist texts and exercises.[51]

For the vernacular schools, Bugenhagen devised a less complex and more practical curriculum. Pupils were to be taught reading, writing, and arithmetic from whatever texts were at hand. They were to memorize the Ten Commandments, the Lord's Prayer, and the Apostle's Creed, and to read Psalms, sing hymns, and learn biblical history. Thereafter they were to learn practical skills of agriculture, commerce, household duties, and the like. Instruction was to be primarily in German, according to the local dialect, though students with special aptitude and interests might also study Greek, Latin, and Hebrew.[52]

The various school ordinances embodying these curricula differed in important respects from the Roman Catholic canon law of schooling. In Lutheran principalities schools were not subject to central ecclesiastical control. The teachers were hired not by ecclesiastical authorities but by the local city or village authorities. The new public schools were Lutheran in their religious orientation. The Bible was a central object of study. All children were invited to attend. To be sure, many of them—perhaps most of them—could not, because their parents could not spare them from work or else because they could not afford to pay the fees that were charged; many of the Lutheran school ordinances, however, provided for financial assistance to needy students.[53]

The transfer of the administration of education from the Roman Catholic priesthood, operating under papal and episcopal legislation, to local political authorities and lay teachers, operating under territorial and urban legislation, is usually described as a process of secularization of education. In a more fundamental sense, however, it was part of a process of spiritualization of the role of secular authorities, and especially of the territorial prince, who under Protestantism became the ultimate source of public school legislation. As "the father of his country," the prince was responsible for the spiritual education of his subjects. Similarly, the extension of the opportunity of education to the public as a whole, as contrasted with its earlier confinement largely to those preparing for one of the clerical professions, is also usually viewed as a process of secularization. But it, too, in a more fundamental sense, was part of a process of spiritualization of the laity. In John Witte's words, "The general calling of all Christians was to replace the special calling of the clergy as the *raison d'être* of education."

Moral Discipline

Contained often in church ordinances, though also sometimes promulgated independently, disciplinary ordinances *(Zuchtordnungen)* were enacted by Lutheran city councils and princes to enforce morality by secular authority. As in the case of liturgy, marriage, and schooling, so in the case of morals, the Lutheran civil authorities replaced the Roman Catholic papal hierarchy as the ultimate source and the ultimate enforcer of the new spiritual legislation; but again, it was Lutheran theologians, often law-trained, who not only inspired but also drafted that legislation and presented it to the civil authorities for enactment.

The types of moral offenses proscribed by the Lutheran disciplinary ordinances were, for the most part, the same as those that were proscribed by the Roman Catholic canon law. As Witte writes:

> New Sabbath-day laws prohibited all forms of unnecessary labor and uncouth leisure on Sundays and holy days and required faithful attendance at services. New spiritual laws prohibited blasphemy, sacrilege, witchcraft, sorcery, magic, alchemy, false oaths, and similar offenses. New sumptuary laws proscribed immodest apparel, wasteful living, and extravagant feasts and funerals. New sexuality laws forbade "unnatural" sexual relationships such as incest, bigamy, polygamy,

homosexuality, and prostitution, and "undignified" sexual acts such as masturbation, bestiality, sodomy, pornography, exhibitionism, and the like. New entertainment laws placed strict restrictions on public drunkenness, boisterous celebration, wild dancing, and gambling and other games that involved fate, luck, and magic. Neither the state's emphasis upon these moral offenses nor its definition of them strayed far from the formulation of the canon law.

Although Lutheran theology agreed with Roman Catholic theology that what made these acts sinful was that they were prohibited by God, and that the commission of them alienated the sinner from God, the two theologies differed sharply as to the responses that should be made to them by the ecclesiastical and civil authorities. Under Roman Catholic canon law, the sinner was required to confess his sins to a priest at least once a year and to receive absolution, conditional on performing satisfaction through penitential deeds. By completing the sacrament of penance, the sinner avoided condemnation to hell and mitigated the temporal punishment of purgatory. Failure to submit to the requirements of confession and penance was itself a mortal sin. Lutheran theology, by contrast, denounced the sacrament of penance as an unconscionable interference by the priesthood in the relationship of the penitent believer to God. According to Lutheran theology, the visible church should discipline the sinner, but only in order to punish and deter sins in the earthly kingdom and not for the sake of ultimate reconciliation with God—"not," as it was put in the Apology of the Augsburg Confession, "for the sake of heaven." The Apology attacked Roman Catholics for "superstitiously imagin[ing] that [penances] avail not for discipline before the church but for appeasing God."[54]

Moreover, Roman Catholic canon law divided enforcement of moral discipline between the "internal forum," of which the jurisdiction of the priest in confession was the chief example, and the "external forum" of the ecclesiastical court of the bishop or archbishop or pope. The external forum was invoked to punish sins whose gravity raised them to the level of ecclesiastical crimes—such as murder committed by a cleric, stealing church property (whether by a cleric or by a layman), heresy, witchcraft, and other offenses to which more severe sanctions were applicable, including, in appropriate cases, imprisonment in a monastery for long periods of time, or even for life, and in extreme cases of heresy, as well as in cases of ecclesiastical crimes that also constituted capital offenses under secular law, such as witchcraft, transfer to the secular power to be hanged or even burned at the stake.

The Lutheran disciplinary ordinances established quite a different regime for punishment of moral offenses. In the first place, Lutheran confession was different in character from the Roman Catholic. Weekly Saturday vesper services included a general penitential service followed by individual confessions to the pastor, but in such confessions enumeration of specific sinful acts was not encouraged; instead, the penitent was encouraged to confess in general terms his violations of individual commandments of the Decalogue, and the pastor might provide instruction on the meaning of those commandments and on how better to follow them. Penances might be imposed, but they were not for the redemption of the sin, which could be accomplished only by the sinner's spiritual reconciliation with God through his own faith and by God's grace.[55] The most severe ecclesiastical sanction that could be imposed for violation of moral discipline was the "small ban," that is, exclusion from the Lord's Supper. Even then, the sinner was still invited to worship in the church and to listen to the preaching of God's Word. The key to the disciplinary ordinances was "discipline before the church," that is, justice and reconciliation within the parish community.

Second, Lutheran theology placed strict limits on the jurisdiction of the consistory or other ecclesiastical tribunal within each bishopric. It could indeed hear cases of minor moral offenses and could impose small fines and some forms of corporal punishment such as whippings and the pillory. Unlike the Roman Catholic ecclesiastical courts, however, the Lutheran tribunals were not part of an official hierarchy of courts operating under a formal system of substantive and procedural law.[56] Thus a sharp distinction was made between (moral) sin and (legal) crime, and those moral offenses that also constituted crimes or civil offenses were subject to criminal or civil sanctions only in the secular courts. This meant, indeed, the transfer to secular courts of not only the criminal jurisdiction of the former ecclesiastical courts but also some of the jurisdiction of the Roman Catholic internal forum. In fact, the sixteenth-century Lutherans could be as zealous as their rival Calvinists in demanding punishments for moral offenses.

Poor Laws

Prior to the sixteenth century, the Roman Catholic Church not only regulated, through the canon law, the liturgical, marital, educational, and moral life of all the peoples of western Europe but also played the major role in the care of persons in poverty or other material or physical need. Christianity, in all its forms, like Judaism from which it was derived, has from the earliest times emphasized the obligation of all believers to care for the poor, the sick, the homeless, widows and orphans, and other needy persons. In the twelfth century and thereafter, the church fulfilled this obligation through a variety of ecclesiastical institutions.[57] Canon law required the parish priest (or, if he was absent, the resident vicar) to be assigned a sufficient portion of church revenues (the amount to be determined by the diocesan bishop) to care for the poor, the homeless, the sick, and others in need of alms. In addition, monasteries gave food, shelter, clothing, and medical care to the needy. Finally, lay persons—kings and princes, feudal lords, and wealthy merchants, as well as guilds and municipalities—endowed ecclesiastical "hospitals," including not only institutions for providing medical care for the sick but also leper colonies, homes for the aged and destitute, shelters for pilgrims and travelers, orphanages, lying-in hospitals for pregnant women, and other types of charitable institutions.[58] In the early sixteenth century, Roman Catholic canon law required that at least one-fourth of all ecclesiastical income be bestowed on the poor.

The German Revolution transferred from the priesthood and monastic orders—"the spirituals"—to secular authorities the primary obligation to regulate, finance, and administer charitable activities. There had been movement in this direction in the previous century and a half, as the need to find new methods of poor relief was heightened by the great increase in poverty and homelessness and disease resulting partly from the Black Death. Also in the fifteenth century the Roman Catholic theology of poor relief tended to move in a direction which was eventually followed and further developed by Lutheran theology. Nevertheless, both the theology of poor relief and the law of poor relief in German territories underwent fundamental changes under the impact of the German Revolution.[59]

The Lutheran theology of poor relief differed from the earlier Roman Catholic theology in three respects: first, it placed more emphasis on the responsibility of the entire community, from prince down to peasant, to help the needy, and less emphasis on the responsibility of the ecclesiastical authorities; second, it placed on local political authorities the primary moral responsibility to establish, regulate, and administer poor relief; and third, it was less tolerant of the sins of sloth and greed that it identified with various forms of poverty, including begging and vagrancy.

It was, once again, mainly Lutheran law-trained theologians who took the initiative in drafting the many poor laws *(Armenordnungen)* that were adopted by city councils throughout most of Germany from the 1520s on. Having protested against neglect of the poor and needy in his Ninety-five Theses of 1517,[60] and having challenged the political authorities to care for the poor and the needy in his 1520 "Address to the Nobility of the German Nation,"[61] Luther began in the early 1520s to make practical proposals of ways in which municipal authorities could fulfill these Christian obligations. In 1520, with assistance from his fellow Reformer Andreas Karlstadt, he drafted an ordinance for the city of Wittenberg to outlaw begging, on the one hand, and, on the other, to institute a comprehensive program of poor relief. Karlstadt's tract "There Shall Be No Beggars among Christians" was instrumental in securing adoption of the ordinance, which required the municipality to establish a "common chest" *(gemeiner Kasten)* to replace the existing endowments of individual charitable institutions.[62] The common chest, from which funds for all the various charities within a given locality were to be derived, was initially to be financed in large part by resources acquired from the dissolution of monasteries and other former Roman Catholic institutions. A similar ordinance was adopted in Nuremberg in 1522. In 1523 Luther was again the principal draftsman of an "Ordinance of a Common Chest" for the town of Leisnig, which included the requirement that all citizens contribute in proportion to their status as nobles, merchants, peasants, and so on, to cover the cost of distributions from such a community chest.[63] Despite considerable resistance, the Leisnig ordinance was finally adopted in 1529. Between 1522 and 1530 more than twenty-five German cities, upon conversion to Lutheranism, adopted poor laws containing the essentials of Luther's suggestions, including especially the institution of the Lutheran common chest.[64]

Municipal community chests, which were established in the sixteenth century in cities throughout Germany, differed from the traditional charitable endowments of Roman Catholic Europe both in the scope of their responsibilities and in the method of their administration. Thus the Leisnig poor law provided that the directors of the common chest were to make precise case studies of the plight of the poor in the city and villages of the parish and to keep a list of deserving needy persons and to consult weekly concerning their situation.[65] The Leisnig ordinance also provided that

> poor and neglected orphans within the city and villages of our entire parish shall, as occasion arises, be provided with training and physical necessities by the directors out of the community chest until such time as they can work and earn their bread. If there be found among such orphans, or the children of impoverished parents, young boys with an aptitude for schooling and a capacity for arts and letters, the directors should support and provide for them. . . . The girls among the neglected orphans, and likewise the daughters of impoverished parents, shall be provided by the directors out of the community chest with a suitable dowry for marriage. Those individuals in our parish and assembly who are impoverished by force of circumstance and left without assistance by their relatives . . . and those who are unable to work because of illness or old age or are so poor as to suffer real need, shall receive each week on Sunday, and at other times as occasion demands, maintenance and support from our community chest through the ten directors . . . so that no impoverished person in our parish need ever publicly cry out, lament, or beg for such items of daily necessity.[66]

The administrative structure adopted in the Leisnig ordinance was headed by an assembly of the citizens of the town which was to meet annually and from which ten directors were to be elected, two from the nobility, two from the incumbent city council, three from among the common citizens of the town, and three from the rural peasantry. The entire assembly was to meet in the town hall three times a year to hear and discuss the report of the directors and to consider future action.[67]

Other poor laws, drafted by other theologians, followed a pattern similar in some basic respects to the Leisnig model.[68] In virtually all sixteenth-century Protestant territories, both Lutheran and Calvinist, and eventually in some Roman Catholic territories as well, community chests were established. Of special interest in this connection was the influence of Johann Bugenhagen, Luther's own pastor, university colleague, and spiritual adviser, who organized a

Reformation in eight leading cities and territories of northern Germany, including the kingdom of Denmark.[69] In his writings and in the poor laws which he drafted for those eight polities, Bugenhagen developed a theory of poor relief based on a combination of theological, social, and political doctrines. His theology of poor relief, like Luther's, was based on Christ's command "that we bear the burden of our neighbors' needs, as Jesus said (John 13:35): 'So will all people know that you are my followers if you always love one another.' "[70] Such obedience was required, he wrote, not in order to merit grace but in order to be a Christian. "Service to our neighbor," Bugenhagen wrote, must "flow freely from the heart . . . for his sake" and not in order to be saved.[71]

Combined with its theological aspect, the social aspect of poor relief, in Bugenhagen's theory, as in Luther's, was partly its function in combating mendicancy—to use present-day terminology, replacing welfare with workfare. "The 'Holy Poverty' of the monastic ideal, the 'raison d'être' of the Franciscan Order, had no place in Bugenhagen's theological understanding."[72] It was not all poor but "the deserving poor" for whom the new poor laws were designed. Bugenhagen emphasized in his writings, and implemented in his drafts of church ordinances, that the poor who are to be supported from the community chest are "the house poor, artisans, and laborers who do not spend their time in idleness and drunkenness but instead work diligently, lead praiseworthy and upright lives, and still are beset with misfortune which imposes suffering through no fault of their own. Also, those who . . . are not able to support themselves . . . by working. . . . They must lead an upright praiseworthy life and not be blasphemers."[73]

In addition to their theological and social basis, the Lutheran poor laws of the sixteenth century were also based on a political doctrine, namely, that the territorial civil authority, and, more particularly, the municipalities and townships within the territories, had the spiritual task of maintaining a Christian society. Bugenhagen insisted that the poor laws, with their establishment of community chests, be adopted by town and city councils and administered by their townsmen. The townsman, the German burgher, was to be "the best expression of the Christian citizen."[74] Bugenhagen's drafts of poor laws were presented to, and adopted by, the king of Denmark and the duke of Pomerania, but those laws gave the final authority for implementing them to city councils, citizens' committees, and local communities generally. Indeed, in Bugenhagen's law for Braunschweig each large parish within the territory was to have its own common chest.

The Interaction of Secular and Spiritual Law

In present-day German, the meaning of the usual word for "spiritual," *geistlich,* seems to be confined largely to what in English would be called "clerical" or "priestly" matters, having to do with the institutional church, while the closely related German word *geistig* means, in most contexts, "mental," "intellectual," "learned." *Geistige Arbeit* is translated in English as "mental work," *geistliche Arbeit* as "church work." English-German dictionaries do not give a good German translation of "spiritual values," or "a spiritual relationship," or "a spiritual life." It is even more difficult, it would seem, to explain in today's German what Luther meant when he spoke of a divine spiritual law, which governs relationships in the heavenly kingdom, especially relationships of faith and love inspired by divine grace. For Luther, the term "spirit," *Geist,* was linked inextricably with the Holy Spirit, *der heilige Geist.* The mere fact that something—law, for example—has a moral character or a religious character did not make it, for Luther, spiritual. His "spiritual," *geistlich,* should perhaps be rendered today as *heilig,* "holy." And the English word "spiritual," when used broadly to refer to the deepest convictions and loyalties of a person, one's closest personal attachments and deepest inner concerns, should perhaps be rendered in German as *spirituell.* If that is so, then the Lutheran church laws, marriage laws, school laws, moral laws, and poor laws might properly be called *spirituelles Recht.*

The meaning of the term "secular," *weltlich,* has also changed radically in the twentieth century, having come to be associated with political, economic, and social institutions and theories that are thought to be not only not religious in character but also not sacred or spiritual in any sense of those words. As early as 1918, Max Weber spoke of the "disenchantment of the world," which he saw as the end product of the "modern age" of rationalism, individualism, and bureaucratic law.[75] In 1906 his friend and colleague the Protestant theologian Ernst Troeltsch had traced the historical origins of the secularization of society to the Protestant Reformation, which introduced, he said, a religious individualism that ultimately itself became secularized.[76] These early prophecies have been taken up by hosts of sociologists, theologians, historians, philosophers, political scientists, and others, who over the past century have published literally scores of books and many hundreds of articles on the impact of secularism on modern society.[77]

As Hans Blumenberg has written, the concept of secularization has itself become secularized.[78] God is no longer thought to be hidden, *absconditus,* in the secular world. Like Luther, we define the laws handed down by state agencies as secular law partly because they are handed down by the secular state and partly because we do not believe that obedience to them can save souls; but we have broken with Lutheran thought by denying to the law of the state the function of expressly fostering "spiritual gifts" through adoption of theologically determined and theologically formulated church laws, marriage laws, school laws, laws of moral discipline, and poor laws, and by denying to religious authorities the function of expressly guiding the secular state in its regulation of those essentially spiritual activities. We have increasingly privatized the spiritual aspects of social life, on the one hand, and, on the other hand, we have increasingly politicized the secular aspects.

These tendencies have strongly influenced—and distorted—conventional historiography. Historians have characterized the sixteenth century, Luther's time, as the beginning of the "Modern Age," as Luther's followers themselves did; but they have given entirely new meaning to that term. They speak of "modernity" *not* as Lutheran theologians did, to refer to a new time of biblical faith, but, on the contrary, to refer to the rise of secularism—and not Luther's or Melanchthon's or Bugenhagen's secularism, in which God is present, but a secularism that is identified with the predominance of political, economic, and social powers, a secularism that exalts freedom from tradition and authority in the name of rationality and pragmatism.

The use of the term "modernity" to signify secularism has led contemporary historians to underestimate the importance of the spiritual aspects of the Lutheran laws discussed in this chapter. To illustrate this, attention may be called to recent studies of two of the five types of these laws: the laws on moral discipline and the poor laws.

A leading school of "early modern" historiography has characterized the sixteenth-century Lutheran laws on moral discipline as an instrument of political absolutism; the rising absolute monarchies, it is argued, sought through legislation on moral discipline to control the population, to make it obedient to the political authority, to keep order, and thus to enhance the power of the state. A new "paradigm" is proposed—social disciplining, *Sozialdisziplinierung*—to complement Max Weber's "paradigm" of "formal rationality" as the key to the emergence of the modern state.[79]

As so often happens when a new "school" emerges, an opposing "school" has arisen to challenge it—not by saying that it is entirely wrong, but by adding another dimension to it. Thus the opponents argue that social disciplining was only one purpose and only one consequence of the Lutheran disciplinary laws; another purpose, even more important, was "confessionalization" *(Konfessionalisierung)*, the reinforcement of state control of the established religious confessions.[80]

Both schools take for granted that "early modern" German history was characterized by the rise of absolute monarchy. Yet a study of the process by which the disciplinary ordinances came into existence makes it clear that the power of the Lutheran princes and city councils that enacted them was shared, and shared equally, with the power of the Lutheran theologians who drafted them. The German Revolution did indeed lead to the transfer from the Church of Rome to the Lutheran princes jurisdiction over liturgy, marriage, schooling, moral discipline, and poor relief; nevertheless, the secular rulers were dependent on the theology professors, including Luther himself, when it came to the exercise of that jurisdiction.

Moreover, the laws themselves made it clear that the Lutheran princes and their councilors were not "absolute"—not "absolved" from obedience to the laws which they made. Indeed, Lutheran princes believed that the laws made by them were subject to divine law, and that citizens retained a freedom even to disobey a secular law if their Christian conscience told them that it contradicted divine law as revealed in the Bible. That belief was given practical effect by the confederate character of the wider German polity; its multiplicity of principalities made it possible for a conscientious citizen of one German state to move across a very near border to another German state with the same language and culture and historical background.

Similarly, contemporary historians of "early modern" Germany have emphasized that the Lutheran poor laws served to enhance not only the political power of the princes but also the economic power of the ruling classes, since through workhouses cheap labor replaced begging and vagrancy.[81] Again, what is missing from this political, economic, and social analysis is the spiritual side. It is undoubtedly true that persons who do useful work at subsistence wages contribute more both to the political power of the state and to the economic power of the ruling classes than persons who do not work but live on the charity—or the property—of others. But there was also a spiritual side to the matter, namely, whether such persons would be better persons if they worked—better in the eyes of God and of their fellows—than they would be if they remained beggars and vagrants. The theology of the Church of Rome gave a sanctity to mendicancy which Lutheran theology sharply opposed.[82]

The fact that the theology of the Lutheran church tended strongly to support the political power of the Lutheran state has led contemporary "secularists" to the conclusion that the Lutheran state used the Lutheran church to enhance its own political power; and this, too—speaking very generally—is true. But it is also true that the Lutheran *church* used the Lutheran *state* to enhance its own *spiritual* mission. Lutheran theology taught that the state's main function is to support the church in its educational task, a task realized through the preaching of the Gospel and the sacraments and also through its social teachings.[83] Luther made the point dramatically: God is present in the office of the secular magistracy, he said, in order to combat sin and the devil.[84]

We may learn from the interaction of spiritual and secular law in the Lutheran ordinances that in Lutheran principalities the church and the state were considered to be two faces, two aspects, of a single order. These were not "two swords," as in the earlier period when the pan-European Church of Rome interacted with a plurality of secular kingdoms, feudal domains, and autonomous cities. Nor were church and state strictly separated from each other, as they became—in democratic theory—in the late eighteenth century and thereafter. Yet in Germany, at least, this was by no means absolute monarchy, let alone Caesaro-papism. In the words of Rosenstock-Huessy, every public servant "passed through the two jurisdictions of a teaching church and a listening government."[85]

Contemporary social theorists have developed a theory of secularization—or, rather, two theories: one, that political science since the sixteenth century has been a secularization of medieval theology,[86] and the other, that secular modernity has its own world outlook, wholly independent of theology.[87] A third theory of secularization emerges from a study of the German spiritual ordinances of the sixteenth century, namely, that the interaction of the secular and the spiritual, which took one form in the First Modern Age, introduced by the Papal Revolution, was preserved but transformed in the Second Modern Age, introduced by the Protestant Reformation; and that such interaction was effectively symbolized in Germany by the pervasive influence of Lutheran theology in civil legislation concerning the church itself, concerning marriage and the family, and concerning public education, morals, and care of the needy.

Finally, the recognition of these as spiritual causes, and of the law regulating them as spiritual law—regardless of whether it is enacted by "state" or by "church"—adds an important perspective not only to the widespread debate about the impact of secularism on Western society in "modern" and "post-modern" times but also to the less widespread but no less important discussion of the interaction of law and religion in the ongoing history of Western civilization.

In the broadest sense of the word, to be sure, virtually all our laws may be said to have a spiritual aspect. Virtually all our laws are intended to promote right conduct; virtually all have a moral dimension; virtually all purport, at least, to foster right relations among people. Yet some laws are so much more spiritual than others that the difference in degree becomes a difference in kind. Thus laws regulating the marriage relationship differ in kind from laws regulating, for example, a commercial partnership—because marriage, as compared with forms of business organization, is more closely connected with the ultimate values, the ultimate purposes, of human life. The laws of business organization are, indeed, extremely important from an economic viewpoint, from a utilitarian viewpoint, from what in traditional Western terminology is called a material or a secular viewpoint. But laws regulating marriage, or the rights and obligations of parents in bringing up their children, affect much more profoundly the human psyche, the human heart, the human spirit. The same may be said of school laws and of laws forbidding certain types of outrageous moral offenses and of laws giving succor to those in dire need. These laws touch what we hold most sacred in our relationships with others and in our nature and destiny as persons. They touch not only the rational calculations of our minds but also the passions of our hearts.

In the theistic religions of Judaism, Christianity, and Islam, and in many other belief systems as well, the human spirit is closely related to the heart. "Create in me a pure heart and a right spirit," says the Psalmist (Psalm 51), and the prophet Ezekiel extends this petition to the whole people: "A new heart will I give to you," he proclaims, "and a new spirit will I put within you. . . . I will put my spirit within you and cause you to walk in my statutes and keep my judgments and do them" (Ezekiel 36:26–28).

Especially in the twentieth century and into the twenty-first, it has generally been overlooked by scholars that the historical development of law in the West has been the product of a dialectical interaction between, on the one hand, what Toqueville called "the habits of the heart" and Abraham Lincoln, in his Second Inaugural Address, called "the better angels of our nature," and, on the other hand, the practical, the quantifiable, the utilitarian—between the sacred and the profane, the moral and the political, the spiritual and the secular dimensions of social life. For the sixteenth-century Lutheran Reformers, as we have seen, and for the Roman Catholics before them, the material and the psychological, the body and the soul, the time-bound and the eternal—the secular and the spiritual—were in dialectical tension.

In the sixteenth century, the transfer to German territorial and local governments of the responsibility hitherto exercised by the clergy, acting under the canon law of the Roman Catholic Church, to regulate the ecclesiastical liturgy, to define and protect marriage relationships, to establish and administer schools, to define and punish moral offenses, and to care for the poor and the needy was indeed, in one sense, a process of "secularization"; that is, what had been ecclesiastical functions were now transferred to lay authorities. In a deeper sense, however, the law governing these matters remained spiritual law. The secular authorities were given what had previously been called spiritual responsibilities. The law of the secular authorities—in that sense, secular law—was spiritualized. This process of spiritualization of secular law was facilitated by the participation of new spiritual authorities, leading Protestant Reformers, in the promotion and drafting of the new legislation.

It may be that for many persons today the word "spiritual" does not carry implications relating it closely to marriage, to education, to morals, and to relief of poverty. And of course strong monarchy, with a state church, is now virtually obsolete in the West. Yet the impact of the sixteenth-century German Revolution on German law is worth remembering not only by historians and philosophers but also by persons interested in contemporary law relating to family life and schooling and social welfare. These are matters which our secular authorities, following in this respect the sixteenth-century German Lutheran secular authorities, should earnestly take to heart.

II

THE ENGLISH REVOLUTION AND THE TRANSFORMATION OF ENGLISH LAW IN THE SEVENTEENTH CENTURY

CHAPTER 7

The English Revolution, 1640–1689

The English Revolution of 1640–1689, like the German Revolution of 1517–1555, was a European Revolution. It was a response to a European, and not only to a national, crisis. Moreover, it had substantial repercussions in other European countries. It cannot be understood, therefore, solely in terms of English history. Both the German and the English Revolutions were, to be sure, national upheavals, which reflected and ultimately reshaped the national character of Germany and England, respectively. But they also reflected and reshaped the character of Europe.

The European Crisis of the Seventeenth Century

The European character of the English Revolution has been obscured—at least until recent decades—by the emphasis placed by English historians on its uniquely English features to the exclusion of those that it shared with other countries of Europe.[1] This tendency toward insularity has been only partially overcome by the emergence of a school of historians who have studied what H. R. Trevor-Roper called in 1959 "the general crisis of the seventeenth century."[2] Although Trevor-Roper correctly described the crisis in terms of the challenge—both in England and elsewhere—to absolute monarchy, his emphasis was mainly on one aspect of that challenge, namely, the opposition of the landed gentry ("the country") to royal bureaucracy ("the court"). A broader view of the general European crisis must be taken, however, if its relationship to the English Revolution is to be understood.[3]

The crisis was in part a religious crisis, in part a political crisis, and in part a socioeconomic crisis. The *religious crisis* was a consequence of the failure to realize the hopes that had been generated by the settlement reached in the German Peace of Augsburg of 1555 and by parallel settlements reached in France,

England, and elsewhere in Europe in the sixteenth century. The Peace of Augsburg gave each of the territorial princes of Germany the power to establish the religion of his territory—but the choice was to be between Roman Catholicism and Lutheranism only. The exclusion of Calvinists from the settlement became a source of intense conflict as Calvinism spread within the German Empire in the late sixteenth and early seventeenth centuries. Moreover, from time to time Protestant rulers came to power in Catholic principalities and Catholic rulers in Protestant, giving rise to fierce conflict. Most important, the Peace of Augsburg failed to provide adequately for the right of Protestant and Catholic minorities to have their own worship services within territories where the opposite faith prevailed. Similar sources of tension existed in other parts of Europe where the principle was adopted that the religion of the ruler was to be the exclusive religion of his territory. Thus the Netherlands, which was subject to the Roman Catholic Spanish Crown, was de facto sharply divided between Roman Catholic and Protestant (chiefly Calvinist) provinces.[4] In Roman Catholic France, following a series of internal religious wars, Henry IV's Edict of Nantes of 1598 provided protection for (chiefly Calvinist) Huguenots, and in Protestant England under Elizabeth (1558–1603) there was a de facto toleration of moderate forms of Calvinist Puritanism within the Church of England and of private individual Roman Catholic worship services. Nevertheless, the religious situation in both those countries, as in Germany, remained one of great tension, culminating in the seventeenth century in a series of religious wars throughout the continent of Europe that are known collectively as the Thirty Years' War (1618–1648). In France the persecution of Protestants resumed, culminating in the revocation of the Edict of Nantes in 1685. In England the Crown cracked down on the Puritans, who eventually rose up in a civil war.

Closely connected with the religious crisis was a *political crisis* within each of the major political dominions into which Europe was divided, as well as an international political crisis among them. Within the various polities there was a continual tension between the principle of constitutional monarchy and the principle of absolute monarchy. In sixteenth-century Germany the power of the Lutheran prince was limited, on the one hand, by the dictates of Christian conscience, reinforced by pastoral admonition, and, on the other, by the body of high councilors, the *Obrigkeit,* which was also subject to Christian conscience and which shared the prince's sovereignty. Protestants in other countries sought to establish similar limitations on the ruler's power, usually without success. Even in Roman Catholic countries the church came increasingly under royal power and a doctrine of absolute monarchy came to be asserted. A monarch who was "absolute" (in Latin, *absolutus*) was the supreme lawmaker in his kingdom, who at the same time was "absolved" from subjection to all human laws including his own. He was considered to be under a moral obligation to obey divine law and natural law, but there was, by definition, no institutional means to enforce this obligation. In the seventeenth century the doctrine of absolute monarchy came increasingly under attack, first, by international Calvinism, which taught an aristocratic as opposed to a monarchical principle of government,[5] and second, by members both of the landed gentry and of other classes that suffered from real or imagined oppression at the hands of royal courts and their bureaucracies. In the 1640s and 1650s, various countries of Europe experienced antimonarchist revolts roughly parallel to the English Revolution of Parliament against the Crown, although they were on a much smaller scale and were generally abortive.

Both the religious crisis and the political crisis within the various territorial polities were linked with the international crisis that wracked Europe in the seventeenth century. The Thirty Years' War, which directly involved the German Empire, the individual German principalities, Sweden, Denmark, Poland, France, Spain, and the Netherlands, was a European civil war, in which even countries (such as England) that did not directly participate in the fighting were nevertheless deeply involved indirectly.[6] Alliances kept shifting as religious animosities coincided or conflicted with political animosities. Some Protestants tended to favor either constitutional monarchy, as exemplified in certain Lutheran principalities, or republicanism, as exemplified in the Netherlands and in Switzerland, while some Catholics tended to favor absolute monarchy. Similarly, some Protestants tended to favor a confederation of princes within the German Empire, while some Catholics tended to favor a centralized union. These lines, however, were not kept straight; there were absolutist Protestants and constitutionalist Catholics as well as federalist Catholics and centralist Protestants, and the wars themselves degenerated into a naked power struggle—which at the time came to be called *raison d'état,* "reason of state."[7]

The international political crisis was finally resolved in 1648 by the Peace of Westphalia, which asserted the sovereignty and equality of each constituent principality within the empire as well as of each of the other European states that were involved. The Peace of Westphalia established a formal legal foundation of the modern European system of states, in which each state takes its character from its membership in the system. It also gave to Catholics, Lutherans, and Calvinists whose religious faith differed from that established by the ruler freedom of conscience, the right of private worship, and the right of emigration, with the exception that in the dominions which continued to be ruled by the Hapsburgs, not even such limited toleration was granted to non-Catholics. Within the German Empire the Imperial Parliament *(Reichstag)* was given greatly increased powers vis-à-vis the emperor and the prince-electors, and from 1663 it remained in permanent session at Regensburg.[8]

The *social-economic dimension* of the European crisis of the seventeenth century was directly related to the sixteenth-century system of government by royal officials who owed their positions of power and wealth primarily to the will of the monarch rather than, as in the fifteenth century and before, primarily to their clerical and feudal lineages. Under the earlier system, the power of the monarch had been checked and balanced by the church, the feudal nobility, and the cities. Also most of the revenues of the monarch had been derived from his or her own crown lands, from customs duties on imports, and from revenues owed to the king as feudal overlord. In the sixteenth century, however, in most countries of Europe, the church, the feudal nobility, and the cities were increasingly brought under monarchical control. In addition, there emerged in many countries a new class of large landholders without feudal ties, as smaller peasant landholdings were consolidated and as the purchase and sale of land came to be increasingly freed from feudal obligations. Meanwhile, the financial cost of warfare rose dramatically as feudal levies were replaced by mercenaries and as armies increased in size and military campaigns increased in frequency and length. In order to raise money to wage war, monarchs mortgaged crown lands and forfeited them when they lost. With the diminution of revenues from crown lands, the taxes imposed on large landholders and merchants became more and more onerous, and in some countries their resentment against the royal councilors who surrounded the king and the royal officials who effectuated his policies tended to grow accordingly. In England, the seventeenth-century conflict between "court" and "country" ultimately helped to produce the English Revolution.[9]

In France, the Netherlands, and Spain there were parallel movements on a smaller scale. Thus in France during the years 1648–1653 there occurred a series of abortive revolts, known as the Fronde, against the king and his chief councilor, Cardinal Mazarin, conducted largely by various groups of the French landed aristocracy. The example of the contemporary revolution of the English landed gentry was invoked by both sides.[10] In 1640 the Catalonian aristocracy led a revolt against the rule of the Spanish king, Philip II, and in the same year the aristocracy of Portugal led a similar revolt which established the independence of their country.[11] While each of these various revolts had its own character, and only one, the Portuguese, was successful, they all represented *in part* a class conflict between a landed aristocracy and an absolute monarchy bent on conducting wars whose costs were beyond its means. In Germany, however, the incipient class conflict between landholders and *Obrigkeit* was overshadowed by religious and political hostilities among the German principalities.

To speak of the large-scale social-economic dimensions of the general European crisis of the seventeenth century leads to the question of narrower economic causes. A distinguished English Marxist historian has described the crisis of the first half of the seventeenth century as the last phase of the general transition from a feudal to a capitalist economy, whose symptoms included declining populations, declining volume of trade, and contraction of overseas expansion.[12] But such declines did not occur everywhere in Europe, and England for the most part avoided serious economic difficulties.[13] A closer examination of these factors in the context of the English Revolution is postponed until a later chapter. Suffice it to say at this point that none of them is sufficiently significant to account for the magnitude of the crisis and of the political and religious changes that eventually took place. The growth in importance of non-feudal and non-clerical landholding classes, however, and the resistance of those classes to the financial pressures of the monarchy, must, indeed, be viewed—when taken together with religious and political factors—as a major dimension of the general crisis.

That the English Revolution was a response to a European crisis, and not only an English crisis, and that it had European repercussions, is evidenced by the way in which it was understood both in England and elsewhere at the time. "These are days of shaking," said Jeremiah Whittaker in the House of Commons in 1643, "and this shaking is universal: the Palatinate, Bohemia, Germania, Catalonia, Portugal, Ireland, England."[14] The Italian Count Birago Avogadro published in 1653 a book, based on newspaper reports, dealing with the "political revolts" of the previous decade in Catalonia, Portugal, Sicily, England, France, Naples, and Brazil.[15] In 1651 the English Admiral Robert Blake, representing the Cromwell government in Spain, was reported to have stated in the public square in Cádiz that with the example afforded by London, all kingdoms would annihilate tyranny and become republics. England had done so already; France was following in its wake; and as the natural gravity of the Spaniards rendered them somewhat slower in the operations, he gave them ten years for the revolution in their country.[16]

The Periodization of the English Revolution and Its Revolutionary Character

Conventional English historiography does not recognize the events that took place in England between 1640 and 1689 as a Revolution in the large sense of that word. The official English Table of Regnal Years, by which English statutes are dated, records the reign of Charles II from January 30, 1649, when his father was executed; omitted entirely is the "Interregnum" of 1649 to 1660, when first Oliver Cromwell and then briefly his son Richard Cromwell reigned as Lord Protectors, while the heir to the executed king resided on the continent. Although the period from 1640 to 1660 eventually came to be called the Puritan Revolution by many English historians, others continue to deny its revolutionary character and some even insist on calling it (as its enemies called it at the time) "the Great Rebellion."[17]

The period from 1660 to 1688 is universally known as the Restoration, since that is what it was called at the time, and since it marked the return of Charles II to England and thus was, indeed, a restoration of the Stuart monarchy. If, however, as some imagine, it was also a return to the status quo ante 1640, then the Puritan Revolution of 1640 to 1660 must have been an aberration.

As a prominent English historian once remarked, in attacking a book titled *The Causes of the English Revolution,* "We need to remember that no revolution of the size claimed for this one ever so readily stopped short and reversed itself."[18] But if, on the contrary, it is acknowledged that in the period after 1640 England did experience a genuine Revolution—in the sense that the French and Russian Revolutions were Revolutions, and in the sense that the German Reformation of the sixteenth century and the Papal Reformation of the eleventh century were Revolutions, with a capital *R*—then the Stuart Restoration must be viewed partly, to be sure, as a step backward but chiefly as a step forward, a new stage of the Revolution and not a reversal of it. In fact, the government of Charles II carried forward some of the reforms of the preceding period and initiated new ones.

Traditionally, when the English have spoken of "the Revolution," they have usually referred to the events of 1688–89, when Parliament created a new royal dynasty under its own control and formally laid down the conditions of its reign. Although this involved the invasion of England by Prince William of Orange, with fifteen thousand troops, it was marked by relatively little bloodshed and was called at the time "the Glorious Revolution."[19] It can only properly be understood, however, as the dénouement, the final settling down, of the Revolution that commenced in 1640.

Like the German Revolution before it, the English Revolution took two generations to establish itself. Its first, radical phase was succeeded by a second, conservative phase, which in turn was followed by a third phase in which a compromise was effectuated between the first two phases. Eventually the grandchildren of those who fought on opposite sides made peace with each other and the Revolution was accepted as an integral part of a larger ongoing history.

All three stages of the English Revolution—the Puritan stage, the later Stuart stage, and the establishment by Parliament of a new dynasty—were conceived at the time as restorations. The Puritan Revolution was conceived to be a restoration of the ancient liberties of Englishmen as laid down in Magna Carta and other medieval statutes and judicial decisions prior to the usurpation of supreme power over church and state by the Tudor-Stuart monarchy more than a century earlier. The Commonwealth's Great Seal of 1649 was inscribed "The First Year of Freedome Restored."[20] The Stuart Restoration was not only a restoration of the monarchy but also a restoration of revolutionary parliamentary legislation of the 1640s, much of which the Cromwell dictatorship of the 1650s had ignored. The term "Revolution" in the name "Glorious Revolution" signified a revolving of the wheel of history back to the time before James II challenged parliamentary rule and threatened to reestablish Roman Catholicism.[21] Throughout the revolutionary period from 1640 to 1689, England was conceived to be moving into the future with its eyes on the past.

The conservatism, in that sense, of the English Revolution is reminiscent of the conservatism of other Revolutions. In the sixteenth century, Lutheran pastors and princes sought to restore the authority of the Bible and go back beyond papal and imperial power to early Christianity. In the eleventh and twelfth centuries, Pope Gregory VII and the papal party invoked the authority of bishops and church councils prior to the rise of the Carolingian Empire to justify their struggle for "the freedom of the church." The myth of a return to an earlier golden age—of nature, of classless primitive tribes—was also part of the ideology of the French and Russian Revolutions, respectively.

Yet the conservatism of the English Revolution—or, more precisely, of its ideology—goes beyond the myth of a return. It includes also the myth of an unbroken continuity. English historiography has preserved this ideology even to the most recent times. It is especially pronounced in the historiography of English law. The strong tendency toward insularity in the treatment of the English Revolution by many English historians is coupled with an equally strong tendency toward incrementalism. Both these tendencies have roots, to be sure, in earlier English history, but they were not part of the prevailing mind-set of pre-Revolution early Stuart and Elizabethan England.

Before 1640 the form of government in England was that of an absolute monarchy, in which the king ruled in his council and, intermittently when he summoned it, in his parliament. (King Charles I summoned it in 1640 only after eleven years of personal rule without it!) After 1689, the form of government was that of a constitutional monarchy in which Parliament met continuously and was supreme, although the king and his council, with the consent of Parliament, retained substantial power, especially with regard to foreign affairs and overseas colonies. Before 1640, the only church that was recognized as legitimate in England was the Church of England, of which the king, both in law and in practice, was the supreme governor. After 1689, Parliament was the de facto head of the Church of England, and various dissenting Protestant churches were recognized as legitimate, although their members remained under political disabilities. In Parliament, a party system—Whigs and Tories—emerged in the 1660s for the first time. For the first time, too, the House of Commons had greater power than the House of Lords. The landed gentry replaced the titled nobility, "the peerage," as the most important segment of the English ruling class.

There was also a fundamental and lasting transformation of English law during this period. Before 1640, judges served at the will of the monarch; in the period after 1689, they were given independence of the Crown and life tenure. Most of the powerful prerogative courts established by the Tudor monarchs, of which Star Chamber became the most notorious in the early seventeenth century, were abolished and the so-called common law courts were made supreme over all others. The common law itself became the constitutional law of England. Jury trial in criminal and civil cases was transformed; the jury became independent of the judge, and witness proof and rules of evidence were introduced. The English law of property, contract, and tort was modernized. The English doctrine of precedent—the hallmark of the modern English common law—was given its modern meaning.

Thus we may say that the English Revolution of 1640–1689 meets the criteria of the other Great Revolutions of Western history.[22] It marked a fundamental change, a rapid change, a violent change, and a lasting change in the English social system as a whole. It took more than one generation to establish roots. It eventually produced a new system of law which embodied some of the major purposes of the Revolution. It remains to be shown in subsequent sections of this chapter and in subsequent chapters that it meets another criterion of a Great European Revolution as well: the new system of law which it produced both changed the Western legal tradition and ultimately remained within that tradition.

The Background of the English Revolution in the First English Reformation

The Protestant Reformation of the sixteenth century, which came to fruition in the German Revolution, took different forms in different European countries. In general it exalted the office of the monarch, but in Germany it was also associated with the existence of a Protestant League, extending beyond the territorial confines of any one of the various German principalities and opposing the emperor while remaining within the empire. Moreover, the Reformation in Germany was strongly associated with the Lutheran revolt against a visible, hierarchical church based on canon law. The sixteenth-century English Reformation, by contrast, was at first primarily a political movement whose object was the replacement of papal authority in England by that of the monarch. As initiated by King Henry VIII (r. 1509–1547), it involved the Anglicization of Catholicism, with retention of many of the basic features of traditional Roman Catholic theology and liturgy. Only under Henry's Protestant son, Edward VI (r. 1547–1553), and—after a Catholic restoration—his Protestant daughter, Elizabeth (r. 1558–1603), did English monarchs permit some Lutheran and Calvinist doctrines to penetrate Anglican theology.

The assertion of absolute authority over the Church of England by Henry VIII and his successors did constitute, however, as the eminent English historian G. R. Elton has argued, a "genuine revolution."[23] One could indeed speak, in that sense, of the English Revolution of the *sixteenth* century. One would want to include as an integral part of that Revolution, as Elton does, the transformation of the kingship itself, of the king's council, of Parliament, and of the judiciary. These are matters now to be discussed, however, as part of the background of the English Revolution of the *seventeenth* century. It should be clear, then, that England experienced two "Great Revolutions," one in the sixteenth and one in the seventeenth century. The sixteenth-century English reformation of the Roman Catholic Church was, from a European point of view, part of the first Protestant Reformation, which began with Luther's declaration of war against the papacy and which spread from Germany to many countries of Europe, each responding in its own way. The sixteenth-century English exaltation of the authority of the monarch was also a European phenomenon that was connected everywhere with the decline of papal power. Yet it is appropriate to refer to the European Revolution of the sixteenth century, which broke out first and in full force in Germany, as the German Revolution, and the European Revolution of the seventeenth century, which broke out first and in full force in England, as the English Revolution. France also experienced repercussions of the European Revolutions of the sixteenth and seventeenth centuries, yet the name "French Revolution" is reserved for its experience in 1789 and thereafter, when it was the first nation to respond violently to the European crisis of the eighteenth century.

At its outset, the sixteenth-century Henrician Reformation was linked with the German Revolution and with Protestantism chiefly by its monarchical and anti-Roman character. It was not, at the outset, primarily a product of Henry's theological convictions. In 1535 he had Sir Thomas More and Bishop John Fisher, two great men, beheaded for treason—a political, not a theological, crime—because they recognized in the canon law of the Church of Rome an authority over the Church of England higher than that of the English king. Indeed, in 1533 Henry had told his Archbishop Thomas Cranmer, who himself was a committed Protestant, that he, Henry, recognized "no superior on earth but only God," and that he was not "subject to the laws of any earthly creature."[24] In this spirit Henry dissolved the Roman Catholic monasteries and confiscated their property to his own use—including approximately one-fourth of the landed wealth of England. Although he used his parliament to accomplish these objectives, his actions—as even Elton, his chief modern defender, has stated—were "essentially personal" and not "essentially parliamentary."[25]

Henry's violent anti-Roman policy was accompanied at various times by a violent anti-Protestant policy. In 1531, 1533, and again in 1540, he had leading English Lutherans burned at the stake as heretics.[26] Nevertheless, Lutheran theology did make inroads into English thought in this period, and this was tolerated and perhaps even encouraged by Henry for short times, when he hoped for a justification of his first divorce by the theological faculty of Wittenberg University and when he sought alliances with German Protestant princes. In 1535 the Coverdale Bible, the first English translation of both the Old and the New Testaments, was published in England; it owed much to Luther's German translation. In 1538 Archbishop Cranmer and other English theologians met with German Lutheran theologians in an effort to develop a common religious doctrine. Eventually, however, the king put a stop to these contacts, and in 1539 he promulgated—and enforced by burnings and hangings—a new declaration of faith, the so-called Six Articles, which reaffirmed basic Catholic (now Anglo-Catholic) teachings.[27]

Under Edward VI, however, and later under Elizabeth, the English Reformation came increasingly under Protestant influences from Germany. Restrictions on printing, reading, and teaching the English Bible were removed. Priests were permitted to marry. The first Book of Common Prayer, published under Edward VI in 1549 and revised in 1552, whose chief author was Cranmer, owed a great deal to Lutheran influences, as did the forty-two Articles of Faith endorsed by Edward VI shortly before his death.

Since Henry's daughter Mary, who succeeded Edward, was a Roman Catholic, therefore, under the doctrine of royal supremacy, England was returned to the Church of Rome. A new reign of terror was instituted. As a leading historian of the English Reformation, A. G. Dickens, has put it, "the population of the prisons rapidly changed."[28] During the five years of Mary's rule, some 290 persons were burned as heretics, most notably Cranmer, and at least forty Protestants died in prison. More than eight hundred Marian exiles, as they were called, fled to Protestant centers abroad.

The accession of the twenty-five-year-old Elizabeth brought a complete reversal of her older sister's religious policies and a return to those of her brother, Edward. At the same time, Elizabeth's main concern was to accomplish this with a minimum of violence. She immediately summoned a parliament, which in 1559 passed a new Act of Supremacy, naming her "Supreme Governor" of the Church of England, as well as an Act of Uniformity, requiring every person to attend church on Sundays under penalty of fines and imposing on clergy and laity alike a uniform ritual, namely, Edward VI's second Book of Common Prayer (1552). The genius of that book lay partly in what has been called its "studied ambiguity." Thus Anglicanism became hospitable, on the one hand, to moderate Protestants, though not to radical Puritans, and, on the other hand, to Anglo-Catholics, though not to Roman Catholics.

In the 1570s and 1580s the threat of an invasion from Roman Catholic Spain, combined with hostile actions by the papacy, contributed to an intensification of animosities. A papal bull of 1570 excommunicated the queen and urged her subjects to depose her. This was met by a statute of 1571 imposing a fine and imprisonment on any person who said or sang the Roman Catholic Mass or who failed to attend the Church of England on Sundays. A royal proclamation of 1582, followed by a statute of 1585, declared that Jesuits and seminary priests found within Her Majesty's dominions were to be considered traitors and were to be punished by death.[29]

The Puritan challenge to the Elizabethan Settlement in the last decades of the sixteenth century came chiefly from within the kingdom rather than from outside—although it, too, had strong foreign connections. It should be stressed, however, that not all persons who at the time were called Puritans, and certainly not all who later came to be called Puritans, opposed the Elizabethan Settlement. The more serious challenge came from those English Calvinists who, in the late sixteenth century, not only sought to "purify" the Church of England (hence the derogatory name "Puritan") but also carried that desire to the point of practicing and preaching both nonconformity to the Anglican liturgy and a radical reconstruction of the system of church government. Such persons were called at the time Nonconformists. They included those Presbyterians who denied the authority of Anglican bishops and advocated that control of the church should be in the hands of local presbyteries, each consisting of a minister and elders elected by the local congregation. They also included a variety of sects called Separatists or Independents or Congregationalists, who rejected all external authority and denied the legitimacy of a national church.

The Tudor System of Government

In England, as elsewhere in Europe, a strengthening of the monarchy had preceded its break with—or, as in countries that remained Roman Catholic, its assertion of control over—the Roman Church. To a limited extent under Henry VII, and much more dramatically under Henry VIII, the king ceased to draw his retinue and his support chiefly from the clerical and feudal nobility, his vassals and tenants. Instead, like the German princes, he developed an inner circle of councilors, appointed by him primarily on the basis of their loyalty and their merit rather than on the basis of their lineage. In 1536, a so-called Privy Council, consisting of full-time professional civil servants, was created out of the older, oversized King's Council, which had met only periodically. Thomas Cromwell was himself a prototype of the new bureaucrat, being the lawyer son of a clothworker and alehouse keeper who had risen in Cardinal Wolsey's household and had subsequently entered the royal service. The Privy Council, numbering about twenty, consisted chiefly of officers in the royal household (the comptroller, the lord chamberlain, the treasurer of the household, and others) and the "great officers" of state (the archbishop of Canterbury, the lord chancellor, the lord treasurer, the lord admiral, and others). The various officers of the Privy Council had their own professional staffs, which operated for the most part independently of the king's personal household. Thus the earlier system of government by the royal household, which had functioned for centuries, was transformed into a rudimentary cabinet system operating through various departments of state. This was the English counterpart of the sixteenth-century German *Obrigkeit.*

The transformation of the council was accompanied by a transformation of the role and functions of the parliaments. Parliaments in the past had occasionally dispensed royal justice in important cases. They also had occasionally enacted statutes. Their most important functions, however, had been to vote taxes to support the Crown (especially at the accession of a new monarch) and to petition the Crown for redress of grievances. Each parliament was a separate entity, summoned and dissolved at the will of the monarch. Each consisted of a House of Lords, drawn from clergy (bishops and abbots) and hereditary lay peers, and a House of Commons, with two members from each shire (county) and borough (city).

The transitory nature of parliaments, and their dependence on the monarch, did not alter substantially in the sixteenth century. In general, the Crown called parliaments only every two or three years and dismissed them after two or three months.[30] Elizabeth called only ten parliaments during her forty-five-year reign, and they met for a total of less than 140 weeks—an average of one parliament in session for fourteen weeks every four and one-half years! Yet although the Crown dominated parliaments in the sixteenth century, it had greater need of their support as an instrument of national will in order to make more acceptable to the nation as a whole the measures being taken to implement greatly increased monarchical power and monarchical initiatives. With the decline in power of the great feudal dynasties, reflected in the transformation of the King's Council into a professional civil service, and with the nationalization of the church, a political unification of England was taking shape. The monarchy was freed from many of the restraints placed on it by competing forces at the top, but by the same token it was less protected against recalcitrance on the part of those who were below the top.

Tudor parliaments continued to act as a court in some types of cases, and they were sometimes referred to as "the High Court of Parliament." They also continued to grant money and to petition for redress of grievances. Yet most of their activity came to consist in the enacting of laws. They differed, however, in several important respects from the kind of legislature that emerged in the seventeenth century. In the first place, the Tudor monarch was "the head" of each parliament. Parliaments in the sixteenth century were not considered to be bodies that opposed or limited the executive authority of the Crown. Instead, the king was said to rule "in his council in his parliament." In the second place, parliaments were not the sole legislative bodies. The king alone, or the king in council without Parliament, could and did enact laws. Such laws were called proclamations, not statutes, but they were nonetheless laws and were enforced by the courts, as well as by other crown officers, through criminal and civil sanctions. In the roughly 500 months, out of 540, of Elizabeth's reign in which a parliament was not sitting, the queen in council issued many hundreds of such laws. Theoretically, only Parliament could change a statute, but no Tudor parliament and no Tudor court ever defied a royal proclamation.[31]

In addition to transforming the King's Council and the parliament into effective instruments of royal policy, the Tudor monarchs transformed the judiciary by the creation of a series of new courts which would be, on the one hand, more efficient in meeting the new political and economic problems that were confronting England and, on the other hand, more directly responsive to the royal will than the traditional common law courts. These courts were thrown off from the Privy Council, which itself frequently acted as a court. They included the Court of Star Chamber, the Court of Requests, the Courts of the Marches, and the Court of High Commission. Also a new High Court of Admiralty was created. In addition, the chancellor's court was renamed the High Court of Chancery and its jurisdiction was greatly expanded.[32] The new "high" courts—"prerogative courts," as all except Admiralty and Chancery were called—were Romanist in character; that is, they operated to some extent, though by no means entirely, according to doctrines and procedures derived in part from the earlier canon law of the Roman Catholic Church and in part from the secular Romanist law which had been studied for some centuries in the universities of Europe, including Oxford and Cambridge, and which underwent a new systematization throughout Europe in the sixteenth century.

Tensions and Portents of Change

The accession in 1603 of James Stuart, king of Scotland, to the English throne did not mark a fundamental change in the character of the English system of government. There were, however, during his reign and that of his son Charles I, substantial changes in the political, economic, and social conditions on which that system rested. Parallel tensions between Puritans and Anglicans and between country and court gradually increased. In addition, from the beginning of the reign of James I, certain features of royal rule were challenged both by the House of Commons and by the judges of the common law courts. James was thereby provoked to expound systematically—and eventually to publish in book form—a theory of absolute monarchy which his predecessors had wisely left largely implicit and ambiguous. Some historians have warned against exaggerating these tensions and conflicts, especially in the period prior to 1629;[33] and no doubt the civil war in which they culminated in 1642 could have been avoided and a compromise reached if both sides had been more reasonable. Moreover, prior to the final break between Parliament and Crown, the opponents of absolute monarchy—with few exceptions—by no means considered themselves disloyal to the king; they were only urging him to accept what they claimed were traditional constitutional limitations on his power.

Throughout the period of the early Stuarts, the major conflicts between the Crown and its parliaments concerned taxation. Elizabeth had left the new king with a sizable debt of £400,000. By 1606, that debt had increased to £700,000. Relying on the royal prerogative to regulate foreign trade, James imposed extra duties on imports and exports—called "impositions"—beyond the usual customs duties ("tunnage and poundage") granted by the first parliament for the king's lifetime.[34] In the 1610 session of the parliament, James instructed the members that they were not to discuss his right to levy impositions. The Commons then drafted a petition asserting its right "to debate freely all matters which do properly concern the subject."[35] A compromise was reached, but before it could be enacted, James dissolved the parliament. Convoked again in 1614, the House of Commons framed a bill declaring impositions to be illegal and refused to vote revenues generated from direct taxation ("supply") until the king would address this and other grievances. Again James responded by dismissing the parliament and later sent several members to the Tower for licentious speeches made during the session.

During this period, exercise of the royal prerogative received challenges from another quarter, namely, the judges of the courts of Common Pleas and King's Bench. These two courts, together with the Court of Exchequer, were the first professional royal courts to have been created out of the King's Council in the twelfth century. In later centuries they came to be known as "courts of common law"—as distinguished from ecclesiastical courts, manorial courts, feudal courts, urban courts, and mercantile courts, and as distinguished also from the extraordinary "equity" jurisdiction of the chancellor as it developed in the fourteenth and fifteenth centuries. In the sixteenth century the common law judges, faced with the allocation of a substantial portion of the nation's legal business to the new prerogative courts and to the remodeled courts of Chancery and Admiralty, had found ways to adapt their traditional procedures and doctrines to new circumstances and occasionally to defend their jurisdiction against encroachments by other royal courts. Moreover, the sixteenth-century rivalry of the common law courts and the prerogative courts had been contained by rather clear lines of demarcation of their jurisdictional boundaries and by the willingness of the common law courts ultimately to accept the royal policy favoring the supremacy of the prerogative courts in those cases in which there was an apparent conflict of jurisdictions.

Under James I, however, the jurisdictional rivalries of the sixteenth century were transformed into a bitter battle of courts, in which the twelve judges of Common Pleas and King's Bench, under the leadership of Sir Edward Coke, sought to control the jurisdiction of the prerogative courts, one after another, as well as the High Court of Admiralty and the High Court of Chancery. In a series of cases decided between 1606 and 1616, Coke, as chief justice first of Common Pleas and then of King's Bench, proclaimed the supremacy of the common law conceived as an ancient English tradition. He ultimately challenged the authority of the king himself to limit the competence of the common law courts to determine their own competence. In 1616, after a dramatic personal confrontation, James dismissed Coke. Coke's assertion of the independence of the common law courts and of their supremacy over the prerogative courts helped to define one of the main issues which were ultimately fought out in Parliament and on the battlefields of the Civil War: the issue of royal absolutism. Indeed, in the 1640s the Puritan radical John Lilburne would go into the House of Commons with the Bible in one hand and Coke's *Reports* in the other.

Coke himself eventually regained the favor of the king and was elected to the parliament of 1621, where he became chairman of the Committee of Grievances in the House of Commons and led the Commons in an incipient movement to assert its independence.

With the accession of Charles I in 1625, the tensions between Parliament and Crown became even more aggravated. Parliament refused to grant the usual lifetime taxes allowed to a new monarch, and Charles resorted to forced loans, imprisoning those who refused to give them.[36] The 1628 parliament began its deliberations with criticism of the monarch's infringements of "the Subject's Liberty in his Person" through forced loans and the accompanying sanctions. The House of Commons unanimously adopted a resolution condemning imprisonment without lawful cause, denial of the writ of habeas corpus, refusal of release on bail, taxation not authorized by Parliament, billeting of soldiers in private houses, summary trials under martial law, and other measures which the king and the Privy Council had taken to compel subscription to the forced loans. These grievances were then embodied in a Petition of Right, drawn up by Coke, which asked the king to declare that henceforth neither he nor his officers would infringe the rights and liberties specified in it. After much hesitation, Charles eventually confirmed the petition—in the legal form required by the Commons—but insisted that he had in no way yielded any of his prerogative powers. The courts, in turn, read the 1628 Petition of Right as applicable only to the specific matters expressly contained in it and not declaratory of any new constitutional principle.[37]

Between 1629 and 1640 Charles did not call another parliament. This was a longer interval between parliaments than had occurred even under Henry VIII or Elizabeth. Charles's personal rule was also distinguished from that of his predecessors both by the unprecedented measures which he took to raise money from a generally reluctant population[38] and by his enforcement of a religious policy that not only alienated the growing number of Puritans within the Church of England but also met with the disfavor of many orthodox Anglicans. This period was later known as the "Eleven Years' Tyranny."

Charles's taxes were probably less offensive to the population as a whole, or even to the upper classes which had to pay them, than his religious policy. Under William Laud, whom Charles in 1633 named to be archbishop of Canterbury, the Anglican Church introduced certain new theological doctrines and liturgical practices that were not only opposed to English Puritanism but were also identified with features of Roman Catholic theology and liturgy that had been repudiated by Anglicanism. Even more odious than these doctrines and practices was the systematic repression of those who publicly opposed them. Visitations of the clergy were conducted throughout the kingdom. Clergy and laity who remained obstinate were disciplined by the Court of High Commission. Some were subjected to severe penalties by the Court of Star Chamber.[39] In order to escape these oppressions, some twenty thousand English subjects emigrated to the Massachusetts Bay Colony between 1630 and 1640, and an equal or greater number emigrated to the Netherlands. As some Anglican churchmen put it at the time, men "flew out of England as out of Babylon."

The Long Parliament, the Civil War, and the Commonwealth

The combined effect of domestic and foreign crises finally exposed the bankruptcy of Charles's policies. In 1637 he sought to impose an Anglican-style prayerbook upon his subjects in Scotland, large numbers of whom adhered to the Calvinist Presbyterian theology and ecclesiology that had first been introduced into Scotland by John Knox in the sixteenth century. In 1638 the General Assembly of the Church of Scotland voted not only to reject Charles's prayerbook but also to abolish the Scottish episcopacy entirely. Charles responded by sending armies into Scotland, first in 1639 and again in 1640, but both times they were defeated. To raise money to carry on the war he called a new parliament in November 1640. It was this parliament—"the Long Parliament"—of which Winston Churchill wrote, more than three centuries later, that it was "the most memorable Parliament that ever sat in England."[40] It was not formally dissolved until 1659.

The Long Parliament drew lessons from the earlier failure of the Petition of Right. First, it insisted on the release and compensation of persons who had been imprisoned by the Star Chamber and the High Commission. Second, it impeached and sent to the Tower—ultimately to be executed—the two chief architects of the Eleven Years' Tyranny, the earl of Strafford and Archbishop Laud, as well as other lesser figures associated with royal arbitrariness.[41] Third, it enacted a series of statutes establishing its own independence and reducing the royal prerogative. The most important of these statutes, all enacted in 1641, were:

1. The Triennial Act, providing that not more than three years should elapse without a parliament being summoned and that neither house could be adjourned without its own consent until it had sat for at least fifty days; and another act providing that the Long Parliament itself could never be dissolved without its own consent. Henceforth Parliament—now with a capital *P*—was to be a permanent institution of government and not an ad hoc assembly summoned and dismissed at the king's pleasure.

2. Four acts prohibiting the imposition of unprecedented taxes, limiting

tunnage and poundage grants to two months (instead of for the life of the monarch), restoring the boundaries of the royal forests to their earlier limits, and preventing "vexatious proceedings touching the Order of Knighthood." Subsequently the surviving feudal incidents were also abolished. Henceforth Parliament was to have exclusive control of taxation.

3. Two acts abolishing the Star Chamber, High Commission, and other prerogative courts,[42] and depriving the Privy Council of its power to hear civil and criminal cases. These statutes also established the right of release on habeas corpus to determine the justice and legality of the commitment of persons on command of the king or the Privy Council. Henceforth the common law courts were to be supreme in criminal and civil cases.

Parliament's measures to reduce royal power were closely associated with its opposition to the religious policies of the Crown. In the spring of 1641 a bill was introduced in the Commons calling for abolition of the episcopacy "with all its dependencies, roots and branches." The bill commanded substantial support, though it failed to pass. In November 1641, however, provoked by a large-scale Roman Catholic rebellion in Ireland and fears of a "popish plot," both houses—Commons and Lords—very narrowly passed a bill, called the Grand Remonstrance, which, although it did not endorse the Root and Branch Bill, indicted the Crown for its alleged sympathy with Roman Catholicism, called for reduction of the power of bishops in the Church of England and their exclusion from the House of Lords, and demanded that the appointment of the king's ministers be subject to parliamentary confirmation.[43] Even this indictment, however, did not attack the legitimacy of royal authority but only required that it be exercised in partnership with the Parliament. Thus a compromise might conceivably have been reached had not the king overreacted. He sent the serjeant-at-arms to arrest five leading members of the House of Commons on the ground that they had conspired with the Scots to support the establishment of Presbyterianism in Scotland. When the House refused to give up the five members, Charles went in person, backed by four hundred armed men, to take them—but they had fled.[44] That was on January 2, 1641/42.[45] During the next months the Parliament and the king were in open hostility. By August, Parliament had raised its own army, and a civil war broke out which raged from 1642 to 1646 and again in 1648.

During this first, violent stage of the English Revolution, great divisions arose within the ranks of the revolutionaries. Parliament in 1645 adopted Presbyterianism as the national religion; in the same year, however, a more radical Puritan body, whose leaders were not Presbyterians but Independents, took over leadership of the parliamentary army, calling it the New Model Army. The Independents opposed Presbyterian councils of elders (presbyteries), synods, and a General Assembly, and favored complete congregational autonomy. A still more radical party within the New Model Army, called Levellers, issued an Agreement of the People, setting forth a proposed democratic constitution for the country, with substantial legal and economic reforms, including abolition of monopolies, reform of the poor laws, reduction of taxes, religious toleration, and a wider franchise. During October and November 1648 a series of meetings was held by an elected General Council of the Army at Putney, known as the Putney Debates, in which the Agreement of the People and other programs were debated seriously and at length.[46] These debates ended with a Leveller-inspired mutiny among certain army regiments.

In January 1649, Parliament, having been purged of its more moderate members, appointed a special High Court of Justice, consisting of some 135 commissioners, which tried "Charles Stuart, King of England," for high treason. Fifty-nine of the commissioners, including Oliver Cromwell, now commander of the parliamentary armed forces, signed the death warrant, and on January 30, 1649, Charles was beheaded—the first trial and execution of a monarch in the history of Europe.[47] Thereafter the Rump Parliament abolished the monarchy and the House of Lords and declared England to be a Commonwealth.[48] Thus ended the first violent phase of the English Revolution.

The Commonwealth was at first governed—wholly ineffectively—by a Council of State, thirty-one of whose forty members were also members of Parliament. In 1653 Cromwell, having returned after four years from successful campaigns in Ireland and Scotland, led a company of soldiers to Westminster and dissolved the parliament by force. Its passing, he noted, occasioned not so much as the barking of a dog. A new parliament of 140 members, "nominated" by the army's Council of Officers under Cromwell, was called "the Parliament of Saints," or "Barebone's Parliament," after one of its members, a London lay Baptist preacher named Praise-God Barebone. Now radical legal and religious reforms were proposed, including the substitution of Mosaic law for secular law, the abolition of tithes to maintain the clergy, and the legalization of civil marriages, as well as the abolition of Chancery, reduction of pay for army officers, and purges of local governments. Finally, in December 1653, a large number of its more moderate members voted to give its powers to Cromwell, who took the title "Lord Protector of the Commonwealth of England, Scotland, and Ireland" under England's first and only written constitution, called "the Instrument of Government," which was drafted by one of his generals and which he himself promulgated. This document named "Oliver Cromwell, Captain General" to be Lord Protector and provided that he should be assisted by a Council of not more than twenty-one or fewer than thirteen members—to be appointed, apparently, by himself—and that upon his death, his successor was to be elected by the Council. It also provided that the supreme legislative authority of the Commonwealth was to reside in the Lord Protector "and the people assembled in parliament," and that "the laws shall not be altered . . . nor any new law made . . . but by common consent in parliament," and that a parliament was to be summoned at least once every three years and was to meet for at least five months. In fact, the Instrument of Government only barely survived the election in 1654 of the first parliament under it, and it was soon abandoned. Until his death in 1658, Cromwell ruled as virtual dictator, with the aid of the army and various juntas of the House of Commons.

Barebone's Parliament was too radical for Cromwell's purposes and he soon dissolved it. His next parliaments, however, were too weak and indecisive for his purposes, and he dissolved them as well. Thus one of the two major conflicts that had given rise to the Civil War, that is, the conflict between Parliament and Crown, was now transformed into an unresolved conflict between Parliament and the Lord Protector. Moreover, the conflict left both sides paralyzed. Between 1653 and 1660 no significant laws were enacted and no significant changes were made in the system of government.

Likewise, Cromwell's religious policy was unsuccessful. He had envisioned local ecclesiastical self-government and toleration for "tender consciences" that sought to form independent congregational churches. Yet disestablishment of religion would have left most of the clergy, now largely Presbyterian, without their property and without their livings. Torn between religious freedom on the one hand and security of property on the other,[49] Cromwell resisted the efforts of Independents to abolish government taxes to support the clergy. Thus the second major conflict that had given rise to the Civil War, that is, the conflict between Puritanism and Anglicanism, was now transformed into an unresolved conflict between congregational liberty of conscience and a national church.

A less visible but more fundamental source of weakness than either of these conflicts was the lack of legitimacy of Cromwell's rule. Neither Barebone's Parliament nor the succeeding parliaments were legal, since the Long Parliament, elected in 1640, had never been formally dissolved; Cromwell and his councilors simply selected new members. Moreover, the 1653 Instrument of Government, which named him Lord Protector, was never approved by a parliament, and in fact some of its provisions were disregarded from the start. Thus the execution of Charles I and the absence of a hereditary monarchy left a hiatus in the legitimate succession to sovereignty that could not be filled. Parliament in 1657 offered Cromwell the kingship, but he declined it, although he continued to sit on a throne and to be addressed as "Your Highness."

The bankruptcy of the Protectorate became apparent after Cromwell's death in September 1658. His son Richard, named to succeed him as Lord Protector, soon resigned. Under pressure from the army, the rump session of the Long Parliament returned in May 1659 to vote its own final dissolution and to order a new election. In April 1660 a so-called Convention Parliament (there was no king to summon it) was elected, which invited Charles II to return from Holland to take the throne.

Oliver Cromwell and His Legacy

A collateral descendant of Henry VIII's famous counselor Thomas Cromwell, Oliver Cromwell was born in 1599 of gentry parents. His father had served as a member of Parliament and Oliver, in turn, was elected to Parliament in 1628 and again in 1640. During the early years of the Long Parliament he gave numerous speeches and served on various committees, but it was as a leader of parliamentary military forces during the Civil War that he came to great prominence—first as head of a troop of cavalry from his native Huntingdonshire, later as second-in-command of the so-called Eastern Association, still later as head of the New Model Army. He returned to the House of Commons after the first phase of the Civil War, but resumed his generalship in the second phase of 1648. After crushing royalist and Scottish forces, he returned to London and served as one of the commissioners for the king's trial. Thereafter he assumed command of a force to put down a rebellion in Ireland, which he accomplished with great ruthlessness, and in 1650 he took charge of the invasion of Scotland.

Cromwell was not a doctrinaire republican. He spoke against the democratic demands of the Levellers at the Putney Debates and turned against further negotiations with Charles I in 1648 only after the king had rejected all proposals for a constitutional monarchy. He was, however, deeply committed both to biblical faith, in the Calvinist sense, and to liberty of conscience. In the early 1630s he seriously contemplated sailing to New England in order to escape the Laudian anti-Puritan reforms of the Anglican Church.[50] In 1641, as a member of the Long Parliament, he supported the Root and Branch Bill, which would have abolished the episcopacy. At the same time, he was equally opposed to an oppressive Presbyterianism. In 1644 he persuaded the House of Commons to pass a motion calling on the Westminster Assembly, a commission of laymen and clerics established to draft a new form of church government, "to endeavour the finding out some ways how far tender consciences, who cannot in all things submit to the common rule which shall be established, may be borne with, according to the Word, and as may stand with the public peace."[51]

Cromwell's five-year reign as Lord Protector was, by its own standards, a failure. It is a mistake, nevertheless, to suppose that it left no lasting institutional or personal legacy. Institutionally, the Protectorate was the first experience in the entire history of Europe of a national government without a king. Moreover, this experience was embodied in a written constitution, the Instrument of Government, which purported to separate the executive and legislative branches. Other legislation provided for a judiciary independent of both. Parliaments were to be summoned regularly and no laws altered or made without their consent. Because, however, all three branches were to be subordinate to the Lord Protector, the system failed. A similar system was adopted by the later Stuart monarchs—under whom it also ultimately failed. Yet it bore within itself the seeds of a future English parliamentary supremacy and eventually of a future French separation of powers.

The failed religious policies of the Protectorate also left an indirect positive legacy. The concept of an England without a national church, a nation whose religious life was to be left in the care of local Christian congregations, though ultimately rejected on the national level, became acceptable as an alternative on the local level. The choice that had been posed in the 1640s between two different versions of a Church of England, the Anglican and the Presbyterian, could no longer be made at the price of eliminating the nascent congregationalism of the Independent and the Separatist churches. Toleration of dissenting churches became a part of the unwritten English Constitution and, eventually, of the unwritten creed of the Anglican Church itself. Indeed, Cromwell's success in mitigating the punishments meted out to the leading Quakers George Fox and James Naylor, condemned by the House of Commons as "blasphemers," indicates that a policy of broad toleration of Protestant denominations was fundamental to the government of the Protectorate. Jews also were tolerated.[52] Only Roman Catholics continued to be severely discriminated against and, in Ireland, ruthlessly persecuted. Indeed, in 1655, almost three and one-half centuries after King Edward I ordered their expulsion from England, Cromwell's Protectorate Parliament formally invited Jews to return.[53]

Moreover, certain aspects of Cromwell's deep biblical faith became embedded in English religious and political thought. The most obvious of these aspects was his conviction that England was an "elect" nation, a new Israel, predestined by God for moral and political greatness. "One of Cromwell's greatest strengths was his power to communicate to his officers and men his own utter certainty that they were the instruments of a divine plan in which England had a special part to play, as in elect nations . . . they were the shock troops of the people of God."[54] Another of his strengths was his aversion to doctrinaire political ideologies, whether of the left (Leveller) or of the right (royalist). He had no fixed plan of republican government. God, he was sure, would direct those who believed in him to do what is right under the particular circumstances. Contrary to later stereotypes of Puritan dogmatism, Cromwell's Puritanism was highly pragmatic. He believed strongly in a divine providence that would lead the faithful, the elect, "the saints," in ways that could not be predicted in advance. "Man never reaches so high an estate," he said, "as when he knows not whither he is going."[55]

Finally, Cromwell left a legacy of public service, on the one hand, and of concern for underdogs and outcasts, on the other. In a letter to the Speaker of Parliament in September 1650, sent from his military headquarters in Scotland, he urged: "Relieve the oppressed, hear the groans of poor prisoners in England. Be pleased to reform the abuses of all professions and if there be one that makes many poor to make a few rich, that suits not a Commonwealth." Yet concern for the poor often conflicted with the ideal of public service. The latter was the duty of the landed gentleman, whose service to his country, his people, might conflict with his sentiments toward the poor, especially if they were idle poor or the poor of a hostile power. This conflict was resolved mercilessly in favor of public service in Cromwell's military conquest of Ireland, which was carried out with barbaric cruelty. Yet he deeply regretted what he considered to be the necessity of such cruelty. As Antonia Fraser writes, "His actual pardons to priests and friars contrasted strangely with the vicious words in which he denounced the Roman Catholic clergy in his declarations." Similarly, while he relocated tens of thousands of Scottish Presbyterians to Northern Ireland, expropriating Irish Catholic nobles in order to accommodate them, at the same time "his personal interventions were always on the side of mercy for individuals."[56]

The Restoration

With the return of Charles II in 1660, the Puritan phase of the English Revolution was effaced from the official record of English history. The period from the outbreak of the Civil War in 1642 to 1660 was now called "the Great Rebellion," and the period from the execution of Charles I in 1649 to 1660 was now called "the Interregnum," with the reign of Charles II considered to date not from 1660 but from 1649. In reality, however, it was impossible to turn the clock back to the Tudor-Stuart system. In the first place, Charles II supported the reenactment in 1660 of much of the legislation of the Long Parliament in 1641–42, whereby government by royal prerogative was to be abolished. Moreover, before returning to England in 1660, Charles issued the Declaration of Breda, in which he granted "a free and general pardon" to all who would "return to the loyalty and obedience of good subjects"—with the exception of those whom Parliament would later decide not to exonerate. He also declared "a liberty to tender consciences, and that no man shall be disquieted or called in question for differences of opinion in matters of religion which do not disturb the peace of the kingdom; and that we shall be ready to consent to such an act of parliament as, upon mature deliberation, shall be offered to us, for the full granting that indulgence." Also he declared that he would leave it to Parliament to provide for the settling of property disputes arising from the "many grants and purchases of estates" that had taken place "in the continued distractions of so many years and so many and great revolutions." Finally, he declared his readiness to consent to any acts of Parliament for the full satisfaction of all arrears due to officers and soldiers of the armed forces.[57]

Thus lip service, at least, was paid to concepts of parliamentary supremacy and liberty of conscience, two of the fundamental principles on which the

Revolution was based. It was the subsequent violation of those principles both by Charles II and later by his brother, James II, that led eventually to the second and final overthrow of the Stuart dynasty.

Despite these violations, neither Charles II nor James II imagined that they could return to the status quo ante. By their decision not to prosecute—or persecute—those who had fought for a new constitutional order, they reconciled themselves to a policy of bringing some sort of harmony to a nation that remained deeply divided. Charles and his chief adviser the earl of Clarendon vigorously advocated in the Convention Parliament in 1660 the adoption of the Act of Free and General Pardon, Indemnity and Oblivion, whereby the promise of amnesty made in the Declaration of Breda was to be amply fulfilled, with exceptions only for the participants in the Irish Rebellion of 1641 and the Regicides, that is, those who had signed the death warrant or participated in the execution of Charles I; and of the scores of Regicides only thirteen were condemned to death.[58] The 1660 Act of Indemnity gave a civil remedy of damages of £10 payable by any gentleman or person above that rank, or 40 shillings payable by any person below that rank, who during the following three years "shall presume maliciously to . . . object against any other person any name . . . or other word of reproach anyway tending to revive the memory of the late differences or the occasion thereof." Subsequent laws did, however, impose severe disabilities, including criminal penalties on those who did not pay tithes to or worship in the Church of England.

The return of the Stuarts to the throne marked the restoration not only of the monarchy but also of Parliament. Moreover, although the House of Lords was restored, and bishops were restored to it, the legislative supremacy of the House of Commons was preserved, especially through its power to initiate financial legislation.[59] As the tensions between Crown and Parliament once again became exacerbated, two rival parties emerged—the first party system of government in European history—and the Whigs, who were the successors of the Puritan and parliamentarian "Roundheads" of Cromwell's time, came to predominate over the Tories, who were the successors of the Anglican and royalist "Cavaliers." Once when the earl of Clarendon complained to Charles that he was permitting too many Roundheads to be returned to Parliament, Charles replied that if he filled the House of Commons with Cavaliers, in seven years they would all be Commonwealth men. In other words, the Restoration was in one sense a counterrevolution, but in another sense it carried the Revolution forward into a new phase. In the first years of his reign, Charles II was able to keep these two movements—backward and forward—in a peaceful though uneasy equilibrium. In later years, however, and especially under his brother, James II, the counterrevolutionary movement began to predominate, with the result that revolutionary forces were once again set in motion, though this time with less violence and less momentum for change.

Charles's initial policy was to rule not "in" his parliament but "with" it, accepting fully his lack of constitutional capacity to raise taxes without Parliament's assent. Parliament restored to the king full command of the armed forces, but by retaining the power of the purse it limited severely their size and the uses to which they could be put.[60] Moreover, in the first ten years of Charles's reign Parliament was in session every year, and in the second ten years every year but two, and all of these sessions lasted at least two months and usually three months or more.

Charles also accepted—at first—the supremacy of the common law and the common law judges. In 1660, with his encouragement, Parliament confirmed the 1641 legislation abolishing the prerogative courts. Also the Admiralty and Chancery courts remained subordinate to King's Bench and Common Pleas.[61] "His Majesty and the Lords and Commons in parliament assembled" also passed an act in 1660 confirming the validity of all judgments and proceedings of courts, judges, commissioners, and justices during the period from the outbreak of the Civil War to the Restoration, except for sales of estates made by virtue of acts or orders of Parliament and for cases involving charges of treason against royalists between May 1641 and the Restoration. The Restoration government also carried forward certain aspects of the movement for law reform that had been initiated by the common lawyers in the period prior to 1640 and had been championed by many Puritans in the period from 1640 to 1660.

The Glorious Revolution

Like the Long Parliament and Cromwell's Protectorate, the restored Stuart monarchy was incapable of finally resolving the acute political, religious, and social-economic conflicts that had given rise to the Civil War: the political conflict between Parliament and Crown, or republicanism and absolute monarchy; the religious conflict between Puritanism and Anglicanism, or sectarian dissent and orthodox establishment; and the social-economic conflict between country and court, or landed gentry and central bureaucracy. In the 1680s, both Charles II and James II were increasingly driven by external forces as well as by their own temperaments toward a return to the absolutist, High Church, and bureaucratic policies of their father and grandfather, Charles I and James I.[62] The final aggravation was James II's confessed Roman Catholicism and, with the birth of a son to his Roman Catholic wife in June 1688, the threat of a Roman Catholic succession to the throne.[63] Shortly thereafter a group of prominent Whigs and Tories—members of a parliament that James had dissolved—invited the Dutch Prince William of Orange together with his wife, Princess Mary, eldest daughter of James, to come to England to take the throne.

The accession of the new dynasty brought to almost fifty years of bitter strife a political, a religious, a social-economic, and a legal settlement.

The Political Settlement

On November 5, 1688, William invaded with fifteen thousand troops and a fleet of three hundred vessels. He was welcomed by an assembly of surviving members of the House of Commons from the lapsed 1681 parliament of Charles II—the last Stuart parliament.[64] Resistance to the invading army was negligible and ineffectual. In December, James was forced to flee England. In January 1688/89, a new Convention Parliament was constituted—again, as in 1660, without royal authority, since there was no monarch to summon it—in order to offer the crown to William and to set the terms on which he was to govern.[65] Henceforth it was clear that Parliament, in W. S Holdsworth's phrase, had the right to make and unmake kings.

The accession of Prince William of Orange to the English throne as William III was called at the time "a Revolution" and "Glorious" and soon thereafter "the Glorious Revolution."[66] True to the ideology of the common law, the English in 1689 viewed "Revolution" as signifying a return of the wheel to its former position, a restoration, as in 1660 they had also viewed the Restoration of the Stuart monarchy as a Revolution.

The chief symbol of the Glorious Revolution, and the basis of its claim to legitimacy, was the Declaration of Rights and Liberties of the Subject, adopted by the Convention Parliament and formally read to and accepted by Prince William and his wife, Princess Mary, on February 13, 1688/89, in the presence of both Houses. In March the Declaration was enacted as a statute by a new, properly elected Parliament, under the title "Bill of Rights."[67] It starts by listing thirteen examples of abuses whereby "the late King James the Second, by the assistance of diverse evil counsellors, judges, and ministers employed by him, did endeavour to subvert and extirpate the protestant religion and the laws and liberties of this kingdom." It continues by stating that "whereas the said late King James the Second having abdicated the government and the throne being thereby vacant, his highness the prince of Orange (whom it hath pleased almighty God to make the instrument of delivering this kingdom from popery and arbitrary power) did (by the advice of the lords spiritual and temporal and divers principal persons of the commons) cause letters to be written to elect a parliament"—which parliament, having assembled, "do in the first place (as their ancestors in like case have usually done) for the vindicating and asserting their ancient rights and liberties, declare . . ."

There follows a list of fundamental rights—also thirteen in number. The Declaration then goes on to state that the lords spiritual and temporal and commons, "having an entire confidence that his said highness the prince of Orange will . . . preserve them from the violation of their rights which they have here asserted, and from all other attempts upon their religion, rights and liberties . . . do resolve that William and Mary, prince and princess of Orange, be and be declared king and queen of England." It adds that after the Declaration was presented to them, "their said majesties did accept the Crown . . . according to the resolution and desire of the said lords and commons contained in the said declaration," and then goes on to state that it is hereby "declared and enacted that all . . . the rights and liberties asserted and claimed in the said declaration are the true, ancient and indubitable rights and liberties of the people of this kingdom."

Thus the English Bill of Rights gave four legal justifications for the revolutionary transformation of the absolute divine right monarchy of Tudor-Stuart England into a constitutionally limited monarchy under parliamentary control: first, that it had previously been a constitutionally limited monarchy, which James II had changed into "an arbitrary despotic power"; second, that James II having abdicated, the throne was vacant (the implication being that his Roman Catholic heir could not legally rule a Protestant England); third, that Prince William of Orange had made it possible for a new parliament to be elected and that he had agreed to the terms on which that parliament had offered him the English throne; and fourth, that the constitutional limitations on the English monarchy, which William accepted, are rooted in ancient rights and liberties of the English people.

The most important of the rights and liberties stated in the 1689 Bill of Rights were the following:

> that the election of members of parliament ought to be free;
> that freedom of speech in Parliament ought not to be questioned in any court or other place;
> that parliaments ought to be held frequently;
> that it is illegal to suspend laws or the execution of laws by royal authority without the consent of Parliament;
> that it is prohibited to raise or keep any army in time of peace except with the consent of Parliament;
> that "excessive bail ought not to be required nor excessive fines imposed nor cruel and unusual punishments inflicted";
> that jurors should be duly impaneled;
> that fines and forfeitures imposed on particular persons before conviction are illegal.

The Bill of Rights did not expressly restrict all areas of the royal prerogative. It did not in terms limit the king's sole power to determine foreign policy or to appoint and dismiss ministers and judges. Further, it did not repeal the royal power to summon, prorogue, and dissolve parliaments, to pardon officials impeached by Parliament, and to veto parliamentary statutes. Moreover, the king continued to exert influence through the ex officio parliamentary membership of royal officials ("placemen"). Once crowned, William did everything he could to exercise and expand these powers. Nevertheless, the tide ran—albeit slowly—against him in all these respects, for the twin doctrines of parliamentary supremacy and constitutional government were implicit not only in the Bill of Rights but also, paradoxically, in the entire revolutionary—illegal—upheaval which formed the context of its framing and enactment.

Thus, although Parliament in the 1690s was not able to prevent William from relying on Dutch advisers and from subordinating English to Dutch interests, nevertheless the Act of Settlement of 1701, establishing a new royal succession under Princess Anne of Denmark, younger daughter of James II, prohibited the holding of public office by foreigners and required parliamentary consent for wars by a foreign king of England in defense of his foreign dominions. Similarly, the Judges' Bill of 1691–92, passed by both Houses of Parliament, sought to create an independent judiciary which could not be dismissed by the king. William vetoed the measure, but it, too, was revived in the 1701 Act of Settlement, which provided that "judges' commissions be made *quamdiu se bene gesserint* ["during good behavior"—in effect, for life, unless dismissed by Parliament for misbehavior in office] and their salaries ascertained and established, but upon the address of both houses of Parliament it may be lawful to remove them."[68] (In fact, William had voluntarily appointed all judges to serve "during good behavior.")

Among other limitations on royal power that had to wait until the 1701 Act of Settlement in order to be formally legislated were the restriction of the royal pardoning power in cases of parliamentary impeachment and the barring of Roman Catholics from the throne. Indeed, the 1701 act, which was titled "An Act for the further limitation of the Crown and better securing the Rights and Liberties of the Subject," resolved most of the doubts about the ultimate significance of the Glorious Revolution that had been raised by William III's intermittent effort to reassert royal supremacy.

William also opposed legislation that would have limited his power to prevent the election of a new Parliament simply by illegally failing to summon it. He was frustrated in this, too, by the introduction in the 1690s of new parliamentary methods of financing royal expenditures, which had the effect of requiring annual sessions of Parliament to grant the Crown sufficient funds to carry on its civil and military activities. Thus the surviving royal prerogative in foreign affairs was subjected to parliamentary approval, and even in peacetime Parliament had to meet annually if only to approve the military budget. In fact, Parliament, which from November 1685 until November 1689 did not meet at all, and met in only 75 of the entire 130 years of Tudor-Stuart reign, has met every year since 1689.

Perhaps the most important symbol of the shift from a divine right, or absolute, monarchy to a parliamentary, or constitutional, monarchy was the new form of oath which the monarch was required—by Parliament—to swear upon coronation. Previously a new king swore merely to keep the laws and customs granted by his predecessors, making no reference whatever to Parliament. Prince William swore to govern "according to the Statutes in Parliament agreed on, and the Laws and Customs of the same."[69]

Yet the parliamentary supremacy that was won in 1689 was quite different from the parliamentary supremacy that had been first asserted in the 1640s, since it represented not the abolition of the monarchy or even its total subordination but rather the refashioning of the monarchy into a strong executive branch of government, with a strong royal civil service and the creation of a cabinet system. Parliament retained the ultimate power, but it granted the Crown substantial control over certain governmental policies. The royal prerogative was permitted by Parliament to survive, for example, in control of the British colonies abroad.

The Religious Settlement

The religious settlement of 1689 matched the political settlement. The oath taken by Prince William included the promise to the utmost of his power to "maintain . . . the Protestant Reformed Religion established by Law." As republican Whigs and divine-right monarchist Tories came together to establish a political system of parliamentary superiority over the Crown, so did Puritan nonconformists and orthodox Anglicans come together to establish a religious system in which the Protestant Church of England remained the nation's established church but Presbyterians, Independents, Congregationalists, and other trinitarian Protestant denominations were "tolerated," Unitarians and Quakers and some other radical Protestant denominations were only suffered, Jews were severely restricted in their activities, and Roman Catholics remained seriously discriminated against.

Although the Crown continued—for a time—to play an important role and was able to influence and occasionally to frustrate parliamentary policy, henceforth it was Parliament, and not the Crown, which ultimately determined the scope of the religious settlement. Parliament had the power to confirm or reject the Crown's nominees as archbishops and bishops of the Church of England and to approve or disapprove its theological doctrines and religious practices.

One of the first measures of the Dutch Calvinist William of Orange and his Protestant wife, Mary, upon their accession to the English throne, was to issue a decree abolishing the Test Act of 1671, which required all persons, before entering upon any public office, to receive the sacrament of Holy Communion in the Church of England. The effect of this law was to exclude Protestant Nonconformists—indeed, William himself—from all public office. Soon thereafter William also sponsored the enactment by Parliament of a law to render ineffective the other measures against Protestant dissenters enacted under Charles II and James II. Though called the Toleration Act, it did not use the word "toleration" nor did it repeal the earlier legislation making nonconformity illegal.[70] Yet by removing, under certain conditions, the penalties against violators of the earlier legislation, it had the effect of introducing de facto toleration of diverse Protestant denominations.

The method of introducing the revolutionary principle of limited religious toleration into English law was characteristic of the ideology of the English Revolution as a whole, and especially of the belief in disguising radical change as a continuity with the past. It remained, for example, a statutory offense under laws enacted in the reigns of Elizabeth I and James I not to attend Sunday church services in the Church of England; one who was absent was liable to pay a fine of one shilling for every Sunday absence and £20 for continuous absence for a month. Under the Act of Toleration, however, violators were exempt from these penalties if they took oaths acknowledging their allegiance to the Crown and its supremacy over the Church of England and renouncing the Roman Catholic doctrine of transubstantiation of the bread and wine of Holy Communion into the flesh and blood of Christ, and if they attended church services at a trinitarian place of worship officially registered as such. Similarly, dissenting preachers were exempt from the penalties of the Act of Uniformity if they subscribed to all of the Thirty-nine Articles except those that relate to the government of the church and to infant baptism. Finally, Nonconformists who were appointed to public offices or to offices in private corporations, and who refused to take the requisite oath or to receive the requisite Church of England sacrament, came to be relieved of any disability or penalty by the practice of enacting every year an act indemnifying them. "A curious English practice," the great legal historian F. W. Maitland called it. "It amounts to saying, 'We will not repeal the law, but it is understood that nobody need keep it, for every year an act will be passed indemnifying those who have not kept it.'"[71]

Under Charles II it was unclear whether Jews should be subjected to severe disabilities as religious dissenters, like Roman Catholics and nonconforming Protestants, or as alien resident merchants, subject to onerous taxes both individually and collectively. James II issued several Declarations of Indulgence stating that lawsuits seeking to harass Jews should cease and that they should "quietly enjoy the free exercise of their Religion, whilst they behave themselves dutifully and obediently to his Majesty's Government."[72] This policy was continued and strengthened under William III when some Jews moved into trusted positions and others were among the arms merchants who supplied William with munitions. At least one Jew was knighted a peer of the realm in this period, and a "grandiose new synagogue" was opened for worship in

1701.[73] Nevertheless, Jews remained barred from civil, political, and military office by the Corporation Act and the Test Act and were subjected to continuing legal harassment of various forms. It was only in the nineteenth century that they were admitted to the English universities and only in 1860 that they received full rights and liberties by enactment in that year of the Jews Act Amendment Bill.[74]

CHAPTER 8

The Transformation of English Legal Philosophy

It should not be surprising that before the Protestant Reformation, books on law written by English canonists and English Romanists, and courses in canon law and Roman law taught in the English universities, reflected a legal philosophy hardly distinguishable from that of canonists and Romanists of other European countries; or that pre-Reformation English theological and philosophical writings were basically similar to those of French, German, Italian, or other European theologians and philosophers. The canonists and Romanists and theologians and philosophers of all parts of Western Christendom in those centuries formed a single community, with a common Roman Catholic religious faith and a common Latin language. One might, to be sure, expect to find distinctive features of English legal philosophy reflected in pre–sixteenth-century writings about the law applied in the royal courts of Common Pleas, King's Bench, and Exchequer, inasmuch as that law differed in many respects from the various types of law applied in royal courts of other European countries. It is, indeed, conventional doctrine that distinctively English concepts of the nature of law and of its sources and its purposes can be traced back to the early history of the English common law in the twelfth and thirteenth centuries.[1] No doubt the pride that various English writers took in the law applied in the English royal courts—from Glanvill and Bracton in the twelfth and thirteenth centuries to Sir John Fortescue and Christopher St. German in the fifteenth and early sixteenth—has some philosophical implications. Yet even books written, like Fortescue's, "in praise of the laws of England" hardly differed in their underlying philosophy from books in praise of German or French or Italian secular law written by German, French, and Italian jurists.

Fortescue, to be sure, has been hailed as an important precursor of the distinctive historicism that came to dominate English legal thought in the seventeenth century. Fortescue did, indeed, trace English law to immemorial custom, dating back to pre-Roman times. Nevertheless, the "laws of England," which he "praised" in a fictitious dialogue between a young exiled English prince and his lord chancellor, were not conceived by him to be essentially different in their fundamental nature, sources, and purposes from the customary laws of other countries, except in their antiquity. They included, he wrote, not only specific English customs but also "universal principles, which teachers of the laws of England call maxims . . . and which the civilians call rules of law."[2] Moreover, Fortescue's principal work on legal philosophy was strictly in the school of natural law represented by Thomas Aquinas, which emphasized the ultimate source of law in divine reason and its ultimate purpose as promotion of the common good.[3] Other English jurists of the fifteenth and early sixteenth centuries were strongly influenced by the "voluntarist" school of natural law, of which the fourteenth-century philosopher William of Ockham was the leading exponent; yet Ockhamist philosophy, which emphasized the ultimate source of law in divine will rather than divine reason, was no more "English" than that of Aquinas, which it opposed, was "Italian."[4]

The name of St. German is also invoked as one of the founders of modern English jurisprudence; and indeed, his *Doctor and Student,* written in 1531 on the eve of the English Reformation, in which the "student" defends the English common law against a "doctor of divinity," showing its correspondence with fundamental principles of justice, does contain some seeds of later developments in English legal theory. Basically, however, St. German remained within the tradition of sixteenth-century European legal philosophy as it began to separate itself from earlier Roman Catholic theology and from the scholastic method. Reiterating theories similar to those of Aquinas but also drawing specifically on the writings of the fifteenth-century French Ockhamist philosopher-theologian Jean Gerson, St. German stressed that all law, including English law, has its ultimate sources in the natural law of reason, the eternal law of God, general customs, and general legal principles ("maxims"). At the same time, he explained peculiarities of English law by distinguishing between "the law of primary reason" and the "law of secondary reason." "The law of primary reason" consisted of general principles applicable at all times and places, such as the elements that constitute murder or perjury or breaking the peace. "The law of secondary reason," by contrast, consisted of uniquely English laws that were the product both of reason and of particular English customs. St. German divided these into "the laws of secondary reason general," consisting of legal customs that are common to the whole world, and "the laws of secondary reason particular," consisting of the unique legal customs of a given polity such as England.[5] Thus, like Fortescue, and, indeed, like French and other legal humanists of the sixteenth century, St. German was concerned to give a universal legitimacy to the customary laws of the national polity.

It was the Anglican theologian and political philosopher Richard Hooker who, in the 1590s, in his multivolume work *Of The Laws of Ecclesiastical Polity,* laid the theological and philosophical foundations for what in the seventeenth century became the first distinctively English jurisprudence. Hooker's book was written in part to defend the Anglican Church against the assaults of radical Puritans; its spirit, however, was one not of sharp confrontation but rather of conciliation with the more moderate elements within the Calvinist ranks. It was also written in part to defend royal supremacy over the Anglican Church against both Puritan and Roman Catholic attack; nevertheless, it also emphasized the autonomy of the church and the subjection of the monarch to the "law of the Commonweal."[6] Finally, Hooker was concerned to identify his own Anglican philosophy with the traditional Aristotelian and Thomist philosophy that prevailed in the Roman Catholic Church;[7] at crucial points, however, he departed radically, albeit respectfully, from Aristotelian and Thomist thought. In short, he well earned the sobriquet "the judicious Hooker," although he did not deserve the distortions of his philosophy committed by various later writers who seized on one part of it or another and neglected its subtlety, its integrity, and its comprehensiveness.[8]

Hooker had a strong premonition that the religious conflicts which divided England would lead to acute civil strife. In the opening words of the preface to his book he wrote that his sole purpose in writing it was "that posterity may know we have not loosely through silence permitted things to pass away as in a dream." He wrote as a postrevolutionary, that is, as one who looked back on the impending transformation and sought to reconcile it with what had gone before; it is not accidental that his book only became the classical statement of Anglican theology and of English political philosophy a century after it was written, as the English Revolution was drawing to a close. John Locke drew heavily on it in his *Second Treatise of Government,* written in the 1680s. In the eighteenth and early nineteenth centuries, Hooker's book continued to reflect mainstream English political and religious thought to a far greater extent than did the works of writers of "liberal" or "Enlightenment" persuasion.

For Hooker, law was founded in reason and morality and in man's natural sociability; to that extent he adhered to classical scholastic natural law theory. But he also asserted that law is founded in will and politics and in the corruption of human nature, which requires, for the sake of sociability itself, submission to the commands of a political authority. Government is the result of man's natural inclination to sociability; all particular forms of government, however, are the result of man's express or tacit consent to submit to those particular forms, and it is such initial consent from which the binding character of the positive law of a particular government is derived.[9] Thus there is a strong element of voluntarism in Hooker's theory as well as a strong implication that the legitimacy of a particular government is rooted historically in the consent of the people. A century later Locke read into Hooker's work a theory of social contract that would justify revolution against a tyrannical government. In fact, however, Hooker understood the initial agreement of men to form a civil society not as a social contract in the Lockean sense but as an expression of universal consent to a permanent status of subjection to political authority.[10] The permanence of the status was related, in Hooker's exposition, to the corporate nature of the political community in time. "The act of a public society of men done five hundred years since," he wrote, "standeth as theirs who presently are of the same societies, because corporations are immortal; we were then alive in our predecessors, and they in their successors do live."[11]

Thus the laws laid down by the political authority in the past remain binding in the present—binding on the entire commonwealth, including its rulers. They may, of course, be changed, but only lawfully, since that was implicit in the initial consent of the people to form a lawmaking government. "Laws they are not, therefore, which public approbation hath not made so."[12] Such approbation exists where the laws are enacted by the representatives of the people acting in their name. Laws of absolute monarchs, according to Hooker, are also binding, because such monarchs enjoy their authority either by divine appointment or, as in England, by consent of the people.

Hooker's "judiciousness" found expression in his repeated distinction between beliefs or practices that are "necessary" and those that are only "probable." The Puritans, he charged, often insisted on the "necessity" of certain rituals or doctrines which in fact were not in themselves objectionable but which were, at the same time, only of "probable" value, that is, they were what Melanchthon had called *adiaphora,* matters of indifference. Similarly, Hooker left open the matter of specific forms of government, requiring only that they be based either on divine institution or on consent of the people or both. Applying the same distinction to legal institutions, Hooker attributed to natural law (or, as he called it, the law of reason)[13] the requirement that theft, for example, be punished, but left to the positive law of individual polities the type and degree of punishment to be applied.[14] His tendency was to reduce substantially the necessary requirements of true Christian faith and of a just political and legal order. Implicit was a constitutional theory: that the sovereign political authority is bound by fundamental law but that its subsidiary laws may vary according to the needs of particular times and places.

Hooker's *Laws of Ecclesiastical Polity* set the stage for the debates that raged in the seventeenth century concerning the nature, sources, and purposes of law. In the first decades of the century, however, it was overshadowed by another legal philosophy, namely, that of King James himself, who not only wrote an important book setting forth his theory of law and government but also effectively enforced that theory against those who dared openly to oppose it.

The Legal Theory of Absolute Monarchy: James I and Bodin

King James presented a coherent philosophy of the interrelationship of divine law, natural law, and positive law. In *The Trew Law of Free Monarchies,* written in 1598, when he was king only of Scotland, as a rebuttal of Calvinist antimonarchical views as well as of Roman Catholic claims of papal supremacy, James met head-on the pre-Reformation theory that it is the law that makes the king, and not the king the law, and that therefore the king is under the law. His answer was that God, as the creator of the universe, that is, of the natural order, appoints monarchs to carry out his will on earth. Thus kings derive their power directly from God and not through a social contract with their people. As divine law is the will of God revealed in Scripture and tradition, so human law is the will of the supreme ruler. Through law the ruler keeps order in society just as through law God keeps order in nature. Reason, in King James's philosophy, is not immanent in nature and in society, as it was believed to be by most scholastic theologians and philosophers ever since Saint Anselm and Abelard. Reason, according to King James, is a standard to which will ought generally to conform, as well as a means through which will ought generally to be effectuated, but ultimately it is the will of the ruler which determines what reason is and what it requires; and in exceptional cases the ruler, like God, may act arbitrarily, against reason, and none may call him to account. Kings are God's representatives on earth, endowed by him with divinity itself.[15]

The reason to which the king's will ought to conform was found by King James in those principles that correspond to the nature of God and that are therefore necessary to the preservation of human nature. Thus in a state of nature, kingship is necessary because otherwise society would consist simply of a headless multitude. The relationship of the king to his subjects, James wrote, is a natural relationship comparable to that of the queen bee to her subjects in the hive or the father to the other members of the family. James also compared absolute monarchy to the natural relation between a soul and a body. Kingship, in his theory, is the soul of the body politic.

This theory was not, of course, original with King James but was in fact the prevailing theory of those who supported absolute monarchy in the Europe of his time. James derived many of his ideas from the influential sixteenth-century French political and legal philosopher Jean Bodin, who had argued that as in nature God rules the universe as an absolute monarch, so in human society sovereignty should be exercised in each political territory by an absolute monarch. According to Bodin, God has "established sovereign princes as his lieutenants for commanding other men."[16] Theories of limited sovereignty had been developed by others in the sixteenth century, and the concept of absolute monarchy—that is, monarchy superior to, and hence "absolved" from, the laws—had been put forward by lawyers and debated and qualified in earlier centuries as well. Bodin, however, was the first major writer to develop a systematic theory of an indivisible sovereignty—not merely a superiority but a total supremacy, a single ultimate human lawmaking authority from which all other human lawmaking authority is derived; and he was the first major writer to develop a systematic theory of the total absolution of the sovereign authority—by definition—from subservience to the laws that it made. Anticipating by almost a century the writings of Thomas Hobbes, Bodin postulated that in every stable political order there must be an ultimate power, whether it be a single person or a group of persons, which makes the laws and therefore stands above them. This differed from Hobbes's positivist jurisprudence chiefly in its postulate of a divine source of the state's lawmaking power.

Bodin's major work, *The Republic,*[17] published in 1576, was directed in part against French Huguenot doctrines of divided sovereignty, legal limitations on monarchical authority, and a right of resistance to monarchs who defy such limitations. In general the Huguenots, following Calvin, advocated the Bible-based right and duty not of every person (as John of Salisbury had advocated in the twelfth century) to kill a tyrant,[18] but of the responsible leaders of the Christian community, the elders or magistrates, to overthrow a monarch who persecutes adherents of the true faith. In attacking this theory Bodin did not exclude the possibility of an aristocratic order; he argued, however, that monarchy was far preferable.[19] Indeed, Bodin elaborated a complex mathematical system to show that religious upheavals follow certain cycles and that only the force exerted by an absolute monarch can counter such disturbances. He also argued that certain climates lead to certain types of human behavior, and that absolute monarchy is appropriate to the climate of Europe.[20]

In England, the philosopher and scientist Francis Bacon, King James's faithful attorney general, also argued that government is a natural thing, and that as nature requires and produces government, so government requires and produces law. Bacon told Parliament in 1621 that forms of government other than absolute monarchy "are apt to dissolve."[21] Forty years later Hobbes made a similar argument, defending absolute monarchy as that form of government which corresponds to the laws of motion followed by physical bodies.

Thus the theory that the monarch, ruling by divine law ("divine right"), is the final source of positive laws, and that at the same time he himself is ultimately absolved from them, was closely linked with the scientific and philosophical thought of the time. A major characteristic of that thought was its assumption that the entire universe is based on a single explanatory model, that all phenomena—stars, billiard balls, forms of government—follow the same basic principles. Bodin, Bacon, Descartes, Hobbes, Filmer, and others were all obsessed by this reductionist view.

Bodin's absolute monarch—and King James's—was not supposed to be a despot. Quite the contrary: as God's representative, he was supposed to rule by just laws. Bodin, himself a lawyer by training, shared the almost universally held belief that kings are required by God to fulfill the divine commandment to maintain justice in their kingdoms and to observe the principles of natural law, that is, the principles of reason and conscience. Indeed, in his coronation oath the monarch—in England as well as in the other countries of Europe—swore to carry out not only the moral obligations but also the legal obligations of his office. What made him absolute, according to Bodin, and later according to King James, was his lack of accountability to anyone other than God himself: that was what was "modern" in Bodin's constitutional theory. The sovereign's oath was to God alone. If he violated that oath, and was a tyrant, his subjects were required nevertheless to obey him and patiently to suffer his despotic rule, albeit with prayers, sighs, and tears, recognizing that he was sent by God as a punishment of the people for their sins.

The monarch could indeed, and should, share with others the exercise of his powers. Legally, however, he could not, even if he wanted to, divest himself of any part of his indivisible supremacy, nor could he grant to others the lawful power to challenge a revocation by him of any jurisdiction that he had previously bestowed upon them. In Bodin's words, "As to control by way of law [*voie de justice*], the subject has no jurisdiction over his prince, since it is from him that all power and authority to command derives, and not only may he revoke all the power and jurisdiction of every magistrate, but in his presence the power and jurisdiction of all magistrates, guilds, and corporations, estates, and communities, entirely lapses."[22]

As Julian Franklin has put it:

> In the constitutional conflicts of the seventeenth century, Bodin was to provide the English royalists with a ready-made arsenal of arguments, or, more precisely, with a model for developing their arguments. [Bodin's] *République* would help to show how all the medieval checks on royal power could be deprived of binding force—how review by the courts [of the legality of royal statutes and proclamations] could be reinterpreted as a mere administrative function, how the work of Parliament could be understood as merely advisory or, at the most, corroborative, and how all charters and engagements by the king could be construed as conditional and temporary. Mutatis mutandis, Bodin's recipe, devised primarily for France, could be applied to England also.[23]

When the seventeenth-century English common lawyers invoked as an "inheritance" judicial or parliamentary powers to limit the royal prerogative, King James would reply that they were merely granted by earlier monarchs as a "toleration" and could therefore be revoked at his discretion.

Thus James also added to his philosophical argument a historical one: that there were kings before there were any estates or parliaments or laws, and it was kings who distributed the land and established the forms of government. "And so it follows of necessity," he wrote, "that the kings were the authors and makers of the laws and not the laws of the kings." The only "fundamental laws" were those maintaining the succession to the crown. Once a king's hereditary right is established, he is above the law and in no way bound to obey it, though he may and should do so "of his good will and for good example-giving to his subjects."[24] The monarch alone is "free." All branches of his government are responsible to him, not he to them. Parliament is "nothing but the head court of the king and his vassals."[25] To illustrate these propositions he drew heavily on Tudor precedents. His language, however, was far less diplomatic than that of the Tudors. Elizabeth I would not have said—she could not have said—what James said in his address to his first English parliament in 1603: "I am the Husband and the whole Isle is my lawful Wife: I am the Head, and it is my Body."[26]

No doubt many members of Parliament were startled to hear from their new sovereign so blunt a statement of the theory of absolute ("free") monarchy. That theory, however, was by no means new to England but for some seventy years had been implicit, and often explicit, in the language of supporters of the Tudor monarchy. Previously the rhetoric had been somewhat softer, especially during the forty-five-year reign of Elizabeth; the first two Stuart kings of England were entirely lacking in the tact that enabled Elizabeth to hold together a people whose unity was continually threatened by gathering Puritan forces on the left and surviving Roman Catholic forces on the right. But basically, the underlying Stuart theory of government and law did not differ in its essentials from that which had prevailed under the Tudors. Indeed, James continually emphasized the consistency of his theories with previous Tudor practice.

Moreover, James I—and later his son Charles—did have, despite the bluntness of their theories of sovereignty and absolutism, a deep respect for English law, including the English common law, and a strong desire to preserve it. Faced throughout their reigns with challenges by common lawyers on the bench and in Parliament, of whom Sir Edward Coke was the most prominent, both James and Charles repeatedly affirmed their intention to abide by the precedents of the past and to maintain intact the legal tradition which they had inherited from their Tudor predecessors.

Sir Edward Coke, Leader of His Majesty's Loyal Opposition

There is a further point to be added, which bears directly on the matter of legal philosophy, namely, that neither Coke nor his allies—except for the Puritans among them and those who secretly adhered to the outlawed Roman Catholic doctrines—challenged the basic theoretical concepts and principles of government and law that were articulated by James I. Coke himself accepted without question the theory of absolute monarchy. He loved the common law and fought for it against those who would curtail its scope and jurisdiction, including the king himself, but he never denied the truth of their philosophical premises. He agreed with them that it is the king's natural duty to safeguard the community, that the king is the supreme lawgiver, and that the king has absolute power to appoint and remove judges. As Elizabeth's attorney general, in upholding her Act of Supremacy over the church, he had himself stated that "by the authority of many acts of Parliament the kingdom of

England is an absolute monarchy."[27] Coke did not believe in Puritan concepts of scriptural authority, congregationalism, and rule by inspired elders. He was no Calvinist. At the same time, he did not believe in the Roman Catholic doctrine of a secular monarchy limited by ecclesiastical authority. He was, in fact, an Anglican and a monarchist through and through. For him, the king was head of both state and church, and for him, reason of state was divorced from both Puritan and Roman theology. Yet as chief justice from 1606 to 1616 and later as a member of Parliament, Coke fought stubbornly to limit the king's prerogative powers and to subject them to the common law and to parliamentary control.

If Coke accepted King James's premises, how was he able to avoid King James's conclusions? The answer lies partly in the character of the man and partly in the historical situation in which England found itself. But it also lies partly in Coke's philosophy of law.

A profound ambiguity in King James's—and, for that matter, Bodin's—political and legal philosophy lay in the various meanings attached to the words "law" and "king," not only by them but also, and especially, by those whom they addressed. The king was indeed said to be above the law, in the sense, first, that he was the supreme maker of the law, and second, that none could challenge him if he himself failed to observe the law that he had made. Yet those who were charged with the duty of interpreting and enforcing the law could not, and were not supposed to, look into the king's mind in each case in order to determine what the law said and what it meant. For them, the law necessarily consisted of concepts, principles, rules, and procedures that had been laid down or established in the past, whose meaning was conveyed by the language in which they were expressed. This, indeed, is a paradox inherent in the very concept of law: that rules laid down yesterday remain binding today—that the prevailing law is, in effect, a memorial of the past. Similarly, "the king," who in James's philosophy was the ultimate source of the law, was not only the person sitting on the throne at a given moment but rather a succession of royal personages who lived in earlier times and who will live in the future. For Coke, "the king's" laws included not only the laws of the reigning monarch but also the laws of his predecessors: the Tudors, the Plantagenets, and the earlier Norman and even Anglo-Saxon rulers, who in and through their councils and their parliaments and their courts had, over the centuries, created a legal system that had duration in time and carried with it meanings remembered from the past. This, too, is a paradox of the law: that earlier lawmakers bind later lawmakers, at least presumptively. Thus it was entirely possible, and in a sense necessary, for Coke, appointed by the king to be chief justice of the common law courts, to consider that he was indeed best serving his monarch when he decided cases according to principles of the common law laid down by the courts and parliaments of "the king" in earlier centuries and not thereafter repealed or modified.[28]

It was precisely Coke's belief that the laws of James's predecessors remained in force that was the chief bone of contention between him and the king. When members of Parliament in 1621 challenged the king's policies with respect to Spain and the Roman Catholic Church, and James forbade them to discuss it further, Coke and others insisted that the freedom of speech of members of Parliament, like the powers of the courts and the liberties of the subject generally, were privileges inherited from previous reigns. James replied that "your privileges were derived from the grace and permission of our ancestors and us, for most of them grow from precedents, which show rather a toleration than an inheritance." At Coke's suggestion, the House of Commons entered into its journals a "Protestation" stating "that the liberties, franchises, privileges and jurisdictions of Parliament are the ancient and undoubted birthright and inheritance of the subjects of England." It was for this that James removed Coke from the Privy Council and had him committed to the Tower of London, where he remained in close confinement and virtual isolation for seven months.[29]

Thus Coke was able, with integrity, to accept King James's basic theory of government and law and yet boldly challenge specific uses of the royal prerogative, first, because of his unwavering personal dedication to the law, and second, because of the ambiguity of the concepts of law and kingship in King James's theory itself. One may find parallels in authoritarian regimes of the past century, when courageous persons have stood up against arbitrary dictatorships, challenging them to live up to their own previously enacted laws. There was a third factor, however, in seventeenth-century England, namely, the historical situation of a people which had, three generations before, decisively repudiated a four-hundred-year-old Roman Catholic heritage, in which church and state checked and balanced each other, in favor of an Erastian sovereignty in which church and state were under a single head, but which found itself in the early 1600s still torn by acute internal religious conflicts, on the one hand, and, on the other hand, by a profound uncertainty concerning the ultimate source of the legitimacy of monarchical rule. In that situation, Coke did not quarrel with the Stuart monarchy's theory of the source of its legitimacy in divine right, but he sought to support that legitimacy, and to condition it, in a way which the king found troublesome, to say the least. That is, Coke justified judicial decisions and parliamentary positions that had the effect of limiting royal power on the ground that they were dictated by the historical precedents of English law—precedents endorsed by previous monarchs. The king could not object in principle to such a justification, since he, too, justified his own actions partly on the basis of their consistency with English legal precedents endorsed by his royal predecessors.

Thus Coke accepted his monarch's philosophy of law, and yet he founded a new school of English legal philosophy diametrically opposed to it! This paradox may be resolved by distinguishing between a theory of law, such as James's (and Bodin's), and a theory of *English* law.

A theory of law addresses directly universal questions concerning the nature of law, the sources of law, the relation of law to morals and to politics, fundamental legal concepts of rights and responsibilities, and other related matters of a general nature. A theory of English law, by contrast, addresses such questions only indirectly and in the context of a particular legal system, posing questions concerning the nature of English law, the sources of English law, the relation of English law to morals and politics, et cetera. A study of seventeenth-century English legal philosophy in the first of these two senses would require an analysis of the philosophical writings of Thomas Hobbes, Robert Filmer, John Locke, James Harrington, and other political and legal philosophers whose theories did, to be sure, reflect their English political and legal heritage, but whose focus, in their philosophical writings, was on politics and law in general, and not only English politics and English law in particular. Coke, however, was concerned above all to explain not law in general but English law, and to identify the factors that gave English law its particular character. The more general unarticulated philosophical and political implications of his analysis were subordinated to its more narrowly legal aspects, which he viewed in historical terms.

Coke's legal philosophy was not only narrowly focused on English law, but also was even more narrowly focused on one branch of the law by which England was governed, namely, the English common law, that is, the law that traditionally was applicable chiefly (though not exclusively) in the royal courts of Common Pleas, King's Bench, and Exchequer. Coke did not attempt to develop a theory of the canon law of the Anglican Church, which was applicable in the English ecclesiastical courts, or the mixture of Romanist and canonist rules and procedures applied in the wide variety of other English courts. He was entirely familiar with the canon law and Roman law applicable in various types of cases in these other courts, but he considered them—as they later came to be considered by most English legal historians—"foreign" law.[30] It is to Coke more than to any other single person that we owe the widespread notion that "English law"—"the law of the land"—means above all, and has always meant above all, the English common law, and not equally (as his opponents correctly argued) "the Law of the Chancery, the Ecclesiastical Law, the Law of the Admiralty . . . the Law of the Merchants, the Martial Law, and the Law of State."[31]

Thus Coke's answer to the free monarchists' general theory of government and law was—no theory at all! He did not deny the validity of King James's version of natural law theory, that law is founded on Reason. Nor did he deny the validity of the king's version of what later came to be called legal positivism—that law is founded on Will, the will of the lawmaker. He merely shifted the jurisprudential focus from law in general to English law, and more especially the English common law, which he then defined in historical terms. His answer to James was History, which he saw largely in terms of Tradition and Precedent. He could get away with this just because it was not—at that time—a theory, and because English monarchists themselves, and above all King James, continually insisted that the English precedents—which they interpreted quite differently—should be respected. For they, too, felt the need of a historical basis for the legitimacy of the monarchy.

To say that Coke did not have a legal philosophy, in the sense of a general theory of law, is not, however, to say that his theory of English law did not have important philosophical implications.[32] Of major philosophical importance was his conception of artificial reason, that is, reason that is brought into being not by nature but by human effort and human art.[33] In a passage often quoted, Coke wrote that law is "perfect reason, which commands those things that are proper and necessary and which prohibits contrary things."[34] On its face, this definition was perfectly acceptable to King James, as it would have been to Thomas Aquinas. Indeed, the king said to Coke, in a famous colloquy, that since the law is reason, and since the king has at least as much reason as any of his judges, therefore his interpretation of the law is entitled to as much weight as the interpretation of Coke or of those whom Coke cited. Coke responded that God had indeed endowed His Majesty with great intellectual capacity but that the reason of the law is not the natural reason of any person but rather the artificial reason of the law itself.[35] "The common law," Coke wrote, "is nothing but reason; which is to be understood [as] an artificial perfection of reason gotten by long study, observation, and experience." The common law "by many succession of ages . . . hath been . . . refined by an infinite number of grave and learned men, and by long experience grown to such a perfection for the government of this realm, [that] the old rule may be justly verified of it, *Neminem opportet esse sapientiorem legibus:* no man out of his own private reason ought to be wiser than the law, which is the perfection of reason."[36]

Coke's conception of the English common law as the embodiment of the reasoning of many generations of learned men represented a different concept of reason from that which had previously prevailed in Western legal philosophy as well as in Western philosophy generally. Both the scholastic philosophers of the twelfth to fifteenth centuries and the humanist philosophers of the sixteenth century had understood reason to be a God-given natural faculty of the human mind, a capacity to understand and to form judgments. Reason was contrasted with will, which was understood to be a natural faculty of the emotions, motivating a person to direct his or her mind or conduct to desired goals or otherwise to control thoughts and actions. Scholastic legal philosophers had contended that reason not only enables a person to distinguish between justice and injustice but also dictates that justice is preferable. Reason, they argued, naturally tends toward promotion of the common good, and hence positive laws that are contrary to reason have no claim to observance. Thus they identified reason with timeless moral principles inherent in human nature itself—not with the laws of any particular nation but with a universal natural law applicable in all nations. Humanist legal philosophers, both Catholic and Protestant, did not fundamentally change this concept of natural law but added to it a greatly increased emphasis on the importance of rationalizing and systematizing legal rules in order better to effectuate sound public policy. Thus for the humanist legal philosophers, who for the most part had less confidence in reason—and more confidence in will—than did their scholastic forebears, moral reason was linked with an overriding political reason, which, however, was also conceived to be a faculty of human nature capable of being analyzed in general terms applicable universally.

Coke did not doubt the existence of natural reason and of natural law, as defined by the moral and political philosophers, but he juxtaposed to it a different kind of reason, which might be called historical reason. The "reason" on which the English common law was based, he argued, is the *reasoning* of English lawyers, that is, the way the "grave and learned men" of English law, over the centuries, have traditionally reasoned about legal matters. This was not the reason implanted by God in human nature as such. It was not to be found in the "private reason" of individuals. It was the practical prudential reason of the experts, persons of experience, who have made a special study of their subject, who know their history, and who build on the learning and wisdom of many generations of other experienced persons. They will know—even in the most complicated circumstances—what is reasonable and what common sense requires.[37] They will therefore be able to solve problems that will baffle the layman or amateur. More particularly, they will seek solutions to problems within the contours of the subject itself. They will look for its reason, its internal logic. In law, they will look for the logic, the reason, the sense, the purposes of the law itself—the law as a whole and the law in all its parts.

Coke's concept of the artificial reason of the law was, however, even narrower than this, since he was concerned not with law in general but with the English common law. His concept of artificial reason might, indeed, be applied to other types of law—canon law, Roman law, or, for that matter, natural law or divine law—since in all such subjects the trained expert, the person of learning and experience in the subject, will be better able than others to understand its inherent reason, logic, sense, and purposes. But for Coke, the artificial reason of the English common law was the unique reason, logic, sense, and purposes of the historically rooted law of the English nation, a repository of the thinking and experience of the English common lawyers over many centuries. Therefore it had to be understood in the light of that history. Natural law was part of it: in *Calvin's Case,* Coke advanced the express proposition that the law of nature is part of the common law.[38] In *Bonham's Case,* Coke held that the principle that no man may be judge of his own cause is a tenet of "common right," that is, of common law.[39] In his *Institutes,* Coke wrote that the right to be heard in one's own defense is a principle of divine justice, and he quoted favorably the words of a fifteenth-century chief justice of Common Pleas: "To those laws which Holy Church hath out of Scripture we ought to yield credit; for that . . . is the common law upon which all laws are founded."[40] Thus Coke did not deny the validity of natural law, and he believed that it was incorporated into the English common law.

Positive law was also part of the common law. Coke never doubted the binding force of legislation, but he viewed legislation within the historical context of the precedents of the English common law courts, the historical common law statutes of Parliament such as Magna Carta, and, more generally, the understandings of the bench and the bar concerning the vast complex of concepts, principles, rules, procedures, and institutions that constitute the numerous branches of the law—constitutional law, administrative law and procedure, criminal law and procedure, civil law and procedure, and the rest. These, taken together, were in Coke's view the product of the history of the English people, their political and economic values viewed in the perspective of many centuries, their fundamental morality; and only one steeped in this age-old law was qualified to understand even relatively recent legislation and to apply it to particular cases.

Thus Coke established in the English context the first principle of the historical school of jurisprudence, which was developed further by his English followers in the seventeenth and eighteenth centuries and which ultimately blossomed into a full-scale general theory of law, taking its place alongside natural law theory and legal positivism. That first principle consisted in the proposition that a nation's law is to be understood above all as the product of that nation's history—not merely in the obvious sociological sense that existing institutions are derived from preexisting institutions but also in the philosophical sense that the past history of a nation's law both has and ought to have a normative significance for its present and future development. From this standpoint, the primary sources of law, to which one should look first in making a legislative or judicial or administrative decision, or in determining the meaning of a legal concept or principle or rule or procedure, are custom and precedent. Other sources of law, especially universal moral concepts of justice (which take precedence under a theory of natural law) and political considerations of legislative will or legislative policy (which take precedence under a theory of legal positivism), should, according to the historical school, be viewed in the light of, and as subordinate to, the historical development and historical circumstances of the particular legal system under consideration.

The historical school of legal theory is itself divided between a conception of past history as a series of fixed points—in law, fixed rules and decisions—to be preserved and reiterated, which may be called *historicism,* and a conception of past history as a process of adaptation of past experience to changing needs, which may be called *historicity.* Jaroslav Pelikan has made a similar distinction between *traditionalism,* which he calls the dead faith of the living, and *tradition,* which he calls the living faith of the dead.[41] The tension between these two versions of historical jurisprudence is strikingly apparent in contemporary American constitutional adjudication, in which some judges rely solely on the original intent of the framers of the Constitution while others interpret constitutional texts in the light also of the changing meanings of their words over the intervening generations and centuries.

Sir Edward Coke is sometimes classified, from this point of view, as a *traditionalist,* since he repeatedly challenged particular exercises of the royal prerogative as innovations, holding up particular ancient laws and court decisions as authoritative. And it is indeed true that he often seemed to invoke the authority of a fixed event of the past, and called for it to be repeated, for its own sake. He glorified the antiquity of the English common law and the immemorial character of its basic principles. He repeated with relish Chaucer's proverb "Out of the old fields must spring and grow the new corn."[42] At the same time, he has been severely criticized by many historians, and was challenged in his own day, for his use of historical precedents in ways that could hardly have been contemplated when they were first introduced. Both his resort to precedent and his apparent abuse of it must be understood, however, in the light of his situation: for the most part, he could not, without forfeiting his public office and risking imprisonment (though also he apparently had no inclination to), challenge abuses of the royal prerogative except on the ground that they violated ancient statutes and decisions. But whatever his motives, Coke was no mere antiquarian who viewed the past in static terms. His belief that the English common law was based on "immemorial custom," going back to Anglo-Saxon times, did not blind him to the many changes that had taken place in it over the centuries. At the same time, he did not view the past, as many do today, as a mere datum or cause or precondition of subsequent events. On the contrary, he saw purposes in it, and norms. Moreover, the past for Coke was not primarily the immediate past but, above all, the ancient past, which meant primarily the pre-Tudor past, the past especially of Bracton and the Year Books. That was what made his conservatism—in its historical context—revolutionary.

John Selden's Legal Philosophy

It took two generations of Coke's followers to develop his philosophy of English law into an English philosophy of law. In the first of those generations, the leading figure in that development was John Selden (1584–1654). In the second, the leading figure was Matthew Hale (1609–1676). The links among the three men were very strong. Selden at age thirty-seven worked with the sixty-nine-year-old Coke in drafting the House of Commons' Protestation of 1621, for which both men were subsequently sent to the Tower. Later Selden himself was elected to Parliament, where he joined his older colleague in drafting and securing enactment of the 1628 Petition of Right—for which he was once again sent to the Tower.[43] In the 1630s and 1640s Selden, in turn, became the mentor and close friend of the young Hale, whom he eventually appointed to be one of the executors of his will. Ultimately, Hale reorganized Coke's *Institutes* to make them more systematic and to draw out their philosophical implications. All three men started their careers as practicing lawyers. All three were deeply involved in the great constitutional struggles of their times. All three were dedicated and prolific scholars.

Selden's scholarship was much broader than Coke's. He was a historian of the first rank, the acknowledged master of the leading English historical society of the time, the Society of Antiquaries. He was also an accomplished biblical scholar, Orientalist, and philosopher. John Milton called him "the chief of learned men reputed in this Land."[44]

Selden carried Coke's historicism one giant step forward beyond the conception of an immemorial past and an unchangeable fundamental law to the conception of an evolutionary past and an evolving fundamental law. Coke had fully understood that the common law had changed over the centuries; his whole emphasis, however, was on its continuity; he viewed the changes as incidental to that continuity. Selden, coming at a later stage in the prerevolutionary and revolutionary conflict, reaffirmed the continuity but also emphasized the changes. He stressed development, growth. He believed in the immemorial and permanent character of basic English constitutional institutions and principles, such as government by assemblies of notables and judicial responsibility to law. But he saw the changes that occurred periodically as examples of the gradual development of those basic institutions and principles.

Above all, Selden attached to the historical development of English law a normative significance. For example, he traced a development of the Germanic *wapentakes* described by Tacitus into the *witans* of the Anglo-Saxons, which in the thirteenth century became parliaments;[45] and he found, in that development, principles—norms—applicable to parliamentary government in his own day. At the same time, humanist scholarship led him to recognize breaks in the evolution of English law, for example, that the Norman Conquest brought substantial changes, including the introduction of feudal law and the strengthening of the independence of bishops' courts. Yet he also stressed elements of continuity with Anglo-Saxon institutions in the post-Conquest period. He treated the ancient British, the Saxon, and the Norman periods of English history as three distinct phases of a single historical development, whose common elements were successively refined. Although most of the ancient laws were superseded, their fundamental structure not only survived but also underwent improvement.

Moreover, Selden's historical jurisprudence was much more than a theory of English law. All legal systems, he wrote, are to be understood as historical in character. He postulated as an immutable law of human nature that men are civil creatures, who, when they first people a land, "plant a common society." In succeeding ages, however, they add to, interpret, and limit natural law according to "the several conveniences," that is, the particular wants and needs, "of divers States." The relative quality of the law of a people, therefore, including (by implication) the common law of England, must be judged not by its superior antiquity (as Coke, following Fortescue and St. German, would have it), since all systems of law are equally ancient, but by the extent to which it "best fits" the wants and needs of the particular people. At the same time, the diverse customs of diverse peoples, which are the source of their respective systems of civil law, though rooted in a common human nature, are subject to a continuous organic process of change, by which natural law is specified and altered. Thus the relative quality of the law of a people must be judged also by the extent to which it remains faithful to the organic continuity of its past—the extent to which, like a ship or a house whose materials have over time been entirely replaced, it is to be accounted the same ship or house.[46]

Selden did not deny—indeed, he affirmed—the source of all civil law in "Nature," that is, in the nature of God's creation, including above all the moral nature of man. In an important book on natural law,[47] he developed at length the theory that the ultimate source of both moral and legal obligation is in divine command, which he found revealed primarily in Scripture, especially the covenant between God and Noah whereby God imposed and Noah accepted certain prohibitions. According to Talmudic tradition, these were prohibitions against idolatry, blasphemy, homicide, incest, theft, the eating of live animals, and disobedience to civil laws. Selden stressed the importance not only of the covenantal, or contractual, nature of the Noachite obligations but also of God-given human conscience in fulfilling them.[48] His entire analysis thus followed the prevailing theological and philosophical tendencies of contemporary Protestant, and especially Calvinist, thought.[49] Perhaps his most distinctive contribution was his interpretation of the contractual character of moral obligations generally: it is not only breach of a prohibition that is offensive to God, and punishable by him, but also breach of a covenant. Indeed, for Selden the most important rule of natural law appears to have been the rule that contracts are to be kept, *pacta sunt servanda,* which he applied not only to divine contracts but also to human contracts generally.[50] His strong conception of the absolute obligation to keep one's contracts was related to his conception of the binding force of customary law, which he viewed as essentially consensual in nature.

What was most distinctive in Selden's thinking, and what was of decisive importance in the development of English legal philosophy, was his historical and sociological concept that legitimate diversities among national legal systems have their source in the diverse customs of diverse peoples. Just as individuals differ from one another, he wrote, so nations differ, and those differences give rise to differences in their customary law. This concept gave a new meaning to the principle—previously emphasized by Hooker—that the ultimate source of the legitimacy of human laws lies not only in their correspondence to divine law, including the law of reason and conscience, and not only in their correspondence to the will of the legitimate lawmaking authority, but also in their conformity to the consent of the people. Selden gave to the doctrine of government by consent of the people—which all the conflicting parties of the time advocated, though each gave it its own meaning—a new legal dimension: consent, in Selden's view, was manifested in custom, that is, in the patterns and norms of behavior tacitly or expressly accepted by the community. He argued that all law originates, historically, in customary law. Indeed, the English common law was itself conceived by him and his colleagues to be essentially an evolving customary law, in the sense that it was the embodiment of the patterns and norms of behavior developed by the common lawyers over many generations and centuries in response to changing circumstances.

Sir Matthew Hale's Life and Works

Selden was twenty-five years old and Coke was fifty-seven when Matthew Hale was born in 1609, but Coke lived another twenty-five years and Selden another forty-five, and both had a profound influence on Hale. It does not appear that Hale ever met Coke, but as a student in the 1620s he must surely have followed Coke's activities in Parliament, and subsequently he was an avid reader of Coke's *Institutes* and *Reports.* Selden became his close personal friend, despite the difference in their ages. In his scholarship as well as in his legal career, Hale followed in the footsteps of both these men, and in many ways even surpassed them.[51]

It was Hale who first articulated a general theory of historical jurisprudence which was implicit in Coke's portrayal of the English common law and in Selden's historical and philosophical studies. In contrast, however, to the schools of historical jurisprudence that flourished in the nineteenth and early twentieth centuries, Hale—here, too, building on both Coke and Selden—integrated his historical theory with its two major competitors, natural law theory and legal positivism.

Hale's extraordinary character justifies a more extensive account of his personal life than has been given here of Coke's or Selden's. His mother died when he was three years old and his father, who gave up the practice of law because of moral scruples against the then required practice of submitting false pleadings, died when he was five. Under the guardianship of a relative of his father, Hale was first instructed by the local vicar, a Puritan minister, and was later sent by his guardian to Oxford to be educated by a leading Puritan theologian. The young Hale himself intended to become a minister, but his youthful attraction to sports, the theater, fine clothes, and partying seems to have distracted him from that goal. He turned instead to the study of law, entering Lincoln's Inn at the age of nineteen. His studies included Roman law and also mathematics, optics, medicine, philosophy, and theology.[52]

While he was at Lincoln's Inn a dramatic experience, in which he witnessed a friend drink himself almost to death (Hale thought he had indeed died), led him to a radical change of life. He gave up drinking except at meals and turned to wearing common clothes instead of fancy gentlemen's clothing. He worked indefatigably to prepare himself for a blameless life of public service. He avoided speaking ill of anyone. He methodically gave one-tenth of his earnings to the poor as well as additional gifts to people in need. These and related qualities remained characteristic of him throughout his life. As a judge he refused not only bribes, which it was then common for judges to accept, but also gifts or favors of any kind, even from the highest nobility, and when certain extra emoluments were privately paid to judges in such a way that it was difficult to refuse them, Hale would send his—anonymously—to be given to the poor. Although people who occupied his position in public life were almost invariably wealthy, Hale lived very modestly and died leaving only a relatively small estate.

His absolute integrity was acknowledged by virtually everyone who came in contact with him.[53] It characterized not only his personal relations with people but also his public life—as legal counsel, for example, to leading royalists tried for treason in the 1640s and 1650s and as intercessor on behalf of Puritans charged with treason under Charles II in the 1660s;[54] as head of an important parliamentary law reform commission in 1652 and as a judge of the Court of Common Pleas from 1653 to 1657 under Cromwell; and under Charles II as chief baron of the Exchequer and, from 1671 until just before his death in 1676, as chief justice of the King's Bench.

Hale's integrity and the profound religious convictions on which it was based help to explain his ability to maintain an essentially neutral political stance throughout a long period of revolutionary upheavals and to serve in high places under successive opposing regimes. Charles Gray is undoubtedly right in attributing Hale's political neutrality to his allegiance to the common law. "Regimes come and go, the common law abides," writes Gray, noting that for Hale, "legal continuity was vital for civic identity."[55] It must be added, however, that his devotion to the continuity of the common law is itself to be explained at least partly by his intense religious beliefs. As a Puritan in spirit who remained, as many Puritans did, a devout member of the Church of England, Hale believed that not only legal continuity but also religious continuity was vital for civic identity. He believed, moreover, that the continuity of the English common law was grounded in English religious faith—a faith that transcended the sharp differences in doctrine and ritual that divided the different branches of Protestant Christianity. It is characteristic of Hale that in the late 1660s he introduced a bill into Parliament to admit Presbyterians to be members of the Anglican Church—not as a matter of toleration but as a matter of their "comprehension" within the Church of England.[56] Hale was also an early advocate of "toleration" of the other dissenting sects, including even the Quakers.[57]

Hale's strong personal character, his devotion to the common law, and his religious convictions—all three—help to explain not only his career as a lawyer in public life but also his intellectual life, which, though devoted chiefly to legal scholarship, included the natural sciences, philosophy, and theology as well. He was an active member of the Royal Society, England's élite circle of scientists and philosophers, and he numbered among his close friends the leading Puritan theologian Richard Baxter as well as other prominent theologians. He was a master of political and legal history and the author of the first history of English law ever written.[58] His writings on English criminal and civil law represent systematic studies in those fields.[59] Moreover, he was a serious student of Roman law and also wrote tracts in the fields of mathematics, natural science, philosophy, and theology.[60]

Hale's religious beliefs profoundly affected both his motivation to be a scholar and his effort to make sense, as a scholar, of the history and system of common law. His habits of prayer led him to ask deep questions concerning the meaning of life and the purposes of human history. His intense devotion to scholarship and his prolific writings seem to have been inspired chiefly by his personal relationship to his Maker and only secondarily by a sense of social or political obligation. Indeed, of the dozens of books and articles that he wrote and circulated to friends and acquaintances, he allowed only two scientific tracts to be printed during his lifetime, and forbade all but a few short works on various subjects to be published after his death.[61] Fortunately he did not destroy the others. Gray writes, "Perhaps Hale's drive to grasp general principles and clarify particulars was primarily a need to make sense to himself, to render a private accounting of the intellectual milieu of the law in which he passed his worldly life."[62] Gray adds, "Rendering an account of oneself to God could easily pass over into accounting intellectually to oneself."[63] Hale's remarkable essay on the office of a judge and his rules for judging—written in his diary in 1668 while he was sitting on circuit and published for the first time in 1988—is an example both of an intellectual accounting to himself and of a personal testimony to God.[64] It would appear that Justice Hale had a strong sense of the presence of God in his courtroom.

It was also characteristic of Hale that no one of his written works constitutes an adequate statement of his legal philosophy. Each, in fact, is incomplete and fragmentary in nature. His *History of the Common Law* was the first attempt to give a comprehensive portrayal of the historical origins and growth of English law, and it remained the standard book on early English legal history until the late nineteenth century. Yet it carried most of the details of the story only through what Hale considered to be its formative era in the twelfth and thirteenth centuries and cited no laws whatever of the Tudor-Stuart period. More important, Hale's effort in it to portray English legal history in philosophical terms, and to articulate its underlying theory, was only partly successful.[65] In another important work, *The Analysis of the Law,* Hale presented the English common law as a coherent system; yet in the preface he admitted that English law was too complex for him alone to "reduce to an exact logical method."[66] He did once give to friends an outline sketch of such a systematization of the law, but said that to carry it out was a work that would have to be undertaken by order of the state together with other men learned in the law.[67] Nevertheless, he did succeed in completely reorganizing the extensive scattered annotations of Littleton in the first volume of Coke's *Institutes* and in extracting their broader philosophical implications. (It was chiefly from Hale's edition that subsequent generations of lawyers read "Coke on Littleton.") Similarly, his *Reflections on Mr. Hobbes's Dialogue of the Law,* in which he responded to Hobbes's attack on Coke, laid the basis of a full-blown jurisprudence, but its approximately seven thousand words, printed (for the first time) in 1921, did not allow room to build a structure on that foundation.[68] His more technical legal writings also contain remarkable insights into the nature of English law and of law in general, but once again, they leave it to the reader to develop from them their general philosophical implications.[69]

It is nevertheless possible by a study of the entire corpus of Hale's writings to reconstruct the coherent legal philosophy that underlies them. One may conclude from such a study that that legal philosophy, when understood in the context of Hale's biography, represents the philosophy which dominated English legal thought in the late seventeenth, eighteenth, and early nineteenth centuries and which still plays an important part in the intellectual outlook of many, if not most, English (and American) practicing lawyers and judges, though not—any longer—of many English (or American) writers on legal philosophy.

Hale's Legal Philosophy

The various schools of legal philosophy that competed for acceptance in all the countries of Europe in the sixteenth and early seventeenth centuries may be grouped under two main headings: natural law theory, which treats law essentially as the embodiment in legal rules and concepts of principles derived from reason and conscience, and positivism, which treats law essentially as a body of rules laid down ("posited") and enforced by the supreme lawmaking authority, the sovereign. The former theory views law as rooted primarily in morality ("reason and conscience"); the latter views law as rooted primarily in politics ("the will of the lawmaker"). Positivists do not deny that law *ought* to serve moral ends, the ends of justice, but argue that what law *is* is a political instrument, a body of rules manifesting the policies of the legitimately constituted political authorities, and only after it is established what law is may one ask what it ought to be. Naturalists, if one may so call them, believe, by contrast, that one cannot know what the law is unless one considers at the same time what it ought to be, since, they argue, it is implicit in legal norms that they have moral (*including* political) purposes and are to be analyzed, interpreted, and applied in the light of such purposes. The naturalist will deny the validity—indeed, the legality—of a rule or action of the political authority that contradicts fundamental principles of justice.

In the four centuries preceding the Protestant Reformation, various natural law theories predominated, of which that of Thomas Aquinas (1225–1274) eventually became the best known. William of Ockham's belief in the priority of will over reason, at both the divine and human levels, referred to earlier, was indirectly connected with the belief of Marsilius of Padua, and later of Machiavelli, in the quintessentially coercive character of all government and law. In the sixteenth century, Lutheran political and legal theory found support in such "voluntarist" doctrines, although Lutherans combined positivist theories with natural law theories and lived with the tension between them.

These philosophical issues concerning the nature of law had, however, a historical dimension, which remained largely unarticulated. Ever since the early formation of discrete modern Western legal systems in the twelfth century, it had been taken for granted that a legal system has an ongoing character, a capacity for growth over generations and centuries. This was a uniquely Western assumption: that a body of law, a system of law, contains—and should contain—a built-in mechanism for organic change and that it survives—and should survive—by development, by growth. Thus the new profession of jurists, coming out of the universities that were founded from the late eleventh century on, developed the newly discovered Roman law texts, and to a somewhat lesser extent the various new systems of royal law, urban law, feudal law, manorial law, and mercantile law, progressively, each generation building on the work of its predecessors. The changes were thought to be part of a pattern of changes and, at least in hindsight, to reflect an inner logic, an inner necessity. The law was thought to be not merely ongoing; it had a history. It told a story.

This historical dimension of Western systems of law did not, however, despite its crucial practical importance, attract the attention of Western philosophers sufficiently to affect their jurisprudence: prior to the seventeenth century, they remained adherents either of natural law theory or of positivism or of an uneasy mixture of the two. There did emerge in the sixteenth century, most prominently in France, a historicist school of legal thought that held up the ancient Germanic and Frankish customary law as a model to be opposed to "foreign" Romanist and canonist legal traditions.[70] This nationalist historicism was invoked against royal "innovations," although in England, sixteenth-century "free monarchists" also invoked ancient English traditions and precedents to support their policies. Prior to Sir Edward Coke, however, it is hard to discover in Europe a legal philosopher who argued that the history of a legal system embodies a basic constitutional norm, which not only does govern but should govern all subsequent developments and which binds the sovereign political authority itself. But Coke was not, properly speaking, a philosopher. As we have seen, he limited his attention chiefly to English law and did not attempt to develop a system of general propositions that would be applicable to all legal systems. Moreover, Coke stressed the element of continuity in English legal history from the earliest times and did not attempt to characterize the many historical changes that had taken place over the centuries, although he was entirely familiar with them. He was not, properly speaking, a historian. Selden was, indeed, both a philosopher and a historian. Yet he, too, writing in the prerevolutionary period of struggle between the common law courts and the prerogative courts, emphasized the ancient tradition of limitations on the royal prerogative. It was left to Hale—building on Selden—to emphasize not only the ancient roots of the English legal tradition but also its capacity to evolve and to adapt itself to new needs. Laws must change with the times, he wrote, or they will lose their usefulness.

Hale developed the outlines of a third major theory of jurisprudence, the historical theory, which two centuries later competed for supremacy with the natural law theory and the positivist theory, but which Hale put forward in conjunction with, rather than in opposition to, the other two theories. Hale's historical theory treats law *partly*—in the nineteenth century, historicists would say it should be treated *primarily*—as a manifestation of the historically developing ethos, the historical ideals and traditions, the evolving customs of a people or society whose law it is. By virtue of its source in this ethos, law imposes limitations both on the sovereignty of the lawmaking power, the political "is," and on the authority of reason and conscience, the moral "ought to be."

Hale's legal philosophy may be divided into several parts. One is his conception of the relationship of what may be called historical law, that is, law in its historical dimension, to natural law, that is, law in its moral dimension, and to positive law, that is, law in its political dimension. A second is his conception of the nature of the historical development of a legal system. A third is his elaboration of the concept of artificial reason that Coke had first adumbrated. A fourth is his theory of sovereignty and of the nature of sovereignty in England. I take these up in turn.

The Historical Dimension of Natural Law and Positive Law

Hale believed that natural law, like positive law, constitutes a distinct body of law, and that it is binding upon states. This traditional Western conception differed from Coke's view that natural law is binding in England only to the extent that it has been made part of the English common law. Thus Hale wrote that there are many offenses that are prohibited by natural law and therefore both are and should be universally proscribed by criminal law. These, he said, may also be proscribed by divine law, which (like other Protestants) he confined to biblical law. Homicide and theft, he wrote, are contrary both to divine law and to the law of nature and are and should be made criminally punishable by all states, whether Christian or heathen.

Hale nevertheless limited the scope of both divine law and natural law. Some crimes proscribed by the Bible, he wrote, were fitted only to the Israelite state and hence are not obligatory for other states. Moreover, the kinds and measures of punishment, he wrote, "are not determined by the law of God or of nature but are left (for the most part if not altogether) to the positive laws and constitutions of the various states." Those positive laws of various states relating to punishment are to be studied and understood, so far as possible, in terms of their historical development. From a detailed study of laws of the Hebrews, the Greeks, the Romans, and the Anglo-Saxons, Hale concluded that

> penalties seem to be *juris positivi* and *non naturalis,* as to their degrees and applications, and therefore in different ages and states have been set higher or lower according to exigencies of the states and wisdom of the lawgiver. Only in the case of *murder* there seems to be a justice of retaliation, if not *ex lege naturali* yet at least by a general divine law given to all mankind, Gen. ix. 6. . . . In other cases, the *lex talionis* in point of punishments seems to be purely *juris positivi,* and although among the Jewish laws we find it instituted, Exod. xxi. 24, 25, "Eye for eye, tooth for tooth, hand for hand, foot for foot, burning for burning, wound for wound, stripe for stripe," yet inasmuch as the party injured is living and capable of another satisfaction of his damage, which he is not in case of murder, I have heard men greatly read in the Jewish lawyers and laws affirm that these taliones among the Jews were converted into pecuniary rates and estimates to the party injured.[71]

Thus divine law, in Hale's view, is found in those biblical precepts that are intended to have universal application, such as the Ten Commandments. Natural law includes such divine law as well as other legal principles and institutions that are in fact common to all nations. Divine law and natural law are binding on all rulers. Positive law is distinct from natural law in that it is subject to the discretion of the lawgiver, although the wise lawgiver will act according to reason and will do what is socially useful under the historical circumstances.

When Hale turns to an analysis of English criminal law, however, he views historical experience as not only instructive but also normative. Thus in arguing that the canonists are wrong in saying that capital punishment should not be inflicted for theft, Hale wrote that not only may utility require so drastic a punishment "when the offence hath grown very common and accompanied with enormous circumstances," but also in England the law—historically considered—had so developed as to require in his time the death penalty for theft, leaving almost no discretion to the judge.[72] He recognized a certain relativity in that regard. "If we come to the laws and customs of our own kingdom," he wrote, "we shall find the punishment of theft in several ages to vary according as the offence grew and prevailed more or less."[73] In contrast to Coke, Hale thus presented a historical jurisprudence with a changing content.

With respect to criminal punishment generally, Hale took the utilitarian view—against the natural law theory—that

> the true or at least the principal end of punishments is to deter men from the breach of laws . . . and the inflicting of punishments in most cases is more for example and to prevent evils than to punish. When offences grow enormous, frequent and dangerous to a kingdom or state, . . . or highly pernicious to civil societies, and to the great insecurity and danger of the kingdom and its inhabitants, severe punishment, even death itself, is necessary to be annexed to laws in many cases by the prudence of law-givers, though possibly beyond the single demerit of the offence itself simply considered.[74]

On the one hand, such a view of the "true or at least principal" purpose of punishment is congenial to a positivist theory of law, which subordinates both the moral and the historical dimension of law to the political dimension. On the other hand, Hale's view of the nature of the offenses to be prohibited by criminal law reflected his belief in the moral dimension of law and is congenial to a natural law theory. He combined these two theories in his analysis of particular legal systems, and especially the English legal system, whose historical experience determined the limits and the interrelations of their political and moral aspects. Thus Hale may be said to have articulated in a new way the integrative jurisprudence which was implicit in the Western legal tradition from the time it was formed, although the legal philosophers had tended (as legal philosophers often do) to assert the supremacy of one theory or the other.

The Historical Development of a Legal System

Hale did not advance a sophisticated theory of the historical development of legal systems, as Savigny, Maine, Durkheim, Max Weber, and other legal historicists and sociologists did in the nineteenth and early twentieth centuries.[75] He did, however, have a profound knowledge of the history of a number of foreign legal systems, which enabled him to make some generalizations about the history of law and to apply those generalizations to the particular character of the history of English law. Thus he wrote that it is in the nature of laws "to be accommodated to the conditions, exigencies and conveniences of the people, for or by whom they are appointed, [and] as those exigencies and conveniences do insensibly grow upon the people, so many times there grows insensibly a variation of laws, especially in a long tract of time."[76] This wholly unremarkable statement had the importance of enabling Hale to accept the differences between the common law doctrines as described by Glanvill in the time of Henry II and those discussed by Bracton in the time of Henry III. It enabled him to show the importance of legislation under Edward I, "the English Justinian," who was in many ways the hero of Hale's *History*—and, more generally, to stress the great role played by legislation throughout English legal history. Coke had minimized legislative changes, though he knew them well, and had stressed judicial continuity. Hale, however, who himself headed the famous Hale Commission for law reform under Cromwell, not only had a different personal background from that of Coke but also, more important, lived in a period of revolutionary upheaval. Like Selden, Hale viewed the history of the English common law as a process of adaptation to changing needs. In a long perspective, he saw such adaptation as a process of gradual improvement and self-perfection. In the eighteenth century this view was captured in Lord Mansfield's expression, "The common law works itself pure."[77]

It was the nature of legal change in England, however (and here Hale agreed with both Selden and Coke), that the basic constitutional framework of the law remained constant. Hale accepted the doctrines of the partisans of the common law and of parliamentary independence that parliamentary institutions had prevailed from the days of the Anglo-Saxon witans and moots, that trial by jury antedated—in a different form—the Norman grand and petty assizes, and that, in general, neither the Norman Conquest nor any subsequent upheavals represented a fundamental break in English constitutional history, although (in contrast to Coke) Hale recognized that the Conquest brought enormous legal changes in property law and other fields.[78] In this, as in other matters, Hale built on the insights of Selden.

Hale's conception of the balance between continuity and change in English legal history is captured by his striking analogies of the ship of the Argonauts and the biography of a human being:

> But tho' those particular Variations and Accessions have happened in the Laws, yet they being only partial and successive, we may with just Reason say, They are the same English Laws now, that they were 600 Years since in the general. As the Argonauts Ship was the same when it returned home, as it was when it went out, tho' in that long Voyage it had successive Amendments, and scarce came back with any of its former Materials; and as Titius is the same Man he was 40 Years since, tho' Physicians tells us, That in a Tract of seven Years, the Body has scarce any of the same material Substance it had before.[79]

This paradox of identity despite change was more than a restatement of a philosophers' conundrum. In the context of the Western legal tradition, it was a new way of addressing the problem of the reality of universals. The reality of the unwritten English constitution consisted above all in the growth of the English common law, its successive accommodations to the exigencies and conveniences of the people "as those exigencies and conveniences do insensibly grow upon the people." The alternatives to this middle course between philosophical realism and philosophical nominalism were, on the one hand, the Platonic notion of the reality of abstract principles of justice, characteristic of extreme versions of natural law theory, and the Machiavellian notion of the unreality of anything except particular decisions of a sovereign will, characteristic of extreme versions of legal positivism. The nature of the historical development of the English legal system, according to Hale, is that the constitution as a whole—the ship of state—is itself constituted by the successive changes in its parts experienced over centuries.

The Common Law as Artificial Reason

Hale accepted and developed further, in more general terms, Coke's concept that the common law is itself artificial reason, that is, that its internal logic, the coherence of its structure and functioning, consists of the reasoned experience of the lawyers and judges and legislators who have made it in the course of many centuries. Hale defended Coke's thesis against a direct attack by Thomas Hobbes. In doing so, Hale articulated the philosophical underpinnings of the thesis, so that it became part of Hale's version of an integrative jurisprudence.

Hobbes's attack on Coke was contained in the form of a dialogue between a philosopher, who presents largely, though not entirely, the thought of Francis Bacon and of Hobbes himself, and a lawyer, who relies largely, though not entirely, on the writings of Coke.[80] Hobbes wrote that Coke's conception of law as artificial reason was both untrue and obscure. It was, in the first place, untrue, since in fact law originates not in lawyers' or judges' reasoning, or indeed in reason at all, but in the will of the sovereign. To require that the sovereign's laws, in order to be enforceable, must conform to reason, whether or not "artificial," would, according to Hobbes, lead to disobedience on the part of every man (or in the case of artificial reason, by inference, every lawyer or judge) who claims to be more reasonable than the law itself. The concept of artificial reason is, in the second place, obscure, Hobbes wrote, since it does not clarify the relationship between lawyers' and judges' reasoning and the actual laws, that is, commands of the sovereign, which judges only interpret and apply in particular cases. "It is not Wisdom but Authority that makes a Law," says the philosopher.

Hale—without mentioning Coke by name—does not answer these charges directly but instead starts, characteristically, with a definition of Reason. Here he distinguishes between, on the one hand, the reason in things, their congruity or fit of interdependence, what we might call their internal logic, as when we say that "the reason" a watch runs is because of the interrelationship of the spring and the hands, or "the reason" an apple falls from a tree is because of the force of gravity, and, on the other hand, the human faculty of reasoning, which connects cause and effect or perceives the proportion between lines and surfaces, or otherwise understands phenomena. Hale calls this faculty "ratiocination, a faculty common to all reasonable creatures." The most important kind of reason is the combination of these two kinds of reason, "when the reasonable faculty is in conjunction with the reasonable subject, and habituated to it by use and exercise, and it is this kind of reason, or reason thus taken, that denominates a man a mathematician, a philosopher, a politician, a physician, a lawyer."[81]

"The reasonable faculty," the capacity to reason, is present in all people, but the reason inherent in various subjects, or various activities, differs, and therefore to be a *good* engineer or *good* surgeon or *good* mathematician requires "the application of the faculty of reason to the particular subjects . . . by particular methods." Thus one man's reason may be suited to one subject but not to the other. "Tully that was an orator, and a good moralist, was but an ordinary statesman and a worse poet." Hale wrote. "And . . . commonly those that pretend to a universal knowledge are but superficial and seldom pierce deep into any thing."

Of all subjects, law is the most difficult for the faculty of reason to understand, Hale wrote, since it deals "with the regulation and ordering of civil societies and with the measurement of right and wrong, when it comes to particulars." Moral actions are infinitely complex, and in applying moral principles to particular moral actions it is impossible to establish the kinds of certainty and of proof that are found in the natural sciences. Consequently, even the most intelligent people disagree concerning particular applications of common notions of justice to particular instances and occasions. Indeed, moral philosophers, who are accustomed to "high speculations and abstract notions touching justice and right . . . differ extremely among themselves when it comes to particular applications [and] are most commonly the worst judges that can be, because they are transported from the ordinary measures of right and wrong by their over fine speculations, theories, and distinctions above the common staple of human conversations."

Having established that, as one might say today, different methods are appropriate to different sciences, depending on the kinds of subject matter under investigation, and therefore that a general faculty of reason cannot in itself give one an understanding of the science of law, and still further, that moral philosophers (including, by implication, Hobbes) are peculiarly unfitted to understand law, which involves not only general principles but concrete applications of general principles by particular persons in particular situations, Hale concludes that in order to avoid instability, uncertainty, and arbitrariness in the application of reason to particular instances, "and to the end that men might understand by what rule and measure to live and possess, and might not be under the unknown, arbitrary uncertain judgment of the uncertain reason of particular persons," "the wiser sort in all ages have agreed" to institute particular laws and particular rules and methods of administration of justice.

The need for certainty, however, is not fully met by the establishment of laws and procedures for enforcing them, since there still remains the problem of applying such rules and procedures in a multitude of particular cases. There must therefore be an elaboration of the laws in order to meet enormously diverse circumstances. No individual can, by his own reason, determine what these laws should be. Even if he thinks he knows what it is right to do in a particular type of case, he must recognize that his knowledge may be inferior to that of others more experienced in such matters. "It is reasonable," Hale writes, "for me to prefer a law made by a hundred or two hundred persons of age wisdom experience and interest, before a law excogitated by myself"; and, "Again, it is a reason for me to prefer a law by which a kingdom hath been happily governed four or five hundred year than to adventure the happiness and peace of a kingdom upon some new theory of my own, tho' I am better acquainted with the reasonableness of my own theory than with that law." He gives the following illustration:

> It is a part of the law of England that all the lands descend to the eldest son without a particular custom altering it. That a freehold passeth not without livery [of] seisin, or attornment by an act in pais, but where statutes have altered [the former rules] that an estate made by deed to a man for ever passeth only for life without the word heirs and infinite more of this kind. Now if [even] the most refined brain under heaven would go about to enquire by speculation, or by reading of Plato or Aristotle, or by considering the laws of the Jews, or other nations, to find out how lands descend in England, or how estates are there transferred, or transmitted among us, he would lose his labour, and spend his notions in vain, till he acquainted himself with the laws of England, and the reason is because they are institutions introduced by the will and consent of others implicitly by custom and usage, or explicitly by written laws or acts of Parlement.

Thus Hale comes finally to Coke's artificial reason against which Hobbes had inveighed:

> And upon all this that hath been said it appears that men are not born common lawyers, neither can the bare exercise of the faculty of reason give a man a sufficient knowledge of it, but it must be gained by the habituating and accustoming and excercising that faculty by reading, study and observation to give a man a complete knowledge thereof.

In contrast to Coke, however, Hale answered Hobbes not primarily by an argument from the particular history of the English common law, but primarily by an argument from the nature of law generally, which is illustrated in English legal history but which is also illustrated in the history of other legal systems. Hobbes had sought timeless answers to timeless questions. His philosophy was unhistorical, and he opposed Coke's historicism on the ground that no truths, no lessons, could be derived from it. "Experience concludeth nothing universally," Hobbes wrote. To this Hale replied, in effect, as Coke might have replied, that a single important experience may be invoked to disprove a universal proposition, and further, that from universal experience one may indeed draw certain universal conclusions.

Hobbes had said that Coke's argument was, first, false because it failed to recognize that law consists of rules which reflect the will of the sovereign, and second, obscure because it defined law as the decisions of judges, whereas judges actually only interpret and apply the sovereign's rules in particular cases. In fact, it was Hobbes's argument that was false, because it failed to recognize that in England, at least, the sovereign inherits its law from the past and can change it only within limits set by the past; and with respect to obscurity, Hobbes simply erred in supposing that Coke defined the common law as the will of the judges. In fact, Coke cited judicial precedents as evidence of an age-old professional customary law that grows out of the reasoning of many generations of learned jurists.

In Hale's terms, what Coke called artificial reason is the combination of the reason inherent in law itself and the reasoning of experienced students and learned practitioners of law. Hale differed from Coke in attributing such reason (without using the term "artificial") not only to the English common law but also to law generally; and not only to its historical dimension but to its political and moral dimensions as well. Thus not only historical reason but also political reason and moral reason—in Aristotelian terms, all practical reason, as contrasted with pure reason—are, in Hale's view, a product of the application of the faculty of reasoning to the reason inherent in the subject matter, its own internal logic.

The Nature of Sovereignty

The second part of Hale's response to Hobbes is titled "Of Sovereign Power" (the first part is titled "Of Laws in General and the Law of Reason"). Hobbes had defined sovereignty as the supreme factual power in a state; he postulated a purely theoretical initial condition of anarchy in the world, a war of each against all, leading those living in such a "state of nature," through the exercise of "natural reason," to enter into a social contract whereby a commonwealth was formed and a sovereignty instituted, whether of one or of many. Given human nature, he contended, it is only through sovereign power that it is possible to obtain habitual obedience and thus to maintain peace in society. The sovereign may exercise his will through laws, which, however, cannot bind him, since otherwise he would lose his supreme power to keep order. "A law," wrote Hobbes in a famous passage, "is the command of him or them that have the sovereign power [over] them that be his or their subjects, declaring publicly and plainly what every one of them may do and what they must forbear to do." The characteristic form of law is therefore statute law. "Statutes," says the philosopher in Hobbes's *Dialogue,* "are not philosophy as is the common law and other disputable arts, but are commands or prohibitions which ought to be obeyed because assented to by submission . . . to whosoever [has] the sovereign power."[82] Coke had said it is the nature of law to be reasonable, and that the test of reasonableness is its ability to withstand the test of time.[83] As D. E. C. Yale has put it, "Hobbes could not admit reasonableness as a criterion either of the nature of law or of its obligatory force, for if men . . . might question the validity of laws on grounds of unreasonableness, how could there be habitual obedience?"[84]

Hale's critique of Hobbes's conception of sovereignty takes the form, principally, of a legal analysis of the nature of political power under the English constitution. From a Hobbesian point of view, this misses the mark. Hobbes did not purport to describe any existing polity; his Leviathan was a model—an "ideal type," in Max Weber's terminology. Yet as in all such ideal types, behind the ideal lay an existing reality, however much the idealization might differ from it; otherwise it would not be an ideal type, a model, but only a utopia, a "nowhere." The Weberian interprets the reality as an example of the ideal type. If, however, it is objected that the reality does not correspond to the ideal type, the Weberian will respond by saying that the ideal type is only an ideal type, a model.[85] Hale understood full well that Hobbes defined sovereignty as factual power, supreme and indivisible. He also understood, however, that Hobbes prescribed this model for an England which had been torn by two decades of civil strife and was still in the turmoil of the aftermath. Hale therefore countered Hobbes's ideal type not only with moral and political arguments but also with the reality of English constitutional history, to which he attached normative significance.

Hale began—in his usual way—with definitions, in this case with definitions of different kinds of power. There is, first, coercive power *(potestas coercive).* The king is not under the coercive power of the laws, though his subjects are. (This was written before 1689, when the king was, in fact, subjected to the coercive power of the laws under a new sovereign power, that of Parliament.) There is also, however, second, directive power *(potestas directiva).* The king has taken a solemn oath at his coronation to observe the fundamental law, including especially laws that concern the liberties of his subjects. He may not be coerced to observe these laws, but they nevertheless have directive power—they direct him. Third, there is a *potestas irritans,* an invalidating power, in the laws themselves, that is, the power to make acts void if they are against the law. Thus the sovereignty of the king exists *within* a legal framework.

Hale lists six great "powers of sovereignty" that inhere in English kingship: the power to make peace and declare war, the power to give value and legitimation to the coin of the realm, the power to pardon persons who have committed public offenses, the power to determine the jurisdiction of courts, the power to raise military forces by land and sea, and the power to make laws. He also identifies, however, certain qualifications even of this limited list of powers. He cites ancient statutes providing that the king cannot force anyone to go out of the kingdom or impose certain taxes without the consent of Parliament, and that, more generally, he cannot make laws without the advice and assent of the two houses of Parliament.

Hale holds up these realities of English constitutional law against Hobbes's argument that—in his model of sovereignty—there can be no qualifications or modifications of the power of a sovereign prince, and that the prince may make, repeal, and alter any laws he pleases, impose any taxes he pleases, derogate from his subjects' property how and when he pleases, and meet all public dangers in any way he thinks fit. "These wild propositions," Hale states, "are 1. Utterly false. 2. Against all natural justice. 3. Pernicious to the Government. 4. Destructive to the common good and safety of the Government. 5thly Without any shadow of law or reason to support them."[86] He takes up each of these objections in turn.

Hale's contention that Hobbes's conception of sovereignty is "false," that is, untrue, reflects his historical jurisprudence. One may ask, How can a "model" be untrue? Hale's answer is that "in things of this nature the best measures of truth or falsehood are not imaginary notions or reasons at large, but the laws and customs of this kingdom which have determined reason at large and bound it up within the bounds of such laws and usages." Here Hale pierces the veil of sovereignty as a model, or ideal type, and looks behind it to the historical reality of sovereignty in a particular place and time. In Hobbes's theory, sovereignty is a hypothetical factual power. Hale, on the contrary, argues that, as a matter of truth or falsehood, sovereignty is not hypothetical (an "imaginary notion") but real, and that it is not necessarily merely factual power but may be power constrained by a legal framework, and, finally, that the truth of these propositions is proved by English historical experience.

It is characteristic of Hale that he did not rely solely on a historical justification of his position but combined it with a moral and a political justification. Natural justice, he wrote, binds princes to carry out their pacts with their people: *pacta sunt servanda*—contracts must be kept. To this obligation, he wrote, "is superadded . . . the great solemnity of the oath which [the king] takes at his coronation to observe and keep those laws and liberties. And tho' it is true that the king's person is sacred, and not under any external coercion . . . yet no man can make a question whether he be not in the sight of God and by the bond of natural justice obliged to keep it."

Similarly, political considerations, expressed in the positive laws, whether of England or of other countries, normally limit and divide sovereign power. It is a fiction to say that the sovereign may not irrevocably delegate some of his powers to others. Hobbes had argued that the prince cannot be bound by laws because an invasion or rebellion or other emergency might occur which would require him to act contrary to them, and if he could not do so, his subjects would lose the benefit of that protection for which his sovereignty was initially established. Hale answers that "it is a madness to think that the model of laws or government is to be framed according to such circumstances as very rarely occur. Tis as if a man should make agarike and rhubarb his ordinary diet, because it is of use when he is sick which may be once in 7 years." Here Hale meets Hobbes on his own positivist and utilitarian ground. Independently of historical and moral considerations, with law understood as the will of the sovereign expressed in statutory commands, "it is better to be governed by certain laws tho' they bring some inconvenience at some time then under arbitrary government which may bring many inconveniences that the other doth not."

English Historical Jurisprudence and Seventeenth-Century Religious Thought

The legal philosophy of such men as Coke, Selden, and Hale must be understood as an integral part of their total philosophy, including their religious philosophy and their philosophy of the natural sciences. Indeed, the term "natural philosophy" was used in the seventeenth century to embrace knowledge of the divine nature, the nature of man, and the nature of the physical world—all three; and knowledge of the nature of man embraced the sciences of politics and law. It was understood, of course, that the science of law differed from, say, the science of astronomy, or optics, or other physical sciences, both in its method and in the certainty or degree of probability of its conclusions. Nevertheless, all the sciences were considered to be "of a sociable nature," dwelling side by side with one another in a common fellowship.

It should not be surprising, then, that Coke, Selden, Hale, and many of their colleagues of the bench and the bar were steeped in knowledge not only of law but also of theology and of the physical sciences, that their views of each of these branches of knowledge were related to their views of the others, and that the revolutionary changes which they introduced into legal philosophy in the seventeenth century paralleled the revolutionary changes that were taking place contemporaneously in virtually all aspects of "natural philosophy." In fact, Hale's historical jurisprudence paralleled in remarkable ways the Calvinist Puritan belief system in which he was trained in his youth, and it also drew heavily on the empirical method which constituted one important component of the new developments in the natural sciences which he discussed and wrote about as a member of the Royal Society.

Despite the many differences among different branches (and, indeed, different congregations) of persons called Puritans, they shared certain basic Calvinist beliefs which ultimately became part of an English world outlook and which found reflection in the historical jurisprudence expounded by Hale and his colleagues. Six such basic religious beliefs are listed here, together with their jurisprudential counterparts.

One was the belief that history is a revelation of divine providence, a spiritual story of the unfolding of God's own purposes, and, more particularly, that God works in history, in part, through his elect nation, England, which is historically destined to reveal and incarnate God's mission for mankind. This belief undergirded the conviction—shared by leading Puritans and leading common lawyers alike—that the English common law had unfolded over many centuries, gradually perfecting itself, and that it was peculiarly English and superior, at least for England, to any "foreign" law.

A second basic Puritan belief was that the reformation of the world is a religious commitment, commanded by God. This belief undergirded the strong emphasis on public spirit and civic virtue which was a hallmark of parliamentary and judicial rule by the English aristocracy and which helped to give English law its legitimacy as a system of justice.

A third basic Puritan belief was that God is a God of law, who inspires his followers to translate his will into legal precepts and institutions. The historical jurisprudence of Coke, Selden, and Hale found a secular equivalent of biblical law in the pre–sixteenth-century heritage of the English common law, which they invoked in order both to delegitimize the exercise of the royal prerogative by the Tudor-Stuart dynasty and to provide a basis for substantial reformation of the common law itself.

A fourth element of Puritan theology was its strong social dimension based on covenant and its belief in the corporate character of the local community of the faithful. This religious teaching found secular expression in the strong emphasis of historical jurisprudence on the central importance of custom in the development of the common law—the customs of the local community and the customary common law developed by the close-knit judiciary and bar.

A fifth characteristic of this belief system was its stress on hard work, austerity, frugality, reliability, discipline, and vocational commitment—what came to be called the Puritan ethic. In subtle but important ways this divinely commanded ethic undergirded the emphasis of English historical jurisprudence on case law and, more particularly, on the necessity of the most meticulous examination of the facts of previous analogous cases in order to determine the applicability of a legal rule or doctrine. As is apparent from his diary entry (quoted in note 64) concerning the enormous responsibility and burden of judging and the need to "turn every stone, weigh every answer, every circumstance" before reaching a decision, Hale—like Oldendorp in Germany a century before—considered judging to involve a deep search by the judge of his own conscience. At the same time, the differences between Oldendorp and Hale in this regard reflect differences in their theories of the sources of law. The specifically English heavy reliance on analysis and analogy of cases, as contrasted with the German-Lutheran—and Romanist-canonist—heavy reliance on analysis and analogy of concepts and of doctrines, is an integral part of English historical jurisprudence. For Hale, as a century later for Lord Mansfield, it was "the reason and spirit of cases" that made law, "not the letter of particular precedents,"[87]—but also not primarily the reason and spirit of an elaborately systematized body of legal concept and doctrines. Thus for Hale, it was not only the conscience of the individual judge but also the collective conscience of the judiciary, the conscience embodied in the line of previous cases, that was crucial.

Finally, Puritan theology undergirded important changes in various branches of the common law—changes which were thought to have roots in its historical development. Thus the Puritan emphasis on the innate sinfulness of all persons, including the judge himself, was strongly reflected not only in Hale's philosophy of judging but also in his theories of criminal law. Of special interest in this connection was Hale's statement of a presumption of innocence and his justification of it in religious terms: that although God requires the judge to convict the guilty and acquit the innocent, where the evidence of guilt is not conclusive the judge should acquit, even though he thereby risks acquitting the guilty, since God himself is the final judge, and, moreover, the guilty person who has mistakenly been acquitted may repent and reform. Similarly, the Puritan emphasis on the source of community in divinely inspired covenants undergirded new doctrines of strict liability for breach of contract. Also biblical authority was invoked for expanded rights of private property. In each of these developments, the common lawyers found—or invented—historical authority that paralleled biblical authority.

English Jurisprudence and Seventeenth-Century Scientific Thought

That English historical jurisprudence—in Hale's time and place—was closely linked with the Puritan religious reformation is easier to show than that it was closely linked with the contemporaneous reformation of the natural sciences. In some ways the changes in the natural sciences and the changes in legal philosophy were, and were recognized to be, contrary to each other. In other ways, however, the premises and methods of the two bodies of thought ran parallel to each other.

Not one but two radical changes in Western scientific thought took place successively in the seventeenth century. The first was reflected in the biographies and writings of Galileo Galilei (1564–1642) and René Descartes (1592–1650). Galileo shattered the Aristotelian view of the universe by his skepticism concerning the possibility of arriving at certain truth through the evidence of the senses and his resort to mathematics as the primary method of achieving certain knowledge of physical nature. The universe, Galileo wrote, is an "open book . . . written in the language of mathematics and the letters are triangles, squares, and other geometric figures."[88] "God hath made all things," he wrote, "in number, weight, and measure."[89] A generation later Descartes built his rationalist philosophy on Galileo's skepticism regarding sense perception and his mathematical method, calling for "clear and distinct ideas" as the sole method of achieving certainty in all fields of knowledge. Eventually Hobbes, Leibniz, and Spinoza also adopted what was called the "geometrical way" of reaching certainty in matters of political and moral philosophy. The geometrical way was to posit a hypothesis concerning the nature of the problem or object under investigation, then by an elaborate system of classification to break it down into a complex of separate simple elements, and finally to apply to the analysis of each of those elements mathematical measurements designed to describe the matter and the motion of which they consist. Through such a deductive method Galileo had proved the truth of Copernicus's hypothesis that the earth moved around the sun. The sequence could also be reversed: like Francis Bacon, one could start with discrete facts and by a series of gradual inductions arrive at proof of the certainty of the general truths which they reflect. Also, of course, the deductive and the inductive method could be combined, as they were by Galileo himself and later by Newton and others. The main point was that the universe was now thought to be a mechanical structure made up "essentially" of matter and motion, and these were thought to be discoverable by the mathematical method, whether solely or in combination with empirical proof.

This method, moreover, was thought to be applicable not only to knowledge of the physical universe but also to all other branches of knowledge. As Descartes wrote, "All the disciplines are so interconnected that it is much easier to study them all together than to isolate one from all the others."[90] Indeed, throughout the West there appeared books and articles in which all the various branches of what continued to be called "philosophy" were juxtaposed—physical, human, and divine. It was generally accepted, however, that "philosophy" meant certain knowledge—as contrasted with knowledge that is only probably true. Therefore, there could be no "philosophy" of history, for example, because (it was said) a knowledge of history is based only on memory, that is, on testimony from the past, which was considered unreliable.[91] Whether or not there could be a "philosophy" of law was debatable. Francis Bacon believed that such a philosophy was possible since law could be rendered certain if properly classified under a limited number of broad "maxims"—universal principles—whose truth could be tested by examples of specific rules drawn from all parts of the legal system.

The first scientific revolution of the seventeenth century proceeded on Galilean and Cartesian, and to a lesser extent Baconian, lines. Truth was identified with what the mind can weigh, measure, and count, which in turn presupposed the total objectivity of the observer. The identification of causation, in one of its aspects, with purposes, as in the Aristotelian concept of "final causes," was rejected in favor of a reduction of all forms of causation to what Aristotle had called "efficient causes," now viewed also in Platonic terms of rational necessity. The Aristotelian conception of a purposive and organic universe was rejected in favor of a morally neutral and mechanical universe.[92]

In the course of the seventeenth century, however, a sharp split developed between the mathematical method and the empirical method. The empirical method came to be viewed by many—especially in England—not in Baconian terms of inductive logic, designed to yield truth that is mathematically certain, but rather in probabilistic terms: the experimental method, it was asserted, could only yield "moral" certainty, that is, a high degree of probability. The Galilean postulate that the conclusions of natural science, being founded on mathematics, are objectively certain and do not depend on human judgment underwent modification, insofar as scientific experimentation came to be understood in terms of trial and error. The use of experiments to confirm hypotheses believed to be mathematically true and a matter of rational necessity was adapted to include the use of experiments to establish the degree of probability of hypotheses believed to be possibly but not necessarily true.[93]

This was a revolutionary change, which was reflected especially in the biography and the writings of Isaac Newton (1642–1727) and John Locke (1632–1704), each of whom denied altogether the capacity of the human mind to achieve absolute truth and instead emphasized various empirical methods of achieving various degrees of probability in various fields of knowledge. The postulate that sense perception and, more broadly, experience, including the collective experience of professional communities, can establish maximum probabilities made possible the development of a new paradigm not only of the natural sciences but also of various other types of sciences based on various other methodologies.

This last point is important for an understanding of the legal revolution of the seventeenth century, since the historical jurisprudence of Matthew Hale and his colleagues had close links with the empirical method used by contemporaries working in the natural sciences, but it was essentially in conflict with the mathematical method espoused by Galileo and Descartes.

It is sometimes supposed that the empirical method of the common lawyers has little or nothing to do with the empirical method of natural scientists, since the latter is based on the principle of hypothesis and falsification whereas the former, while deriving general rules from examination of decisions in individual analogous cases, treats the rules not as hypotheses but rather as authoritative statements to be adhered to even if they subsequently prove unsatisfactory. This view of law, however, looks only at the form of legal rules and disregards their purposes and their consequences; hence it neglects the processes by which legal rules are modified as their validity is tested in new applications. There are, to be sure, crucial differences between, on the one hand, the process of analysis of the facts of reported cases in the courts in order to determine the rules implicit in the judicial decisions and, on the other hand, the process of analysis of the facts of experiments in the natural sciences in order to test hypotheses concerning the causes and effects of physical occurrences. Nevertheless, there are also certain important similarities between the two processes, especially in their underlying philosophical implications.

The philosophical implications of the experimental method in the natural sciences were the subject of a series of polemical debates between one of the great seventeenth-century practitioners of that method, Robert Boyle, and none other than—once again—"the Philosopher" Thomas Hobbes.[94] Philosophy, Hobbes wrote (today we would say "science"), is "such knowledge of effects or appearances as we acquire by true ratiocination from the knowledge we have first of their causes or generation: And again, of such causes or generations as may be from knowing first their effects." Since the aim of philosophy, Hobbes argued, is the highest degree of certainty that can be obtained, therefore fallible sensory knowledge cannot constitute its foundations. Sense and memory, he wrote in opposition to Boyle, constitute knowledge, but because they are not given by reason, "they are not philosophy." Experience is "nothing but memory," and no general truths can be derived from it. Hobbes therefore denied that Boyle's invention of an air-pump designed to create an artificial vacuum, and his subsequent use of the invention to test hypotheses concerning the motion of light, could in themselves contribute to the kind of certainty that constitutes "philosophy." On the contrary, as Boyle himself admitted, they could only generate probable truth.

Boyle and his supporters (including his friend Matthew Hale) did not regard their search for probable truth as a regrettable retreat from more ambitious goals. On the contrary, they regarded the quest for absolute certainty as both a failed and a dangerous project—failed because all scientific knowledge, they contended, is probabilistic, and dangerous because the quest for absolute certainty leads to a dogmatism that tolerates no dissent.

But if the truths derived from the experimental method are always probable and never certain, how is the validity of an experiment to be proved? Boyle's answer was that its validity depends on its verification by other members of the scientific community. Witnesses of the experiment must be multiplied. If the experience of it can be extended to many persons, and in principle to all, then the result may be treated as a fact, that is, as a truth having the highest degree of probability. Thus Boyle anticipated the social theory of scientific knowledge that has been widely expounded since the latter part of the twentieth century: that scientific truth is that which is accepted as truth by the scientific community.[95]

Boyle also made it a requirement of the experimental method that its practitioners should avoid introducing speculations concerning first causes. Natural philosophers, he wrote, can legitimately disagree about the causes of natural effects. Here again his enemy was Hobbes, for whom dissent—disunity—was the greatest evil.

It is no accident that Hale sided with Boyle in this debate, and that he viewed Boyle's philosophy of natural science as having a close affinity with his own philosophy of law. For Hale, the validity of legal principles, like the validity of the principles of natural science, depended on repetition and verification by the community of trained practitioners. The common lawyers' "artificial reason" itself represented a kind of empiricism, different from but parallel to the experimental empiricism of the natural scientists.

That for many centuries law in the West had developed historically, with each generation consciously building on the experience of its predecessors, was, of course, a well-known fact. Prior to the seventeenth century, however, it had not risen to the level of a theory. Now Coke, Selden, Hale, and their followers ascribed a philosophical dimension to the history of the English common law. They asserted, in effect, the normative character of historical experience, putting custom and precedent on a level with equity and legislation as sources of law. They thus laid the foundations of a historical jurisprudence that occupied an equal place with natural law theory and legal positivism.

It was their understanding—more fully developed in Hale than in Selden, and more fully developed in Selden than in Coke—that law in this large sense has both a moral character (its purpose is to do legal justice) and a political character (its purpose is to maintain legal order), but it also has a historical character (its purpose is to preserve and develop the legal traditions of the people whose law it is). It was at least implicit in their writings that these three purposes, or aspects, of law should be integrated, and, more particularly, that conflicts which inevitably arise between the moral and political purposes of law can and should be resolved in the context of legal history. Thus law, they might have said, is the balancing of morality and politics in the light of history; it is the balancing of justice and order in the light of experience.[96]

CHAPTER 9

The Transformation of English Legal Science

In the late seventeenth and early to mid-eighteenth centuries, the English legal system underwent fundamental changes in its method, that is, in the basic principles by which it operated. The new emphasis on the historicity of English law, that is, on the normative character of its historical development over generations and centuries, was manifested in new ways of systematizing it.

The most obvious methodological manifestation of the new historical jurisprudence was the emergence of the modern doctrine of precedent. Related methodological changes included the transformation of some of the historical forms of action into modern remedies for the protection of rights of property and for enforcement of obligations of contract, tort, and unjust enrichment. Closely connected both with the transformation of the forms of action and with the doctrine of precedent was the resort to legal fictions as a device for adapting older doctrines and procedures to new purposes.

Other changes in legal method were closely connected not only with the new emphasis on the historicity of law but also with new philosophical concepts of truth and justice that grew out of older jurisprudential theories of natural law and positivism. These included the increase in the independence of the jury as a trier of fact and law, the expansion of the rights of the accused in criminal trials, the introduction of the adversary system of presentation of evidence, and the establishment of new criteria of proof in civil and criminal cases.

Finally, the transformation was reflected in a new type of legal literature, namely, modern legal treatises analyzing and systematizing English law as a whole as well as some of its individual branches.[1]

These topics—doctrine of precedent, forms of action, legal fictions, jury trial, rights of the accused, adversary system, evidence, treatises—may seem at first to be only a list of diverse features of the Anglo-American legal system. They may also be seen, however, and are treated in this chapter, not only as legal data but also as interlocking ways in which legal data were understood—that is, as important constituent parts of a coherent body of knowledge about law, and in that sense as elements not only of a legal method in the more technical sense but also of a legal science in the more theoretical sense. Indeed, in the sixteenth and seventeenth centuries the words "method" and "science" were often used interchangeably, bringing together mode of operation and theory.[2]

To speak of legal science, or a science of law, is to risk serious misunderstanding on the part of those who assume that the only true sciences are the natural sciences, and especially the "hard" natural sciences such as physics and chemistry. This is a contemporary Anglo-American usage; in most other languages, "science" (in German *Wissenschaft,* in French *science,* in Russian *nauka*) has retained its older, broader meaning of a coherent, systematic body of knowledge, combining particular facts with general principles, and is applied not only to the exact natural sciences but also to the less exact social and other humane sciences, including the science of law *(Rechtswissenschaft, science de droit, pravovaia nauka).*

There is, however, another more serious ambiguity in the application of the word "science" to law, namely, that legal science may refer not only to a body of knowledge about law generated by legal scholars (as the word "physics," for example, refers to a body of knowledge about matter and motion generated by physicists, or the word "geology" to a body of knowledge about the formation of the earth generated by geologists), but also to a body of knowledge generated by the law itself, defining its functions and the ways in which it operates. To say that a given system of law may itself contain, in that sense, a science is by no means to deny that (like medicine, for example) it is also, in its application, an art; it is only to say that principles laid down by its authors and practitioners—legislators, judges, administrators, and others—may expressly define its character, that such principles may be not only statements *about* law but also statements *of* law, and that in the Western legal tradition, at least, they are understood to constitute a coherent, systematic body of knowledge relating particular rules and decisions, particular modes of operation, to general legal theories. Even the simplest legal rules—for example, that a certain type of agreement is a legally binding contract, or that to kill another person intentionally and with malice aforethought constitutes the crime of murder—connote general principles of the legal system, such as the principle that contracts give rise to civil obligations enforceable by courts, the principle that some types of homicide are more severely punishable than others, and that certain kinds of distinctions are to be made between civil law and criminal law, et cetera; and these principles are officially declared to be necessary to the achievement of the purpose of law to promote justice and to maintain order. This is only to say that the science of law, like other social sciences, and like the science of language itself, differs from the natural sciences insofar as the participants in legal activities, that is, those who make or apply or administer or practice law, themselves articulate the nature of those activities, and their articulations are an essential part of the science itself. Indeed, in the Western legal tradition the legal actors themselves have for many centuries consciously ascribed to their own declarations of what they themselves are doing the qualities of a systematic, objective, verifiable body of knowledge, a meta-law by which the legal system itself may be analyzed and evaluated.

On the one hand, the rules and principles of English law of the late seventeenth and early to mid-eighteenth centuries may thus be said to have constituted its *internal* science. The new treatise literature of that period, on the other hand, generated by legal scholars, not only recapitulated the internal legal science but also analyzed, classified, systematized, and evaluated English legal institutions according to criteria drawn partly from within but also partly from outside those institutions, and thus may be said to have constituted an *external* science of English law.[3] The frequent references to "legal science" made in that literature did not, however, expressly distinguish between its internal and its external aspects. William Blackstone, for example, in initiating in 1753 the first course on English law ever offered in an English university, said that "law is to be considered not only as a matter of practice but as a rational science," grounded on "general principles" inherent in the law itself, and that it is the task of the legal scholar to discern those principles.[4] At the same time, Blackstone followed a method of analysis and synthesis of English law that had been introduced three generations earlier by Matthew Hale,[5] a method that was drawn partly from philosophy, theology, and the natural sciences, as well as from the entire body of Western legal scholarship. Blackstone referred indirectly to that external aspect of the science of law in writing that the teaching of English legal science had been "committed to his charge to be cultivated, methodized, and explained," and that English law should be studied "in a solid, scientifical method."[6] Indeed, if only the internal mode of operation of the English legal system were to be taught, without external theoretical analysis and evaluation, it would hardly make sense to teach it in a university course designed, as he said, as part of the general education of "every gentleman and scholar."[7]

It must also be noted that the authors of the first treatises on English law were not professors but judges and practicing lawyers, and their treatises in fact strongly affected the fundamental structural and institutional changes in the English legal system that took place in the late seventeenth and early to mid-eighteenth centuries. Indeed, a principal source of the differences between the new English legal theory and the legal theory that had prevailed previously in the West was the fact that the earlier legal theory was primarily professorial in its origin and nature, whereas the new English legal theory was primarily judicial in its origin and nature. The English Revolution exalted the role of the legal profession as guardian not only of the positive law but also of legal science. This fact, too, contributed to the integration of the internal and external aspects of English legal science—its method in the narrower sense and its theory in the broader sense.

The Emergence of the Modern Doctrine of Precedent

In the earliest stages of the development of adjudication by English royal courts, and especially after the introduction of written records of court proceedings, there also developed an interest in judicial decisions as guides to what the law is. Casuistry was, indeed, also a hallmark of the contemporary systems of canon law and Roman law, but it flourished especially in the English royal courts, whose law was not a university discipline and was only occasionally subjected to theoretical treatment in learned books. Casuistry, however, treats cases not as authoritative precedents but merely as examples of the application of principles and rules of law; in none of the legal systems that prevailed in the West prior to the seventeenth century did judicial decisions have normative force not merely for the parties in the cases but also as a source of law; on the contrary, they were considered to be only particular examples of how the law was applied in particular cases—examples that might or might not be followed in later analogous cases. Thus, although Bracton's great thirteenth-century *Treatise on the Laws and Customs of England* refers to some five hundred decided cases, and Bracton also wrote a *Note Book* containing digests of some two thousand cases, he did not espouse a doctrine of precedent, and indeed the word "precedent" is absent from his vocabulary.

Bracton's attitude toward cases reflected the canonist rule—which he repeated in his *Treatise*—that "one must judge not by examples but by reasons" ("non exemplis sed rationibus adjudicandum est"). Judicial decisions could be used to illustrate legal principles but were not themselves an authoritative source of law. In England in the period of the "Year Books" (ca. 1290–1535), which were law students' reports of judicial sessions they attended, cases were sometimes discussed in oral argument, and in procedural matters a series of similar decisions might be considered to be evidence of the existence of the custom of the judges *(mos judiciorum),* but even such a custom was regarded as having only persuasive and not binding authority. If a judge did not approve of a previous decision, or even of a previous custom of the court, he might say that it was wrong and disregard it.

With the end of the Year Books, private reports of cases began to be published, some of them much like the Year Books. Usually named for some distinguished lawyer or judge, the reports of the sixteenth and early seventeenth centuries consisted of a mixture of the facts of the cases, the statements of judges and of counsel, and the comments and notes of the reporters. As historical records, they were often quite unreliable. They did, however, serve to reinforce a newly emerging principle that in matters of procedure and pleading, the common law courts would adhere to their custom—and, in that sense, their precedents. This principle was not ironclad; in 1557, in perhaps the first recorded use of the term "precedent," a case was reported in which it was said that judgment was given, "notwithstanding two presidents."[8] Moreover, the principle was largely confined to procedural matters, including matters of judicial competence, and was probably related to the necessity of maintaining lines of separation between the jurisdiction of the common law courts and that of the other types of courts.[9]

The doctrine of precedent—that judicial decisions are an authoritative source of law, binding on courts in later analogous cases—requires that a distinction be made between statements by a judge that are necessary to the decision in the case and those that are not necessary. Only those reasons that are necessary to a given decision can constitute the legal principle or principles for which the case "stands." Whatever a court says in its opinion in a given case that is not necessary to the decision is said to be only "dictum," something that was only "said," and hence is not binding on courts in later analogous cases. What is binding are the "holdings" of the cases, namely, those reasons on which the decisions are necessarily based, that is, reasons that are essential to an explanation of the decision in the case. It is the holdings of cases that constitute rules of law which are binding in future analogous cases.

The earliest attempt to develop the distinction between dictum and holding was that of Chief Justice Vaughan of the Court of Common Pleas in 1673. Vaughan stated: "An opinion given in Court, if not necessary to the judgment . . . but . . . [the judgment] might have been as well given if no such or a contrary opinion had been broached, is no . . . more than a *gratis dictum.*" Vaughan did not consider, however, that the holding in any particular case was necessarily to be followed in subsequent cases. "If a judge conceives a judgment given in another Court to be erroneous," Vaughan stated, "he being sworn to judge according to law, that is, in his conscience, ought not to give the like judgment."[10]

In Matthew Hale's words: "The decisions of courts of justice . . . do not make a law properly so-called (for that only the King and Parliament can do); yet they have a great weight and authority in expounding, declaring, and publishing what the law of this kingdom is, especially when such decisions hold a consonancy and congruity with resolutions and decisions of former times, and though such decisions are less than a law, yet they are a greater evidence thereof than the opinion of any private persons, as such, whatsoever."[11]

Noteworthy in this statement is Hale's emphasis on the consistency of decisions in analogous cases over time. A line of judicial decisions consistently applying a legal principle or rule to various analogous fact situations is "evidence," in Hale's formulation, of the existence and the validity of such a principle or rule. The decisions are not only "examples" of the principle or rule but also "proof" of its reception by the judiciary and hence a source of its binding force.[12] Judges, to be sure, do not "make" laws but "find" them in the received legal tradition and "declare" them. This "declaratory theory," as it is called, means that the source of law in precedent is itself linked to the source of law in custom, which in turn is linked to the source of law in "reasonableness," as the moral element in law was then called for the first time. The link with reasonableness leaves room for courts to overrule even long-practiced error. Yet reasonableness itself, in the seventeenth-century English concept of it, had a historical dimension. "The conviction of the reasonableness of the law," as Gerald Postema has said, writing of the origins of the "traditionary" doctrine of precedent (as he aptly called it) in the late seventeenth and early eighteenth centuries, "does not rest, as in classical natural law theory, on the conviction that the law conforms to some set of transcendent standards of reason or justice. . . . It rests, rather, on two other convictions: (1) a sense of the historical appropriateness of the precedent and of the body of law as a whole, and (2) the belief that its component decisions are the products of a disciplined process of reasoning and reflection on common experience."[13]

Thus the traditionary concept of precedent should not be confused with the strict doctrine of *stare decisis* that first emerged in the nineteenth century, under which the holding of a particular case is treated as binding on a court in a later similar case. The strict doctrine was a product of the nineteenth-century mind, and is associated with different concepts from those which predominated in the late seventeenth and early eighteenth centuries. The strict doctrine builds, to be sure, on the distinction between holding and dictum which was established in the earlier period. But the doctrine of precedent of the earlier period was more closely related to the concept of *mos judiciorum*, the custom of the judges; it was a line of cases, rather than a single decision, that ought not to be overturned in the absence of very weighty reasons. Lord Mansfield could still say, in 1762, that "the reason and spirit of cases make law; not the letter of particular precedents."[14]

As shown in the previous chapter, the traditionary doctrine of precedent was founded on the theory of scientific knowledge expounded in the late seventeenth century by the chemist Robert Boyle, the physicist Isaac Newton, the jurist Matthew Hale, and other prominent members of the Royal Society.[15] That theory was subsequently developed in the mid-eighteenth century by David Hume. Hume traced our knowledge of truth to our mental habits of testing truth, and he traced those mental habits to social conventions handed down from the past. This was a metaphysical version of Boyle's theory that the ultimate source of knowledge in both the natural and social sciences is professional verification and acceptance of empirical observation. The traditionary doctrine of precedent treated the judiciary's repeated application of previous holdings to analogous cases as the best evidence of their probable validity, just as the repeated confirmation of the results of scientific experiments by the community of physicists and chemists was treated as proof of the probable truth of their findings.

The Transformation of the Forms of Action

As the earlier casuistry of the English common law was transformed in the late seventeenth and early eighteenth centuries into a new doctrine of precedent, so the earlier system of civil remedies based on forms of action was transformed into a new system of substantive civil law in which the forms of action were revised to correspond to general categories of property, contract, tort, and unjust enrichment.

In establishing, in 1178, the Court of Common Pleas as the first permanent professional English royal court, Henry II had limited its civil jurisdiction to types of complaints for which the chancellor would issue a writ. At first these were chiefly complaints alleging certain types of "trespasses" (as they came to be called) against rights of possession of land and chattels as well as against the bodily security of the person. Later the chancellor also granted writs of "debt" for the payment of money which the plaintiff claimed belonged to him, writs of "detinue" to recover damages for the wrongful detention of the plaintiff's chattels, writs of "replevin" for the return of chattels pledged for an obligation that had been fulfilled, writs of "covenant" for breach of a sealed instrument containing a promise, and various others. By the year 1300 there were dozens of different types of such "forms of action" commenced by a royal writ issued to local royal officials (sheriffs), ordering them to have the defendant before the judges of Common Pleas or King's Bench to answer the charges stated in the writ. In the fourteenth and fifteenth centuries, however, very few new types of writs were issued, although one of them, "trespass on the case," was of great importance, since it gave a legal remedy for certain types of harm to persons or property caused "indirectly" and also for certain types of harm caused by failure to perform an act which the defendant had specially undertaken to perform ("special assumpsit").[16] In the sixteenth century a new form of trespass-on-the-case called "indebitatus assumpsit," or "general assumpsit," gave a remedy for breach of certain types of obligations where no undertaking was expressly given but one could be implied since the defendant was "indebted," as where the defendant had received something of value from the plaintiff and, in the absence of an agreement on the price, would not pay for the benefit he had obtained.

Each of the various forms of action was relatively narrowly defined, and together they constituted a highly formal system of civil remedies. Moreover, different trial procedures were sometimes applicable to different forms of action. If the plaintiff obtained from the chancellor a writ of detinue when in fact a writ of debt was appropriate, or a writ of debt when a writ of general assumpsit was appropriate, he lost his case. It was partly because of the relative narrowness and formalism of civil remedies applicable in the royal courts of Common Pleas and King's Bench that the Tudor monarchs created new prerogative courts to handle new types of civil cases. Similarly, the relative narrowness and formalism of criminal remedies available in the older royal courts was one of the factors that led to the expanded criminal jurisdiction of the prerogative courts. At the same time, rivalry with the new prerogative courts led the older courts to expand the scope of various forms of action in order to attract litigation. Thus in the late sixteenth and early seventeenth centuries, they expanded the remedy of special assumpsit to include new types of undertakings—for example, certain types of executory contracts, that is, exchanges of promises of future performance, and also promises by one party given in return for the other party's act or forbearance to act, provided that the act or forbearance was of value.[17] Despite these changes, however, the common law of contracts remained relatively undeveloped, and the system of pleading and proof remained highly formal, so that only a relatively few types of contract disputes found their way into the common law courts during this period.[18]

The "formulary procedure," as it was called, of the older royal courts of Common Pleas and King's Bench reflected a different legal science from that of the newer "high courts" created by royal prerogative in the sixteenth century, including the renamed High Court of Chancery and the renamed High Court of Admiralty as well as the King's Council sitting as the High Court of Star Chamber, the supreme ecclesiastical court called the High Commission, the Court of Requests, the Court of Wards, and others. Not only the procedure and substantive law of Chancery, for example, differed substantially from that of the older courts, but also the criteria by which legal arguments were advanced and justified and decisions reached. The chancellor's "equity" was not only a different body of rules but also a different kind of legal reasoning—not totally different, of course, but different enough to be distinguishable. Similarly, Star Chamber, High Commission, Admiralty, and the other newer courts had their own distinctive legal methods. There was, to be sure, a common English legal tradition, which was part of the common Western legal tradition, but within each of those legal traditions there were plural, albeit interrelated, legal systems with plural legal methods and theories.

With the suppression of Star Chamber, High Commission, and other prerogative courts by the Long Parliament in the 1640s, and the eventual supremacy of the common law over Chancery, Admiralty, and the ecclesiastical courts, the common law courts took over much of the civil jurisdiction and almost all of the criminal jurisdiction of their erstwhile rivals. Inevitably, the forms of action had to be either (1) abandoned, (2) confined to the older causes of action to which they had traditionally been applied, or (3) expanded to provide remedies previously available only in the rival courts. The third possibility was the one most consistent with the belief in the historicity of English law and the traditionary doctrine of precedent, and it was the one that was adopted.

The Use of Legal Fictions to Establish Rights of Ownership

In some instances the forms of action were transformed by use of legal fictions. Two striking examples were the transformation of the possessory action of ejectment to protect the right of ownership, and not merely the right of possession, of land and the transformation of the possessory action of trover to protect the right of ownership, and not only the right of possession, of goods.

The action of ejectment had become available in the thirteenth century to protect persons in possession of land, especially lessees, against dispossession by persons who unjustifiably claimed a better right of possession, including their lessors. At that time, and for several centuries thereafter, a supreme right in land, including the full right of use and disposition and not only a superior right of possession, had very limited applicability and could be vindicated only by a very cumbersome procedure. Indeed, the common law of real property had consisted largely of the law of feudal tenures and had not developed a clear concept of ownership. In the seventeenth century, however, there was a felt need to adapt the simpler forms of possessory actions to the protection of full ownership. The extraordinary solution devised by the common lawyers to meet this need was to transform, by a series of fictions, the possessory action of ejectment into an action to try title to land. Thus the claimant in an action of ejectment (we may call him Smith) alleged that he had leased the land to a fictitious lessee, John Doe, who, while occupying the land, was ejected by a fictitious lessee of the other party, Richard Roe, and that Richard Roe had notified the other party (we may call him Saunders) that John Doe had brought an action of ejectment against him, Roe, to which he did not intend to make any defense, and that Saunders should appear in court and apply to be made the defendant in the action. Thus there was a fictitious lease by Smith to Doe, a fictitious entry by Doe, and a fictitious ouster of Doe by Roe, and a fictitious notification of Saunders that Roe would not defend the suit, so that, in form, the only point left to be decided by the court was whether Smith or Saunders had the better right to lease the land. The action to try this point was entitled *Doe d. [= on the devise of] Smith v. Saunders,* and in form Smith was suing Saunders for the "ejectment" of Smith's lessee. In substance, however, the defendant Saunders was allowed to set up the title of a third person, and public notice of the proceeding was given so that any other claimant to the land could appear. Thus although the actual dispute was between two parties, Smith and Saunders, each of whom claimed ownership of the land, and third persons who claimed ownership could appear as parties, the procedure was in the form of a dispute over the right to lease the land, since at common law that was the only convenient procedural form available.

A similar fiction was involved in the transformation of the action of trover—or, more precisely, the action of trespass-on-the-case for trover and conversion—from an action for damages brought against a possessor of a chattel by one who claimed a better right of possession into an action to try the right of full ownership of the chattel. In its initial form, the plaintiff alleged that the defendant had found a chattel ("trover" is from the French *trouver,* "to find") belonging to the plaintiff and, intending to deceive him, refused to return it but instead converted it to his own use. The remedy was damages for the conversion; the defendant in possession of the chattel was not required to return it (as he would be in an action of replevin) but to pay its value. In the sixteenth century the allegations of a finding and of intent to deceive the plaintiff were treated as irrebuttable and were not tried. These fictions were introduced in order to avoid the need to bring the action of detinue, whose archaic procedure ("wager of law") was cumbersome and unreliable and whose remedies were unsatisfactory.[19] The issue to be tried, however, was at that time similar to the issue in detinue: Was the defendant wrongfully exercising rights of possession of the chattel—rights that belonged to the plaintiff? In the late seventeenth and eighteenth centuries, however, an additional substantive fiction was added to the procedural fictions: not only the superior right of possession as between the parties but also the full right of ownership, valid against all possible claimants, was decided by the action.[20] And again, as in ejectment, this was accomplished by permitting the defendant to raise the defense that title was not in the plaintiff but in a third party, and by advance notice to the public that the action was pending.[21]

Ejectment and trover are dramatic examples of a number of fictions by which the changes in substantive law were accomplished by English common law courts in the seventeenth and eighteenth centuries. At first blush it may seem that the use of such fictions was completely arbitrary. Rules were applied to situations to which by their very terms they were wholly inapplicable. It is one thing to interpret a rule broadly, to "stretch" it to include something not originally intended to be covered, as when it is said that a seller's "warranties" cover certain contingencies that he did not expressly affirm, although originally the word "warranty" ("guaranty") was understood to mean an express affirmation. This is a metaphorical use of the word "warranty" that does not seem to do violence to the language, at least so long as the seller is permitted expressly to disaffirm the particular contingencies. But to say that a seller who has expressly disaffirmed a warranty is nevertheless "deemed" to have made it—that it is "implied in law" although it does not exist (even by implication) in fact—is another matter. As a matter of fact, it is not true that he made it. As a matter of fact, it is not true—to take other contemporary examples—that a corporation is a "person" (and therefore may sue and be sued), or that a child who enters land without permission and is injured by a hidden source of danger on the land is an "invitee" (and therefore has greater rights than those to be accorded to a "trespasser").

Yet legal fictions are not lies. They are not intended to deceive. To that extent, at least, the term "fiction" is very apt, for it applies equally to literature.

Like a literary work of fiction, a legal fiction is not meant to be taken as true in fact. It is, however, true in another sense: it is true in law.

Legal fictions do, indeed, especially offend literalists such as the great eighteenth-century iconoclast Jeremy Bentham, who believed that every word should have a single fixed, objective, value-neutral meaning. "Fiction," Bentham wrote—"Fiction, tautology, technicality, circuity, irregularity, inconsistency remain [in English law], but above all, the pestilential breath of Fiction poisons the sense of every instrument it comes near."[22] Yet if historical traditions (for which Bentham had no use) are to be preserved, and yet adapted to new conditions, then ambiguities and sometimes even contradictions in individual words or concepts or rules are not necessarily repugnant; they may—in some instances—be both useful and enlightening.

The utility of legal fictions introduced into the English common law in the late seventeenth and eighteenth centuries was that they applied to new rules procedural and substantive law embodied in older rules. Thus new situations were converted into familiar terms of the past.[23] This, indeed, is the chief virtue of legal fictions generally; in the words of the great nineteenth-century German jurist Savigny, the new rule expressed in a legal fiction "is joined directly on to an old and existing institution and in this way the certainty and development of the old is procured for the new."[24] In late-seventeenth- and early-eighteenth-century England this had not only a practical but also a theoretical virtue: it reinforced the belief in the tradition of the common law. The resort to legal fictions by English judges was closely related to their resort to the doctrine of precedent. Both are ways of making new law—fictions directly and openly, precedent indirectly and more subtly. Both preserve continuity with the past—precedents directly and openly, fictions indirectly and more subtly.

Expansion of the Forms of Action to Cover the Major Types of Civil Obligations

Partly by resort to fictions, but chiefly through reasoning by analogy of cases and analogy of doctrine, the common law courts in the late seventeenth and early eighteenth centuries expanded the forms of action to cover the three major sources of civil obligations that were at that time identified in the Western *jus commune* as obligations arising from breach of contract, from wrongful conduct (delict, tort), and from unjust enrichment.[25] Thus the action called "special assumpsit" was expanded to give the common law courts jurisdiction over a wide variety of contracts which previously had been subject to the jurisdiction of Chancery, Admiralty, High Commission, and Star Chamber. This had the effect of unifying the English law of contract. At the same time, it introduced a greater strictness into contract law—not in comparison with the older common law, but in comparison with the Roman law and canon law of the other courts. Parliament's enactment of the Statute of Frauds in 1677 was one sign of this new strictness: many oral contracts previously enforceable in the other courts now required a writing to be enforced in any court.

The expansion of the common law remedy of special assumpsit to cover kinds of contracts previously enforceable in other courts was accompanied by the acceptance of some of the contract doctrines of those other courts and the rejection of others. Perhaps the most important change in the law of contracts was the introduction of the English doctrine of absolute liability for breach of contract regardless of impossibility of performance. Here the leading case was *Paradine v. Jane,* decided by the King's Bench in 1647, in which the defendant lessee, being sued for nonpayment of rent, pleaded that the invading army of the German Prince Rupert had driven him off the land so that he could not enjoy it or take the profits from it.[26] The court summarily rejected this defense. Counsel for the defendant had argued that by "the law of reason" he ought not to be charged with the rent, since it was through no fault of his own that he could not occupy the premises, and that "the civil-law and canon-law and moral authors do confirm this," and further, "neither by martial law is the defendant chargeable, and that is the law of nature as well as of nations." The court, however, was unimpressed with these authorities, stating that by the common law of England "when the party by his contract creates a duty or charge upon himself, he is bound to make it good . . . notwithstanding any accident by inevitable necessity, because he might have provided against it by his contract."[27] Thus a rule which might have been justified if confined to leases of land was transformed into a new doctrine of liability without fault applicable to contracts generally.[28]

The adoption of the doctrine of absolute contractual liability reflected a Puritan belief in the sanctity of covenants as well as a mercantile emphasis on security of bargained transactions. These ideological and policy considerations should not obscure, however, the significance of the method by which the new doctrine was articulated. In the context of a suit for nonpayment of rent due under a lease of land, the court, in explaining its decision, stated a principle which it declared to be applicable to contracts generally. Moreover, that principle had the effect of distinguishing contractual liability from liability in tort, in which inevitable necessity was often a valid defense.

The separation of contract from tort in the common law (they had long been separated in the law applied in Chancery, Admiralty, Star Chamber, and other royal courts) had significant consequences for the English science of tort law as well. Above all, it marked the first steps in the development of the modern theory that liability under the various common law forms of action for wrongful injury to persons or property must be based either on the intentional causing of harm or on the negligent causing of harm, or, in certain cases, on the causing of harm without intent or negligence (so-called strict or absolute liability). The distinction between trespass and trespass-on-the-case, which had emerged in the fourteenth century, was retained: trespass chiefly for "directly" causing harm, trespass on the case for "indirectly" causing harm; and in many types of trespass actions, "inevitable accident" was a defense, to be proved by the defendant, while in trespass-on-the-case, the fact that the defendant acted "negligently" often had to be alleged and proved by the plaintiff. These precursors of the modern doctrine of tort liability based on fault became much more highly developed in the late seventeenth and eighteenth centuries. A striking example is Lord Holt's analysis of the law of bailment in *Coggs v. Bernard* in 1703.[29] Expressly drawing on doctrines of maritime and mercantile law previously applied in Admiralty and other non–common law courts, Lord Holt distinguished between those types of bailment in which the bailee's liability for loss or damage to the goods is to be based on "neglect," those in which "gross neglect" must be proved, and those in which there is strict liability save for "Act of God and the King's enemies," a phrase drawn from maritime law. He also drew expressly on rules, doctrines, and concepts of Roman law, citing at length the *Institutes* of Justinian as well as Bracton and other English authorities that supported and amplified the Roman law sources.[30] The influence of outside sources was also felt in the incorporation into the common law, during this period, of the doctrine of the vicarious liability of employers for harm caused by negligent acts of their servants *(respondeat superior)*—a form of strict liability that is closely related to negligence.[31]

The conventional view of legal historians that the law of negligence was a creature of the nineteenth century[32] has failed to take seriously enough the developments in English legal science in the late seventeenth and eighteenth centuries in which the doctrine of negligence was secreted, so to speak, in the interstices of the forms of action. In Plucknett's words, "The trees were familiar to English lawyers long before they formed an idea of the wood, and not until 1762 did it occur to the compiler of an abridgment to collect material under the heading of 'action on the case for negligence.'"[33]

The use of legal fictions and of analogy of cases and doctrine, as well as the importation of principles derived from outside the common law, were also present in the expansion of the remedy of *indebitatus assumpsit,* into the English common law equivalent of the "Roman law" doctrine of unjust enrichment. As indicated earlier, that remedy was initially introduced into the English royal law in the late fifteenth and early sixteenth centuries as appropriate in certain types of cases where there was not an express contractual undertaking, although an underlying contractual relationship existed either expressly or by implication in fact.[34] Thus if one party delivered goods to another without specifying the terms and the recipient kept the goods without paying for them, or if one party performed valuable services for another without an agreement on the price, or if one party received money from another without an agreement as to the terms on which it should be repaid, in these specific instances and in certain others—eight all told, called "the common counts"—the other party was held liable to pay for what he had received.[35]

What happened in the latter seventeenth and early eighteenth centuries was that the action of general assumpsit was extended to cover not only such implied-in-fact contractual obligations but also obligations arising from the receipt of benefits in certain types of cases where there existed no contractual relationship at all, express or implied, as, for example, where money was paid by mistake to a stranger who innocently took it and now could be required to restore the amount of the enrichment to the person at whose expense he was enriched. An important difference between the two kinds of obligation—one contractual, the other noncontractual—becomes apparent when one considers the extent of the obligation. Normally, one who is under a contractual obligation to pay for a benefit that he has received is liable to do so whether or not he remains benefited at the time payment is due, whereas one who is under no contractual obligation to pay for a benefit that he has received at the expense of another is liable, if he is liable at all, only if it is unjust for him to retain the benefit. Thus if the benefit is lost—for example, the money paid by mutual mistake is stolen from the innocent recipient—he is no longer enriched and no longer liable to restore it. Furthermore, if the obligation is a contractual one—for example, if the defendant has received products with the understanding that he will pay for them, or the plaintiff has rented rooms to the defendant with a similar understanding—and the price of the goods or services is not specified in the contract, then the court may fix the amount at the market price, or at the price the parties would or should have agreed to, whereas if the obligation is noncontractual, the amount to be restored is measured by the actual enrichment of the defendant, which may be more or less than the market price or a hypothetical agreed-upon price.

In the seventeenth and early eighteenth centuries, common law courts and common law writers began to speak of the remedy in general assumpsit as "quasi-contractual." "Quasi-contract" is a term drawn from Roman law; its literal meaning is "as if [there were] a contract." An action "in quasi-contract" *(quasi ex-contractu)* presupposes that there is in fact no contract, either express or implied, but that there is liability based on some other source. What that other source might be is not indicated, except that it is related to contractual liability in some fictitious "as if" way.

In the mid-eighteenth century the court of King's Bench under Lord Chief Justice Mansfield gave a broad construction to the term quasi-contract, stating that the quasi-contractual obligation to restore "money had and received" in an action of general assumpsit is based on "natural justice" and "equity."[36] This, in effect, was a reception of the doctrine of unjust enrichment into the common law. Lord Mansfield's broad view, though endorsed by Blackstone, was later rejected.[37] Nevertheless, the English courts continued to imply in law a contractual relationship in traditional cases of general assumpsit where no contractual relationship existed, even by implication. And finally, in the latter half of the twentieth century, English courts came around to full acceptance of the doctrine of unjust enrichment.

The earlier rejection by the English courts of a general doctrine of unjust enrichment and the confinement of the doctrine of quasi-contract to certain limited classes of cases, "the common counts," like the extension of the doctrine of absolute obligation to contracts generally, may be explained as a reflection both of Puritan morality and of mercantile economics. They must also be explained, however, in terms of the new legal science that accompanied the triumph of the common law courts over their rivals. The common law action of general assumpsit was itself an innovation of the late sixteenth and early seventeenth centuries, based on the assumption that where there is a debtor-creditor relationship, there is an implied undertaking on the part of the debtor to pay for what he has received from the creditor. Outside the common law—in Admiralty, Chancery, Star Chamber, High Commission, and Requests—the broader doctrine of unjust enrichment had been accepted. In the late seventeenth and eighteenth centuries, the common law courts, now supreme over all others, expanded the remedy of general assumpsit to cover cases—within the limits of the so-called common counts—where no contractual obligation could be implied in fact. Their refusal, however, to go beyond the specific types of cases covered by the common counts, or to adopt a general remedy called unjust enrichment, is to be explained not only by moral and economic considerations but also by methodological considerations: the doctrine of unjust enrichment lacked discernible boundaries; one could measure the "enrichment," but the "injustice" of retaining it was too general a concept to be easily workable in the case method of the common law. "Absolute obligation in contract," however, though an equally broad generality, was technically acceptable, since the action of special assumpsit had already been expanded conceptually to include all types of valid contracts, and therefore the rule that impossibility of performance was not a good defense in an action for breach of a contract of lease could be extended by analogy to other types of contracts as well.

The Transformation of Civil and Criminal Procedure

In its infancy, the English common law did not provide for a judicial hearing of civil and criminal cases. Instead, an inquest, consisting of twelve sworn men *(jurati),* reported to the royal judges on circuit whether or not the defendant had committed the offense with which he was charged in the chancellor's writ (in a civil case) or in the grand jury's presentment or indictment (in a criminal case). The jurors were supposed to have gathered the evidence, and to know what the verdict should be, in advance of the judicial proceeding. Scholars characterize the jury in this period as the "active" or "self-informing" jury. In criminal cases a surprisingly high percentage of indictments resulted in acquittal.[38] The only sanction available to coerce juries to give verdicts satisfactory to the royal judges was the attaint, an extraordinarily complicated and rarely used procedure available only to challenge jury verdicts in civil cases.

In the course of time, certain kinds of evidence began—very gradually—to be presented to the jury in the judicial proceeding. From the early thirteenth century, witnesses to certain disputed civil transactions, such as transfer of title to land (so-called deed witnesses), were summoned to give testimony before the jury. By the fifteenth century, juries in civil cases sometimes listened to statements made by the parties, and occasionally by witnesses, in answer to questions put by the judge on the jurors' behalf; and in criminal cases statements were also sometimes made in court, in answer to judges' questions, by private accusers, including the victim and the victim's kin, as well as by crown officials such as the coroner and the constable. By the middle of the sixteenth century, the appearance of witnesses in civil cases was not uncommon, and in criminal cases an elaborate system had been developed for the production of evidence both at the stage of grand jury indictment, when justices of the peace examined suspects and witnesses, and at the trial stage, when in certain types of cases crown prosecutors, and not only judges, interrogated the accused and called witnesses. In the early seventeenth century, jurors usually did not investigate the facts of the case before trial, although it was not until the eighteenth century that they were forbidden to consider personal knowledge gained out of court.[39]

Thus the first stages of the transformation of the "active" jury into the "passive" jury occurred before the English Revolution, chiefly under the auspices of the Tudor monarchy. Indeed, the introduction of evidence in jury proceedings in the sixteenth century was part of the general movement toward increased rationalization of secular civil and criminal procedure which took place throughout Europe at that time and which was closely connected with the Protestant Reformation and the rise of strong monarchies.[40] In England, the increased rationalization of jury trial in the sixteenth century was also needed to support the common law courts in their rivalry with the new prerogative courts, in which trial was not by jury but by professional judges who interrogated the parties and the witnesses.

The principal changes that occurred in the late seventeenth and early eighteenth centuries in the wake of the triumph of the common-law courts over their rivals were (1) the establishment of the independence of the jury as trier of both fact and law; (2) the establishment of substantial procedural rights of the accused in criminal trials; (3) the introduction of the adversary system of presentation of evidence; and (4) the development of new criteria for proof of guilt in criminal cases and of liability in civil cases. Each of these points will be examined in turn.

Establishment of the Independence of the Jury

With the increased use of witness proof in the common law courts in the sixteenth and early seventeenth centuries, and the gradual transformation of the "active" jury into the "passive" jury, the jury lost a great deal of its former independence. Now the judge in civil cases would know as much about the case as the jurors did. And now the judge in criminal cases had before him an indictment founded on evidence submitted to a grand jury in an extensive pre-trial proceeding before justices of the peace and also, in many cases, a crown prosecutor who presented the evidence that had been introduced to support the indictment. Now stringent sanctions—heavy fines and confinement under harsh physical conditions—came to be imposed on recalcitrant juries by the trial judges in criminal cases.

During the 1640s and after the restoration of the monarchy in 1660, the coercion of juries by royal judges was strongly attacked by the opponents of royal supremacy, as the Crown increasingly resorted to criminal prosecutions of political and religious dissenters in the common law courts and as juries of their peers increasingly resisted instructions by royal judges to impose sanctions on them. A cause célèbre was the prosecution in 1670 of the young Quaker radicals William Penn and William Mead for "preaching seditiously and causing a great tumult of people . . . to be gathered together riotously and routously . . . to the great terror and disturbance [of the king's subjects]." Despite threats by the judge to deprive them of food and water and otherwise to subject them to humiliating conditions until they brought in a verdict of guilty, the jurors refused to convict. The judge fined each of them forty marks for refusing to obey his instruction and then had them imprisoned for failing to pay the fines.[41] One of the jurors, Edward Bushell, obtained a writ of habeas corpus from the Court of Common Pleas, which held, after a hearing, that jurors may not be fined or imprisoned for their verdict even if it contradicts the instructions of the judge.[42] In freeing the prisoners, Chief Justice Vaughan reasoned that jurors have the responsibility of deciding according to their own judgment, and the fact that the judge, having heard the same evidence, may reach a different conclusion does not diminish that responsibility, since, as he stated in his opinion, "the Judge and jury might honestly differ in the result from the evidence, as well as two Judges may, which often happens."[43]

Bushell's Case held that the jury was the final trier of fact. It did not expressly hold that the jury was also judge of the law—that is, that it had the right to reject the judge's instructions on the law. That question remained a vexed one, which was answered differently in criminal and in civil cases. In civil cases, a judge could direct a jury verdict or could give a judgment notwithstanding the verdict. In criminal cases the judge could, in effect, direct a verdict of acquittal by dismissing the indictment, or he could reprieve the prisoner after a verdict of guilty and recommend that the Crown grant a pardon; but *Bushell's Case* established that he could not overturn the jury's verdict of acquittal even if it clearly nullified the legal rule stated in his instructions. This led to the widespread view that the jury was equally equipped to determine the law applicable to the case before it.[44] In his widely read treatise on jury trial, first published in 1680, John Hawles enlarged upon Vaughan's reasoning in *Bushell's Case.* "The office of the juryman," he wrote, "is conscientiously to judge his neighbor, and he needs no more law than is easily learnt to direct him therein."[45] Similarly with respect to indictment by grand jury, Hawles in another widely read treatise argued that the grand jury, too, is independent and should not bow to a zealous prosecutor. It should not only look to the facts, he wrote, but also "take upon itself the knowledge of the law."[46]

That the establishment of the independence of the jury was a fact of great political importance, and also of great philosophical importance, should not obscure its equal importance for legal science. In *Bushell's Case,* Chief Justice Vaughan stated that he doubted

> whether any thing be more common than for two men, students, barristers or Judges, to deduce contrary and opposite conclusions out of the same case in law. . . . Is anything more frequent in the controversies of religion, than to press the same text for opposite tenets? How then comes it to pass that two persons may not apprehend with reason and honesty, what a witness, or many, say? . . . [M]ust therefore one of these merit fine and imprisonment, because he doth that which he cannot otherwise do, preserving his oath and integrity, and this often is the case of the Judge and jury.[47]

On the one hand, the principal purpose of a criminal trial is to determine the truth of the allegations contained in the indictment, including the allegations of fact and the allegations of violations of law. On the other hand, different people may reasonably reach different conclusions from the same evidence and from the same premises. The decision to place the outcome in the hands of the jury, strongly guided but not dominated by the court, was based in part on the belief that the anonymous collective judgment of twelve persons, representing the community, is more trustworthy than the judgment of one or more specially trained officials.

Establishment of Procedural Rights of the Accused

The changes in criminal procedure introduced in the sixteenth century had not only reduced substantially the independence of the jury but also restricted severely the rights of the accused. Conversely, the movement in the late seventeenth century to free the jury from judicial domination also substantially increased the rights of the accused.

The position of the accused in a criminal case in the period before 1640 may be summarized as follows.[48] First, the accused was usually kept in close confinement prior to trial. He was examined by the justices of the peace or other local officials, and his answers were written down and available for use by the prosecution at trial, but he was given no opportunity to prepare his own defense.[49] Second, he was not shown the indictment, nor was he given notice beforehand of any of the evidence to be used against him at trial. Third, he had no absolute right to counsel either before or at trial, and counsel were very rarely allowed to appear. Fourth, he was not told who would be on the jury. Fifth, at trial he could be questioned by the jury or by the judge on the jury's behalf and by the prosecution, without rules limiting the questions that could be asked and without rights of refusal to answer. Sixth, prosecution witnesses were not required to confront the accused but could have their written depositions read to the jury in their absence. There was no proper cross-examination of those prosecution witnesses who did appear. The accused was given the opportunity to contest their testimony, but when he did, the trial often became simply a loose altercation between him and those who testified against him.[50] Finally, the accused had no right to have witnesses summoned by the court and was usually not allowed to call witnesses himself. When witnesses were called by the accused, they were not examined under oath, as were the prosecution witnesses, so their testimony had less credibility. Also the accused had no way of ascertaining in advance what witnesses would say. The accused himself or herself was not allowed to testify under oath.

In the course of the English Revolution and in the decades thereafter, this picture changed drastically. In the words of James Fitzjames Stephen:

> From the year 1640 downwards, the whole spirit and temper of the criminal courts . . . appear to have been radically changed from what it had been in the preceding century to what it is in our own day. In every case, so far as I am aware, the accused person had the witnesses against him produced face-to-face, unless there was some special reason (such as sickness) to justify the reading of their depositions. In some cases the prisoner was questioned but never to any greater extent than that which it is practically impossible to avoid when a man had to defend himself without counsel. When so questioned, the prisoners usually refused to answer. The prisoner was also allowed not only to cross-examine the witnesses against him if he thought fit, but also to call witnesses of his own. These great changes in procedure took place apparently spontaneously, and without any legislative enactment.[51]

Stephen was referring, in this passage, to the period after 1640 but before persons accused of felony had the right to be represented by counsel at trial. That right, which had previously existed in cases of misdemeanors,[52] was introduced by statute in 1696 in cases of treason and in the 1730s was extended by the courts to felonies generally.

The Treason Trials Act of 1696 has been termed "a by-product of the Revolution of 1688 [which] belongs with the Bill of Rights and the Toleration Act to the class of postrevolutionary remedial measures,"[53] and which "completed the transition from Tudor-style judicial procedures to essentially modern ones."[54] It provided (among other things) that a person accused of treason could have two counsels to assist him before trial and at trial; that five days before arraignment he was to receive a copy of the indictment, with ample time before trial to prepare his defense, and two days before trial he was to receive a copy of the jury panel; that at trial no overt act not included in the indictment could be offered in evidence against him; and that he could not be convicted unless two witnesses testified under oath to his having committed one or more overt acts of treason.[55]

At the time of its enactment, many argued that its provisions should be expressly made applicable not only to treason (which itself was very broadly defined) but also to felonies, which at that time comprised capital crimes other than treason. Although this argument did not prevail, courts in the next decades, without benefit of statute, did gradually extend to felony cases the right of the accused to know in advance of trial the charges against him and to have time, with the assistance of counsel, to prepare a defense, the right to consult counsel during trial on questions of law, and eventually, by the 1730s, the right to be represented by counsel in the examination and cross-examination of witnesses. Also by statute defendants were given the right to have witnesses summoned by the court and the right to have such witnesses testify under oath.[56]

It is worth emphasizing that these rights were first granted to persons charged with political crimes. For two hundred years, England had experienced an almost continual series of dramatic criminal trials of political figures first under the Tudors and the early Stuarts, then under the Puritans and the later Stuarts. Papists and Protestants, royalists and parliamentarians, Whig leaders and Tory leaders, or just simply ardent opponents of the ruling powers—all had been successively charged with "high treason." Prominent persons so accused had protested against the injustices to which they were subjected under the common law, whose inquisitorial procedures of that time were particularly well suited to the purging of political enemies. Thus in 1603 Sir Walter Raleigh, being tried for treason on trumped-up charges, requested the court to call to the witness stand the man whose highly problematic out-of-court confession of complicity was the chief item of evidence introduced by the prosecution. The presiding judge, none other than Sir Edward Coke, refused Raleigh's request. Raleigh argued, "The common trial of England is by jury and witnesses." Coke replied, "No, by examination: if three conspire a treason and they all confess it, there is never a witness, yet they are condemned."[57]

With the Glorious Revolution of 1689, pressure to introduce a new kind of procedural justice in political cases inevitably carried over to nonpolitical crimes as well. Again, as in the case of trial by jury, English criminal law chose as a model a procedure that protected the accused against possible official prejudice and corruption. Indeed, the independence of the jury in criminal cases could be realized in practice only by giving the accused sufficient rights to protect him against judicial and prosecutorial bias in the presentation of evidence. This was a matter not only of politics and morality but also of the integrity of the legal system—a matter of legal science.

Introduction of the Adversary System

To speak of "the adversary system" of procedure and its rival, "the inquisitorial system," is to raise sharp questions of comparative law. After the French Revolution, criminal procedure in France, Germany, and elsewhere on the European continent was transformed by the establishment of a procedure—which in broad outline still exists—for the impartial investigation of crimes leading to indictment: an impartial examining magistrate (the French *juge d'instruction,* the German *Untersuchungsrichter*) questions witnesses, gathers evidence, interrogates the person charged by police or other administrative authority, and, if there is sufficient evidence to justify a trial, issues an indictment containing a full report of the evidence on which it is based. The indictment is shown to the accused and presented to a court. At trial, the burden is on the prosecution to prove the facts charged in the indictment. The court—constituted differently in different European countries but in criminal cases usually sitting with a lay jury of one kind or another—normally interrogates first the accused and then the witnesses. The prosecution and defense counsel ask supplementary questions. The prosecution is limited to the evidence contained in the indictment, while the defense may challenge that evidence and may introduce other evidence. The procedure is called "inquisitorial" because it is an "inquiry" or "inquest" into the facts of the case—an investigation or, as Coke called it in the case of Sir Walter Raleigh, an "examination." Most countries of the world use something like this method of investigation and trial of crimes.

"The adversary system," in contrast, which has been characteristic of English criminal procedure since the English Revolution, and which was inherited in the various parts of the British Empire, including the American colonies, shares certain features of the inquisitorial system, just as the inquisitorial system shares certain features of the adversary system. (Indeed, in the twentieth century in most countries the two systems drew increasingly close to each other.) Principal distinguishing features of the English adversary system, however, are (1) that indictment is by a grand jury and is based solely on evidence presented by the prosecution, that is, evidence tending to show guilt; (2) that at trial, the prosecution first presents its witnesses, whom the defense may cross-examine in turn, and at the close of "the prosecution's case" the defense may present its case, that is, its witnesses, whom the prosecution may cross-examine in turn; and (3) that the accused may not be summoned to testify by the prosecution or the court and need not testify at all if he does not so choose. As in the continental system, the burden of proof of guilt is on the prosecution. In the nineteenth century this came to be referred to in England as the presumption of innocence, but the widespread notion that it is absent in continental European systems is quite false. There is this difference, however: in those systems the accused, summoned by the court and standing before the judge, must respond to his questions and be judged in part by such responses, whereas in the English system no adverse inferences may be drawn from the decision of the accused not to testify. He is not to be convicted "out of his own mouth" or out of his own silence. (If he does decide to testify on his own behalf, however, he may be cross-examined by the prosecution.) Also in the English system the questioning of witnesses, including the accused if he "takes the stand," is primarily conducted by counsel and not, as in the various continental European systems, primarily by the court.

If we compare the system of criminal procedure that emerged in England in the late seventeenth and early eighteenth centuries with that which developed in the late eighteenth and nineteenth centuries, it is apparent that many adversarial features that emerged in the later period were absent in the earlier period. This has led some scholars to conclude that the English inquisitorial procedure of the late sixteenth and early seventeenth centuries survived until the nineteenth century.[58] In this context, reference is often made to the Prisoner's Counsel Act of 1836, which expanded substantially the rights of counsel for the accused.[59] Yet if one compares the development that took place in the century and a half after 1640 with what went before it instead of with what came after it, it becomes apparent that one can properly speak of the emergence after 1640 of the adversary system. Indeed, the sponsors of the Prisoner's Counsel Act themselves paid tribute to the Treason Trials Act of 1696 as the source of many of its principles.[60]

The principal feature that characterizes the adversary system at the trial stage, namely, presentation of evidence by prosecution and defense rather than elicitation of it solely by the court, was an innovation of the late seventeenth century. Before then, English judges—like continental European judges today—examined the accused on evidence contained in the prosecution's indictment and the depositions of prosecution witnesses. Indeed, as was pointed out earlier, the accused was not informed of such evidence before trial. The trial was a judicial investigation, the accused being asked to respond to the various allegations made against him. When prosecution witnesses were called by the court, the accused was once again asked what he had to say in response to their charges. He rarely had witnesses of his own, and, as indicated earlier, when he did, he was not prepared to interrogate them. Even after the introduction of defense counsel in felony trials, the English judges dominated the trial proceedings.[61] In comparison with most American judges, they still do. But the fact that the judge may play an active role in questioning parties and witnesses does not negate the adversary character of the proceedings. In the first place, the accused (though not the witnesses) could—and often did—refuse to answer the judge's questions. In the second place, the accused now had the right to call his own witnesses. Finally, and most important, counsel for the accused (or, in the absence of counsel, the accused himself) now had the right to examine defense witnesses and to cross-examine prosecution witnesses. The witnesses were the parties' witnesses, not, as in other European countries, the court's witnesses. The emergence in the early eighteenth century of rules of cross-examination of hostile witnesses by opposing counsel was an important element in the development of the adversary system in both criminal and civil procedure.[62] It represented a new method of arriving at the truth of a matter—not directly, by asking questions relevant and material to the ultimate issue of guilt or innocence, but indirectly, by restricting questions of opposing counsel to those matters that are relevant and material to the testimony elicited on affirmative examination of the particular witness.

New Criteria for Proof of Guilt and Liability

The establishment of the independence of the jury, the expansion of the procedural rights of the accused in criminal cases, and the introduction of the adversary system of presentation of evidence were closely related to the development of new criteria of proof in both criminal and civil cases. These were four interconnected elements in the modernization of common law trial procedure.

The new criteria of proof were based on the new philosophical and scientific theory that all evidence, whether of physical phenomena or of social phenomena, must be met initially by doubt and that initial doubts can be overcome only by tests of probability. This was a new theoretical source of the doctrine that the burden of proof of any proposition is on the one who asserts it. Such proof, however, could not be required—or expected—to yield absolute certainty but only, at best, what was called at the time "moral certainty," which in turn was equated with maximum probability. Carried over into law, these postulates meant that the burden of proof in criminal and civil cases rested on the prosecution and the civil plaintiff, respectively, and that the evidence introduced to support the assertion of guilt or liability must have more probative force than the evidence introduced to negate it. In criminal cases, since the consequences of a conviction were very severe—in cases of treason and felony, death by hanging—it followed, as Matthew Hale wrote, and as William Blackstone repeated after him, that it is better that ten guilty men be acquitted than that one innocent man be convicted.[63] Hale, indeed, as previously noted, spoke expressly of a presumption of innocence.[64] In civil cases, the consequences of error being less severe, and usually falling equally on one or the other of the parties, liability could properly be made to depend on a lower standard of probability. It was not until 1770 (so far as scholarship has revealed) that the precise criminal standard of "proof beyond a reasonable doubt," and not until even later that the precise civil standard of "proof by a preponderance of the evidence," were first announced by English courts;[65] nevertheless, both of these standards were implicit in the judicial instruction commonly given to juries in the late seventeenth and early to mid-eighteenth centuries, namely, that they were to give a verdict against the defendant only if their conscience was satisfied that he was guilty, or, in civil cases, legally liable. A "satisfied conscience" at that time was founded not only on the general concept of probabilities but also on newly developed specific concepts concerning the valuations to be placed on various kinds of proofs.[66]

The concept of probability lay at the heart of the common law of evidence as it was first systematically expounded in the late seventeenth and early eighteenth centuries. Sir Jeffrey Gilbert's treatise *The Law of Evidence,* written in the early 1700s but published later, which was the first systematic English-language work on that subject, starts by stating that it will treat of "the Evidence that ought to be offer'd to the Jury, and by what Rules of Probability it ought to be weigh'd and consider'd."[67] The author then refers to the observation of "a very learned man"—the reference is to John Locke, with whom Gilbert was closely associated—"that there are several Degrees from perfect Certainty and Demonstration, quite down to Improbability and Unlikelihood, even to the Confines of Impossibility; and there are several Acts of the Mind proportion'd to these Degrees of Evidence, which may be called the Degrees of Assent, from full Assurance and Confidence, quite down to Conjecture, Doubt, Distrust, and Disbelief."[68] Building on Locke's *Essay Concerning Human Understanding,* Gilbert goes on to state that a person may be most certain of what he perceives with his senses, and that in legal matters such certainty may occasionally be achieved by "demonstration" founded on sense perception (he gives the example of the record of a transfer of land from J. S. to J. N. from which, in a dispute between the two as to whose land it is, the necessary inference may be drawn from perception of their conduct that it belongs to J. N.). Most matters of civil life, however, Gilbert continues, are not capable of such "strict demonstration," and "therefore the Rights of Men must be determined by Probability." One step down from direct sense perception is "that Faith and Credit to be given to the Honesty and Integrity of credible and disinterested Witnesses, attesting any Fact under the solemnities and Obligation of Religion and the Dangers and Penalties of Perjury"; their testimony "cannot have any more Reason to be doubted than if we ourselves had heard and seen it; and this is the Original of Tryals, and all manner of Evidence." Gilbert then moves from these generalizations to what he terms the first and most important rule in the law of evidence, namely, "That a Man must have the utmost Evidence [which] the Nature of the Fact is capable of."[69]

This "best evidence" rule is a key to the analysis of various kinds of testimony and to the weight to be given to each in the context of the facts to be proved. The body of the treatise, then, is presented not by the topical method of the German professors but by the case method characteristic of English judges and practicing lawyers. The initial impression is of a handbook for practitioners and judges: what can and what cannot be given in evidence in jury trials of various types of civil and criminal cases. But in fact there is a method and a system and a science in the law of evidence as Gilbert presents it. It is an empirical method; it is also a coherent system of evaluation of evidence on the basis of its probative force in given types of cases; and, finally, such evaluation rests on a science of probabilities—not an abstract or mathematical science but a distillation of what experience has shown to be the most convincing forms of proof in jury trials.

The Emergence of Scientific Legal Treatises

The transformation of English legal science in the late seventeenth and early eighteenth centuries was also reflected in the emergence of comprehensive treatises on several individual branches of English law and on English law as a whole. Mention has already been made of Gilbert's substantial treatise on the law of evidence applicable to jury trials. Gilbert also wrote separate treatises on more than fifteen other branches of English law, including *Devises, Tenures, Uses and Trusts, Dower, Debt,* and *Ejectment,* as well as *Common Pleas, Exchequer, Forum Romanum (Chancery),* and *King's Bench.*[70] But the most impressive of the treatises on a particular branch of the law was Hawkins's massive *Pleas of the Crown,* a comprehensive analysis of English criminal law, written at about the same time as Gilbert's treatise on evidence.

Prior to the triumph of the common law over its rivals, a comprehensive analysis of the law of evidence or the law of crimes in England would have had to be divided into the different kinds of proof and the different kinds of criminal law applicable in the different kinds of secular and ecclesiastical jurisdictions The only previous example of a comprehensive treatise on a particular branch of English law was Littleton's *Tenures,* on land law, written in Law French in the sixteenth century and translated and extensively commented on by Sir Edward Coke in the early seventeenth century, but this was an exception made possible by the monopoly of the common law courts over disputes concerning freehold land tenure. As for a treatise on English law as a whole, prior to the mid-seventeenth century it would have required a division into English canon law, the Romanist law of the English civilians applicable in the prerogative courts, maritime law, law merchant, and equity, in addition to the so-called common law of the courts of King's Bench, Common Pleas, and Exchequer. It was the revolutionary establishment of the supremacy of the "common law" over its rivals that made it possible to speak accurately of that law as *the* law of England.

The first book purporting to present an analysis of the entire body of the English common law as a whole was Matthew Hale's pathbreaking work *The Analysis of the Law,* subtitled *A Scheme or Abstract of the Several Titles and Partitions of the Law of England, Digested into Method.*[71] Hale drew partly on the topical method introduced by the sixteenth-century German systematizers of the *jus commune,* with its emphasis on divisions into genus and species, and partly on the terminology of Justinian's *Institutes,* but he adapted that method to the peculiarities of the English common law.[72] Thus in the preface of the book, in which he set forth what he called his "analytical method," Hale divided English laws into two kinds, "the Civil Part" and "the Criminal Part." Thereafter he divided the Civil Part into "civil rights or interests," "wrongs or injuries relating to those rights," and "relief or remedies applicable to those wrongs." "Civil rights or interests" are then subdivided into "rights of persons" and "rights of things," and "rights of persons" are further subdivided into those that concern persons themselves and those that relate to their goods and estates. Then "persons" are subdivided into "natural persons" and "corporations" (including "bodies politics"), which in turn are further subdivided. Eventually "wrongs" and "remedies" are also broken down into their respective species, and the entire work follows the "method" thus set forth.

The "criminal part" of English law is omitted from Hale's *Analysis* only because, as he states in the last paragraph of that book, he had already written a treatise on the criminal law, "which I shall add to this in due time." That earlier work was titled *Pleas of the Crown or A Methodical Summary of the Principal Matters Relating to that Subject.*[73] It is divided into two parts: the kinds of offenses and the incidents of the various kinds. The kinds of offenses are divided into common law crimes and statutory crimes, and these in turn are divided into capital and non-capital offenses. Common law capital offenses are divided into offenses against God (heresy and witchcraft) and offenses against man (treason and felonies). Felonies are said to be of four kinds: against life, against goods, against habitation, and against public justice. Various common law felonies (all capital) are defined (murder, manslaughter, various forms of larceny, robbery, piracy, burglary, arson, breach of prison) and various statutory capital offenses are listed. Non-capital common law offenses are also listed, such as failure to report a felony ("misprision") and breach of the peace. Non-capital statutory offenses "are many and not here to be treated of."

This relatively short book of approximately 45,000 words (plus front matter and index) was the first "methodical" presentation of the English law of crimes applicable in the common law courts. It formed the basis, less than two generations later, of William Hawkins's great work *A Treatise of the Pleas of the Crown: A System of the Principal Matters relating to that Subject, digested under the proper Heads.*[74] Hawkins expanded Hale's "summary" to a comprehensive two-volume "system" of approximately 375,000 words, which for a century remained the authoritative textbook of English criminal law.

A distinctive feature of Hale's analytical method was the implicit rejection of the sharp distinction drawn in the European literature on the *jus commune* between public law and private law. Hale treated legal powers of "bodies politic" under the law of artificial persons. He stated that the king is, in his political capacity, a corporation sole.[75] This had the effect of placing government within, and not above, the legal order. Substantial limitations of the rights, powers, prerogatives, and jurisdiction of the Crown and of subordinate magistrates (including Parliament and the judiciary) are set forth in some detail. The king's power to make statute laws, Hale wrote, is "only a qualified and coordinate power," requiring the consent of both houses of Parliament, and although he has the power to issue proclamations "which in some instances are to be taken for law, as in calling Parliaments, declaring war, etc . . . yet the king cannot by these introduce a new law, so as to alter or transfer properties, or impose new penalties of forfeiture beyond what are established by statute or common law."[76] This was, indeed, a substantial limitation of the royal power to issue proclamations as it had previously existed.[77]

In general, Hale's analysis did for English law what the sixteenth- and seventeenth-century systematizers of the European *jus commune* had done for the Western legal tradition as a whole. As they had set forth a comprehensive method of analysis applicable to the entire ensemble of the autonomous legal systems that previously had coexisted within each of the various European principalities, so Hale set forth a comprehensive method of analysis applicable to the various parts of the English common law, including both judge-made law and statute law. In contrast, however, to the *jus commune,* Hale's "common law" focused on only one of the legal systems that had prevailed in England in the earlier period, namely, the law applicable in the royal courts of Common Pleas, King's Bench, and Exchequer Chamber. Hale treated only cursorily ecclesiastical law, maritime law, mercantile law, and the law of the staple towns, and omitted entirely that branch of English law, called equity, that was applied in Chancery. Indeed, the equitable remedies of the chancellor's court are not even included in the sections of Hale's work that deal with remedies.

Hale's treatise is less important for what it contained than for what it inspired, and particularly for its enormous influence on English legal scholarship in the two generations after it was first published in 1713. William Blackstone, in his *Analysis of the Laws of England* (1753) and his four-volume *Commentaries on the Laws of England* (1765–1769), fully acknowledges his debt to Hale's "science" of English law.[78] As Hawkins had expanded Hale's summary of English criminal law, so Blackstone expanded Hale's analysis of English civil law—expanded it, indeed, into three large volumes. His fourth volume, on criminal law, was based largely on Hawkins's treatise, and thus only indirectly on Hale's *Pleas of the Crown.*

Blackstone's two treatises embodied the new science of English law that had emerged out of the English Revolution. His purpose, he wrote, was "to mark out a Plan of the Laws of ENGLAND, so comprehensive, so that every Title might be reduced under some one of its general Heads, which the student might afterwards pursue to any Degree of Minuteness; and at the same time so contracted, that the Gentleman might with tolerable Application contemplate and understand the Whole."[79]

To "understand the Whole," it was necessary not only to classify the various parts of the law under their appropriate "heads" but also to explain the relationships of the heads to one another and of the parts to the whole. Those relationships might derive from the concern to maintain the rationality of the system, including not only its logical consistency but also its moral purposes. They might derive also, or alternatively, from the concern to effectuate the will, the policies, of the lawmaker. And they might derive also, or alternatively, from the concern to maintain the continuity, the tradition, the historicity of English law. Blackstone, like Hale and others before him, adhered to all three of these sometimes conflicting goals, which legal philosophers have classified as natural law theory, legal positivism, and historical jurisprudence. Blackstone's genius, however, lay not in legal philosophy but in the systematic exposition of the ways in which the English legal system worked, that is, in what he called the science of English law. His science was, to be sure, an empirical one,[80] but at the same time he recognized as an empirical fact that the English legal system as a whole, and every rule of law or legal institution within that system, contains a political aspect, a moral aspect, and a historical aspect. He recognized, and did not hesitate to say, that some of the laws were arbitrary and that some parts of the legal order lacked a coherent structure;[81] nevertheless, it was his task as a scientist, a "methodist," to identify the standards of reasonableness and coherence by which the objects of his science were to be analyzed and judged. Blackstone's great contribution, like Hale's, was to examine objectively the data, the phenomena, of English law—the cases, the statutes, the rules and procedures, the institutions—and to discern within them the underlying principles and regularities, the method, by which the system was intended to operate, the meta-law which was embodied in the law itself.

The principal "heads" of the law, that is, the topics which formed the basic categories under which particular institutions, principles, rules, and procedures of English law were to be analyzed, were drawn by Blackstone (following Hale and others) partly from the terminology of the Roman law of Justinian, especially from his *Institutes*, and more particularly from a statement in the *Institutes* that the entire civil law was divided into three parts: the law of persons, the law of things, and the law of actions. Thus Book 1 of Blackstone's *Commentaries* is devoted largely to "The Rights of Persons," Book 2 is titled "The Rights of Things," and Book 3, though titled "Private Wrongs, or Civil Injuries," is devoted chiefly to civil actions to remedy such wrongs or injuries. Apart, however, from the name "Institutes" and from the use of the words "persons," "things," and "actions," there is very little connection between Justinian's *Institutes* and the legal writings of Hale, Blackstone, and other English so-called "Institutionalists" of the seventeenth and eighteenth centuries.[82] In the first place, despite the initial statement of the author of Justinian's *Institutes* that his subject, civil law, was to be divided into the law of persons, the law of things, and the law of actions, his book is not so divided: the classical and post-classical Roman lawyers were not conceptualists or synthesizers.[83] In the second place, in Justinian's "civil law," public law was entirely omitted, and his law of persons was devoted primarily to distinctions between the law of slaves and the law of free men, whereas Hale's and Blackstone's "civil law," like that of contemporary continental "Institutionalists," contained much of what the Romans would have called public law, including, under the heading of "persons," the rights and duties of the persons of the monarch, members of Parliament, and other "magistrates." In the third place, Justinian was concerned with "the law"—*jus*—of persons and of things *(jus personarum, jus rerum)*, whereas Hale and Blackstone, like their continental counterparts, were concerned with "the rights"—*jura*—relating to persons and things *(jura personarum, jura rerum)*. The concept of subjective rights as contrasted with objective right, or law, hardly existed in the classical Roman law but was first developed by the European jurists of the twelfth century.[84]

Thus in Book 1 of the *Commentaries*, titled "The Rights of Persons," Blackstone starts by setting forth the "absolute rights" of "natural persons" to enjoy personal security, personal liberty, and private property. He then analyzes the "relative rights" of (1) "public persons," including legislators (Parliament), the executive (the king and the royal family), and certain others (aliens, civil servants, the military), and (2) of "private persons," including master and servant, husband and wife, parent and child, guardian and ward. Finally, "The Rights of Persons" concludes with a section on corporations. Surely there is nothing of the method of Justinian here, though there is a good deal of the method of the sixteenth- and seventeenth-century European *jus commune* adapted to the English legal tradition.[85]

The Empirical Method of the New Legal Science

In both its internal aspect and its external aspect, the new English legal science of the late seventeenth and early to mid-eighteenth centuries bore a close relation to the second scientific revolution of the seventeenth century. The doctrine of precedent, for example, was closely related to the empirical method that was used in other sciences. There are, to be sure, crucial differences between, on the one hand, analysis of experiments in the natural sciences in order to test hypotheses concerning the causes and effects of physical occurrences and, on the other hand, analysis of facts of reported cases in the courts in order to determine the rules implicit in the judicial decisions. Nevertheless, there are also important parallels between the two processes. Just as consistency in the results of experiments in the natural sciences helps to establish truth, so consistency of judicial decisions in analogous cases helps to establish both truth and justice: the truth that the cases are in some important sense alike, and the justice of the principle that like cases be decided alike. Moreover, both the coherence of a system of legal rules and predictability in their application are enhanced by the probability that courts will do in future cases what they have done in past analogous cases.

There is, moreover, a striking methodological similarity between the empirical method in the natural sciences, as described by Isaac Newton, and the case method of legal reasoning reflected in the doctrine of precedent. Newton stated that his method of investigation of the laws governing gravity and other active forces in nature involved three major steps: (1) the derivation of general principles ("laws") from empirical evidence, (2) the extension of those principles by mathematical procedures, and (3) the deduction of as yet unaccounted for facts from the general statement of the theory. He called the first step "analysis" and the last step "synthesis." Such synthesis, or explanation, he stated, was always to be understood as subject to revision in the light of new evidence. "Reacting to the aprioristic method of Descartes, Newton repeatedly insisted on the empirical nature of scientific statements, and he fully realized that the price for empirical grounds was the loss of metaphysical certainty."[86] Similarly, in applying the doctrine of precedent, English judges looked to the empirical evidence of previous decisions in analogous cases and sought to derive from them general principles. They then elaborated those principles by logical (though not, to be sure, mathematical) procedures, in order to apply them to the case before them. Finally, they would sometimes then take a third step of deducing from the general theory, that is, the holding, its application to cases other than the one before them. The decision in the case at hand would serve as a precedent for future analogous cases, although such new cases might cast doubt on the validity of the principles previously stated, which would then be subject to revision. Because it was "case law," it could never achieve certainty. It was a science, albeit a science of probabilities.

The parallel between the new legal science and the revolution in the natural sciences is also illustrated in the new criteria of proof that were introduced in criminal and civil cases. The requirement that to convict in a criminal case, or to find for the plaintiff in a civil case, the jury's "conscience" must be "satisfied" that the evidence meets specific standards of probability is a clear example of the application to law of the new epistemology that prevailed in the natural sciences as well as in theology and philosophy. The "satisfied conscience" was identified in law, as in moral theology and philosophy, with the mind whose initial doubts have been overcome by probative evidence and which has been fully persuaded.[87] While to achieve absolute certainty was considered to be beyond the capacity of the human mind, one could be convinced of a person's guilt "to a moral certainty," or in John Locke's terminology, "to the highest degree of probability."[88] Similarly, arrests were to be made only if there was "probable cause" to believe the suspect to be guilty—not the "highest degree of probability" such as was required to convict after trial, but sufficient probability to warrant a trial.[89] Indeed, as noted earlier, a whole new science of evidence was developed on the basis of Newtonian and Lockean concepts of probability.

The relation between the new science of English law and other sciences was not a one-way street. The legal concept of "fact," or "matter of fact," as something usually to be left to the jury to decide, as contrasted with "law," or "matter of law," to be declared (though in criminal cases not finally imposed) by the judge, had an influence on the concept of "fact" in other sciences.[90] In the other sciences, as in law, facts are to be proved by the evidence of witnesses, whereas theories, like principles of law, are to be found in authoritative writings and developed by experts. Other elements of the language of evidence, such as "testimony," "circumstantial evidence," and "hearsay," also passed over into the literature of the natural sciences. The great chemist Robert Boyle compared the probative value of repeated experiments in the natural sciences with the probative value of the testimony of multiple witnesses in a law court. "Though the testimony of a single witness shall not suffice to prove the accused party guilty of murder," he wrote, "yet the testimony of two witnesses, though but of equal credit, that is, a second testimony added to the first, though of itself never a whit more credible than the former, shall ordinarily suffice to prove a man guilty, because it is thought reasonable to suppose that, though each testimony single be but probable, yet a concurrence of such probabilities . . . may well amount to a moral certainty."[91] Similarly, Boyle argued, if an experiment in chemistry, for example, is repeated by other chemists with the same results, the probability of its truth is increased not merely because of the multiplication of testimony but because of the amount of independent probative evidence for the proposition in question. Indeed, "probability" in the natural sciences, like "probability" in law, "had the qualitative meaning 'worthy of approbation,' and not today's quantitative meaning expressed by degrees of likelihood."[92]

Above all, the seventeenth-century English concept of "reasonableness," which English legal science originally received from theology, went back from theology and law into other disciplines and into general speech. It is a word that is almost untranslatable into other languages; neither the French *raisonnable* nor the German *vernünftig* captures its meaning, since they imply not what in English is called "common sense," which is partly intuitive, but rather the kind of rationality that comes solely from ratiocination. The English word "reasonable" eventually came to be used in a multitude of contexts. English lawyers came to speak not only of reasonable doubt but also of reasonable care, reasonable reliance, reasonable risk, reasonable mistake, reasonable delay, reasonable force—and, of course, "the reasonable man."[93] As George Fletcher has shown, the virtual absence of this terminology from French, German, and other continental legal systems reflects an important difference between Anglo-American and continental European legal science.[94]

Finally, the methodology of the modern English legal treatise, pioneered by Matthew Hale and consummated by William Blackstone, also bore a strong relationship to the new methodology of the second scientific revolution of the seventeenth century.

Because the English writers of legal treatises were for the most part judges and practicing lawyers, it was natural for them to focus a great deal of their attention on the reflection of English law in judicial decisions and legal practice. One therefore finds in the English legal treatises many of the same connections between legal science and other sciences that were built into the law itself: the empirical character of judicial reasoning from precedent, the emphasis on probability in the law of evidence, a concept of facts heavily influenced by the sharp division between matters of fact and matters of law, and an emphasis on reasonableness. Legal science in England tended to be primarily a judicial legal science rather than primarily a professorial legal science, as in Germany.[95]

This contrast should not, however, be overdrawn. In all stages of the development of Western legal science, the professors, the judges, and the legislators have all played important parts. In the first stage, from the late eleventh through the fifteenth centuries, there was a striking symbiosis among the three branches of the profession; especially among the canonists, many bishops, archbishops, and popes were all three—legal scholars, judges, and legislators. With the Lutheran Reformation, a greater separation was wrought between the role of the supreme legislator, now the prince, and the respective roles of the professors and the judges. In legal science, the professors' role predominated—especially in Germany. In sixteenth-century England as well, the professors played the leading role in the legal science of Roman law, which alone, at that time, could be taught in the universities. With the English Revolution, however, the role of the judges of the common law courts was greatly enhanced. They not only decided cases but also, in their judicial opinions, explained at some length the basic principles on which their decisions rested. When early-eighteenth-century efforts to introduce a course in English law into the universities finally succeeded, the mantle fell on Blackstone, a practicing lawyer who himself later became a common law judge and whose lectures inevitably focused on the law as it appeared to judges. To this day, most English (and American) law professors have devoted their scholarship largely to analyzing, criticizing, and building on the explanations given by judges in decided cases.

English legal science of the seventeenth and early to mid-eighteenth centuries, being primarily a judge-made rather than primarily a professorial legal science, added to the dialectical method of the twelfth through fifteenth centuries and to the topical method of the sixteenth and early seventeenth centuries the historical method which was embodied in the doctrine of precedent and in other basic principles of English law. This inevitably tended to make English legal science more a particular science of English law and less a general legal science, just as English historical jurisprudence was more a particular jurisprudence of the historical development of English law and less a jurisprudence of the nature and development of law generally. That is not to say, however, that English legal science and English legal philosophy were provincial; on the contrary, both proclaimed a belief in the universal validity of their particularist orientation.

The New English Legal Science and the English Revolution

Every legal system, wrote the noted comparatist Otto Kahn-Freund, requires a unifying element, and that unifying element in England is "the fiction of historical consistency," whereas in continental Europe it is "the fiction of logical consistency." He added:

> If law can be called a science it is [in England] an empirical science. It is an answer—primarily—to the question: "what was done previously?" [rather than] a logical process untrammelled by previous attempts to grapple with a similar situation. . . . The axiom that the law is a logical system, self-sufficient, comprehensive, without "gaps," arose on the Continent as a response to the needs of the growing civil service state. . . . The modern continental systems were developed in the universities by legal scholars for the use of officials. . . . It was due to political factors, to the failure of the absolute monarchy in England, to the aristocratic structure of the body politic . . . that the administration of the law remained in the hands of the [common] lawyers' guilds. With some exaggeration one might say that it was the Revolution of 1688, not the refusal to "receive" Roman Law that, in [England], sealed the fate of systematic legal science in the continental sense.[96]

The emergence of the new English legal science was part of the aftermath not just of the Glorious Revolution of 1688, as Kahn-Freund suggests, but of the entire English Revolution of 1640–1689, commencing with the revolt of a Puritan-dominated parliament against the king and culminating in 1689 in the Bill of Rights. It is generally recognized that that larger Revolution was not only a constitutional transformation, establishing for the first time the supremacy of Parliament over the Crown and of the common law courts over their "Romanist" rivals, as well as a two-party system of Whigs and Tories, but also a social-economic transformation, establishing the predominance of the landed gentry ("the country") and a rising merchant class over the royal nobility ("the court"), and a religious transformation, establishing the legitimacy of Calvinist belief systems alongside a more liberal ("latitudinarian") Anglicanism. This was a Great European Revolution in the classical sense, similar in scope to the Lutheran and monarchical German Revolution of the previous century and the Deist and democratic French Revolution of the following century. Each of these successive upheavals was characterized by civil war, class struggle, and an apocalyptic vision of a new era. Each produced fundamental constitutional, social-economic, and religious change.

Less well recognized, however, are the connections between the Great Revolutions and the fundamental changes in legal philosophy, legal science, and criminal and civil law that inevitably accompanied or followed them. And in the case of the English Revolution, a central element of whose ideology was a radical belief in the organic continuity of English history from early times, broken only by Tudor-Stuart despotism, most historians have accepted an essentially Whig version of the development of English law, namely, that it did not undergo fundamental change during the late seventeenth and early eighteenth centuries, that the English "common law" was always supreme over the "foreign" legal regimes that once coexisted with it, and that the constitutional reforms of the late seventeenth century did not substantially affect the incremental development of the law applicable in the royal courts. Indeed, except for criminal law, the fundamental changes in English law in the period, from the late seventeenth to the late eighteenth century have been greatly neglected.[97] T. F. T. Plucknett, one of the two or three most outstanding English legal historians of the twentieth century, even spoke of "the remarkable continuity and stability of English law during the vicissitudes of the seventeenth century."[98] Presumably Plucknett meant by "English law" the English common law rather than constitutional law, and by the English common law the civil law rather than the criminal law, and by the civil law its formal rules and doctrines, often preserved only by fictions, rather than its method and theory.

Once it is recognized that English law underwent substantial changes in the seventeenth and eighteenth centuries, the question arises: How were these related to the "vicissitudes" of that time? More particularly, what was the relationship of the new English legal science to the constitutional, social-economic, and religious transformations that preceded and accompanied it? In fact, it was closely connected, in its causes and its consequences as well as in its character, with the totality of the changes of the time. Thus with respect to the constitutional transformation, the new doctrine of precedent and the independence of the jury, both of which provided a protective armor against direct political interference in the decisions of the courts, were intimately connected with the establishment of the supremacy of the common law courts over their rivals and their independence of the Crown (and eventually, in 1701, by virtue of the life tenure of judges, of the Parliament itself).[99] With respect to the social-economic transformation, the enhanced rationalization and systematization of the law of property, contract, tort, and unjust enrichment ("quasi-contract") was both a consequence and a cause of the enhanced protection of landed estates and the security of commercial transactions. At the same time, the entrusting of legal science largely to judges and members of the bar, who were drawn chiefly from the landed gentry, rather than primarily to university professors, led to the specific kind of systematization that distinguished it from the legal science of other European countries. With respect to the religious transformation, most of the legal changes mentioned earlier have sources in the various forms of neo-Calvinist Puritanism that marked the first phase of the Revolution; and new standards of proof in criminal and civil cases and the new theories of evidence expounded by the common lawyers, and, more generally, the adversary system of trial procedure, were also closely related to the rise of the new latitudinarian Anglicanism, which denied the possibility of achieving absolute certainty in some matters of religious doctrine, and which consequently advocated tolerance of certain kinds of dissent within limits of probable truth.

If the transformation of legal science is seen in the context of the total English Revolution, and not only in the context of the general transformation of scientific thought, light may be shed also on the vexed question of the relationship of the English Revolution to that larger scientific revolution. Some students of the history of science have linked the transformation of the natural sciences in the seventeenth century to the Puritan phase of the English Revolution, when English scientists in various fields, many of them with Puritan sympathies, founded the Royal Society and espoused empiricism as the foundation of scientific knowledge.[100] The sociologist Robert Merton, following Max Weber's interpretation of the Calvinist work ethic, argued that the Puritan millenarian dedication to the reformation of the world, coupled with the Puritan emphasis on the salvific value of industry and enterprise, created the necessary environment for the new scientific method of experiment and observation.[101] Other scholars have traced the source of the new scientific "paradigm" to later phases of the Revolution, namely, the Restoration and the Glorious Revolution, and especially to the acceptance, during those later decades, of a more liberal Anglicanism, which was less dogmatic than Puritanism and more accepting of the positive value, for science itself, of the clash of opposing positions.[102] Still others have found sources of the new science in a dialectical interaction between the Puritan and the reformed Anglican phases of the Revolution.[103] The transformation of legal science gives evidence that supports the latter position. It also confirms, and supplements, the broader thesis advanced by Merton that there is an "interplay" between culture and science and, more particularly, an "interdependence" between scientific knowledge and "institutional" developments in the fields of economy, politics, and religion.[104]

Perhaps the closest connection between the transformation of English political, economic, and religious institutions in the late seventeenth century, on the one hand, and, on the other hand, the transformation of the sciences, including both the natural sciences and legal science, was the strong emphasis placed on the corporate character of both action and thought. It has become customary to attribute to the seventeenth century, especially in England, the rise of individualism in all spheres of social life, after a long "medieval" age of communitarianism.[105] In fact, the English Revolution was marked in all its phases by the formation of close-knit religious, political, economic, professional, and other communities. The connection between this kind of communitarianism and the development of the natural sciences is apparent in the thesis advanced by Robert Boyle, and accepted by scientists to this day, that scientific truth in a particular field is established by the successive confirmation of the results of experiments by the community of scientists working in that field. Its connection with legal science is apparent in the similar thesis advanced by the common lawyers: that the validity of legal rules and doctrines is established by their confirmation by the close-knit profession of judges and lawyers in applying them to analogous cases. The verdict of the professional community in an individual case must, however, itself be justified in terms of the entire science. The particularism of the process rests on the recognition that there is an underlying interdependence and interaction of the findings, or the holdings, with the entire "body" of the science. That individual laws—whether in the sense of laws of motion or in the sense of laws of contracts—form part of a system of such laws is a fundamental premise on which both natural science and legal science rest.

CHAPTER 10

The Transformation of English Criminal Law

The fact that English criminal law underwent a rapid and fundamental transformation in the late seventeenth and early eighteenth centuries has been obscured by the ideology of the English Revolution itself, which proclaimed the unbroken continuity of English legal history at least from the time of the Norman Conquest.[1] It has also been overshadowed over the past century by the extensive researches of legal historians into the reformation of English criminal law in the sixteenth and early seventeenth centuries, on the one hand,[2] and into the reforms of the late eighteenth and nineteenth centuries, on the other.[3] Strangely, the intervening century from the 1640s and 1650s to the 1760s and 1770s has been largely neglected by those who have explored major turning points in the transition from "medieval" to "modern" English criminal law. Only in the 1980s did legal historians begin to publish important works on the changes in English criminal law during that time, but even those works have not attempted systematically to relate the changes they analyze to the political, socioeconomic, and religious revolution of which they were a part.[4] Social historians, by contrast, especially those of Marxist orientation, have stressed the connection between the rise to power of the landed gentry and certain important changes in English law, including certain changes in criminal law, without, however, examining the fundamental transformation of the system of criminal law as a whole.[5]

Criminal law in England did, to be sure, undergo substantial changes in the sixteenth and early seventeenth centuries. There was not, however, prior to the late seventeenth century, one all-embracing system that could be called "the" English system of criminal law. Different systems of criminal law continued to be administered in the ecclesiastical courts as well as in the various secular courts themselves: royal, feudal, local, manorial, mercantile, urban. In the sixteenth century the Tudor monarchs created a whole new set of royal courts, called prerogative courts, to operate alongside the older royal common law courts of King's Bench, Common Pleas, and Exchequer; each of these new courts had its own criminal jurisdiction and its own substantive criminal law and criminal procedure. As will be shown in the present chapter, the abolition of the prerogative courts in the English Revolution, and the concentration of criminal jurisdiction in the common law courts, were accompanied by revolutionary changes in both the substantive and the procedural common law of crimes. The focus will be on the relationship of those innovations to the English Revolution itself, that is, to the total upheaval—political, religious, social, economic, and legal—which began with the revolt of the Long Parliament against the Crown in 1640–41 and culminated in the final establishment of parliamentary supremacy and the adoption of the Bill of Rights in 1689.

The chapter is divided into four topics:

1. the coexistence and competition of diverse systems of criminal law in England from the twelfth to the early seventeenth century;
2. the effect of the triumph of the English common law courts over their rivals on the development of English criminal law in the late seventeenth and eighteenth centuries;
3. the effect of the triumph of the landed gentry on the development of English criminal law in the late seventeenth and eighteenth centuries; and
4. the effect of the triumph of a Calvinist moral theology on the development of English criminal law in the late seventeenth and eighteenth centuries

The Coexistence and Competition of Diverse Systems of Criminal Law

Very few traces of the Anglo-Saxon criminal law of the sixth to eleventh centuries survived the legal reforms that followed—everywhere in western Europe—in the aftermath of the Papal Revolution.[6] Like their counterparts elsewhere, the Norman rulers of England replaced the older system of settlement of blood feud and private compensation of victims with a new system of judicially supervised trial by ordeal, with guilty persons punished by death or mutilation.[7] With the effective abolition of ordeals by decision of the Fourth Lateran Council in 1215,[8] however, the English kings introduced trial by jury for certain types of violent crimes, as they had introduced it fifty years before for certain types of civil cases involving forcible breaches of the king's peace. English royal judges, traveling on circuit, summoned grand juries to present persons suspected of having committed so-called felonies during the preceding period, and then summoned petty juries to declare whether the indicted persons were guilty or innocent.[9] There was no presentation of evidence; the jurors were supposed to have informed themselves in advance whether the accused were innocent or guilty of the crimes charged. The self-informing jury was an important element of English local government which, over the course of succeeding centuries, sometimes frustrated royal policy. A great many accused persons were acquitted.[10] At the same time, jury participation in the decision of criminal and civil cases helped to make royal justice acceptable in the localities.[11]

The substantive criminal law administered by the royal judges through local juries consisted of a limited number of types of capital offenses, chiefly murder, mayhem, rape, arson, burglary, and robbery, called felonies, as well as certain serious nonviolent crimes, notably larceny and treason. Minor criminal offenses, called misdemeanors, subject to fine, corporal punishment, or short periods of imprisonment (usually for no more than one year), could also be submitted to juries by royal judges ("indictable trespasses"), but more often they were prosecuted by local (county) authorities rather than in the royal courts. Also feudal courts attended by lord and vassals, manorial courts attended by lord and peasants, urban courts established in the chartered cities and towns that were founded in England (as elsewhere in Europe) from the twelfth century on, and mercantile courts attended by merchants at fairs or in cities all had, in addition to their civil jurisdiction, a criminal jurisdiction over certain types of offenses and all followed their own types of procedure.

In addition, the system of criminal justice administered by the ecclesiastical courts ranked in importance with the various systems of secular criminal justice—and was far more sophisticated. Operating according to the canon law of the Roman Church, English ecclesiastical courts had at least concurrent jurisdiction over all kinds of crimes committed by clerics (a large class that included, for example, university students) and exclusive jurisdiction over a great variety of crimes committed by laymen, including heresy, sacrilege, sorcery, witchcraft, usury, defamation, and sexual and marital offenses, as well as any crime whatever committed by a laymen against a cleric or against church property.[12] Ecclesiastical sanctions included alms, amends, fasting, good works, degradation from church office, long-term physical confinement, and ultimately excommunication. Under canon law procedure, ecclesiastical judges took testimony under oath, including sworn written interrogatories and depositions from parties and witnesses. Appeals from decisions of a bishop's court could be taken to the court of the appropriate archbishop (in England, the archbishop of Canterbury or the archbishop of York), as well as to the papal court in Rome.

Certain features of the various systems of criminal law that emerged in England in the twelfth and thirteenth centuries were unusual, while other features were typical of contemporary Western legal systems generally. Typical were the systems of criminal law administered by the English ecclesiastical courts, feudal courts, manorial courts, urban courts, and mercantile courts. Such courts also flourished in other European countries and administered similar types of substantive and procedural law. Unusual, however, was the English royal system of indictment by a grand jury and verdict by a self-informing jury. In other countries—for example, the German principalities—laymen also participated in the trial of criminal cases, but they heard evidence in open court before rendering a verdict; moreover, indictments could be brought and defendants prosecuted by officials.[13] Unusual also was the wide scope of the criminal and civil jurisdiction of the English royal courts, compared to that of central tribunals in other kingdoms. Other European countries during this period also lacked a developed system of professional royal judges traveling on circuit to hear criminal and civil cases.

The systems of criminal justice established in England in the twelfth and thirteenth centuries underwent significant development in the fourteenth and fifteenth centuries. Feudal and manorial courts substantially declined in importance while the jurisdiction of the urban and mercantile courts gained in importance.[14] The ecclesiastical courts also continued to flourish, though royal parliaments occasionally issued laws designed to protect the royal courts from what were increasingly viewed as papal encroachments. The criminal jurisdiction of the royal courts (especially the Court of King's Bench) gradually expanded and, partly in connection with that, evidence of certain types of witnesses slowly began to be introduced into grand jury and petty jury proceedings. With the decline of the manors, a new class of landed gentry began to acquire powers of local government; commissioned by the Crown as justices of the peace, prominent members of the landed gentry enforced criminal law in the localities, subject to periodic control by royal judges on circuit.[15] In short, the system of criminal justice instituted in the twelfth and thirteenth centuries evolved incrementally in the fourteenth and fifteenth centuries, with important but not fundamental changes.

The first mutation in this process of evolution occurred with the assertion by King Henry VIII of royal supremacy over the church and the establishment of new royal courts with jurisdiction over many types of matters that previously had been the province of the ecclesiastical and other courts. Of the new courts, the Privy Council and the Court of High Commission had the largest criminal jurisdiction, but the new High Court of Admiralty, Court of Requests, and High Court of Chancery also exercised the power to fine and imprison. All these courts applied a substantive and procedural criminal law markedly different from that applied by the older courts of common law, although they also applied the common law in cases where their jurisdiction overlapped that of the common law courts.[16]

The new Tudor Privy Council, carved out of the older King's Council, was not only the chief executive arm of the king, with ultimate control of the entire system of courts, but was also itself a judicial body. The Privy Councillors often held court in a room with a starred ceiling, called the Star Chamber *(camera stellata)*, and in time their judicial sessions in Star Chamber were distinguished from their other business as the Privy Council. When the Privy Council sat as the High Court of Star Chamber, as it came to be called, the chief justices of the King's Bench and Common Pleas also participated, though they were not Privy Councilors. The chancellor, a leading member of the Privy Council, would usually preside over these judicial sessions, which heard both criminal and civil cases. Except in rare cases when the king chose to interfere personally, Star Chamber could not impose the death sentence and could not determine rights in freehold land; these were reserved to the common law courts. Therefore Star Chamber normally had no jurisdiction over felonies and treason, since these involved capital punishment and escheat of land. Instead, its normal punishments were fines, imprisonment (up to life), loss of ears or nose or tongue (not eyes or legs), whipping, the pillory, and public confessions (sometimes accompanied by the wearing of a paper specifying the offense—for example, "For lewd [i.e., seditious] words").[17] In contrast, courts of common law were limited in cases of felony to sentences of death by hanging, mutilation of eyes or legs, escheat of land, forfeiture of chattels, and outlawry, and in cases of lesser crimes to relatively small fines and imprisonment up to one year.

The procedure in Star Chamber was adapted from the canon law and in general was considerably more sophisticated than that of the common law courts of the time. In contrast to common law procedure, accusation was either by a private accuser or on information of the attorney general, not by grand jury presentment or indictment; parties and witnesses were examined by sworn written deposition and orally under oath; a civil remedy could be given to the victim in a criminal case.[18]

The difference between prerogative justice and that administered by the common law courts may be illustrated by sixteenth-century criminal cases in the Privy Council, not expressly identified as sitting in Star Chamber, in which the court required twenty-five booksellers to report purchases and sales within the previous three years, subject to fines for importing books "of ill matter," and imprisoned one bookseller for delivering to be printed a certain "erroneous" religious book titled *A Postilla upon the Gospels and Pistols;*[19] ordered a defendant to be put in the pillory, with his ear nailed until it was torn off, for uttering "lewd"—that is, treasonous—words;[20] set at liberty with a reprimand a man who had been "roving about the country in a kind of frenzy" but who after being committed had "come to himself, repenting of his folly, declaring to have been seduced for the love of a woman";[21] and ordered the royal justices and the justice of the peace in the county of Surrey to dismiss an indictment against one of Her Majesty's gentleman pensioners, since their lordships had found that the accusation was false and had committed the person who made it to prison.[22]

Reports of other cases in the latter sixteenth and early seventeenth centuries, labeled "In Star Chamber, before the Council," include one in 1596 in which the defendant was charged with falsely stating that the earl of Essex had searched the Lord Admiral's ship and had found gunpowder barrels filled with ashes, dust, and sand and had called the Lord Admiral a traitor before the queen. He was sentenced to lose an ear on the pillory and to be whipped and to have a paper on his head showing his offense and to be imprisoned "during pleasure" and to be fined £20—"which should have been far greater but for his baseness, being a peasant and a boy."[23] Other Star Chamber cases of the late sixteenth and early seventeenth centuries involved seditious words in contempt of justices of the peace and the council for alleged miscarriages of justice.[24]

It should not be thought, however, that Star Chamber was concerned primarily with political and ideological crimes. Its criminal jurisdiction also included extortion, forgery, riot, subornation of perjury, maintenance, vexatious litigation, libel, fraud (including impersonation), and conspiracy. These were "sophisticated crimes, unlike the ancient felonies which were all . . . crimes of force rather than crimes of cunning."[25] Only in the early seventeenth century did Star Chamber earn its reputation as an instrument of political and ideological oppression. Prior thereto, Sir Edward Coke himself, the great champion of the common law against the excesses of the royal prerogative, wrote that the High Court of Star Chamber "is the most honourable court (our parliament excepted) that is in the Christian world, both in respect of the judges of the court, and of their honourable proceeding according to their just jurisdiction. . . . This court . . . doth keep all England in quiet."[26]

The contrast between "crimes of force" and "crimes of cunning" reflects a fundamental difference between the overriding (though by no means exclusive) concern of the common law courts with the specific criminal act (or, in tort cases, with the specific tortious act), viewed objectively in terms of its physical characteristics, and the overriding (though by no means exclusive) concern of the Star Chamber with criminal (and, in civil cases, tortious or contractual or other civil) intent. Ordinary royal jurisdiction over certain types of crimes, first asserted in the twelfth and thirteenth centuries, was founded chiefly on, and justified chiefly by, the need for a central authority to repress violence, and had been limited chiefly to manifest acts of "force and arms." Moral offenses that lacked manifestations of violence were left largely to the ecclesiastical courts and in some cases also, in the fourteenth and fifteenth centuries, to the court of the chancellor, who was usually a bishop or archbishop or even a cardinal.[27] As late as 1640, the common law did not punish the crimes of bribery, extortion, forgery, perjury, fraud, libel, sedition, or conspiracy. It did not have a doctrine of criminal attempt. It hardly distinguished between principals and accessories. It was only in the late seventeenth and early eighteenth centuries, after the triumph of the common law courts over their rivals, that these branches and elements of criminal law were received into the common law—not, as is often supposed, because previously English legal theory and English legal institutions were not sufficiently sophisticated, but because previously these branches and elements of criminal law were within the province of other types of English courts.

Operating under the supervision of the Privy Council and Star Chamber, the Court of High Commission, like the ordinary ecclesiastical courts, had original jurisdiction over immorality and violations of ecclesiastical laws by the clergy as well as over heresy, schism, and nonconformity committed by either the clergy or the laity. These offenses were defined very broadly. "The quarreling of two old women in church was schism, witchcraft was heresy, and the failure of the parson to read prayers on Wednesday because he was reaping his harvest was non-conformity."[28] The procedure of the court permitted it to summon persons on suspicion and to examine them under the notorious ex officio oath.[29] Lawyers who appeared before it were trained in the Roman law and the canon law, and in the tradition of the canon law the judges took evidence by sworn written interrogatories and depositions. Unlike the ordinary ecclesiastical courts, however, it had the power to fine and imprison. As Holdsworth has put it, "The Court of High Commission stood to the . . . ordinary ecclesiastical courts somewhat in the same relation as the Council and Star Chamber stood . . . to the ordinary courts of the state, central and local."[30] To this must be added, however, that in view of royal supremacy, both High Commission and its subordinate ecclesiastical courts were—equally with "the ordinary courts of the state"—bound by the instructions and decisions of the Privy Council and the Star Chamber. For example, in 1613 High Commission was given the power to enforce the Star Chamber rules concerning censorship of the press, a power which it continued to exercise until the revolutionary Puritan-controlled Long Parliament dissolved both it and the Star Chamber.

Other prerogative courts also had criminal jurisdiction, and also operated under rules of procedure derived ultimately from the canon law of the ecclesiastical courts. The High Court of Admiralty, whose jurisdiction was mainly civil, nevertheless had large powers of fine and imprisonment for crimes committed on the seas. The High Court of Chancery and the Court of Requests, whose jurisdiction was also mainly civil, could impose fines and imprisonment for disobedience to their decrees.[31]

It is important to note that the criminal jurisdiction of the common law courts also expanded in the Tudor-Stuart period. Parliamentary statutes added somewhat to the number of capital crimes—and except in extreme political cases, like that of Thomas More, the common law courts retained their monopoly over the death penalty. Legislation creating new capital crimes often also imposed penalties of escheat of land and/or mutilation of eyes and legs, and the infliction of these, too, were within the exclusive competence of the common law courts. Why the Star Chamber and High Commission were not given the power to inflict capital punishment or other common law penalties on traitors or witches or heretics is not obvious; they could, after all, and sometimes did, torture suspects and accused persons—which the common law courts did not do, if only because it would be awkward to torture a suspect or witnesses before a grand jury or a defendant or witnesses before a petty jury. Perhaps it was deeply felt that a person should not be put to death, at least for a nonpolitical crime, without a judgment of his peers. But if that was the reason, why could not Star Chamber have instituted trial by jury in its own preceedings? Perhaps because it was too primitive a process. How could a jury examine witnesses? And if witnesses were to be examined by judges, or possibly lawyers, in front of the jury, would there not have to be rules of evidence? But perhaps these considerations were less important than the felt need to preserve some continuity in the common law of crimes, in view of the radical changes taking place under the Tudor monarchs in other departments of church and state.

Whatever the reason, the common law courts retained their virtual monopoly over the death sentence, and in other courts judges continued to sit without a jury and to examine witnesses under oath, using written interrogatories and depositions and applying sophisticated rules of evidence. Nevertheless, there was interaction between the two systems, and this had consequences for both. The judges of the prerogative courts were entirely familiar with the common law; indeed, as was noted earlier, the chief justices of King's Bench and Common Pleas sat in cases heard in Star Chamber. Also the judges of the common law courts were familiar with the substantive criminal law and the criminal procedure applicable in the prerogative courts. To mutual knowledge must be added the effect of competition between the two systems. In particular, the common law courts were jealous of their powers and sought, through writs of habeas corpus, prohibition, and other devices, to resist encroachments of the prerogative courts.

Some of the changes in the common law in the sixteenth and early seventeenth centuries anticipated the transformation of English legal philosophy and English legal science which took place during and after the English Revolution. Some also constituted important steps toward the later modernization of the common law of crimes, which is the principal subject of the present chapter. In considering those earlier changes, however, one must bear in mind that the criminal law applied in the common law courts during the sixteenth and early seventeenth centuries remained part of a pluralist structure of systems of criminal law, in which the supreme power and the chief initiative for change had come to fall upon the Privy Council. It was, above all, the Privy Council that controlled both the expansion of the competence of the common law courts and the principal changes in their procedure, as they controlled the competence and the procedure of the other prevailing systems of courts.[32]

The Triumph of the Common Law Courts over Their Rivals

The abolition of the prerogative courts in 1640, and the transfer of most of their criminal jurisdiction to the courts of common law, as well as the subordination to the ultimate control of the common law courts of the limited criminal jurisdiction of the non–common law courts that remained, had enormous consequences for the substance of the English criminal law. It meant that to be tried for any serious crime a person must have been indicted by a grand jury on the basis of evidence presented to it, and that to be sentenced he must have been tried and convicted by a petty jury, with both the indictment and trial conducted under the supervision of a court of common law. To the relatively short list of common law felonies with which a person could have been charged in the fifteenth and sixteenth centuries, Parliament in the late seventeenth and early eighteenth centuries added a host of others, drawn in part from the suppressed jurisdictions of the prerogative courts. As felonies, these now became crimes punishable by death, unless Parliament determined that they should be punished by other sanctions.[33] Other offenses previously prosecuted in the prerogative courts were reclassified as common law misdemeanors, with the consequence that the competence of the common law courts to impose fines and imprisonment was greatly enlarged. Among the capital crimes created by statute in the century after 1640 were adultery, various forms of aggravated assault, forgery, piracy, poaching, and new forms of complicity in larceny.[34] Misdemeanors first made punishable after 1640 included a variety of forms of gambling proscribed by statute as well as nonsupport of family members, previously punishable in the prerogative courts.[35] Trial of misdemeanors remained, as before, largely within the competence of the justices of the peace, but the constant scrutiny of their activities by Star Chamber was eliminated, leaving them subject only to supervision of their decisions by the justices of King's Bench sitting on circuit.[36]

It is also to be emphasized that in contrast to criminal proceedings in the prerogative courts, prosecution at common law was carried out not by an official royal prosecutor but by private persons (usually the victim or his close relatives) or by representatives of newly formed organizations concerned with enforcement of public order or morals. Moreover, it was very rare for defense counsel to be present in trials at common law; the accused normally conducted his own defense.

The new role of the common law courts in criminal cases is graphically illustrated in the following report of the case of *The King v. Sir Charles Sidley*, tried in the King's Bench in 1664:

> Sir Charles Sidley was indicted at common law for several misdemeanors against the peace of the King which were to the great scandal of Christianity, and the cause was that he showed his nude body in a balcony in Covent Garden to a great multitude of people and there did these things and spoke these words etc. [stating the particulars of his misbehavior] and this indictment was openly charged to him in Court and he was told by the justices that since there was no longer at this time any Star Chamber they would have him know that this Court is guardian of the morals [*custos morum*] of all the subjects of the King,

> and it is now high time to punish such profane actions done against all modesty, which are so frequent that not only Christianity [b]ut all morality [text garbled]. [The case was continued to the end of Michaelmas term.] The Court having required his trial at the Bar, he submitted himself to the Court and confessed the indictment. Therefore the Court considered what judgment to render, and since he was a gentleman of a very ancient family (now of the county of Kent) and his estate was encumbered (not intending his ruin but to reform him) they fined him only 2,000 marks and that he be imprisoned for a week without bail and on good behavior for three years.[37]

It may be noted that, as exemplified in this case, the Court of King's Bench acquired not only the jurisdiction of Star Chamber over moral offenses but also its competence to impose heavy fines, imprisonment, and post-imprisonment probation.

The Effect of the Triumph of the Landed Gentry and Wealthy Merchants

The English Revolution of 1640 to 1689 established the supremacy of Parliament over the Crown and of the landed gentry and the wealthy merchants over the royal nobility. It is not surprising, therefore, that in the late seventeenth and early eighteenth centuries a large percentage of the many new statutory capital crimes had the effect of protecting the property rights of the landed gentry and the merchant classes. For example, the common law felony of larceny was extended to a wide variety of economic offenses that had previously not been punishable in the common law courts at all or else were punishable there only as misdemeanors. Thus a statute of 1731 extended (capital) larceny to include the stealing of gates, railings, and other objects attached to buildings, while other statutes made it larcenous to steal trees, fruits, and vegetables from a landed estate—all of which offenses had previously been treated as incidental to non-felonious trespasses and hence only as misdemeanors.[38] The most notorious of the new laws imposing the death sentence for such economic crimes was the Black Act of 1723, which purported to be directed against poaching game but which also included a host of other offenses.[39]

After the Norman Conquest, the Crown had arrogated to itself certain tracts of land as game preserves and had asserted the right to prohibit the hunting of game anywhere in England by any persons to whom the Crown had not issued hunting franchises. By the end of the sixteenth century, however, the royal forest laws had lost much of their effectiveness. Under James I there was a resurgence of royal claims over forests and game; to purchase licenses to hunt deer, partridges and pheasants, or rabbits, even on one's own land, one had to possess a freehold or leasehold worth a very substantial amount.[40] In addition, Charles I revived portions of ancient game laws concerning the Crown's franchise rights as a means of collecting revenues. Violations were punishable as misdemeanors.

In the wake of the Puritan Revolution and the Restoration, control over forest lands and hunting shifted from the Crown to the landed gentry.[41] In 1671 Parliament enacted a Game Act granting the right to hunt and to preserve game to an owner of a freehold worth at least £100 or of a leasehold worth at least £150. The 1671 act did not, however, impose new criminal penalties on poaching but left in force older penalties. It was the Black Act of 1723, enacted after a series of depredations by bands of poachers amounting virtually to class war, which in effect codified the criminal law concerning not only poaching (called "blacking," since poachers often blackened their faces in order to disguise themselves) but also many other types of related crimes against landed property.

The Black Act made it a capital offense for any person armed or with his face blackened or otherwise disguised merely to be present in places where deer or hares or conies "were or are or are to be" usually kept. The act also listed a wide variety of specific capital crimes: hunting, wounding, or stealing red or fallow deer; poaching hares or fish; cutting down trees planted in any avenue or growing in any garden or orchard; setting fire to any house, barn, or haystack; sending anonymous letters demanding "money, venison, or other valuable things"; and many others. Willfully and maliciously shooting at any person—in any dwelling or any other place—was made punishable by death, even if the victim survived. Thus attempted homicide or attempted maiming—by anyone, anywhere—was made punishable equally with the completed act, and the older law, which made assault with intent either to maim or to murder only a misdemeanor, was silently repealed. Similarly, a section of the act imposing the death penalty for breaking down the mound of a fish pond had the effect of replacing a 1568 statute which imposed for that specific offense imprisonment for three months and triple damages plus the finding of sureties for good behavior for another seven years. In addition, the provisions of the act extended not only to principal offenders but also to their associates, including accessories after the fact.[42]

The harshness of the sanctions under the Black Act is discussed in the next section of this chapter. Emphasized here is the fact that the scope of its coverage reflected a new policy of increased protection of the property rights of the landed gentry. This was clearly class legislation. In that connection it should also be noted that control of enforcement, which under the Tudors and early Stuarts had been largely in the hands of Crown officials or persons under royal supervision, was now transferred, under the system of private prosecution, largely to the landed gentry itself.

The newly emerging wealthy mercantile class was also the beneficiary of new criminal legislation. Piracy, from which shippers and traders were at particular risk, was the subject of comprehensive legislation in the year 1700. Any "commander or master of any ship or any seaman or mariner" who should "betray his trust and turn pirate, enemy or rebel" was made liable to capital punishment. Similarly, any ship's master or crewman who should "yield [the ship's goods] up voluntarily to any Pirate, Enemy, or Rebel, or shall bring any seducing Messages from any Pirate, Enemy, or Rebel, or consult, combine, or confederate with or attempt to corrupt any Commander, Master, Officer, or Mariner to yield up or run away with Ship, Goods, or Merchandizes, or turn Pirate, or go over to Pirates" was also guilty of piracy and subject to capital punishment. In order to expedite the trials of pirates, the statute empowered the officers of English ships—naval as well as merchant—to assemble a court of seven members to hear piracy cases and, in appropriate cases, impose the death penalty.[43]

Banking also received increased protection by a series of statutes relating to the forgery, larceny, and embezzlement of various types of banknotes, bonds, debentures, bills of exchange, and other commercial instruments. In 1724 it was made a capital felony to forge banknotes or bills, and in 1725 it was made a capital felony to forge East India and South Sea bonds;[44] previously such forgery had been punished as a misdemeanor in Star Chamber and, after the abolition of Star Chamber, as a misdemeanor in the common law courts.[45] In 1729 it was made a felony to steal various types of commercial instruments from the custody of persons holding such instruments;[46] previously, this offense was characterized not as larceny but only as a misdemeanor, since the holders of the documents did not have property rights in the underlying claims represented by them and there was therefore no trespassory taking. In 1742 Parliament went further and made embezzlement of various types of commercial instruments a felony when committed by officers or servants of the Bank of England. Later embezzlement statutes extended the crime to servants of the South Sea Company and the Post Office.[47]

The Effect of the Triumph of Calvinist Moral Theology

We owe to Douglas Hay a dramatic account of the paradox that in the late seventeenth and early eighteenth centuries there was, on the one hand, an extraordinary proliferation of capital offenses—the number rose from about thirty prior to 1640 to at least two hundred a century and a half later—and at the same time a substantial decline in the percentage of indictments for capital offenses that resulted in hangings.[48] This was due partly to the fact that juries would often acquit persons accused of capital crimes or else convict them of lesser included offenses that were not punishable by death, and partly to the fact that judges would sometimes reduce indictments for capital crimes to charges of lesser offenses or, alternatively, would offer the condemned person the possibility of a royal pardon conditioned on accepting transportation overseas, chiefly to North America to work in indentured servitude or, more rarely, in penal colonies. In 1718 Parliament enacted a Transportation Act that regularized this practice, allowing judges to impose transportation for seven years on persons convicted for the first time of a "clergyable" felony, and fourteen years on persons convicted of a "non-clergyable" felony.[49] Thus Parliament kept legislating capital punishment, but the proportion of executions to prosecutions kept declining.

Hay's explanation of this phenomenon is that judges, private prosecutors, and jurors tended to be members of the ruling class of landed gentry, which could exercise either terror or mercy depending on the impression it wanted to convey to the lower classes. The threat of the death penalty, especially in cases of property crimes, deterred many prospective criminals and helped to keep alive the belief in the sanctity of property; at the same time, discretion in its application was used by men of property to reinforce community sentiments of the objectivity and majesty of the law and hence loyalty to the class system.

Much of Hay's explanation has been challenged by John Langbein, who has shown by hard evidence, first, that contrary to Hay's assertions, most of the persons accused of capital crimes in this period were not destitute victims of the economic system but rather hardened criminals, often quite successful in their profession; second, that a large majority of the victims who prosecuted the crimes were not from the propertied classes but were either farmers, tradesmen and artisans, or laborers; and third, that the minimum property qualification for jury service of £10 per year hardly resulted in panels drawn from England's social elite.[50] As Langbein states, "[Hay's] theory of ruling-class conspiracy is impossible to reconcile with the reality of jury discretion."[51]

Although he refutes Hay's avowedly Marxian interpretation of the paradox, Langbein does not offer his own interpretation. That is, he does not attempt to explain either the extraordinary increase in the number of statutory capital crimes in this period of English history or the strong tendency toward jury leniency in the application of the death penalty or the relationship between these two phenomena. Indeed, Langbein's emphasis on the more plebeian character of juries, as compared with the more aristocratic character of members of Parliament, might suggest the possibility of a class analysis only slightly different from Hay's: that the landed gentry in Parliament wanted to have all the scoundrels executed, but the local villagers and townsmen on the juries had some sympathy for them. Such an explanation, however, would have to account for the fact that the upper-class judges and members of Parliament were willing to leave the application of the law to unfettered lower-class juries. Still another explanation, and one more in keeping with Langbein's own analysis, would focus on the character of the system of criminal procedure in the common law courts in the late seventeenth and eighteenth centuries, under which the procedure for taking evidence was weighted against the defendant, who was not allowed to testify under oath and was not represented in court by counsel. Under those circumstances the jury might take very seriously the requirement that guilt be proved beyond a moral certainty or, as it later came to be called, a reasonable doubt.[52] As early as the 1670s Matthew Hale wrote in his diary, "If . . . the scales are even . . . it is safer to err on the side of sympathy than severity" and "Where the evidence is obscure, innocence is presumed."[53] In the late eighteenth century this would come to be called the presumption of innocence.[54]

None of these explanations, however, fully resolves the paradox. One cannot assume that Parliament wanted something which the judicial system—for which Parliament was ultimately responsible—would not accommodate. One must start, at least, from the assumption that both the statutes enacted by Parliament and the decisions reached in the common law courts reflected a shared outlook, a shared set of values, a shared belief system.

A key to the paradox lies in the Calvinist moral theology that prevailed in sixteenth- and early-seventeenth-century English Puritanism and eventually penetrated Anglicanism in the late seventeenth and eighteenth centuries.[55] That theology encouraged the maximum severity of criminal sanctions as a matter of law,[56] in the formal meaning of the word "law," that is, as a matter of stated legal rules, coupled, however, with a high degree of humaneness and conscientiousness in the application of those rules to concrete cases.

In the sixteenth century, outstanding German Lutheran legal scholars had defined law as a combination of two distinct elements: rules, which they considered to partake of the sinfulness of the earthly kingdom, since they are general in character and thus fail to distinguish the unique features of every person and every situation, and the application of rules to particular cases, in which the judge should immerse himself in the unique circumstances of the case and seek to do justice to the parties, searching his conscience and seeking the guidance of divine inspiration.[57] Calvinism, in its English form, accepted the Lutheran distinction between (sinful) rules and (conscientious) application of rules. It went even further than Lutheranism, however, in its advocacy of maximum strictness and severity of rules, on the one hand, and maximum conscientiousness and mercifulness in their application, on the other. These contrasting principles were related to three Calvinist doctrines which found expression in Anglican moral theology, namely: (1) the calling of every Christian to lead a holy life, coupled with the possibility of salvation of sinners by faith alone; (2) the distinction between punishment for sins of willfulness and punishment for sins of infirmity; and (3) community responsibility to apprehend and correct those who commit sins and, if their acts constitute crimes, to institute criminal prosecutions. I consider these three theological doctrines in turn and then trace their relationship to the transformation of English criminal law and procedure.

The Holy Life and Salvation by Faith

Traditional Roman Catholic theology distinguishes between the so-called evangelical precepts that are binding on all persons, such as the duty to love God and one's neighbor and not to kill or steal or commit adultery or otherwise violate divine law, and, on the other hand, the so-called counsels of perfection intended for those persons who accept a call to lead a perfect life. The counsels of perfection include chastity, poverty, and obedience, which correspond to the three traditional vows of the monastic life. In traditional Roman Catholic moral theology, only the church's spiritual elite are expected to conform their lives to the counsels of perfection. Others, however, can be "saved," that is, made holy in the sight of God, if through confession and penance they are entirely cleansed from their sinfulness.

Both Luther and Calvin rejected the hierarchical moral division between a spiritual elite and a sinful majority. In both traditional Lutheran and traditional Calvinist thought, all believers, and not only a monastic or priestly elite, are called to lead "the holy life," unblemished by sin. Concomitantly, all sinful acts, large or small, are said to be punishable, in principle, by eternal damnation. At the same time, salvation—released from damnation—is available by faith alone. Seventeenth-century English Calvinists, both Puritan and Anglican, carried to an extreme this dual doctrine of the duty of all Christian believers to lead lives of moral perfection and the possibility of salvation, by God's grace, of even the most sinful among them. In words of Jeremy Taylor, a leading Anglican theologian, "all Christians must be not only holy but eminently holy."[58] That meant that the Roman Catholic distinction between big sins and little sins—so-called mortal sins, punishable ultimately by condemnation to hell, and venial sins, requiring only temporal punishment—was rejected. Such a distinction, according to Bishop Taylor and other leading English moral theologians of the mid- and late seventeenth century, debases the concept of holiness and encourages people to continue in their course of sinning. Moreover, it was associated with the offensive Roman Catholic doctrine of purgatory and the accompanying practice of granting indulgences. According to Calvinist theology, all sins, even those that do no harm to others, were punishable by eternal damnation in hell, and for the true believer all sins, even the most harmful, could be forgiven by divine grace.[59]

At first blush, these doctrines seem to provide no basis for distinguishing between degrees of guilt in the commission of sins. In fact, however, Calvinist moral theology, as reflected in the writings of seventeenth-century English scholars and preachers, did make such a distinction. It was based, however, not on the degree of gravity of the sinful act but on the degree of depravity of the sinful will. Sinful acts committed from motives of malice were said to reflect a perversion of the will of the actor, and hence not to be pardonable, whereas sinful acts committed not from motives of malice but from the actor's personal weakness of mind or spirit, being less "willful," were said to be pardonable. The fact that they were pardonable or not pardonable did not imply that they would in fact be pardoned, since actual pardons depended in all cases on true faith and divine grace. Nevertheless, the distinction between pardonable and not pardonable sins was used to distinguish degrees of sinfulness, which in turn were measured by the degree to which the will of the sinner was perverted.[60]

Sins of Willfulness and Sins of Infirmity

The distinction between sins of willfulness and sins of infirmity may have played an important part in motivating the decisions of eighteenth-century English juries in felony cases whether to convict or acquit of the felony, whether to convict of a lesser crime than that charged, and whether to impose death or a lesser penalty such as transportation overseas. Peter King, in analyzing sentencing and pardoning policies in reported cases of felony prosecutions in England in the eighteenth century, has stated that "the great majority" of decisions in such cases "were based on the following criteria: the prisoner's youth or infirmity, his good character and previous conduct, his prospects of employment or reform, the destitution of his family, the possibility of his innocence, the nature and surrounding circumstances of his crime, or the respectability of his background." Within these criteria, King adds, "respectability was the least frequently mentioned [in judicial reports] and most ambivalently treated factor." Judges not only noted these factors, he states, but "also acted on these criteria in a systematic way." He attributes these policies to "a strong element of practical, and in some senses Christian, humanity."[61]

Of the criteria listed, the prisoner's youth or infirmity, his good character, his prospects of reform, and the nature of his crime relate specifically to the Calvinist concept of sins of infirmity. Consideration of them reflects what King calls "in some senses Christian humanity." Other criteria—prospects of employment, the destitution of his family, the possibility of his innocence, the respectability of his background—may constitute what King calls "a strong element of practical . . . humanity." What is noteworthy, and what is Calvinist, is that while a great variety of willful acts are made punishable by death, the character of the offender plays a dominant role in the decision to pardon him or to reduce his sentence.

Community Responsibility for the Repression of Sin

The twin theological doctrines that all believers are called to lead a holy life but may be saved even if they fail to achieve that goal, and that sins of willfulness are generally to be punished more severely than sins of infirmity, were associated with a third theological doctrine, that God has imposed on the community a responsibility to assist individual believers in their efforts to achieve righteousness. Contrary to the assumptions of many twentieth-century social theorists, not individualism but communitarianism was a dominant feature of the prevailing belief system of late-seventeenth-century and early-eighteenth-century England. In the words of Robert Sanderson, a leading seventeenth-century Anglican bishop: "God hath made us sociable creatures, contrived us into poli[t]ies and societies and commonwealths; made us fellow-members of one body and every one another's members. As, therefore, we are not born, so neither must we live, to and for ourselves alone; but our parents and friends, and acquaintances, nay, every man of us hath a kind of right and interest in every other man of us, and our country and commonwealth in us all."[62]

Puritan solicitousness for the moral improvement of the community, which found reflection in the seventeenth-century English concept of public spirit as the legitimizing factor in political action, also carried with it the Puritan concern that one's neighbors not be led into sin and that those that are so led be properly corrected. Especially after 1689, many feared that popular immorality, which had become not only widespread but also widely accepted in the Restoration period, would bring a divine judgment upon England, jeopardizing the new religious settlement. Invoking biblical imagery such as that of Jonah preaching in Nineveh and the fall of Sodom, preachers and others encouraged their hearers to reform their neighbors' lives in order to forestall such a divine judgment.[63]

These three theological doctrines help to explain the paradox of a penal policy in which criminal statutes provided for maximum severity of sanctions, namely, the death penalty, for a dramatically increasing number of offenses, while juries increasingly refused to apply the death penalty in prosecutions brought under those statutes but instead often either acquitted defendants or else convicted them of lesser offenses included in the indictments to which the death penalty was not applicable. From this theological standpoint, Parliament could be justified in declaring that the malicious poacher who on one occasion has killed a single rabbit should be subject to punishment no less severe than the malicious poacher who has repeatedly killed a large number of deer. They both have fallen below the moral standards set for Christian Englishmen. Nevertheless, since the evil which merits punishment is the depraved will, the judge and the jury, in applying the statutory rules, must conscientiously examine all the circumstances of the case, including the background and character of the defendant, in order to determine whether he acted out of malice or whether his will was weak and infirm. The first offender may have been induced by hardened criminals to join them, and may have succumbed to their blandishments because of intellectual and moral frailty. Other circumstances may have mitigated the defendant's guilt. As God himself may by his grace remit damnation for even the most grievous sins, so the judge or the jury, in their discretion, may withhold the death penalty for even the most heinous crime—if the offender, being penitent, gives promise of overcoming the burden of an infirm will. Judges increasingly recommended royal pardon for persons convicted of capital offenses, and upon the granting of such pardon would impose transportation overseas; eventually Parliament itself authorized the imposition of transportation instead of hanging for many offenses.[64]

Connected with jury discretion was the belief in the community's responsibility for sustaining individual believers in the holy life and for repressing and correcting sin. The jury was considered to represent the collective judgment of the community. Jury service was an expression of the theological doctrine expressed by Bishop Sanderson, namely, that "God hath made us sociable creatures, contrived us into polities and societies and commonwealths [and] made us fellow-members of one body and every one another's members." By convicting the guilty, the jury fulfilled the community's responsibility to repress and correct sin. By acquitting, or by convicting of a lesser crime, it served to control that responsibility by its judgment as to the nature and circumstances of the alleged sin.

Closely related to theological doctrines of sociability was the formation of voluntary associations of public-spirited citizens whose purpose was to initiate criminal proceedings against violators of the law. In the absence of a professional police force, and with the abolition of prosecutions in the prerogative courts by royal prosecutors, prosecution at trial was left to the victim or victims of the crime or their relatives. Such private prosecutions were expensive; only in the 1660s did the Crown establish ad hoc rewards for those who undertook them, and only after 1689 did Parliament establish a regular system of payments to reimburse their expenses.[65] But even with reimbursement, private prosecution was haphazard. Beginning in the 1690s and early 1700s, local Societies for the Reformation of Manners were formed, which hired informants to collect evidence of moral offenses such as prostitution, drunkenness, gambling, and violation of Sunday laws. Officers of the societies would swear out warrants that local constables would serve in order to bring offenders before local justices of the peace. These societies flourished for almost fifty years; although they diminished in number in the 1730s and apparently died out in the 1740s, they were revived on a smaller scale in the 1760s and continued into the early 1800s.[66]

Thus in the formation of prosecution associations, theological doctrines of sociability and of community responsibility for the repression of sin were reinforced by the social and economic interests of the landed gentry.[67] As in the case of the paradox of harsh laws and lenient application, one must look not only to morality but also to politics and economics for an explanation. And one must look also to history, including the history of law itself, for it was the triumph of the common law courts over their rivals that formed the context and created the conditions that made the subsequent transformation of English criminal procedure both possible and necessary.

The Impact of Calvinist Moral Theology on Substantive Criminal Law

New moral conceptions were also reflected in the development of the English law of homicide, the creation of the independent crime of conspiracy, and the introduction of imprisonment and transportation as major criminal sanctions.

Homicide

Together with the proliferation of new statutory crimes, the judge-made law of homicide underwent substantial change in the aftermath of the English Revolution. A striking manifestation of that change was the emergence of the felony-murder rule and the misdemeanor-manslaughter rule. In addition, defenses available to reduce the charge of murder to manslaughter came to be articulated by the courts in terms of so-called provocations. These developments, too, can be explained partly by the influence of Calvinist moral theology on English legal thought in the late seventeenth and early eighteenth centuries.

Under the felony-murder rule, a person who in the course of committing any felony causes a death is liable for murder, even though the death was entirely unforeseeable. Under the misdemeanor-manslaughter rule, a person who in the course of committing any misdemeanor causes a death is liable for manslaughter, even though the death was unforeseeable. These two rules, which remain law in England and America today, are viewed in most other countries as irrational and unjust. Why should a person who intended to commit, say, a burglary be liable for murder if, contrary to all his expectations, a stranger who unexpectedly appeared in the house suddenly saw the burglar and in his fright died of a heart attack? This result is, to be sure, more anomalous today than it was in the seventeenth and eighteenth centuries, when most felonies, including both burglary and murder, were equally subject to punishment by death.[68] The misdemeanor-manslaughter rule, however, was at that time even harsher than it is today, since manslaughter (negligent homicide), as a felony, was, like murder (intentional homicide), in principle punishable by death, while misdemeanors were in principle punishable only by imprisonment up to one year and/or a fine. Thus a relatively minor offense was raised to the level of a capital crime because of its objective consequences, however unforeseeable.[69]

The emergence of the judge-made felony-murder rule in the late seventeenth century may be explained, at least in part, by the same Calvinist belief system that motivated Parliament to multiply the number of statutory capital crimes. That belief system, as noted earlier, measured the degree of sinfulness of the defendant's conduct not by the type of act that he or she committed but by the degree of depravity of the actor in committing it. Both the act of stealing and the act of killing, for example, were violations of divine law laid down in the Ten Commandments, and hence in principle deserving of death. In the particular case, however, the felon—even though he murdered—might deserve only to be transported to servitude abroad or perhaps even convicted of a lesser offense and let off with imprisonment and/or a fine. Conversely, if the burglary or rape or larceny accidentally caused a death, then—if the sinfulness of the actor in committing the act was great enough—he or she might justifiably be considered punishable as a murderer.

Prior to the seventeenth century, the difference between murder and manslaughter in English law had rested on the distinction between premeditated killing ("malice prepense," "malice aforethought") and sudden killing ("chance medley" or "misadventure"). In the early seventeenth century, however, premeditation came to be presumed; as a result, many persons who previously would have been convicted of manslaughter were convicted of murder.[70] With the emergence, in the late seventeenth century, of the definition of manslaughter as negligent homicide, the common law of murder was left without even a formal division into various degrees of murder and without clear doctrines of justified and excused homicide. English lawyers of the late seventeenth and early eighteenth centuries must have been aware of these deficiencies, since the prerogative courts had derived from the canon law a sophisticated body of learning on such matters. Canonist ("Romanist") doctrines were derived, however, from a quite different theology from that which prevailed in England after 1640. For the canonists, the distinctions between various types of crimes reflected distinctions between various types of sinful acts. What was to be punished in the external forum was the offensive act, and punishments were to be measured according to the gravity of the type of act. Guilt was determined by the defendant's state of mind with respect to that type of act—especially his or her direct or indirect intent to cause the prohibited result or, if intent were lacking, his or her fault in failing to foresee that it would occur. Canonist procedures for trying criminal cases were well adapted to implementing these doctrines, while the common law system of jury trial, at this stage of its development, was not.

With the submergence of the Romanist courts, the dramatic increase in the number of common law crimes, both felonies and misdemeanors, and the adoption of the felony-murder and misdemeanor-manslaughter rules, the Court of King's Bench was confronted with the need to find new ways of distinguishing between different kinds of homicide. It held in a series of cases that defendants charged with murder should be convicted of manslaughter, and punished for the first offense by only a year's imprisonment and/or a fine, if it appeared that they were "provoked" to kill the victim under circumstances that diminished their guilt. The new doctrine of provocations was not elaborated systematically but was gradually amplified case by case. Ultimately it was summarized by William Hawkins, who concluded that one who commits homicide in "heated blood," that is, in a state of extreme anger or agitation, is guilty not of murder but of manslaughter.[71]

The doctrine of provocations performed functions similar to those performed in canon law and in other legal systems by doctrines of justification and excuse and by distinctions between various degrees of criminal homicide. Yet it performed those functions in a way that reflected a Calvinist rather than a Roman Catholic moral theology. Essentially, the jury was given the primary responsibility of weighing the moral quality of the defendant's conduct, under the particular circumstances of the case, against the general rule that felonies are, in principle, punishable by death. Not the sinfulness of the type of act as such, but the sinfulness of the defendant in committing it, was to be judged, and his or her lack of sinfulness in committing the act could overcome the harshness of the general rule.

Conspiracy

The modern English doctrine of conspiracy, which prevails also in the United States, first emerged in decisions of the King's Bench in the late seventeenth and early eighteenth centuries. Unique among Western legal systems in its breadth, the doctrine makes punishable as a crime the mere agreement of two or more persons to commit an unlawful act or, indeed, an act which is not in itself unlawful but is so immoral as to become unlawful when done by two or more persons jointly. In some other legal systems, as in England prior to the late seventeenth century, agreements to commit certain types of serious crimes may, indeed, themselves constitute crimes—notably agreements to commit certain types of crimes against the state such as treason. Generally, however, in other Western legal systems an agreement to commit a crime is not itself criminal unless it is followed by a concrete act in furtherance of the agreement—at the very least, an act of preparation of the crime, and in most legal systems an attempt to commit it or concealment of it after its commitment. The gist of such an offense is not "conspiracy" but "complicity," that is, participation of two or more persons in the carrying out of a criminal act. Moreover, the agreement and the attempt must be directed to the commission of a crime, and not merely the commission of a civil offense.

In England, the name "conspiracy" was given at an early time to subversion of the judicial process by bringing false charges against a person.[72] Prior to the early seventeenth century, such a "conspiracy" was not punishable unless as a result the victim was indicted and subsequently acquitted. In 1611, however, in a case decided by the Star Chamber in which the defendants had plotted to give false evidence of a criminal act but the grand jury refused to indict the person against whom they had plotted, the court nevertheless found the defendants guilty of conspiracy.[73] In 1615 the King's Bench extended the crime of conspiracy still further, to include repeated efforts by a prominent citizen of the city of Plymouth, together with others, to ruin the good name of the mayor of that city.[74] In both these cases, acts were performed to carry out the nefarious agreement. Nevertheless, Sir Edward Coke's report of these decisions included broad language to the effect that "a conspiracy with others to do a thing prejudicial to the public good" is a crime "even if the offenders do nothing to execute the agreement." In 1664 this dictum was repeated in a prosecution brought against some of the brewers of London who had agreed among themselves not to produce a cheap alcoholic beverage in order to deprive the Crown of revenue that accrued from its sale.[75] The King's Bench held the brewers guilty; an act in pursuance of such an agreement, it was said, was not needed. In all these cases, however, the defendants apparently had in fact, in addition to agreeing, taken some steps to carry out their agreement. At least the requirement of an "overt act," in addition to a "bare conspiracy," continued to be asserted.[76] Finally, Lord Holt, in 1705, settled the matter by stating that "if [as in the case before him] two or three persons meet together, and discourse and conspire how to accuse another falsely of an offense, it is of itself an overt act and is of itself an offense indictable. . . . [T]he very assembling together was an overt act."[77] Thus the issue was resolved by a fiction—one that has persisted in Anglo-American case law until the present day.[78]

In other cases the doctrine was elaborated that a criminal conspiracy exists not only when there is an agreement to commit a criminal act but also when there is an agreement to commit a tortious act or, indeed, an act that is neither criminal nor tortious but immoral. Thus William Hawkins, in *Pleas of the Crown* (1716), was able to state that "there can be no doubt but that all confederacies whatsoever, wrongfully to prejudice a third person, are highly criminal at common law."[79] In 1721 the King's Bench held that the mere agreement of certain defendant journeymen tailors to withhold their services unless they received higher pay was in itself criminal, the justices stating that "a conspiracy of any kind is illegal, although the matter about which they conspired might have been lawful for them, or any of them, to do, if they had not conspired to do it."[80] In 1724 the King's Bench stated that "a bare conspiracy to do a lawful act to an unlawful end is a crime, though no act be done in consequence thereof."[81]

The emergence of the notorious English doctrine of criminal conspiracy in the late seventeenth and early eighteenth centuries reflected the new role of the courts of common law as custodians of the morals of the English people. As shown earlier in this chapter, they took over that role, in part, from the defunct Star Chamber. As illustrated by the case of the journeymen tailors, the morality that the courts enforced was one that served the interests of the new ruling classes—the landed gentry and merchants. At the same time, Anglo-Calvinist concepts of public morality and public spirit played an important part in the extension of the criminal law to cover not only socially harmful acts but also offensive motivations manifested in collective agreements. In Lord Mansfield's words, "Whatever is contrary [to] *bonos mores et decorum* the principles of our law prohibit, and the King's Court, as general censor and guardian of the public manners, is bound to restrain and punish."[82]

Penal Sanctions

Calvinist and neo-Calvinist theology also had a profound influence in the creation of two new types of sanctions for felony, namely, imprisonment and transportation.

Imprisonment for felony was first introduced in England by a statute of 1706.[83] Previously English kings had often put their enemies in prison for indefinite periods, and in the sixteenth century the new royal prerogative courts had put persons in prison for refusing to obey their orders (civil contempt). Also in the sixteenth century so-called houses of correction, or "Bridewells," appeared, first in England's urban areas and later in outlying parts of the country, as a means of housing and putting to work the homeless, the destitute, and "sturdy beggars."[84] The common law courts, however, could impose the sanction of imprisonment only for quite short terms in order to restrain accused persons prior to trial, to compel payment of outstanding debts, and to punish persons convicted of certain misdemeanors.[85]

The 1706 statute did not make imprisonment an alternative to, or a substitute for, the death penalty. Rather it made imprisonment a punishment applicable to persons convicted for the first time of so-called clergyable felonies, that is, felonies for which punishment of first offenders had previously been limited to branding on the thumb. Now a minimum term of imprisonment for six months and a maximum term of two years could be added to the branding, at the discretion of the court.

The Transportation Act of 1718, discussed earlier in connection with the tension between severe rules and lenient application of them, provided that those to be transported were to be bound over to contractors, who were to assume the cost of transporting them but who were allowed to sell or otherwise assign the contracts to third parties in the American colonies.

Both imprisonment and transportation were served under conditions of hard labor, and no doubt favored the economic interests of the landed gentry and merchants who benefited from such labor. At the same time, they reflected a theological belief that arduous work may be not only a form of penance and a means of rehabilitation, as in Roman Catholic theology, and not only a Christian calling, as in Lutheran theology, but also a sign of predestined salvation. Hard work is, in any case, in Calvinist theology, a responsibility imposed by the divine "covenant of works," which "instituted basic human relationships of friendship and kinship, authority and submission," and established "basic values of devotion and piety, honesty and honor, discipline and diligence, humility and charity."[86] It is no accident that where Calvinism flourished in the seventeenth and eighteenth centuries—in England and America, in Holland, among the French Huguenots—hard work, sobriety, frugality, and other qualities of the so-called Puritan ethic also flourished.[87] In addition, a strong theological doctrine of the tension between divine justice and divine mercy supported the development of punishments that would be, on the one hand, more severe than a mere branding of the thumb or, in the case of a royal pardon, a total exoneration, and, on the other hand, less severe than the death sentence.

Such tension between justice and mercy was, indeed, a major theme of the sermons preached at the assizes to crowds assembled to attend the executions of felons. As noted earlier, no distinction was made between small offenses and great offenses; both might be equally punishable by death. Yet a first offender was subject to correction. The distinction between divine justice and divine mercy was reflected in the distinction between human law and human equity. In the words of the Reverend Zachariah Mudge, preaching at the assizes at Exeter Caster in 1732, because of the imperfect quality of human justice there "arises room for equity,"[88] which is "a power to stop the course of justice under the notion of mercy."[89] Mercy, said Mudge, makes it possible to distinguish among different offenses and different offenders when applying the law.[90] But mercy is also shown by severely punishing the guilty, since justice for the guilty is mercy for the innocent—that is, for the innocent victims of their crimes and for the community generally.[91]

CHAPTER 11

The Transformation of English Civil and Economic Law

The principal purposes of this chapter are, first, to recount and interpret fundamental changes in the law of property, of contracts, and of corporations that took place in the seventeenth and early eighteenth centuries in the wake of the establishment of the political supremacy of Parliament, the economic dominance of the landed gentry and leading merchants, and an Anglo-Calvinist moral theology; and second, to relate the changes in civil law to the accompanying transformation of commercial and financial law, notably the elimination of royal monopolies, the introduction of modern forms of credit, the rise of the modern stock market, the emergence of what has been called the "tax state," the creation of the modern system of patent law, and the introduction of marine and other forms of insurance.

In analyzing changes in basic legal concepts of property, contract, and corporations, attention is focused primarily on substantive law, as distinguished from related jurisdictional and procedural reforms transferring to the common law courts various types of civil disputes that had previously been dealt with in other courts and expanding common law civil remedies. These jurisdictional and procedural reforms have been treated in earlier chapters on the transformation of English constitutional law and English legal science. It is a widespread view among legal historians that despite such far-reaching jurisdictional and procedural changes during this period, basic concepts and principles of substantive civil law remained fundamentally the same as in the preceding period and developed only incrementally.[1] It is submitted that that view is refuted by the evidence presented in the discussion that follows.

Property

In the law of real property—land law—key events in the late seventeenth and early eighteenth centuries were (1) the abolition of so-called feudal tenures requiring services or payments to superior lords or requiring their consent to various forms of use or disposition of the property, resulting in the de facto replacement of the tenurial system by the modern law of land ownership; (2) the elimination of restraints on the enclosure movement and the carrying out of thousands of enclosures, resulting in the aggregation of landholdings and the replacement of copyhold tenure by long-term leases; (3) the invention of the so-called strict settlement, permitting landed estates to be preserved intact in the same family over many generations, while preserving rules against restraints on alienation of land not included in such settlements; and (4) the development of a law of trusts and mortgages, facilitating the establishment of a market in transfers of real property. Each of these events is discussed in turn.

The Abolition of Feudal Land Tenure

By resolutions in 1641 and 1645 and by a statute enacted in 1656, the Long Parliament abolished preexisting forms of tenure of land held of the Crown by tenants-in-chief, and after the restoration of the monarchy these actions were confirmed by the Tenures Abolition Act of 1660.[2] The immediate effect of this legislation was to deprive the Crown of the power unilaterally to impose certain kinds of feudal dues on landholders—chiefly, so-called knight-service and wardship.[3] One must say "so-called," because that was the language of feudal institutions that had long since ceased to exist. Indeed, the duty of a vassal to furnish his lord with knights to do battle had begun to be commuted to money payments ("scutage") as early as the twelfth century, and with the virtual disappearance of lord-vassal relationships in the fourteenth and fifteenth centuries, scutage itself, together with other feudal dues, most of which were payable upon descent or other transfer of freehold land, also virtually disappeared. It was the Tudor monarchs who artificially revived them in the sixteenth century in order to raise money for the Crown, and it was their Stuart successor Charles I who converted them into forced loans that enabled the monarchy to operate for eleven years without summoning a parliament to vote ordinary taxes.

The Tenures Abolition Act had the effect of subjecting the entire taxing power of the Crown to the will of Parliament. It also had the effect of converting virtually all types of freehold land tenure into "free and common socage." Previously, the strange term "socage" had been applied to various forms of landholding with various forms of obligatory service other than knight-service.[4] The 1660 act converted socage tenure into a freehold tenure with no obligation to perform services or make payments to a superior and with no requirement of consent by a superior to various forms of use and disposition—in effect, though not in name, ownership in the modern sense.

Elimination of Restrictions on Enclosures

Related to the liberation of freehold landholdings from obligatory payments and services to higher lords and to the Crown was the elimination of restrictions on the acquisition of lands held by villagers in common and used principally for pasturing sheep or grazing cattle. Such acquisitions were called enclosures because they were carried out by enclosing the commons with a fence, a hedge, or a ditch.

Enclosures had been infrequent in the heyday of the manorial system of agriculture from the twelfth to the mid-fourteenth century. Under that system, peasants held parcels of land ("strips"), usually scattered in various parts of the manor, "of" the lord of the manor, and the rights and obligations associated with such parcels, as well as rights in the commons, were based on manorial custom. With the decline of the manorial system in the late fourteenth and fifteenth centuries, especially after the Black Death of 1348–49, peasants generally retained their customary tenures as described in copies of the old manorial records, and these miscellaneous tenures were called by the general name "copyhold." But just as the gradual disappearance of the lord-vassal relationships changed the character of feudal tenures, so the gradual disappearance of lord-peasant relationships changed the character of manorial tenures. In the fifteenth century there emerged in the villages well-to-do peasants (yeomen), who acquired parcels of arable land from poorer peasants and who sometimes made inroads on the commons in order to obtain large areas of contiguous pastureland, chiefly for grazing sheep. One consequence was to drive numbers of peasants away from the land.

As enclosures increased in number in the late fifteenth and early sixteenth centuries, they aroused great opposition not only on the part of the poorer peasantry but also on the part of the Crown and the nobility, who, on the one hand, considered themselves the peasants' protectors and, on the other hand, were not favorably disposed toward the emerging class of prosperous yeomen. In 1515 Thomas More, in his *Utopia,* wrote of the enclosures that "sheep are eating men,"[5] and in 1517 Cardinal Wolsey appointed a commission of inquiry into depopulations caused by enclosures, which resulted in prosecutions of offenders in the High Court of Chancery for the next twenty years.[6] In the course of the sixteenth and early seventeenth centuries, legislation severely restricted the enclosure movement, which had become an important factor in the rise of the landed gentry. The repeal of anti-enclosure legislation was proposed by Sir Edward Coke and others—unsuccessfully—in the 1624 parliament of James I.[7] In the 1630s Charles I vigorously prosecuted violations of that legislation, and in 1644 one of the charges that resulted in the execution of Archbishop Laud was that he had supported the ruthless suppression of enclosures.

During the Commonwealth period and thereafter the enclosure movement was given full endorsement by Parliament. It was eventually subjected to certain judicial and parliamentary controls; in particular, as hundreds of private bills authorizing specific enclosures came to be enacted in Parliament, it became customary to include in them provisions granting some protection of persons likely to be adversely affected by them.[8]

The enclosure movement, which was accompanied by the "engrossing"—that is, the combining—of separate strips in the open fields, made inroads upon the system of copyhold tenures, the protection of which had been one of the aims of the Tudor-Stuart legislation restricting enclosures. Slowly in the sixteenth century, and rapidly in the seventeenth century, especially after enclosures became legalized, there developed a practice of transforming copyhold tenures into leasehold tenures. The holder of the dominant freehold to which the copyhold estate was subordinate would enter into an agreement with the copyholder whereby the latter would pay an initial sum of money, called an entry fine, and would then agree to pay annual rents under a long-term lease. Such negotiated leasehold tenures replaced earlier customary manorial copyhold tenures just as free socage tenures replaced earlier customary feudal tenures. As the holder in socage tenure was, in effect, no longer a tenant but an owner, so the long-term leaseholder was no longer a peasant but a farmer, whose property right was acquired by contract with the landlord. Indeed, the fiction that all land continued to be "held" of the Crown only disguised the fact that a "fee simple" now constituted ownership and that a "leasehold" was a contractual relationship which established certain property rights in the lessee.[9]

Strict Settlement

That drastic changes in land law in the late seventeenth and early eighteenth centuries reflected the interests of the landed gentry is also well illustrated by the so-called strict settlement, a method by which holders of landed estates could lawfully secure the descent of their property intact within the same family over many generations.

Freedom to dispose of freehold land by will or by contract or gift inter vivos had been actively fostered in the twelfth to sixteenth centuries, in the first instance by the Roman Catholic Church, which chiefly by such devises and gifts had acquired approximately one-third of the land of Europe. Land held by the Church "in free alms," however, almost invariably remained in the Church. Donors of land to others also often desired that further disposition of the devise, gift, or sale be restricted in particular ways, while the legatee or donee or his or her successor often desired otherwise. English law responded to this dilemma by creating a highly complicated set of rules to accomplish a wide variety of specific objectives. Certain forms of words in the devise or gift could be used to control further disposition of the land to particular persons. For example, a devise or gift of land "to A for life, and after A's death in tail to B and his heirs" would give A a "life estate," without the right to dispose of the land by will, but would give to B, if he were alive at A's death, full power to dispose of the land as he wished. Similarly, if A gave or devised land to B, with the condition that after B's death it should pass to B's first son who shall reach the age of twenty-one, then B could frustrate the donor's intention by disposing of the land at any time before he had a son who reached the age of twenty-one. The "contingent remainder," as it was called, that is, the minor son's future interest in the land, could be destroyed. The technical reason given for this rule was that if B should die before his eldest son reached twenty-one, no one would have property rights in the land—that is, there would be an "abeyance of seisin"—and this would be an intolerable situation. The rule extended to such hypothetical contingent remainders generally. A gift to S, a son, for life, with remainder to his eldest son, was at the mercy of S until a son was born to him in whom the remainder could vest.

The sense in the technical rule against abeyance of seisin—which is still law in England (as well as in the United States)—is that since a failure of the contingency to materialize would frustrate the intention of the testator or donor, the choice thereafter would lie between transferring the property to his heirs-at-law and giving full power of disposition of it to the intermediate legatee or donee of the life estate. The latter alternative is at least as likely as the former to correspond to what the testator or donor would have chosen, and it is more sound economically than the former since the alienability of land increases its value. Indeed, there was a strong tendency in the late-seventeenth-century common law to remove most surviving restraints on alienation of land.

Nevertheless, the rule that a purely hypothetical contingent remainder gave the holder of a life estate full power to alienate the land threatened to prevent the holders of great landed estates, who formed the ruling aristocracy of England, from preserving those estates intact over more than two generations. The problem was solved in the 1670s by Sir Orlando Bridgman, considered at the time to be the most outstanding member of the bar, among whose clients were the wealthiest and most prominent landed gentlemen of England. Sir Orlando had the genius to invent a device, called the strict settlement, by which the sense in the law of contingent remainders could be preserved while at the same time its impact on the great families which sought to preserve their dominant position over generations and centuries could be avoided. He created a trust to stand between S, the son, and G, the grandson, the trustees being charged with preserving contingent remainders; and the trustees' estate vested—that is, took effect—immediately upon the gift to S. The formula was a highly complex one: to S for life, remainder to trustees for the life of

S in trust for S for life and to preserve contingent remainders, remainder to S's first son in tail male (i.e., to descend in the male line), with successive remainders in tail male to the other sons of S. By this scheme the son, S, is deprived of his power to convey the land prior to the birth of his own son (the grandson, G), since there is a vested estate *in the trustees;* and any attempt by the trustees to dispose of the land contrary to the trust will be void. When the grandson, G, is born, his remainder vests. And when G reaches majority, S, in the pithy words of two great scholars of an earlier generation,

> has reached his forties or fifties and feels himself the guardian of the family honor, tradition, and estate. G may be rebellious and undisciplined, but he cannot disentail and thereby acquire a fee simple in remainder, because disentailment is possible only for a tenant in tail in possession; so, no matter what wild and radical ideas G may have at the age of 21, he can do the family estates no damage. It was at this point that, traditionally, S called G in for a chat. He explained to him that, having arrived at manhood's threshold, G would be wanting to make the Grand Tour of the continent, and present himself at the London season; this would take money, but there were family funds, controlled by S, available for members of the family who showed that they had the family interests at heart. S further explained that one of the important interests of the family was the continuation of the family estates and that there were a few papers to be signed to that end, now and at once. Thus gently nudged, it was traditional for G to sign as requested and thus make available to himself those advantages which flow from a generous parental allowance [10]
>
> Thus the basic pattern was pushed forward one generation. S could now rest easy in the confident belief that G would have no power to put the estates out of the family until he had a son 21 years old; and by that time G in his turn would be settled down, devoted to a shire life of farming and fox hunting, and determined to see that the family estates were preserved. You will, of course, realize that this little narrative is a simplification and to some extent a fictionalization and that for various family contingencies other devices were required; but this was the fundamental process. By this method thousands of estates . . . were kept substantially intact for centuries; if you care to get a notion the extent to which this went, look at copies of Burke's Peerage and Burke's Landed Gentry for any period during the nineteenth century.[11]

This system, whereby the estates of the great landed families remained intact for many generations, lasted until 1925, when it was ended by new legislation on taxation of property and inheritance.[12]

Development of Trusts and Mortgages

Although the right of one who held land in fee simple to sell it without the consent of his superior lord existed in English law from 1290, such sales were greatly inhibited in practice by the survival of feudal and manorial services and payments.[13] Where other tenures existed, namely, in the cities, land and buildings were indeed bought and sold from an early time.[14] In the late seventeenth century, with the final disappearance of most feudal and manorial tenures in the countryside, a flourishing market began to develop also in agricultural land, including landed estates. Indeed, it was to resist the temptations of such a market that many of the landed gentry tied up the descent of their estates through the strict settlement. Many of the same landed gentry, however, were willing to sell at least parts of their land, and these were often purchased by leading merchants and others who had acquired wealth through the expansion of commerce. It was a mark of the social success of such a city dweller to purchase a landed estate and to join the ranks of the landed gentry, while also maintaining his lucrative commercial connections in London or elsewhere.

Among the ways in which English law responded in the late seventeenth century to the greatly increased demand to make land marketable, perhaps the most important was the creation of a distinction between two types of title, one called "equitable" (and hence enforceable only in a court of equity, namely, Chancery), the other called "legal" (and hence enforceable only in a court of common law, namely, Common Pleas or King's Bench). The creation of the concept of equitable title involved a transformation of the law of trusts, whereby the grant of land to A in trust for B meant that both A and B became owners of the land, but owners for different purposes and with different rights and obligations. B was the "equitable" owner; A was the "legal" owner. B, not A, had the right of possession, use, and disposition of the land, but only within the limits of the trust instrument, which may have required that he use it in certain ways and dispose of it only with the consent of the trustee. By contrast, A, the trustee, as legal owner, was not to violate the rights of B, the beneficiary, and claims of creditors of A, unlike claims of creditors of B, were not to be enforced against the land.

The distinction between equitable and legal title to land was part of a fundamental transformation of equity—the body of law administered by the Court of Chancery—which took place in the late seventeenth century under the leadership of Lord Nottingham.[15] That transformation led also to the development of a new law of mortgages, which greatly facilitated the creation of a market in land, including both urban and agricultural land. The common law of "gage"—that is, pledge—of land as security for a debt goes back in time to the twelfth century, when the creditor, the mortgagee, occupied the debtor's land until the debt was paid.[16] Rules were developed that permitted the creditor to take the land if the debt was not repaid within a certain agreed-upon time. The law of mortgages was part of the common law, but in exceptional cases the chancellor would intervene to do equity. Thus Chancery would permit the mortgagor in default subsequently to repossess the land if he repaid the debt at a certain time after the initially agreed-upon time had expired ("the equity of redemption"), and would also grant other forms of relief to the mortgagor in default where there were exceptional circumstances.

What was needed, however, in the seventeenth century, if the law of mortgages was to serve the emerging markets in land, was not equitable relief in cases of hardship but a new concept of the mortgagee's relationship to the land. The older concept was that under the common law he was a pledgee of the land, and that upon repayment of the debt, he was to restore the land to the mortgagor. This concept had been watered down over the centuries by the practice of leaving the mortgagor in possession of the land and also by the development of equitable remedies in Chancery in exceptional cases. Nevertheless, persons who wanted to borrow money in order to purchase real property, or for other purposes, would hesitate before subjecting themselves to the terms of such a pledge.

The solution was found, once again, in the new law of equity that developed in the late seventeenth century. The mortgagor retained equitable title to the property, yielding to the mortgagee the legal title. As legal owner, the mortgagee had only subordinate rights in the possession and use of the land, namely, to prevent substantial deterioration of its value, and controlled the disposition of it only to the extent necessary to ensure that the payment of the debt would not be put at risk. In other words, the mortgage became, for the first time, simply a security for repayment of a debt. As such, it played a critical role in the new dynamic of transfers of real property.

Contract

As there was a highly developed body of sophisticated property law in England, and in Europe generally, from the twelfth century on, so there was also a highly developed body of sophisticated contract law. This was, in the first instance, the canon law of contracts, which drew on, but radically transformed, the Roman law of contracts found in the *Digest* of Justinian and taught in the universities.[17] There also existed a body of customary contract law applied throughout Europe, including England, in markets and fairs and in cross-border trade—the *lex mercatoria,* or "law merchant," as it was called.[18] The urban courts of the thousands of European cities and towns also resolved contract disputes, often turning to canon law and Roman law (and, in England, to English royal law) and to their own charters and statutes, as well as to the law merchant and their own customary law, as sources of their decisions.[19]

The early English common law, however—that is, the law applied in the royal courts—had only limited remedies for contractual disputes, resolving them chiefly through the common law actions of debt, detinue, account, deceit, covenant, and trespass on the case. None of these were contract actions in the proper sense, that is, actions to enforce agreements as such. Trespass on the case came closest to a contract action when it became applicable in "assumpsit," that is, when the defendant had undertaken ("assumed") to do something and did it negligently, causing harm to the plaintiff. In the fourteenth and fifteenth centuries, when the common law courts, King's Bench and Common Pleas, were unwilling to develop new types of remedies for breach of contract, the chancellor acquired a wide jurisdiction over contracts in cases which fell outside the common law (such as many types of oral promises and claims of third-party beneficiaries) or which the common law courts were unable to decide fairly (for example, because of inadequacy of common law remedies). In enforcing contracts in these limited kinds of cases, the chancellor's "court of conscience" drew upon canon law, Roman law, mercantile law, and its own ingenuity and sense of fairness.[20]

In the sixteenth and early seventeenth centuries, the English law applicable to contracts underwent significant development. The Tudor prerogative courts, including the Court of Requests and also the reformed High Court of Chancery and High Court of Admiralty, exercised a greatly expanded jurisdiction, applying to commercial cases the traditional law merchant as well as many rules and concepts derived from canon law and from Romanist legal science. Partly in order to meet the new competition, and partly in the spirit of the times, the common law courts also began to reform the action of assumpsit, making it available not only, as before, in cases of harm caused by faulty performance of the undertaking ("misfeasance") but also in certain types of cases of simple nonperformance ("nonfeasance"), and also simplifying their procedures in order to make the action a less unwieldy instrument for settling commercial disputes. In *Slade's Case* (1602), assumpsit was made available in cases of half-performed contracts and half-performed sales of goods, which previously had been subject to the archaic remedies of debt and detinue. By that time, the common law courts had also elaborated a doctrine of consideration, similar in effect to doctrines of equity and of the canon law, by which the validity and enforceability of an undertaking—whether in the case of the half-completed exchange or in the case of a simple promise—was tested in terms of the circumstances which caused or motivated it.[21]

Despite such significant changes, the underlying presuppositions of contractual liability in all the legal systems that prevailed in England, including the common law, remained basically the same, in the sixteenth and early seventeenth centuries, as they had been in the earlier period. Breach of a promise was actionable, in the first instance, because—if—it was a wrong, and in the second instance, because—if—the promisee had a right to require its enforcement in view of its reasonable and equitable purpose. With some qualifications, the common lawyers accepted these premises no less than the canon lawyers. Prior to the latter part of the seventeenth century, assumpsit was essentially an action for breach of a (unilateral) promise, not breach of a (bilateral) contract in the modern sense, and the required consideration was conceived in terms of the moral justification and purpose of the promise. The common law action of covenant, by contrast, was not a contractual remedy in the proper sense but rather an action for breach of a sealed document; duress in procuring the document was a defense, but fraud in the inducement was not, although relief in some cases might be obtained from the chancellor. The fact that the common law courts used distinctive procedures in enforcing certain kinds of promises, applied distinctive technical rules (often required by the different procedures), and gave only limited contract remedies reflected the division between the ecclesiastical and secular spheres and the subdivision of the secular sphere into plural jurisdictions. These divisions and subdivisions were themselves associated with the specific worldview that had first emerged in the eleventh and twelfth centuries.

With the victory of the common law over its rivals, the vast increase in the number and variety of commercial cases that came before the common law courts required an expansion and revision of their remedies and doctrines. Especially after 1660, when some of the most important reforms of the Puritan period were confirmed under a restored, chastened, and limited monarchy, the common law courts gradually adopted a great many of the remedies and rules that had been elaborated in the previous hundred years by the prerogative courts and by Chancery. Other changes, however, in the common law of contracts as it developed in the latter seventeenth and eighteenth centuries cannot be attributed to the adoption or adaptation of doctrines previously elaborated in rival jurisdictions. There was, in fact, a decisive shift in some of the basic presuppositions of contract law that had developed over the previous five centuries. This shift may be summarized in three interrelated propositions:

First, the underlying theory of liability shifted from breach of promise to breach of a bargain. The emphasis was no longer placed primarily on the sin, or wrong, of the defaulting promisor but rather on the binding character of an agreement as such and the disappointment of the expectations of the promisee. This change raised more acutely than before the question whether the promises of the two sides were to be treated as independent or interdependent. Previously, they had generally been treated as independent, so that the failure of one party to perform his promise was not a defense to his action for the other party's breach but had to be the subject of a subsequent suit. The tendency of the courts in the century from 1660 to 1760 was to treat the two promises as mutually interdependent.[22]

Second, the emphasis on bargain was manifested in a new conception of the doctrine of consideration. Stated broadly, that doctrine refers to the mutuality of a contractual relationship: A's promise to B is binding if it is given "in consideration" of some benefit to A. The older conception that the "consideration" underlying the contract is its purpose or motive or justification (analogous to the canonists' conception of *causa*) gave way in the latter seventeenth century to a conception of consideration as the price paid by the promisee for the promise of the promisor. This change raised more acutely than before the question of the adequacy or relative value of the consideration. The tendency of the courts in the century after the Puritan Revolution was increasingly to enforce bargained agreements regardless of the inadequacy of the consideration.[23] The payment of a pound by the promisee could be sufficient consideration to support the contractual obligation of the promisor to perform services worth a hundred pounds: it showed that the parties intended their agreement to be legally binding.

Third, the basis of liability shifted from fault to absolute obligation. The promisee was entitled to compensation for nonperformance in accordance with the terms of the bargain itself, regardless of the intervention of unexpected circumstances that made performance excessively burdensome or impossible; excuses for nonperformance were to be confined, generally speaking, to those provided for within those terms.

The shift from a promise theory to a bargain theory of contract is well illustrated in the famous case of *Paradine v. Jane*, decided in 1647, discussed in an earlier chapter. At the height of the Civil War, the lessee of a landed estate, ousted from occupation of it by an invading army, was sued by the lessor for nonpayment of rent. The lessee raised the defense that performance of the contract was frustrated by unforeseen circumstances beyond his control, citing canon law, Roman law, military law, moral law, the law of reason, the law of nature, and the law of nations. Indeed, an English court today might in a similar case decide that "natural justice" would excuse the defendant from liability, although the matter is complicated by the fact that under English law to this day contracts of lease are enforced more strictly than other types of contracts. In Paradine v. Jane, the court enunciated a broad principle of strict contractual liability. It said that where a duty is created by law, the party will be excused if he is not at fault, "but when the party by his own contract creates a duty or charge upon himself he is bound to make it good, if he may, notwithstanding accident or inevitable necessity, because he might have provided against it by his contract."[24]

One may find earlier cases that suggest a doctrine of strict contractual liability. Indeed, one may show that all the doctrinal ingredients of the modern action for breach of contract were present in embryo in the action of assumpsit as it developed in the late 1500s and early 1600s.[25] In tracing the history of legal doctrine, it is usually not difficult to find in some earlier decision or text a source for every new development. Yet it is fair to say that before *Paradine v. Jane* no English court had ever laid down a theory of absolute obligation for breach of a bargained exchange, namely, that obligation in contract is distinguished from obligation in tort by the fact that the parties to a contract set their own limits to their liability; and moreover, that after *Paradine v. Jane* that theory was never effectively challenged. It remains a general rule in the English (and American) common law today that unless it is otherwise provided in the terms of the contract, liability for breach will not depend on proof of fault.

Historians of English law, however, have said that it "was not until the eighteenth century that a serious search for a general theory of contract was undertaken,"[26] and that it was not until the nineteenth century that there emerged a bargain theory of contract, based on agreement of the wills of autonomous parties.[27] These statements depend for their validity on a special meaning of the phrase "general theory of contract." It can hardly be maintained that prior to the eighteenth century contractual liability under English law was not considered to be based on a coherent set of principles, including the principle of the binding force of a bargained agreement expressing the intent of the parties.

The emergence of the doctrine of strict liability for breach of contract is strikingly illustrated in the development of the law of negotiable instruments. As James Steven Rogers has shown, the middle of the seventeenth century is a dividing line in the history of bills of exchange in English law, when for the first time there was declared to be an absolute obligation to honor a negotiable promissory note or draft on a third person, without regard to the validity of the underlying sales or services or other transaction which gave rise to its initial issuance.[28] Prior to the mid-seventeenth century, an action for nonpayment brought against the indorsee or drawee or drawer of a bill of exchange required proof of the nature of the "underlying obligation" for which the bill was issued; it was the entire commercial transaction, rather than the commercial paper itself, that gave rise to rights and liabilities regarding payment. Rogers properly relates the later change in the law to the transition in the seventeenth century from a town economy to a national economy, when English merchants began to trade on a large scale through permanent representatives in London and other locations in England "and thereby acquired credits in distant lands on which they [could] draw bills of exchange."[29] It was also related, however, to the newly developing concept that a bargained promise is binding regardless of the justness of the underlying transaction. Strict liability to honor a negotiable bill of exchange is not, to be sure, based on its nature as a bargained promise. It may or may not have been issued or indorsed for a "consideration." The legitimating role of the bargain is fulfilled, however, by certain formal requirements, including the strict requirement that certain words, including "to the order of" the payee or indorsee, be inserted, in order to show the intent to make the instrument an independent source of rights in the hands of whoever properly holds it.

Corporations

As the Calvinist ethic influenced the development of English contract law in the late seventeenth and eighteenth centuries, it also influenced the development of the law of corporations. This was not, however, the Calvinist ethic portrayed by Max Weber in his famous work *The Protestant Ethic and the Spirit of Capitalism.* Weber focused attention on what he called the "ascetic" aspect of sixteenth- and seventeenth-century Calvinism, that is, its commitment to a life of self-discipline, austerity, and hard work, which, he said, created "a feeling of unprecedented inner loneliness of the single individual."[30] According to Weber, it was the doctrine of predestination, and the obsessive desire continually to prove to oneself and to the community that one is a member of the elect, that led the English Calvinists not only to advance their entrepreneurial economic interests with an enthusiasm previously not seen on the world stage but also to create the belief system that supports the social structure of modern capitalism.

Weber developed his theory without any reference to the legal institutions that prevailed in the societies that came under Calvinist influence—especially England and Holland. In fact, his thesis is not only not supported but refuted by seventeenth-century developments in English law, which reflected not an individualist but a communitarian ethic and spirit.

A striking example is the emergence of the joint-stock company as a device for bringing together a group of prominent persons to constitute a business or charitable enterprise, on the one hand, and a large number of shareholders to raise the capital needed to finance it, on the other. In his analysis of the spirit of capitalism, Weber did not take account of the communitarian character of such important seventeenth-century joint-stock companies as overseas trading enterprises, which were designed not only to make a profit but also to serve public causes. An example is the 1692 act of Parliament granting a corporate charter to a Company of Merchants of London to carry on trade with Greenland, which recited the great importance of such trade, how it had fallen into the hands of other nations, and the need to regain it by the joint efforts of many persons.[31] Similar recitals of a public purpose marked the corporate charters of other joint-stock companies. These were, to be sure, entrepreneurial activities intended to be profitable to the shareholders, and the new corporate form permitted venturers to limit their risks to the proportion of their subscriptions to the jointly held stock. At the same time, the enterprise depended on the close cooperation of many like-minded people, who were motivated partly by a desire to participate with others in a joint venture serving a public cause.

Nothing is more symbolic of the communitarian spirit of English economic life in England in the late seventeenth century than the creation of the joint-stock company called the Bank of England, which was founded by act of Parliament in 1694 principally in order to finance the government's war against France. Under the act, commissioners were appointed by the Crown to receive subscriptions, and the Crown was empowered to incorporate "subscribers and contributors, their heirs, successors, or assigns, to be one body politick and corporate."[32] Shareholders were required to identify their collective interests with the welfare of the English economy. Some 1,300 persons subscribed £1.2 million to support the war—and to receive profits from increases in the value of their shares, which were backed in part by government subsidies derived from customs duties. Subscribers included leading merchants and landed gentry, among them many members of Parliament. Of the first twenty-six members of the Court of Directors, six subsequently became Lord Mayors of London. The bylaws of the bank required the Court of Directors to meet every week and the General Court of the shareholders to meet twice a year "for considering the general state and condition of this Corporation and for the making of dividends . . . according to their several shares."[33]

The late seventeenth century also witnessed the creation of another important legal institution which served communitarian as well as private purposes, namely, the modern law of trusts.[34] Like the joint-stock company, the trust device facilitated the formation of business and charitable associations embracing numerous members in common endeavors.

The roots of English communitarianism of the seventeenth and eighteenth centuries, as reflected in these new legal institutions, are not in what Max Weber called the ascetic aspect of the Protestant ethic, derived from the more individualistic doctrines of predestination and calling, but in its collectivist aspect, derived from the more communitarian doctrines of covenant and covenanted communities.

Economic Law Reforms

Closely related to changes in the civil law of contracts, property, and corporations were fundamental reforms of economic law, including (1) the elimination of all grants of monopolies over production and distribution of particular products; (2) reform of private and public finance, including the introduction of new forms of credit transactions, the rise of the modern stock market, and the introduction of new forms of state taxation; (3) the introduction of patents on inventions and copyright of literary works; and (4) the introduction of new methods of insurance against loss of or damage to property. Except for elimination of grants of monopolies, in which the legacy of Sir Edward Coke played an important role, these reforms are usually neglected in the historiography of English law; in recent years, however, they have been analyzed by economic historians, who have increasingly recognized the importance of legal institutions in facilitating economic growth.

The Attack on Monopolies

An important feature of royal power in the Tudor and early Stuart period had been the granting of economic monopolies by the Crown to its favorites.

Through so-called letters patent the Crown would grant to individuals an exclusive right to manufacture and market particular products. Some of these private monopolies were challenged in court in the late 1500s and early 1600s. and in 1624 Charles II's rambunctious House of Commons (of which Sir Edward Coke was a leading member) enacted the Statute on Monopolies, requiring that such ordinances and bylaws be approved by Parliament before they could take effect. Parliament did not then dare, however, entirely to forbid the establishment of monopolies by royal letters patent. Such royal power had indeed been challenged in the courts in a case in 1603, but the holding of that case was a narrow one.[35] The later report of it by Sir Edward Coke, however, attributed to the common law a deep hostility to such restraints on trade, and after the Glorious Revolution, Coke's view came to prevail as an interpretation of the common law.[36]

The outlawing of royal grants of monopolies served to protect the traditional system of production and distribution of goods and services by the various craft guilds. For centuries, members of each of the various crafts—wool weavers, silversmiths, goldsmiths, coppersmiths, glassmakers, shoemakers, tanners, butchers, bakers, and many others—had banded together in close-knit associations that set standards of quality and price and regulated relations between masters and journeymen. The craft guild policed its members' professional practices, and guild courts heard complaints of poor workmanship, unfair competition, and the like. Guilds had first been formed throughout the West in the twelfth century and constituted a principal mode of production until the eighteenth century. In seventeenth-century England the Puritan community ethic complemented the ethos of the guild with the language of covenant and calling, and guilds seem to have supported the Puritan cause in the 1640s and 1650s as well as the parliamentary cause in the 1680s.[37]

New Methods of Private and Public Finance

The great increase in monarchical power in the sixteenth and early seventeenth centuries, associated in part with royal supremacy over the church in Protestant countries as well as the increase in royal power over the church in countries that remained Roman Catholic, had led to chronic religious warfare among the monarchical states, fought largely by mercenary armies, and this in turn tended to exhaust the financial resources derived by monarchs from their royal properties and from occasional special levies. In England, as recounted in a previous chapter, the early Stuart monarchs had to resort to extraordinary measures to exact payments from their subjects in order to fight their wars, which was one of the immediate causes of the Revolution of Parliament.[38]

With the Glorious Revolution and the accession of William and Mary, Parliament began to devise a new system of finance, drawing partly on earlier Dutch experience with which the new king was entirely familiar. One source of public finance was through the establishment of the Bank of England as a joint-stock company, out of whose resources loans could be made to the Crown to finance wars in England and on the European continent. The Bank of England was authorized to sell bonds backed by the Crown, thus acting as an agent of public finance, borrowing from the well-to-do in order to finance government operations. Also, in accordance with new banking practices that were becoming prevalent in the Netherlands as well, the Bank of England added to the traditional banking functions of receiving deposits and clearing depositors' checks the relatively new function of discounting promissory notes, that is, purchasing them at a discount measured by the interest that would accrue between the time of such purchase and the time when they became due. Indeed, the issuance of promissory notes by the British treasury was introduced in 1696 as a means of financing the war against France. Further, the Promissory Notes Act of 1704 made it possible for both the Crown and private persons or enterprises to issue negotiable commercial paper, that is, bills and notes transferable by endorsement and in the hands of holders in good faith free of personal defenses such as fraud or incompetence of the initial maker.[39]

In the late 1680s and early 1690s the modern stock market, a relatively new institution that had emerged in the Netherlands, was also established in England, whereby joint-stock companies could acquire financing through the sale of transferable shares. Regular lists of stock prices were published in London commercial periodicals, and standard contracts of purchase and sale were printed.[40] Stock brokers, as they were now called, meeting with clients in coffeehouses, developed a whole new vocabulary of subscription, underwriting, puts, and refusals.[41] On the one hand, the new institution of the liquid stock market generated income to commercial enterprises and individual merchants upon which and upon whom the Crown, through the Bank of England, could draw for loans and upon whose resources Parliament could draw by way of taxation. On the other hand, the Crown itself could invest in joint-stock companies serving a public purpose, including joint-stock companies financed by the Crown for overseas exploration and colonization.

New in the 1690s was the emergence of a regular market for trading in shares, namely, liquidity and transferability.[42] Share transfers were controlled by a special committee appointed by Parliament, and foreigners were forbidden to hold shares. Moreover, ownership of shares in chartered companies such as the East India Company and Hudson's Bay Company was concentrated among a few persons. This was not democratic bourgeois capitalism. This was aristocratic mercantilism, controlled by representatives of the landed gentry and leading merchants elected to the House of Commons.

The transformation of the financial system was coupled with the institution of new methods of taxation, on the one hand, and the introduction of a national debt, on the other. The Crown no longer lived chiefly on the hereditary resources of the royal family. With the great expansion of commercial activity,

England, like other European states, multiplied taxes on virtually all consumer goods as well as materials used in their production, and also on building materials, houses, horses and carriages, and virtually everything that was bought or sold or made. The rich paid taxes on luxuries—wigs, tobacco, playing cards, and dice. The poor—the great majority—also paid taxes on virtually everything they purchased. Taxes on land ("feudal dues," as they continued to be called) and taxes on exports and imports continued to be levied. Together these various taxes supported colonization of North America and India and the other increased activities of what economic historians have called the "tax state."

Patents and Copyright

Letters patent, used in sixteenth-century England to grant monopolies of manufacture and distribution of goods, also came to be used occasionally at that time to give exclusive rights in an invention to the inventor. It is from that usage that our modern legal term "patent," denoting rights of exclusive use of an invention, is derived. Prior to the late seventeenth century, however, monopoly of the use of an invention, like monopolies of the manufacture and distribution of goods, was a prerogative of royal patronage occasionally granted by the Tudor and early Stuart monarchs. In England, as in other parts of Europe, such prerogatives were granted to persons whose skills served the economic or political interests of the ruling authorities—the monarchy, the court, the nobility, and the civil service.[43]

The 1624 Statute of Monopolies, which subjected royal grants of monopolies to parliamentary review, allowed an exception for grants of letters patent, valid for fourteen years, to "the true and first inventor" of new manufactures that provided economic benefit to the realm.[44] It was only in the latter half of the seventeenth century, however, that a patent gradually came to be viewed not primarily as a royal grant of a monopoly but primarily as a legal property right of the inventor. After the Glorious Revolution patents were granted regularly for new inventions. The 1690s saw a boom in English patents, connected in part with the rise of the stock market.[45]

Underlying the new patent law was the fundamental principle that the inventor of a new product or a new process should have ownership of it, with the right to possess, use, and dispose of it, but that that property right should be limited to a given period of years, so that eventually the new product or process would be made freely available to all. What had formerly been, in law, a royal prerogative to dispense patronage to favorites became a privilege of the inventor, and of those with whom he shared it, during the lifetime of the patent.

The same principle was extended to authors of literary and artistic works. Before the seventeenth century it had been chiefly royal authorities who had occasionally by letters patent granted exclusive rights to copyists and book dealers, and later to printers, to produce copies of written or artistic works. In England, Henry VIII granted many such exclusive printing rights, and in 1530 a copyright was given for the first time to an author, though limited to seven years. Although in 1649 Parliament enacted the first copyright statute, it was directed to protection not of authors as such but of licensed printers against piracy by other printers, providing for the forfeiture of presses that published materials licensed to another. In 1662 the requirement was added that copies of copyrighted materials be deposited at the king's library and at each of the two universities. This licensing act was on the books until 1694, when it was allowed to lapse because of abuses by the persons to whom the exclusive licenses were granted. Without a licensing law, however, piracy of published works flourished. Finally in 1710 Parliament enacted a statute giving the author of an existing work or his assigns the sole right of publication for twenty-one years and the author of a work not yet published the sole right of publication for fourteen years. The author's right, like that of the patentee, was a privilege granted for a limited time, subject to the covenanted community's eventual interest in sharing the benefits of the author's creative work.[46]

Insurance

Some forms of insurance, including especially marine insurance, had existed throughout Europe ever since the first commercial revolution of the twelfth and thirteenth centuries. New in the seventeenth century, however, was the application of mathematics to the development of a science of forecasting and of calculation of the relationship of the risk of loss to the cost of insurance premiums. The new science of risk management was a product of the new science of probability that had been pioneered in physics, chemistry, and other natural sciences by Newton, Boyle, and others, and had greatly influenced legal science. The modern marine insurance industry was born in the coffeehouses of London in the late 1680s and 1690s, where so-called underwriters, using new methods of statistical analysis to calculate odds on the safe transit of merchandise overseas, met with their merchant customers.[47]

The first marine insurance companies, called assurance corporations, were established in the early eighteenth century by royal charter, but private underwriters continued to operate alongside them. Then as now, persons seeking insurance would go to a broker, who would find a risk-taker who would cover losses in return for a premium, writing his name under the terms of the contract (hence the term "underwriter"). Apart from marine insurance, many other kinds of insurance became available in the course of the eighteenth century, including insurance of the risk of damage to property, robbery, death, fire, and other contingencies. Eventually, seventy-nine of the underwriters who did business at the London coffeehouse established in the 1670s by

Edward Lloyd subscribed £100 each and joined together in the Society of Lloyd's, "an unincorporated group of individual entrepreneurs operating under a self-regulated code of behavior." These and later other members of Lloyd's "committed all their financial capital to secure their promise to make good on their customers' losses."[48]

The development of the insurance industry was closely connected with the birth and refinement of theories of probability in the middle decades of the seventeenth century. John Graunt's book *Natural and Political Observations Made upon Bills of Mortality* (1662), which drew heavily on the mathematical science of probability developed in the 1650s and 1660s,[49] provided the foundation of the reasoning that has come to be known as actuarial science.

Many historians have emphasized the connection between the creation of new economic institutions in England in the late seventeenth and early eighteenth centuries and the previous development of similar institutions in Holland, without, however, noting that in the seventeenth century both Holland and England were under the strong influence of Calvinism, and that many of the English economic developments came after the Glorious Revolution of 1688, when the Dutch Calvinist William of Orange was on the English throne. It is customary to ignore the Calvinist influence or, occasionally, to follow Max Weber in focusing on only one aspect of it, namely, the alleged dedication of Calvinist businessmen to a calling of acquisition of wealth that would presage their being chosen by God to be among the elect. Much more important than the doctrine of predestination, or, indeed, of the famous Protestant work ethic, was the Calvinist theology of covenant. The critical innovations in the economic institutions of the late seventeenth and early eighteenth centuries, both in Holland and in England, were based on the creation of new types of credit transactions. Underlying the stock market, underlying the national debt, underlying the tax state, underlying the negotiability of promissory notes—underlying all of these was credit, which was itself based on trust, which in turn presupposed a community of fellow subjects bound together by a shared covenant, a shared belief in an overriding obligation to honor one's commitments, to keep one's word.

CHAPTER 12

The Transformation of English Social Law

As in sixteenth-century Protestant German principalities, so in sixteenth-century Protestant England in the First English Reformation, a state church was established to which all English subjects were required by law to belong. Under the supremacy of the Tudor and early Stuart monarchs, the Church of England, like the Lutheran churches of German principalities, was governed by royal statutes regulating matters that had previously been within the competence of the Church of Rome. That the state took over the regulation of such matters is usually characterized as a process of secularization of institutions previously considered to be of a spiritual nature. It may also be viewed, however, as a process of spiritualization of the state's jurisdiction, which previously had been limited chiefly to the secular sphere. The Tudor and early Stuart monarchs, together with the councils and parliaments under them, took it upon themselves not only to proclaim the laws of God,[1] but also to enact human laws governing what were previously called, and what still may be called, spiritual relationships. In particular, changes in sixteenth-century English laws relating to church liturgy, marriage, moral offenses, education, and poor relief, matters which previously had been under the almost exclusive jurisdiction of ecclesiastical authorities subordinate to Rome, were similar in important respects to the changes that law underwent in Protestant Germany under the impact of Lutheranism.

As in Germany, though not to the same extent, the liturgy of the Anglican Church, in contrast to the Roman Catholic liturgy previously applicable in English churches, gave more scope to congregational participation in the worship service. The Latin missal was replaced by the Book of Common Prayer adopted by King Edward VI and amended slightly by Elizabeth and her Stuart successors.[2] Written in majestic English, the Book of Common Prayer gave wide scope to congregational recital of prayers, and passages from the newly translated English Bible were also required to be read in various parts of the services.[3] Congregational singing was stimulated by the introduction of metrical psalmody, although it was not until the eighteenth century that hymnody in the German style was widely introduced.[4] In some Tudor and Stuart churches, as in Lutheran and Calvinist lands, inspired preaching came to play a central role in the worship service.[5]

The new English liturgy, like the Lutheran liturgy adopted by German princes, reduced the number of sacraments from seven to two—baptism and Holy Communion—and the nature of the latter was defined in a new way. As in Lutheranism, marriage, no longer a sacrament, became a social estate, although in contrast to Lutheranism, full divorce was not permitted and a marital ceremony was not required if the couple exchanged vows of marriage and lived together as man and wife.

Also in England, as in Lutheran principalities, moral offenses came to be identified chiefly by royal law rather than, as before, by Roman Catholic canon law; in contrast to Lutheran German monarchs, however, Tudor and Stuart monarchs left jurisdiction over many such offenses to ecclesiastical courts, which remained much more active in England than in Germany. And with respect to education, there was in England, as in Germany, a movement to make schools more widely available to the laity, and the teachers, in contrast to teachers in the earlier time, were mostly lay persons rather than clerics; but in contrast to the Lutheran German law, England required all teachers in the sixteenth and early seventeenth centuries to obtain a license to teach from their diocesan bishop.

Finally, sixteenth- and early-seventeenth-century English poor laws, like the German, denounced mendicancy and established workhouses for "the deserving poor." Unlike the German poor laws, however, Tudor and early Stuart legislation left it to local parish officers and vestry to collect alms and taxes for poor relief, although in so doing they acted under the supervision of lay justices of the peace.

Thus the highest English secular authority—the king in his council in his parliament—drew more heavily on bishops and church parishes for the administration of spiritual law than did the Lutheran German princes. Also both the royal theology and the royal law of Tudor-Stuart England remained closer to the earlier Roman Catholic theology and law than did the theology and law of Lutheran German principalities. The First English Reformation was thus a less radical version of Protestantism than the Lutheran Reformation of Germany.

In the mid-seventeenth century, however, the Second English Reformation—what the great poet-philosopher John Milton, writing in the midst of it, called "the Reformation of the Reformation"—turned against the concept of a monarchical state church to which all English subjects were required to belong. Building on the Calvinist theology of the left wing of the German Revolution, English Puritanism first penetrated parts of the Anglican Church, then in the 1640s and 1650s overthrew it, and ultimately, after Anglicanism was restored in the 1660s, helped to subordinate it to Parliament and at the same time to introduce a policy of toleration for so-called dissenting churches. After 1689, the Anglican Church was no longer the state church, to which all subjects were required to belong; it remained the established church, which meant that it was a privileged church, supported by the state, but English subjects became free to worship at other "tolerated" Protestant churches—especially the Presbyterian, the Congregational, the Baptist, and later the Quaker and the Methodist.[6]

With the coexistence of plural religious denominations, what was to become of spiritual law? Liturgy, to be sure, could be determined independently by each of the various tolerated denominations, but what about marriage? sanctions for moral offenses? school laws? poor laws? If England was to remain a Christian nation, how was Parliament, in regulating these spiritual causes, to reconcile the different theories and policies of the various Christian churches concerning them?

Liturgy

Technically, the Crown remained the governor of the Church of England; formally, Elizabeth I's Act of Supremacy continues in force until this day, insofar as archbishops and bishops of the Church of England are still appointed by the Crown and subject to royal regulation. In fact, however, after 1688 parliamentary statutes provided that the prime minister, taking into consideration recommendations of appropriate ecclesiastical bodies, shall submit to the Crown nominations of bishops and archbishops of the Church of England, and by constitutional custom the Crown must accept the prime minister's nominees.[7] Similarly, the Crown may alter the Book of Common Prayer only with the consent of Parliament, and since 1689 neither Crown nor Parliament has introduced any such alteration.

Parliament's policy of noninterference in the liturgy of the churches permitted the established Church of England to adopt a policy of inclusion within Anglicanism of a variety of liturgies, which came to be characterized as either "Low Church" or "High Church." At the same time, tolerated dissenting churches were largely exempt from the network of laws that regulated worship and belief.

An important part of the Puritan cause in the sixteenth and early seventeenth centuries had been the reform of the Anglican worship service, including the elimination of kneeling when taking communion, of special clothing—"vestments"—worn by clergy at church services, of the use of incense and the chanting of the service, as well as of other ceremonies that reflected, in the Puritan view, false theological doctrines. Indeed, after the Restoration, when Charles II convened a large number of persons of various ecclesiastical backgrounds in order to discuss possible changes in the Book of Common

Prayer, Richard Baxter, a leading Puritan, stated that if the Puritan demand to eliminate the requirement of kneeling and vestments had been granted, the Civil War could have been avoided![8] Nevertheless, Charles did not yield to the reiteration of this demand by Baxter and others. Thus it may be said that it took not only a Civil War but also a change of royal dynasty, plus a parliamentary statute instituting toleration of dissenting Protestant churches, to make the Church of England sufficiently "comprehensive" to accommodate within its own ranks both Anglo-Calvinist and Anglo-Catholic liturgies.

Marriage

The English law of marriage did not yield so easily to the Protestant belief system underlying England's two Reformations. The Tudor and Stuart regimes accepted the Protestant view that marriage is not a sacrament; nevertheless, they called it "a sacramental," and they preserved the Roman Catholic prohibition on full divorce with the right to remarry (Henry VIII's divorces were all accomplished under the guise of annulments), and they also preserved the earlier Roman Catholic rule—repealed in 1580 by the Council of Trent—that it was words of consent to be united as man and wife that constituted marriage and that an ecclesiastical ceremony was not necessary. Thus clandestine marriages, sometimes spurious or fraudulent, continued to be lawful in England in the sixteenth and early seventeenth centuries. As Christopher Lasch has put it, "Because it upheld marriage as an antidote to lust, the Catholic Church made it easy to marry and almost impossible to obtain a divorce."[9] Although Anglican theologians and English popular sentiment turned against this view of marriage, stressing both the character of marriage as a social estate and the central importance of the loving companionship of the spouses,[10] nevertheless the law of marriage during England's First Reformation remained basically the same as it had been under the canon law of the Roman Catholic Church.[11]

Moreover, although there were substantial changes in the English law of marriage during the Commonwealth period, including the requirement of public registration of marriages either in parish churches or in the marketplace, and including the right of divorce for cause to be granted by a civil court, these reforms were repealed after the Restoration. Indeed, even after parliamentary supremacy was finally established in 1689, it took much agitation over a period of more than sixty years to enact a law—Lord Hardwicke's Marriage Act of 1753—that required marriages to be advertised in advance by publication of notices ("banns") in the parish church of the vicinity where the parties resided, or if they resided in different parishes, then in the churches of both parishes.[12] Thus clandestine marriages, which the Roman Catholic Church itself had outlawed at the Council of Trent almost two centuries earlier, were finally outlawed also in England. Moreover, under Lord Hardwicke's Act, openly living together as man and wife no longer in itself constituted marriage; indeed, it was required by the act that all marriages except those of Quakers and Jews be performed in the Church of England according to the Anglican rite in the presence of a clergyman and two witnesses. Thus, as far as the formation of marriage was concerned, toleration extended only to Quakers and Jews! Moreover, a full divorce, as contrasted with separation from bed and board, continued to be forbidden, except that in rare cases full divorces were granted to favored persons by Parliament itself.[13] Finally, various types of legal questions involving marital relations remained under the jurisdiction of Anglican ecclesiastical courts.

Thus the transfer of jurisdiction over marital relations from the Roman Catholic Church to Protestant secular authorities—first the Crown and later Parliament—did not result in fundamental changes in marriage law. It was not until the Marriage Act of 1836, under the influence less of Lutheran or Calvinist Protestantism than of democratic individualism, that English law permitted marriages to be solemnized "according to such form of ceremony as the parties may wish to adopt," required marriages to be registered in government offices, made full divorce available on the ground of adultery, and transferred jurisdiction over questions of marriage and divorce to the civil courts.[14]

Moral Offenses

As in the case of marital relations, so in the case of moral offenses, parliamentary legislation during the First English Reformation largely reiterated provisions of the canon law of the Roman Catholic Church previously applicable in England and left prosecution and punishment largely to the ecclesiastical courts. Such offenses included unnatural sexual acts, adultery, incest, sorcery, witchcraft, misbehavior in church, failure to attend church services, profaning the Sabbath, blasphemy, swearing, drunkenness, defamation, usury, and others. During this period, however, Parliament occasionally enacted statutes making one or more of such offenses a crime, thereby removing ecclesiastical jurisdiction over it. Thus in 1553 unnatural sexual acts, in 1541 witchcraft, and in 1603 bigamy were made felonies, punishable only in the royal courts. Statutes of 1624 made drunkenness and profane cursing and swearing punishable in the local justice of the peace courts by fines or placing in stocks, and a statute of 1625 added fines or stocks for violating Sunday laws and tippling in alehouses or other public places.[15] Also sexual and other moral offenses were sometimes prosecuted in the courts of the justices of the peace as disturbances of public order. Nevertheless the scope of ecclesiastical jurisdiction remained wide.[16]

In 1641 the Puritan parliament abolished the criminal jurisdiction of the ecclesiastical courts. Although that jurisdiction was restored after the Restoration, the Court of High Commission, which had been the supreme ecclesiastical court, was not revived, nor was the Court of Star Chamber, which had also had a wide jurisdiction over moral offenses. Now the Court of King's Bench began to take jurisdiction as *custos morum,* guardian of morals, over moral offenses that previously had been within the competence of the ecclesiastical and the prerogative courts. Moreover, Restoration parliaments also enacted laws giving justices of the peace and the common law courts jurisdiction to impose criminal penalties for various moral offenses, including doing business on Sundays and engaging in gambling.[17]

It was in the 1690s and early 1700s, however, after the consummation of the Revolution, that Parliament began gradually but systematically to substitute the criminal jurisdiction of the justices of the peace and the courts of common law for the ecclesiastical jurisdiction in matters of moral offenses. Statutes imposing fines and confinement in stocks for profane cursing and swearing were enacted in 1694 and 1746.[18] A statute of 1697/98 imposed similar penalties on persons who, having been educated in the Christian religion or having made profession thereof, denied the divinity of any one of the persons of the Holy Trinity or denied the truth of the Christian religion or that the Holy Scriptures were of divine authority.[19] Statutes prohibiting gambling, including lotteries of various descriptions, were enacted in 1698, 1710, 1711, 1722, and 1733. In 1739 it was enacted that games of chance called ace of hearts, pharaoh, basset, and hazard were covered by these statutes.[20] An act of 1740 laid down the conditions under which horse races were to be run and provided that only two racetracks might be authorized to conduct horse racing that involved wagering.[21]

The regulation of theatrical and other forms of public entertainment, much of which had been licentious, had been a matter of royal prerogative until the Commonwealth period, when a regime of Puritan morality was introduced. The Restoration unleashed an even more licentious period against which the legislation of the restored royal prerogative proved quite ineffectual. It was not until 1737, when Parliament imposed comprehensive regulations governing the theater, including licensing of plays and of players and defining certain categories of unlicensed actors to be "rogues and vagabonds," that theatrical performances began to meet the higher moral standards that Crown, Parliament, and a host of writers had been proclaiming.[22]

More important, however, than parliamentary legislation in transforming Tudor-Stuart English gaiety into Puritan and post-Puritan English sobriety was the emergence in the 1690s of voluntary associations in the form of Societies for the Reformation of Manners. In the words of Dudley Bahlman, these societies constituted "the army of reform," which played a key role in what Bahlman rightly calls "the moral revolution of 1688." He writes: "Neither the

Church nor the State furnished the army of reformers. Its ranks did indeed include justices of the peace, constables, and clergymen, but the army was a private army, making its own rules, appointing its own leaders."[23] The societies started as small groups of persons who came together to find ways of improving what they called the "manners" of their local communities. They quickly grew in number and in size, and formed committees to adopt bylaws and to commission "stewards" to carry out their programs. Their bylaws declared it to be their purpose to close "houses of lewdness and debauchery," to combat "drunkenness, swearing and cursing, and profanation of the Lord's day," and to "inquire into the behavior of constables and other officers" charged with enforcement of the laws prohibiting such moral offenses. Treasurers, recording secretaries, and others were appointed, and networks of paid informants were formed.

Although neither church nor state initiated or controlled the movement, both supported its cause. In 1691 Queen Mary, at the suggestion of the prominent latitudinarian Bishop Stillingfleet, wrote a famous letter to the justices of the peace of Middlesex urging them to be especially diligent in prosecuting offenders against the moral laws. King William issued an entire series of royal proclamations urging officers of the law to be diligent in prosecuting moral offenses. These royal pronouncements had the effect of encouraging constables, magistrates, and other officers of the law to join the societies, of which by 1701 almost twenty had been formed in London alone. Throughout the country the number grew rapidly in the first two decades of the eighteenth century. In the Isle of Wight there was a society made up almost entirely of Anglican clergymen, and in Wiltshire a parson formed a society consisting of elderly people. There were two societies in Portsmouth, one consisting of the mayor, justices of the peace, and aldermen, the other consisting of twenty-three tradesmen. Bahlman writes: "To many Englishmen this reformation was the most important aspect of the revolution, since only through a reformation of manners could the revolution endure. King William's work would go for nothing, as he himself recognized in his proclamations, unless England had God's blessing, and in order to have God's blessing a reformation of manners was indispensable."

Although popular participation in the enforcement of criminal sanctions against moral offenses was hardly new in the Western legal tradition, and hardly unique to England, there was, indeed, something radically new in the self-mobilization of lay persons in local communities throughout the country to form small associations, with formal structures, to help overcome the deterioration of moral behavior that had characterized the post-Cromwellian Restoration of 1660 to 1688. Previously, the Anglican clergy had been primarily responsible for prosecuting moral offenses such as those now being investigated and reported by the Societies for the Reformation of Manners; and in fact many "High Church" bishops of the Anglican clergy, together with Tories in Parliament, spoke against the lay societies, which were largely supported—successfully—by latitudinarian and dissenting clergy and Whigs.

The legal, though unofficial, character of the societies was dramatically reflected in the publication of 1700 of a pamphlet, titled *A Help to a National Reformation,* setting forth rules for the proper conduct of informants hired by them. Informers were instructed to be certain that they had actually witnessed a breach of the law. Various rules were laid down for apprehension and prosecution of drunkenness, of profanity, of selling goods on Sunday, and of other specific crimes. One section was titled "Prudential Rules for the Giving of Information to Magistrates." Despite the intense unpopularity of the paid informants, many of whom were beaten or threatened with violence, the pamphlet urged that earnest men undertake the task, a charge supported by justices of the peace, who stressed "the common duty of all good subjects to endeavor by timely information" to put the laws against vice into execution, and by clergy, who in sermons compared the reformers to ancient martyrs and saints.

The societies also played an important role in influencing magistrates and legislators to support the cause of moral reform. They published broadsides listing penalties to which officials were subject for failing to perform their duties in this respect, and petitioned the House of Commons to improve the law under which the societies brought prosecutions.

The effectiveness of the societies in combating moral offenses was hotly debated at the time and is impossible to measure. "Manners" certainly continued to need "reformation." Indeed, one index that can be measured, the consumption of alcohol, seems to have increased greatly. Certainly a very large number of prosecutions were brought by the societies—by their surviving account books, over 100,000 in the forty-four years from 1694 to 1738—but this proves only that the societies were active, not that they were effective. To judge their effectiveness, one would need to know how many moral offenses subject to their prosecution would have been committed if the societies had not existed—a question for which there is no answer.

Similarly, no adequate answer has been given to the question why they declined in the 1730s and virtually ceased to exist after 1738[24]—but then were later revived on a smaller scale in the late 1750s by Methodist leaders, including John Wesley, and later by William Wilberforce and other leading reformers.[25] The vicissitudes of the societies were accompanied by efforts to strengthen official law enforcement by constables and other peace officers and by the eventual establishment of full-time professional police forces in various localities.[26]

Thus the Puritan principle of voluntary collective local responsibility to apprehend and correct moral offenders survived in England for over a century after the end of the Puritan phase of the English Revolution—interrupted by the Restoration but resumed after the accession of William III and the establishment of parliamentary supremacy. The formation of voluntary associations to prosecute moral offenses was connected with the assumption by Parliament of the responsibility to define such offenses and to authorize punishments to be applied by justices of the peace—a responsibility that had previously belonged chiefly to the clergy and to ecclesiastical courts. One may view these developments the way they have conventionally been viewed, as a process of secularization of ecclesiastical responsibilities; but one may also view them as a process of spiritualization of secular responsibilities. In terms of the Western legal tradition, it was part of the impact of Protestantism (in this case not Lutheran but Calvinist) on the reception of the canon law of the church (in this case not the Roman Catholic Church but the Church of England) by the state (in this case not the German prince and his high magistracy but the English Parliament and the local communities led by public-spirited Christians of various denominations).

Elementary Education: The Charity Schools

The English Revolution brought in its aftermath radical changes in the English system of elementary education, changes derived to a large extent from the Calvinist moral theology that prevailed not only in the dissenting churches but also among latitudinarian Anglicans, who constituted a substantial portion of both the leadership and the membership of the Church of England. These changes were directed toward education of the children of the laboring classes and to vocational training, and were effectuated largely by voluntary associations of persons drawn in the first instance from gentry and leading merchants and eventually supported by tradesmen and shopkeepers as well. They helped, therefore, to strengthen the system of class relations established by the English Revolution.

In the century before the outbreak of the English Revolution, the Protestant Church of England, like the Protestant churches of the Lutheran German principalities, had emphasized the desirability of bringing a reading knowledge of the Bible to the widest number of people. The English translation of the Bible was to be read, together with the English-language Book of Common Prayer, in Anglican church services that all Christian subjects were required to attend regularly. All were to hear these English texts and, if they could, to read them; and this was not only for the salvation of their souls but also for the fostering of their loyalty to their country and to the Crown, for church and state were now united under the supremacy of the Protestant monarch, whose greatest enemy, both at home and abroad, was a "foreign" Roman Catholicism.

Also in Tudor-Stuart England, as in other Protestant lands, the political authorities drew much more heavily on the laity for their councilors and civil servants than had their Roman Catholic predecessors. In England this stimulated the founding of many so-called grammar schools that educated future community leaders not only in the Protestant faith but also in the classics and humanities.[27] A great emphasis was placed on preparing the children of the ruling elite for higher education in the universities and in the Inns of Court.

In the sixteenth and early seventeenth centuries, secular authorities in England played for the first time a leading role in the organization of schooling. The Roman Catholic monastic and chantry schools were replaced by schools established by municipal and other local authorities and by private endowments. Yet the Church of England also played a great role in secular education—greater than the role of the clergy in Lutheran German principalities. To be permitted to be a teacher in England, whether in a school or as a private tutor, required the authorization of the diocesan bishop, which was given only after a searching examination of each candidate. The Tudor-Stuart church was able, through its licensing power, to exercise practical control of education throughout the country.[28]

Nevertheless, the increased scope of the education of the upper classes of the gentry and merchants in the sixteenth and early seventeenth centuries, despite its sponsorship and control by the Tudor-Stuart monarchy, helped to produce a class of persons who brought about its overthrow. As Lawrence Stone has noted, many schoolmasters and dons in this period were religious dissidents, and their stress on freedom of conscience found a receptive audience even among English elites. Moreover, Stone notes, the lawyers, who eventually played an important part in bringing about the Revolution, were taught in the course of their studies at the Inns of Court that the common law was supreme over both Crown and church. And it was university-trained gentry, sensitive to their privileges, who dominated the local governmental bodies that selected representatives to the early Stuart parliaments.[29]

Radical changes in English schooling that took place after the accession of William and Mary in 1688 were presaged in the 1640s and 1650s in the works of prominent Puritan writers.[30] These writers stressed, in the words of John Dury, that "the main scope of the whole work of education, both in boys and girls, should be none other but this: to train them up to know God in Christ, that they may walk worthy of him in the Gospel and become profitable instruments of the Commonwealth in their generations." The first aim, to train for "Godliness" (as Dury called it), was traditional, except that it was to be Godliness as understood by reformed schoolmasters rather than by High Church Anglican clergy. The second aim, to train for "Serviceableness" (as Dury called it), was new; Dury defined it as "Serviceableness towards the society wherein they live, that they may be enabled, each in their sex respectively, to follow lawful callings for profitable uses; and not become a burden to their generation by living in idleness and disorderliness, as commonly those do who come from the school of this age."[31] Thus a vocational aim was added to the theological aim—to cultivate in children of both sexes and all classes not only an understanding of Protestant Christian faith through rigorous study of the Bible and the creed but also a body of useful secular knowledge that they might take with them into the world of work.

Not only the purposes but also the methods of schooling were to be informed by the Puritan ethic. Strict measures were to be adopted in the education of girls to eliminate "whatsoever . . . doth tend only to foment pride and satisfy curiosity and imaginary delights," such as dancing, hairdressing, and putting on of apparel. Instead they were to be taught "through the fear of God to become good and careful housewives, loving towards their husbands and their children when God shall call them to be married." At the same time, "such as may be found capable of tongues [i.e., languages] and sciences . . . are not to be neglected, but assisted towards the improvement of their intellectual abilities." "As for the boys," Dury continued, "the same rule is to be observed . . . both for tongues, sciences, and employment. . . . [A]ll the unprofitable exercises of their mind and body . . . shall be altered into profitable employments which may fit them for [work] in husbandry, in necessary trades, in navigation, in civil offices for the administration of justice; in peace and war; and in economical duties by which they may be serviceable to their own families, and to their neighbors."[32] A rigorous discipline was to be imposed on pupils, including long hours of classes and severe corporal punishment for delinquency.

Puritan efforts to reform English schooling, which were only partially realized during the Commonwealth period, were officially repudiated during the Restoration, when Nonconformists were forbidden to teach under the very heavy statutory penalty of £40.[33] Calvinist educational theories were revived, however, after the Glorious Revolution and underlay the radical changes that took place in the 1690s and the early 1700s.

What the Puritans started in the mid-seventeenth century was carried out in the early eighteenth century not only by Presbyterians, Congregationalists, Methodists, and other newly "tolerated" Calvinist denominations, but also by Anglicans, both Low Church and High Church. The emphasis on education of all classes—an emphasis that had roots both in Calvinist and in Lutheran theology—was implemented not primarily by school ordinances or other legislation, as in Protestant German principalities, but primarily by the coming together of public-spirited persons in local communities to form voluntary associations to establish, maintain, and finance schooling for the poor, with emphasis on schooling in useful trades.

The most important such associations were the Societies for the Propagation of Christian Knowledge (SPCKs), the first of which was founded in March 1698/99 by five residents of London, including an outstanding clergyman and four prominent lay members of the Church of England, some of whom were High Church and some Low Church in theology, some Tory and some Whig in political sympathies.[34] Their purpose was to sponsor local associations of public-spirited persons, at first in London and eventually throughout Great Britain, that would establish so-called charity schools for the children of the laboring classes. Within two years the number of subscribing members of the London Society had expanded to ninety. Within a generation there were hundreds of such societies throughout England and over a thousand charity schools.[35] Each local society was a separate autonomous entity, although all adhered to the same bylaws.

The SPCKs were important not only because of their profound influence on the content of English elementary schooling over the next century but also because of their internal corporate structure and their method of self-governance. Subscribing members, who gained admission only by recommendations, paid an annual subscription and enjoyed voting rights at society meetings.[36] Thus the societies operated on two fundamental principles that also characterized the recently founded Bank of England and other joint-stock enterprises: first, the economic principle that numerous "subscribers," each of whom contributes a relatively small amount of money, can thereby establish a relatively large capital fund that can be used in more productive ways than the sum total of the various amounts spent separately; and second, the legal principle that such subscribers, by discussion and vote at subscribers' meetings, can effectively direct the activities of the association in ways that serve its purposes.

In addition to SPCK-sponsored charity schools established and financed by subscriptions of members, a great many charity schools were established and financed by endowments of wealthy persons and were governed by the terms of the trusts that established them. As charitable trusts, these were technically under the supervision of the Crown, and their funds and their administration were vested in the trustees. In many cases, however, the trustees named in the endowment were local landholders, town officials, and other prominent persons of the same class as the subscribers in the subscription type of charity schools. As Mary G. Jones has written, in most respects "the majority of the endowed and subscription elementary schools of the eighteenth century were alike."[37]

The SPCKs were initially linked closely with the Church of England, and their bylaws required that the teachers in schools supported by them be observant Anglicans.[38] Also legislation restricting all teaching to Anglicans remained on the books. In fact, however, the SPCKs were initially closely linked with the Societies for the Reformation of Manners, which openly included members of Presbyterian, Congregationalist, and other dissenting denominations; and in the early 1700s the legislative restrictions on teaching by Nonconformists were rendered ineffective by decisions of the courts.[39] Thus teaching in charity schools came to be open in fact to members of the "tolerated" churches.

Moreover, SPCKs served as a model for the formation of other types of voluntary associations that arose to found schools in the local parishes into which England was divided. Thus in many parishes either the local pastor or one or more lay members of the parish would announce that the formation of a local school was needed, and several others would join to make a plan for such a school, and then subscribers would make contributions to a fund to hire teachers. Parishioners might agree to contribute small monthly payments for the upkeep of such a school, and would then meet periodically to discuss its successes and failures, and if they disapproved of its methods of operation or the quality of the teachers, the annual subscriptions might decline.[40]

Much that was good and much that was questionable in Calvinist moral theology was reflected in the system of schooling of children of the laboring classes that came to prevail in England in the last decade of the seventeenth century and the first half or more of the eighteenth. On the questionable side was the exaggerated emphasis on discipline. These were usually four-year schools for children approximately seven to eleven years of age, who were required to be in class six hours a day. Great emphasis was placed on punctuality, correctness of behavior, memorization of texts, and concentration of attention, and delinquency in any respect—not only more serious offenses such as truancy but also lack of attention, lack of preparation, even playful distractions or impoliteness—was severely punishable, including by harsh flogging of girls as well as boys. Indeed, the children were required to fill out daily forms indicating any "faults" that they had committed.[41] The prevailing ethic was well expressed in a 1708 *Account of the Charity Schools Lately Erected:* "Children are made tractable and submissive by being early accustomed to awe and punishment and dutiful subjection. From such timely discipline the public may expect honest and industrious servants."[42]

Also on the questionable side was the tendency to teach down to the students, as members of a lower class. Thus *Rules for the Good Order and Government of Charity Schools drawn up by the Trustees of these Schools,* issued in 1724 under the direction of the bishop of London, advised teachers that the children were not to be taught anything "to set them above the conditions of servants, or the more laborious employments."[43] What this meant in practice was that emphasis on training in the practical arts—sewing, knitting, and the like for girls, shoemaking, gardening, and the like for boys—tended to increase, and education in "tongues and science" was often confined solely to the Bible and the catechism, plus reading and arithmetic. Much, of course, depended on the quality of the teachers, some of whom were of considerable attainments. Also some prominent voices were raised on behalf of more advanced instruction. In practice, however, the opinion seems generally to have prevailed that "the children were to be rescued from idleness and vagrancy, washed and combed, and instructed in their duties by the catechism, that they might become good men and women and useful servants. The schools did not exist to develop their intellectual powers, nor to steer them towards equality of opportunity."[44]

On the good side of the Calvinist moral theology that was reflected in the charity schools was its emphasis on tempering discipline with a strong sense of social responsibility. The failure of the schools in many instances to achieve the goal of true charity was countered by their success in achieving that goal in some instances. There were some schools where discipline was practiced without brutality and where dedicated, sensitive, and able teachers had the love and respect of their pupils and of their pupils' parents.[45] It is also of some significance that there were as many girls in charity schools as there were boys, and further, that some of the graduates of the schools, having learned to read and write, went on to higher callings and prominent careers.[46]

Most important was the reflection of Calvinist moral theology in the emphasis on the Christian responsibility of the laity, and especially of its public-spirited leaders, its "elders," to care for the spiritual welfare of their less fortunate neighbors. The establishment of charity schools for the poor, to be financed and guided by the subscribing members of local associations, gave a new dimension to what has been called the "laicisation of religion,"[47] or, as it is called in this chapter, the spiritualization of secular law.

Poor Relief

From the twelfth through the fifteenth centuries, in England as elsewhere in Europe, relief of the poor, including the sick, the infirm, the aged, orphans, widows, and others unable to earn a living, was conducted almost entirely by Roman Catholic ecclesiastical institutions and was financed almost entirely by church taxes (tithes) and by individual voluntary contributions to the church's charitable foundations. In the late fourteenth and fifteenth centuries, however, the gradual dissolution of the manorial system of agriculture and the transformation of arable land into pastures for sheep led to widespread emigration of peasants to the towns and eventually put a heavier burden on poor relief than almsgiving alone could bear. As in Germany and elsewhere in Europe, large numbers of vagrants and vagabonds lived by begging or else by plundering. In England, as elsewhere, secular legislation during this period imposed criminal sanctions on idleness and vagrancy—in the words of Sidney and Beatrice Webb, "not Poor Laws, that is, measures for relief of the poor, but laws against the poor and the rights of labor . . . tempered, it is true, by the charity of the Church."[48]

As in Lutheran principalities, so in sixteenth-century England. The abolition of the Roman Catholic Church was the occasion for the establishment of a new system of poor relief in the form of "common chests," financed through municipal taxes and charitable contributions as well as through resources of confiscated religious foundations.[49] Begging was prohibited and the mendicant orders were dissolved, and in various places workhouses were established to give relief to the "deserving poor" as well as to reform idlers and settle vagrants. In some Roman Catholic territories similar methods of poor relief—especially common chests and workhouses—were instituted although monastic and other charitable foundations continued to be maintained and mendicancy continued to be permitted.

As in the case of other spiritual causes—liturgy, marriage, moral offenses, and education—so in the case of poor relief, English legal institutions during the sixteenth and early seventeenth centuries remained somewhat closer in character to those of the Roman Catholic past than did parallel legal institutions in other Protestant countries. Many charitable responsibilities that had previously been carried out by the Roman Catholic Church were now transferred to the Church of England. It was only during and after the English Revolution of 1640 to 1689 that responsibility for relief of poverty was transferred almost entirely to civil authorities and at the same time a new theory of poor relief was introduced as well as a new motivation—a theory and a motivation that were more closely associated with Calvinist forms of Protestantism than with Lutheran.

The major change in the English law of poor relief during the sixteenth and early seventeenth centuries, introduced by a series of statutes initiated by the Privy Council, was the assignment of responsibility for such relief to officers of the thousands of individual church parishes into which the territory of England was divided.[50] The parish at that time was both an ecclesiastical and a political unit. As an ecclesiastical unit it was headed by a priest—the incumbent rector or vicar ("the incumbent")—who was assisted by lay churchwardens elected from among the householders of the parish at an annual meeting (called "town meeting" and later "vestry"). The chief officer of the parish was the justice of the peace, appointed by the Crown, who was almost always the local country squire of one or more parishes.[51] In addition, a constable, a surveyor of highways, and overseers of the poor, like the churchwardens, were chosen annually from among the householders of the parish. The constable, who was chosen by the justices of the peace of the county of which the parish was a part, apprehended persons suspected of crimes (there being no organized police force in England until the nineteenth century) and presented them to the county justices of the peace at sessions that met every three months (called quarter sessions). The surveyor of highways, who in many parishes was chosen by the constable and churchwardens, was responsible for maintenance of roads in the parish. Under a statute of 1536, overseers of the poor, normally two per parish, were chosen annually by justices of the peace.[52]

The extraordinary fact about this system of local government is that of the six types of officers—the incumbent, the churchwardens, the justice of the peace, the constable, the surveyor of the highways, and the overseers of the poor—only one, the incumbent, was not a layperson and only he received payment for his services. Moreover, all except the incumbent and the justice of the peace were chosen annually, usually through a system of rotation. These were local persons who held the land on which they lived by freehold, copyhold, or leasehold tenure—called "householders"—performing civic obligations imposed on them by the Crown as head of both church and state.

The justice of the peace—the squire—was under strong pressure from the Crown to make sure that the poor of the parish were supported. Under Elizabethan legislation, in the words of Sidney and Beatrice Webb, "the nobles and gentry who owned the land were made responsible, as Justice of the Peace and masters of the parish, not only for maintaining order and repressing crime, but also for ensuring an adequate supply of food with low prices, with a greater regularity of employment, and, more lastingly, by insisting on the levy and expenditure of a poor rate for preventing unemployment among the able-bodied, and destitution among the orphans, the sick, the aged and the infirm."[53] Especially in the period from 1590 to 1640, the Privy Council enforced this policy through a series of orders and proclamations addressed to the county justices of the peace at quarter sessions. As the Webbs write, "To the landless man or indigent widow, the King in Council may have appeared as the Father of his people."[54]

The overseers of the poor were charged with the duty of taking a census of those residents of the parish in need of various kinds and degrees of relief, estimating the annual cost of such relief and, together with the incumbent and churchwardens, and above all the local justice of the peace, fixing the rate—called the poor rate—at which the householders should be taxed for that purpose. The respective functions and powers of the various offices as well as methods of selection were determined largely by local custom and differed in different parishes.

In addition to relying on local parishes to care for the indigent, the English Crown also sought to curb vagrancy and vagabondage by establishing workhouses—as in other countries of Europe—where a strict work regimen was to cure idlers of their wicked tendencies. The first of these was established in 1557 in London, in response to a proposal made in 1552 by King Edward VI and the bishop of London.[55] It was located in a former residence of King Henry VIII called Bridewell; within decades, some two hundred other such "Bridewells," as they were called, operating with a prison-like discipline, were established in virtually all parts of England. Constables of the parishes could present vagrants to quarter sessions for commitment to a Bridewell.[56]

Royal revenues and local taxation could not in themselves, however, suffice to raise the funds necessary for relief of the indigent in England in the sixteenth and early seventeenth centuries, and in fact such funding was substantially supplemented by individual charitable donations, both inter vivos and testamentary, to establish so-called hospitals and other forms of sustenance for the destitute.[57]

It was the English Revolution of 1640–1689 that transformed English poor law from a system administered largely by individual local parishes into a more or less integrated national system and at the same time shifted its main emphasis from relief of indigence and correction of idleness to employment of the able-bodied poor in productive and profitable work—that is, as one would say today, from welfare to workfare.

Under the earlier system of poor relief, the amount of the poor rate, as well as the extent and nature of relief, inevitably differed substantially among the different parishes, some of which were much smaller than others and some of which were much poorer than others. One of the main problems that this created was that many people who desired relief resorted to parishes where relief was the most abundant. To meet this problem a series of laws were enacted in the sixteenth and seventeenth centuries, called Laws of Settlement, whose purpose was to restrict the granting of relief within a parish to those who had resided there for a given period of time, or who had property there of a given value, or whose family had lived there, or who otherwise had a claim to be counted as a member.[58] When strictly enforced, these laws could keep a needy person confined to a single parish for his or her entire life. Also it came to be recognized that restrictions on mobility of labor and disparities in the amount of relief available in different parishes had a substantially deleterious effect on the English economy as a whole.[59]

Moreover, the earlier system had come to be resented by large numbers of the landed gentry, who were a chief source of the taxes needed to provide relief for the poor in their parishes. It is likely that one of the grievances that led many landed gentry to support the parliamentary cause in the Civil War was the pressure put on them by the Crown to pay taxes for poor relief. Moreover, the Bridewells were for the most part neither efficient workhouses nor effective houses of correction. Many of them were, in effect, simply prisons.[60]

In the 1640s, in the first phase of the English Revolution, leading Puritans called for the establishment of a new type of workhouse that would stress, in the words of Samuel Hartlib, "inculcation of those moral values associated with Puritan godliness and self-advance," and that would house not only adult poor but also children, whom it would "civilize and train in their books, so by degrees to trades, that so they may be fit servants for the Commonwealth."[61] Hartlib and others called for the formation of associations of leading citizens to establish and supervise workhouses dedicated to such purposes, which would not be "houses of correction" like the Bridewells but would serve as productive and profitable enterprises. In 1647, in the midst of the Civil War, the first such official association was formed, called the London Corporation of the Poor, and in 1649 it established in London the first such workhouse.[62]

In 1662, in the Restoration phase of the Revolution, the London workhouse was replaced by another of the same kind and the establishment of Corporations of the Poor was reauthorized.[63] The London workhouse served as a model for others. Persons were not required to work in them, and those working in them could leave at any time. The emphasis on "godliness and self-advance" was retained, but it was combined with an increased emphasis on productivity and profitability. Charitable relief and Bridewells were retained, but a statute of 1723 gave parishes the right to deny aid to able-bodied poor persons who refused an offer to work in the new workhouses.[64]

The 1723 act also provided that children of the poor could be educated in the workhouses and that the sick and the aged could be maintained there. In addition, it substituted long-term salaried administrators for the unpaid and annually changing personnel of the earlier system. The act left it to future legislation, however, in the form of local acts, to authorize the establishment of Corporations of the Poor, and consequently workhouses, in various localities. It is estimated that in the first half of the eighteenth century, a network of some seven hundred such workhouses was created by local Corporations of the Poor, through such local acts.[65]

The 1723 Workhouse Act also allowed the creation of joint workhouses by several parishes. This was a response to the strong criticism leveled against the earlier system of parochial poor relief. Among the critics were such leading figures as the jurist Matthew Hale,[66] as well as the merchant and economist Josiah Child.[67] These and others advocated that a network of workhouses be established throughout the country, under control of Corporations of the Poor, to carry out training and work programs that would bring the unemployed into the mainstream of profitable production of goods for the market. As Josiah Child wrote, "The radical error I esteem to be leaving it to the care of every parish to maintain their own poor."[68] ("The subtle Dutch," he added, "do not ask persons who seek work where they come from.")[69] Between 1696 and 1711, unions of urban parishes had been allowed for fourteen towns by local acts of Parliament, and this number was greatly increased by the 1723 Workhouse Act. Eventually unions of rural parishes were also authorized, although such unions were often successfully resisted by the local gentry. In fact a substantial percentage of the parishes continued to operate independently as they had done before.

The parish itself, however, changed radically in the course of and after the English Revolution. On the one hand, the ecclesiastical hierarchy, the clergy, at the central, the intermediate, and the local levels, ceased to play an official role in the political and economic life of the parish. On the other hand, religious convictions, spiritual values, continued to be of great importance in determining political and economic policy—indeed, with respect to poor relief, of decisive importance. The religious convictions of members both of the Anglican Church and of the dissenting churches, strongly influenced by Calvinist moral theology, motivated them to support the reforms of English poor law that were made in the period from the mid-seventeenth to the mid-eighteenth century; and with respect to the religious significance of both the duty to work and the duty to give aid to the needy, there was in that period no substantial difference between Anglican and Puritan belief systems.[70]

Moreover, to give aid to the needy required not only the establishment of workhouses for the able-bodied but also the establishment of new sources of charitable relief that could supplement, if not replace, the older system of scattered individual donations. This was forthcoming in a new form of funding of charitable activity by the combined subscriptions of large numbers of benefactors.[71] In the late seventeenth and eighteenth centuries, for the first time, large numbers of donors would subscribe jointly to the founding of "hospitals" of various kinds, not only for the sick but also for children of the poor, for foundlings, for the aged, and for other persons in dire need. Such "associated philanthropy," as it has been called, was modeled on the example of joint-stock companies, which also came into existence and flourished on a large scale in this period.[72] In addition, hundreds of so-called "friendly societies" sprang up in the century after 1640, to provide mutual protection for their members against illness and misfortune. In the words of Paul Slack, "The language of charity and the language of entitlements and obligations under the law were different, and could sometimes be in tension with one another, but the second would have been inconceivable without the first"[73]—to which it may be added that the first would have been unworkable without the second.

To stress the spiritual motivations that underlay the transformation of the English law of poor relief in the late seventeenth and early eighteenth centuries is to take seriously what the authors of that transformation wrote about their motivations,[74] but at the same time to run counter to the main body of twentieth-century historical scholarship on the subject. In the vast literature on the history of English poor laws, the overwhelming emphasis since the 1920s has been on the connections between the laws of poor relief and the rise of capitalism, and more specifically, the laws are said to be based on economic motivations to protect the capitalist class. Perhaps the strongest statement of this interpretation is that of the distinguished neo-Marxist historian of sixteenth- and seventeenth-century England, Christopher Hill, who wrote in 1997 that "the fundamental reasons for the revolution of thought that took place in England between the Reformation and the Restoration were economic. . . . But it is very much nicer for a business man to be told that his actions are in accordance with the will of God. So ideas lubricate economic processes."[75] Hill has characterized the Puritan belief system as a "bourgeois" and "individualist" ideology and the poor laws of the sixteenth and seventeenth centuries as a means whereby an emerging capitalist class of merchants and industrialists exploited the working underclass. In this he carries to a sharp conclusion the views of many if not most historians of the period. Thus in Bronislaw Geremek's masterly study of the history of poverty in Europe, the author repeatedly discounts religious motivations and emphasizes as the chief cause of the programs of poor relief in the sixteenth and seventeenth centuries "the emergence of industrial capitalism."[76]

The truth is that the English program of poor relief in the late seventeenth and early eighteenth centuries was neither capitalist nor individualist nor bourgeois. The capitalists of the closing decades of the seventeenth century and the opening decades of the eighteenth, in particular the city merchants and the emerging class of manufacturers, viewed the new workhouses as a source of unfair competition, which used cheap labor, supported by taxpayers' money, to flood the market with inferior goods at low prices.[77] Subsidized workfare was no more "capitalist" than the earlier charitable welfare; and certainly the formation of (unpaid) Corporations of the Poor, of associations of joint subscribers to charitable causes, and of friendly societies for mutual protection cannot be explained as a manifestation of "individualism"; in fact, these groups were manifestations of a Calvinist communitarianism. And finally, the principal support for the new system of poor relief came not from the bourgeoisie, the urban middle class, or the merchants but from the aristocratic landed gentry, which in the English Revolution wrested supreme power from the royal nobility and established itself as the ruling class and chief source of power in Parliament, in the judiciary, and in the civil service. The English Revolution was not a "bourgeois" revolution but an aristocratic revolution. Parliamentary policies were determined not primarily by the public opinion of the urban business and professional classes but by the public spirit of the ruling landed elite, which formed close-knit associations to establish and supervise workhouses for the able-bodied and to found hospitals for the infirm, the aged, orphans, and others unable to work. Commercial capitalism did, indeed, benefit in the long run from these policies, but industrial capitalism, still in its infancy, was hardly an important factor in their formulation.

Those who established the English system of poor relief during and after the English Revolution considered it to be first a response to the will of God, second an act of common humanity, and third an instrument of sound social policy. Matthew Hale—hardly a bourgeois capitalist—began his *Discourse Touching Provision for the Poor* with the following words:

> A due care for the relief of the poor is an act, 1. Of great Piety towards Almighty God who requires it of us: He hath left the Poor as his Pupils and the Rich as his Stewards to provide for them. . . . [God] hath scattered the Poor among the rest of Mankind as his Substitutes and Receivers.
>
> 2. It is an act of greatest Humanity among men. Mercy and Benignity is due to the very Beasts that serve us, much more to those that are partakers of the same common nature with us.
>
> 3. It is an act of great Civil Prudence and Political Wisdom: for Poverty . . . makes men tumultuous and unquiet. Where there are many very Poor, the Rich cannot long or safely continue such.

These words echo those of earlier Roman Catholics as well as of Lutherans and of Christians of all other denominations. They also reflect the Lutheran view that it is not only for the church but also for the civil authority—and, indeed, primarily for the civil authority—to care for the poor. But later in his *Discourse* Hale distinguishes two kinds of charity: *relief* of the "impotent poor," the infirm who are unable to support themselves, and *employment* of the able-bodied poor, which, Hale writes, is "a charity of greater extent, and of very great and important consequence to the public Wealth and Peace of the Kingdom as also to the benefit and advantage of the Poor."[78]

Thus as in Lutheran Germany, the English civil authority was given the spiritual responsibility, as God's "stewards," of providing for the poor as God's "substitutes and receivers." But on Calvinist principles, the civil authority was to do so not primarily through governmental establishment of community chests and workhouses for relief of the incapacitated and the indigent but also, and primarily, through the formation of voluntary associations of public-spirited persons whose concern was not only to care for the disabled and the needy but also to provide training and ultimately profitable employment for the able-bodied who had not found work on their own initiative.

What has been recounted in this chapter is often characterized as a process of secularization, which has traditionally meant the transfer of responsibilities and activities from ecclesiastical to civil institutions, whether governmental, communal, or private. In England, as has been shown, this institutional process went through two stages. The English Reformation of the sixteenth century was partly a secularization in this sense but partly also a transfer of ecclesiastical responsibilities and activities from one church to another—from the Church of Rome to the Church of England. The Church of England, however, was itself, "secularized" insofar as it was placed under the supreme authority of the Crown acting chiefly through its Privy Council and its parliaments. Only during and after a second English Reformation, the English Revolution of 1640–1689, were certain basic spiritual responsibilities and activities of the ecclesiastical authorities—prosecution of moral offenses, education, and poor relief—transferred in large part to secular institutions.

It is submitted that—contrary to the usual interpretation—such transfer in both the German and the English Revolutions should be understood not only, and not primarily, as a process of secularization of ecclesiastical responsibilities and activities but also, and primarily, as a process of spiritualization of secular responsibilities and activities. This, at least, is how it was understood by its Protestant authors—especially in sixteenth-century Germany and in seventeenth-century England. The Lutheran doctrine that all Christian believers constitute a priesthood, a spiritual body, and the Calvinist doctrine that it is the Christian mission of the elect to reform the world, led inevitably to what from Protestant perspectives was the spiritualization of the secular. In Protestant countries large parts of the spiritual law of the Roman Catholic Church were appropriated and transformed by the secular power and administered not by the clergy but by the laity.

Beginning in the twentieth century, however, social theorists have given "secularism" a much broader meaning than suggested thus far in this analysis. It has come to refer to a decline in religious beliefs altogether and the substitution of other beliefs. These other beliefs include, in Ernest Gellner's words,

> [the] rejection of supernatural or 'spiritual' explanations of phenomena; . . . explanations of phenomena in terms of the structure and activity of matter; a positive expectation that everything in nature and man can be explained in natural intramundane terms; determinism; empiricism in epistemology; hedonism and/or egoism in psychology; belief in reason as the guide and arbiter of life; rejection of the authority of tradition; utilitarianism in ethics, and utilitarianism and/or democracy in politics; pragmatism with regard to the theory of truth; relativism."[79]

Max Weber in the early 1920s called the triumph of secularism "the disenchantment of the world." Secularism had itself become secularized.

Among historians of modern Europe, the source of such a secularized secularism has sometimes been traced—mistakenly—to sixteenth- and seventeenth-century Protestantism. Thus C. John Sommerville attributes what he calls a secularization of space and time, of concepts of history, of political theory, of education, of language, of culture itself, in sixteenth- to eighteenth-century England, chiefly to Protestantism, which, he writes, "has, by its nature, a secularising tendency." Even religion, he argues, became secularized in early modern Protestant England insofar as it "became something to be explained rather than the basis of all explanations." Sommerville goes so far as to trace to sixteenth- and seventeenth-century Protestantism the emergence of rationalism, individualism, and privatization of religion. "The privatization of religion," he states, "is the reverse side of [secular] institutionalization." The triumph of secular institutions under Protestantism had "the effect of confining religion to ever fewer areas of life," since such institutions "will always have a less religious (more 'secular') character." Sommerville gives as an example "the English State's assumption of poor-relief activities," which, he states, "might be termed profanation, since it involves something formerly regarded as sacred into the area of the profane, literally, outside the temple."[80]

This statement poses sharply the differences between the Roman Catholic view of the church as a visible hierarchical institution ("the temple") and the Lutheran and Calvinist view of the institutional church as itself a secular ("earthly") body and of the invisible church as a spiritual ("heavenly") community of the faithful, "the priesthood of all believers," "the communion of saints." Yet the continuity between the two main branches of Western

Christianity is reflected in the continuity of legal regulation of spiritual matters. It represented, in its time, a strengthening, not (as Sommerville argues) a weakening, of English "religious culture" that Parliament replaced ecclesiastical authorities as the ultimate source of English law governing liturgy, marriage, moral offenses, education, and poor relief, and further, that the regulation of these spiritual matters on the ground, so to speak, came increasingly into the hands of the laity.

CONCLUSION

CONTEMPORARY scholars in all the relevant fields—historians, theologians, philosophers, social scientists, lawyers—have with few exceptions paid little attention to the enormous impact of sixteenth- and seventeenth-century Protestantism on the development of Western legal institutions. Indeed, they have largely neglected to consider the impact of belief systems generally on law—the influence of Roman Catholicism on the formation of the Western legal tradition in the late eleventh and twelfth centuries, the influence of Lutheran and later Calvinist Christianity on the development of national legal systems in the sixteenth, seventeenth, and early eighteenth centuries, the influence on law of Enlightenment beliefs in Deism and rationalism and individualism in the late eighteenth and nineteenth centuries, the influence on the Western legal tradition of atheism and agnosticism and of various secular social and political belief systems in the twentieth century. Nor have they, again with few exceptions, recognized the continuity of the Western legal tradition despite—and because of—these transformations.

It is the thesis of this book that the evolution of the Western legal tradition is founded on an evolving Western belief system, and that it was, above all, the failure of belief systems to change in time, and thus to provide a foundation for necessary changes in the existing legal systems, that was a precondition for the periodic resort to violent action, Great Revolutions, which transformed the original apocalyptic vision partly in order to bring about such changes. Eventually, however, in each case, after more than a generation of strife and upheaval, the Revolution came to an end and a legal settlement was reached that reconciled its utopian vision with some of the legal institutions that it had initially overthrown.

With the end of each of the Great Revolutions, the old law and the new law came together in a new ensemble. The German Revolution outlawed the Roman Catholic Church in territories that came to be ruled by Lutheran princes and subjected the entire ecclesiastical jurisdiction to the secular authority; yet a considerable amount of the substance of the Roman Catholic canon law was reintroduced by the secular German lawmakers and courts as well as by Lutheran ecclesiastical tribunals. Indeed, a considerable amount of the law of all countries of the West, including the United States, is derived historically from the canon law of the Roman Catholic Church. In legal philosophy, basic questions concerning the nature of divine law and of natural law and their relationship to the positive law of the state remained basically the same after the Lutheran Reformation as before, although the answers of Lutheran jurists to those questions were different from the answers of their Roman Catholic predecessors. A new meaning was giving to the word "conscience" and to the concept of "equity." The monarch's legal rules prevailed, but they were to be applied in the light of the purposes of law, equitably, by resort to the God-given conscience of the court. In legal science as well, the older so-called scholastic method was attacked by Lutheran jurists and a new topical or conceptual method of systematization was introduced, but again, much of the earlier dialectical method of reconciling contradictions in authoritative texts was in fact carried over into the new topical method. Now, however, it was the university law professors who played a decisive role in maintaining the integrity of the whole legal system, both through their treatises and through their power of decision of difficult cases. In the light of the new Lutheran legal philosophy and legal science, the older criminal and civil law was systematized and reformed but not abandoned. The codification of criminal law, though accomplished by Schwarzenberg before his conversion to Lutheranism and adopted by the Roman Catholic emperor after the Lutheran faith had come to prevail in many German principalities, embodied both the legal philosophy and the legal science of the Lutheran Reformation and the German Revolution.

The impact of Protestant belief on German civil and economic law is less obvious than its impact on legal philosophy and legal science and less obvious also than its impact on criminal law. Yet it is not a mere coincidence that among the territorial rulers the Protestant princes were the most active in promoting the reform of civil law in their territories. Nor was it merely coincidental that the Protestant emphasis on the role of the laity in matters such as enforcement of morals and schooling and poor relief was accompanied by an emphasis on the refinement and systematization of the law of contracts so as to give added protection to persons engaged in commercial and other contractual relationships, and of the law of property so as to make more secure the transfer of rights of possession and use of land to persons to whom the land was leased. The German Revolution was fought in the name of a biblical faith that entailed a biblical morality, which in turn was to infuse legal relations among believers at all levels. What Lutheran Protestantism brought to civil and economic law was not a set of legal rules that differed essentially from those that Roman Catholics could also support, but rather a strong motivation to systematize such rules through royal legislation and scholarly treatises, and to enforce them through secular courts and a secular bureaucracy.

Among the greatest changes in sixteenth-century German law were those in what may be called spiritual law, that is, in branches of law that had previously been a virtual monopoly of the church, namely, the law governing ecclesiastical liturgy, marriage, moral offenses, education, and poor relief. In some of these matters, the beliefs of Roman Catholics and Lutherans differed sharply, and the transfer of competence over them from the Roman Catholic Church to the Lutheran state had a most important effect. The liturgy was translated into German and included popular hymns sung by the congregation. Marriage was no longer a divine sacrament and much more a social and a family event. Many types of moral offenses that had previously been punished within the internal forum of the church were now punished in the secular courts. In modern terms, workfare supplemented welfare as a principal method of poor relief. Still, this was a transformation, not a new creation, not the "new heaven and new earth" that radicals of the first apocalyptic and antinomian phase of the Revolution had anticipated.

Similarly, the English Revolution of the seventeenth century, though in its first radical phase it called for the abolition of the monarchy, the abolition of the Church of England, the institution of a democratic government, a written constitution, and the legislative codification of criminal and civil law, finally settled for a constitutional monarchy subject to parliamentary supremacy, a "comprehensive" Anglicanism with toleration of dissenting Protestant churches, government under a two-party system of Whigs and Tories supported by an aristocratic class of landed gentry and wealthy merchants, and a reformed and more systematized body of common law developed by an independent judiciary and applied in both criminal and civil cases by an independent jury. England's First Protestant Reformation of the previous century had been in some respects a later version of the German Lutheran Reformation, in that much of the competence of the Roman Catholic Church in spiritual matters, including legal regulation of ecclesiastical liturgy, marriage, moral offenses, education, and poor relief, had been transferred by the royal ruler to the newly nationalized Church of England, of which the monarch was the supreme head. A century later, the impact of the Second English Reformation, and of the English Revolution of which it was a part, was to increase substantially the role of the laity in these matters, as in Germany more than a century earlier, with this difference, which is characteristic of the differences between the two Revolutions: that in Germany it was the territorial prince and the high magistracy, the state, that invoked and controlled the participation of the laity in matters of moral offenses, schooling, and poor relief, whereas in England, more than a century later, voluntary associations of leading public-spirited citizens in charitable corporate organizations took the initiative and provided the necessary financial support. Here Anglo-Calvinism, called at the time Puritanism, with its emphasis on the mission of the local community to be "a city on a hill," played an important role.

At the heart of the transformation of English law in the seventeenth century was the Anglo-Calvinist belief that God had made a covenant with the English people, that England was an elect nation, chosen, as the children of Israel had once been chosen, to be "a light to all the nations." To this belief in a divine covenant was added the Calvinist doctrine that history is wholly within the providence of God, and that the history of the English people, including the history of their institutions, was the heritage on which their constitutional law was founded and which gave guidance for its future development. Calvinism in its English form also contributed to the revolt against royal absolutism and the establishment of the supremacy of a parliamentary aristocracy. John Calvin himself had written a century earlier that the best form of government is aristocracy, or, in some instances, aristocracy tempered by democracy. This concept also supported the abolition of the Tudor-Stuart courts of royal prerogative and the supremacy of the common law courts.

Connected with the concept of the historicity of English law was the introduction of the doctrine of precedent as a central element in English legal science. Parliament was the supreme lawgiver, and theoretically there were—and are—no limits on its competence; but judges also were to play a creative role in adapting parliamentary legislation, and, indeed, the unwritten English constitution, to the changing needs of society as they are reflected in criminal and civil litigation. Not only parliamentary legislation but also judicial precedents were to govern the dramatic development of civil and economic law.

Perhaps the most dramatic change in the procedure of the English common law courts in the late seventeenth century was the transformation of jury trial through the introduction of witness proof at the trial stage. Now judge and jury heard the same evidence, and might disagree in interpreting it. As we have seen, a relativist concept of truth, one that corresponded to the new scientific method of the time, was enunciated to resolve the question of which interpretation should prevail, namely, that in such cases it should not be presumed that one or the other interpretation of the facts was true, but that, on the contrary, reasonable persons could differ as to the truth, and that consequently the judge, in most cases, may not overrule a jury verdict since it is in order to find the facts that the jury is instituted. In authoritatively deciding this question, Chief Justice Vaughn, speaking for the Court of King's Bench, specifically noted that even in such important matters as religion, reasonable persons can differ. Some thirty years later this view prevailed in Parliament's adoption of the Toleration Act.

The story of the gradual evolution of the Western legal tradition over a period of ten centuries, on the one hand, and, on the other, of the periodic mutations in that evolutionary process brought about by the Great Revolutions of the sixteenth to twentieth centuries, constitutes a striking challenge to (1) conventional Western historiography, (2) conventional social theory, and (3) conventional legal philosophy.

(1)

The history of law in the West contradicts the conventional periodization of Western history into medieval and modern, a periodization that has survived despite the attacks on it by distinguished professional "medievalists" (as they are still called) for over eighty years.[1] Perhaps the inclusion of legal history in the historiographical curriculum would compel general historians also to revise their periodizations. "Modern" English, German, French, Italian, Swedish, Dutch, Polish, and other national European legal systems were initially formed in the twelfth and thirteenth centuries under the influence, first, of the new canon law of the newly independent hierarchical Roman Catholic Church, which governed the wide variety of "spiritual causes" in all the territories of Western Europe; second, of the discovery in the late eleventh century in a library in Pisa of the sixth-century texts of the Eastern Roman emperor Justinian's Roman law, which provided a largely new legal language to the canonists as well as to legal scholars advising territorial rulers; and third, of the parallel origin and development of systems of royal or princely law, feudal law, urban law, and mercantile law—covering matters of royal, feudal, urban, and mercantile legal relations that were not covered by canon law. The formation of secular legal systems was partly in response to the emergence of canon law. The secular legal systems competed with canon law in matters where there was concurrent jurisdiction of ecclesiastical and secular jurisdiction, and also competed with one another, again in matters where there was concurrent jurisdiction.

One can, of course, always trace origins back to earlier times. Nevertheless, in the history of law it is a crucial fact that many basic legal institutions and concepts that characterized the Western legal tradition in the period of its early formation survived transformations of that tradition in subsequent periods of revolutionary change. For example, the elaborate rules of contract law and of credit transactions that were developed in both the new Roman law and the new canon law in the twelfth and thirteenth centuries survived successive economic changes and were an essential foundation of the laissez-faire capitalist economy that emerged in the nineteenth century. Similarly, the corporate form of association that was originally linked with twelfth-century ecclesiastical foundations, guilds, and universities became an essential basis of the development of the modern business corporation. Similarly, the development of political democracy in the West is unthinkable without the survival and adaptation of "medieval" concepts of the supremacy of law in a polity based on the coexistence and competition of plural jurisdictions. The twelfth-century principle of a rational judicial procedure, based on rules designed to secure a fair hearing of opposing parties by an impartial tribunal, served as a foundation for the seventeenth-century development of a rational parliamentary procedure, based on the debates of opposing political parties, and of the late-eighteenth- and nineteenth-century development of a rational procedure for the democratic election of both the legislative and executive branches of government. Other basic legal concepts that have survived since the twelfth century include the concept of hierarchy of offices, with reciprocal rights and duties between superior and subordinates in the hierarchy.

Moreover, starting in the late eleventh and early twelfth centuries, Europeans in the Roman Catholic West began to describe the times in which they lived as a new age, the "modern age," a time of "modernity." Then, for the first time, historians, as contrasted with the earlier chroniclers, saw history as moving from the past, through stages, into a new future. In this they reflected the spirit of Europe's first revolutionaries, those who fought under the banner of Pope Gregory VII to liberate the clergy from domination by emperors, kings, and feudal lords and to establish the Church of Rome as an independent corporate, political, and legal entity, under the papacy.

The term "modern" and "modernity" were also invoked in subsequent ages of radical reform. "We are at the dawn of a new era," exclaimed Martin Luther, and it was his followers who adopted the term "Middle Age" *(Mittelalter)* to refer to the period between early Christianity and themselves. Today "modern history" is dated in our universities from the so-called Enlightenment of the eighteenth century, and a school of historiography has arisen that rejects the rationalism, individualism, and capitalism identified with that age and that calls itself "postmodern." Whatever justification there may be for these contemporary periodizations, they cannot apply to the history of law in the West, which shows elements of remarkable continuity over ten centuries.

The periodization of history has, of course, strong political connotations. The word "medieval" was pleasing not only to Protestants but also to Roman Catholics, since it implied that Protestantism was an innovation and that Roman Catholicism had an unbroken continuity from early Christianity on. The concept "Middle Ages" was also convenient for nationalists, since it seemed to define the period between the decline of the Roman Empire and the rise of the modern sovereign state. By the same token, however, both Roman Catholics and Protestants should welcome a new periodization, derived from legal history, which treats the era of Protestant Reformations in the sixteenth and seventeenth centuries as an era of transformation, a second stage of modernity. And both the nationalists and the internationalists have cause to welcome such a periodization, since it traces each of the national legal systems of the West to a common transnational formative era, but at the same time stresses the emergence from that common basis of the European system of national states.

(2)

Social theorists of the nineteenth and twentieth centuries have used the division into "medieval" and "modern" to distinguish between an era of so-called feudalism and an era of so-called capitalism. In emphasizing this distinction they have usually overlooked the enormous expansion of commerce and the rise of cities in Europe in the heyday of so-called feudalism, and the fact that not only capitalism but also bureaucratism, rationalism, and indeed "modernity" in all its forms were characteristic of European society to one degree or another from the twelfth century on.

Karl Marx, writing in the middle of the nineteenth century, may be excused for his failure to take account of the radical economic changes that took place in the middle of so-called medieval history, since the existence of those changes was not recognized by the historians of his time. Max Weber, writing in the early 1900s, would have a feebler excuse for dating the origin of "the spirit of capitalism" to the seventeenth century, namely, that he was describing "ideal types" of social orders. More important is the fact that both erred in underestimating the independent role of legal institutions in effectuating economic and political change.

Marx found in economic class struggle the basic source of social change from "medieval" to "modern" times. In the medieval period of Western history, he wrote, and in comparable periods of the history of other civilizations, feudal lords controlled the production and distribution of goods carried out by their subordinates, chiefly serfs; in modern times—since approximately the sixteenth century—capitalists came to control the production and distribution of goods produced by the workers in their factories. Law, under this theory, is a means whereby the ruling class maintains its domination over its subordinates, and belief systems, called ideologies, are rationalizations that explain and justify economic class consciousness; indeed, in the form of religions they are an "opiate" that induces the exploited classes to accept their inferior position. Both law and religion, in Marxist terminology, are part of the ideological "superstructure" that is built on the economic "base" of social development.

Weber and his followers accepted the Marxian historiography that traces the development of society from feudalism to capitalism (with the implicit assumption of a future development from capitalism to socialism), but traced the fundamental causes of social development not only to economic factors but also to political factors. For Weberians, as for Marxists—and, indeed, for a great many non-Weberians and non-Marxists as well—law is primarily an instrument of power. Weber differed from Marx, however, in tracing the "superstructure" of law and ideology to a "base" primarily in the competition for political power rather than primarily in the economic class interest of those who control the means of production.

If, as in this book, one traces the impact of two Great Revolutions, the German and the English, on the development of law in the West, and stresses the role of two belief systems, two versions of Christianity, sixteenth-century German Lutheranism and seventeenth-century English Calvinism, in the transformation of a legal tradition that had emerged earlier under the powerful influence of a different version of Christianity, Roman Catholicism, one finds more links with Weberian than with Marxian social theory. Such a study differs markedly, however, from both Marxist and Weberian theory in placing both law and religion at the base of the historical changes. It differs especially from Marxism in viewing the princes and high magistracy, the secular *Obrigkeit,* as the class that drew power away from the Roman Catholic clergy in the sixteenth century, and the landed gentry, not the capitalist bourgeoisie, as the class that drew power away from king and court and nobility in the seventeenth century. It differs especially from Weberian theory in deriving fundamental changes in political power in the sixteenth and seventeenth centuries from fundamental changes in the belief systems and changes in law, rather than deriving fundamental changes in the belief system and changes in law from fundamental changes in political power.

Reference was made in an earlier chapter to the fact that contemporary economic historians, in seeking to explain the extraordinary level of economic development in the West, as compared with other parts of the world, have traced periods of economic growth in the West from the eleventh and twelfth centuries to the present, and that some among them have attributed an important role to legal developments and especially to periodic changes in property law, which provided the security needed for rapid economic development. It may be added to this important insight that changes not only in property law but also in other branches of law such as the law of contracts and of business associations, and, indeed, changes in the legal system as a whole, including legal philosophy and legal science, have all played a decisive role in stimulating or inhibiting economic growth. And as soon as the inquiry into the interrelationship of economics and law is so broadened, it becomes necessary to explore not only the dependence of economic growth on law but also the dependence of law on the underlying belief system of the society whose law it is. One may hope that someday a Nobel Prize will be awarded to a legal historian who undertakes that further exploration.

(3)

Not only certain fallacies of conventional historiography and conventional social theory but also certain fallacies of conventional legal philosophy are exposed by a study of the origin and development of the Western legal tradition.

Contemporary legal philosophers have continued in different guises the age-old debate between so-called positivism and so-called natural law theory. Is the law, above all, an expression of the will of lawmakers, expressed in rules of positive law laid down by them and enforced by state sanctions, as positivists say? Or is law, above all, as theorists of natural law believe, an expression of moral principles that exist in human nature, known through reason and conscience and expressed in fundamental standards of justice, to which legal rules declared by lawmakers must conform or else lose their validity as law? This is certainly a legitimate argument, although missing from both theories in the past century, with rare exceptions, is an analysis of the religious foundations on which not only natural law doctrine but also positivism were originally founded.

Missing also is their connection with a third theory, which in the nineteenth century came to be called historical jurisprudence, or the historical school, which subordinated both the "will" dimension of law and the "reason and conscience" dimension to the "experience" dimension, that is, to the historical traditions of the society whose law it is. The historical school combines the other two, but stresses that at any given time both the political will that declares and enforces legal rules and the moral reason that holds such rules to standards of a higher justice must be evaluated historically, that is, in terms of the traditions and the values of the society whose law it is. An impressive specific example given in 1814 by the great German jurist Friedrich Carl von Savigny, in his pathbreaking essay that founded the historical school, was that a proposal being prominently made at the time that Germany enact a Civil Code, as France had done a decade before, was misguided, not because of either political or moral considerations but because historically the German people, German legal traditions, and the German legal language itself were not ready for such a code. Law, Savigny wrote, drawing on the writings of Edmund Burke, is the product of a people's culture viewed historically over generations and centuries, and must be evaluated according to its correspondence to what he called the *Volksgeist,* the "spirit" or "mind," one might say the belief system, of the society.

An earlier chapter has told the story of the establishment in England, in the seventeenth century, of historical jurisprudence as the implicit jurisprudence of the courts, through the doctrine of precedent and of the belief in the historicity of the English common law. In the nineteenth century, partly under the influence of Savigny, historical jurisprudence found many adherents among legal scholars in various countries of Europe as well, and also in the United States. Indeed, the historicity of law is implicit in the American Constitution, whose written language requires continual reinterpretation over a period of centuries, so that one can understand it only in the light of how it came to be and what it is tending to become. Yet among contemporary writers on legal philosophy, both in America and in Europe, the historical school, with its belief in the normative character of tradition, is hardly represented. The story of the normative character of the Western legal tradition, with its successive transformations, supports an integrative jurisprudence, in which history plays an equal role with politics and morality, helping to resolve tensions between them.

Some may say, "But history and tradition are two different things." It is true that a legal tradition is something more than history in the usual sense, just as it is something more than law in the usual sense. Yet neither law nor history can be understood, and more than that, neither can be preserved, if the legal tradition of which they are both part is forgotten or rejected.

The role of the Protestant Revolutions in transforming, and thus preserving, the Western legal tradition is not simply an academic topic. The issue was put sharply by the historian C. John Sommerville, who contends that Protestantism led to dissent, which led to relativism, which led to Deism, which led to atheism—which presumably is fatal to the preservation of Western culture, including the Western legal tradition. Should we attribute to the founders of a new era the distortion of their beliefs by their successors? Or should we return with some pride and some humility to their achievements in overcoming the evils that gave rise to their new beliefs and their initiative in incarnating them in new institutions?

In the early twenty-first century, the Western legal tradition is no longer alive and well. Some critics have said that in making that argument, and in viewing history from that perspective, the earlier volume of *Law and Revolution* departed from history into prophecy. But there is an element of prophecy in all historiography. It has been well said that a historian is a prophet in reverse! But even if references to what has happened during the past century may seem, at first, to be out of place in books on earlier centuries, it surely is plausible, on reflection, that the present can illuminate the past—and that the decline of the Western legal tradition in our century illuminates the nature of that tradition in the centuries in which it flourished. At the same time, the past can illuminate the future. Indeed, in the words of the great historian and prophet Alexis de Tocqueville, "When the past no longer illuminates the future, the spirit walks in darkness."

NOTES

ACKNOWLEDGMENTS

INDEX

NOTES

The following abbreviations are used in the notes.

CCC	Constitutio Criminalis Carolina
CR	*Corpus Reformatorum*, 28 vols. (Frankfurt am Main, 1834–1860)
LW	*Luther's Works*, ed. Jaroslav Pelikan, 55 vols. (St. Louis, 1956)
WA	Martin Luther, *Werke: Kritische Gesamtausgabe* (Weimar, 1883)

Introduction

1. Harold J. Berman, *Law and Revolution: The Formation of the Western Legal Tradition* (Cambridge, Mass., 1983) (hereafter Berman, *Law and Revolution*).
2. See Jaroslav Pelikan, *The Vindication of Tradition* (New Haven, 1984), p. 65.
3. See Edward Shils, *The Virtue of Civility: Selected Esays on Liberalism, Tradition, and Civil Society* (Indianapolis, 1997), p. 107. Cf. idem, *Tradition* (Chicago, 1981).
4. See Ilan Rachum, *"Revolution": The Entrance of a New Word into Western Political Discourse* (Lanham, Md., 1999), p. 230. Rachum traces to Italian sources of the fourteenth and fifteenth centuries the use of the word "revolution" to signify important abrupt changes, including important abrupt political changes. His principal thesis is twofold: first, that long before the seventeenth and eighteenth centuries, contrary to what many have maintained, "revolution" came to mean change forward, not a cyclical return—not a "revolving"—to a previous position; and second, that many such changes in the political sphere were called revolutions. Rachum ignores, however, the very strong evidence presented by Eugen Rosenstock-Huessy that the first use of the word to represent not just "a" political change but a fundamental transformation of the entire political and social order was in England in 1688, when not just "a" revolution but "the Glorious Revolution" was understood by the Whigs, who effectuated it and named it, as the inauguration of a new era in English history, though disguised in the terminology of a "restoration" of the ancient rights and liberties of Englishmen. See Eugen Rosenstock-Huessy, *Out of Revolution: The Autobiography of Western Man* (1938; reprint, Providence, 1993), pp. 304–305, 340–341. See also W. A. Speck, *Reluctant Revolutionaries: Englishmen and the Revolution of* 1688 (Oxford, 1988), p. 1 and n. 1. Rosenstock-Huessy's great work has been almost totally ignored by historians of the European Revolutions. Norman Cantor counted four "world revolutions," namely, the Papal Revolution, the Protestant Reformation, the French Revolution, and the Russian Revolution, but omitted the English Revolution and the American Revolution. See Norman Cantor, *Medieval History: The Life and Death of a Civilization* (New York, 1968). Crane Brinton, in *The Anatomy of Revolution*, rev. ed. (New York, 1965), analyzed the English Revolution, the American Revolution, the French Revolution, and the Russian Revolution, but omitted both the Papal

Revolution and the German (Protestant) Revolution. More recently, Charles Tilly, in *European Revolutions: 1492–1992* (Oxford, 1993), examines causes and outcomes of "abrupt wide-reaching, popular change in a country's rulers" in Spain and the Netherlands in the sixteenth century, Britain in the seventeenth century, France in the eighteenth century, and Russia in the twentieth century. Theda Skocpol, in *States and Social Revolutions: A Comparative Analysis of France, Russia, and China* (Cambridge, Mass., 1999), focuses on the causes and consequences of the outbreak of the French, the Russian, and the Chinese Revolutions in the first few years, that is, in their most radical phases. R. I. Moore, by contrast, in *The First European Revolution: c. 970–1215* (Oxford, 2000), portrays political, economic, and social changes, including changes in law, that took place during the century before the Papal Revolution and the century after it. At the same time he minimizes the significance of the violence and rapidity that characterize the climax of the revolutionary upheaval and that establish it in the historical memory of the society. None of these other authors trace, as Rosenstock-Huessy does, the continuity of European history from the twelfth to the twentieth century, preserved and transformed by periodic revolutionary upheavals that take two or three generations to run their course.

5. Reference here and throughout is to the Bolshevik Revolution of October 1917, as contrasted with the peaceful establishment in Russia of the so-called Provisional Government in February 1917, after the tsar's abdication, which is called "the February Revolution," and the uprising of the populace in 1905, leading to the establishment of the first Russian parliament (Duma), which is called "the 1905 Revolution." The first two upheavals, though called revolutions, turned out to be preludes to the third, which alone of the three had substantial European and, indeed, worldwide repercussions.
6. See Berman, *Law and Revolution,* pp. 94–107.
7. "Rex non debet esse sub homine sed sub deo et sub lege, quia lex fecit regem." Henry de Bracton, *De Legibus et Consuetudinibus Angliae (On the Laws and Customs of England),* vol. 2, ed. George E. Woodbine, trans. Samuel E. Thorne (Buffalo, N.Y., 1968), p. 33.
8. "Gott ist selber Recht, deshalb ist ihm Recht lieb." This quotation is repeated often in literature on the *Sachsenspiegel* but without citation of the edition and page number, and copies of the book itself are difficult to obtain. See, for example, Christoph Hinckeldey, ed., *Justiz in alter Zeit* (Rothenburg ob der Tauber, 1984), p. 10.
9. Myron Gilmore, *The World of Humanism, 1453–1517* (New York, 1952), p. 135.
10. More general ordinances, covering various fields, were called *Polizeiordnungen,* "policy ordinances."
11. See Jean Bodin, *On Sovereignty,* ed. and trans. Julian H. Franklin (Cambridge, 1992). Bodin's work strongly influenced the thought of King James I of England, who himself authored a defense of absolute monarchy.
12. The term "aristocracy" is used here, as elsewhere in this book, to refer to what Aristotle called "the rule of the few," as contrasted with monarchy, "the rule of one," and democracy, "the rule of the many." In England, however, the term is generally applied to the titled nobility, called "the peerage," but not to the landed gentry, called "the squirearchy." Cf. Lawrence Stone, *The Crisis of the Aristocracy: 1558–1641* (Oxford, 1965), p. 13.
13. The first use of the term is generally ascribed to Immanuel Kant, who called the philosophy of the French "lights" *die Aufklärung,* "the Enlightenment."

14. See James F. Traer, "From Reform to Revolution: The Critical Century in the Development of the French Legal System," *Journal of Modern History* 49 (1977), 73–88; idem, *Marriage and the Family in Eighteenth-Century France* (Ithaca, N.Y., 1980). For a general survey of private law legislation of the period preceding the drafting of the "Code civil," see Phillippe Sagnac, *La legislation civile de la révolution française* (Paris, 1989).
15. See Declaration and Resolves of the First Continental Congress, in *Documents of American History,* vol. 1 (to 1898), ed. Henry S. Commager and Milton Cantor, 10th ed. (New York, 1988), pp. 82–85. In the Resolutions of the Stamp Act Congress (1765), a similar demand had been made on the British Government: "His Majesty's liege subjects in these colonies are intitled to all the inherent rights and liberties of his natural born subjects within the kingdom of Great Britain" (ibid., p. 58).
16. French ministers writing of the American situation in the mid-1770s spoke of "les révolutions des empires" in referring to colonial agitation in the New World. This term was taken up by Gouverneur Morris in 1776, who wrote to his mother concerning the American Revolution that "great revolutions of empire are seldom achieved without much human calamity." See Rosenstock-Huessy, *Out of Revolution,* p. 646. Subsequently the term "Revolution" was invoked to compare and contrast the American and French experiences. See Friedrich von Gentz, *The Origin and Principles of the American Revolution Compared with the Origin and Principles of the French Revolution* (Delmar, N.Y., 1977), published in German in 1800 and translated soon after into English by John Quincy Adams, who made use of the work as a pamphlet in his father's reelection campaign. Cf. Robert R. Palmer, *The Age of the Democratic Revolution: A Political History of Europe and America, 1760–1800,* vol. 1 (Princeton, 1959), pp. 187–188 (discussing the significance of this pamphlet in American politics). Historians continue to be divided between those who treat the American Revolution as a revolutionary upheaval and those who see it as a War of Independence to gain for the colonists the ancient rights of Englishmen. Thus, Gordon Wood—who classifies himself with the former—distinguishes between progressive historians, such as Carl Becker, who stress the class tensions and social struggle inherent in the Revolution, and conservatives, such as Bernard Bailyn, who see the Americans as concerned "not with the need to recast the social order but with the need to purify a corrupt constitution and fight off the apparent growth of prerogative power." See Gordon S. Wood, *The Radicalism of the American Revolution* (New York, 1992), pp. 3–5, quoting Bernard Bailyn, *The Ideological Origins of the American Revolution* (Cambridge, Mass., 1967), p. 283.
17. Quoted in Joseph Story, *Commentaries on the Constitution of the United States,* vol. 1, 3rd ed. (Durham, N.C., 1858), p. 105 n. 1.
18. "Society is indeed a contract. . . . [B]ut the state ought not to be considered as nothing better than a partnership agreement in a trade of pepper and coffee, calico, or tobacco . . . to be dissolved by the fancy of the parties. . . . It is a partnership in all science, a partnership in all art; a partnership in every virtue and in all perfection. As the ends of such a partnership cannot be obtained in many generations, it becomes a partnership not only between those who are living, but between those who are living, those who are dead, and those who are to be born." Edmund Burke, *Reflections on the Revolution in France* (1790), ed. J. G. A. Pocock (Indianapolis, 1987), pp. 84–85.
19. In the 1770s, Benjamin Franklin proposed that the Deistic Society of London, which he had been instrumental in creating, be transformed into a "church" re-

plete with liturgy and a "priest of nature." The Society flourished throughout much of the late 1770s and early 1780s, and included as participants such figures as Thomas Paine, Dupont de Nemours, and, in all likelihood, the English radicals Richard Price and Joseph Priestley. David Williams, who served as a "priest of nature," preached regularly in the Society's "chapel." On the activities of this Society, see Nicholas Hans, "Franklin, Jefferson, and the English Radicals at the End of the Eighteenth Century," *Proceedings of the American Philosophical Society* 98 (1954), 406.

20. The surprising fact that both sides in this great religious-philosohical and political-legal debate could appeal to the writings of John Locke is due to the neglected fact that those writings could be construed either as a justification for the aristocratic, traditionalist, and communitarian English Revolution or as a foundation of the democratic, rationalist, and individualist program eventually embodied in the French Revolution.
21. See Vincent Ostrom, *The Meaning of American Federalism: Constituting a Self-Governing Society* (San Francisco, 1991). Ostrom shows the depth of the meaning of federalism as understood in late-eighteenth-century America, including its basis in the religious concept of covenant *(foedus)*. The theory of federalism reflected in *The Federalist,* he writes, challenged traditional concepts of sovereignty and reflected instead "a theory of concurrent, compound republics that enables democratic societies to reach out to continental proportions" (p. 97).
22. The same Russian word, *vospitat'*, means "to educate" and "to nurture or nourish." On the Soviet concept of the educational or nurturing role of law, see Harold J. Berman, *Justice in the U.S.S.R.* (Cambridge, Mass., 1963), pp. 277–284.
23. On Karl Llewellyn's use of the term "parental law," see ibid., p. 284.
24. See Harold J. Berman, "Atheism and Christianity in the Soviet Union," in Lynn Buzzard, ed., *Freedom and Faith: The Impact of Law on Religious Liberty* (Westchester, Ill., 1982), p. 127.
25. Quoted in Nathan Gardels, "An Interview with Czeslaw Milosz," *New York Review of Books,* February 27, 1986, p. 34.
26. See Manlio Bellomo, *The Common Legal Past of Europe,* trans. L. G. Cochrane (Washington, D.C., 1995). As Bellomo writes (p. xvii), a study of the sixteenth- and seventeenth-century pan-European *ius commune,* or "common law," as it was called, is particularly timely in an age when a reader might easily imagine "a future in which national barriers will be in great part dismantled, in individual minds and in collective awareness, and in which specific structures will become either anachronisms or a special province for speculation and fiscal legerdemain." Traditionally the unique features of English law have been stressed by legal historians and comparatists, and books and articles are written contrasting the English "common law" with the continental European "civil law." Reinhard Zimmermann has been in the forefront of those who have exposed as a "myth" the autochthonous character of English law, stating that "in reality . . . ever since the Norman conquest continuing international contact has left a definitive and characteristic mark on English law." See Reinhard Zimmermann, "Civil Code and Civil Law: The Europeanization of Private Law within the European Community and the Re-emergence of a European Legal Science," *Columbia Journal of European Law* 1 (1994), 87–88; idem., "Der europäische Charakter des englischen Rechts: Historische Verbindungen zwischen Civil Law und Common Law," in *Zeitschrift Fur Europaisches Privatrecht* 1 (1993), 4; idem, "Das römisch-kanonische *ius commune* als Grundlage europäischer Rechtseinheit," *Juristenzeitung* 47 (1992), 8. Historical links between English law and the law of other European countries are discussed infra in Chapters 7 through 12.

27. See Rosenstock-Huessy, *Out of Revolution,* p. 707.
28. The term "middle age" originally referred to the concept of an intermediate period between an "ancient" period whose progress had been interrupted and a "modern" period which in some respects was returning to that earlier time. Although I have found no evidence that the term "middle age" was applied to the period preceding the Papal Revolution of the late eleventh and early twelfth centuries, partisans of the Papal Revolution claimed that it introduced a new "modern" age (see Berman, *Law and Revolution,* p. 112 and sources cited p. 581 n. 35), and they looked back to pre-Carolingian canons and patristic writings to justify their claim that the intervening centuries of imperial domination of the church were a "time of usurpation." See citations to Augustin Fliche, *La réforme gregorienne,* in Charles J. Reid, Jr., "The Papacy, Theology, and Revolution: A Response to Joseph L. Soria's Critique of Harold J. Berman's *Law and Revolution,*" *Studia canonica* 29 (1995), 473–475. The first use of the term "middle age" that scholars have found was in the early fifteenth century, and then it was said to refer to the centuries between the so-called fall of Rome in the West and the rise of self-governing Italian city-states some seven centuries later. See Alison Brown, *The Renaissance,* 2nd ed. (London, 1999), pp. 7–8. Later in the fifteenth century, the term was used by Italian humanists to refer to the period between the classical writers of Greek and Roman culture and themselves, roughly from the fifth to the late fifteenth century. None of these uses of the term "middle age," however, had the same degree or the same kind of influence as its subsequent use by early-sixteenth-century followers of Luther to refer to the period between the Protestant Reformation and the early biblical Christianity to which Protestantism was returning. The Lutheran concept of "middle age" (or, in English usage, "middle ages") had a religious and political significance, linking it with the hegemony of the Roman Catholic Church. Marxists later came to identify it with "feudalism."
29. See Berman, *Law and Revolution,* pp. 112 and 581 n. 35.
30. As Marc Bloch wrote concerning the French Declaration, "How could one thenceforth deny the reality of a system which it had cost so much to destroy?" Quoted in Berman, *Law and Revolution,* p. 42. With similar irony, F. W. Maitland wrote: "Now were an examiner to ask who introduced the feudal system into England? One very good answer, if properly explained, would be Henry Spelman. . . . If my examiner went on with his questions and asked, when did the feudal system attain its most perfect development? I should answer about the middle of the [eighteenth] century." Quoted in S. F. C. Milsom, introduction to Sir Frederic Pollock and F. W. Maitland, *History of the English Law before the Time of Edward I* (Cambridge, 1969), p. xxviii.
31. The use of the word "Renaissance" to characterize a historical period, namely, the late fifteenth and early sixteenth centuries in Italy, was introduced by the French historian Jules Michelet in the mid-nineteenth century and taken up shortly thereafter by the Swiss historian Jacob Burckhardt to signify an age of great achievements of artists and writers in that time and place. Otherwise it was a time and place of the greatest political and religious corruption and scandals. Despite the fact that virtually all scholars would agree with George Holmes that the term "Renaissance" is "an elastic term which has been used with a dozen different meanings" (*Renaissance* [London, 1996], p. 7), it keeps being used, and different authors, like Holmes, give it their own different meaning. It should simply be dropped.
32. Douglass C. North has been in the forefront of those economic historians who have emphasized the importance of legal institutions in facilitating the economics

of the West over the centuries. It is the principal theme of his voluminous writings on the economic history of the West—writings that have earned him the Nobel Prize in economics—that "well-specified and enforced property rights [are] a necessary condition for economic growth," and further, that it was the periodic establishment of secure property rights that accounts for the "rise of the West." See his essay "The Paradox of the West," in R. W. Davis, ed., *The Origins of Modern Freedom in the West* (Stanford, 1995), pp. 7–34. Among his major works are Douglass C. North and Robert Paul Thomas, *The Rise of the Western World* (Cambridge, 1973); Douglass C. North, *Structure and Change in Economic History* (New York, 1981); idem, *Institutions, Institutional Change, and Economic Performance* (Cambridge, 1990); Douglass C. North, Paul R. Milgrom, and Barry R. Weingast, *The Role of Institutions in the Revival of Trade: The Law Merchant, Private Judges, and the Champagne Fairs* (Stanford, 1990).

33. The original German title was *Die Protestantische Ethik und der "Geist" das Kapitalismus,* published in two parts in 1904 and 1905. The quotation marks around the word "spirit" *(Geist)* were omitted in the standard English translation by Talcott Parsons.
34. Max Weber, *Economy and Society: An Outline of Interpretive Sociology,* ed. Guenther Roth and Claus Wittich (New York, 1978), p. 53.
35. "Time is money. . . . Money can beget money, and its offspring can beget more. . . . He that murders a crown, destroys all that it might have produced even scores of pounds." Ibid., pp. 48–49.
36. Both Michael Walzer and Herbert Luthy, although they challenge Weber's thesis in many respects, endorse his belief that "asceticism" was carried over from sixteenth- and seventeenth-century Puritanism to nineteenth-century industrial capitalism. See Michael Walzer, *The Revolution of the Saints: A Study in the Origins of Radical Politics* (Cambridge, Mass., 1982), pp. 303–304; Herbert Luthy, "Variations on a Theme by Weber," in Menna Prestwich, ed., *International Calvinism, 1541–1715* (New York, 1985), pp. 382–384. The problem lies partly in the word "ascetic," which was originally applied to monastic life (Weber's "inner-worldly asceticism"), and which has come to mean austere, severe, disciplined, self-denying. As I have indicated, Weber applied it to the capitalist's alleged dedication to an "outer-worldly" calling to earn more and more money while avoiding all other enjoyments. But Weber himself recognized that authentic Calvinism, like other forms of Christianity, denounces greed as a mortal sin. Moreover, there is abundant evidence that sixteenth- and seventeenth-century Puritans, although they denounced drinking, gambling, and theatergoing, thoroughly enjoyed music, art, literature, athletics, and good food. Puritanism did stress hard work and did value success, but that did not distinguish it fundamentally from other branches of Christianity.
37. On the act incorporating the Greenland Company, see Samuel Williston, "History of the Law of Business Corporations before 1800," *Harvard Law Review* 2 (1888), 111. On the economic and legal history of the English joint-stock company, see William Robert Scott, *The Constitution and Finance of English, Scottish, and Irish Joint-Stock Companies to 1720,* 3 vols. (1912; reprint, Gloucester, Mass., 1968). See also Frank Evans, "The Evolution of the English Joint-Stock Limited Trading Company," *Columbia Law Review* 8 (1908), 339–361, 461–480. Unfortunately, these works do not discuss, but take for granted, the strong communitarian character—and philosophy—of this form of economic and legal enterprise.
38. 5 & 6 William & Mary c. 20 (1694).
39. See John Giuseppi, *The Bank of England: A History from Its Foundation in 1694*

(London, 1966), pp. 9–14 (discussing the origins of the Bank and the social backgrounds of its first investors and directors); *Rules, Orders, and By-Laws for the Good Government of the Corporation of the Governor and Company of the Bank of England,* reprinted in *Bank of England: Selected Tracts, 1694–1804* (Farmborough, Hants., 1968), p. 11 (on the weekly meetings of the Court of Directors) and p. 19 (on the biennial meetings of the General Court of shareholders). As in the case of the joint-stock company, so in the case of banking and other forms of crediting, there exists a large economic and legal literature which traces the origins of the modern form of these institutions to the latter half of the seventeenth century but which takes for granted, without stressing, their strong communitarian character. See, for instance, Frank T. Melton, *Sir Robert Clayton and the Origins of English Deposit Banking, 1658–1685* (Cambridge, 1986); P. G. M. Dickson, *The Financial Revolution in England: A Study in the Development of Public Credit, 1688–1756* (London, 1967); and James Steven Rogers, *The Early History of Bills and Notes: A Study of the Origins of Anglo-American Commercial Law* (Cambridge, 1995).

40. See Max L. Stackhouse, "A Premature Postmodern," *First Things* (October 2000), 20.

1. The Reformation of the Church and of the State, 1517–1555

1. In *The Age of Reform, 1250–1550* (New Haven, 1980), Steven Ozment writes: "Europeans suffered the worst famine of the Middle Ages between 1315 and 1317, and recurring poor harvests kept resistance to disease low when bubonic plague, following the trade routes from the east into and throughout western Europe, struck in mid-century. Many areas lost half of their population, and the overall decrease has been estimated at two-fifths of the previous total. By 1500 these losses had been fully recovered, and the sixteenth century became a period of steady, almost universal population growth. By gross estimate the Empire, France, and Italy were the largest countries, with 12 million people in the Empire, and 10 million in both France and Italy. There were 7.5 million in Spain and 3.5 million in England. By 1600 the population in the Empire had risen to 20 million, in France to 15 million, in Italy to 13 million, in Spain to 10 million, and in England to 5.5 million. Europe's overall population grew to an estimated 85 million by 1600 and stabilized in the seventeenth century at about 100 million.

"Cities and towns contained only a small fraction of the total population; an estimated nine out of ten Europeans lived in rural areas. This generalization is somewhat deceptive, however, for urban density could be greater in some areas (Germany, the Netherlands, and Italy) than in others (Spain). In Saxony, where the Reformation began, one in five was a townsman by 1550. Reflecting the general population growth, many cities and towns doubled in size during the sixteenth century, among them Naples (possibly Europe's largest city, with 200,000 in 1500), Seville, London, Milan, Cologne, and the three major Reformation centers, Augsburg, Nuremberg, and Strasbourg. Even areas like France, where religious and civil warfare took the lives of thousands, still registered population increases in the sixteenth century. Whereas only five cities could boast more than 100,000 people in 1500 (London, Paris, Florence, Venice, and Naples), at least a dozen could do so by 1600.

"Germany especially teemed with small towns. Of some 3,000 German towns at the turn of the century, 2,800 had populations under 1,000 and only fifteen could boast more than 10,000. Augsburg and Cologne, with populations between

25,000 and 30,000, were the largest. Wittenberg, the birthplace of the Reformation, was by comparison a small town of only 2,500. Zürich, the home of Zwinglian Protestantism, had a population of 6,000, and Geneva, where Calvinism began, held about 15,000 people within its walls when John Calvin arrived in 1536" (pp. 191–192). (For somewhat different population estimates of non-German European cities, see n. 68).

2. The eighth-century Latin translation of the original name for what is called in modern English "German," and in modern German "Deutsch," was *theodisca,* from which is derived the Italian *Tedeschi.* On the derivation of "Deutsch," see Eugen Rosenstock, "Unser Volksname Deutsch und die Aufhebung des Herzogtums Bayers" (1928), in Hans Eggers, ed., *Der Volksname Deutsch* (Darmstadt, 1970), pp. 32–102. The word *theod* was apparently a rendition of the native word for "people," or "folk," and was applied to the Carolingian imperial armed forces.
3. Previously the pope had been called vicar of Saint Peter and the emperor had been called vicar of Christ. See Berman, *Law and Revolution,* pp. 92–93.
4. Ibid., p. 503.
5. See C. P. Magill, *German Literature* (Oxford, 1974), pp. 1–17.
6. See Berman, *Law and Revolution,* pp. 503–505, 632–633.
7. Ibid., pp. 371–380.
8. Ibid., pp. 199–254. The swearing of an oath or a pledge of faith to perform an obligation would suffice to give the ecclesiastical court jurisdiction.
9. These figures are derived from the *Reichsmatrikel* (federal tax schedule) of the 1521 Diet of Worms, reproduced in Gerhard Benecke, *Society and Politics in Germany, 1500–1750* (London, 1974), pp. 382–393. It is not possible to determine a precise count of all the territorial units within the empire at any given time. Benecke himself states that the list is incomplete.
10. For a summary of German territorial law in the twelfth and thirteenth centuries, especially in Bavaria, see Berman, *Law and Revolution,* pp. 505–510 and sources cited therein. For the fourteenth and fifteenth centuries, see Karl Kroeschell, *Deutsche Rechtsgeschichte,* 8th ed., vol. 2 (1250–1600) (Opladen, 1992), pp. 59–125.
11. Universities were established at Prague (1348), Vienna (1365), Heidelberg (1386), Cologne (1388), Erfurt (1392), Leipzig (1409), Rostock (1419), Greifswald (1456), Freiburg (1457), Basel (1460), Ingolstadt (1472), Mainz (1476), and Wittenberg (1502). For data on Germans studying in France, Italy, and Germany from the fourteenth through the seventeenth centuries, see Adolf Stölzel, *Die Entwicklung des gelehrten Richtertums in den deutschen Territorien,* vol. 1 (1872; reprint, Aalen, 1964), pp. 45–111; Jacques Verger, *Les universités françaises au Moyen Age* (Leiden, 1995), pp. 122–173; and Marcel Fournier, "La nation allemand à l'Université d'Orléans au XIVe siècle," *Nouvelle revue historique de droit français et étranger* 12 (1888), 386–431.
12. See Karl Zeumer, *Quellensammlung zur Geschichte der Deutschen Reichsverfassung in Mittelalter und Neuzeit,* 2 vols. (Tübingen, 1913), vol. 1, pp. 173–176.
13. See Eugen Rosenstock-Huessy, *Out of Revolution: The Autobiography of Western Man* (1938; reprint, Providence, 1993), p. 374. Many of the insights of the present chapter, as of subsequent chapters in this book, are drawn from Rosenstock-Huessy's pioneering work, a revision of his earlier work in German titled *Die Europäischen Revolutionen: Volkscharaktere und Staatenbildung* (Jena, 1932).
14. In the eleventh century, with the Papal Revolution, popes asserted the power to distribute merits in purgatory equivalent to the time period of penance that would be required on earth to expiate the penitent's sins. These were "partial indulgences," normally given in terms of years, months, days, or "quarantines"

(Lenten periods). The term of indulgence referred not to the time of punishment but to the time of penance; that is, an indulgence of six years corresponded in value to six years lived under the penitential disciplines of the church. A "plenary" indulgence remitted the full temporal punishment incurred by a sinner. See Paul F. Palmer, *Sacraments and Forgiveness: History and Doctrinal Development of Penance, Extreme Unction, and Indulgences* (Westminster, Md., Newman Press, 1960), pp. 329–367 and 398–401. In the 1476 bull *Salvator Noster,* Pope Sixtus IV extended plenary indulgences for the first time to souls already in purgatory. B. J. Kidd, *Documents Illustrative of the Continental Reformation* (Oxford, 1911), pp. 3–4. This allowed the living to purchase indulgences on behalf of their deceased loved ones suffering in purgatory for sins not yet fully expiated.

15. The "treasury of merits" was the infinite reservoir of good works accumulated by Christ, the Virgin Mary, and the saints. It was administered by the pope. The theory of the treasury of merits was formalized in the 1343 bull *Unigenitus* of Clement VI. See Kidd, *Documents Illustrative of the Continental Reformation,* pp. 1–3.
16. See Martin Luther, *Address to the Christian Nobility,* vol. 44 of *Luther's Works* (Philadelphia, 1966), pp. 142–143.
17. John Wyclif (1320–1384) was a master at Oxford University whose views on religious doctrine foreshadowed those of Luther. Wyclif denied that the pope had authority over all Christendom, preaching instead a priesthood of all believers who stood in a direct relation to God. Like Luther, he translated portions of the Bible into the vernacular. Like Luther, he also rejected the church's eucharistic doctrine of transubstantiation. See Kenneth B. McFarlane, *John Wycliffe and the Beginnings of English Non-Conformity* (New York, 1953); Anthony Kenny, *Wyclif* (Oxford, 1985). Although Wyclif's followers, known as Lollards, were persecuted by English kings and put down in a 1414 revolt, small communities of Lollards survived until the Reformation reached England in the sixteenth century. See John A. F. Thomson, *The Later Lollards, 1414–1520* (London, 1965).
18. Jan Hus (1369–1415), a dean at the University of Prague who was ordained in 1400, studied Wyclif's writings and was strongly influenced by his reform ideas. In his principal work, *De Ecclesia* (1415), he asserted, as did Wyclif, a priesthood of all believers and a church in which Christ, not the pope, was the head. Condemned as a heretic, Hus went to the Council of Constance to defend his views. Despite a letter of safe conduct from the emperor Sigismund, the council condemned Hus to be burned at the stake in 1415. See Matthew Spinka, *John Hus' Conception of the Church* (Princeton, 1966), and *John Hus, A Biography* (Princeton, 1968). Hus's death made him a martyr for Czech nationalism. In 1420 the emperor preached a crusade against the Hussites, as the adherents of reform had become known. The first Hussite Wars (1420–1434) ended in a compromise which established an autonomous Bohemian church and secularized monastic lands. Later outbreaks occurred periodically until 1571. In the sixteenth century, Bohemia proved fertile ground for both Lutheranism and Calvinism. See Josef Macek, *The Hussite Movement in Bohemia* (Prague, 1958), and Howard Kaminsky, *A History of the Hussite Revolution* (Berkeley, 1967).
19. See Henry Kamen, *The Spanish Inquisition: An Historical Revision* (London, 1997), pp. 174–213. At this time a series of Roman pontiffs were more concerned with consolidating their power in local Italian politics and commissioning grand works of art than tending to the spiritual well-being of the church. The Fifth Lateran Council (1512–1517), convened under Julius II and Leo X with the avowed purpose of reforming Christendom, succeeded in little more than establishing a new concordat with France and reasserting the doctrine of immortality. It ended

seven months before Luther posted his Ninety-five Theses. See Hubert Jedin, *A History of the Council of Trent,* vol. 1 (New York, 1949); Richard J. Schoeck, "The Fifth Lateran Council: Its Partial Successes and Its Larger Failures," in Guy Fitch Lytle, ed., *Reform and Authority in the Medieval and Reformation Church* (Washington, D.C., 1981), pp. 99–126.

20. The German text is reproduced in Heinrich Koller, ed., *Reformation Kaiser Siegmunds* (Stuttgart, 1964); an English translation is provided in Gerald Strauss, *Manifestations of Discontent in Germany on the Eve of the Reformation* (Bloomington, Ind., 1971), pp. 3–31. For commentary and discussion, see Lothar Graf zu Dohna, *Reformatio Sigismundi: Beitrag zum Verständnis einer Reformschrift des fünfzehnten Jahrhunderts* (Göttingen, 1960).

21. Reforms of municipal laws, called reformations, took place in Cologne (1437), Nuremberg (1479), Hamburg (1497), Worms (1499), and Frankfurt (1509). See Franz Wieacker, *A History of Private Law in Europe, with Particular Reference to Germany,* trans. Tony Weir (Cambridge, 1995), pp. 143–167 (hereafter Wieacker, *History of Private Law*).

22. Myron Gilmore, *The World of Humanism,* 1453–1517 (New York, 1952).

23. Marsilius proposed that the church be governed by a general council of clergy and laity. Also his theory of penance anticipated Luther's in its rejection of the priestly power of absolution. See Alan Gewirth, *Marsilius of Padua: The Defender of Peace,* vol. 1 (New York, 1951), pp. 260, 262, 265–268, and 283–292.

24. Article 36: "Any Christian whatsoever who is truly repentant enjoys plenary remission from penalty and guilt, and this is given him without letters of indulgence." Article 37: "Any true Christian whatsoever, living or dead, participates in all the benefits of Christ and the Church; and this participation is granted to him by God without letters of indulgence." Article 76: "We assert to the contrary, and say that the pope's pardons are not able to remove the least venial of sins as far as their guilt is concerned." A translated text of the Ninety-five Theses is printed in John Dillenberger, ed., *Martin Luther: Selections from His Writings* (Garden City, N.Y., 1961), pp. 489–500.

25. Luther's writings to which this discussion refers may be found in Dillenberger, *Martin Luther;* Thomas M. McDonough, *Law and Gospel in Luther: A Study of Martin Luther's Confessional Writings* (London, 1963); and Heinrich Bornkamm, *Luther's Doctrine of the Two Kingdoms in the Context of His Theology,* 2nd. ed. (Philadelphia, 1966).

26. "A Commentary on St. Paul's Epistle to the Galatians" (1531), trans. in Dillenberger, *Martin Luther,* pp. 144–145.

27. See Martin Luther, *D. Martin Luthers Werke: Kritische Gesamtausgabe* (hereafter *WA*) (Weimar, 1883), p. 390.

28. See Martin Luther, "The Sermon on the Mount," in Jaroslav Pelikan, ed., *Luther's Works* (hereafter *LW*), 55 vols. (St. Louis, 1956), vol. 21, esp. p. 108 (arguing that "it is the duty and obligation of those who participate in this earthly regime to administer law and punishment, to maintain the distinctions that exist among ranks and persons, and to manage and distribute property"); Martin Luther, "Whether Soldiers, Too, Can Be Saved," in J. M. Porter, ed., *Luther: Selected Political Writings* (Lanham, Md., 1974), esp. pp. 1–5 (asserting that "there is no doubt that the military profession is in itself a legitimate and godly calling and occupation"). See also Martin Luther, "On War against the Turk," in Porter, *Luther,* pp. 124–125 (proposing "to teach . . . how to fight with a good conscience").

29. See Martin Luther, "Secular Authority: To What Extent It Should be Obeyed"

(1523), in Dillenberger, *Martin Luther,* pp. 382–392; Martin Bucer, "De Regno Christi," in Wilhelm Pauck, ed., *Melanchthon and Bucer* (Philadelphia, 1969), bk. 2, chap. 1 ("By What Ways and Means the Kingdom of Christ Can and Should Be Reformed by Devout Kings").

30. *WA,* 32: 394.
31. See Luther, "Secular Authority," p. 366; and idem, "An Appeal to the Ruling Class of German Nationality as to the Amelioration of the State of Christendom," in Dillenberger, *Martin Luther,* p. 411.
32. See Jean Bodin, *On Sovereignty: Four Chapters from Six Books of the Commonwealth,* ed. and trans. Julian H. Franklin (Cambridge, 1992), p. 23 ("the main point of sovereign majesty and absolute power consists of giving the law to subjects in general without their consent"); Glenn Burgess, "The Divine Right of Kings Reconsidered," *English Historical Review* 107 (1992), 837, 842 ("the essential feature of absolutism was its claim that the king alone was superior to the positive law and not bound by it"). See generally Julian H. Franklin, *Jean Bodin and the Rise of Absolutist Theory* (Cambridge, 1973); cf. Michael Stolleis, *Geschichte des öffentlichen Rechts in Deutschland, Erster Band: Reichspublistik und Policeywissenschaft,* 1600–1800 (Munich, 1988), pp. 172–186.
33. See Luther's exegesis of the Fourth Commandment in his *Large Catechism,* in *WA,* 30:132–182.
34. Posted by Luther in October 1917, the Theses reprinted in Magdeburg and Leipzig in November. A German translation appeared in Basel in December. Bernd Moeller can find no records of contemporary translations of the Theses into vernacular languages other than German. See Bernd Moeller, "Luther in Europe: His Works in Translation, 1517–46," in E. I. Kouri and Tom Scott, eds., *Politics and Society in Reformation Europe* (London, 1987), pp. 237–238. Thus the principal direct impact of the Theses outside Germany would have been confined to audiences reached by persons able to read Latin. Yet the literate classes in Europe probably read Latin as much as they read the vernacular, and the non-literate could be reached by Latin-reading preachers and scholars. Moeller states (pp. 24–25): "The theses struck an extraordinarily responsive chord. In retrospect Luther later said that they 'almost raced through all of Germany in fourteen days.' Even if this assertion is tempered somewhat by the relatively small number of reprintings, still the success of this piece of scholastic and scholarly writing is thoroughly remarkable." Moeller also cites Luther's contemporary Oecolampadius, who stated that the Theses "were distributed with amazing speed throughout Germany and were welcomed with special favor by all of the learned." See Bernd Moeller, *Imperial Cities and the Reformation: Three Essays* (Philadelphia, 1972), p. 24 and n. 10.
35. See Ozment, *Age of Reform,* p. 401.
36. See Roland H. Bainton, *Here I Stand: A Life of Martin Luther* (Nashville, 1950), pp. 185–186.
37. De Lamar Jensen, *Confrontation at Worms: Martin Luther and the Diet of Worms* (Provo, Utah, 1973), pp. 75–111.
38. See generally Steven Ozment, *When Fathers Ruled: Family Life in Reformation Europe* (Cambridge, Mass., 1983).
39. Robert Scribner, "Incombustible Luther: The Image of the Reformer in Early Modern Germany," *Past and Present* 110 (1986), 47–50.
40. Cf. Ozment, *Age of Reform,* p. 231.
41. "Distinguished alike in the translation of the Bible, the composition of the cate-

chism, the reform of the liturgy, and the creation of the hymnbook, Luther was equally great in the sermon preached from the pulpit, the lectures delivered in the class hall, and the prayers voiced in the upper room. His versatility is genuinely amazing. No one of his own generation was able to vie with him." Bainton, *Here I Stand,* p. 346.

42. In his earlier years Luther wrote in a more friendly way about Judaism, hoping thereby to facilitate conversion of Jews to Christianity. In this respect he appears to have been less antagonistic to them than the Roman Catholics on the whole had been in earlier centuries, and especially in the period of the late-fifteenth-century Inquisition in Spain, Portugal, and Italy. Under both Roman Catholicism and Protestantism, Jews who converted to Christianity were not discriminated against, and Jews who did not so convert were permitted to undertake certain types of economic activities and were often protected therein by both ecclesiastical and secular authorities. The vast majority of Jews, however, were required to live in ghettos and to wear distinctive yellow badges on their clothing and were treated as outcasts from the prevailing civil society. Indeed, they were periodically expelled from particular countries or, within a country, from particular cities. Luther's later vitriolic and inflammatory attacks on Jews, as on Turks, although they fed the overt racist culture of the time, should be taken as religiously rather than racially motivated. As Heiko Oberman has said: "The harshness of those attacks may be explained by the fact that in his later years he spoke out of a pressing eschatological belief that he was living in an end-time, in which the true Church was threatened by three powerful enemies, namely, aberrant Christians led by the Bishop of Rome, infidel Turks then at war with Christians in the Balkans, and Jews, the chosen people, who refused to acknowledge Jesus as the Messiah." See Heiko A. Oberman, *The Roots of Anti-Semitism in the Age of Renaissance and Reformation* (Philadelphia, 1984), pp. 104–105. A somewhat contrary view is that of Mark U. Edwards, *Luther's Last Battles: Politics and Polemics, 1531–1546* (Ithaca, N.Y., 1983), p. 31. See also Salo W. Baron, *A Social and Religious History of the Jews,* 2nd ed. rev. and enl., vol. 13 (New York, 1965), pp. 253ff.; Ronnie Po-Chia Hsia, "Jews," in Hans Joachim Hillerbrand ed., *The Oxford Encyclopedia of the Reformation,* vol. 2 (Oxford, 1996), pp. 340ff. See also Chapter 4.
43. See David V. N. Bagchi, *Luther's Earliest Opponents: Catholic Controversialists, 1518–1525* (Minneapolis, 1991); John S. Oyer, *Lutheran Reformers against Anabaptists: Luther, Melanchthon, and the Anabaptists of Central Germany* (The Hague, 1964), esp. pp. 114–139.
44. See Berman, *Law and Revolution,* p. 94; Orville Prescott, *Lords of Italy: Portraits from the Middle Ages* (New York, 1972), p. 43.
45. On October 31, 1517, Luther wrote to the archbishop of Mainz, asking him to revoke his instructions concerning indulgences. Included in the letter was a copy of the Ninety-five Theses. The latter provoked strong reaction, in particular from the Ingolstadt theologian Johann Eck. Luther responded to attacks on him by writing a set of "Resolutions," in which he elaborated the Ninety-five Theses. He gave a copy of the Resolutions to be forwarded to Pope Leo X, asking for the pope's support against the pope's Dominican "inquisitors." See Martin Brecht, *Martin Luther: His Road to Reformation* (Philadelphia, 1985), pp. 190–192, 218–219.
46. Ibid., p. 369.
47. In notifying Duke Frederick the Wise that he was leaving his Wartburg Castle, Luther wrote sharply to him, saying: "I have no mind to ask for Your Grace's protection; nay, I hold that I could protect Your Grace more than he could protect me . . . he who believes most will protect most; and because I believe that Your

Grace is still weak in the faith, I cannot by any means think of Your Grace as the man who could protect or save me." The letter is quoted in full in Rosenstock-Huessy, *Out of Revolution*, pp. 388–389.

48. See Hans Hillerbrand, *Landgrave Philipp of Hesse* (St. Louis, 1967).
49. These included Andreas Karlstadt (1486–1541), who taught at Wittenberg with Luther but eventually broke with him over infant baptism and the Eucharist; Thomas Müntzer (ca. 1491–1525), who was present in Wittenberg in 1517–18 and began to preach the Reformation in 1519, but who sided with the peasants during the Peasants' War and was captured and executed in May 1525; and the Swiss priest Huldrych Zwingli (1484–1531), who began to preach the Reformation in Zürich in 1519 but who rejected Lutheran teaching on baptism and the real presence of Christ in the Eucharist. He died in fighting that broke out among the Swiss cantons in 1531. On Karlstadt, see Calvin Augustine Pater, *Karlstadt as the Father of the Baptist Movements: The Emergence of Lay Protestantism* (Toronto, 1984). On Müntzer, see Hans-Jürgen Goertz, *Thomas Müntzer: Apocalyptic, Mystic, and Revolutionary*, trans. Jocelyn Jaquiery, ed. Peter Matheson (Edinburgh, 1993). On Zwingli, see Joachim Rogge, *Anfänge der Reformation: Der junge Luther (1483–1523), der junge Zwingli (1484–1523)*, 2nd ed. (Berlin, 1985); and W. Peter Stephens, *The Theology of Huldrych Zwingli* (Oxford, 1985).
50. On the reformations in the cities, see generally Steven E. Ozment, *The Reformation in the Cities: The Appeal of Protestantism to Sixteenth-Century Germany and Switzerland* (New Haven, 1975); and Bernd Moeller, *Imperial Cities and the Reformation: Three Essays*, ed. and trans. H. C. Erik Midelfort and Mark U. Edwards, Jr. (Philadelphia, 1972), pp. 41–115.
51. See William P. Hitchcock, *The Background of the Knights' Revolt, 1522–1523* (Berkeley, 1958); Hajo Holborn, *Ulrich von Hutten and the German Reformation* (New Haven, 1937).
52. See Bernd Moeller, "The German Humanists and the Reformation," in *Imperial Cities*, p. 23 (documenting Luther's criticism of Erasmus). Moeller states: "In general, one can conclude that the humanists, unlike Luther, stood on the foundations of medieval Catholicism" (p. 29).
53. On relations between Luther and Calvin, and on similarities and differences between Lutheran and Calvinist theology, see Chapter 7.
54. See Franz Lau and Ernst Bizer, *A History of the Reformation in Germany to 1555*, trans. Brian A. Hardy (London, 1969), p. 78.
55. On the actions of the Schmalkaldic League in the 1530s and 1540s, see Hajo Holborn, *A History of Modern Germany*, vol. 1, *The Reformation* (New York, 1959), pp. 215–217; Lewis W. Spitz, *The Protestant Reformation, 1517–1559* (New York, 1987), pp. 117–121.
56. For the text of the Peace of Augsburg, see Sidney Z. Ehler and John B. Morrall, eds., *Church and State through the Centuries* (London, 1954), pp. 164–173. The peace did not extend to "non-German" parts of the empire, including the Netherlands, Switzerland, and Franche-Comté.
57. See Herman Tuchle, "The Peace of Augsburg: New Order or Lull in the Fighting," in Henry J. Cohn, ed., *Government in Reformation Europe, 1520–1560* (London, 1971), p. 155.
58. This provision was issued as a supplement to the text and was not recognized as imperial law. The staunchly Catholic Emperor Charles V could not in good conscience recognize the apostasy of bishops and archbishops who had abandoned the "ancient Christian and Catholic religion." The inevitability of such a recognition led him to entrust authority over the Augsburg Diet to his brother Ferdinand

and ultimately to abdicate to him the imperial throne. See Tuchle, "Peace of Augsburg," pp. 147–148.

59. Ibid., p. 166.

60. Henry J. Cohn, "The Territorial Princes in Germany's Second Reformation, 1559–1622," in Menna Prestwich, ed., *International Calvinism, 1541–1715* (Oxford, 1985), pp. 135–166.

61. Of the seven imperial electors, only those of Saxony and Brandenburg were Protestant in 1555. The conversion of the elector of the Palatinate in 1556, however, added a third, leaving only four Catholic electors—the three ecclesiastical electors and the king of Bohemia. The possibility of a Protestant majority among the electors arose first in the early 1580s, when the Roman Catholic archbishop-elector of Cologne married according to the Lutheran rite and was deposed. Also, the assumption of the Bohemian crown by the elector of the Palatinate in 1616 again temporarily tipped the balance in favor of a Protestant majority. In none of these instances, however, was there a vacancy to be filled.

62. In terms of the political struggle in Germany itself, the following results were reached. All of northern Germany east of the Weser River, including Prussia, was Protestant. The Protestant principalities of Hesse, Nassau, and Saxony dominated the central regions. Although southern Germany remained largely Roman Catholic, Protestantism had made inroads in the Palatinate, Ansbach, and Württemberg. Although both Roman Catholicism and Lutheranism were tolerated in all the imperial free cities, the majority of them chose Lutheranism, and of the major ones only Aachen and Cologne remained largely Roman Catholic. Enclaves of Catholic rule survived in three regions: to the east and south, Austria and Bavaria; in central Germany, the three Main River bishoprics of Bamberg, Mainz, and Würzburg, together with the abbey of Fulda in Franconia; and in the west, most of the ecclesiastical territories in the Rhineland and Westphalia, including the archbishoprics of Trier and Cologne and the bishoprics of Münster, Paderborn, and Strasbourg. Yet even in these Catholic territories Protestantism continued to win converts.

63. A. G. Dickens, *The German Nation and Martin Luther* (New York, 1974), p. 5.

64. Ibid., p. 182.

65. See generally Steven Ozment, *Protestants: The Birth of a Revolution* (New York, 1992).

66. R. W. Scribner, in attempting to "provide a brief sociology of the reform movement," states, "To say that it found adherents among all social groups is an unhelpful truism." R. W. Scribner, *The German Reformation* (Atlantic Highlands, N.J., 1986), p. 25. He goes on to say: "What we need to know for an adequate sociology is whether its adherents were drawn disproportionately from one social group or another, and whether there were significant differences in how each group understood its message. We should also examine any differences between leaders and followers, and whether there was any differential appeal in terms of age, gender, occupation or profession and wealth." Scribner concedes that "at this stage of the research, it is difficult to provide firm answers to all these questions." Nevertheless, "we now have enough case-studies to risk a crude sketch." Scribner's sketch does not, however, effectively challenge the thesis that virtually the entire German people was involved in the Reformation on one side or another and that by their reciprocal interactions all groups, including the vanquished as well as the victors, made it what it was. If one is seeking to tell the story of *what* happened, and *how* it happened, this is by no means an "unhelpful truism," even though

it does not fully answer the question of *why* it happened. That question itself, however, points not only to its causes but also to its consequences, which, indeed, substantially affected "all social groups."

67. See n. 1. See also Paul Bairoch, Jean Batou, and Pierre Chèvre, *The Population of European Cities: Data Bank and Short Summary of Results* (Geneva, 1988), pp. 6–68, where it is stated that Paris in 1500 had 225,000 souls, Naples had 125,000, Milan and Venice 100,000 each, and Prague and Grenada 70,000 each, and that other cities with populations over 50,000 included Lisbon, Tours, Rome, London, Ghent, Bordeaux, Lyon, Bologna, Florence, Genoa, Palermo, and Verona.
68. Ozment, *Age of Reform*, p. 192; see also Ozment, *Reformation in the Cities*, pp. 121–131; Robert M. Kingdon, *Transition and Revolution: Problems and Issues of European Renaissance and Reformation History* (Minneapolis, 1974), pp. 53–107; Lewis W. Spitz, "Humanism in Germany," in Anthony Goodman and Angus MacKay, *The Impact of Humanism on Western Europe* (London, 1990), pp. 202–219 (documenting the fifteenth-century dissemination of humanist ideals into Germany).
69. See Moeller, *Imperial Cities*, pp. 41–42.
70. See Peter Blickle, *The Revolution of 1525: The German Peasants' War from a New Perspective*, trans. Thomas A. Brady, Jr., and H. C. Erik Midelfort (Baltimore, 1981), p. 165.
71. Ibid., pp. 187–188. In Freiburg, however, and perhaps in some other cities, serious rifts existed between peasant rebels and poor urban dwellers. See Tom Scott, *Freiburg and the Breisgau: Town-Country Relations in the Age of Reform and Peasants' War* (Oxford, 1986), pp. 212–213.
72. See Blickle, *Revolution of 1525*, p. 195. The report of the twelve Articles is drawn largely from Blickle's account.
73. See ibid., pp. 148, 189, 192–193.
74. See ibid., pp. 165–169.
75. See ibid., pp. 170–180.
76. Steven E. Ozment, *Protestants: The Birth of a Revolution* (London, 1993), p. 30.
77. See the essays collected in Ole Peter Grell, ed., *The Scandinavian Reformation: From Evangelical Movement to Institutionalisation of Reform* (Cambridge, 1995). Religious toleration was only introduced in Sweden and Finland in 1781, in Denmark in 1844, in Norway in 1845, and in Iceland in 1874.
78. The Ninety-five Theses were preached in Gdansk in the summer of 1518. By the 1550s, however, Polish Protestantism was badly fractured, and featured a strong radical, anti-trinitarian element, known as the Polish Brethren, existing side by side with mainstream Lutherans and Calvinists. See Stanislas Lubieniecki, *History of the Polish Reformation and Nine Related Documents*, trans. George Huntston Williams (Minneapolis, 1995); George Huntston Williams, *The Radical Reformation* (Philadelphia, 1962), pp. 404–416 and 639–669. Cf. Paul Fox, *The Reformation in Poland: Some Social and Economic Aspects* (Baltimore, 1924). It was primarily the divided nature of Polish Protestantism that allowed the Roman Catholic reaction to score a number of successes in Poland beginning in the 1560s and caused the collapse of Polish Protestantism by the middle decades of the seventeenth century. See George Huntston Williams, *The Polish Brethren: Documentation of the History and Thought of Unitarianism in the Polish-Lithuanian Commonwealth and in the Diaspora, 1601–1685*, Harvard Theological Studies, no. 30, 2 vols. (Missoula, Mont., 1980). The Teutonic order was dissolved elsewhere later. Bohemia, the present-day Czech Republic, had been the scene some one hundred years

before of Jan Hus's Czech religious movement, and substantial Hussite sympathies were still detectable in 1517.

79. The name "Huguenots" seems to have been derived from a French shortening of the German word *Eidgenossen,* "confederates," used by Protestant opponents of the duke of Savoy in the 1520s.
80. On the development of Lutheranism in France, see Denis Crouzet, *La genèse de la réforme française, 1520–1560* (Paris, 1996); and Mark Greengrass, *The French Reformation* (Oxford, 1987). On the Edict of Nantes, see Bernard Cottret, 1598, vol. 1, *Édit de Nantes, pour en finir avec les guerres de religion* (Paris, 1997).
81. On the Dutch Inquisition, see Edward Grierson, *The Fatal Inheritance: Philip II and the Spanish Netherlands* (Garden City, N.Y., 1969), pp. 55–56 and 66–72.
82. For analysis of the use of the terms "Counter-Reformation" and "Catholic Reformation," see H. Outram Everett, *The Spirit of the Counter-Reformation* (Cambridge, 1968), and Hubert Jedin, *Katholische Reformation oder Gegenreformation? Ein Versuch zur Klärung der Begriffe* (Lucerne, 1946).
83. Francisco Ximenes de Cisneros, *Biblia Complutensis* (Rome, 1983).
84. In 1536 Vitoria founded a famous school at Salamanca, whose pupils included such future "greats" as Soto, Lessius, Molina, and Suarez. Vitoria himself published nothing, but his pupils published under his name what he had taught them. Vitoria taught in vain that the Spanish repression of conquered peoples of South America was a violation of international law. His conception of the relationship of the Old World to the New was based "upon the fundamental principle that possession should follow discovery to confer a title, and that the barbarians held title to their 'principalities' . . . upon an equality with the kingdoms of Spain and France." See James Brown Scott, *The Spanish Origin of International Law: Francisco de Vitoria and His Law of Nations* (Oxford, 1934), pp. 106–107. Scott rightly emphasized the importance of Vitoria's insistence that the conquered "barbarians" of Latin America were entitled to full rights under the law of nations. The notion, however, that Vitoria's writings on this and other subjects constituted the origin of modern international law has been shown to be untrue, although it was widely accepted until the last decades of the twentieth century. Grotius, who is usually considered to be the founder of modern international law, did indeed draw on the works of Vitoria and other sixteenth-century Spanish jurists, but no more than he drew on the work of many others, and the doctrine of the universality of international law and its extension to non-Christian peoples was widely held as early as the twelfth and thirteenth centuries. See Brian Tierney, *The Idea of Natural Rights: Studies on Natural Rights, Natural Law, and Church Law* (Atlanta, 1997), pp. 333–342. Tierney points out that Grotius employed a vocabulary that originated with the twelfth-century canonists. See also Landau, "Der Einfluss des kanonischen Rechts," pp. 50–52.
85. On the similarities and differences between sixteenth-century Spanish neo-scholastic and sixteenth-century German Lutheran legal philosophy and legal sciences, see Chapter 2, n. 144, and Chapter 3.
86. See Wolfgang Reinhard, "Konfession und Konfessionalisierung in Europa," In Wolfgang Reinhard, ed. *Bekenntis und Geschichte: Die Confessio Augustana im historischen Zusammenhang* (Munich, 1981), pp. 165–189; cf. Wolfgang Reinhard, "Reformation, Counter-Reformation, and the Early Modern State: A Reassessment," *Catholic Historical Review* 75 (1989), 383, 390, and n. 24 (summarizing subsequent research on the issue of confessionalization).
87. See Ronald H. Asch, *The Thirty Years' War: The Holy Roman Empire and Europe, 1618–1648* (New York, 1997), p. 76.

88. See Leo Gross, "The Peace of Westphalia, 1648–1948," *American Journal of International Law* 42 (1948), 20, 21–22 (reviewing the religious provisions of the treaty); and Herbert Langer, 1648*: Der Westfälische Frieden. Pax Europaea und Neuordnung des Reiches* (Berlin, 1994), pp. 11–69 (reviewing the structure of the Peace).
89. See Martin Luther quoted in Gerald Strauss, *Law, Resistance, and the State: The Opposition to Roman Law in Reformation Germany* (Princeton, 1986), p. 14.
90. See Owen Chadwick, *The Reformation* (Grand Rapids, Mich., 1965), p. 189.
91. Steven Ozment, *Protestants: The Birth of a Revolution* (New York, 1992), p. 29.
92. That the transition from the *Ständestaat* to the *Fürstenstaat* took place, and that the prince's officialdom took charge, may be judged from the mass of complaints that were made against their bureaucratic rule. See Gerald Strauss, *Luther's House of Learning: Indoctrination of the Young in the German Reformation* (Baltimore, 1978), p. 159: "Protests from all over Germany accused *Amtleute, Vögte, Pfleger, Keller, Schergen, Schosser, Schreiber, Landsknechte, Knechte, Unterknechte* of high-handed behavior." These are all names for various kinds of officials.
93. See Otto Brunner, *Lord and Lordship,* trans. James van Horn Melton (Philadelphia, 1992).

2. Lutheran Legal Philosophy

This chapter draws partly on an article written by the author jointly with John Witte, Jr., titled "The Transformation of Western Legal Philosophy in Lutheran Germany," *Southern California Law Review* 62 (1989), 1573–1660. See also Harold J. Berman, "Conscience and Law: The Lutheran Reformation and the Western Legal Tradition," *Journal of Law and Religion* 5 (1987), 177–202.

1. Ernst Cassirer, quoted in Herman Dooyeweerd, *Rechtsphilosophie und der Rechtswetenschap* (Amsterdam, 1946), p. 93.
2. Two fairly recent books in which sixteenth-century Lutheran jurists are discussed briefly are Ian Maclean, *Interpretation and Meaning in the Renaissance: The Case of Law* (Cambridge, 1992), and Donald R. Kelley, *The Human Measure: Social Thought in the Western Legal Tradition* (Cambridge, Mass., 1990). Neither author, however, relates the theories of the Lutheran jurists to Lutheranism. Maclean identifies theories of Lutheran jurists such as Christoph von Hegendorph, Johann Apel, and Johann Oldendorp as "humanist" and links them with those of non-Lutheran humanists such as Cantiuncula, Alciato, and Hotman. The name "Luther" and the word "Reformation" do not appear in his index. Kelley discusses briefly various Lutheran theological and political beliefs, and also makes scattered references to Lutheran legal thinkers such as Apel, von Hegendorph, and Konrad Lagus, but he does not draw connections between the theories of the Lutheran jurists and Lutheran theological and political doctrines. Neo-Thomist jurisprudence in sixteenth-century Spain has been treated in many works, again, however, without reference to contemporary Protestant legal thought. See, for example, James R. Gordley, *The Philosophical Origins of Modern Contract Doctrine* (Oxford, 1991), dealing with the contributions to the philosophy of contract law of Vitoria, Molina, Soto, and other sixteenth-century neo-Thomist Spanish theologians. On the relation of sixteenth-century neo-Thomist Spanish legal philosophy to sixteenth-century Lutheran German legal philosophy, see n. 144.
3. Franz Wieacker notes in a cryptic paragraph that Luther at first denied man's ability to have knowledge of natural law but that "when Lutheran theology subse-

quently returned to natural law, it linked up with the Aristotelianism of the Thomists, although with an emphasis on Ciceronian thinking which betrays the influence of Melanchthon's humanism, and a stronger focus on the Decalogue, which testified to the progress of the Reformation." Wieacker, *History of Private Law,* p. 209; see also p. 471. Wieacker devotes a few paragraphs to the Lutheran jurist Oldendorp's theory of natural law (pp. 224–225), and two short paragraphs to Luther's colleague Johannes Apel (p. 117), but he treats them more as humanists than as Lutherans and nowhere spells out what is distinctive in Lutheran legal thought. Likewise Helmut Coing, in *Europäisches Privatrecht,* Band 1, *Älteres Gemeines Recht (1500 bis 1800)* (Munich, 1985), pp. 229–232, deals only cursorily with Lutheran jurisprudence, although he does analyze briefly Lutheran ecclesiastical law and family law. Coing also refers briefly to Oldendorp's topical method (p. 21) and devotes a short paragraph to Apel's application of the distinction between proximate cause and remote cause to property transfers (p. 179). Neither Coing nor Wieacker, who are generally considered to be the two leading historians of German law in the second half of the twentieth century, mentions Vigelius, Kling, and other great Lutheran jurists. They mention Melanchthon in passing but ignore his writings on law.

Similarly, Hans Hattenhauer's massive history of European law deals only cursorily with the impact of the Reformation on law, stating that "if one asks of [the sixteenth-century Protestant churches] what consequence the Reformation had for civil and criminal law, the law of the common man, the answer of the Lutherans, above all, would turn out to be thin [*düftig*]. . . . [Luther's] follower, the jurist Oldendorp (1480–1567), undertook to write a book about equity in the year 1529. But if one looks for significant jurists who came from the Lutheran Reformation and brought forth something fundamentally new, the result is modest. Luther created no effective impulse in jurisprudence for the whole of Europe. Great European theologians and musicians, poets and educators, came forth from his teaching, but the jurists of his school influenced very little of Europe's law. The center of gravity of European jurisprudence shifted from Rome not to Wittenberg but to France and Bourges." Hans Hattenhauer, *Europäische Rechtsgeschichte* (Heidelberg, 1992), p. 367. Hattenhauer mentions only one of Oldendorp's many works and none by Apel, Lagus, Kling, Vigelius, or even Melanchthon.

4. See Ernst Troeltsch, *Protestantism and Progress: A Historical Study of the Relation of Protestantism to the Modern World,* trans. William Montgomery (Boston, 1958), p. 101.
5. See Berman, *Law and Revolution,* pp. 143–151 and 275–276.
6. Schuerpf (1481–1554) served as the "best man" at Luther's wedding. He stood by when Luther burned the canon law books in 1520, and he accompanied Luther to the Diet of Worms in 1525 and spoke there on his behalf. It was Schuerpf's example most of all, Luther wrote later in his life, that "inspired me [in 1517] to write of the great error of the Catholic Church." Quoted by Theodor Muther, *Aus dem Universitäts- und Gelehrtensleben im Zeitalter der Reformation* (Erlangen, 1866), p. 190. For further information on Schuerpf, see ibid.; Roderich von Stintzing, *Geschichte der deutschen Rechtswissenschaft,* 3 vols. (Munich, 1880–1884), 1:267–268 (hereafter Stintzing, *Geschichte der Rechtswissenschaft*); and Melanchthon's panegyric, *Oratio de Vita Clarissimiviri Hieronymi Schurffi,* in *Corpus Reformatorum,* 28 vols. (Frankfurt am Main, 1834–1860) (hereafter *CR*), 12:86. Stintzing and Muther were the two leading historians of German law in the latter half of the nineteenth century.

   Apel (1486–1536) attended Luther's wedding, strongly endorsed Luther's writings on marriage and the family, and, after leaving the university in 1529, frequently corresponded with him. Luther had come to Apel's aid in 1523 when Apel was imprisoned for marrying a former nun in violation of the canon law and in defiance of his archbishop. He, in turn, strongly endorsed Apel's tract *Defensio pro Suo Coniugio* (1524) and wrote a foreword to an amicus curiae brief submitted to the local ecclesiastical tribunal on Apel's behalf. For further information on Apel, see Stintzing, *Geschichte,* pp. 287ff.; Muther, *Aus dem Universitäts,* pp. 455ff.; Theodor Muther, *Doctor Johann Apel: Ein Beitrag zur Geschichte der deutschen Jurisprudenz im sechszehnten Jahrhundert* (Königsberg, 1861); Franz Wieacker, *Gründer und Bewahrer: Rechtslehrer der neueren deutschen Privatrechtsgeschichte* (Göttingen, 1959), pp. 44ff.

Luther was also a friend of other lawyers, including Basilius Monner (ca. 1501–1566), Melchior Kling (1504–1571), Gregor Brueck (n.d.), Hieronymous Baumgartner (d. 1565), and Johannes Schneidewin (1519–1568). These friendships did not, of course, prevent Luther from berating the legal profession of his day for its avarice, apathy, and indifference to the demands of justice and the needs of society. See Hermann Wolfgang Beyer, *Luthers und das Recht: Gottes Gebot, Naturrecht, Volksgesetz in Luthers Deutung* (Munich, 1935), pp. 51–54; Karl Köhler, *Luther und die Juristen: Zur Frage nach dem gegenseitigen Verhältniss des Rechts und der Sittlichkeit* (Gotha, 1873); Gerald Strauss, *Law, Resistance, and the State: The Opposition to Roman Law in Reformation Germany* (Princeton, 1986), pp. 215–218.

7. See the collection of quotations in Jaroslav Pelikan, *Spirit versus Structures: Luther and the Institutions of the Church* (New York, 1968), pp. 20–24.
8. Luther's writings on social and political questions, their titles here translated into English, include: "Shorter Sermon on Usury" (1519); "Longer Sermon on Usury" (1520); "An Appeal to the Ruling Class of German Nationality as to the Amelioration of the State of Christendom" (1520); "On Married Life" (1522); "A Sermon from the Gospel on the Rich Man and the Poor Lazarus" (1523); "On Temporal Authority: To What Extent It Should be Obeyed" (1523); "Against Wrong and False Imperial Mandates" (1523); "A Letter to the Mayor, Council, and Community of the City of Muehlhausen" (1524); "To the Council Members in the Cities of German Territories" (1524); "That Parents Should Not Compel Their Children to Marriage" (1524); "On Trade and Usury" (1524); "Against the Rapacious and Murdering Hordes of Peasants" (1525); "Whether Soldiers Too Can Be Saved" (1527); "On the Keeping of a Community Chest" (1528); "Concerning War against the Turks" (1529); "A Sermon on Keeping Children in School" (1530); "On Marriage Matters" (1530). For his correspondence with jurists, see Hans Liermann, "Der unjuristisches Luther," *Luther-Jahrbuch* 24 (1957), 69–85.
9. For further discussion of Luther's legal and political views, see W. D. J. Cargill Thompson, *The Political Thought of Martin Luther,* (Totowa, N.J., 1984); Johannes Heckel, *Lex Charitatis: Eine juristische Untersuchung über das Recht in der Theologie Martin Luthers* (Munich, 1963); Paul Althaus, *The Ethics of Martin Luther,* trans. Robert C. Schultz (Philadelphia, 1972), pp. 25–35, 112–154; Beyer, *Luther und das Recht;* Ferdinand Edward Cranz, *An Essay on the Development of Luther's Thoughts on Justice, Law, and Society* (Cambridge, Mass., 1959).
10. Although Luther often deprecated Roman law, he occasionally also gave it unstinted praise. See, e.g., *WA,* 30:557 ("our government in these German lands shall and must adhere to the Roman imperial law, which is the wisdom and reason inherent in all politics, and a gift of God") and 51:242 (Roman law is a paradigm of "heathen wisdom"). Nevertheless, Luther continued to criticize specific provisions of Roman law, such as those relating to slavery, marriage and family, and

property. See, e.g., *WA*, 12:243ff.; 16:537; 14:591, 714. For more general treatments, see Strauss, *Law, Resistance, and the State*, pp. 201–202; Heckel, *Lex Charitatis*, pp. 82–85.

11. *WA*, 40:305; see also 51:242 ("natural law and natural reason form the heart and source of all written law"); cf. 17:102.
12. *WA*, 51:242–243. Luther's exaltation of reason in matters of law and politics, and his detraction of reason in matters of doctrine and belief, is predicated on the two kingdoms theory, which separates the spiritual knowledge and activity of the heavenly kingdom, based on faith, from the temporal knowledge and activity of the earthly kingdom, based on reason. This ontological distinction allows Luther, on the one hand, to dismiss reason as "the devil's whore" and "Aristotle's evil brew" when it intrudes on the heavenly kingdom and, on the other hand, to treat it as "a divine blessing" and "an indispensable guide to life and learning" when it remains within the earthly kingdom. See, generally, Bernhard Lohse, *Ratio und Fides: Eine Untersuchung über die ratio in der Theologie Luthers* (Göttingen, 1958), pp. 70–72; Brian Albert Gerrish, *Grace and Reason: A Study in the Theology of Luther* (Oxford, 1962), pp. 10–27, 57–68, and 84–99.
13. Bernhard Lohse writes: "Since the days of high scholasticism a distinction had been made on the basis of earlier linguistic usage between between *synteresis* and *conscientia* in connection with what we call conscience. In general, *synteresis* was regarded as an ability of the soul, not entirely corrupted by the Fall, to incline toward the good, whereas *conscientia* makes practical application of the principles of *synteresis*. Whether, following Thomas [Aquinas] or Duns [Scotus], *synteresis* is primarily associated with the reason or, following Bonaventura [or Ockham], with the will . . . makes little difference. In any case, the basic design remained the same." See Bernhard Lohse, "Conscience and Authority in Luther," in Heiko Obermann, ed., *Luther and the Dawn of the Modern Era: Papers for the Fourth International Conference for Luther Research* (Leiden, 1974), p. 159.
14. See Emmanuel Hirsch, *Luther studien*, vol. 1 (Gütersloh, 1954), pp. 127–128.
15. Quoted in Friedrich Julius Stahl, *Die Kirchenverfassung nach Protestanten*, 2d ed. (Erlangen, 1862), p. 37.
16. Cf. Luther, "Secular Authority: To What Extent It Should be Obeyed," in John Dillenberger, *Martin Luther: Selections from His Writings* (Garden City, N.Y., 1961), pp. 368–369.
17. On Luther's doctrine of the uses of the law *(usus legis)*, see John Witte, Jr., and Thomas Arthur, "The Three Uses of the Law: A Protestant Source for the Purposes of Criminal Punishment," *Journal of Law and Religion* 10 (1994), 433–465; Frank Alexander, "Validity and Function of Law: The Reformation Doctrine of Usus Legis," *Mercer Law Review* 31 (1980), 514–519; Cranz, *Essay on the Development of Luther's Thoughts*, pp. 94–112; Wilfried Joest, *Gesetz und Freiheit: Das Problem des Tertius usus legis bei Luther und die neutestametliche Parainese* (Göttingen, 1956); Werner Elert, "Eine theologische Faelschung zur Lehre von Tertius usus legis," *Zeitschrift für Religions- und Geistesgeschichte* 2 (1948), 168–170.
18. *WA*, 10:454.
19. Although Luther generally spoke of the "civil use" as the "first use of the law," and the "theological use" as the "second use of the law" (see, e.g., *WA*, 10:454, 40:486ff.), nevertheless "for Luther the primary emphasis is on the theological use of the law . . . particularly later in his career." Alexander, "Validity and Function of Law," p. 515.
20. *WA*, 15:302.

21. *WA,* 4:3911, 4733ff.
22. Romans 7:7–25; Galatians 3:19–22. See Dillenberger, *Martin Luther,* pp. 14ff., and discussion in Cranz, *Essay on the Development of Luther's Thoughts,* pp. 112ff.
23. See, generally, Adolf Harnack, *History of Dogma,* trans. Neil Buchanan, vol. 7 (New York, 1958), p. 206; Joest, *Gesetz,* pp. 196ff.; Werner Elert, *Law and Gospel,* trans. Edward H. Schroeder (Philadelphia, 1967), pp. 38ff.; Gerhard Ebeling, *Word and Faith,* trans. James W. Leitch (Philadelphia, 1963), p. 75. For a discussion of the controversy over the place of the third use of the law in early and later Lutheran theology, see Ragnar Bring, *Gesetz uns Evangelium und der dritte Gebrauch des Gesetzes in der lutherische Theologie* (Berlin, 1943).
24. See, for example, *Apology of the Augsburg Confession* (1529), art. 4, in *Triglot Concordia: The Symbolic Books of the Ev. Lutheran Church* (St. Louis, 1921), pp. 127, 161, 163, where Melanchthon speaks of the virtues that the law teaches. In the 1535 edition of his *Loci Communes Rerum Theologicorum* (written four years later), Melanchthon describes this "legal instruction in virtue" as the third use of the law. See *CR,* 21: 405–406. Luther approved of both these writings by Melanchthon. In several places in his writings, Luther also suggests the idea of, if not the term, the pedagogical use of the law. Cf. *WA,* 10: 454; see also the collection of maxims under the rubric "Of Princes and Potentates," in *The Table Talk or Familiar Discourse of Martin Luther* trans. William Hazlitt (London, 1848), pp. 135–136. It is clear from these and other passages that for Luther, law could serve not only as a harness against sin and an inducement to grace but also as a teacher of Christian virtue.
25. H. Fild, "Justitia bei Melanchthon" (Diss., Erlangen, 1953), p. 150.
26. Wilhelm Dilthey, *Weltanschauung und Analyse des Menschen seit Renaissance und Reformation: Gesammelte Schriften* (Leipzig, 1921), p. 193.
27. Cf. K. Hartfelder, *Philip Melanchthon als Praeceptor Germaniae* (1889; reprint, Nieuwkoop, 1964); James William Richard, *Philip Melanchthon, the Protestant Preceptor of Germany* (New York, 1898).
28. See Philip Melanchthon, "De Corrigendis Adolescentiae Studiis," in Robert Stupperich, ed., *Melanchthons Werke in Auswahl,* 7 vols. (Gütersloh, 1955–1983), 3:29–42.
29. For further biographical information on Melanchthon, see Hartfelder, *Philip Melanchthon;* Wilhelm Maurer, *Der junge Melanchthon zwischen Humanismus und Reformation,* 2 vols. (Göttingen, 1967–1969).
30. A number of earlier scholars have argued that since Melanchthon achieved fame not only as a theologian but also as a humanist, his outlook differed in important respects from that of Luther. Thus Otto Ritschl dismisses Melanchthon as a "distorter of pristine Lutheran doctrine." See Otto Ritschl, *Dogmengeschichte des Protestantismus: Grundlagen und Grundzüge der theologischen Gedenken- und Lehrbildung in den protestantischen Kirchen,* 4 vols. (Leipzig, 1908–1927), 2:39. See also Franz Hildebrandt, *Melanchthon: Alien or Ally?* (Cambridge, 1946). For a survey of this genre of literature, see Robert Stupperich, *Melanchthon,* trans. Robert H. Fischer (Philadelphia, 1965), pp. 128–135; and Wilhelm Hammer, *Die Melanchthonforschung im Wandel Jahrhunderte: Ein Beschriebendes Verzeichnis* (Gütersloh, 1967). More recent writers, however, have lauded Melanchthon as the greatest systematizer of Lutheran doctrine. Thus Ernst Troeltsch wrote: "It was not Luther, but Melanchthon who determined fully what the exact consistency of Lutheranism was to be. He was the chief teacher and instructor, the scholarly publicist, and the theological diplomat of Lutheranism; as such he passed Luther's ideas through the sieve of his formulations." Quoted in Michael Rogness, *Philip Me-*

lanchthon: Reformer without Honor (Minneapolis, 1969), p. vii. See also Sachiko Kusukawa, *The Transformation of Natural Philosophy: The Case of Philip Melanchthon* (Cambridge, 1995), p. 4: "Melanchthon saw in natural philosophy a potent response to issues which he believed to be seriously jeopardizing Luther's cause; he reinterpreted classical and contemporary authors along Lutheran principles; and he made natural philosophy an integral part of a pedagogy which was aimed at establishing and consolidating Luther's message."

31. Concerning Melanchthon's chief theological writing, the *Loci Communes Rerum Theologicarum,* Luther wrote: "We possess no work wherein the whole body of theology, wherein religion is more completely summed up than in Melanchthon's *Loci communes;* all the Fathers, all the compilers of sentences, put together, are not to be compared with this book. It is after the Scriptures the most perfect of works." Luther, *Table Talk,* p. 21. After Luther's death, Lutheran theologians became divided for a time between so-called Phillipists, who were followers of Melanchthon, and so called Gnesio-Lutherans, who opposed the Phillipists. The differences between them were not great, and after the publication of the *Book of Concord* in 1580 the two groups came together.
32. See Adolf Sperl, *Melanchthon zwischen Humanismus und Reformation* (Munich, 1959), pp. 141–170.
33. For analysis of Melanchthon's jurisprudence, see Guido Kisch, *Melanchthons Rechts- und Solziallehre* (Berlin, 1967); C. Bauer, "Melanchthons Rechtslehre," *Archiv für Reformationsgeschichte* 42 (1951), 64–100. See also Kusukawa, *Transformation,* pp. 165–167 and 176–178.
34. See Heinrich Bornkamm, "Melanchthons Menschenbild," in Walter Elliger, ed., *Philip Melanchthons Forschungsbeiträge zur Vierhundertsten Wiederkehr seines Todestages* (Berlin, 1961), pp. 76–90.
35. See Karl Gottlieb Bretschneider and Heinrich Ernst Bindseil, eds., *Philippi Melanchthonis Opera Quae Supersunt Omnia, CR,* 13:150 and 647. In *CR,* 21:712, Melanchthon calls these elements of knowledge "a natural light in the intellect [*naturalis lux in intellectu*]," "a light of the human faculty [*lux humani ingenii*]," "a divine light ingrafted on the mind [*lumen divinitus insitum mentibus*]."
36. Melanchthon writes: "For just as there are in theoretical disciplines, such as mathematics, certain common principles, common concepts, or assumptions, such as that 'the whole is greater than the parts,' so there are in morals certain common principles and first axioms which constitute the ground rules of all human functions. These you will rightly call the laws of nature." *CR,* 21:117. Melanchthon connects these first principles to an inborn awareness of the first principles of the Ten Commandments: "[The term] law of nature signifies natural elements of knowledge concerning morals, that is, practical principles and right axioms and necessary consequences arising from these principles. These elements of knowledge are revealed in their best and most appropriate form in the Decalogue, which is the epitome and summary of the law of nature." Quoted in Stupperich, *Melanchthons Werke,* 3:208.

    Melanchthon describes his general theory of the inborn elements of knowledge in greater detail in his *Compendaria Dialectices Ratio* (1520), *CR,* 20:748; and *De Loci Communibus Ratio* (1526), *CR,* 20:695. See also Dilthey, *Weltanschauung,* p. 162. Dilthey describes Melanchthon as "the middle link [*Mittelglieder*] who . . . combined the natural knowledge of God and the world as revealed in the renewed classics with faithful piety as revealed in the renewed Christendom. In this universal spirit a balance was struck between Humanism and Reformation." Dilthey, *Weltanschauung,* p. 162.

37. Melanchthon, quoted by Dooyeweerd, *Rechtsphilosophie,* 2:58.
38. See Dilthey, *Weltanschauung,* pp. 175–176. Cf. Berman, *Law and Revolution,* p. 175.
39. See *CR,* 16:70–72.
40. See *CR,* 13:547–555; and 21:116–117 and 399–400. Melanchthon distinguished, however, between theoretical principles *(principia theoretica),* which he defined as the principles and axioms of geometry, arithmetic, physics, dialectics, and other (what we would today call) exact sciences, and practical principles *(principia practica),* which he defined as the principles and norms of ethics, politics, law, and theology, arguing that man's rational knowledge of theoretical principles is far less distorted by sin than is his rational knowledge of practical principles. *CR,* vol. 21, cols. 398–400 and 711–713.
41. In his *Annotationes in Evangelium Matthei,* in Stupperich, *Melanchthons Werke,* Melanchthon states that "natural and divine law order man to do that which the power of human nature is incapable of doing. . . . Nor can the law bring us to those things which satisfy the law . . . [for] sin holds us fast." Elsewhere, Melanchthon adduces in support of his view the strong language of Saint Paul in Romans 1:18–20: "For the wrath of God is revealed from heaven against all ungodliness and wickedness of men who by their wickedness suppress the truth. For what can be known about God is plain to them, because God has shown it to them. Ever since the creation of the world his invisible nature, namely his eternal power and deity, has been clearly perceived." *CR,* 21:401–402.
42. *CR,* vol. 16, col. 23.
43. Ibid., col. 24.
44. Melanchthon states: "In order more easily to understand natural laws, the best method is to use the Decalogue. It is to the Decalogue that we must accommodate the laws of nature." *CR,* vol. 21, col. 392. Elsewhere, he states: "Why then did God proclaim the Ten Commandments? . . . Answer: There are many important reasons for this open magisterial proclamation, but two are especially important. [First,] in the wake of sin, the light in human reason was not as clear and bright as before. . . . Against such blindness, God not only proclaimed his law on Mount Sinai but has sustained and upheld it since the time of Adam in his Church. . . . The second reason is that it is not enough that man know that he is not to kill other innocent men, nor rob others of their wives and goods. One must first of all know God's nature and know that God earnestly wants us to be like him, and that he is enraged against all sin. Therefore he proclaims his commandments himself, that we may know that they are not only in our minds but are God's law, that God is the judge and executor against all sin, that our hearts may recognize God's wrath and tremble before it. . . . God also proclaims his law because human reason without God's word soon falls into error and doubt. If God himself had not graciously proclaimed his wisdom, men would fall still further into doubt about God's nature, right and wrong, order and disorder." *CR,* vol. 21, cols. 256–257. Cf. Maurer, *Der junge Melanchthon,* 1:288–290; and Bauer, "Melanchthons Rechtslehre," pp. 67–71.
45. Like Luther, and like the earlier scholastics, Melanchthon distinguished three types of biblical laws—the ceremonial, judicial, and moral laws. Only the moral law (which was summarized in the Decalogue, as well as in the Golden Rule, the Beatitudes, and various injunctions in Paul's letters) remained in effect after Christ. The ceremonial laws (dealing with sacrifices, rites, feasts, and similar matters) and judicial laws (dealing with forms of Old Testament monarchical government, law, and similar matters) were no longer binding. See *CR,* vol. 21, cols.

294–296 and 387–392. See also Wilhelm Pauck, ed., *Melanchthon and Bucer* (Philadelphia, 1969), pp. 53–57 (translating Melanchthon's treatment of the ceremonial laws in the *Loci Communes*).

46. There are at least three traditions for numbering and arranging the Ten Commandments: the Judaic tradition, the Greek Orthodox tradition (also followed by some non-Lutheran Protestant groups), and the tradition established by Saint Augustine, which is followed both in the Roman Catholic Church and by Lutheran theologians. In the Augustinian tradition, which Melanchthon followed, the first three commandments are assigned to the first table of the Decalogue, and the last seven to the second table. (In the Hebrew Bible the commandments are not numbered at all, and there is no punctuation to separate their various parts. See Exodus 20:1–17; Deuteronomy 5:6–21. Indeed, they are called not "commandments" but "words," *d'vorim.*) For a more detailed treatment of the three traditions of numbering, and references for further reading, see Berman and Witte, "Transformation of Western Legal Philosophy," pp. 1619–20, n. 114.
47. Thomas Aquinas, *Summa Theologiae,* pt. I–II, qu. 98, art. 5.
48. See, for example, Angelus de Clavasio, *Summa Angelica de Casibus Conscientiae* (Venice, 1481), section on "Poenitentia." See also Rudolf Weigand, *Die Naturrechtslehre der Legisten und Dekretisten von Irnerius bis Accursius und von Gratian bis Johannes Teutonicus* (Munich, 1967), pp. 220, 438–439 (discussing Huguccio, Laurentius, and Raymond de Penafort on the Ten Commandments). Steven Ozment states, concerning fourteenth- and fifteenth-century Catholic views of the Ten Commandments: "In the late fourteenth and the fifteenth centuries, the Ten Commandments replaced the Seven Deadly Sins as the main guideline for oral catechesis and confession. This was an important shift which enlarged the areas of religious self-scrutiny of and by the laity. At no other time were the Ten Commandments so zealously promoted and carefully expounded." Steven E. Ozment, *The Reformation in the Cities* (New Haven, 1975), p. 17.
49. See Martin Luther, *Large Catechism,* in *Triglot Concordia,* pp. 166–215; and Melanchthon, *CR,* vol. 22, col. 220.
50. *CR,* vol. 22, col. 153.
51. *CR,* vol. 21, col. 716.
52. See Clyde L. Manschreck, ed. and trans., *Melanchthon on Christian Doctrine: Loci Communes,* 1555 (New York, 1965), p. 123; *CR,* vol. 22, col 250.
53. See *CR,* vol. 22, col. 250.
54. Ibid., col. 151.
55. See Manschreck, *Melanchthon,* p. 122; *CR,* vol. 22, col. 249.
56. See *CR,* vol. 21, cols. 69–70 and 250–251.
57. Melanchthon makes clear that not only the divine law (i.e., the Ten Commandments) but also the civil law serves both to make men aware of their depravity and to impel them to grace. Thus, "all punishments through the [Obrigkeit] and others should remind us of God's wrath against our sin, and should warn us to reform and better ourselves." Manschreck, *Melanchthon,* p. 56; cf. *CR,* vol. 22, col. 152.
58. *CR,* vol. 21, col. 250. For Melanchthon's theory of the uses of the law, see Philip Melanchthon, *Epitome Renovatae Ecclesiasticae Doctrinae, CR,* vol. 1, cols. 706–709; *Oratio de Legibus, CR,* vol. 11, col. 66; and Manschreck, *Melanchthon,* pp. 122–128. The doctrine of the threefold uses of the law was repeated in later sixteenth-century Lutheran confessions and catechisms, notably *The Formula of Concord,* pt. 6 ("of the Third Use of the Law"), in *Triglot Concordia,* p. 805: "The law was given to men for three reasons: first, that thereby outward discipline

might be maintained and wild and intractable men may be coerced by certain rules; second that men thereby may be led to the knowledge of their sins; third, that men who have already been reborn . . . may on this account have a fixed rule according to which they can and ought to form their whole life." The doctrine also found a prominent place in Calvinist theology. See John Calvin, *Institutes of Christian Religion,* chap. 7.

59. See Pauck, *Melanchthon and Bucer,* pp. 138–140. Luther sets forth his thesis that man is at once saint and sinner *(simul iustus et peccator)* in *LW,* 21:205. See also *LW,* 5:50, where Luther states: "Man has a twofold nature, a spiritual one and a bodily one. According to the spiritual nature, which men refer to as the soul, he is called a spiritual, inner, or new man. Accordng to the bodily nature, which men refer to as the flesh, he is called the carnal, outer, or old man."
60. Manschreck, *Melanchthon,* p. 127.
61. See *CR,* 1:706–708.
62. Ibid., at cols. 707–708. Cf. Köhler, *Luther und die Juristen:* "The emphasis on the pedagogical character [of the state and its law] is much stronger in Melanchthon than in Luther. Initially, Melanchthon had maintained Luther's view that the *Obrigkeit* exists to punish crimes and to maintain peace. Subsequently, however, he modified his position: the *Obrigkeit* should serve not only to preserve external peace and harmony [in society] but also to ensure that persons live properly [within this society]. Instruction *(disciplina)* and a sense of obligation *(pietas)* are the goals which the *Obrigkeit* must seek to attain through the instrument of the positive law." See also Strauss, *Law, Resistance, and the State,* p. 228: "[For Melanchthon,] law is part of a *paedagogica politica* capable of mending public mores."
63. See Werner Elert, "Zur Terminologie der Staatslehre Melanchthons und seiner Schüler," *Zeitschrift für systematischen Theologie* 9 (1932), 522–534.
64. See *CR,* vol. 11, cols. 69–70, and vol. 21, col. 1011; Manschreck, *Melanchthon,* pp. 328–331.
65. See *CR,* vol. 21, cols. 611–612: "But I say rational laws, that is, those that follow the natural law which God has created in people. That one should honor virtue and punish vice." See also *CR,* vol. 16, col. 230, where Melanchthon speaks of the "rationes iuris positivi."
66. *CR,* vol. 16, col. 87 ("magistratus est custos primae et secundae tabulae legis"). See also *CR,* vol. 22, col. 286: "The worldly *Obrigkeit* . . . should be a voice of the Ten Commandments" within the earthly kingdom.
67. See *CR,* vol. 16, cols. 87–88, and vol. 22, cols. 615–617; Manschreck, *Melanchthon,* p. 335.
68. *CR,* vol. 22, cols. 617–618.
69. *CR,* vol. 22, col. 610.
70. The concept *Gemeinnutz,* or "common good," was a dominant theme of sixteenth-century German law reform. A German scholar has written that for Melanchthon, "the common good becomes the model for the religious and moral education which church and state have to undertake. The state is a teacher of virtue *(paedogogium virtutis),* its policy is directed to facilitating progress *(foelicitatis progressum),* its final goal is eternal blessedness. . . . For Melanchthon the political order *(ordo politicus)* is synonymous with common weal *(salus publica)* . . . and history is viewed optimistically as progress." Ludwig Zimmerman, *Der hessissche Territorialstaat im Jahrhundert der Reformation* (Marburg, 1933), pp. 384, 386.
71. *CR,* vol. 22, col. 615.
72. Ibid., col. 224.

73. For Melanchthon's discussion of contracts, see *CR,* vol. 16, cols. 128–152, 251–269, 494–508 *(Dissertatio de contractibus);* Manschreck, *Melanchthon,* p. 116; and Stupperich, *Melanchthons Werke,* 2:802–803.
74. For Melanchthon's views of marriage and the family, see *CR,* vol. 16, col. 509; vol. 21, col. 1051; vol. 22, col. 600; vol. 23, col. 667. See also Stupperich, *Melanchthons Werke,* 2:801–802. For a detailed treatment of the Lutheran theory and law of marriage in the sixteenth century, see John Witte, Jr., *From Sacrament to Contract: Marriage, Religion, and Law in the Western Tradition* (Louisville, Ky., 1997), pp. 42–73.
75. Quoted by Emil Sehling, *Kirchenrecht* (Leipzig, 1908), pp. 36–37. Cf. Philip Melanchthon, *Instruction to Visitors,* ibid., vol. 1, pt. 1, pp. 149–152 and 163–165.
76. See *CR,* vol. 16, cols. 241, 469, 570; vol. 22, cols. 227 and 617; and Sehling, *Kirchenrecht,* vol. 1, pt. 1, p. 149. Melanchthon writes in summary, in *CR,* vol. 22, cols. 617–618: "God-fearing rulers are obliged for the properties of the Church to supply necessary offices, pastors, schools, church buildings, courts, and hospitals. It is not right to allow these properties to be squandered by idolatrous, idle, immoral monks and canons. Also it is not right for rulers to take possession of these properties unless they decree proper assistance for pastors, schools, and courts." For further discussion, see P. Meinhold, *Philip Melanchthon, der Lehrer der Kirche* (Berlin, 1960), pp. 40, 94; Hans Liermann, *Deutsches evangelisches Kirchenrecht* (Stuttgart, 1933), pp. 150ff.; Richard Nürnberger, *Kirche und weltliche Obrigkeit bei Melanchthon* (Würzburg, 1937); Wilhelm Maurer, "Überden Zusammenhang zwischen Kirchenordnungen und christlicher Erziehung in den Anfängen lutherischer Reformation," in *Die Kirche und ihr Recht: Gesammelte Aufsätze zum evangelischen Kirchenrecht* (Tübingen, 1976), pp. 254–278.
77. *CR,* vol. 21, cols. 223–224.
78. Romans 13:1–7.
79. *CR,* vol. 22, col. 613. Cf. Manschreck, *Melanchthon,* p. 333.
80. See particularly *CR,* vol. 11, col. 66. For further discussion, see Kisch, *Melanchthons Rechts- und Soziallehre,* p. 86; Köhler, *Luther und die Juristen,* p. 103; Albert Haenel, "Melanchthon der Jurist," *Zeitschrift für Savigny Stiftung für Rechtsgeschichte* (hereafter *ZSS*) *(Rom. Abt.)* 8 (1869), 249–270.
81. Quoted by Kisch, *Melanchthons Rechts- und Soziallehre,* p. 177. See further discussion in *CR,* vol. 11, cols. 73 and 552.
82. See *CR,* vol. 11, cols. 921–922.
83. See *CR,* vol. 11, cols. 218ff., 357ff., 630ff., and 922ff.
84. See particularly Philip Melanchton, *De Irnerio et Bartolo Iurisconsultis Oratio Recitata a D. Sebaldo Munsero* (1537), in *CR,* vol. 11, col. 350. For further discussion, see Kisch, *Melanchthons Rechts- und Soziallehre,* p. 117; and Haenel, "Melanchon der Jurist."
85. For an account of Melanchthon's connections with numerous leading German jurists, as a teacher, colleague, and/or correspondent, see Guido Kisch, "Melanchthon und die Juristen seiner Zeit," in *Mélanges Philippe Meylan* (Lausanne, 1963), 2:135.
86. Quoted by Kisch, *Melanchthons Rechts- und Solziallehre,* pp. 113ff.
87. *CR,* vol. 11, col. 358 ("Romanum ius . . . quandam philosophiam esse").
88. Köhler, *Luther und die Juristen,* p. 125: "Melanchthon in particular was held in the highest regard by jurists both within and without Germany. Leading legal scholars recommended strongly his *Elements of Ethical Doctrine* to young students, for nowhere else were the sources of law so clearly set forth. Especially in Witten-

berg there was formed under the personal influence of [Melanchthon] a school of jurists who in their lives and in their jurisprudence strongly manifested the new religious movements of the time."

89. P. Macke, "Das Rechts- und Staatsdenken des Johannes Oldendorp" (Inaugural diss., n.d.; date of oral examination May 25, 1966). Most of the biographical material presented here is derived from Hans-Helmut Dietze, *Johann Oldendorp als Rechtsphilosoph and Protestant* (Königsberg, 1933). See Erik Wolf, *Grosse Rechtsdenker der deutschen Geistesgeschichte,* vol. 3 (Tübingen, 1951), pp. 129–132; Sabine Pettke, "Zur Rolle Johann Oldendorps bei der offiziellen Durchführung der Reformation in Restock," *ZSS (Kan. Abt.)* 101 (1984), 339–348. Cf. Otto Wilhelm Krause, *Naturrechtler des sechszehnten Jahrhunderts: Ihre Bedeutung für die Entwicklung eines natürlichen Privatrechts* (Frankfurt am Main, 1982), pp. 115–125.
90. Stintzing, *Geschichte der Rechtswissenschaft,* p. 311. Stintzing called Oldendorp "the most significant of the German jurists of the middle of the sixteenth century." Ernst Troeltsch described him as the "most influential jurist" ("massgebendster Jurist") of the age of the Reformation. Ernst Troeltsch, *Die Soziallehren der christlichen Kirchen und Gruppen,* Bd. 1 of *Gesammelte Schriften* (Tübingen, 1912), p. 545, n. 253.
91. The year of Oldendorp's birth remains a point of controversy. The date 1480 is accepted by Stintzing (*Geschichte der Rechtswissenschaft,* p. 311). More recently, however, Wieacker (*History of Private Law,* p. 283) has given Oldendorp's birthdate as 1486. Macke, "Rechts- und Staatsdenken des Oldendorp," has adopted the date 1488. Even later dates have been argued by other historians. Either 1486 or 1488 seems more plausible in light of Oldendorp's career.
92. Macke, "Rechts- und Staatsdenken des Oldendorp," p. 9; Dietze, *Johann Oldendorp,* p. 59; and Köhler, *Luther und die Juristen,* p. 127.
93. See Stintzing, *Geschichte der Rechtswissenschaft,* p. 323. Oldendorp's full response to the Landgrave is instructive: "First, Your Eternal Princely Grace, the Praise, the Honor, and the Betterment of this land and the entire German nation—the study of law (which after God's word is the most important pursuit and study) should be organized not only in light of the Word, but in accordance with it in deed; the Word must be its starting point and its guide. And when the true teaching of virtue through written laws and equity is required (as I have seen some do and Philip Melanchthon surely helps in this), [Your Eternal Princely Grace] and other estates will be relieved of much deception and aversion."
94. Oldendorp wrote at least fifty-six separate tracts, of which three are in Old German and the rest are in Latin. The German writings are among the earliest. The fullest bibliography of Oldendorp's writings is given in Dietze, *Johann Oldendorp,* pp. 18–21. Macke's bibliography ("Rechts- und Staatsdenken des Oldendorp," pp. viii–xi), while not as exhaustive as Dietze's, includes six works not found in Dietze. Two of the German works have been translated into modern German and published in Erik Wolf, *Quellenbuch zur Geschichte der deutschen Rechtswissenschaft* (Frankfurt am Main, 1949). These are *Was billig und recht ist* (1529) (hereafter *Billig und recht*) and *Ratmannenspiegel* (1530). A number of Oldendorp's Latin works have been reprinted as Johann Oldendorp, *Opera,* 2 vols. (Aalen, 1966), including the *Isagoge Iuris Naturalis Gentium et Civilis* (1539) (hereafter *Isagoge*) and many of his studies of Roman law. The *Isagoge* and the *Divinae Tabulae X Praeceptorum* (ca. 1539) are reproduced in edited form in Carl von Kaltenborn, *Die Vorläufer des Hugo Grotius* (Leipzig, 1848), pp. 1–25. (Kaltenborn

mistakenly identifies the *Divinae Tabulae* as Title 5 of the *Isagoge,* though the two works were written separately.) Subsequent citations of the *Isagoge* are to Kaltenborn's edition. More than twenty of Oldendorp's works are to be found in the Treasure Room, Langdell Library, Harvard Law School.

95. Oldendorp wrote: "Ius . . . idem est quod lex" (Law . . . is the same as a law). "Law [*Recht*], or the laws [*Gesetze*], is [sic] twofold: written and unwritten" ("Recht, oder die Gesetze . . . ist zweierlei, geschrieben und ungeschrieben"). Under written law he included the civil law (Roman law) and positive law, and under unwritten law he included custom, the law of nations, and natural law. See also *Isagoge,* p. 57, where he put customary law on an equal level with enacted law.

96. Conscience, for Oldendorp, is a form of reason. Cf. Krause, *Naturrechtler,* p. 118: "*Ratio* and revelation are two independent ways of ascertaining the natural law. Oldendorp, however, saw *ratio* as the first source of natural law. Only when *ratio* fails should man resolve his doubt through the Decalogue, and here again, it is reason that we use to draw conclusions from the divine commandments. Equating the Decalogue with natural law unmistakably separated Oldendorp from the teachings of Melanchthon. Oldendorp tried to show that *ratio* is a divine spark in a spoiled human nature and that this was the primary source of natural law. Oldendorp, however, was still very far from being a typical rationalist, nor did he believe in the supremacy of reason because in the end . . . reason is free [only] so long as it does not contradict divine commandments." Krause also points out that for Oldendorp the Decalogue "built an ideal order and foundation for human coexistence, but contained no concrete rules of law, only very general principles." Krause is wrong, however, in suggesting that Melanchthon did not "equate" the Decalogue with natural law. See the discussion of Melanchthon and natural law earlier in this chapter.

97. See Oldendorp, *Isagoge,* p. 15: "The divine tables restore and describe law [*ius*] and the law of nature [*lex naturae*] with such a sure testimony that there can be no variation [between them]." See also *Divinae Tabulae,* p. 17: "Since . . . the natural elements of knowledge in persons have been obscured because of original sin, a merciful God has restored and described them on tables of stone so that there would be a sure testimony that these laws of nature are confirmed by the word of God, which he has also inscribed on the souls of men."

98. Quoted in Macke, "Rechts- und Staatsdenken des Oldendorp," pp. 30–31: "Natura: hoc est, Deus creator omnium." See also *Isagoge,* p. 6: "Nature [stands] for God himself, who is the first cause from whom all causes flow."

99. *Billig und recht,* p. 57. I have substituted "natural law" for the word "equity" *(Billigkeit)* in the original quotation; Oldendorp uses the two synonymously.

100. Quoted in Dietze, *Johann Oldendorp,* p. 81.

101. *Divinae Tabulae,* pp. 15–25. See the further discussion in *Naturrechtler,* pp. 118–122.

102. See Oldendorp, *Opera,* 2:286–288. In these pages Oldendorp adopts not only the Aristotelian analysis of "causes" but also the Aristotelian concept of liberality as "the wise disposition of a person's resources, giving to the right people the right amounts and at the right time," and the Aristotelian concept of commutative equality as the equivalence in value of the resources exchanged. On the application of these Aristotelian concepts to contract law by sixteenth-century Spanish jurists, see James Gordley, "Contract Law in the Aristotelian Tradition," in Peter Benson, ed., *The Theory of Contract Law* (Cambridge, 2001), pp. 265, 297, and 307.

103. *Isagoge,* p. 13.

104. Ibid., pp. 12–13. See also the collection of quotations from other works of Oldendorp in Macke, "Rechts- und Staatsdenken des Oldendorp," pp. 49–50. Of slavery,

Oldendorp writes: "Although slaves are by all means men, created in the image of God, they are driven into the rank of brute beasts; . . . all these [rules] concerning strict servitude were introduced into civil law against natural law. Therefore they are not to be obeyed" (p. 50). A similar quotation appears in the *Isagoge,* p. 13.

105. See *Billig und recht,* pp. 60–62. Oldendorp urged citizens "to enhance the common good as the highest ideal. For by serving the common good, you help not only one person but many."

106. Immanuel Kant, *Critique of Pure Reason,* trans. Norman Kemp Smith (London, 1929), A/32–B/71, A/34–B74, and discussion in Ken Kress, "Legal Indeterminacy," *California Law Review* 77 (1989), 283, 332–333. This is similar to the position Lon L. Fuller took in his classic debate with H. L. A. Hart, "Positivism and Fidelity to Law: A Reply to Professor Hart," *Harvard Law Review* 71 (1958), 630, 669–670. Hart's position was that each rule has "a core of settled meaning," and that it is only in the "penumbral" cases that it becomes unclear how to apply the rule. See H. L. A. Hart, "Positivism and the Separation of Law and Morals," *Harvard Law Review* 71 (1958), 593, 606–608. Fuller contended that rules are not to be applied by cataloguing those situations to which their words clearly refer and those to which they refer less clearly. He proposed instead that in every case they should be applied according to their purposes. Translated into Oldendorp's terms, this means that rules are always to be applied "equitably."

107. *CR,* vol. 16, cols. 72–81. See also Melanchthon's discussion of equity *(epiekeia)* in *CR,* vol. 21, col. 1090.

108. *CR,* vol. 16, cols. 72–81. The same statement is made by Justice Oliver Wendell Holmes, Jr., in his dissent in *Lochner v. New York,* 198 U.S. 45, 76 (1905) ("General propositions do not decide concrete cases. The decision will depend on a judgment or intuition more subtle than any articular major premise").

109. *CR,* vol. 16, cols. 66–72 and 245–247; Stupperich, *Melanchthons Werke,* vol. 2, pt. 1, p. 159; Manschreck, *Melanchthon,* pp. 332–333; *CR,* vol. 11, cols. 218–223. For further discussion of Melanchthon's theory of equity, see his *In Quintum Librum Ethicorum Aristotelis Enarrationes Philippi Melanchthonis,* in *CR,* vol. 11, col. 262. See Kisch, *Melanchthons Recht- und Soziallehre,* pp. 168–184.

110. Manschreck, *Melanchthon,* p. 333.

111. "Equity is the judgment of the soul, sought from true reason, concerning the circumstances of things which pertain to moral character, since [these circumstances] indicate what ought or ought not to be done" ("Aequitas est iudicium animi, ex vera ratione petitum, de circumstantiis rerum, ad honestatem vitae pertinentium, cum indicunt, quid fieri aut non fieri oporteat"). Oldendorp, *De Iure et Aequitate, Forensis Disputatio* (Cologne, 1541), p. 13. Justice Joseph Story cited this very language in his *Commentaries on Equity Jurisprudence.* After discussing various rules of equitable interpretation of laws "according to their nature and operation, whether they are remedial, or are penal laws; whether they are restrictive of general right, or in advancement of public justice or policy; whether they are of universal application, or of a private and circumscribed intent," Story cited Grotius and others, adding: "There are yet other senses in which equity is used, which might be brought before the reader. The various senses are elaborately collected by Oldendorpius in his work *De Jure et Aequitate Disputatio;* and he finally offers, what he deems a very exact definition of equity, in its general sense, Aequitas est judicium animi. . . . ," quoting in full the Latin passage reproduced here. (Story, however, renders "indicunt" as "incidunt," and inserts immediately thereafter the words "recte discernens.") Joseph Story, *Commentaries on Equity Jurisprudence, As Ad-*

ministered in England and America, 12th ed., rev. Jairus Ware Perry (Boston, 1877), p. 7, n. 2. Story had a copy of Oldendorp's book in his library.

112. See Aristotle, *Ethics*, in *The Ethics of Aristotle: The Nicomachean Ethics*, ed. and trans. J. A. K. Thomson (London, 1953), bk. 5, chap. 12, p. 10: "Equity, though just, is not the justice of the law courts but a method of restoring the balance of justice when it has been tilted by the law. The need for such a rectification arises from the circumstance that law can do no more than generalize, and there are cases which cannot be settled by a general statement. . . . So when a case arises when the law states a general rule, but there is an exception to the rule, it is then right when the lawgiver owing to the generality of the language left a loophole for error to creep in to fill the gap by such a modified statement as the lawgiver himself would make, if he was present at the time, and such an enactment as he would have made, if he had known the special circumstances." See also Aristotle, *The Art of Rhetoric*, trans. John Henry Freese (London, 1926), bk. 1, chap. 12, secs. 13–19.

113. See Harold J. Berman, "Medieval English Equity," in *Faith and Order: The Reconciliation of Law and Religion* (Atlanta, 1993), pp. 55–82. See also the sources listed in Berman and Witte, "Transformation of Western Legal Philosophy."

114. See Oldendorp, *Disputatio* 72: in *De Jure et Aequitate Disputatio* (1541) "The highest law is sometimes simply law, at other times it is the apex of law, inflexible law, general definition, subtlety of words, firm law, strict law, [all of which are contrasted with] equity, the good and equitable, *epieikeia*, or suitability, good faith, natural justice, etc."

115. Oldendorp writes: "Natural law and equity are one thing" ("Natürlyk Recht und Billigkeit ist ein Ding"). Quoted by H. Dietze, *Naturrecht in der Gegenwart* (Bonn, 1936), p. 71. Cf. Wolf, *Quellenbuch*, p. 161. Guido Kisch hails Oldendorp as the first great humanist jurist to transform traditional Aristotelian concepts of equity. See Guido Kisch, *Erasmus und die Jurisprudenz seiner Zeit: Studien zum humanistischen Rechtsdenken* (Basel, 1960), p. 228. Kisch's exposition of Oldendorp's theory of equity does not make clear, however, the nature of that transformation. Dietze writes that in Oldendorp, "thesis and antithesis stand over against each other unreconciled: the thesis [that] equity and law are two types of value, the antithesis [that] both are one and the same." See Dietze, *Johann Oldendorp*, pp. 88–89. It would be more accurate to say that Oldendorp in fact reconciles these contradictory propositions by stating that law and equity—the rule and the conscientious application of the rule—are two different parts of a single whole, and that if they seem to conflict, it is equity that prevails.

116. See Macke, "Rechts- und Staatsdenken des Oldendorp," pp. 63–66.

117. Here, too, Oldendorp's concept of natural law is sharply distinguished from that of Aquinas, who speaks of natural law as a middle stage between divine and human law. See Aquinas, *Summa Theologiae*, pt. II–II, pp. 93–95.

118. Macke, "Rechts- und Staatsdenken des Oldendorp," p. 151, rightly charges both Erik Wolf and Franz Wieacker with oversimplifying Oldendorp's conception of natural law (or equity). The same charge can be leveled against Carl von Stachau Kaltenborn, *Die Vorläufer des Hugo Grotius auf dem Gebiete des iusnaturae et gentium Sowie der Politik im Reformationszeitalter* (Leipzig, 1848), pp. 233–236, on whom both Wolf and Wieacker partly rely. Wolf says that natural law for Oldendorp consists of unchangeable principles derived from natural reason, which are above human law; this characterization is derived from Oldendorp's *Billig und Recht*, and does not take into account Oldendorp's other writings. See Wolf, *Quellenbuch*, p. 161. Wieacker, relying on Oldendorp's *Isagoge*, describes natural law

as a divine source of legal norms, equivalent to the Decalogue. See Wieacker, *History of Private Law,* pp. 283–284. Kaltenborn, also relying on *Isagoge,* describes Oldendorp's natural law as a divine source of legal principles from which the positive law is derived and by which it is tested. In this view, the Decalogue merely aids human reason to understand and apply the natural law. Such a misunderstanding of Oldendorp stems, in part, from Kaltenborn's unwarranted reduction of Oldendorp's *Divinae Tabulae* to a mere title of *Isagoge.* Macke, relying on the totality of Oldendorp's writings, argues convincingly that his complete conception of natural law can be derived only from his concept of nature as God himself, creator of all things *(deus creator omnium).* Natural law, therefore, includes both God-given legal norms (the Decalogue), from which civil legal norms are derived, and principles derived from God-given reason, but it also includes much more, namely, the capacity of conscience, implanted in man by God, to apply norms and principles equitably to concrete circumstances.

119. *Isagoge,* pp. 6–11; *Billig und recht,* pp. 58–67. Oldendorp drew on an earlier scholastic conception of conscience, insofar as he defined it as an aspect of practical reason through which general moral principles are applied to concrete circumstances. Thomas Aquinas had developed the conception of conscience as an act of applying knowledge of good and evil to a particular case. See Eric D'Arcy, *Conscience and Its Right to Freedom* (New York, 1961), p. 42; Michael Bertram Crowe, *The Changing Profile of the Natural Law* (The Hague, 1977), pp. 136–141. Aquinas, however, had not translated—as Oldendorp did—this moral concept into a legal concept. Moreover, Oldendorp, in contrast to Aquinas, accepted the Lutheran conception of conscience as pertaining to the whole person of man, including his faith, and not simply to his intellectual and moral qualities.

120. D'Arcy, *Conscience,* p. 42.

121. "Faith redeems, protects and preserves our consciences," Luther wrote in *On the Freedom of the Christian* (1522), quoted by Michael G. Baylor, *Action and Person: Conscience in Late Scholasticism and the Young Luther* (Leiden, 1977), p. 247.

122. Oldendorp, *Disputatio,* quoted in Dietze, *Johann Oldendorp,* p. 173; see also pp. 78–89, 126–131; Macke, "Rechts- und Staatsdenken des Oldendorp," pp. 67–72. There are striking parallels between Oldendorp's theory of judgment and that developed in the following century in England by the great Puritan Anglican judge Sir Matthew Hale.

123. Quoted in Macke, "Rechts- und Staatsdenken des Oldendorp," p. 121.

124. See Dietze, *Johann Oldendorp,* pp. 11–13. In his legal dictionary *Lexicon Juris* (Frankfurt, 1553; Venice, 1555), which was widely used in the sixteenth and seventeenth centuries, Oldendorp defines the civil polity *(civitas)* as "a corporation of citizens brought together so that it may prosper by right of partnership" ("universitatis civium, in hoc collecta, ut iure societatis, vivat optimo").

125. Oldendorp, *Lexicon Juris,* p. 272: "magistrata . . . legum ministri sunt." Cf. *Divinae Tabulae,* p. 19; and *Ratmannenspiegel,* pp. 73–77.

126. Quoted in Macke, "Rechts- und Staatsdenken des Oldendorp," pp. 79–80: "Falsum igitur est simpliciter asserere, principem habere potestatem contra ius. Decet enim tantae maiestati, . . . servare leges."

127. See ibid., p. 85.

128. See ibid., pp. 85–92.

129. Oldendorp, *Lexicon Juris.* See also Macke, "Rechts- und Staatsdenken des Oldendorp," p. 92.

130. Macke, "Rechts- und Staatsdenken des Oldendorp," pp. 92–94.

131. Ibid., pp. 80–82.

132. Ibid., p. 110.
133. Oldendorp, *Lexicon Juris,* p. 249: "Iuris finis est, ut pacifice transigamus hanc vitam umbratilem, ac perducamus ad Christum et aeternam vitam."
134. Ibid. See also Macke, "Rechts- und Staatsdenken des Oldendorp," p. 13.
135. See, for example, *Isagoge,* pp. 9–10: "To be sure, the nature of man has been corrupted through the fall of Adam; so that just sparks remain, by which nevertheless it is possible to recognize the magnificent bounty of divine and natural law" ("ceterum natura hominis ex Adae lapsu adeo corrupta fuit, ut vix igniculi remaneant, ex quibus tam magnifica divini et naturalis iuris bonitas agnosci posset").
136. A detailed analysis of the character of the Roman Catholic Church as the first modern state and of the rise of secular states after the Papal Revolution may be found in Berman, *Law and Revolution,* pp. 113–115 and 275–276.
137. "The central problem of late medieval intellectual and religious history was the mentality that had given birth to the synthesis of reason and revelation, the presumptuous seductive vision of high medieval theology." Steven Ozment, *The Age of Reform,* 1250–1550 (New Haven, 1980), p. 21.
138. See the collection of quotations by Jaroslav Pelikan, *Reformation of Church and Dogma (*1300–1700*)* (Chicago, 1989), p. 20.
139. On the Anglo-American concept of jury equity, see the important article by George E. Butler II, "Compensable Liberty: A Historical and Political Model of the Seventh Amendment," *Notre Dame Journal of Law, Ethics, and Public Policy* 1 (1985), 595, 713–720. Butler shows that in the development of trial by jury in England and America, with its sharp distinction between rules of law stated by judges and application of the rules by the jury, the term "jury equity" is applied to the process of decision making in concrete cases. Jury equity is to be distinguished from jury nullification, which developed after courts began to lay down rules in absolute terms instead of provisionally, and thus attempted, in effect, to restrict the jury's ultimate power.
140. *WA,* 32:390; see also 38:102.
141. *CR,* vol. 16, col. 436.
142. On the development of the German *Rechtsstaat* theories in the nineteenth and twentieth centuries, see Otto von Gierke, *Johannes Althusius und die Entwicklung der naturrechtlichen Staatstheorien,* 5th ed. (Aalen, 1958), pp. 264ff. ("Die Idee der Rechtsstaat"); Herman Dooyeweerd, *De Crisis der humanistischen Staatsleer in het Licht eener calvinistische Kosmologie en Kennistheorie* (Amsterdam, 1931), p. 40. On the contributions of Lutheranism to the modern idea of the state, see James D. Tracy, ed., *Luther and the Modern State in Germany* (Kirksville, Mo., 1986); Günther Holstein, *Luther und die deutsche Staatsidee* (Tübingen, 1926).
143. Thomas Aquinas, *Summa Theologiae,* pts. I–II, qu. 90, art. 4.
144. Lutheran legal philosophy has sometimes been caricatured by its opponents as based on the twin concepts that the fundamental sinfulness of fallen man renders him incapable of observing natural law and that human law is inherently a reflection not of inborn reason but of the will of the lawmaker. These concepts have been contrasted with those held by Roman Catholic contemporaries of Luther, and especially the sixteenth-century "late scholastic" Spanish jurists, who developed a legal philosophy based on the natural law theory of Thomas Aquinas. Thus in an otherwise distinguished book, James Gordley writes: "Lutherans and Calvinists claimed that the Fall had so debased man that he could neither discover nor do what is good. Princes claimed that the law depended on their will alone. The antidote was Thomism with its confidence in natural reason, and particularly

Thomistic ideas of natural law." James Gordley, *The Philosophical Origin of Modern Contract Doctrine* (Oxford, 1991), p. 70. As shown in this chapter, however, Lutheran theologians and jurists, despite their diminished optimism concerning human nature, did indeed believe that God plants in the human mind knowledge—*notitiae*—of fundamental moral principles and, further, that God has revealed fundamental legal principles in the Ten Commandments, summarized by Jesus as the commandment to love God and to love one's neighbor as oneself. Although Melanchthon had less confidence than Thomas in the capacity of human reason to understand the fundamental principles of natural law, he at the same time had more confidence in the capacity of human conscience, guided by faith and inspired by grace, to apply those principles equitably. Moreover, although Lutheran jurists were more explicit than Thomists in saying that because of human weakness, and the consequent need for political order, it was necessary sometimes to obey some laws that conflict with fundamental principles of natural law, Thomas, too, qualified his dictum that a human law that conflicts with the law of nature "is no longer a law"—saying at one point that such a law might "perhaps" be obeyed "in order to avoid scandal or disturbance," though not if it conflicts not only with natural law but also with divine law. See Thomas Aquinas, *Summa Theologiae,* pts. II–II, qu. 96, art. 2.

In fact there were many similarities between the legal philosophy of the Lutherans and that of the Spanish neo-Thomists. As shown earlier, Oldendorp adopted Aristotelian concepts of liberality and commutative justice as "causes" of law, concepts that (as Gordley emphasizes) were fundamental to neo-Thomist legal thought. At the same time, the Spanish neo-Thomists departed from classical Thomism and moved toward Protestantism in their frequent reliance on the Decalogue and other biblical sources of legal (and not only moral) doctrine. Also, both Spanish neo-Thomist and German Lutheran jurists built on the humanism of the late fifteenth and early sixteenth centuries, with its revival of sources from classical antiquity. And both were monarchist, emphasizing the source of both secular and spiritual law in royal legislation, for Spain at that time exalted royal authority over the church despite its nominal subordination to the papacy. Where Lutheran legal philosophy differed most sharply from that of the Spanish neo-Thomists was in its teaching that (1) equity is not merely to be applied, as Aristotle had taught, in the exceptional case in which a strict application of a rule would work injustice, but is embedded in the rules themselves and is therefore to be applied in every application of every rule; (2) that the ultimate source of equity is not reason but conscience; and (3) that the ultimate source of conscience is, again, not reason but a combination of faith and grace.

It may be noted also that in legal science, as distinct from legal philosophy, the Spanish neo-Thomists did not adopt the topical method of the Lutheran jurists, discussed in the next chapter, but continued to organize their materials, as the earlier scholastics had done, around cases *(disputationes),* issues *(questiones),* and arguments *articuli*), leading to resolutions.

3. The Transformation of German Legal Science

This chapter draws partly on an article written by the author jointly with Charles J. Reid, Jr., "Roman Law in Europe and the *Jus Commune:* A Historical Overview with Emphasis on the New Legal Science of the Sixteenth Century," *Syracuse Journal of International Law and Commerce* 20 (1995), pp. 1–27.

1. See Berman, *Law and Revolution,* pp. 123–151.
2. The Digest was one part of the body of legal writings assembled at the order of Justinian in the early sixth century. Running to some 1,200 pages in a modern English translation, the Digest contains a wide miscellany of passages from the leading jurists of the preceding centuries, chiefly in the form of rules of law probably derived from decisions or arguments in particular cases. Other works that constituted what in the sixteenth century came to be known in the West as the *Corpus Juris Civilis* are the Institutes, intended as an introductory text for students, the Codex, consisting of the imperial legislation of Justinian's predecessors, and the Novellae, the "New Laws," consisting of Justinian's own legal decrees.
3. See Winfried Trusen, *Anfänge des Gelehrten Rechts in Deutschland: Ein Beitrag zur Geschichte der Frührezeption* (Wiesbaden, 1962). Despite the uncontroverted truth of Trusen's thesis, leading legal historians continue to date the "practical reception" of Roman law in Germany from the fifteenth-century.
4. The 1495 ordinance specified that at least half the members of the new court, called the Imperial Chamber Court *(Reichskammergericht),* should be learned in the law. The higher princely courts in the German territories followed this example, and by the middle of the sixteenth century, university-educated jurists trained in Roman law and canon law dominated the entire German upper judiciary, with a trickle-down effect on the personnel of lower tribunals as well. See Wieacker, *History of Private Law,* pp. 133–135.
5. The term "humanists" was used in the fourteenth century to refer to university students of grammar, rhetoric, poetry, history, and moral philosophy, as contrasted with the more standard curricula of theology, law, and medicine. In the fifteenth and early sixteenth centuries, the term "humanist" came to be applied to the revival of studies of classical Latin and Greek literature in a number of fields. Widely varying philosophical outlooks could be encompassed within the terms. Thus Petrarch, Erasmus, and Melanchthon could all qualify as humanists. At the same time, it was characteristic of humanism in all of its stages to attack the earlier so-called scholastic orthodoxies of church and state. See Philip P. Wiener, ed., *Dictionary of the History of Ideas,* vol. 2 (New York, 1973), pp. 515–523.
6. These and similar charges are quoted in Paul-Émile Viard, *André Alciat, 1492–1550* (Paris, 1926), p. 119, nn. 1–9.
7. For an analysis of Valla's influence on legal science, see Donald R. Kelley, *Foundations of Modern Historical Scholarship: Language, Law, and History in the French Renaissance* (New York, 1970), pp. 19–52. Cf. Myron P. Gilmore, *Humanists and Jurists: Six Studies in the Renaissance* (Cambridge, Mass., 1963), pp. 3ff.; Quentin Skinner, *The Foundations of Modern Political Thought,* vol. 1 (Cambridge, 1978), pp. 201ff.; Ernst Andersen, *The Renaissance of Legal Science after the Middle Ages: The German Historical School No Bird Phoenix* (The Hague, 1974), pp. 31ff.
8. Kelley, *Foundations,* p. 31. See also Lisa Jardine and Donald R. Kelley, "Lorenzo Valla and the Intellectual Origins of Humanist Dialectic," *Journal of the History of Philosophy* 15 (1977), 143–164.
9. Cf. Kelley, *Foundations,* p. 40. Valla's "anti-Tribonianism" played an important role in the scholarship of sixteenth-century French jurists, including Charles Dumoulin, François Hotman, Jacques Cujas, Pierre Pithou, and others. See Stintzing, *Geschichte der Rechtswissenschaft,* pp. 375–381; Julian Franklin, *Jean Bodin and the Sixteenth-Century Revolution in the Methodology of Law and History* (New York, 1963), pp. 36ff.; Andersen, *No Bird Phoenix,* pp. 103ff.
10. Kelley, *Foundations,* p. 41.

11. Theodor Viehweg, *Topics and Law: A Contribution to Basic Research in Law,* trans. W. Cole Durham (Frankfurt am Main, 1993), pp. 61–63; Karl H. Burmeister, *Das Studium des Rechts im Zeitalter des Humanismus im deutschen Rechtsbereich* (Wiesbaden, 1974), pp. 241–251; Stintzing, *Geschichte der Rechtswissenschaft,* pp. 121–129.
12. Lorenzo Valla, *Contra Bartolum Libellum Cui Titulus de Insigniis et Armis Epistola* (1518), quoted and discussed in Gilmore, *Humanists and Jurists,* pp. 31–32, and in Domenico Maffei, *Gli inizi dell'umanesimo giuridico* (Milan, 1956), pp. 38–41. These charges against Bartolus, communicated by Valla in a letter to a friend which later became public, caused such an uproar at the University of Pavia that Valla was forced to resign from his chair and flee the city.
13. In the fourteenth century, Lucas de Penna stated that "God gave law to humankind by means of the Roman Emperors," and that "we should believe that the Holy Spirit is located in [the Roman statutes]." Quoted in Walter Ullmann, *The Medieval Idea of Law, as Represented by Lucas de Penna: A Study in Fourteenth-Century Legal Scholarship* (London, 1946), pp. 75–76.
14. Andersen, *No Bird Phoenix,* pp. 30–121; Hans Erich Troje, *Graeca Leguntur: Die Aneignung des byzantinischen Rechts und die Entstehung eines humanistischen Corpus iuris civilis in der Jurisprudenze des 16. Jahrhunderts* (Cologne, 1971); idem, "Die Literatur des gemeinen Rechts unter dem Einfluss des Humanismus," in Helmut Coing, ed., *Handbuch der Quellen und Literatur der neueren europaischen Privatrechtsgeschichte: Neuere Zeit,* vol. 2 (1500–1800) (Munich, 1977), pt. 1, pp. 615, 640–671. The most famous exposure was of the Donation of Constantine, which purported to refer to a grant by Emperor Constantine to Pope Sylvester of exclusive spiritual and substantial temporal authority over Christendom. The document had been regarded by papalists since the ninth century as an important historical basis for expanding papal authority. In 1433 Nicholas of Cusa had offered some evidence that the Donation was a forgery. In 1440 Valla provided conclusive philological proof of the forgery. Valla's proof, though circulated privately, was not published until 1517 and was used by Luther and other reformers in their attack on canon law and papal authority. Cf. Andersen, *No Bird Phoenix,* pp. 31ff.
15. Particularly in France, Romanist legal thought remained largely antiquarian in the sixteenth century, thereby contributing to the movement to restore the "Gallic" roots of contemporary French law. For an account of the French jurists' philological reconstruction of ancient legal texts, see particularly Andersen, *No Bird Phoenix,* pp. 33ff.; Coleman Phillipson, "Jacques Cujas," in John MacDonnell and Edward Manson, eds., *Great Jurists of the World* (Boston, 1914), pp. 83–108; and Ernst Spangenberg, *Jacob Cujas und seine Zeitgenossen* (Frankfurt am Main, 1967). Cujas is generally considered to have been the most outstanding of the French jurists of the sixteenth century. He did not, however, develop a systematic jurisprudence. His principal contribution consisted rather in searching out, editing, and annotating a large number of ancient manuscripts of Roman law. On the antiquarian accomplishments of the humanist legal scholars, see Kelley, *Foundations,* 151–216; Hans Troje, "Die Literatur des gemeinen Rechts unter dem Einfluss des Humanismus," in Coing, *Handbuch,* vol. 2, pt. 1, pp. 615–795; Michael H. Hoeflich, "A Seventeenth-Century Roman Law Bibliography: Jacques Godefroy and His Bibliotheca Iuris Romani," *Law Library Journal* 75 (1983), 514–527. In the seventeenth century they came to be called "the Elegant School." See Peter Stein, "Elegance in Law," *Law Quarterly Review* 77 (1961), 242–256.
16. See Maffei, *Inizi,* p. 56.
17. For a discussion of changes in the teaching method and curriculum of the law faculties of the German universities, see Burmeister, *Studium des Rechts,* pp. 17ff.,

73ff., 251ff. Cf. also Helmut Coing, "Die juristische Fakultät und ihr Lehrprogram," in Coing, *Handbuch,* vol. 2, pt. 1, pp. 30–49, 59–61, and Otto Stobbe, *Geschichte der deutschen Rechtsquellen,* Bd. 1 (Aalen, 1965), pp. 9–43.

18. See Erasmus, letter to Charles Sucquet, July 2, 1529, in P. S. Allen and H. M. Allen, eds., *Opus Epistolarum Des. Erasmi Roterdami,* 12 vols. (Oxford, 1906–1958), 8:221.

19. Budaeus studied Greek, philology, philosophy, theology, and medicine at the University of Paris. He also studied law for a short time at the University of Orléans. For general studies of his life and work, see Louis Delaruelle, *Guillaume Budé: Les origines, les débuts, les idées maîtresses* (Geneva, 1970), and Jean Plattard, *Guillaume Budé et les origines de l'humanisme français* (Paris, 1923).

20. *Udalrici Zasii Censura Interpretationis Petri Stellae,* col. 247, quoted in Michael L. Monheit, "Passion and Order in the Formation of Calvin's Sense of Religious Authority" (Ph.D. diss., Princeton University, 1986), p. 46. Zasius's diatribe against Budaeus is discussed at some length in Roderich von Stintzing, *Ulrich Zasius: Ein Beitrag sur Geschichte der Rechtswissenschaft im Zeitalter der Reformation* (Basel, 1857), pp. 196ff.

21. See Godehard Fleischer, "Ein europäischer Streit über einer bereicherungsrechtlichen Frage" (Diss., Freiburg im Breisgau, 1966), pp. 60–62; and Monheit, "Passion and Order," p. 41.

22. For biographical studies of Zasius, see Steven Rowan, *Ulrich Zasius: A Jurist in the Renaissance* (Frankfurt am Main, 1987); Stintzing, *Geschichte der Rechtswissenschaft,* pp. 155–174; Erik Wolf, *Grosse Rechtsdenker der deutschen Geistesgeschichte,* vol. 2 (Tübingen, 1944), pp. 55–91; Guido Kisch, *Erasmus und die Jurisprudenz seiner Zeit: Studien zum humanistischen Rechtsdenken* (Basel, 1960), pp. 317–343; Hans Winterberg, *Die Schüler von Ulrich Zasius* (Stuttgart, 1961).

23. Zasius's writings, including some eight hundred legal opinions (*responsa* and *consilia*), his lectures on the Digest, and many of his letters, are collected in his *Opera Omnia,* 6 vols. (Lyon, 1550). See also Hans Thieme, ed., *Aus den Handschriften Ulrich Zasius* (Freiburg im Breisgau, 1957).

24. Preface to *Intellectus Juris Civilis Singulares* (1532), quoted in Wolf, *Grosse Rechtsdenker,* p. 22.

25. *Lucubrationes Aliquot Sane Quam Elegantes, Nec Minus Eruditae* (1518), p. 69, quoted in Wolf, *Grosse Rechtsdenker,* p. 17.

26. On Alciatus's life and career, see Coleman Phillipson, "Andrea Alciat and His Predecessors," in MacDonnell and Manson, *Great Jurists of the World,* pp. 58–82. On his works and their significance, see Roberto Abbondanza, "La vie et les oeuvres d'André Alciat" and "Premières considérations sur la méthodologie d'Alciat," in *Pédagogues et Juristes* (Paris, 1963), pp. 93–106, 107–118; Vincenzo Piano-Mortari, "Pensieri di Alciato sulla giurisprudenza," in *Apollinaris: Studia et documenta historiae et juris* 33 (1967), 189–220; Maffei, "André Alciat," in *Inizi,* pp. 132–136; Kelley, *Foundations,* pp. 87–115.

27. Some eight hundred such *consilia* and *responsa* appear in the 1582 edition of Alciatus's works *(Opera).*

28. Hans Erich Troje, "Alciats Methode der Kommentierung des '*Corpus iuris civilis,*'" in August Buck and Otto Herding, eds., *Der Kommentar in der Renaissance* (Boppard, 1985), p. 60. Troje's judgment, though cast only on Alciatus, is equally applicable to the writings of Zasius.

29. This judgment is ultimately supported by Viard, *André Alciat,* p. 164, and Maffei, "André Alciat," p. 132. Piano-Mortari, "Pensieri di Alciato," p. 219, goes so far as

to say that Alciatus's "ideal" consisted of "avoiding original ideas, of being simply a part of the patrimony conveyed by the legal-philosophical thought of the ancients and the medievals."

30. Such jurists included Claudius Cantiuncula (Claude Chansonnette) (ca. 1490–1560), Christophus Hegendorphinus (1500–1540), Matthaeus Gribaldus Mopha (n.d.), Franz Frosch (d. 1540), Sebastian Derrer (d. 1541), Joachim Hopperus (d. 1576), and others. See Burmeister, *Studium des Rechts,* pp. 251 ff., and Troje, "Die Literatur des gemeinen Rechts," pp. 718–730. Their primary concern, however, was pedagogic: to restructure, simplify, and abbreviate legal education. Stintzing, *Geschichte der Rechtswissenschaft,* pp. 242–260, describes the work of these earlier jurists as the "Methodological and Systematic Experimentation Stage" of German legal science. Likewise Theodore Muther, in *Doctor Johann Apel: Ein Beitrag zur Geschichte des deutschen Jurisprudenz im sechszehnten Jahrhundert* (Königsberg, 1860), pp. 7–8, identifies this earlier phase of legal science as the "time of preparation" for the great systematic writings of the latter two-thirds of the sixteenth century.

Several recent writers have challenged this conclusion and have not distinguished these earlier writings from the later stage. Thus Troje ("Die Literatur," p. 734), identifies Hegendorf's *Libri Dialecticae Legalis Quinque* as the "first high point" of the new legal science. Franz Wieacker (*History of Private Law,* pp. 162–165) treats the works of Cantiuncula, Derrer, Frosch, Drosaus, Apel, Lagus, and others simply as different expressions of a humanist legal science inspired by a new concern for legal pedagogy and language and a new interest in the Institutes of Justinian. Guido Kisch argues that Cantiuncula was a "pathbreaker" in the development of German legal science, who "dethroned the commentators" and inaugurated a "fresh appreciation for the sources." Guido Kisch, *Claudius Cantiuncula: Ein Basler Jurist und Humanist des 16. Jahrhunderts* (Basel, 1970), pp. 57–71. Hans-Peter Ferslev, "Claudius Cantiuncula: Die didaktischen Schriften" (Thesis, Cologne, 1967), contrasts the "philological-historical school of Alciat, Zasius, and Budaeus" with the "dialectical-synthetical school of Cantiuncula, Apel, and Hegendorf," arguing that each of the members of the latter school offered a new synthesis of law: Cantiuncula (and Nicolaus Everardus) on the basis of Ciceronian topics and Hegendorf and Apel on the basis of Melanchthonian dialectics (pp. 35–40). While it is true that later writings of some of these jurists, such as Cantiuncula and Hopper, contributed to the development of a full-fledged systematic legal science, their early writings, which recent authorities cite in support of their propositions, reflect what I have called the second stage of legal science. Christophus Hegendorphinus's *Libri Dialecticae Legalis Quinque* (Paris, 1531; 1549 ed.), for example, which Troje and others have described as the first comprehensive systematization of the law, is, in fact a thirty-two-page compilation of previous opinions about various legal categories and doctrines loosely modeled on the dialectical categories of Rudolph Agricola. See n. 38.

31. In response to a letter from Joannes Fichard requesting his opinion of the call for a new systematic genre of legal science, Zasius urged his former student simply to study the Digest itself. "I do not thereby seek to persuade you," he writes, "that the law has no principles or dividing points. It certainly has them: they are extensive, though not infinite." But to adopt a method which concentrates on these principles, he warns, is ultimately fruitless. "In conclusion, do not worry about questions of method: the fifty books of the Digest can be both your method and text." Letter of ca. 1530 in Rieggerus, *Udalrici Zasii, jc Friburg Quondum Celeberrimi, Epistolae ad Viros Aetatis sive Doctissimus* (Ulm, 1774), p. 382. Stintzing,

Geschichte der Rechtswissenschaft, pp. 108ff., discusses similar sentiments in some of Zasius's other writings and correspondence.

32. In addition to Apel, Lagus, and Oldendorp, Luther befriended and corresponded with many other German jurists who were influential in developing the new systematic legal science, including Joachim von Beust (1522–1597), Henning Gode (1450–1521), Kilian Goldstein (1499–1568), Joachim Hopper (d. 1576), Melchior Kling (1504–1571), Basilius Monner (ca. 1501–1566), Christoph Scheurl (1498–1542), Johannes Schneidewin (1519–1568), Hieronymous Schurpf (1481–1554), and Michael Teuber (1522–1597). Also among Luther's friends and associates was a substantial group of Lutheran theologians who helped to draft new imperial, territorial, and urban codes, as well as church ordinances. These included Johannes Brenz (1498–1570), Martin Bucer (1491–1551), Johannes Bugenhagen (1485–1558), Johannes Oecolampadus (1482–1531), and Andreas Osiander (1498–1552). For a general survey of Luther's relations with the jurists of his day, see Karl Köhler, *Luther und die Juristen: Zur Frage nach dem gegenseitgen Verhältniss und der Sittlichtkeit* (Gotha, 1873). For biographical and bibliographical information on each of these jurists and theologians, see *Allgemeine Deutsche Biographie,* 56 vols. (Leipzig, 1875–1910).

    On Zasius's attitude toward Luther and Lutheranism, see Stintzing, *Geschichte der Rechtswissenschaft,* pp. 216–255. On Alciatus's attitude toward Luther and Lutheranism, see Phillipson, "Jacques Cujas," p. 72. They were reformers both in law and theology, but would not go the whole way.

33. For an account of Melanchthon's activities at Wittenberg as a law teacher and his relationship with numerous jurists at Wittenberg and beyond, see, inter alia, Guido Kisch, *Melanchthons Rechts- und Soziallehre* (Berlin, 1967), pp. 60ff.; Stintzing, *Geschichte der Rechtswissenschaft,* pp. 287ff. Theodor Muther, *Aus dem Universitäts- und Gelehrtensleben im Zeitalter der Reformation* (Erlangen, 1866), emphasizes Melanchthon's admiration of, and friendship with, Hieronymous Schuerpf.

34. Revisions were published in 1525, 1535, 1544–45, and 1555, with minor changes in the title. On the significance of these changes see Quirinius Breen, "The Terms '*Loci communes*' and '*Loci*' in Melanchthon," *Church History* 16 (1947), 197, 203–204; Muther, *Aus dem Universitäts- und Gelehrtensleben.*

35. Melanchthon defines method as "the right way or order of investigation and explication, either of simple questions or of propositions . . . that is, *Methodus* is a habit *(habitus),* which is to say a science *(scientia)* or an art *(ars),* making a pathway by means of certain reasoning *(ratio).*" Melanchthon, *Erotemata Dialectices* (n.d.), p. 573.

    In 1534, in an early edition of the *Erotemata Dialectices,* titled *Dialectices Philippi Melanchthonis Libri II,* under the heading *De Demonstrationibus,* p. 112, Melanchthon wrote: "The term Method, of which we have spoken above, should be fitted especially to this way of teaching, [namely,] when we use demonstration, when we give definitions, when we seek causes, when we draw effects and proper functions from the causes, when we show the origins and sources of the arts. For [certain] principles, certain common judgments, are born with us. For God has impressed on our minds certain elements of knowledge *(notitiae)* which are like rules in judging concerning nature and concerning civil customs, of whatever kind they are." This passage from the 1534 *Dialectices* clearly identifies "Method" as a way of demonstrating and judging and not only a way of classifying, investigating, and explicating.

36. Melanchthon, *Erotemata Dialectices,* pp. 573–578.
37. Melanchthon's method developed in the *Loci Communes* of 1521 and in subsequent works must be contrasted with the *loci* method developed in certain legal tracts in the years shortly before, most notably Peter Gammarus, *Legalis Dialectica* (1514); Nicolaus Everardus, *Topicorum Seu de Locis Legalium Liber* (1516; reprint, 1552); and Claudius Cantiuncula, *Topica Dialectices* (1520), reprinted in *Primum volumen tractatuum ex variis iuris interpretibus collectorum,* 2nd. ed. (Lyon, 1549), pp. 253–271. In these tracts the *loci* are treated, in Stintzing's words, as "mnemonic devices . . . in which arguments and materials are organized for quick reference." Stintzing, *Geschichte der Rechtswissenschaft,* pp. 114–115. Each locus is a subject, such as usury, intestacy, or liberation of slaves, drawn from the Digest, the glosses, the Commentaries, or elsewhere (in the first edition of Everardus's work, there are 131 such *loci*). Under each subject heading, there is a cryptic summary of the discussion of this subject in the Roman law texts and their glosses and commentaries, as well as in the writings of the Greek and Roman philosophers, the Church Fathers, the Christian councils, and the scholastic theologians and canonists. These summaries of traditional teachings, though comprehensive, were largely eclectic and uncritical. There was little attempt made to resolve the tensions or contradictions between certain texts or to purge them of obsolete or impractical teachings. Stintzing concludes that the *loci* method of these jurists provided convenient summaries of traditional teachings but did little to advance legal science. "A scientific advance is evident," writes Stintzing (*Geschichte der Rechtswissenschaft,* pp. 119, 121), "only insofar as [these writers] became aware of the need to reform dialectical loci. But [they] did not achieve this reform but continued down well-worn scholastic paths. . . . All this work bore little fruit for the development of topical science. These topical writings can be regarded not as the start of a new movement but only as a vestige of the moribund scholastic tradition."
38. See, e.g., Neal W. Gilbert, *Renaissance Concepts of Method* (New York, 1960), pp. 127–128, who dismisses Melanchthon's dialectical writings as "superficial doctrine" and his analytical questions as a "mélange." "Melanchthon," Gilbert writes, "still dealt with method in the finding part of dialectic, while Ramus's signal, and most controversial, innovation was the placing of method into judgment." Walter J. Ong, *Ramus, Method, and the Decay of Dialogue: From the Art of Discourse to the Art of Reason* (1958; reprint, Cambridge, Mass., 1983), takes a similar view, arguing that Ramus was the first to make method the key to scientific truth and, further, that Melanchthon did not discuss method at all prior to his *Erotemata* of 1547. In fact, however, Melanchthon, in his *Dialectices Libri II* (1534), had already identified *methodus* with right, reason, science, and true knowledge. Neither Gilbert nor Ong refers to the passages from the earlier work. (Gilbert remarks that "the inaccessibility of earlier editions prevents us from determining whether doctrines of method appear in earlier versions of [the *Erotemata*]"; p. 126, n. 13. Ong, in a short essay on Ramism, published in 1973, seems to have modified his position when he writes: "Between the years 1543 and 1547 all three [Ramus, Sturm, and Melanchthon] introduced sections on method into their textbooks on dialectic or logic. (Melanchthon had done a bit with method slightly earlier.)" Walter J. Ong, "Ramism," in Philip Wiener, ed., *Dictionary of the History of Ideas,* vol. 4, *Studies of Selected Pivotal Ideas* (New York, 1973), p. 43. In a letter to the author, however, written in 1994, Ong acknowledged that he had overestimated the originality of Ramus and that Melanchthon's much earlier elaboration of the topical method was far more significant. More recently, an important book by Ian

Maclean on legal interpretation and legal language in the sixteenth century also attributes advances in the topical method chiefly to Ramus, mentioning Melanchthon only in passing. See Ian Maclean, *Interpretation and Meaning in the Renaissance: The Case of Law* (Cambridge, 1992). Although, following Ong, Maclean associates Ramus's method with Calvinism and Melanchthon's method with Lutheranism, he nevertheless attributes Ramus's method to Freigius (Johan Thomas Frey), without noting that Freigius was Lutheran (pp. 42–43). He neglects to point out that the graphs he reproduces from Freigius's book (*Partitiones Juris Utriusque* [Basel, 1571]) were almost identical in style to those being produced by the Lutheran jurists more than a generation earlier.

The position taken in the text, namely, that Melanchthon from an early time placed method in the judgment part of dialectic, and that he was the first to do so, is supported both by Paul Joachimsen, "Loci Communes: Eine Untersuchung zur Geistesgeschichte des Humanismus und der Reformation," in *Luther-Jahrbuch* (1926), 85, and by Ernst Wolf, *Phillipp Melanchthon: Evangelischer Humanismus* (Göttingen, 1961). See also Quirinius, "The Terms *'Loci communes'* and *'Loci'* in Melanchthon," and Adolf Sperl, *Melanchthon zwischen Humanismus und Reformation: Eine Untersuchung uber den Wandel des Traditionverständnisses bei Melanchthon und die damit zusammenhängenden Grundfragen seiner Theologie* (Munich, 1959), p. 34.

Melanchthon seems to have dropped almost entirely out of late-twentieth-century German legal historiography. Thus Helmut Coing, in a highly condensed summary of the topical method, whose origin and development he sees as a line from Rudolf Agricola (1444–1485) to Peter Ramus (1515–1572), limits his discussion of Melanchthon's contribution to a single sentence, stating that "the theoretical writings of Melanchthon had the same significance in Lutheran territory as those of Ramus had in Calvinist territory." See Coing, *Handbuch*, pp. 24–25. Similarly, Hans Hattenhauer, in a comprehensive study of European legal history, notes in a single sentence that Melanchthon and Luther were the source of "binding interpretations of Bible and law for the Lutheran world." See Hans Hattenhauer, *Europäische Rechtsgeschichte* (Heidelberg, 1992), p. 367. In his book on the logical legal method of the sixteenth century, Vincenzo Piano Mortari does refer often to Melanchthon's work, but almost always as indistinguishable from that of Agricola and always as that of a humanist, never a Lutheran. See Vincenzo Piano Mortari, *Diritto logica metodo nel secolo XVI* (Naples, 1978). Also Paul Koschaker, in his pathbreaking study of the influence of Roman law on European history, not only fails to mention Melanchthon but also states that legal science itself *(Rechtswissenschaft)* is a nineteenth-century invention of the German historical school, "Made in Germany." See Paul Koschaker, *Europa und das römische Recht* (Munich, 1947), p. 210. One can only explain this historiographical blind spot as a repudiation of the religious sources of the Western legal tradition.

39. Ramus claimed that his method of classification, which was essentially mathematical in nature, yielded truth, but a careful reading of Ong confirms that in fact Ramus did not prove anything new or important. See Ong, *Ramus*, pp. 171–195.

40. In the opening passages of the *Loci Communes* of 1521, Melanchthon distinguishes traditional scholastic theological *loci*, which, he wrote, are "incomprehensible," "stupid discussions" that "argue more accurately for certain heresies than they do for the Catholic doctrines." Such expositions, he wrote, do not inspire and form the basis of true "Christian knowledge: to know what the law demands, where you may seek power for doing the law and grace to cover sin, how you

may strengthen a quaking spirit against the devil, the flesh, and the world, and how you may console an afflicted conscience. Do the Scholastics teach those things? In his letter to the Romans when he was writing a compendium of Christian doctrine, did Paul philosophize about the mysteries of the Trinity, the mode of incarnation, or active and passive creation? No! But what does he discuss? He takes up the law, sin, grace, [loci] on which the knowledge of Christ exclusively rests. How often Paul states that he wishes for the faithful a rich knowledge of Christ! For he foresaw that when he had left the saving [*loci*], we would turn our minds to disputations that are cold and foreign to Christ. Therefore, we shall draw up some account of those [*loci*] which commend Christ to you, strengthen the conscience, and arouse the mind against Satan." Melanchthon, *Corpus Reformatorum,* 22:83–85, translated in Wilhelm Pauck, *Melanchthon and Bucer* (Philadelphia, 1969), pp. 20–22.

41. For biographical and bibliographical information on Apel, see Muther, *Aus dem Universitäts- und Gelehrtensleben;* Stintzing, *Geschichte der Rechtswissenschaft,* pp. 270ff.; idem, "Johann Apel," in *Allgemeine Deutsche Biographie;* F. Merzbacher, "Johann Apels dialektische Methode der Rechtswissenschaft," *ZSS* (Rom. Abt.) 55 (1958), 364ff.; Franz Wieacker, *Humanismus und Rezeption: Eine Studie zu Johannes Apels Dialogus oder Isagoge per Dialogum in IV Libros Institutionum* (1940), reprinted in *Grunder und Bewahrer: Rechtslehrer der neueren deutschen Privatrechtsgeschichte* (Göttingen, 1959), pp. 44–104; Gerhard Theuerkauf, *Lex, Speculum Compendium Iuris, Rechtsaufzeichnung und Rechtsbewusstsein in Norddeutschland vom 8. bis 16. Jahrhundert* (Cologne, 1968), pp. 202ff. A comprehensive list of Apel's works is provided in Muther, *Aus dem Universitäts- und Gelehrtensleben,* pp. 455–487.
42. *Methodica Dialectices Ratio ad Iurisprudentiam Accomodata, Authore Iohanne Apello* (Nuremberg, 1535). Apel's epilogue is dated July 31, 1533. See Troje, "Die Literatur des gemeinen Rechts," p. 734.
43. *Isagoge per Dialogum in Quatuor Libros Institutionum Divi Iustiniani Imperatoris, Autore Ioanne Apello* (Bratislava, 1540).
44. Apel, *Methodica,* fol. 272r. ibid., B. 4; also D. 8. See also Stintzing, *Geschichte der Rechtswissenschaft,* pp. 289–90.
45. Stintzing, *Geschichte der Rechtswissenschaft,* p. 289. A similar judgment is offered by Ferslev, "Claudius Cantiuncula," p. 36, who writes that Apel "was the first to carry through logically the rational treatment of the legal material." See also Muther, *Doctor Johann Apel,* pp. 34–35 ("Apel's dialectical method as a whole is the Melanchthonian method; the juridical examples are his own"), and Wieacker, *Humanismus und Rezeption,* pp. 64–67.
46. Quoted by Wieacker, *Humanismus und Rezeption,* pp. 62–63.
47. Ibid.
48. For an overview of these basic principles of Lutheran theological hermeneutics, see Joachim Beckmann, "Die Bedeutung der reformatorischen Entdeckung des Evangelium für die Auslegung der Heiligen Schrift," *Luther-Jahrbuch* 34 (1963), 20ff.; Edward H. Schroeder, "Is There a Lutheran Hermeneutic?" in Robert W. Bertram, ed., *The Lively Function of the Gospel: Essays in Honor of Richard R. Caemmerer* (St. Louis, 1966), pp. 81–98. On the broader significance of Lutheran theological hermeneutics, see Karl Holl, "Luthers Bedeutung für den Fortschritt der Auslegungkunst," in *Gesammelte Aufsatze zur Kirchengeschichte,* 6th ed. (Tübingen, 1932), 1:544ff.; Alfred Voigt, "Die juristische Hermeneutik und ihr Abbild in Melanchthons Universitätsreden," in Carl Joseph Hering, ed., *Staat-Recht-Kultur: Festgabe für Ernst von Hippel zu seinem 70. Geburtstag* (Bonn, 1965), pp. 265ff.

49. On the development of the concept *ius ad rem,* see Harry Dondorp, "*Ius ad rem* als Recht, Einsetzung in ein Amt zu Verlangen," *Tijdschrift voor Rechtsgeschiedenis* 59 (1991), 285–318; Peter Landau, "Zum Ursprung des '*Ius ad Rem*' in der Kanonistik," in Stephan Kuttner, ed., *Proceedings of the Third International Congress of Medieval Canon Law* (1971), 81–102. The term *ius ad rem* was coined in the twelfth century primarily to describe the legal status of a party who had been invested with a fief or a benefice but had not yet taken physical possession. The party did not have full rights in the property *(ius in re)* but had only a right against the lord of the fief or the ecclesiastical superior to be given actual possession at a future time. The development of the concept *ius ad rem* was part of a broader development of *ius* as a subjective right. Prior thereto, the word *ius,* in Roman law, referred only to objective right, that is, law. The law, *ius,* imposed duties and obligations, but in classical Roman law there was no word for subjective rights. The twelfth-century canonists used the word *ius* for the first time to designate the law-based claim of one to whom a duty is owed, reflecting "a zone of human autonomy" and "a neutral sphere of personal choice." See Brian Tierney, *The Idea of Natural Rights: Studies on Natural Rights, Natural Law, and Church Law,* 1150–1625 (Atlanta, 1997), pp. 66–67. In the thirteenth century the new understanding of subjective right was integrated into the whole body of the canon law. See Charles J. Reid, Jr., "The Canonistic Contribution to the Western Rights Tradition: An Historical Inquiry," *Boston College Law Review* 33 (1991), 37–92; and Charles J. Reid, Jr., "Thirteenth-Century Canon Law and Rights: The Word *Ius* and Its Range of Subjective Meanings," *Studia Canonica* 30 (1996), 295–342.
50. In making this division Apel acknowledges, early in the *Isagoge,* his indebtedness to a manuscript he discovered in Königsberg, which he mistakenly regarded as an early edition of Justinian's Institutes but which, in the eighteenth century, was identified as an early edition of the twelfth-century *Brachylogus Juris Civilis,* a product of the glossators. Several editions of the *Brachylogus* after 1551 included Apel's *Isagoge* as an appendix. See Stintzing, *Geschichte der Rechtswissenschaft,* pp. 292–293; and Theuerkauf, *Lex,* p. 195. The scholastic jurists did not, however, make the division between *dominium* and *obligatio* the basis for a synthesis of legal doctrine. Indeed, the *Brachylogus* simply includes *dominium* and *obligatio* in a list of several dozen legal topics, largely drawn from and arranged in accordance with Justinian's Institutes, and provides only a rudimentary taxonomy of law. It makes no attempt to define the relations among the legal topics, and offers only cryptic definitions and illustrations—frequently less than one hundred words—of each topic. A 1557 edition of the *Brachylogus,* published in Lyon, occupies but 123 pages, with fewer than two hundred words per page. Such a work stands in sharp contrast to the writings of Apel, both in organization and in comprehensiveness.
51. In his *Methodica,* Apel stated that in terms of both its material cause (that is, its subject matter) and its formal cause (that is, its form), law *(ius)* is divided into public law and private law, and private law, in turn, into written law and unwritten law. In terms of its efficient cause (that is, its source), Apel divided law into natural law, law of nations, and civil (i.e., Roman) law. Thus unwritten private law was derived from natural law and written private law from civil law. Although this classification did not exclude the derivation of public law partly from civil law, Apel's analysis of civil law tended to focus primarily on its private law aspects.
52. On the divisions between public law and private law in Roman law and earlier

canon law, see Hans Mullejans, *Publicus und Privatus im römischen Recht und im alteren kanonischen Recht unter besonderer Berücksichtigung der Unterscheidung Ius publicum und Ius privatum* (Munich, 1961). Mullejans concludes from his careful study of the sources that the Roman lawyers and the early ecclesiastical lawyers "made no clear distinction" between a "*ius publicum,* that is, a law pertinent to the affairs of the state or of the ecclesiastical domain" and "a *ius privatum,* that is a law governing the private affairs of persons" (pp. 1–3, 187–188).

53. Apel, *Methodica,* fol. 27sr. Johann Oldendorp adopted these distinctions in his *Lexicon juris civilis* (1547). See Stintzing, *Geschichte der Rechtswissenschaft,* p. 296. Apel's systematization is sharply criticized by Wieacker, *Humanismus und Rezeption,* pp. 84–86. To Wieacker, Apel's system was based on he "illusion" that the law could be reformed with "sterile mechanical dialectics." Wieacker adds, "A new systematization of law could have been obtained only on the basis of a new form of community and society and thus also a newly directed fundamental idea of justice." Contrary to Wieacker, I contend that it was precisely the "new form of community and society" introduced by the Protestant Reformation and also the "newly directed fundamental idea of justice" associated with Protestantism that are reflected in Apel's "new systematization of law."

54. Wieacker, *Humanismus und Rezeption,* p. 69.

55. Among other important sixteenth- and seventeenth-century works by German and Dutch authors exemplifying the new systematic method of law are the following (arranged alphabetically according to author and dated according to the date of the first available published edition): Johannes Althusius (ca. 1556–1638), *Iurisprudentiae Romanae Methodicae Digestae Libri Duo* (1586); idem., *Dicaeologicae Libri Tres, Totum et Universum Ius, Quo Utimur, Methodice Complectentes* (1618); Benedict Carpzov (1595–1666), *Practicae Novae Imperialis Saxonicae Rerum Criminalium* (1703); Balthasar Clammer (d. 1578), *Compendium Iuris* (1591); Hermann Conring (1606–1681), *Opera Iuridica Historica, Politica et Philosophica* (1648); Christoph Ehem (1528–1592), *De Principiis Iuris Libri Septem* (1556); Gerhard Feltmann (1637–1696), *Institutiones Juris Novissimi* (1671); idem, *De Jure in Re et ad Rem* (1672); Johann Thomas Freigius (1543–1583), *Methodica Actionum Iuris Repetitio ad Ordinem Iurisconsulti Triboniani Instituta* (1569); idem, *Partitiones Juris Utriusque* (1571); Ludwig von Freudenstein Gremp (1509–1583), *Codicis Justinianei Methodica Tractatio* (1593); Hugo Grotius (1583–1645), *De Iure Belli ac Pacis Libri Tres* (1646); Johann Gottlieb Heineccius (1681–1741), *Elementa Juris Civilis Secundum Ordinem Pandectarum* (1731); Joachim Hopperus (1523–ca. 1580), *De Iuris Arte Libri Tres* (1553); Joannes Kahl (d. ca. 1552), *Jurisprudentiae Romanae Synopsis Methodica* (1595); Melchior Kling (1504–1571), *Das gantze Sechsisch Landrecht mit Text und Gloss in eine richtige Ordnung gebracht* (1572); Samuel Pufendorf (1632–1694), *De Officio Hominis et Civis Juxta Legem Naturalem Libri Duo* (1673); Mattaeus Stephani (1576–1646), *Exegesis Iuris Civilis, Quotimur, ad Methodum Institutionum Justiniani Imperatoris Concinnata et Secundum Tria Iuris Objecta, Tribus Partibus Comprehensa* (1617); idem, *Tractatus Methodus de Arte Juris et Eius Principiis* (1631); Samuel Stryk (1640–1710), *Institutiones Juris Civilis cum Notis* (1703); idem, *Specimen Usus Moderni Pandectarum* (1708); Christoph Sturtz (ca. 1555–1603), *Methodus Logica Universi Iuris Civilis in Quatuor Institutionum, Quinquaginta Pandectarum et Novem Libros Codicis, Iusta Ratione Continuationis Omnium Titulorum Anima-adversa et Proposita* (1591); Nicolaus Vigelius (1529–1600), *Methodus Iuris Controversi* (1579); idem, *Methodus Juris Pontifici* (1577); idem, *Methodus Observatium Camerae Imperialis* (ca. 1579); idem, *Methodus Universi Iuris Civilis Absolutissima* (1561); idem, *Partitiones Iuris Civilis: Digestorum Suorum*

Rationem et Ordinem Breviter Demonstrates (1571); idem, *Praefatio Apologetica: Methodus Duplex Commentariorum Tiraquelli* (1586); Hermann Vultejus (1555–1634), *Iurisprudentiae Romanae Justiniano Compositae Libri Duo* (1590).

56. Of the later sixteenth-century German and Dutch jurists Udo Wolter writes that "by far the greatest number were Protestant." Udo Wolter, *Ius Canonicum in Iure Civili: Studien zur Rechtsquellenlehre in der neueren Privatrechtsgeschichte* (Cologne, 1975), p. 59. Of the authors listed in n. 55, apparently only Hopper and Freigius remained loyal to the Roman Catholic Church.

57. For biographical and bibliographical information on Konrad Lagus, see Theodor Muther, *Zur Geschichte der Rechtswissenschaft und der Universitaten in Deutschland* (Jena, 1876), pp. 299ff.; idem, "Lagus, Konrad," in *Allgemeine Deutsche Biographie;* Stintzing, *Geschichte der Rechtswissenschaft,* pp. 296ff.; Theuerkauf, *Lex,* pp. 183ff.; Hans Erich Troje, "Wissenschaftlichkeit und System in der Jurisprudenz des 16. Jahrhundert," in Jürgen Blühdorn and Joachim Ritter, eds., *Philosophie und Rechtswissenschaft: Zum Problem ihrer Beziehungen im 19. Jahrhundert* (Frankfurt am Main, 1969), pp. 76ff.

58. Konrad Lagus, *Protestatio Adversus Improbam Suorum Commentariorum de Doctrina Iuris Editionem ab Egenolpho Factam* (Danzig, 1544), A.4v. Cf. Theuerkauf, *Lex,* p. 201, n. 74; and Troje, "Wissenschaftlichkeit und System in der Jurisprudenz des 16. Jahrhundert," p. 76. Troje properly relates this insight to the thought of Melanchthon: "Konrad Lagus . . . sought to write a juridical pendant to Melanchthon's *Loci communes theologici.* His methodological obsevations and excursions are very clearly inspired by Melanchthon."

59. Lagus, *Protestatio,* A.4v.

60. Lagus's *Juris Utriusque Methodica Traditio* was reprinted frequently throughout Europe: in Frankfurt (1543, 1552, 1565), in Paris (1545), in Lyon (1544, 1546, 1562, 1566, 1592), in Louvain (1550, 1552, 1565), and in Basel (1553).

61. Lagus, *Juris Utriusque Methodica Traditio,* B.lv.

62. Theuerkauf, *Lex,* p. 206; see also Gilbert, *Renaissance Concepts,* p. 112 and sources cited therein.

63. Lagus, *Methodica,* B. I. "All the so-called *loci ordinarii* of the law," he wrote, "were never brought together [by the scholastic jurists] into an ordered relationship. Through the structuring of this relationship a student may readily see what the connection is [between *loci*] and how they reveal, to a certain extent, a compendium of all legal knowledge. One can find some progress towards this in the so-called *Summae,* particularly those of Azo and Hostiensis. But the summists did not attempt to divide the whole body of the law into distinct principal members. They were only concerned to describe dialectically (or dogmatically) the content of specific titles in given ordinances that they found in the Justinian Code or the Decretals. They were far more concerned with the individual titles than with a *methodum juris.*"

64. Lagus, *Methodica,* B.lv. Cf. Theuerkauf, *Lex,* p. 201, n. 73. Stintzing writes: "Lagus's *Methodica* . . . is indeed the oldest comprehensive compendium of the law." Stintzing, *Geschichte der Rechtswissenschaft,* p. 300.

65. Theuerkauf, *Lex,* p. 206, states that "it may be supposed" that Lagus "had learned of Apel's attempts to apply dialectics to jurisprudence," and that "perhaps" Lagus was familiar with the 1535 edition of Apel's *Methodica* and the 1540 edition of his *Isagoge,* but that any influences "cannot be proved." He then states specifically that the fact that Lagus made a fundamental division of the civil law into ownership and obligation "must not be traced back to Apel's influence but can much

rather rest immediately on the Institutes of Justinian." A similar interpretation was offered earlier by Otto von Gierke, who wrote: "Lagus, to be sure, was the first to carry through the idea of a systematic legal textbook, but he retained the essential order of the Institutes." Otto von Gierke, *Johannes Althusius und die Entwicklung der naturrechtlichen Staatstheorien,* vol. 5 (Aalen, Scientia Verlag, 1958), p. 38. These conclusions are unfounded. In fact, the Institutes of Justinian gives no basis for Lagus's—and Apel's—division of civil law into two fundamental parts, the one constituting *dominium* (or *res*) and the other *obligatio.* On the contrary, the Institutes proposes, but does not follow, a classification into persons, things, and actions, which Apel rejected and Lagus criticized and transformed. The Institutes defines *dominium* as ownership *in re* but does not distinguish it from rights *ad rem.* For further discussion of the separation of the law of ownership from the law of obligations, see Chapter 5.

In accounting for the important similarities in the writings of the two men, one must start with the fact that for many years they were colleagues at the University of Wittenberg, teaching very similar subjects, and that they were both ardent followers of Luther and Melanchthon. It was usual at that time for authors not to cite the works of other contemporary authors. Lagus's dependence on his Wittenberg colleagues as well as his advance beyond them, is explained incisively by Muther, *Aus dem Universitäts- und Gelehrtenleben,* pp. 308–309. "While Apel placed all his emphasis on the dogmatic dialectical treatment of individual legal data and only later advanced to a systematic treatment of these data, Lagus had from the beginning placed foremost emphasis on the system. Until that time, one had always sharply separated the sources of Roman and canon law and lectured separately on the contents of these texts. It was Lagus who first undertook to combine these sources and bodies of law into a whole and to depict dogmatically in a systematic compendium a Roman law modified by canon law. I believe I do not err when I point to Melanchthon as the model whom Lagus sought to emulate in this regard. In 1521 this praeceptor of Germany first published his *Loci Communes,* a systematic summary of theology which can be regarded as the first compendium of Protestant dogma. The great success which this book achieved, the important influence which it had on the study of theology, stirred other disciplines, particularly jurisprudence, to seek to imitate it."

66. This "causal" analysis is drawn from Lagus, *Methodica* (Lyon, 1544), pp. 9–12, 24–26.
67. Ibid., p. 68.
68. See Theuerkauf, *Lex,* p. 201.
69. The canonists had to know some Roman law; the great twelfth-century canonist Hostiensis wrote a treatise on Roman law. The Romanists, by contrast, usually ignored canon law, although the great thirteenth-century jurist Baldus was both a Romanist and a canonist and wrote extensively on each law. The two subjects were taught separately, and books were written on the differences between them. See nn. 70 and 71.
70. Cf. Muther, *Aus dem Universitäts- und Gelehrtenleben.* On the separation of Roman law and canon law in legal education and in legal literature prior to the sixteenth century, see Wolter, *Ius Canonicum,* pp. 1–52. Wolter (pp. 50–51) writes: "The glossators occupied themselves only superficially with the canon law. Only on specific questions of marriage law and the law of interest was the primary value of canon law acknowledged." The commentators, such as Bartolus and Baldus, he continues, building on their comparative studies of canon law and Roman law,

made increasing use of certain canon law concepts and prescriptions in the areas of marriage and family law, protection of property interests, and bona fide contracts. They also used concepts of canonical equity to mitigate against the rigor of the law in individual cases. "But the overlap of canon law and civil law," even among the commentators, Wolter concludes, "consisted only in the adoption of individual statutory prescriptions of the *Corpus Juris Canonici* and remained thereby only sporadic."

71. A similar method was used by Oldendorp in his important work *Collatio Iuris Civilis et Iuris Canonici* (A Collation of Civil Law and Canon Law); for an excellent example of this "bringing together" of the Roman law and canon law, see Lagus's discussion "De Obligationibus Quae ex Quasi Contractu Oriuntur," in *Methodica,* pp. 364–367.
72. Theuerkauf, *Lex,* p. 208. Lagus's *Methodica* was last published in 1592.
73. Konrad Lagus, *Compendium Juris Civilis et Saxonici: In grundlicher ordentlicher ausszug/begriff und einhalt des Keys- und Sachsischen Rechten* (first published in Magdeburg in 1597 and again in 1603). Unlike the *Sachsenspiegel,* Lagus's compendium treated only the *Landrecht,* not the *Lehnrecht.* See Theuerkauf, *Lex,* pp. 281, 284–287, 290–291.
74. For biographical and bibliographical information on Vigelius, see Stintzing, *Geschichte der Rechtswissenschaft,* pp. 424–440; A. London Fell, *Origins of Legislative Sovereignty and the Legislative State,* vol. 2 (Cambridge, Mass., 1983), pp. 111–113; idem, "Nicolaus Vigelius," in *Allgemeine Deutsche Biographie,* 39:693.
75. Vigelius produced other "methodical" treatises during his long life. See Stintzing, *Geschichte der Rechtswissenschaft,* pp. 428–440. His *Digesta,* published between 1568 and 1571 in Basel, is a massive seven-volume work, of which the first volume is devoted to public law. He begins it with a chapter on "definitions and divisions" of law, in which he analyzes law in terms of the four Aristotelian causes in a manner similar to that of Lagus. He also produced a systematic commentary on the *Carolina* in German and in Latin; this was the first systematic treatise on German criminal law. See Chapter 6.
76. For biographical and bibliographical information on Althusius, see Stintzing, *Geschichte der Rechtswissenschaft,* pp. 468–477; idem, "Althusius, Johann," in *Allgemeine Deutsche Biographie;* von Gierke, *Johannes Althusius.*
77. See von Gierke, *Johannes Althusius,* pp. 37–49; Stintzing, *Geschichte der Rechtswissenschaft,* pp. 468–477.
78. The following sixteenth- and seventeenth-century authors from Spain, France, and England are among those who contributed important works to the European jus commune: Diego de Covarruvias y Leyva, *Variarum ex Iure Pontificio Regio, et Caesario Resolutionum Libri Tres* (1545); Francisco Suarez (1548–1617), *Jurisprudentiae Romanae a Justiniano Compositae Libri II* (1590); Hugues Donellus (1527–1591), *Commentariarum Juris Civilis* (1576); Sir Arthur Duck (1580–1648), *De Usu et Authoritate Juris Civilis Romanorum in Dominiis Principum Christianorum* (1653).
79. *Utrumque jus* is usually translated "both laws." Other possible translations are "each law" and "one and the other law." To this day European legal scholars may receive the degree J.U.D., standing for *juris utriusque doctor,* "doctor of both laws," meaning doctor of both Roman law and canon law.
80. A typical example is the work of the Spanish Roman Catholic jurist Covarruvias, cited n. 78, which, on the one hand, states in its table of contents that the *ius commune* consists of general principles drawn from canon and Roman law, but which on the other hand devotes the third of its three main parts *(libri)* to royal and feudal law as part of the *ius commune.* Similarly, the sixteenth-century English

Romanist legal scholar Sir Arthur Duck included the *Libri Feudorum,* a twelfth-century digest of feudal law, as a category within the *jus commune.* See Peter Stein, "A Seventeenth-Century English View of the European *Jus Commune,*" pp. 719–720.

81. Martin Lipen, the eighteenth-century bibliographer, created a category for this literature titled *Differentiae Juris.* See Martin Lipen, *Bibliotheca Realis Juridica* (Hildesheim, 1746). Under Lipen's general heading "Differentiae inter Jus Canonicum et Civile," there are twenty-one titles, the oldest dated 1535, the most recent dated 1746. A list of dozens of books written from the twelfth to the early sixteenth centuries concerning differences between Roman and canon law, and a report of their tables of contents, is given in Jean Portemer, *Recherches sur les "Differentiae juris civilis et canonici" au temps du droit classique de l'Église* (Paris, 1946). There seems to be a sharp contrast between the earlier *differentiae* literature and the later, arising from the fact that the earlier literature was directed to two separate jurisdictions, the ecclesiastical and the secular, while the later was directed to a single secular jurisdiction in which the earlier canon law still survived. It is this combining of the two species under a single genus that has led modern historians to speak of the sixteenth-century European *jus commune* as being based on "Roman-canon" law. The emergence of the later sixteenth-century *differentiae iuris* literature occurred against the backdrop of what Luigi Moccia has identified as the first stage of the emergence of the discipline of comparative law. The purpose of comparative law during this phase, Moccia states, was to provide "a way of searching for concordances among state legal systems." See Luigi Moccia, "Historical Overview on the Origins and Attitudes of Comparative Law," in Bruno de Witte and Caroline Forder, eds., *The Common Law of Europe and the Future of Legal Education* (Cambridge, Mass., 1992), p. 613.
82. Thus Johann Oldendorp, in defining *jus commune,* states that it "represents the natural law [*pro iure naturali*]" (*Lexicon Juris* [1546], p. 250). Oldendorp himself wrote a book titled *Collatio Juris Civilis et Canonici, Maximum Afferens Boni et Aequicognillinem* (Cologne, 1541), in which he emphasized not the "differences" but the "collation," that is, the common features of the two systems. See Heinz Mohnhaupt, "Die Diffentienliteratur als Ausdrsuck eines methodischen Prinzips früher Rechtsvergleichung," in Bernard Durand and Laurent Mayali, eds., *Exceptiones Iuris: Studies in Honour of André Gouron* (Berkeley, 2000), pp. 439–458. Mohnhaupt emphasizes (p. 450) the role of Oldendorp in using the comparison of Roman and canon law "not only for the exposure of the differences between [them] but also to elaborate what they have in common." Oldendorp did not write a "scientific *Methodica*" of law, similar to those of Apel, Lagus, and Vigelius, which built on Melanchthon's *praecipui juris loci,* but he did write in 1541 a philosophical *Loci Iuris Communes,* building on Melanchthon's universal topics.
83. For discussion of the sixteenth-century French contribution to legal science, see Kelley, *Foundations,* pp. 53–148; Andersen, *No Bird Phoenix,* pp. 112–122; Phillipson, "Jacques Cujas"; and Coing, *Handbuch,* pp. 56–58, 238–242, 756–759, 786–787, 902–926.

4. The Transformation of German Criminal Law

1. See John H. Langbein, *Prosecuting Crime in the Renaissance: England, Germany, France* (Cambridge, Mass., 1974) pp. 129–209; Eberhard Schmidt, *Einf ührung in die Geschichte der deutschen Strafrechtsplege* (Göttingen, 1965); Robert von Hippel, *Deutsches Strafrecht,* Bd. 1 (Berlin, 1925), pp. 159–220.

2. "The problem of poverty and vagrancy had reached an acuteness probably never before encountered." Thorsten Sellin, *Pioneering and Penology: The Amsterdam Houses of Correction in the Sixteenth and Seventeenth Centuries* (1942), p. 8, quoted in John H. Langbein, *Torture and the Law of Proof: Europe and England in the Ancien Régime* (Chicago, 1977), p. 33. See Robert Jütte, *Poverty and Deviance, in Early Modern Europe* (Cambridge, 1994), pp. 143–157.
3. See Berman, *Law and Revolution,* pp. 371–380, 503–510.
4. Ibid., pp. 57–58. See also Robert Bartlett, *Trial by Fire and Water: The Medieval Judicial Ordeal* (Oxford, 1986), and the sources cited therein.
5. Although John Langbein follows Schmidt and others in terming this system "Roman-canon *Inquisitionsprozess,*" he nevertheless acknowledges that it was "considerably more canon than Roman in its sources" and that "the notoriously ill-defined Justinian sources could not and did not sustain the extensive medieval elaboration." See Langbein, *Prosecuting Crime,* pp. 129, 138. In fact, hardly any of the Roman law of procedure, whether criminal procedure or civil procedure, survived in the West.
6. There is considerable disagreement among scholars concerning the time when the inquisitorial procedure was introduced into German practice. Some say the fifteenth century, some say the fourteenth, some say the thirteenth or twelfth. One source of confusion is the fact that there was no German national state in those centuries but rather, on the one hand, a Holy Roman Empire of the German Nation, which had very limited criminal jurisdiction, and, on the other hand, a large number of German "lands" *(Länder),* each of which had its own system of courts. Another source of confusion is the almost universal practice among nineteenth- and twentieth-century medievalists of treating the canon law of the Roman Catholic Church as foreign law—indeed, foreign not only to Germany but to all other countries of Western Christendom as well. Cf. Schmidt, *Einführung,* pp. 28–29. Thus Langbein writes that inquisitorial procedure "did not harden in Germany until the sixteenth century"—apparently meaning by "Germany" the empire and at that point overlooking both the law of the church in Germany and the law of the German territories. Langbein does not deny that in both the empire and the territories, church courts were applying inquisitorial procedure from the twelfth century on, and that these German church courts were staffed by German canon lawyers. The inquisitorial procedure which they applied was gradually adopted, with modifications, in the various German territorial courts from at least the thirteenth century. See Udo Wolter, *Ius Canonicum in Iure Civili* (Cologne, 1975), pp. 8–9.
7. Cf. U.S. Constitution, art. 3, sec. 3: "No Person shall be convicted of Treason unless on the Testimony of two Witnesses to the same overt act, or on Confession in open Court." The two-witness rule was a creation of the canonists and Romanists, utilizing both Roman law and scriptural authority as sources. Perhaps the fact that it was a product of their own conscious deliberation contributed to their willingness to carve out exceptions to it. See Richard Fraher, "Ut nullus describatur reus prius quam convincatur: Presumption of Innocence in Medieval Canon Law," in Stephan Kuttner and Kenneth Pennington, eds., *Proceedings of the Sixth International Congress of Medieval Canon Law* (Vatican City, 1985), p. 494. Cf. H. van Vliet, *No Single Testimony: A Study on the Adaptation of the Law of Deuteronomy 19:15 into the New Testament* (Utrecht, 1956) (exploring the scriptural origins of the two-witness rule).
8. See Langbein, *Torture and the Law of Proof.* Writing of the reaction to the abolition of ordeals, Langbein states (p. 7): "The Roman-canon law of proof solved the

problem of how to make the judgment of men palatable. That judgment was to rest on certainty. It was to rest upon standards of proof so high that no one would be concerned that God was no longer being asked to resolve the doubts." This view has been challenged by Richard Fraher, "Conviction According to Conscience: The Medieval Jurists' Debate Concerning Judicial Discretion and the Law of Proof," *Law and History Review* 7 (1989), 23–88; and by Mirjan Damaska, "The Death of Legal Torture," *Yale Law Journal* 87 (1978), 860–884 (reviewing Langbein). Damaska argues that Langbein exaggerates the rigidity in this new system of proofs (pp. 865–866). Cf. Walter Ullmann, "Reflections on Medieval Torture," *Juridical Review* 56 (1944), 123–137 (outlining the rules and principles that guided the application of torture in the thirteenth through fifteenth centuries).

9. On those immune from torture, see Langbein, *Torture and the Law of Proof*, p. 13.
10. Ibid., p. 7.
11. See Fraher, "Conviction According to Conscience," pp. 37–38. Under the system of "legal proofs" or "statutory proofs," one eyewitness would constitute a half proof, as would evidence of admissions of guilt made to others before arrest, and taken together these two half proofs would add up to a full proof. Testimony of a witness rather than an eyewitness might constitute quarter proof. See J. P. Levy, *La hiérarchie des preuves dans le droit savant du moyen age* (Paris, 1939).
12. See Fraher, "Conviction According to Conscience," p. 52. Laura Stern makes much the same observation concerning fifteenth-century Florence: "Most crimes had a set amount of proof which was required to condemn. . . . [T]his would seem to limit the discretion of the judge and make his decisions automatic, again tending to give justice a formulaic character. However, judgments did not function like this in practice. If a litigation was contested, the proof was weighed by all the judges and the rector. In practice, there was a great deal of inexactitude concerning the quality of proof and the ways different qualities of proof could be combined. In the trials of many crimes, the judge was given a great deal of discretion, even in the proof stage." See Laura Ikins Stern, *The Criminal Law System of Medieval and Renaissance Florence* (Baltimore, 1994), pp. 31–32. Cf. Walter Ullmann, "Medieval Principles of Evidence," *Law Quarterly Review* 62 (1946), 82–83 ("The conception of the judge as a seeker after truth entailed that strict and binding rules of evidence were out of the question. . . . [The judge] was at complete liberty in sifting and evaluating the evidence. In other words, the jurists would not allow this freedom to determine the relative value of conflicting evidence to be restricted by a strait-jacket of fixed and rigid rules. Truth, they thought, is obtainable in many a way, and the discovery of truth would certainly not be furthered by forcing the judge to observe certain classes or rules of evidence."
13. Thus the fourteenth-century canonist William Durantis defined *pene occultum* crime: "It is said 'almost,' that is *quasi* secret, because since a few know it, perhaps two or three, or even five, it can thus nevertheless be proven." William Durantis, *Speculum Iudicialis*, pars iii, rubric, Quid sit occultum? (Lyon, 1574). See Fraher, "Conviction According to Conscience," pp. 48–51 (discussing the views of canonists Durantis, Hostiensis, and Johannes Andreae on the distinction between *pene occultum* crimes and "manifest" or "notorious" offenses).
14. Quoted in Harold J. Berman, "Law and Belief in Three Revolutions," *Valparaiso Law Review* 18 (1984), 581–582, n. 13.
15. See Herbert L. Packer, "Two Models of the Criminal Process," *University of Pennsylvania Law Review* 113 (1964), 1–68. This conflict had important parallels in earlier canonist and Romanist literature. The thirteenth-century canonist Hos-

tiensis argued that the "public interest" permitted the ecclesiastical courts to dispense with a number of procedural formalities for the sake of controlling crime, while Pope Innocent IV, writing privately as a canonist and not in his capacity as pope, argued that "due process" safeguards ought nevertheless to be observed. Richard Fraher has argued that eventually the "public interest" model of Hostiensis became the prevailing philosophy of criminal prosecution in both civilian and canonist circles. See Richard Fraher, "The Theoretical Justification for the New Criminal Law of the High Middle Ages: '*Rei Publicae Interest, Ne Crimina Remaneant Impunita*,' " *University of Illinois Law Review* (1984), 581–589.

16. See Erik Wolf, *Grosse Rechtsdenker der deutschen Geistesgeschichte*, 4th ed. (Tübingen, 1963), p. 102, reprinted in Friedrich-Christian Schroeder, ed., *Die Carolina: Die peinliche Gerichtsordnung Kaiser Karls V von 1532* (Darmstadt, 1986), pp. 120–184. See also Stintzing, *Geschichte der Rechtswissenschaft*, pp. 612–617; Hippell, *Deutsches Strafrecht*, pp. 196–199; Langbein, *Prosecuting Crime*, pp. 163–165.
17. See Otto Stobbe, *Geschichte der deutschen Rechtsquellen*, Bd. 2 (Aalen, 1965), pp. 242–243. Schwarzenberg headed a group of experts, but Wolf states that we do not know who they were and what they contributed. See Wolf, *Grosse Rechtsdenker*, pp. 115–118.
18. After the establishment in 1495 of the first professional imperial court, the *Reichskammergericht*, it was felt immediately that additional legislation was needed to define its criminal jurisdiction and the procedure by which it was to operate in criminal cases. See Stintzing, *Geschichte der Rechtswissenschaft*, pp. 622ff. At the *Reichstag* at Freiburg in 1497–1498, it was recommended that there be prepared "a common Reformation and Statute [*Ordnung*] as to how one should proceed in criminal matters." At the Augsburg *Reichstag* of 1500 this recommendation was raised to a decision to be executed by the *Reichsregiment* with the advice and help of the *Kammergericht*. But the matter was dropped and only taken up again at the Mainz *Reichstag* of 1517, when the estates adopted a memorial *(Denkschrift)* to the emperor in which existing evils were depicted. Still nothing happened. In January 1521 the *Reichstag* at Worms appointed a committee to draft a statute on capital crimes, which it promptly did, and in April 1521 the estates transmitted the draft to the *Reichsregiment* for consideration and revision. The *Reichsregiment* then appointed a committee, headed by Schwarzenberg, to prepare the legislation. By then the Bambergensis had received very wide circulation, having been printed as a handbook, and it was adopted as the working draft by the committee. It went through a number of subsequent drafts before final adoption in 1532. See nn. 23 and 24.
19. "Roughly a fifth of the Bambergensis articles did not find their way into the Carolina; and a handful of Carolina articles have no Bambergensis counterparts. The Carolina not infrequently revises a Bambergensis provision. However, in the perspective of the whole work, the revisions are minor. The Carolina is effectively a version of the Bambergensis." Langbein, *Prosecuting Crime*, p. 163, n. 96. Cf. Stintzing, *Geschichte der Rechtswissenschaft*, p. 629.
20. See Heinrich Zoepfl, ed., *Die Peinliche Gerichtsordnung Kaiser Karls V neben der Bamberger und der Brandenburger Halsgerichtsordnung*, 3rd synoptic ed. (Leipzig, 1883), in which the Bambergensis, the 1521 and 1529 drafts of the Carolina, and the final 1532 version are placed side by side in parallel columns, with footnote references to minor variations in the Brandenburg version of the Bambergensis. These are all in the original Old German, there apparently being no modern German translation. There have been subsequent translations into French, Latin,

Polish, Low German, and Russian (1967). Langbein, *Prosecuting Crime,* p. 140. Langbein notes that Peter the Great is said to have studied the Carolina in preparing a code of military law, and that substantive provisions of the Carolina were cited by German courts as late as the 1870s.

21. Azo, in about 1210, wrote glosses on the criminal law provisions of Justinian's Codex; other Romanists who wrote summaries of the criminal law included William Durantis and Albert Gandinus, whose *Tractatus de Maleficiis,* published in 1299, greatly influenced fourteenth- and fifteenth-century criminal law. These and other authors are listed in Wolf, *Gross Rechtsdenker,* p. 105. Wolf, like many others who write on the history of criminal law in this period, lists Romanists but omits canonists, who in fact were even more influential at the time. This omission is corrected by Fraher, "Conviction According to Conscience," who discusses, among other thirteenth- to fifteenth-century canonists who wrote influential works on criminal law, Tancred, Johannes Andrae, and Angelinus Aretinus.
22. For German *Halsgerichtsordnungen,* prior to 1507, see Stobbe, *Geschichte der deutschen Rechtsquellen,* Bd. 2, pp. 237–241. These earlier statutory enactments are much more primitive than the Bambergensis. The Nuremberg *Halsgerichtsordnung* of 1481, for instance, briefly lists only a few crimes, such as theft and murder. Ibid., p. 240.
23. See Georg Dahm, *Untersuchungen zur Verfassungs- und Strafrechtsgeschichte der italienischen Stadt im Mittelalter* (Hamburg, 1941), pp. 42–56; and Carlo Calisse, *A History of Italian Law* (Boston, 1928), pp. 173–179. The Library of Congress holds the texts of the *statuti* of over forty Italian city-states in its collection. These include large cities, such as Turin, Bologna, Cremona, Viterbo, and Trent, and many smaller municipalities, such as Apricale, Aviano, Celle, Fondi, and others. The city of Florence also produced a major codification of the law. See Josef Kohler and G. degli Azzi, *Das florentiner Strafrecht des XIV. Jahrhunderts mit einem Anhang über den Strafprozess der italienischen Statuten* (Mannheim, 1909). See also the discussion later in this chapter.
24. Gerhard Schmidt, "Sinn und Bedeutung der Constitution Criminalis Carolina als Ordnung des materiellen und prozessualen Rechts," *ZSS* (Germ. Abt.) 83 (1966), 239, 252–253.
25. Reinhart Maurach, *Deutsches Strafrecht,* 4th ed. (Karlsruhe, 1971), p. 47. Maurach lists territorial codifications in Hesse (1535), Kurpfalz (1582), Hamburg (1603), and Bavaria (1616), adding that "all these laws are connected but nevertheless constituted *das gemeine deutsche Strafrecht.*"
26. See Emil Brunnenmeister, *Die Quellen der Bambergensis: Ein Beitrag zur Geschichte des Deutschen Strafrechts* (Leipzig, 1879).
27. Wolf, *Grosse Rechtsdenker,* p. 109. Cf. Constitutio Criminalis Carolina (hereafter CCC), art. 104.
28. Friedrich Karl von Savigny, *Of the Vocation of Our Age for Legislation and Jurisprudence,* trans. Abraham Hayward (New York, 1975), pp. 68–69.
29. Carlo Calisse, for instance, has stated, regarding criminal punishments in Italy of the fourteenth and fifteenth centuries: "The penalty aimed both to punish the criminal and, by inspiring terror, to prevent repetition and imitation. Such a system produced very cruel penalties. There was death, made terrible in many ways: mutilation, blinding, torture, flogging, exposing in cages, unspeakable prisons—all with a view to instill fear." See Calisse, *History of Italian Law,* p. 175.
30. CCC, art. 6. See August Schoetensack, *Der Strafprozess der Carolina* (Leipzig, 1904), pp. 96–97.

31. CCC, arts. 12–15.
32. CCC, art. 12.
33. Langbein, in *Prosecuting Crime,* translates *redliche Anzeigung* as "legally sufficient indication" and characterizes it as "something close to the Anglo-American law's idea of probable cause" (p. 161). It should be noted, however, that in non-capital cases, "legally sufficient indication" was enough not only to accuse but also to convict. In capital cases, however, a distinction was made between "sufficient indication" to justify examination under torture and "sufficient proof" to justify conviction without torture.
34. Thus Article 23 provides that "every sufficient indication upon which it is sought to examine under torture shall be proven with two good witnesses, as described below in several articles concerning sufficient proof." Article 25 then lists eight "matters which raise suspicion" and thus may justify investigation, although Article 27 cautions that "none of these matters of suspicion alone suffices as legally sufficient indication upon which basis torture may be employed." Article 27 goes on to state that when two or more of eight previously listed matters of suspicion are present, the person responsible for conducting torture "shall determine whether the aforementioned . . . matters of suspicion really constitute sufficient indication" for "examination under torture." Articles 29–32 then establish general principles to guide the investigators as to when torture may licitly be employed. Articles 45–47 establish rules for the proper conduct of examinations under torture, while Article 33 provides special rules where an allegation of murder is being investigated. The translations of the Carolina used herein are drawn, for the most part, from Langbein, *Prosecuting Crime,* pp. 266–308.
35. CCC, art. 20.
36. CCC, art. 69.
37. CCC, art. 59.
38. Bambergensis, art. 33.
39. CCC, art. 37.
40. CCC, art. 43.
41. CCC, art. 52.
42. CCC, arts. 71, 74, 65. Cf. art. 67: "When a crime is proved with at least two or three credible good witnesses, who testify from a true knowledge, then there shall be process and judgment of penal law according to the nature of the case."
43. CCC, arts. 41, 137. Cf. Schoetensack, *Strafprozess der Carolina,* p. 79, discussing the orality of the process.
44. See Langbein, *Prosecuting Crime,* p. 172.
45. Quoted and discussed ibid., p. 172.
46. Langbein (ibid., pp. 172–174) contends that these provisions show the draftsman's "astounding distrust of the competence of the courts for which he was legislating," and that they also work against the goal of narrowing the arbitrariness of criminal law, in effect authorizing definitions of crimes beyond the statute, "contrary to the modern principle of strict construction *(nulla poena sine lege).*" He goes on to say, however, that "what reconciles such discretion with the commitment to a criminal law of rules is the effort to have the discretion be rule-guided and professionally administered." The discretion provided for is not, he indicates, "discretion to proceed by fiat."
47. See Langbein, *Torture and the Law of Proof,* p. 57, summarizing Adolf Friedrich Stölzel, *Die Entwicklung des gelehrten Richtertums in deutschen Territorien: Einerechtsgeschichtliche Untersuchung mit vorzugswieser Berücksichtigung der Verhältnisse im Gebiet des ehemaligen Kurfürstentums Hessen,* Bd. 1 (Stuttgart, 1872), pp. 349, 355ff.

48. The Carolina goes a long way toward distinguishing between a general and a special part, although such a division is not complete. Thus Articles 106–136 deal with the punishments inflicted for various types of crime. Article 137 concerns "undisputed killings which occur in circumstances such that the punishment is excused," and is followed by treatments of self-defense (arts. 138–145), accidental deaths (145–146), and those who kill in fights and brawls (147). Articles 149–150 then address the "several sorts of homicide, which may also be subject to exculpation." Similarly, theft is divided into clandestine and public theft (arts. 156–157); first, second, and third offenses (158–161); aggravating circumstances (162); and circumstances that mitigate or excuse the theft, such as youthfulness or hunger (see art. 163, on youthfulness, and 165, on "genuine distress of hunger").
49. Exceptions are the crimes of arson (art. 125) and robbery (art. 126), for which only the penalties are prescribed. It is possible that Schwarzenberg and his colleagues assumed that in such cases the definitions of the old law should be applicable.
50. Three limited exceptions include definitions of some crimes in the Tyrolean territorial criminal procedure ordinance of 1499, the Radolfzell ordinance of 1506 (which, together with the Tyrolean law, made up the Maximilianischen Halsgerichtsordnungen), and the Wormser Reformation of 1498. See Eberhardt Schmidt, ed., *Die Maximilianischen Halsgerichtsordnungen für Tirol (1400) und Radolfzell (1506) als Zeugnisse mittelalterlicher Strafrechtspflege* (Bleckede/Elbe, 1949). The Wormser Reformation is unavailable in modern editions.
51. Thus Article 127 of the Carolina, repeating Article 152 of the Bambergensis, provides that "one who makes an evil uprising of the common people against the high magistracy [*Oberkeit*]" shall be beheaded or flogged or banished. References to civil penalties may be found in Articles 138, 158, and 167 of the Carolina. See also Schoetensack, *Strafprozess der Carolina*, pp. 37, 38.
52. CCC, art. 109.
53. Wolf, *Grosse Rechtsdenker*, p. 149.
54. CCC, art. 140.
55. See Langbein, *Prosecuting Crime*, p. 171.
56. See Stintzing, *Geschichte der Rechtswissenschaft*, pp. 623–624, 628, 267. Eleven years after Schwarzenberg's death, Luther wrote that to achieve certain results, "one would have to summon from all lands people who were thoroughly learned in Holy Scripture . . . including some from the secular estate . . . who would also be understanding and upright, as if Hans van Schwarzenberg still lived, whom one knew to trust." *WA*, pp. 50, 622, 11–16 (*Von den Konzilien und Kirchen*, 1539).
57. Thus Langbein's impressive study of the Carolina ignores entirely its relation to the Reformation. Neither the names of Melanchthon and Luther nor the analytical category "Reformation" appear in his index. Langbein sees the story entirely as the sixteenth-century triumph of an *Inquisitionsprozess* that began to develop as early as the thirteenth century in the courts of the canon law. See Langbein, *Prosecuting Crime*, pp. 154–155. In this respect he follows the traditional course of German legal historiography of the late nineteenth and twentieth centuries.
58. Carl Güterbock, *Die Entstehungsgeschichte der Carolina auf Grund archivalischer Forschungen* (Würzburg, 1872), p. 207.
59. See Stintzing, *Geschichte der Rechtswissenschaft*, p. 628.
60. Wolf writes: "Little of the theological studies and religious struggles that filled Schwarzenberg's life come to expression in the Bambergensis. . . . Its [concept of] justice could not yet be that of the Reformation. One can only call Schwarzenberg 'a legal thinker of the Reformation' insofar as [the Bambergensis]

gives evidence of the basic spiritual mood [*geistige Grundstimmung*] of the time." Erik Wolf, "Johann Freiherr von Schwarzenberg," in Schroeder, *Die Carolina,* p. 151.

61. See Wolf, "Johann Freiherr von Schwarzenberg," pp. 131–132, 135.
62. CCC, art. 11.
63. Wolf, "Johann Freiherr von Schwarzenberg," p. 146.
64. Stintzing, *Geschichte der Rechtswissenschaft,* pp. 620–621.
65. See Langbein, *Prosecuting Crime,* p. 168.
66. See ibid., pp. 171–172. See also Wolf, *Grosse Rechtsdenker,* pp. 126–127.
67. Wolf, "Johann Freiherr von Schwarzenberg," pp. 150–151.
68. Wieacker, *History of Private Law,* p. 100.
69. An analysis of the "general parts" of a few *statuti* demonstrates the large differences between these documents and the Carolina. The Italian "general parts" consist largely of exhortations and declarations of general purposes. Thus the third rubric of the *statuta* for Cremona, its "general part," consists of a single long paragraph admonishing the residents of the city to keep the peace. It states that one of the purposes of law is to keep the city in strength and vigor and that the peace of the ruler is promulgated and ordained in order to defend and conserve the people in their rights. See Gino Solazzi, ed., *Statuta et ordinamenta Communis Cremonae* (Milan, 1952), p. 11. Book 3 of the *statuta* of Teramo (1440) (including the town of Assisi), also a "general part," opens with a declaration of the authority by which the judge proceeds in criminal cases. Paragraph 1 declares that the judge exercises the power he has in order that the people might live honestly and the public interest in criminal prosecution be preserved. See Francesco Savini, ed., *Statuti del Commune di Teramo del 1440* (Florence, 1889), p. 104. The *proemium* of the *statuti* of Celle (1414) begins by invoking the Blessed Virgin, the angels, the apostles, and the saints to provide guidance to the city and then admonishes all concerned to obey the law. See Maddalena Cerisola, ed., *Gli statuti di Celle* (Bordighere, 1971), pp. 23–24.
70. This analysis is confirmed by an examination of the *statuti* of nineteen northern Italian cities held by the Library of Congress in Washington, D.C. Although these *statuti* widely in character, it may be said that generally their similarities to the Bambergensis and Carolina in procedure are more frequent than their similarities in substantive law. Thus some of these *statuti* place limitations on private prosecution through imposition of heavy fines on accusers who fail to prove their cases; cf. *Statuta et ordinamenta Communis Cremonae* (1389), pp. 39–40 (imposing fines on unsuccessful accusers), and *Statuti di Aviano del 1403* (requiring accuser to post security). Also some of these *statuti* contain restrictions on torture similar to those of the Bambergensis and Carolina. Thus the *Statuta Castra Serrae* (1473) requires "legitime probata inditia et sufficientia" (lawfully proved and sufficient indicia) before subjecting an accused person to torture. Even with reference to procedure, however, these *statuti* are quite skimpy with respect to such matters as the examination of witnesses, and none go so far as to distinguish hearsay from direct evidence.

    With respect also to substantive law, the Bambergensis and Carolina are far more comprehensive and sophisticated than the nineteen *statuti* under consideration. For example, although the *statuti* sometimes make mention of complicity and attempt, they do not define those terms, and they omit entirely general concepts such as necessary defense. They do speak of intent, usually identified as *irato animo* (with aroused mind) or *scienter* (knowingly), as an element of particular crimes, and they also occasionally provide for the reduction of punishment in the event of a spontaneous confession of wrongdoing (see *Statuti del Commune di Teramo del 1440,* pp. 131–132). Nothing is said, however, in the *statuti* under consideration about such matters as the exoneration of an accused person on the ground of an infirmity that causes lack of understanding. Although there are occasional references to appeals to higher courts, no procedure is provided for referring difficult cases to learned jurists—probably because the Italian judges themselves were supposed to be learned jurists, who sat without the presence of laymen and who were presumably familiar with the scholarly literature on criminal law written by Romanist and canonist jurists.

71. See Langbein, *Prosecuting Crime,* pp. 222 and 248–249 on the French ordinance and pp. 130–131 and 204ff. on the Marian statutes. The central points of his book are surely valid, namely, that there were certain common features in the substantial statutory reforms of criminal law that took place in major European countries in the sixteenth century, and that at the same time those reforms necessarily differed in some important respects because of differences in the preexisting national legal systems.

72. Friedrich Engels, *Der Deutsche Bauernkrieg* (1850), in Karl Marx and Friedrick Engels, *Werke,* Bd. 7 (Berlin, 1969), pp. 327, 332.

5. The Transformation of German Civil and Economic Law

1. The term "civil law" is used here in its contemporary sense, embracing chiefly the law of property, contract, tort, business associations, commercial transacations, and related fields, and not in the original Roman meaning of *jus civile,* "the law of [Roman] citizens," as contrasted with *jus gentium,* "the law of [all] peoples." In the period from the eleventh through the fifteenth centuries, Europeans called the entire body of Roman law *jus civile.* Large parts of that law, however, including Roman civil and criminal procedure, most of Roman substantive criminal law, Roman family law, Roman law relating to sacred rites, and Roman constitutional and administrative law, were largely ignored by the European Romanists. Sixteenth-century legal treatises, for the first time, made a sharp distinction between *jus publicum* and *jus privatum,* and what today is called civil law was classified largely under the heading of *jus privatum.* Continental European jurists, in contrast to English and American, still strongly emphasize the classification of law into "public law" and "private law." Thus what is treated in this chapter as civil law is often characterized by German legal historians as private law, although, as will be shown, much of it was heavily regulated by public authorities. The peculiar use of the term "civil law system" by contemporary Anglo-American legal scholars to characterize continental European legal systems, and to distinguish them from the Anglo-American "common law" system, is here rejected as wholly unhistorical. The term "economic law" is used here to identify those aspects of civil law that relate most closely to trade, investment, and finance and to economic development generally.

2. An important early example is the treatise of Hostiensis in the late-thirteenth-century *De Pactis,* "Concerning Agreements." Hostiensis includes the making of truces and the making of peace, the settlement of litigation for the purpose of avoiding judgment, and also commercial transactions. See *Summa Domini Henrici cardinalis Hostiensis* (1537; reprint, Aalen, 1962).

3. See Klaus-Peter Nanz, *Die Entstehung des allgemeinen Vertragsbegriffs, im 16. bis 18. Jahrhundert* (Munich, 1985), pp. 104ff.
4. Ibid.
5. Coing notes that the various contract doctrines of the sixteenth-century *jus commune* were "foreign to ancient Roman law," implying that they were new, without indicating that many of them had existed for centuries in the canon law of the church. Helmut Coing, *Europaisches Privatrecht*, Bd. 1, *Älteres Gemeines Recht (1500 bis 1800)* (Munich, 1985), p. 412.
6. See Gustaf Klemens Schmelzeisen, *Polizeiordnungen und Privatrecht* (Münster, 1955). Schmelzeisen is exceptional in analyzing the effect of territorial German policy ordinances, which regulated customary property and contract relations, on doctrines of private law.
7. See Matthias Weber, *Die Schlesischen Polizei- und Landesordnungen der frühen neuzeit* (Cologne, 1996), p. 222.
8. Otto Feger and Peter Ruster, *Das Konstanzer Wirtschafts- und Gewerberecht zur Zeit der Reformation* (Constance, 1961), pp. 55–56.
9. See Württemberg *Landesordnung* II (3) (1).
10. In Roman law, *Codex*, bk. 4, title 32, established the rules for taking interest on a loan. The term regularly used to describe such interest was *usura*, meaning "that which will be gained by use." There was no general prohibition of excessive interest, although Roman emperors from time to time did establish maximum limits on the amount that might be charged. See Adolf Berger, *Encyclopedic Dictionary of Roman Law* (Philadelphia, 1953), pp. 753–754. The Latin verb *interesse*, which meant "to have an interest in," did not designate interest due on a loan but rather signified the appropriate measure of damages when a contract had been broken. Thus in *Digesta* 13.4.2.8, the verb *interesse* referred to damages due when one who agreed to pay a fixed sum at Ephesus paid at Carthage instead. The late-twelfth-century Romanist Azo was apparently the first to use *interesse* as a noun, although his usage still conveyed the traditional Roman meaning of a measure of damages. See John T. Noonan, Jr., *The Scholastic Analysis of Usury* (Cambridge, Mass., 1957), p. 106. In the mid- or late thirteenth century, however, canonists used the term *interesse* to signify the lawful amount due a lender as compensation for his labor, his risk, or his potential loss of future profits, as distinct from amounts exceeding such compensation, to which the term *usura* then came to be confined. (pp. 112–115).
11. See Raymond de Roover, "The Concept of the Just Price: Theory and Practice," *Journal of Economic History* 18 (1958), 418–434; John W. Baldwin, *The Medieval Theories of the Just Price: Romanists, Canonists, and Theologians in the Twelfth and Thirteenth Centuries* (Philadelphia, 1959); Joel Kaye, *Economy and Nature in the Fourteenth Century: Money, Market Exchange, and the Emergence of Scientific Thought* (Cambridge, 1998), pp. 87–101.
12. See Terence P. McLaughlin, "The Teaching of the Canonists on Usury, Part II," *Mediaeval Studies* 2 (1940), 21, n. 204 (referring to secular statutes providing for the punishment of usurers).
13. The widely held Weberian theory that the doctrines of usury and just price were anti-capitalist in their nature and consequences (see n. 21) has been effectively refuted by John T. Gilchrist and John F. McGovern, among others. See John T. Gilchrist, *The Church and Economic Activity in the Middle Ages* (New York, 1969), pp. 274ff.; and John F. McGovern, "The Rise of New Economic Attitudes in Canon and Civil Law, A.D. 1200–1550," *Jurist* 32 (1972), 44–55.
14. See de Roover, "Concept of the Just Price," pp. 427–428.

15. Although a contrary view is often expressed, it is not supported by the evidence. See also Kaye, *Economy and Nature,* pp. 80–88. Jurists made particular use of two doctrines drawn from the law of damages—"out-of-pocket" expenses *(damnum emergens)* and "expectancy damages" *(lucrum cessans)*—to fashion rules for the charging of lawful interest on a loan. See Noonan, *Scholastic Analysis of Usury,* pp. 118–128 and 249–256. Richard Helmholz has shown that in England the charging of excessive interest was rarely prosecuted in the church courts but was to be confessed in the internal forum of the church and, if it constituted the sin of greed, subjected to penance. See Richard H. Helmholz, "Usury and the Medieval English Church Courts," *Speculum* 61 (1984), reprinted in Helmholz's *Canon Law and the Law of England* (London, 1987), pp. 323–339.
16. This view was supported by references to Aristotle's theory that money, being a measure of the value of goods, was essentially unproductive ("sterile" or "barren"), and therefore for a lender to value it differently at different times is to distort its character. Thomas Aquinas argued that although the purchasing power of money may change, such change is not due to the fault of the borrower, and hence the lender may not take advantage of it. See Noonan, *Scholastic Analysis of Usury,* p. 56. This view, though followed by successive generations of moral philosophers, conflicted sharply with the economic and legal realities of the period. Writing about the commercial revolution of the eleventh and twelfth centuries, Robert Lopez stresses that "unstinting credit was [its] great lubricant." See Robert Lopez, *The Commercial Revolution of the Middle Ages,* 950–1350 (Cambridge, 1976), p. 72. A useful account of commercial banking practices in the twelfth and thirteenth centuries is found in N. J. G. Pounds, *An Economic History of Medieval England,* 2nd ed. (London, 1994), chap. 9 ("The Commercial Revolution,"), pp. 407–442.
17. See Robert B. Ekelund, Jr., et al., *Sacred Trust: The Medieval Church as an Economic Firm* (Oxford, 1996), p. 118. In loaning money at interest, the papacy often cloaked the true amount of the interest by assessing fees *(servitia)* for the services rendered. Ibid., p. 119. The church also sponsored the creation of *monti di pietà,* charitable funds which had as their purpose the lending of "money to the poor at the lowest possible interest to alleviate immediate distress." See Geoffrey Parker, "The Emergence of Modern Finance in Europe, 1500–1700," in Carlo M. Cipolla, ed., *The Fontana Economic History of Europe,* vol. 3 *The Sixteenth and Seventeenth Centuries* (Glasgow, 1974), p. 534.
18. Carlo M. Cipolla, *Money, Prices, and Civilization in the Mediterranean World: Fifth to Seventeenth Century* (Princeton, 1956), pp. 63–65.
19. Ibid., p. 65. The Zürich rate is cited in Karl Marx, *Capital,* vol. 3, chap. 36. See Karl Marx, *On Religion,* ed. Saul K. Padover and The Karl Marx Library, vol. 5 (New York, 1964), p. 135.
20. Max Weber explained the Roman Catholic Church's attack on usury, in which he included all interest charges, as a "conscious protest" against the impersonal character of the emerging market economy. "What [was] involved," Weber wrote, "[was] a struggle in principle between ethical rationalization and the process of rationalization in the domain of economics." See Max Weber, *Economy and Society: An Outline of Interpretive Sociology,* ed. Guenther Roth and Claus Wittich, vol. 2 (New York, 1968), pp. 584–585. This struggle changed, according to Weber, with the rise of capitalism and the spread of the Protestant ethic in the sixteenth century. Benjamin Nelson, starting expressly from Weber's analysis, argued that the Roman Catholic ethic, which, he stated, forbade usury in relations between Christians but permitted it to be practiced in relations between Christians and

Jews, was replaced in the sixteenth and seventeenth centuries by a Calvinist ethic, which, according to Nelson, permitted usury within the Christian brotherhood. See Benjamin Nelson, *The Idea of Usury: From Tribal Otherhood to Universal Brotherhood,* 2nd ed. enl. (Chicago, 1969). Nelson's analysis, like Weber's, is flawed owing to his belief that the distinction between excessive and lawful interest was "post-medieval" in origin" (p. 17, n. 34). In fact, Jewish moneylenders were also prohibited by a decree of the Fourth Lateran Council of 1215 to "extort oppressive and excessive interest charges [*usurarias*] from Christians." See *Decrees of the Ecumenical Councils,* ed. Norman P. Tanner, S. J., vol. 1 (London, 1990), p. 265, Concilium Lateranense IV, 1215, 67, *De usuris Iudaeorum.* On Calvin's views, see n. 23. Similar misunderstandings of the history of usury both before and after the Protestant Reformation continue to inform contemporary treatments of the subject. See Edward L. Glaeser and Jose Scheinkman, "Neither a Borrower nor a Lender Be: An Economic Analysis of Interest Restrictions and Usury Laws," *Journal of Law and Economics* 41 (1998), 25–26.

21. *LW* 45:248.
22. See William J. Wright, *Capitalism, the State, and the Lutheran Reformation: Sixteenth-Century Hesse* (Athens, Ohio, 1988), pp. 17–21. Lutheran doctrine, like the Roman Catholic, made an exception in the case of noncommercial loans, such as loans to relatives or friends. Thus Melanchthon distinguished between a loan that is required by a duty *(officiosa mutuatio),* such as family interest, and a loan that is made for some other reason *(non officiosa mutuatio),* such as money put to an "economic use," as when kings borrow from citizens. The former type, he wrote, is the subject of the scriptural text "lend freely, expecting nothing in return." In an *officiosa mutuatio,* Melanchthon permitted the taking of interest on the basis of actual loss or loss of profits (*damnum emergens* or *lucrum cessans*), but such loss, he wrote, must be significant *(insigne).* See Philip Melanchthon, *Dissertatio de Contractibus, CR,* vol. 16, cols. 505–506.
23. See Noonan, *Scholastic Analysis of Usury,* pp. 365–367, and W. Fred Graham, *The Constructive Revolutionary: John Calvin and His Socio-Economic Impact* (Richmond, Va., 1971), pp. 90–94.
24. Hans Liermann, *Deutsches evangelisches Kirchenrecht* (Stuttgart, 1933), p. 254 (estimated rise in prices of 50 percent in Germany in the first half of the sixteenth century).
25. See "Population in Europe, 1500–1700" in Cipolla, *Fontana Economic History of Europe,* p. 15 (estimated 25 percent growth in population from 12 to 15 million).
26. See Wright, *Capitalism,* pp. 30–32.
27. See Fernand Braudel, *The Wheels of Commerce,* trans. Siân Reynolds, vol. 2 of *Civilization and Capitalism, Fifteenth to Eighteenth Centuries* (New York, 1982), pp. 232–249.
28. On the first commercial revolution, see Robert S. Lopez, *The Commercial Revolution of the Middle Ages, 950–1350* (Englewood Cliffs, N.J., 1971); on the development of commercial law in the twelfth and thirteenth centuries, see Berman, *Law and Revolution,* pp. 333–356.
29. See Wright, *Capitalism,* p. 3. See also Ludwig Zimmermann, *Der ökonomische Staat Landgraf Wilhelms IV: Der hessische Territorialstaat im Jahrhundert der Reformation* (Marburg, 1933), pp. 389–393.
30. See Wright, *Capitalism,* pp. 3–5.
31. See, e.g., Eli Heckscher, *Mercantilism,* vol. 1 (London, 1955), pp. 19–30.
32. See Immanuel Wallerstein, *The Modern World System: Capitalist Agriculture and the Origins of the European World Economy in the Sixteenth Century* (San Diego, 1974), pp. 137–143.

33. See Richard Ehrenberg, *Capital and Finance in the Age of the Renaissance: A Study of the Fuggers and Their Connections,* trans. H. M. Lucas (London, 1928), pp. 79–86; cf. Paul Kennedy, *The Rise and Fall of the Great Powers: Economic Change and Military Conflict from 1500 to 2000* (New York, 1988), pp. 54–55.
34. See Raymond de Roover, *L'évolution de la lettre de change, XIVe–XVIIIe siècles* (Paris, 1953), pp. 23–42.
35. A summary of units of account used in sixteenth-century Europe is found in Marie-Thérèse Boyer-Xambeu, *Private Money and Public Currencies: The Sixteenth-Century Challenge,* trans. Azizeh Azadi (Armonk, N.Y., 1994), p. 107; cf. Cipolla, *Money, Prices, and Civilization,* pp. 42–43.
36. See Cipolla, *Money, Prices, and Civilization,* p. 38.
37. A leading European economic historian wrote in 1977 that legal historians have shown "no interest" in sixteenth- and seventeenth-century economic history. See Slicher von Bath, "Agriculture in the Vital Revolution," in *The Cambridge Economic History of Europe,* vol. 5, *The Economic Organization of Early Modern Europe* (Cambridge, 1977), p. 42. This situation hardly changed in the following decades.
38. See Ernst Meynial, "Notes sur la formation de la théorie du domaine divise (domaine direct et domaine utile) du XIIe au XIVe siècles dans les romanistes," in *Mélanges Fitting,* vol. 2 (Montpellier, 1908), pp. 409–461. Cf. Berman, *Law and Revolution,* p. 239.
39. See Berman, *Law and Revolution,* pp. 242–245.
40. Ibid., pp. 453–457 (England), 475–476 (France).
41. Hugo Kress, *Besitz und Recht: Eine civilrechtliche Abhandlung* (Nuremberg, 1909), p. 10.
42. Helmut Coing, *Privatrechtsgeschichte, Handbuch der Quellen und Literatur der neueren-europäischen* (Munich, 1973), pp. 277ff.
43. See Kress, *Besitz und Recht,* pp. 9–10. Cf. Coing, *Privatrechtsgeschichte,* pp. 272, 277ff. Coing (p. 272) notes in passing the influence of the canon law remedy for dispossession of land and goods (the *actio spolii*).
44. See *Bernhard Walthers Privatrechtliche Traktats aus dem 16. Jahrhundert,* ed. Max Rintelen (Leipzig, 1937), p. 1.
45. See Johan Apel, *Methodica Dialectics Ratio ad Iurisprudenti Accommodate, Authore Johanne Apello* (Nuremberg, 1535); Johan Apel, *Isagoge per Dialogum in Quattuor Labors Institutum divi Iustiniani Imperatoris, Autore Johanne Appel* (Bratislava, 1540).
46. In his first major work, published in 1536, Apel wrote that there are two species of property rights *(jura in re),* as distinct from rights arising from contract and other obligations *(iura ad rem),* namely, *proprietas,* or full ownership, and *ius in re specificum,* the latter term referring to the *ususfructus,* that is, the right of use and benefit, of a thing that is owned by another. See also Apel, *Methodica,* leaf 274 rb–277 rb. In his later work, the *Isagoge,* published posthumously in 1540, Apel repeats the substance of this analysis with a slightly different terminology, substituting "*dominium* and its affines" for *ius in re,* and *obligatio* for *ius ad rem.* See Stintzing, *Geschichte der Rechtswissenschaft,* p. 295. Stintzing notes that "in both writings, Apel warned expressly against interchanging and mixing contract and the methods by which ownership is acquired." Cf. Theodor Muther, *Doctor Johann Apel: Ein Beitrag* (Königsberg, 1861), pp. 54ff.
47. The distinction between the two forms of *dominium,* direct and beneficial, did not, however, survive the dogmatism of late-nineteenth-century Romanist jurisprudence, which held that ownership was absolute and unitary or else it was not ownership. Thus the terminology of *dominium utile* was rejected. This development, too, had been anticipated by another leading sixteenth-century jurist, Hugo Donellus (1527–1599), who was undoubtedly familiar with Apel's work. French

by birth and upbringing (his name in French was Hugues Doneau), Donellus for many years taught and wrote at Bourges, the great sixteenth-century French center of legal scholarship. He was, however, like some other leading French jurists, a Protestant, who felt personally threatened after the Saint Bartholemew's Day massacres of 1572 and thereafter accepted invitations to teach in Germany, where he remained until his death. See A. P. Th. Eyessell, *Doneau: Sa vie et ses ouvrages* (Geneva, 1970). For the term *dominium utile,* Donellus substituted the phrase *jura in re aliena* (rights in the property of another). See Robert Feenstra, "*Dominium* and *ius in re aliena:* The Origins of a Civil Law Distinction," in Peter Birks, ed., *New Perspectives in the Roman Law of Property: Essays for Barry Nicholas* (Oxford, 1989), pp. 111–122. Feenstra discusses Apel's earlier analysis, noting that the concept of divided ownership, espoused by Apel but rejected by Donellus, corresponded to the realities of the time. In fact, Donellus's *jus in re aliena* is essentially Apel's *usufructus.* Nevertheless, Apel has been more or less forgotten by most modern writers. Cf. Peter Stein, "Donellus and the Origin of the Modern Civil Law," in *Mélanges Felix Wubbe: offerts par ses collègues et ses amig à l'occasion de son soixante-dixième anniversaire* (Fribourg, 1993), pp. 439–452. Stein attributes to Donellus the origin of the distinction between the law of property and the law of obligations and designates him "the founder of the modern civil law" (p. 452). Even Feenstra, who recognizes that Apel's works preceded by a generation that of Donellus, and were widely circulated in France and other countries, refers to Apel as one of "some rather obscure German jurists of the sixteenth century."

48. See Johann Oldendorp, *Actionum Forensium Progymnasmata,* in *Opera,* 2 vols. (Aalen, 1966), 2:588–589.
49. Christopher Zobel, *Differentiae Iuris Civilis et Saxonici* (Leipzig, 1598). Zobel reproduced 70 "differences" originally listed by Ludwig Fachs and 273 "differences" originally listed by Benedict Reinhard, adding his own commentary, partly in German, partly in Latin. Reinhard's work, which appeared in handwritten form as early as 1549, was later combined with an apparently still earlier work of Fachs, and the combined works were published in 1567 and later republished in 1573 and 1582. The Fachs-Reinhard *differentiae,* written in Latin, were translated into German and published in 1586, 1595, and 1598, with comments and additions, by Georg Schwarzkopff under the title *Ludovici Fachsi et Benedicti Reinharti Differentiae Iuris Civilis et Saxonici.* The eighteenth-century bibliographer Martin Lipen, in *Bibliotheca Realis Juridica* (Leipzig, 1746), listed approximately fifty titles of such *Differentiae Juris,* in addition to twenty-one titles of *Differentiae inter Jus Canonicum et Civile* and five titles of *Differentiae Juris Hebraica.* Among the most important of the sixteenth-century books on differences was that of Bernhard Walther (see Chapter 3), written in German, which analyzes the differences between the *jus commune* and the territorial laws of lower Austria under fifteen headings, including servitudes, administrative prerogatives, preemptive rights or relatives, intestate succession, family relationships, bail and other forms of security, wills, and feudal estates.
50. Coing, *Privatrechtsgeschichte,* p. 366.
51. The English equivalent of the Latin *census* and French *rente* and German *Zins* was the mortgage, which came to be attached to the lease of land for a term of years and eventually to copyhold tenure. See Charles Montgomery Gray, *Copyhold, Equity, and the Common Law* (Cambridge, Mass., 1963); R. W. Turner, *The Equity of Redemption* (Cambridge, Mass., 1931); Charles J. Reid, "The Seventeenth-Century Revolution in English Land Law," *Cleveland State Law Review* 43 (1995), 221ff.

52. See *Martin Luther: Works,* trans. H. E. Jacobs, 6 vols. (Philadelphia, 1915–1932), 4:96–97; Benjamin Nelson, *The Idea of Usury* (Chicago, 1969), p. 33.
53. In Württemberg, for a *Rentenkauf* transaction involving a purchase price above a certain amount, the permission not of the court but of the prince's chancery was required. See Robert von Hippel, *Deutsches strafrecht* (Berlin, 1925), Bd. 1.
54. See William J. Wright, *Germany: A New Social and Economic History* (London, 1996), p. 181: "Capitalism emerged during the 'long sixteenth century' (1450–1610)." Wright recognizes the importance of partnership as a means of pooling capital and engaging in economic activity, and notes (p. 183) that Hanseatic shipping "came to be dominated by partnerships." He also emphasizes the use of long-distance agents, including family members as plenipotentiaries and factors as agents who received a percentage or salary (p. 184). Of bourses, Wright notes (p. 186) that they were frequent gatherings of merchants of different nationalities in order to do business without exhibiting, delivering, or paying for goods at the same time. What was new in bourses of the fifteenth and sixteenth centuries, Wright states, as contrasted with merchant fairs of the twelfth to fourteenth centuries, was the performance of banking services, and this, he states, was very important for capitalist developments. Yet apart from the performance of banking services at bourses, all of these factors were present in European commerce in earlier centuries.
55. Wright relies on a work of Bruno Kuske in asserting that "the idea of the joint-stock company" was in existence in the sixteenth century (ibid.). The work of Kuske that he cites, however, contains little about joint-stock companies, and it seems that Wright mistook for joint-stock companies profit-sharing arrangements among lenders who put up risk capital for joint ventures.
56. Heckscher is quoted in Wright, *Capitalism, the State, and the Lutheran Reformation,* p. 3. In this work Wright emphasizes the strong economic role played by the princes of Hesse as "architects of a mercantilist state," and also the important influence of their Lutheran faith in their attempt to protect the needs of the poor against economically progressive interests, even to the detriment of their own needs as rulers. Among many other similar measures, peasants were given preemptive rights to buy food and wool at market prices before entrepreneurs could buy up those products and later sell them at exorbitant prices, and peasants and weavers were protected against oppressive credit arrangements and foreclosures. At the same time, importation of foreign cloth was restricted, trade was taxed as a major source of revenue, and other controls were placed on market transactions.

6. The Transformation of German Social Law

1. See Peter Brown, "St. Augustine," in Beryl Smalley, ed., *Trends in Medieval Political Thought* (Oxford, 1965), p. 11.
2. *The Confessions of St. Augustine,* trans. E. B. Pusey (New York, 1907), pp. 317–318; Saint Augustine, *The Trinity,* ed. Roy Deferrari, trans. Stephen McKenna (Washington, D.C., 1963), pp. 271–289, 308–309. Cf. Leonardo Boff, *Trinity and Society,* trans. Paul Burns (Maryknoll, N.Y., 1988), p. 56; Harold J. Berman, "Law and Logos," *De Paul Law Review* 44 (1994), 149–150.
3. See Berman, *Law and Revolution,* pp. 92–93, 581–582. Although priests generally were called "spirituals," the priesthood itself was divided between "secular" clergy, incardinated in particular dioceses and subject to the discipline of the local bishop, and "regular" clergy, who were members of religious orders and subject to the orders' rules *(regulae).* In addition, the name "spirituals" was appropriated

by the radical wing of the Franciscan movement in the late thirteenth and fourteenth centuries.

4. Pope Gregory VII to Bishop Hermann of Metz, March 1081, quoted in ibid., p. 110.
5. Although canon law as a whole was called *jus spirituale,* a division was made between those aspects of the canon law that dealt with strictly secular matters, called *jus temporale,* and other temporal matters which were connected to spiritual causes, called *jus annexum spiritualibus.* For example, the law of patronage, which dealt with the power of laymen to present candidates for ecclesiastical office, was said to be "not spiritual but annexed to the spiritual." Hostiensis, *Commentaria,* x.1.6.28.
6. Thus the great fourteenth-century Italian jurist Baldus, who was both a Romanist and a canonist, wrote that in cases of conflict involving spiritual or mixed causes, canon law should be preferred since it is connected to divine law. See Giuseppe Ermini, "Ius Commune e Utrumque Ius," *Acta Congressus Iuridica Internationalis* 2 (1935), 522, n. 32.
7. Luther stated that marriage is "the source of the economy and the polity and the seed-bed of the Church." Quoted in Johannes Heckel, *Lex Charitatis: Eine juristische Untersuchung über das Recht in der Theologie Martin Luthers* (Munich, 1953), pp. 101–102.
8. Cf. Christoph Strohm, "*Ius divinum* und *ius humanum:* Reformatorische Begründung des Kirchenrechts," in Gerhard Rau, Hans-Richard Reuter, and Klaus Schlaich, eds., *Das Recht der Kirche,* Bd. 2, *Zur Geschichte des Kirchenrechts* (Guterslöh, 1994), p. 145. Strohm states that the law of the invisible church ("the church as a creature of the word and the spiritual community of love") is "Law sui generis" and that its uniqueness "lies above all in the fact that in its obligatory character it can be really known and recognized by those to whom faith has awarded the promise of salvation" (p. 145, n. 108). See also Heckel, *Lex Charitatis.*
9. See D. Gerhard Ebeling, "Zur Lehre vom triplex usus legis in der reformatorischen Theologie," in *Wort und Glaube,* Bd. 1 (Tübingen, 1960), pp. 50–68; John Witte, Jr., and Thomas C. Arthur, "The Three Uses of the Law: A Protestant Source of the Purposes of Criminal Punishment?" *Journal of Law and Religion* 10 (1993–94), 433–465.
10. These specific types of *Ordnungen* were sometimes incorporated into large "policy ordinances" *(Polizeiordnungen).* See Gustav K. Schmelzeisen, *Polizeiordnung und Privatrecht* (Münster, 1955).
11. See Harold Berman and Charles J. Reid, Jr., "Roman Law in Europe and the *Jus Commune,*" *Syracuse Journal of International Law and Commerce* 20 (1995), pp. 1–30.
12. The theologians included Luther, Melanchthon, Johannes Bugenhagen, Antonius Corvinus, Kaspar Cruciger, and many others. See Anneliese Sprengler-Ruppenthal, "Kirchenordung, evangelische," in *Theologische Realenzyklopädie,* Bd. 18 (Berlin, 1989), pp. 679–681.
13. Church, marriage, disciplinary, and other ordinances promulgated in Calvinist cities and principalities are not included in the present discussion.
14. See Sprengler-Ruppenthal, "Kirchenordnung," pp. 670–707 and sources cited therein. Private confession and absolution from sins was retained by the Augsburg Confession of 1530. It eventually ceased to be obligatory.
15. The chief Lutheran modifications in the liturgy of the Roman Catholic Church are reviewed by Timothy George, *Theology of the Reformers* (Nashville, 1988), pp. 92–95 and 145–158.

16. See Hans J. Hillerbrand, ed., *The Oxford Encyclopedia of the Reformation,* vol. 2 (1996), pp. 439–441 ("Protestant Liturgy").
17. *LW* 35:501.
18. *LW* 35:53–54.
19. Carter Lindberg, *The European Reformations* (Oxford, 1996), p. 116.
20. Ibid., pp. 116, 117.
21. Luther, "The Order of Baptism," *LW* 53:95–103.
22. Quoted in John Tonkin, "Luther's Understanding of Baptism: A Systematic Approach," *Lutheran Theological Journal* 11 (1977), 101–102.
23. See Paul Nettl, *Luther and Music,* trans. Frida Best and Ralph Wood (Philadelphia, 1948), p. 82.
24. See Johannes Riedel, *The Lutheran Chorale: Its Basic Traditions* (Minneapolis, 1967), pp. 35–38. Luther intended that his hymns, through reliance on traditional German folk melodies and strong, simple vernacular language, would reinforce popular belief in Evangelical theology. Music, Luther said, "makes people milder and more gentle, more civil and more sensible" (p. 36). A leading interpreter of the Lutheran Reformation has written that "music was the audible symbol of a church struggling against too much clarity and too much visibility." Eugen Rosenstock-Huessy, *Out of Revolution: The Autobiography of Western Man* (1938; reprint, Providence, 1993), p. 423.
25. This hymnal was called *Achtliederbuch* (Eight Song Book). See Frank C. Senn, "Liturgy," in Hillerbrand, *Oxford Encyclopedia of the Reformation,* 2:441.
26. Ulrich Leupold, ed., *Liturgy and Hymns,* in Helmut T. Lehmann, ed., *Luther's Works,* vol. 53 (Philadelphia, 1965), p. 194.
27. In addition to the Creed and the Sanctus, other parts of the Mass for which Luther introduced congregational hymns were the Introit, the Gradual, and the Agnus Dei. See Robin Leaver, "Theological Consistency, Liturgical Integrity, and Musical Hermeneutics in Luther's Liturgical Reforms," *Lutheran Quarterly* 9, n.s. (1995), 117–138.
28. Letter to Georg Spalatin, quoted in James F. Lambert, *Luther's Hymns* (Philadelphia, 1917), p. 15.
29. *LW* 53:225.
30. Quoted in Nettl, *Luther and Music,* p. 75.
31. Leupold, *Liturgy and Hymns,* p. 225.
32. See Rosenstock-Huessy, *Out of Revolution,* p. 417.
33. Lambert, *Luther's Hymns,* pp. 441–50; Nettl, *Luther and Music,* p. 53.
34. George, *Theology of the Reformers,* p. 91, citing *LW* 39:22, *WA* 6:75.
35. Quoted in George, *Theology of the Reformers,* p. 92. The references were to Johann Bugenhagen, Justus Jonas, and Philip Melanchthon, respectively. (Jonas, who taught law at the University of Erfurt, graduated from Wittenberg in 1514 and was an early member of Luther's circle.)
36. Luther, "A Reply to the Twelve Articles," *LW* 4:223.
37. As late as 1527, Luther spoke out against official persecutions of Anabaptists, stating: "It is not right, and I am deeply troubled that poor people are so pitifully put to death, burned, and cruelly slain. Let everyone believe what he likes. If he is wrong, he will have punishment enough in hellfire. Unless there is sedition one should oppose them with Scripture and God's word. With fire you will accomplish nothing." Quoted in Roland Bainton, *The Travail of Religious Liberty* (New York, 1958), p. 61. In 1536, however, he endorsed a memorandum recommending the death penalty for Anabaptists (p. 64). See also Nikolaus Paulus, *Luther und die Gewissensfreiheit* (Munich, 1905).

38. See Ulrich Nembach, *Predigt des Evangeliums: Luther als Prediger, Pädagoge und Rhetor* (Münster, 1972), pp. 25–59.
39. Quoted in Annaliese Sprengler-Ruppenthal, "Das kanonische Recht in Kirchenordnungen des 16. Jahrhunderts," in Richard H. Helmholz, ed., *Canon Law in Protestant Lands* (Berlin, 1992), p. 49. See also idem, "Bugenhagen und das protestantische Kirchenrecht," in *ZSS* 88 *(kan. Abt.)* (1971), 205–207.
40. See the Calenberg-Göttinger *Kirchenordnung* of 1542, in Emil Sehling, ed., *Die evangelischen Kirchenordnungen des XVI Jahrhunkerts,* Bd. 6, vol. 2 (Aachen, 1955), p. 732, discussed in Sprengler-Ruppenthal, "Das kanonische Recht," p. 50.
41. Sehling, *Kirchenordnungen,* pp. 91–92.
42. See generally John Witte, Jr., *From Sacrament to Contract: Marriage, Religion, and Law in the West* (Louisville, Ky., 1997), chap. 2; Hartwig Dieterich, *Das Protestantische Eherecht in Deutschland bis zur Mitte des 17. Jahrhunderts* (Munich, 1970). See also John Witte, Jr., "The Transformation of Marriage Law in the Lutheran Reformation," in John Witte, Jr., and Frank S. Alexander, eds., *The Weightier Matters of the Law: Essays on Law and Religion—A Tribute to Harold J. Berman* (Atlanta, Ga., 1988), pp. 57–98.
43. See Witte, "Transformation of Marriage Law," p. 70; see also pp. 76–94 (analyzing some of the chief reforms of the marriage law found in the *Eheordnungen*). See also Dieterich, *Das Protestantische Eherecht,* passim.
44. See Dieterich, *Das Protestantische Eherecht,* pp. 147–166, 177–180.
45. This section draws in part on John Witte, Jr., "The Civic Seminary: Sources of Modern Public Education in the Lutheran Reformation of Germany," *Journal of Law and Religion* 12 (1996), 173–223.
46. For Italy, see Paul F. Grendler, *Schooling in Renaissance Italy: Literacy and Learning, 1300–1600* (Baltimore, 1989); idem, *Books and Schools in the Italian Renaissance* (Brookfield, Vt., 1995). Some two dozen German cities (chiefly of the Hanseatic League) had established both Latin and vernacular schools to train officials and businessmen; also some large craft and merchant guilds maintained their own schools, and there were in addition some private boarding and day schools run by one or more lay teachers. See Witte, "Civic Seminary," pp. 182–183.
47. See ibid., p. 186. In asserting the importance of education, Luther was following Jesus' last instruction to the apostles, "Go ye therefore and teach all nations, baptizing them in the name of the Father, and of the Son, and of the Holy Ghost: teaching them to observe all that I have commanded you" (Sermon on the Mount 28:18–20).
48. Quoted in Witte, "Civic Seminary," p. 187.
49. Quoted ibid., p. 188.
50. This set of concepts found expression as early as 1520 in Luther's revolutionary *Appeal to the Ruling Class of German Nationality as to the Amelioration of the State of Christendom,* in which he advocated compulsory universal public schooling as a Christian responsibility of the local civil magistrate. See Witte, "Civic Seminary," pp. 191–192.
51. See Gerald Strauss, *Luther's House of Learning: Indoctrination of the Young in the German Reformation* (Baltimore, 1978), pp. 194–198.
52. Ibid.
53. See William J. Wright, "The Impact of the Reformation on Hessian Education," *Church History* 44 (1975), 183, stating that "the scholarship system was . . . a Lutheran idea."
54. See Apology of the Augsburg Confession, in *Concordia Triglotta* (1921), art. 6, p. 287.

55. See David W. Myers, *"Poor Sinning Folk": Confession and Conscience in Counter-Reformation Germany* (Ithaca, N.Y., 1996), pp. 63–76.
56. See Werner Heun, "Konsistorium," in *Theologische Realenzyklopädie,* Bd. 19 (Berlin, 1990), pp. 483–488.
57. See Brian Tierney, *Medieval Poor Law: A Sketch of Canonical Theory and Its Application in England* (Berkeley, 1959).
58. Ibid., pp. 84–86. The word "hospital," derived from the Latin *hospites,* meaning "guests," referred to various types of places where people went for succor.
59. This analysis draws on data presented in Robert Jütte's important book *Poverty and Deviance in Early Modern Europe* (Cambridge, 1994) and Bronislaw Geremek's masterly work *Poverty: A History,* trans. Agnieszka Kolakowska (Cambridge, Mass., 1994). It differs substantially, however, with Jütte's view that there was no substantial shift from Roman Catholic to Protestant policies of poor relief, and that such shift as did take place was not due to changes in religious beliefs. Thus Jütte states (p. 105): "Today historians see little or no religious influence, either of Catholicism or Protestantism, in the development of the characteristic features of sixteenth-century poor relief organization." In supporting this view, which is widely shared by other contemporary historians, though not by their predecessors, Jütte points to several examples of Roman Catholic precursors of Lutheran policies and methods of poor relief as well as to several examples of Roman Catholic adoption of such policies and methods during and after the Lutheran Reformation. He states (p. 108): "We have shown that the Reformation created neither the communal nor the governmental system of poor relief, since both had their counterparts in Catholic countries." Yet immediately after that statement he adds: "But there can be no doubt that the discussion of Luther's principles of relief and their effects in the sixteenth century shaped the centralized poor relief system not only in Germany but elsewhere in Europe. The Reformation paved the way for the development of a new social policy which favoured secular systems of poor relief." And in the conclusion of his book (esp. pp. 194, 198), Jütte emphasizes strongly the influence of Lutheran theological concepts and of parallel changes in Roman Catholic theology in the development of new systems of poor relief.

    Likewise, Natalie Zemon Davis, in her otherwise excellent account of the system of poor relief introduced in 1534 in the predominantly Roman Catholic city of Lyon, discounts the specific influence of preexisting German Protestant models. She attributes the establishment of a common chest in Lyon, effectuating the centralization of charitable activities in the secular municipal authorities, primarily to the "urban crisis, brought about by a conjuncture of older problems of poverty with population growth and economic expansion." Such welfare reform, she states, took place in Protestant and Catholic cities as well as cities of mixed religious composition, and "rested on values and insights common to both groups." Natalie Zemon Davis, "Poor Relief, Humanism, and Heresy: The Case of Lyon," *Studies in Medieval and Renaissance History* 5 (1968), 267. She grants that "Protestant and Catholic religious sensibility and doctrine found their own paths to justify the elimination of begging and the establishment of centralized organizations to provide relief and rehabilitation," but adds that for Catholics in Lyon, and perhaps in other Catholic cities, "the path was ordinarily opened . . . by Christian humanists following an Erasmian program of reform" (p. 268). Only touched on, in Davis's account, is the role of the substantial Protestant population in Lyon in pressing for the reform, and the substantial opposition of Roman Catholic authorities to the reduction or elimination of the Roman Catholic charitable endowments. As for humanism, both Davis and Jütte emphasize the role played by the writings on poor relief of the great Roman Catholic humanist Juan Luis Vives, Spanish exile and friend of Erasmus. But Vives, like Erasmus, was a Roman Catholic reformer, some of whose books were put on the papal Index. Like the Lyon preacher and humanist Jean de Vauzelles, a principal Roman Catholic leader of the Lyonnais reform of poor relief, Vives was a friend of Protestants; indeed he was considered by the Lutheran historian Andreas Osiander to be a secret admirer of Luther. See Carolos G. Norena, *Juan Luis Vives* (The Hague, 1970), p. 3; Jütte, *Poverty and Deviance,* p. 117. Davis is certainly right in saying that Roman Catholics and Lutheran Protestants shared many common values, but the substitution of secular for ecclesiastical control of poor relief came to Lyon only after a bitter struggle with Roman Catholic ecclesiastical authorities, whereas a decade before it had come to Nuremberg and other German cities at the initiative of Lutheran ecclesiastical authorities.

Jütte, Davis, and other contemporary historians who discount the impact of Lutheranism on poor relief in German territories fail to make the proper connections between Lutheran theology and Lutheran politics. They make no connection, for example, between Luther's theology and his advocacy of the establishment by town councils of a common chest for poor relief. Luther himself, however, and his colleagues such as Johann Bugenhagen, saw the common chest as a manifestation of the theological doctrine of the priesthood of all believers. Nor do they take into account the relation between the Lutheran doctrine of secular callings and the Lutheran repudiation of charitable support of able-bodied mendicants.

That there were occasional examples of the establishment of systems of poor relief by royal authorities and local town councils in Catholic countries before, during, and after the Reformation hardly affects these conclusions. The Protestant Reformation, and the accompanying expansion of the powers of the secular authorities, had been increasingly foreshadowed in the preceding century.

60. Thesis 43 states: "Christians are to be taught that one who gives to the poor or lends to the needy does a better deed than one who buys indulgences." See Kurt Aland, ed., *Martin Luther's Ninety-five Theses: With the Pertinent Documents from the History of the Reformation* (St. Louis, 1967), p. 54. See also Carter Lindberg, "Reformation Initiatives for Social Welfare: Luther's Influence at Leisnig," *Annual of the Society of Christian Ethics* (1987), 86.
61. Lindberg, "Reformation Initiatives," p. 87.
62. See Carter Lindberg, "'There Shall be No Beggars among Christians': Karlstadt, Luther, and the Origins of Protestant Poor Relief," *Church History* 46 (1977), 322–323.
63. Luther expressed the desire "that every noble, townsman, and peasant living in the parish shall according to his ability and means, remit in taxes for himself, his wife, and his children, a certain sum of money to the chest each year, in order that the total amount can be arrived at and procured which the deliberations and decisions of the general assembly . . . have determined to be necessary and sufficient." *LW* 45:190. See also Lindberg, "Reformation Initiatives," p. 92.
64. See Jütte, *Poverty and Deviance,* p. 107.
65. See Harold J. Grimm, "Luther's Contribution to Sixteenth-Century Organization of Poor Relief," *Archives for Reformation History* 61 (1970), 228.
66. See Lindberg, "Reformation Initiatives," p. 93.
67. See Grimm, "Luther's Contribution," p. 227.

68. This was the case in Wittenberg and Nuremberg. Ibid., pp. 226 and 229 (discussing Wittenberg) and pp. 229–231 (discussing Nuremberg). But most did not include, as Leisnig did, aid to pastors, artisans, merchants, or others. Cf. Frank Peter Lane, "Poverty and Poor Relief in the German Church Orders of Johann Bugenhagen, 1485–1558" (Ph.D. diss., Ohio State University, 1973), pp. 177–178 (comparing Leisnig's arrangements with those of Braunschweig, Lübeck, Hamburg, and Hildesheim, among other places).
69. "During . . . thirty-seven years Bugenhagen served as the pastor of the city church of Wittenberg (1522–1558) as well as Luther's confessor and spiritual adviser; a university professor at Wittenberg and adviser to the northeastern European reformers; organizer of the reform in Braunschweig, Hamburg, Lübeck, Schleswig-Holstein, Denmark, Pomerania, Hildesheim, and Braunschweig-Wolfenbüttel as well as providing a Low German translation of the Old and New Testaments for northern Germany; a renowned commentator on the Psalms and a harmonizer of the four gospels. Bugenhagen presided over and blessed the marriage of Luther and Catherine von Bora and preached the eulogy at Luther's funeral. He also crowned the king and queen of Denmark, consecrated the first evangelical bishops, refounded the University of Copenhagen, and refused two bishoprics twice." Lane, "Poverty and Poor Relief," pp. 1–2.
70. This is the language of the introduction to the Braunschweig Church Ordinance of 1528, which Bugenhagen drafted. Ibid., p. 141.
71. Ibid., p. 146. Ernst Wolf notes, "The spirit of faith, God's love, and the reliance on Holy Scripture: these three things are the basis of Bugenhagen's church orders." See Ernst Wolf, "Johannes Bugenhagen," in Wilhelm Schmidt, ed., *Gestalten der Reformation* (Wupperthal-Barmen, 1967), p. 62.
72. See Lane, "Poverty and Poor Relief," p. 160.
73. Ibid., pp. 155–156.
74. Ibid., pp. 174–175 (discussing H. Nobbe, "Die Regelung der Armenpflege im 16. Jahrhundert nach den evangelische Kirchenordnungen Deutschlands," *Zeitschrift für Kirchengeschichte* 10 [1889], 574).
75. See Max Weber, "Science as a Vocation," in *From Max Weber: Essays in Sociology,* ed. and trans. Hans H. Gerth and C. Wright Mills (New York, 1958), pp. 138–139. See also Anthony T. Kronman, *Max Weber* (Stanford, Calif., 1983), pp. 166–170.
76. Ernst Troeltsch, *Die Bedeutung des Protestantismus fur die Entstehung der modernen Welt* (1911). Troeltsch the theologian and Weber the sociologist were close friends. Troeltsch's book was an expanded version of a 1906 lecture at a large conference on German history. The lectureship was offered first to Weber but he declined. See Hermann Lübbe, *Säkularisierung: Geschichte eines ideenpolitischen Begriffs,* vol. 2 (Freiburg, 1975), p. 74, n. 2.
77. A bibliography in Heinz-Horst Schrey, ed., *Säkularisierung* (Darmstadt, 1981), contains 368 titles! Two important books on secularization in the sixteenth century in Germany and England, respectively, are Irene Crusius, ed., *Zur säkularisierung geistlicher Institutionen im 16. und im 18./19. Jahrhundert* (Göttingen, 1996), and C. John Sommerville, *The Secularization of Early Modern England: From Religious Culture to Religious Faith* (New York, 1992). The present chapter is the first attempt, so far as I know, to identify as "spiritual" certain branches of law that are directly inspired by what Sommerville refers to as religious faith, whether or not they are promulgated by ecclesiastical authorities.
78. Hans Blumenberg, *The Legitimacy of the Modern Age,* trans Robert M. Wallace (Cambridge, Mass., 1983), pp. 10–11.

79. See Gerhard Oestreich, "Strukturprobleme des europäischen Absolutismus," in *Geist und Gestalt des frühmodernen Staates: Ausgewählte Aufsätze* (Berlin, 1969), pp. 179–197. See also Winfried Schulze, "Gerhard Oestreichs Begriff 'Sozialdiszplinierung' in der frühen Neuzeit," *Zeitschrift für historische Forschung* 14 (1987), 265–302 (critically reviewing Oestreich's thesis).
80. See Michael Stolleis, "'Konfessionalisierung' oder 'Säkularisierung' bei der Entstehung des frühmodernen Staates," *Jus Commune* 20 (1990), 1–23; and Heinz Schilling, "Die Kirchenzucht im frühzeitlichen Europa in interkonfessionell vergleichender und interdisziplinärer Perspektive—eine Zwischenbilanz," in Heinz Schilling, ed., *Kirchenzucht und Sozialdisziplinierung im frühneuzeitlichen Europa* (Berlin, 1994), pp. 11–40.
81. See Robert Jütte, *Obrigkeitliche Armenfürsorge in deutschen Reichsstädten der frühen Neuzeit: Städtisches Armenwesen in Frankfurt am Main und Köln* (Cologne, 1994).
82. On the Roman Catholic theology of mendicancy, see Michel Mollat, *The Poor in the Middle Ages: An Essay in Social History,* trans. Arthur Goldhammer (New Haven, 1986), pp. 119–134.
83. See Wolfgang Huber, *Kirche und Öffentlichkeit* (Stuttgart, 1973), pp. 58–59. The ultimate goal of such collaboration of church and state, Huber writes, is "die Verkirchligung der Öffentlichkeit"—"the churchification of the public."
84. See Heckel, *Lex Charitatis,* p. 45. Cf. the church ordinance of the principality of Lüneberg: "The first and greatest concern of the prince must be that God's Word be preached purely and rightly." "Radtslach to nodtroft der kloster der förstendoms Lüneborch, Gades wort unde ceremonien belangen," in Emil Sehling, ed., *Die evangelischen Kirchenordnungen des XVI Jahrhunderts,* Bd. 6, vol. 1 (1955), p. 586.
85. Rosenstock-Huessy, *Out of Revolution,* p. 369.
86. Karl Löwith, *Meaning in History: The Theological Implications of the Philosophy of History* (Chicago, 1949), published in German under the title *Weltgeschichte und Heilsgeschichte: die theologischen Vorraussetzungen der Geschichtsphilosophie,* 2 vols. (Stuttgart, 1953).
87. See Blumenberg, *Legitimacy of the Modern Age,* orig. *Die Legitimität der Neuzeit (erweiterte und überarbeitete Neuausgabe)* (Frankfurt, 1966). See also idem, *Säkularisierung und Selbstbehauptung* (Frankfurt am Main, 1974). Cf. Robert M. Wallace, "Progress, Secularization, and Modernity: The Löwith-Blumenberg Debate," *New German Critique* 22 (1981), 63–79.

7. The English Revolution, 1640–1689

1. This is not to say, of course, that anything like the English Revolution had ever happened before. It is only to say that, like the German Revolution of the previous century, and like the French Revolution of the next century, it had been prepared by political and religious movements that were pan-European in scope, and it had political and religious consequences that were also pan-European in scope.
2. H. R. Trevor-Roper, "The General Crisis of the Seventeenth Century," *Past and Present* 16 (1959), 31–64. Five years earlier Eric Hobsbawm had argued for a "general crisis" in the European economy in his article "The Crisis of the Seventeenth Century," *Past and Present* 5 (1954), 33–53; 6 (1954), 44–65. In the same year the French historian Roland Mousnier's study *Les XVIe et XVIIe siècles,* 5th ed. (Paris, 1954), described the period 1598–1715 as a "century of crisis." But Trevor-Roper's

article sparked the greatest debate. Cf. *Past and Present* 18 (1960), 8–42; Trevor Aston, ed., *Crisis in Europe*, 1560–1660 (Garden City, N.Y., 1967).

3. An example of a broader approach, treating both the socioeconomic crisis and the political crisis, can be found in Geoffrey Parker and Lesley Smith, eds., *The General Crisis of the Seventeenth Century* (London, 1978). The various authors of this anthology, however, fail to link the socioeconomic and the political crises, and the role of religion is treated only as one possible revolutionary ideology.
4. The Catholic provinces were, in general, loyal to Spain, and revolts against Spain in 1566 and 1572 were ruthlessly crushed. In 1576, however, thirteen of the seventeen provinces signed the Pacification of Ghent, providing for joint action against Spain and the formation of a United Netherlands Estates-General chosen by the various provincial estates. In 1578 an "edict of religious toleration" *(Religionsvrede)* was proposed, which would have allowed freedom of religion to all religious minorities of one hundred families or more in any one place. This was defeated, and the division between Catholic and Calvinist provinces was further intensified. Thus the Netherlands, like Germany, remained within the basic constitutional framework of established churches, without toleration, at the same time that it developed the rudiments of a republican form of government, at both the provincial and the national levels. See Geoffrey Parker, *The Dutch Revolt* (Ithaca, N.Y., 1977).
5. See Winthrop S. Hudson, "John Locke: Heir of Puritan Political Theorists," in George Laird Hunt, ed., *Calvinism and the Political Order* (Philadelphia, 1965), pp. 108–129. See also Menna Prestwich, *International Calvinism*, 1541–1715 (Oxford, 1985).
6. England had a vested interest in the outcome, for the Elector Palatine Frederick V was James I's son-in-law. After Frederick, who was a Calvinist, accepted the offer of the estates of Bohemia to become their king, he was defeated by imperial forces at the Battle of White Mountain (1620) outside Prague, and his principality was occupied by Spanish troops. While members of Parliament advocated vigorous military support for their fellow Protestants on the continent, the monarchy pursued more diplomatic means with the modest goal of mediating the reinstatement of Frederick and James's daughter Elizabeth to the Palatine electorate. English forces were sent to the Palatinate in 1625 and attacks were made on Spain (Cádiz expedition) and France (relief of La Rochelle). The military efforts ended in failure, and peace treaties were made with France (1629) and Spain (1630). During the 1630s England played no active role in the war. See W. B. Patterson, *King James VI and I and the Reunion of Christendom* (Cambridge, 1997), pp. 293–338 (analyzing James's diplomatic efforts to resolve the Thirty Years' War).
7. See Sigfrid Henry Steinberg, *The Thirty Years' War and the Conflict for European Hegemony, 1600–1660* (New York, 1966), pp. 2, 99.
8. Ibid., p. 83.
9. Cf. Perez Zagorin, *The Court and the Country: The Beginning of the English Revolution* (London, 1969); idem, *Rebels and Rulers, 1500–1660*, vol. 2 (Cambridge, 1982), pp. 138–146.
10. Roger Merriman, *Six Contemporaneous Revolutions* (Oxford, 1938), pp. 170–189; P. A. Knaechel, *England and the Fronde: The Impact of the English Civil War and Revolution on France* (Ithaca, N.Y., 1967). Richard Bonney, "The English and French Civil Wars," *History* 65 (1980), 365–382, analyzes the contrasts between the civil wars in the two countries. See also A. Lloyd Moote, "The French Crown versus Its Judicial Officials, 1625–1683," *Journal of Modern History* 34 (1962), 146–160 (analyzing the claims made by the Parlement of Paris justifying an indepen-

dent judicial authority vis-à-vis the Crown). In his book Merriman also discusses the "uprising in Naples" and the "revolution in the Netherlands." The Naples revolt of 1647 was essentially a popular rebellion. The local elite played little role except to support the Spanish Crown in suppressing the revolt. See John Huxtable Elliott, "Revolts in the Spanish Monarchy," in Robert Forster and Jack P. Greene, eds., *Preconditions of Revolution in Early Modern Europe* (Baltimore, 1970), pp. 111, 123–127. In the Netherlands, the revolution began more than a half century before, in the successful struggle for independence from the Spanish Crown and the establishment of a new republic, the United Provinces. The first revolt began in 1566, and official Spanish recognition of the Dutch Republic did not occur until the Peace of Westphalia in 1648. It was therefore a precursor of the English Revolution of 1640–1689. The revolt of 1650, which Merriman includes in his "six contemporaneous revolutions," concerned the form of government the republic was to take: a federation of sovereign provincial republics, with federal authority resting in an Estate-General (dominated by Holland, the largest and most prosperous of the seven provinces), or a single republic, increasingly centralized under the authority of the stadtholder. The death of the twenty-five-year-old stadtholder William of Orange in 1650 allowed Holland to reassert its leadership through the abolition of the office and the strengthening of the powers of the provincial estates.

11. See John Huxtable Elliott, *The Revolt of the Catalans: A Study in the Decline of Spain, 1598–1640* (Cambridge, 1963); idem, "Revolts in the Spanish Monarchy," pp. 109–130; Merriman, *Six Contemporaneous Revolutions,* pp. 10–17.
12. Hobsbawm, "Crisis of the Seventeenth Century," p. 33. Other historians, while avoiding a Marxist framework, have similarly emphasized an overall decline in the production and the rate of growth of the European economy. These works are summarized in Niels Steensgaard, "The Seventeenth-Century Crisis," in Parker and Smith, *General Crisis,* pp. 27–42.
13. England avoided the devastating type of subsistence crisis which occurred with regularity on the continent. Lawrence Stone, *The Origins of the English Revolution* (London, 1972), p. 67. Commerce and trade did slump, however, in the 1620s and 1630s.
14. Quoted in Trevor-Roper, "General Crisis," p. 31.
15. Parker and Smith, *General Crisis,* p. 1. Ralph Josselin, an English vicar, recorded in his diary in 1652: "France is likely to fall in flames by her owne divisions. The Spaniard has almost reduced Barcelona, the chiefe city of Catalonia, and so that kingdom; the issue of that affaire wee waite. Poland is free from warre with the Cossacks but feareth them. Dane and Suede are both quiet, and so is Germany, yet the peace at Munster is not fully executed: the Turke hath done no great matter on the Venetian, nor beene so fortunate and martial as formerly, as if that people were at their height and declining rather." Parker and Smith note that the diary "reveals the wide range of foreign affairs information that came even to a small Essex village." Ibid., p. 2.
16. *Calendar of State Papers, Venetian, 1647–52* (London, 1927), p. 170. The letter of the Venetian ambassador in Spain continues: "Moreover from that end Cardenas reports that after his victory in Scotland, Cromuel wrote to the parliament that through that success they might now consider the affairs of the interior safe, and that for the future they must think of helping other nations to throw off the yoke, and to consolidate their government by establishing republican neighbors." Merriman *Six Contemporaneous Revolutions* (p. 95 n. 4), cites as corroborating evidence of the veracity of this diplomatic correspondence a letter from Edward Hyde to the royal secretary Sir Edward Nicholas, dated February 9, 1651, at Ma-

drid: "That you may see how brave and open dealing your friends of the new commonwealth are, Blake, at his late being at Cadiz, said openly, that Monarchy is a kind of government the world is weary of: that it is past in England, going in France, and that it must get out of Spain with more gravity, but in ten years it would be determined there likewise."

17. Edward Hyde, earl of Clarendon and the first chief minister to Charles II, titled his work, first published in 1702–1704, *History of the Rebellion and Civil Wars in England.* Among modern historians, note Ivan Alan Roots, *The Great Rebellion, 1642–1660* (London, 1966). Cf. J. P. Kenyon, *The Stuart Constitution,* 2nd ed (Cambridge, 1985), p. 7.
18. G. R. Elton in a review of Lawrence Stone's *Causes of the English Revolution* in *Historical Journal* 16 (1973), 207.
19. James R. Hertzler, "Who Dubbed It 'The Glorious Revolution?'" *Albion* 19 (1987), 579–585.
20. See Eugen Rosenstock-Huessy, *Out of Revolution: The Autobiography of Western Man* (1938; reprint, Providence, 1993), p. 761, and, on the three restorations, p. 260.
21. On the term "revolution" in the seventeenth century, see Vernon Snow, "The Concept of Revolution in Seventeenth-Century England," *Historical Journal* 5 (1962), 167–174; and Zagorin, *Court and Country,* pp. 13–16. Both stress the seventeenth-century predominance of the astronomical meaning of the term, an emphasis on circularity in which planetary bodies return to their original place in the heavens. Zagorin states that the French historian François-Pierre-Guillaume Guizot (*Histoire de la révolution d'Angleterre depuis l'avènement de Charles I jusqu'à sa mort,* 2 vols. [Paris, 1826]) was the first to systematically treat the period 1640–1660 as an authentic revolution in the modern sense. Christopher Hill, "The Word 'Revolution' in Seventeenth-Century England," in Pamela Tudor-Craig and Richard Ollard, eds., *For Veronica Wedgewood: These Studies in Seventeenth-Century History* (London, 1986), pp. 134–151, argues that "revolution" in the sense of a break in continuity was used before 1688, with the catalyst being the dramatic developments of the winter of 1648–49. This view is confirmed by the statement of Admiral Blake in Cádiz, quoted earlier in the text.
22. Berman, *Law and Revolution,* p. 19.24.
23. G.R. Elton, *The Tudor Constitution* (Cambridge, 1960), p.327.
24. *State Papers of Henry VIII, 1509–1547,* vol. 1 (London, 1970), p. 392. Cranmer had close relations with leading German Lutherans, including Martin Bucer, and in 1532 married a relative of Luther's friend Andreas Osiander. See Diarmaid MacCullogh, *Thomas Cranmer: A Life* (New Haven, 1996), p. 72.
25. Elton, *Tudor Constitution,* p. 344.
26. See Basil Hall, "Lutheranism in England," in Derek Baker, ed., *Reform and Reformation: England and the Continent* (Oxford, 1979), pp. 111–112.
27. The Six Articles declared that anyone who denied transubstantiation—namely, that the bread and wine of the eucharist become the spiritual body and blood of Christ upon their elevation by the priest in the ceremony of Holy Communion—was a heretic and therefore subject to be burned at the stake, and anyone who maintained opinions contrary to other provisions of the Six Articles was a felon and therefore subject to be hanged. Hall, "Lutheranism in England," pp. 118–119; cf. Edward John Bicknell, *A Theological Introduction to the Thirty-nine Articles of the Church of England* (London, 1944), pp. 12–13. See also Elton, *Tudor Constitution,* pp. 399–401.
28. A. G. Dickens, *The English Reformation,* (New York, 1964), p. 287.

29. Elton, *Tudor Constitution,* pp. 423–442 and documents pp. 197–201.
30. E. B. Fryde et al., eds., *Handbook of British Chronology,* 3rd ed. (London, 1986), pp. 572–574.
31. Elton, *Tudor Constitution,* p. 22, claims that proclamations had no force in the common law courts. This is not true. R. W. Heinze, *The Proclamations of Tudor Kings* (Cambridge, 1976), pp. 63, 262–263, cites proclamations that specifically list the courts of King's Bench, Common Pleas, and Exchequer as places where offenses could be tried. Other proclamations mention or imply that any court of record is a proper venue. See also Frederic A. Youngs, *The Proclamations of the Tudor Queens* (Cambridge, 1976), who states (pp. 39–40): "Regardless of the opinions held by some jurists who would have restricted proclamations to a subordinate role and denied them the right to make law in them, both Mary and Elizabeth used royal proclamations to frame temporary legislation." Proclamations could extend the effect of existing laws; they could define situations as falling within the purview of existing legislation; they could create new offenses directly or by applying penalties designed for principal offenders to accessories as well.
32. Other prerogative courts, that is, courts created by the royal prerogative, included the Court of the Council of the North, the Court of the Council in the Marches of Wales, the Court of the Duchy of Lancaster, and the Court of the Exchequer of the County Palatine of Chester. In fact, though not in theory, the High Court of Admiralty was a new court and a prerogative court, although it had predecessors in the so-called Admirals' Court of an earlier time. Also the High Court of Chancery was in fact, though not in theory, a new court and a prerogative court, although its historical roots in the Chancery jurisdiction of the fourteenth and fifteenth centuries were strong.
33. In the 1970s and 1980s revisionist historians, though they disagreed among themselves on many points, challenged the hitherto almost universally accepted view that a crescendo of constitutional conflict led to the outbreak of the English Revolution in the 1640s. The revisionists minimized the strength of Parliament, the existence of an opposition to the Crown, and the provocative role of Puritanism. They instead emphasized the ineffectiveness of Parliament and the divisions within it, the financial crisis brought on by war expenditures, and the "revolutionary" nature of royal ecclesiastical policy in the 1630s. The outbreak of the Revolution was thus made to appear to be a historical accident brought on by the fiscal, religious, and foreign policy blunders of the monarchy in the decade prior to the Civil War. See Conrad Russell, "Parliamentary History in Perspective, 1604–1629," *History* 51 (1976), 1–27; idem, *Parliaments and English Politics, 1621–1629* (Oxford, 1979); Kevin Sharpe, ed., *Faction and Parliament: Essays on Early Stuart History* (Oxford, 1978); and Howard Tomlinson, ed., *Before the English Civil War* (New York, 1983). The element of truth in these views is that the Revolution was not inevitable; it could have been avoided if both sides had been more understanding and less stubborn. This is true of all the Great Revolutions.
34. "Tunnage and poundage" were customs duties granted to the king since the fourteenth century. Tunnage was a fixed rate assessed on each "tun" (cask) of wine imported. Poundage was a tax proportional to monetary value (pounds) levied on all imported and exported goods. "Impositions" were not a Stuart innovation; they had been introduced in the reign of Mary and were continued under Elizabeth. In 1606 a merchant named John Bate challenged the legality of the imposition on currants. The Court of Exchequer ruled in the king's favor, Chief Baron Gleming holding that "if the king may impose, he may impose any quantity he pleases, [and] this is to be referred to the wisdom of the king . . . and is not to

be disputed by a subject; and many things are left to his wisdom for the ordering of his power, rather than his power shall be restrained." J. R. Tanner, *Constitutional Documents of the Reign of James I* (Cambridge, 1930), p. 342.

35. Ibid., pp. 245–247.

36. The 1621 parliament was dominated by discussions of James's policies relating to the religious wars in Europe and his intention to marry his son Charles to the Catholic Princess Maria of Spain. (Charles later married a different Catholic princess, Henrietta Maria of France.) James rejected parliamentary counsel, declaring that foreign policy was within the royal prerogative and constituted "matters far above [the Commons'] reach and capacity." On December 18, 1621, the Commons adopted a Protestation, stating that it possessed the right to discuss on its own initiative all matters of church and state and that the king may not limit such discussions. This was directly contrary to the principle laid down in 1593, under Elizabeth, that matters concerning the royal prerogative, called "matters of state," could be discussed in a parliament only with the express permission of the monarch. The 1621 Protestation, drafted by Coke, declared "that the liberties, franchise, privileges and jurisdiction of parliament are the ancient and undoubted birthright and inheritance of the subjects of England." On the following day James prorogued Parliament, and on December 30 he sent for the journal of the House of Commons and in the presence of the Privy Council tore out the page on which the Protestation had been entered. Ibid., pp. 274–295. Coke and two other members of the Commons were sent to the Tower, where Coke sat for six months. Some seventy gentlemen were imprisoned for such opposition.

    The "forced loan" had been used as a financial device by the Tudor monarchs, but never on such a large scale and never to overcome parliamentary opposition to a monarch at the beginning of his reign. See Frederick C. Dietz, *English Government Finance, 1485–1558* (Urbana, Ill., 1921), pp. 93–97, 163–166, 211; idem, *English Public Finance, 1558–1641* (New York, 1932), pp. 25–26, 62–63.

37. The Petition of Right is reproduced in Kenyon, *Stuart Constitution*, pp. 68–71. In 1629 a second rancorous session of Parliament ended dramatically when the Speaker, on the king's orders, declared Parliament to be adjourned but the Commons insisted on continuing the session. The Speaker rose to cut off debate, but two members pushed him back down and held him in his seat while another member read three resolutions indirectly criticizing the Crown. The House passed the resolutions and then voted its own adjournment.

38. Without Parliament, Charles resorted to a series of devices to raise money even more extraordinary than the earlier forced loans. See Roger Lockyer, *Early Stuarts: A Political History of England, 1603–1642* (London, 1999), pp. 267–268. The most offensive was "ship money," originally collected from seaport towns and surrounding regions to increase the strength of the navy against foreign enemies and pirates but now extended by Charles to inland counties as well. Charles's ship money was imposed at a higher rate and over a broader class of people than the traditional tax, and many small freeholders and merchants who previously had been exempt from such taxes were now included. In 1637 a joint session of the courts of King's Bench and Common Pleas, in *Hampden's Case*, by a vote of seven to five, upheld the convictions of a group of gentlemen who had refused to pay ship money.

39. Three writers of anti-episcopal tracts (William Prynne, John Bastwick, and Henry Burton) were tried in Star Chamber in 1637 and ordered to have their ears cut off, to pay heavy fines, and to be imprisoned for life.

40. Winston Churchill, *A History of the English-Speaking Peoples*, vol. 2, *The New*

World (New York, 1956), pp. 212–213. In April 1640, before the second Scottish war, Charles had summoned a parliament (the first since 1629), which, however, he dissolved after three weeks (it was called "the Short Parliament") because it refused to grant him money for the war unless he first redressed its grievances.

41. Among the lesser officials impeached were those judges of King's Bench and Common Pleas who in 1637 had supported the monarchy in the seven-to-five vote of *Hampden's Case* (see n. 38). See W. J. Jones, *Politics and the Bench: The Judge and the Origins of the English Civil War* (London, 1971), pp. 139–143, 199–215.
42. The Act for the Abolition of the Court of Star Chamber (17 Charles I, 10) was passed July 5, 1641. It also abolished the other prerogative courts listed in n. 32. The Act for the Abolition of the Court of High Commission (17 Charles I, 11) passed the same day. Both statutes are reproduced in S. R. Gardiner, *Constitutional Documents of the Puritan Revolution*, 1625–1660, 3rd ed. (Oxford, 1958), pp. 179–189. Records of the Court of Requests ceased in 1642. See John H. Baker, *An Introduction to English Legal History*, 3rd ed. (Cambridge, 1990), p. 105.
43. The Grand Remonstrance passed by a vote of only 159 to 148. The document, together with the king's reply, can be found in Gardiner, *Constitutional Documents*, pp. 202–232, 233–236.
44. "Such an event was entirely without precedent. It has been pointed out that the usual entry in the Journals of the House breaks off suddenly, 'as if the excitement of the scene had paralyzed the clerks at their work.' The House itself was stricken with amazement, fury, and shame. 'Such a night of prayers, tears, and groans,' wrote an eyewitness long afterwards, 'I never was present at in all my life.' As one writer said at the time, 'The obedience of his Majesty's subjects hath been poisoned.' The danger which had been dreaded had come at last, and it was now certain, what before had only been suspected, that the King was prepared, even in violation of his pledged word, to throw the sword into the scale. The House appealed to the City for protection, and adjourned its sittings to the Guildhall, and when it returned to Westminster it met under a guard of train-bands." J. R. Tanner, *English Constitutional Conflicts of the Seventeenth Century*, 1603–1689 (Cambridge, 1928), p. 114.
45. In the "Old Style" English calendar, the new year began on March 25. This was not changed until 1751. Thus January 1641/42 refers to both the "Old Style" and "New Style" year.
46. The Putney Debates pitted the more conservative senior army officers against the more radical junior officers and rank-and-file soldiers. Cromwell participated in the debates, but the principal spokesman for the senior officers was his son-in-law Henry Ireton. No consensus was reached. The debates are recorded in A. S. P. Woodhouse, ed., *Puritanism and Liberty, Being the Army Debates*, 1647–49, 2nd ed. (London, 1974).
47. Gardiner, *Constitutional Documents*, pp. 371–374. Charles's defense and the significance of the trial are discussed later in this chapter.
48. Blair Worden, *The Rump Parliament, 1648–1653* (Cambridge, 1974), pp. 306–308.
49. See Austin Woolrych, *Oliver Cromwell* (Oxford, 1964), pp. 46–47.
50. See Antonia Fraser, *Cromwell, the Lord Protector* (New York, 1973), pp. 48–50.
51. See Claire Cross, "The Church in England, *1646–1660*," in G. E. Aylmer, ed., *The Interregnum: The Quest for Settlement, 1646–1660* (Hamden, Conn., 1972), p. 102.
52. Despite King Edward I's order, there is evidence that small numbers of Jews remained in the realm, since conversions from Judaism continued to be recorded throughout the fourteenth and fifteenth centuries. In addition, a small commu-

nity of Spanish Marranos existed in London, although its members took considerable pains to conceal their Jewish identity. The revival of interest in Hebrew in the sixteenth century and the introduction of Hebraic studies at Oxford and Cambridge helped to create a climate that one scholar has labeled "philo-Semitism." In the 1650s, negotiations were opened up with Menassah ben Israel, a leader of the Amsterdam Jewish community, over the return of Jews to England, and in 1655 an invitation was extended to Menassah, who led the return personally. See David S. Katz, *The Jews in the History of England, 1485–1850* (Oxford, 1994), esp. pp. 107–144; cf. idem, *Philo-Semitism and the Readmission of the Jews to England, 1603–1655* (Oxford, 1982) (documenting the changed climate of opinion and its effect on Christian-Jewish relations).

53. On the persecution of Irish Catholics, see Nicholas P. Canny, "The Ideology of Colonization: From Ireland to America," *William and Mary Quarterly* 30, 3rd ser. (1973), 575–598; James Muldoon, "The Indian as Irishman," *Essex Institutes Historical Collections* 111 (1975), 267–289. Cf. Brendan Fitzpatrick, *Seventeenth-Century Ireland: The Wars of Religion* (Dublin, 1988).
54. Austin Woolrych, "Cromwell as a Soldier," in John Morrill, ed., *Oliver Cromwell and the English Revolution* (London, 1990), pp. 93–118; Oliver Cromwell, *Letters and Speeches,* ed. Thomas Carlyle, vol. 1 (London, 1845), pp. 472–473.
55. Quoted in Eugen Rosenstock-Huessy, *Out of Revolution,* p. 358.
56. Fraser, *Cromwell,* pp. 355–357.
57. For the documents quoted in this discussion, see Kenyon, *Stuart Constitution,* pp. 339–344 (Act of Indemnity) and 331–332 (Declaration of Breda).
58. On the Regicides, who they were, and what became of them, see A. L. Rouse, *The Regicides and the Puritan Revolution* (London, 1994).
59. Financial legislation now originated in the House of Commons, and this was used as a means of asserting legislative prerogatives with which the Lords could not interfere. See ibid., pp. 415–419.
60. In the 1670s Charles circumvented the financial restrictions of Parliament with the aid of a £200,000 annual subsidy from Louis XIV, part of the secret 1670 Treaty of Dover, in which Charles promised to help the French in their war against the Dutch and also to convert openly to Catholicism at the earliest possible time. When trade recovered in the late 1670s, the king's revenues increased and he grew more independent of the legislative assembly. "The Restoration financial settlement, which had been designed to restore a balanced constitution in which King and Parliament should cooperate, had opened the way to a second Stuart depotism." Roger Lockyer, *Tudor and Stuart Britain* (New York, 1985), pp. 349.
61. See Baker, *Introduction to English Legal History,* pp. 127–128 (discussing Chancery) and 142–143 (discussing Admiralty).
62. James II, who ascended the throne in 1685, took a number of reactionary steps: he established a court of ecclesiastical commission that resembled the old High Commission too closely for comfort; he dismissed judges for political reasons; he promoted Catholics within the army; and he issued in 1687 a new Declaration of Indulgence which had the effect of lifting all civil penalties against membership in the Roman Church. See Goldwin Albert Smith, *A History of England,* 2nd ed. rev. (New York, 1957), p. 365; and Frederick George Marcham, *A History of England* (New York, 1950), pp. 482–484.
63. Charles II had proclaimed himself a Catholic on his deathbed. See Marcham, *History of England,* p. 481. James II, however, was then a Protestant and only later became a Catholic. Prior to the birth of James's son, it was thought that he would be succeeded by his Protestant daughter Mary, who was married to William of

Orange. The birth of James's son, however, changed this political calculation dramatically. Ibid., p. 484.

64. At the time of William's invasion, his supporters had built a strong constitutional case against James's continued reign. An important constitutional challenge to his authority had been raised when seven of England's leading bishops refused to read from the pulpit his Declaration of Indulgence and petitioned him to revoke the Declaration as illegal. The bishops were tried for seditious libel, but their acquittal in July 1688 in the so-called *Seven Bishops' Case* seriously undermined the legitimacy of James's rule. See Marcham, *History of England,* pp. 483–484.
65. See Howard Nenner, *The Right to Be King: The Succession to the Crown of England, 1603–1714* (Chapel Hill, 1995), esp. pp. 149–247.
66. See Hertzler, "Who Dubbed It 'The Glorious Revolution?'"
67. 1 William III and Mary II c. 36 (1689). See Lois Schwoerer, *The Declaration of Rights, 1689* (Baltimore, 1981).
68. 12 & 13 William III c. 2 (1701). Since 1701, no English judge has been removed from office.
69. 1 William & Mary, c. 6 (1689).
70. 1 William & Mary, c. 18 (1689). The formal title of the Toleration Act was "An Act to Exempt their Majesties' Protestant Subjects Dissenting from the Church of England from the Penalties of Certain Laws."
71. F. W. Maitland, *The Constitutional History of England: A Course of Lectures,* ed. H. A. L. Fisher (Cambridge, 1965), p. 516. (The lectures were originally delivered in 1887 and 1888.)
72. See Katz, *Jews in the History of England,* pp. 151–153.
73. Ibid., p. 201.
74. See ibid., passim; also Abraham Gilam, "The Emancipation of the Jews in England, 1830–1860" (Ph.D. diss., Washington University, 1978), pp. 80–175.

8. The Transformation of English Legal Philosophy

1. This view, which originated in the seventeenth century, acquired even greater support in the heyday of English insularity in the nineteenth and early twentieth centuries. Thus Bishop William Stubbs, a leading English constitutional historian of the Victorian era, described English law as the purest surviving specimen of Germanic customary law, to which he attributed a strong stress on individual freedom and constitutional limitations on the monarch, as opposed to Romanist theories of absolutism. From the time of Henry II, he wrote, the English common law reflected a wholly different philosophy from that of the canon or civil law, to which "there was in England the greatest antipathy." See William Stubbs, *Lectures on Early English History* (London, 1906), p. 257; idem, *Constitutional History of England,* vol. 1 (Oxford, 1891), pp. 584–585. The notion of an age-old conflict between a democratic, individualist, empirical, Anglo-Saxon or Germanic theory of law and government versus an autocratic, collectivist, dogmatic Romanist one was widespread in late-nineteenth-century America as well, and was taught at Harvard University, for example, by Henry Adams. See Henry Adams, *Essays in Anglo-Saxon Law* (Boston, 1905), containing his Harvard lectures.

   Similar views recur even in more recent scholarship. Thus Quentin Skinner, in *The Foundations of Modern Political Thought,* vol. 2 (Cambridge, 1978), pp. 54–55, states that English "nationalist hostility" to the Roman law and the canon lawyers "can be traced as far back as Bracton's defence of custom in the thirteenth century." In fact Bracton, in his great treatise on English law, quoted Roman law favorably in at least five hundred different places; moreover, Bishop Raleigh, the judge for whom Bracton clerked and whose cases he collected in his *Casebook,* was an ardent supporter of the papacy who was called at the time a second Thomas Becket and who had to flee to France to escape the king's wrath. Skinner also wrongly attributes to the fifteenth-century English jurist Sir John Fortescue the view that "the whole of the Roman code is alien to the 'political' nature of the English constitution," and he misreads Fortescue as "xenophobic" toward Romanists and canonists. In fact, at the page cited by Skinner to support these conclusions, Fortescue merely states that English law is as "adapted to the utility of [England] as the civil law is to the good of the Empire." See Skinner, *Foundations,* p. 55; and Sir John Fortescue, *De Laudibus Legum Angliae* (In praise of the laws of England), ed. S. B. Chimes (Cambridge, 1942), pp. 25 and 37.

A prominent contemporary historian of medieval English law, R. C. van Caenegem, makes an argument similar to that of Stubbs and Skinner, and in addition contrasts the empirical, inductive character of the "Germanic and feudal customs and laws of England" in the twelfth century and thereafter with the dogmatic, deductive character of the Roman law of the continental European universities. See R. C. van Caenegem, *The Birth of the English Common Law,* 2nd ed. (Cambridge, 1988), pp. 85–110. But of course the comparison should be between the Germanic and feudal customs of England and the Germanic and feudal customs of the other countries of western Europe, and between the Roman law of the continental European universities and the Roman law of the English universities.

2. Fortescue, *De Laudibus Legum Angliae,* p. 20.
3. See John Fortescue, *De Natura Legis Naturae,* in *Works,* ed. Lord Clermont, vol. 1 (London, 1869). Fortescue submitted this book to the examination of the pope, asking him if he found it right and just to impart it to all the sons of the church or otherwise "to annul it" (p. 332). See George L. Mosse, "Sir John Fortescue and the Problem of Papal Power," *Medievalia et Humanistica* 7 (1952), 89. Fortescue presented the orthodox view, then more or less universally shared in the West, that human law, including the statutes of Parliament, were derived from natural law, which was a reflection of divine law, and that statutes contrary to natural law were void; and further, that the church was the final custodian of divine and human law and the pope the final authority in its interpretation. Indeed, Fortescue goes so far as to say that the secular judge, in interpreting divine law, should "in doubtful matters follow the decree of the supreme Pontiff." See Joan Lockwood O'Donovan, *Theology of Law and Authority in the English Reformation* (Atlanta, 1991), p. 49.
4. See Norman Doe, *Fundamental Authority in Late Medieval English Law* (Cambridge, 1990), pp. 12–19; idem, "Fifteenth-Century Concepts of Law: Fortescue and Pecock," *History of Political Thought* 10 (1989), 257–280.
5. See Christopher St. German, *St. German's Doctor and Student,* ed. T. F. T. Plucknett and J. L. Barton (London, 1974), pp. 8–31. Cf. J. A. Guy, *Christopher St. German on Chancery and Statute* (London, 1985), p. 19 ("Within St. German's framework, the universal laws of God and Nature were shown to be both rationally antecedent to, and harmoniously co-existent with, English common law (the law of man)").
6. See Richard Hooker, *The Laws of Ecclesiastical Polity,* bk. 1, chap. 10, reprinted in *The Works of that Learned and Judicious Divine, Mr. Richard Hooker,* ed. John Keble (1888; reprint, New York, 1970), 1:239. At a later point Hooker wrote that "where the law doth give him dominion, who doubteth but that the king who

receiveth it must hold it of and under the law? According to that axiom, *Attribuat rex legi, quod lex attribuit ei, potestatem et dominium* [the king will give to the law that which the law gives to him, power and dominion] and again *rex non debet esse sub homine sed sub deo et lege* [the king ought to be under God and the law]." Hooker, *Ecclesiastical Polity,* bk. 8, chap. 2, (Keble ed. 3:342). This last expression, drawn from Bracton, is used eleven times by Hooker in his working notes to *Ecclesiastical Polity.* See Arthur S. McGrade, "Constitutionalism, Late Medieval and Early Modern—*Lex Facit Regem:* Hooker's Use of Bracton," in *Acta Conventus Neo-Latini Bononiensis (Proceedings of the Fourth International Congress of Neo-Latin Studies),* ed. R. J. Schoeck (Binghamton, N.Y., 1985).

7. He calls Thomas Aquinas "the greatest amongst the school-divines." Hooker, *Ecclesiastical Polity,* bk. 3, chap. 9 (Keble ed., 1:381). See also Robert K. Faulkner, *Richard Hooker and the Politics of a Christian England* (Berkeley, 1981), pp. 63–72, for a comparison of Hooker with Aristotle and Aquinas.
8. On Hooker's theological comprehensiveness, see John E. Booty, "Hooker and the Anglican Tradition," in *Studies in Richard Hooker,* ed. W. Speed Hill (Cleveland, 1971), pp. 207–239; and John Marshall, *Hooker and the Anglican Tradition: An Historical and Theological Study of Hooker's Ecclesiastical Polity* (Sewanee, Tenn., 1963).
9. See Hooker, *Ecclesiastical Polity,* bk. 1, chap. 10 (Keble ed., 1:239). Cf. E. T. Davies, *The Political Ideas of Richard Hooker* (London, 1946), p. 65.
10. See W. D. J. Cargill Thompson, "The Philosopher of the 'Politic Society': Richard Hooker as a Political Thinker," in Hill, *Studies in Richard Hooker,* p. 39. Cf. Faulkner, *Richard Hooker,* pp. 110ff.
11. Hooker, *Ecclesiastical Polity,* bk. 1, chap. 10.
12. Ibid.
13. Hooker uses the phrase "natural law" or "law of nature" to refer to the phenomena of inanimate nature and of animal and human biology, and the phrase "law of reason" to refer to human moral and intellectual processes. See Davies, *Political Ideas of Hooker,* p. 49.
14. Hooker, *Ecclesiastical Polity,* bk. 1, chap. 10.
15. See *The Trew Law of Free Monarchies,* in *The Political Works of James I,* ed. Charles Howard McIlwain (Cambridge, Mass., 1918), passim. Unlike God, however, a ruler might prove to be evil. Such a ruler is to be tolerated as condign punishment for sins, rather than resisted (p. 67).
16. Jean Bodin, *On Sovereignty,* ed. and trans. Julian Franklin (Cambridge, 1992), p. 46.
17. Jean Bodin, *Les six livres de la République* (The six books on the Republic) (1576). The 1583 text of this work was reprinted in 1961 in facsimile edition by Scientia Verlag (Aalen, Germany). A modern abridgment and translation is Jean Bodin, *Six Books of the Commonwealth,* trans. M. J. Tooley (Oxford, 1955). For a translation of Bodin's central arguments on sovereignty, with commentary, see Bodin, *On Sovereignty.*
18. John of Salisbury, *Policraticus,* ed. C. C. Webb (Oxford, 1909), 3.15. See also *The Statesman's Book of John of Salisbury, Being the Fourth, Fifth, and Sixth Books, Selections from the Seventh and Eighth Books, of the Policraticus,* trans. with intro. John Dickinson (New York, 1963), pp. lxxiii–lxxiv. For analysis of John of Salisbury's political theory, including his doctrine of tyrannicide, see Berman, *Law and Revolution,* pp. 276–288.
19. See Julian Franklin, *Jean Bodin and the Rise of Absolutist Theory* (Cambridge, 1973), pp. 23, 54ff. In his earlier writings Bodin had defended a limited sovereignty,

but in *The Republic* he argued that in every ordered commonwealth there must be a single center of absolute authority, and that apparent constitutional restrictions on monarchical power, such as the monarch's oath to obey the laws of the realm and his establishment of various offices to carry out various governmental functions, are not binding upon him. The sharing of sovereignty among prince, nobility, and people, he wrote, would amount to "anarchy." Ibid., p. 29.

The premises of James's argument for royal absolutism differed from Bodin's insofar as James, perhaps because of his Protestantism, relied heavily on biblical sources, including, in particular, examples of absolute monarchical rule drawn from the books of Samuel, Chronicles, Kings, and Psalms.

20. See Anton Meuten, *Bodins Theorie von der Beeinflussung des politischen Lebens der Staaten durch ihre geographische Lage* (Bonn, 1904).
21. Francis Bacon, "A Speech of the King's Solicitor, Persuading the House of Commons to Desist from Farther Question of Receiving the King's Messages," in *The Works of Francis Bacon,* ed. Basil Montagu, vol. 2 (Philadelphia, 1857), pp. 276, 277.
22. Quoted in Franklin, *Jean Bodin,* p. 93. Bodin did place two theoretical limitations on the absolute power of the monarch, namely, that kings are obliged to honor their contracts and that they may not deprive persons of property without compensation. The latter obligation included a restriction on royal power to impose arbitrary taxes. In view of these limitations, some writers dispute the view that Bodin advocated a theory of absolute monarchy. Bodin did not, however, propose any means for enforcing these limitations on tyrannical power: no agency of government was empowered, in his theory, to oppose the monarch's will and no right of civil disobedience was attributed to the monarch's subjects. Nevertheless, the French monarchy was, as a practical matter, under some significant restraints at the hands of the nobility. See J. Russell Major, *Representative Institutions in Renaissance France, 1421–1559* (Madison, Wisc., 1960).
23. Franklin, *Jean Bodin,* p. 106.
24. James I, *Trew Law of Free Monarchies,* in Charles H. McIlwain, ed., *The Political Works of James I* (Cambridge, Mass., 1918), pp. 62–63.
25. Ibid. Cf. John D. Eusden, *Puritans, Lawyers, and Politics in Seventeenth-Century England* (New Haven, 1958), p. 46.
26. Quoted in McIlwain, *Political Works of James I,* p. xxxv.
27. *Caudrey's Case,* 5 *Coke's Reports,* 1, 8 (K.B., 1595); 77 *Eng. Rep.* 1, 10.
28. Coke's position on this point is set forth in *Calvin's Case* (1608), where he quoted Plowden's statement that "the King has in him two bodies, viz. a body natural and a body politic," the latter "consisting of policy and government" and being "utterly void of infancy and old age and other natural defects and inbecilities." See Ernst Kantorowicz, *The King's Two Bodies: A Study in Medieval Political Theology* (Princeton, 1957), p. 7. Thus the king's law could survive his death.
29. The pretext was that he had at one time failed to pay taxes to the Crown. The common law judges dismissed the complaint, and Coke was thereupon released from custody. Catherine Drinker Bowen, *The Lion and the Throne,* (Boston, 1957), pp. 455–457. Note that the "birthright" theory of the common law became important in the struggle of the American colonies against abuses of the royal prerogative.
30. To assume that the new Roman law and the new canon law were foreign to England in the period from the twelfth century on, one would have to draw the absurd conclusion that they were foreign to all the other countries of Europe as well. Richard Helmholz has noted that Coke "possessed a sizable collection of

works from the Roman and canon law. His professed antipathy toward them did not prevent him from drawing upon what he found in those works." Richard Helmholz, *The Jus Commune in England: Four Studies* (Oxford, 2001), p. 4.

31. This was the objection raised by Serjeant Ashley to the position taken by Coke and Selden and two other spokesmen for the House of Commons at a conference held between the Lords and Commons in 1628—prior to the issuance of the Petition of Right—"concerning the subject's Liberties and Freedoms from Imprisonment." Ashley argued that the phrase *per legem terrae* in Magna Carta must be understood to refer to "divers laws of this realm" and not only to the common law. See *State Trials,* iii, 153. Cf. J. W. Gough, *Fundamental Law in English Constitutional History* (Oxford, 1955), pp. 61–63.
32. Charles Gray has said that Coke had "an ad hoc mind" and that "he did not think philosophically." See Charles M. Gray, "Reason, Authority, and Imagination: The Jurisprudence of Sir Edward Coke," in Perez Zagorin, ed., *Culture and Politics from Puritanism to the Enlightenment* (Berkeley, 1980), p. 28. Gray adds, however, that "in his attitudes the outlines of a jurisprudence are discernible." Ibid.
33. Gray has called Coke's concept of artificial reason "perhaps Coke's main gift to legal theory." Ibid., p. 30. See also J. W. Tubbs, *The Common Law Mind: Medieval and Early Modern Conceptions* (Baltimore, 2000), pp. 162–165.
34. Edward Coke, *The First Part of the Institutes of the Laws of England,* ed. Robert H. Small (Philadelphia, 1853), 319b (p. 15).
35. Coke's version of the colloquy is given at length in *Prohibitions del Roy,* 12 *Coke's Reports* 63 (1608). Although it is highly colored, it does represent accurately the nature of the conflict and many parts of it are corroborated by other sources. It reads as follows:

"Note upon Sunday the 10th of November in this same term, the King, upon complaint made to him by Bancroft, Archbishop of Canterbury, concerning prohibitions, the King was informed that when the question was made of what matters the Ecclesiastical Judges have cognizance, either upon the exposition of the statutes concerning tithes, or any other thing ecclesiastical, or upon the statute 1 Eliz. concerning the High Commission, or in any other case in which there is not express authority in law, the King himself may decide it in his Royal person; and that the Judges are but the delegates of the King; and that the King may take what causes he shall please . . . from . . . the Judges, and may determine them himself. And the Archbishop said it was clear in divinity, that such authority belongs to the King by the word of God in the Scripture.

"To which it was answered by me, in the presence and with the clear consent of all the judges of England, and Barons of the Exchequer, that the King in his own person cannot adjudge any case, either criminal, as treason, felony, etc., or betwixt party and party, concerning the inheritance, chattels, or goods, etc., but this ought to be determined and adjudged in some Court of Justice, according to the law and custom of England, and always judgments are given *ideo consideratum est per Curiam* [thus it was considered by the Court] so that the Court gives the judgment.

"Then the King said that he thought the law was founded upon reason, and that he and others had reason as well as the Judges. To which it was answered by me that true it was that God had endowed His Majesty with excellent science and with great endowments of nature. But His Majesty was not learned in the laws of his realm of England, and causes which concern the life or inheritance or goods or fortunes of his subjects are not to be decided by natural reason but by the artificial reason and judgment of law, which law is an act which requires long study and experience before a man can attain to cognizance of it; that the law was the golden met-wand and measure to try the causes of the subjects, and which protected His Majesty in safety and peace. With which the King was greatly offended and said that then he should be under the law, which was treason to affirm, as he said. To which I said that Bracton saith: *quod Rex non Debet esse sub homine sed sub Deo et lege* [the king ought not to be under man but under God and the law]."

36. Coke, *Institutes,* 97b (p. 1).
37. Indeed, the translation of "reason" into "reasonableness" and the exaltation of "common sense" were English developments of the seventeenth century, to which Coke contributed. To this day it is difficult to find in other languages precise equivalents for the English words "reasonable" and "common sense." The usual translation of "reasonable" into equivalents of "rational" is a distortion; as Lon L. Fuller once said, "To be reasonable is to be not too rational." Likewise, common sense is not the same as public opinion; it is more like the shared moral judgment of the community. Cf. Christopher Hill, "'Reason' and 'Reasonableness' in Seventeenth-Century England," *British Journal of Sociology* 20 (1969), 235–252. See also John Underwood Lewis, "Sir Edward Coke (1552–1633): His Theory of 'Artificial Reason' as a Context for Modern Basic Legal Theory," *Law Quarterly Review* 84 (1968), 330–342. Cf. Michael Lobban, *The Common Law and English Jurisprudence, 1760–1850* (Oxford, 1991), pp. 6–7.
38. See *Calvin's Case, 7 Coke's Reports,* 1a. Cf. Gray, "Reason, Authority, and Imagination," pp. 37, 55 n. 24. In time the phrase "natural justice" came to be used by the English courts more frequently than "natural law," and eventually to replace it.
39. *Bonham's Case, 77 Eng. Rep.* 638, 644 (K.B. 1611), is sometimes taken to stand for the proposition that the courts may annul an act of Parliament if it is in contradiction to the common law. In fact, the holding of the case rested on an interpretation of the statute rather than an annulment of it. See Samuel Thorne, "Dr. *Bonham's Case,*" *Law Quarterly Review* 54 (1938), 543–552, criticizing some conclusions drawn in T. F. T. Plucknett, "*Bonham's Case* and Judicial Review," *Harvard Law Review* 40 (1926), 30–70. But see also Charles M. Gray, "*Bonham's Case* Reviewed," *Proceedings of the American Philosophical Society* 116 (1972), 35–58; and Tubbs, *Common Law Mind,* pp. 154–155. In any event, the line was relatively thin, in 1611, between judicial review of the constitutionality of a statute and judicial interpretation of a problematic statute in order to make it conform to constitutional requirements. If, as Coke assumed, the judges of the common law courts had final power to interpret the common law, then it would require a clear alteration of the common law by Parliament to avoid judicial control in a given case.
40. Coke, *Institutes,* pt. 2, sec. viii (p. 625). See Eusden, *Puritans, Lawyers, and Politics,* p. 124. Cf. Coke, *Institutes,* 11b (the *lex naturae* is one of the "diverse laws within the realm of England.")
41. Jaroslav Pelikan, *The Vindication of Tradition* (New Haven, 1984), p. 65.
42. Sir Edward Coke, preface to *The First Part of the Reports of Sir Edward Coke, KT.* (London, 1727); see Geoffrey Chaucer, *The Parliament of Foules* (ca. 1380), ed. T. R. Loundsbury (Boston, 1877), p. 52: "For out of olde feldys, as men sey,/Comyth al this newe corn from yer to yere."
43. Selden's first term in the Tower of London lasted only five weeks. In his second term, commencing in 1629, he was released early from imprisonment but re-

mained under restraint until early 1635. See David Sandler Berkowitz, *John Selden's Formative Years* (Washington, D.C., 1988), pp. 231–290.

44. John Milton, *Areopagitica,* ed. John W. Hales (Oxford, 1886), p. 16.
45. Berkowitz, *John Selden,* p. 276.
46. See Arthur B. Ferguson, *Clio Unbound: Perception of the Social and Cultural Past in Renaissance England* (Durham, N.C., 1979), p. 295 (quoting Selden, *Ad Fletam Dissertatio*). Richard Tuck has characterized the passage from Selden, quoted in the text, as an expression of "the Burkean theory of English law." See Richard Tuck, *Natural Rights Theories: Their Origin and Development* (Cambridge, 1979), p. 84. Selden's understanding of the Western legal tradition was in many ways superior to that of his successors, even down to the twentieth century. He understood, for example, that the Roman law of Justinian was not simply "received" into European law. He denied the usual English assumption that "the supreme and governing law of every other Christian state (saving England and Ireland) . . . [i]s the old Roman imperial law of Justinian." He insisted that "no nation in the world is governed by [that law]." "Doubtless," he continued, "custom hath made some parts of the imperials to be received for law in all places where they have been studied, as even in England also," but that only means that they have become part of the local law. England is thus not unique in its uniqueness: "Every Christian state hath its own common law, as this kingdom hath." See Richard Helgerson, *Forms of Nationhood: The Elizabethan Writing of England* (Chicago, 1992), p. 68 (quoting Selden, *History of Tythes*).
47. John Selden, *De Jure Naturali et Gentium juxta Disciplinam Ebraerorum Libri Septum* (London, 1640).
48. J. P. Sommerville, "John Selden, the Law of Nature, and the Origins of Government," *Historical Journal* 27 (1984), 440–442.
49. Richard Tuck argues that Selden's political philosophy was highly original and represented a decisive break with much of the theologically based political theory of the time. See Tuck, *Natural Rights Theories,* pp. 90–100. J. P. Sommerville has argued, however, that while Selden was a highly original legal historian (as well as scholar of Hebrew and Greek antiquities), he nevertheless contributed little that was new to contemporary debates on political theory as such. See Sommerville, "John Selden," p. 446. It is argued here that the chief elements of Selden's originality lay in that special part of his political philosophy which was constituted by legal philosophy.
50. See Chapter 11.
51. Holdsworth writes of Hale: "His character and talents made him easily the greatest English lawyer of his day [and] the most scientific jurist that England had yet seen." William S. Holdsworth, *A History of English Law,* 13 vols. (London, 1922–1952), 6: 580–581 (hereafter cited as Holdsworth, *History of English Law*). Elsewhere Holdsworth states: "[Hale] was the greatest common lawyer who had arisen since Coke; and, that, though his influence has not been so great as that of Coke, he was as a lawyer, Coke's superior. The position which they respectively occupy in our legal history is as different as their character and mental outlook. Coke . . . stands midway between the medieval and the modern law. Hale is the first of our great modern common lawyers. . . . He was what Coke never was—a true historian; and, like Bacon, he had studied other things besides law, and other bodies of law besides the English common law." W. S. Holdsworth, "Sir Matthew Hale," *Law Quarterly Review* 39 (1923), 424–425. An excellent comparison of Coke and Hale may also be found in Charles M. Gray, "Editor's Introduction" to Matthew Hale, *The History of the Common Law of England* (Chicago, 1981), pp. xxiii–xxxvii.

52. The classic biography of Sir Matthew Hale remains the one written by his near contemporary Gilbert Burnet, *Lives of Sir Matthew Hale and John Earl of Rochester* (London, 1829). See also Edmund Heward, *Matthew Hale* (London, 1972). Additional biographical data are also found in Holdsworth, "Sir Matthew Hale," and Gray, "Editor's Introduction."
53. Holdsworth, "Sir Matthew Hale," p. 408.
54. Holdsworth indicates that Hale served as counsel to Charles I during his trial and that he advised Charles to plead to the jurisdiction of the newly created "High Court of Justice." Ibid., p. 403. It seems that Hale also advised Strafford on the occasion of his impeachment and provided legal services to Laud as well. See ibid.
55. Gray, "Editor's Introduction," pp. xiv–xv.
56. Hale's bill was "killed stone dead" by the opposition of the Anglican clergy, who feared that it "meant more competition for preferments and livings." Ibid., p. 103.
57. Many examples can be given of specific legal contributions that reflected Hale's religious outlook. As a judge, he set an example of scrupulous fairness to prisoners in criminal cases. He once persuaded a jury, with some difficulty, to acquit a man who had stolen a loaf of bread because he was starving. He shared the overriding Puritan concern with poor relief; his "Discourse Touching Provision for the Poor," written in 1659, contained a detailed plan for providing work for the poor, anticipating reforms that were only carried out a century and a half later. Yet he also shared the Puritan horror of witchcraft and in 1664 imposed the death penalty, as provided by statute, on two women found by the jury to be guilty of bewitching certain children.
58. Hale's *History of the Common Law* was first published in 1713, years after his death. In fact, none of Hale's voluminous legal writings were published in his lifetime, though many of them circulated widely in manuscript.
59. Hale's *History of the Pleas of the Crown,* first published in 1736, was not a history but a textbook on criminal law and procedure dealing with capital crimes. Heward writes (*Matthew Hale,* pp. 133–34): "This book is a tour de force. It is systematic and detailed. . . . Hale succeeded in reducing the mass of material to a coherent account of the criminal law relating to capital offenses." His *Analysis of the Law* divides the law into two main divisions, namely, civil law and criminal law, but itself deals only with civil matters, which it divides into civil rights or interests, wrongs or injuries related to those rights, and relief or remedies applicable to those wrongs. Civil rights are subdivided in the *jus commune* style into rights of persons (chiefly obligations) and rights of things (chiefly property).
60. Although he did not write any tracts on Roman law, Hale admired Roman law and, in the words of his contemporary biographer, Burnet, "lamented much that it was so little studied in England." Quoted in Heward, *Matthew Hale,* p. 26. Hale's systematization of English law was greatly influenced by Romanist legal science as it had developed in the West since the late eleventh century. His systematization of English law was also greatly influenced by his knowledge of the exact and natural sciences, on which he did write several long tracts. He was well acquainted with Boyle and Newton and with some of the founders of the Royal Society of London. Three of his discourses on religion were published after his death by his friend the Puritan minister Richard Baxter. They are summarized ibid., pp. 127–128.
61. Gray, "Editor's Introduction," p. xv.
62. Ibid., p. xix.
63. Ibid., p. xvi.

64. This diary, which is kept in the Beineke Rare Book and Manuscript Library of Yale University, was edited and published by Maija Jansson under the title "Matthew Hale on Judges and Judging," *Journal of Legal History* 9 (1988), 201–213. It reveals Hale's powerful reliance on divine guidance in the performance of his judicial duties. He writes that judging is so "difficult an employment" that "it is a wonder that any prudent man will accept it, and that any man in his right judgment should desire it or not desire to decline or be delivered from it." He lists twelve of its onerous requirements, including that "it requires a mind constantly awed by the fear of almighty God and sense of his presence." Describing his feelings in trying criminal cases, he writes that "it is the grace and goodness of God that I myself have not fallen into as great enormities as those upon which I give judgment. I have the same passions and lusts and corruptions that even those malefactors themselves have. . . . But even while the duty of my place requires justice and possibly severity in punishing the offense, yet the same sense of common humanity and human frailty should at the same time engage me to great compassion to the offender." The judge, Hale writes, must "avoid all precipitancy in examining, censuring, judging, [and must] pause and consider, turn every stone, weigh every answer, every circumstance." These meditations lead Hale to the conclusion that if, in a criminal case, "upon the best inquisition a man can make, the scales are very near even," a judgment of acquittal is fitter than a judgment of condemnation, "for though to condemn the innocent and to acquit the guilty are both abomination unto God, yet that is here a sufficient evidence of guilt appears, but *in obscuris et in evidentibus praesumitur pro innocentia* [both in matters that are obscure and in matters that are clear, innocence is presumed] and I had rather through ignorance of the truth of the fact or the unevidence of it acquit ten guilty persons than condemn one innocent. For the hand of divine justice in the way of His providence may reach in after time a guilty person, or of evidence to convict him, he may hereafter repent and amend; but the loss of the life of an innocent is irreconvertable in this world. But this must be intended where upon a sincere, judicious, impartial, inquiry the evidence is inevident, not where a man out of partiality or vain pity will render use to himself to each himself of doing justice upon a malefactor."
65. Cf. Gray, "Editor's Introduction," p. xviii.
66. Matthew Hale, preface to *The Analysis of the Law,* 2nd ed. (1716), quoted in Barbara Shapiro, "Law and Science in Seventeenth-Century England," *Stanford Law Review* (1969), 746. Shapiro emphasizes that Hale approached both the common law and the civil law as "systems," that is, as "series of interrelated parts" rather than as random assortments of writs or rules (p. 746).
67. Hale's biographer Burnet reports that some persons once said to Hale that they "looked on the common law as a study that could not be brought into a scheme, nor formed into a rational science, by reason of the indigestedness of it, and the multiplicity of cases in it." Hale replied decisively that he "was not of their mind," and he drew on a large sheet of paper "a scheme of the whole order and parts of it . . . to the great satisfaction of those to whom he sent it." Quoted in Holdsworth, *History of English Law,* p. 584.
68. The text is published in *Law Quarterly Review* 37 (1921), 274–303 under the title "Sir Matthew Hale on Hobbes: An Unpublished Manuscript," with a short introduction by Sir Frederick Pollock.
69. Some of Hale's more technical legal writings include *The Jurisdiction of the Lord's House, Considerations Touching the Amendment and Alteration of Laws, A Short*

Treatise of Sheriff's Accompts, and *A Treatise on the Admiralty Jurisdiction.* A full list is given in Heward, *Matthew Hale,* pp. 130–155.

70. See Donald R. Kelley, *Foundations of Modern Historical Scholarship: Language, Law, and History in the French Renaissance* (New York, 1970), pp. 118–120; idem, *François Hotman: A Revolutionary's Ordeal* (Princeton, 1973), pp. 192–197. Cf. Gerald Strauss, *Law, Resistance, and the State: The Opposition to Roman Law in Reformation Germany* (Princeton, 1986). See also Chapter 8.
71. Matthew Hale, *Historia Placitorum Coronae,* ed. Sollom Emlyn, vol. 1 (Philadelphia, 1847), p. 13.
72. Ibid., p. 12.
73. Ibid., p. 11.
74. Ibid., pp. 12–13.
75. Savigny, generally considered to be the founder of the historical school of legal philosophy, viewed the development of law as part of the historical development of the common consciousness of a society. Law, he wrote, is developed first by custom and by popular belief, and only then by juristic activity. As a people becomes more mature, and social and economic life becomes more complex, its law becomes less symbolic and more abstract, more technical, requiring administration and development by a professional class of trained jurists. The professional or technical element should not, however, Savigny wrote, become divorced from the symbolic element or from the community ideas and ideals which underlie both the early and later stages of legal development. Thus Savigny combined a historical and a sociological analysis with a normative one. See Friedrich Karl von Savigny, *Vom Beruf unsrer Zeit für Gesetzgebung and Rechtswissenschaft* (1814), 2nd ed. (Heidelberg, 1840), trans. Abraham Hayward, *On the Vocation of Our Age for Legislation and Jurisprudence* (1831; reprint, New York, 1975).

    Maine also saw a normative element in the development of modern law from its origins in "early" societies, stressing the transition over many centuries from fictions to equity to legislation as the main source of creative legal innovation and from status to contract as the main source of legal obligation. See Henry Sumner Maine, *Ancient Law* (London, 1861) and *Early History of Institutions* (London, 1875).

    Durkheim echoed Savigny in emphasizing the source of law in the moral sense and collective consciousness *(conscience collective)* of a people, and built partly on Maine in tracing a movement of the center of gravity of law from repressive to restitutive sanctions. See Emile Durkheim, *The Division of Labor in Society* (Glencoe, Ill., 1893), and *Durkheim and the Law,* ed. Steven Lukes and Andrew Scull (New York, 1983) (a collection of Durkheim's writings on law and legal evolution). In contrast to Savigny and Maine, however, Durkheim did not expressly attach normative significance to his evolutionary theory. Similarly, Weber, in tracing changes from what he termed charismatic to traditional and to formal-rational types of law, did not attribute a normative character to historical development within each of the particular types of law or from one type to another. See *Max Weber on Law in Economy and Society,* ed. Max Rheinstein (Cambridge, Mass., 1954).
76. Matthew Hale, *The History of the Common Law of England,* ed. Charles M. Gray (Chicago, 1971), p. 39.
77. This expression appears to have been first articulated by Lord Mansfield as solicitor general in the case of *Omychund v. Barker,* 1 Atkyns 32 (1744). At issue was whether the testimony of an Indian, who had sworn an oath in accord with "Gen-

too" (Hindu) religion, could be accepted as evidence in an English court, since a statute of Parliament required the oath to be taken on the Gospels. Mansfield argued that "principles of reason, justice, and convenience" required that the testimony be admitted. In explaining why the court should go beyond the statutory language in this case he stated, "A statute very seldom can take in all cases, therefore the common law, that works itself pure by rules drawn from the fountain of justice, is for this reason superior to an act of parliament." The court subsequently accepted this reasoning. See J. W. Gough, *Fundamental Law in English Constitutional History* (Oxford, 1955), p. 188. Mansfield's view closely approximates Hale's theory of legal development. Michael Lobban has stated, "Hale reconciled the immemoriality of the common law with its flexibility by putting forward a Burkean view: the common law was a body, which grew and adapted itself to the people's needs, ever approaching perfection." Lobban, *Common Law and English Jurisprudence,* p. 3. Lobban quotes Hale's statements that "by use, practice, commerce, study and improvement of the English people, [the laws] arrived in Henry II's time to a greater improvement" and that under Edward I, the "English Justinian," the law "obtained a very great perfection." Hale, *History of the Common Law,* pp. 84 and 101.

78. Whether the Norman Conquest was a decisive rupture in the common law was a question of fundamental importance in the constitutional debates of the late sixteenth and early seventeenth centuries. On the one hand, parliamentarians like Coke, who wished to emphasize the prerogatives of representative institutions vis-à-vis the Crown, argued that the Norman Conquest did not represent a fundamental breach in English law and also maintained that the origins of Parliament itself could be traced back into the mists of Anglo-Saxon times. Royalists like Archbishop Laud, on the other hand, tended to see the appeal to an Anglo-Saxon past as little better than "a stimulus to rebellion." See Christopher Hill, "The Norman Yoke," in *Puritanism and Revolution: Studies in Interpretation of the English Revolution of the Seventeenth Century* (London, 1958), p. 62. Hale, like Selden, took a middle view, asserting, with Coke, a continuity of representative government from Anglo-Saxon times but departing from Coke in tracing the introduction of feudal property law and other related matters to the Normans.
79. Hale, *History of the Common Law,* p. 40. The Argonaut image builds on Selden, discussed earlier in this chapter. The image of the human body is more powerful. Hale also sometimes compared the common law to a river that is fed from many tributaries.
80. See Thomas Hobbes, *A Dialogue between a Philosopher and a Student of the Common Laws of England,* ed. and intro. Joseph Cropsey (Chicago, 1971). The *Dialogue* runs to 115 printed pages. It was first published in 1681, two years after Hobbes's death, and was written after 1661 and before Hale's death in 1676. Hale saw it in manuscript. His reply was also not published until after his death, but, like Hobbes's essay, was no doubt circulated during his lifetime in manuscript form. Hobbes's essay was a shorter but in some respects stronger statement of the political and legal philosophy contained in his famous book *Leviathan,* published in 1651.
81. These and the following quotations are from William Holdsworth, "Sir Matthew Hale on Hobbes," *Law Quarterly Review* 37 (1921), 287–291.
82. Hobbes, *Dialogue,* p. 69. See also D. E. C. Yale, "Hobbes and Hale on Law, Legislation, and the Sovereign," *Cambridge Law Journal* 31 (1972), 123–124.
83. See Lewis, "Coke: His Theory of 'Artificial Reason,'" p. 339.
84. Yale, "Hobbes and Hale on Law, Legislation, and the Sovereign," pp. 121, 123–124.

85. See Harold J. Berman, "Some False Premises of Max Weber's Sociology of Law," *Washington University Law Quarterly* 65 (1987), 759–760.
86. These and the following quotations are from Holdsworth, "Sir Matthew Hale on Hobbes," pp. 297–298 and 302.
87. *Fisher v. Prince*, 97 *Eng. Rep.* (K.B. 1762), p. 876, quoted in Cecil H. S. Fifoot, *Lord Mansfield* (London, 1936), p. 219. Mansfield's concept of "the reason and spirit of cases," as contrasted with "the letter of particular precedents," resulted in attaching authority to a line of similar decisions on a particular matter rather than to the holding of a single case. This was a later development of Hale's concept of the doctrine of precedent, which was expressed in his statement that "the Decisions of Courts of Justice . . . have a great Weight and Authority in Expounding, Declaring, and Publishing what the Law of this Kingdom is, especially when such Decisions hold a Consonancy and Congruity with Resolutions and Decisions of former Times." Hale, *History of the Common Law*, p. 45. Only in the later nineteenth century was this declarative theory of precedent, as it came to be called, replaced—in both England and the United States—by the strict doctrine, called *stare decisis*, "to stand by the decisions," that the holding of a single case whose facts are entirely similar to the facts of a later case is binding in the later case. The later theory reflected a historicism that was quite different from Hale's or Mansfield's conception of historicity. Late-nineteenth-century historicism was associated with a drive toward predictability based on a rational categorization of authoritative legal principles and rules, and was more consonant with late-eighteenth-century Enlightenment concepts and the nineteenth-century codification movement than with the idea of an ongoing tradition of judicially declared law associated with the seventeenth-century English Revolution. See Harold J. Berman, "Law and Belief in Three Revolutions," *Valparaiso Law Review* 18 (1984), 607–608; Harold J. Berman, Samir Saliba, and William R. Greiner, *The Nature and Functions of Law*, 5th ed. (Westbury, N.Y., 1996), pp. 483–485; Rupert Cross and J. W. Harris, *Precedent in English Law*, 4th ed. (Oxford, 1991), pp. 24–36; Charles M. Gray, "Parliament, Liberty, and the Law," in *Parliament and Liberty: From the Reign of Elizabeth to the English Civil War*, ed. J. H. Hexter (Stanford, 1992), pp. 155, 157–60.
88. Galileo Galilei, *Dialogues Concerning Two New Sciences*, trans. Henry Crew and Alfonso DeSalvio (New York, 1914), p. 24.
89. Quoted in John Herman Randall, Jr., *The Making of the Modern Mind* (Boston, 1926), p. 237.
90. René Descartes, *Rules for the Direction of the Mind*, in *Great Books of the Western World*, vol. 31 (Chicago, 1952), p. 1.
91. See Lucien Lévy-Bruhl, "The Cartesian Spirit and History," in Raymond Klibansky and H. J. Paton, eds., *Philosophy and History: Essays Presented to Ernst Cassirer* (Oxford, 1936), p. 191.
92. Of the vast literature on the philosophical implications of the contributions of Galileo (1564–1642) and Descartes (1596–1650), the following studies are pertinent to the present discussion: Maurice Clavelin, *The Natural Philosophy of Galileo: Essays on the Origins and Formation of Classical Mechanics*, trans. A. J. Pomerans (Cambridge, Mass., 1974); Robert E. Butts and Joseph C. Pitts, eds., *New Perspectives on Galileo*, (Dordrecht, 1978); William A. Wallace, ed., *Prelude to Galileo: Essays on Medieval and Sixteenth-Century Sources of Galileo's Thought* (Dordrecht, 1981); Desmond Clarke, *Descartes' Philosophy of Science* (University Park, Pa., 1982).
93. See Barbara Shapiro, *Probability and Certainty in Seventeenth-Century England:*

A Study of the Relationships between Natural Science, Religion, History, Law, and Literature (Princeton, 1983). Shapiro shows that in the thirty to fifty years after Bacon's death, experimental scientists in the Royal Society abandoned his idea that the inductive method could yield certain knowledge and instead adopted a probabilistic view. Cf. Steven Shapin and Simon Schaffer, *Leviathan and the Air Pump: Hobbes, Boyle, and the Experimental Life* (Princeton, 1985). Relying partly on Shapiro's work, Shapin and Schaffer state (p. 24) that "by the adoption of a probabilistic view of knowledge one could attain to an appropriate certainty and aim to secure legitimate assent to knowledge claims. The quest for necessary and universal assent to physical propositions was seen as inappropriate and illegitimate. It belonged to a 'dogmatic' enterprise, and dogmatism was seen not only as a failure but as dangerous to genuine knowledge."

94. This debate is analyzed in depth in Shapin and Schaffer, *Leviathan and the Air Pump*. The quotations and paraphrases of the arguments of Hobbes and Boyle given in the text may be found at pp. 107–108 of that work.

95. See Robert K. Merton, *The Sociology of Science: Theoretical and Empirical Investigations* (Carbondale, 1973); cf. idem, *Science, Technology, and Society in Seventeenth-Century England,* 1st American ed. (New York, 1970). Merton, a pioneer in the discipline called sociology of knowledge, does not expressly state that what he calls "certified scientific knowledge" is ultimately what the scientific community determines it to be; nevertheless, that proposition is assumed by him throughout his work. See *Sociology of Science,* pp. 267–278. He writes that scientific inquiry presupposes an "interplay" between "culture and science," and that there exists an "interdependence" between scientific knowledge and "institutional" developments in the fields of "economy, politics, religion, military, and so on" (pp. ix–x). See also I. Bernard Cohen, ed., *Puritanism and the Rise of Modern Science* (New Brunswick, N.J., 1990) (a retrospective on the contribution of Robert K. Merton to the sociology of knowledge).

That scientific knowledge—"truth"—is not achieved either by individual reason or by divine or other authoritative will ("revelation") but by satisfaction of criteria established by the relevant scientific communities is also the underlying premise of Thomas Kuhn's important conception of scientific revolutions in which scientific communities create new scientific "paradigms." See Thomas Kuhn, *The Structure of Scientific Revolutions,* 2nd ed., enl. (Chicago, 1970). See also Shapiro, *Probability and Certainty,* pp. 15–73, and Shapin and Schaffer, *Leviathan and the Air Pump,* pp. 69–79, for excellent discussions of the seventeenth-century origins of this distinctively twentieth-century approach to scientific knowledge.

96. See Harold J. Berman, "Toward an Integrative Jurisprudence: Politics, Morality, History," *California Law Review* 76 (1988), 797–801. This trinitarian view of law is strikingly parallel to the view of social life generally that seems to have prevailed among seventeenth-century English writers. Thus F. Smith Fussner states that it can be said "with certainty" that "most seventeenth-century [English] writers thought of politics, morality, and tradition (alias history) as forming a kind of trinity." F. Smith Fussner, *The Historical Revolution: English Historical Writing and Thought, 1580–1640* (London, 1962), p. xvii.

9. The Transformation of English Legal Science

1. The designation "legal treatise" is used here in a broader sense than that advanced in A. W. B. Simpson, "The Rise and Fall of the Legal Treatise: Legal Principles

and the Forms of Legal Literature," *University of Chicago Law Review* 42 (1981), 632. Simpson would confine the term "treatise" to a particular type of systematic monograph on individual branches of English and American law, a type which, he contends, "rose" in the 1770s and 1780s and "fell" only in the twentieth century, and would exclude systematic works on English law as a whole, such as those of Bracton in the thirteenth century, on the one hand, and, on the other hand, those of Matthew Hale in the late seventeenth century and William Blackstone in the mid-eighteenth century. For reasons only roughly indicated in his article, Simpson hesitates to designate as "treatises" works on individual branches of English law written in the late seventeenth and early eighteenth centuries, such as the treatise on the law of evidence by Jeffrey Gilbert and the treatise on criminal law by William Hawkins.

2. See the discussion in Chapter 3.
3. H. L. A. Hart draws a similar distinction, though for a different purpose, between the internal and external aspects of legal rules. He describes the internal aspect of legal rules as that which governs persons who are subject to the law, for whom legal rules are "the rules of the game" by which they are bound, and the external aspect as the ways in which the rules appear to an external observer who describes them as binding upon others but who himself is not playing the game. See H. L. A. Hart, *The Concept of Law,* 2nd ed. (Oxford, 1994), pp. 56–57, 88–90, 102–103. It is contended here that external observers are also players in the game.
4. William Blackstone, *Commentaries on the Laws of England,* 4 vols. (1765–1769; reprint, Chicago, 1979), 2:2, 4:5; see idem, *An Analysis of the Laws of England* (1753; reprint, Buffalo, 1997). Cf. Daniel J. Boorstin, *The Mysterious Science of the Law: An Essay on Blackstone's Commentaries* (1941; reprint, Boston, 1958) pp. 20 (characterizing Blackstone's conception of English legal science): "Everywhere in English law 'principles' were waiting to be found."
5. See Matthew Hale, *The Analysis of the Law: A Scheme or Abstract of the Several Titles and Partitions of the Law, Digested into Method* (ca. 1670; first published London, 1713).
6. Blackstone, *Commentaries,* 1:4, 34.
7. Ibid., 1:5–6; cf. 1:33: "The inconveniences here pointed out can never be effectually prevented, but by making academical education a previous step to the profession of the common law and at the same time making the rudiments of the law a part of academical education. For sciences are of a sociable disposition, and flourish best in the neighborhood of each other: nor is there any branch of learning, but may be helped and improved by assistances drawn from other arts."
8. "Et le briefe et judgement *supra* fuit rule per opinionem Curiae de Banco non obstante deux presidents." See C. K. Allen, *Law in the Making,* 7th ed. (Oxford, 1964), p. 204.
9. In the late 1500s and early 1600s, the courts of common law sometimes referred to previous decisions in order to justify their competence in the matter before them. See John H. Baker, "New Light on *Slade's Case,*" *Cambridge Law Journal* 29, pts. 1 and 2 (1971), 51–67, 213–236; idem, *The Common Law Tradition: Lawyers, Books, and the Law* (Hambledon, 2001), pp. 158–164. Other English courts did the same. See Thomas G. Barnes, "A Cheshire Seductress, Precedent, and a 'Sore Blow' to Star Chamber," in Morris S. Arnold et al., eds., *On the Laws and Customs of England: Essays in Honor of Samuel E. Thorne* (Chapel Hill, 1981), pp. 359, 378.
10. *Bole v. Norton* (1673), *Vaughan's Rep.,* 382.

11. Matthew Hale, *History of English Law* (London, 1739) p. 67, cited by C. K. Allen, *Law in the Making,* 6th ed. (Oxford, 1958), p. 206.
12. See Gerald J. Postema, "Some Roots of the Notion of Precedent," in Laurence Goldstein, ed., *Precedent in Law* (Oxford, 1987), pp. 9, 16: "On [Hale's] view, both the meaning or normative content and the authority of the precedential case rest on its being recognized as an integral part of the collective experience (or 'wisdom') of the community, of which the law is the repository"—and of which "the law reports are the public record."
13. Ibid. pp. 16–17.
14. *Fisher v. Prince,* 97 *Eng. Rep.* 876 (K.B. 1762).
15. On the Royal Society, see note 100. On Hume's theory that knowledge is based on habitual experience, see Terence Penelhum, *David Hume: An Introduction to His Philosophical System* (West Lafayette, Ind., 1992), pp. 76–77; Daniel E. Flage, *David Hume's Theory of Mind* (London, 1990), pp. 92–93; cf. Knud Haakonssen, "The Structure of Hume's Political theory," in David Fate Norton, ed., *The Cambridge Companion of Hume* (Cambridge, 1993), pp. 182, 202–203.
16. On the origin and development of the writ system, see F. W. Maitland, *The Forms of Action at Common Law: A Course of Lectures* (1909; reprint, Cambridge, 1965). On the "freezing" of the writs in the fourteenth century and the resulting expansion of the equitable jurisdiction of the chancellor, see T. F. T. Plucknett, *Statutes and Their Interpretation in the First Half of the Fourteenth Century* (Cambridge, 1922), pp. 121, 169; also Harold J. Berman, *Faith and Order: The Reconciliation of Law and Religion* (Atlanta, 1993), chap. 4 ("Medieval English Equity"), pp. 65–67.
17. For other changes in the same direction taken by the common law courts, see John H. Baker, "Origins of the 'Doctrine' of Consideration, 1535–1585," in Arnold et al., *On the Laws and Customs of England,* pp. 336–358.
18. A large proportion of the contract cases in the common law courts in the sixteenth and early seventeenth centuries were suits on so-called recognizances. These were, in effect, penal bonds payable only on default of the timely performance of the contractual obligation. The bonds were usually for at least twice the contract price and were reduced to judgment at the time of contracting, so that on default the debtor could be sued on the judgment. See A. W. B. Simpson, *A History of the Common Law of Contract: The Rise of the Action of Assumpsit* (Oxford, 1987), pp. 125 (indicating that in one sample year, that of 1572, 503 actions were brought on bonds, in contrast to three actions brought in assumpsit).
19. The action of detinue had three principal shortcomings: (1) it permitted wager of law at the option of the defendant, which meant, in practice, that a defendant would prevail if he could muster six or twelve men to swear that his statements were true; (2) the defendant had the option either to return the goods or compensate the plaintiff for the harm which his detention of them had caused him; and (3) where the defendant chose to return the goods, he could deliver them in whatever condition they were in at the time of judgment. See John H. Baker, *An Introduction to English Legal History,* 3rd ed. (London, 1990), pp. 7:441–445. Wager of law was abolished in 1833.
20. Holdsworth confirms the point that the decisive change in trover occurred in the late 1600s, when litigants were allowed to plead the rights of a third party—the *jus tertii*—as a means of demonstrating that the plaintiff lacked property rights in the thing claimed. He states: "At the end of this period [the late seventeenth century] we can see the beginnings of the idea that, if a plaintiff in an action of trover is relying, not on his possession, but on his right to possess, the defendant could . . . meet his claim by proving a *jus tertii.* In other words, the plaintiff must

prove an absolute right good as against all the world." Holdsworth, *History of English Law,* 7:426. Cf. *Cooper v. Chitty,* 1 Burr. 20, 97, *Eng. Rep.* 166 (1756), 172, declaring per Lord Mansfield that the first element of proof in an action of trover is "property in the plaintiff," and holding that an officer to whom goods in a bankrupt estate had been transferred for distribution to creditors must pay the value of the goods to one into whose ownership they had been transferred by the bankrupt prior to his insolvency.

21. Some English legal historians have tended to stress the use of fictions to expand the actions of ejectment and trover in the sixteenth and early seventeenth centuries, and have underestimated the more important changes of the late seventeenth and early eighteenth centuries. The earlier fictions, however, were procedura*l* fictions, to which the common law courts resorted in order to rationalize and enhance their attractiveness in their competition with other courts. See Holdsworth, *History of English Law,* 7:405. In contrast, the resort to substantive fictions in the late seventeenth and eighteenth centuries occurred at a time when the common law courts were supreme and did not need to use fictions to expand their jurisdiction vis-à-vis other courts but did need them in order to maintain the myth of continuity with the past.

22. Jeremy Bentham, "A Fragment on Government," in *The Works of Jeremy Bentham,* vol. 1, ed. J. Bowring (1843), p. 235, n. s. See also idem, "Elements of Packing as Applied to Juries," in *The Works of Jeremy Bentham,* vol. 5, ed. J. Bowring (1843), pp. 92 ("In English law, fiction is a syphilis, which runs in every vein, and carries into every part of the system the principle of rottenness").

23. See Lon L. Fuller, *Legal Fictions* (Stanford, 1967), pp. 63–65. Owen Barfield, English lawyer and poet, has compared legal fictions with metaphors, in which old words receive new meanings. Legal fictions are an extreme example, he writes, of the process of expressing new meanings in preexisting language and, in law, of applying preexisting legal rules to new situations. See Owen Barfield, *The Rediscovery of Meaning and Other Essays* (Middleton, Conn., 1977), pp. 44 ("Poetic Fiction and Legal Diction"), 57.

24. See Friedrich Carl von Savigny, *Vom Beruf unserer Zeit für Gesetzgebung und Rechtswissenschaft,* 2nd ed. (Heidelberg, 1828), pp. 32–33, quoted in Fuller, *Legal Fictions,* p. 59.

25. In Justinian's *Institutes,* obligations *(obligationes)* were divided into four categories: those arising from contract, those arising from delict, those arising "as if from contract" *(quasi ex-contractu),* and those arising "as if from delict" *(quasi ex-delicto).* Although thereafter various types of contractual, delictual, quasi-contractual, and quasi-delictual obligations were identified, there was (as was usual in the classical and post-classical Roman law) no conceptual analysis of the underlying principles that distinguished them from one another. The European Romanists of the twelfth to seventeenth centuries struggled with the nature of those differences and with the division itself. By the seventeenth century, the European *jus commune,* which combined Roman law, canon law, and common features of the laws of secular polities of Europe, had assimilated quasi-delictual to delictual obligations and had attached the concept of unjust enrichment to quasi-contractual obligations. See Reinhard Zimmermann, *The Law of Obligations* (Oxford, 1990), pp. 1–33 and 885–886.

26. Style 47, 82 *Eng. Rep.* 519 (1647); Aleyn 26, 82 *Eng. Rep.* 897 (1647). The report in Aleyn is usually cited or reproduced in American books on contract law. The report in Style, from which the discussion in the text is chiefly drawn, gives a much better account of the losing arguments of the defendant.

27. Style 47.
28. Although it remains true in English and American law that one who breaks a contract is liable even in the absence of fault, the doctrine of absolute liability announced in *Paradine v. Jane* has been generally repudiated in the past century, except that in England, at least, it is still said to be applicable to leases. That is, the risk of impossibility due to unforeseen contingencies is placed on the lessee, in the absence of express terms to the contrary. Also in commercial cases where the parties are of more or less equal bargaining power and they insert into their contract a list of contingencies that will excuse nonperformance, the risk of frustration of the purpose of the contract owing to an unforeseen contingency that is not included in the list will, in certain types of cases at least, be borne by the obligor. See Harold J. Berman, "Excuse for Non-performance in the Light of Contract Practices in International Trade," *Columbia Law Review* 63 (1963), 1413.
29. 2 *Lord Raymond* 909, 92 *Eng. Rep.* 107 (1703).
30. See George W. Paton, *Bailment in the Common Law* (London, 1952), pp. 81–85.
31. This development was also a contribution of Lord Holt, who imported it into the common law chiefly from maritime law, which was then understood as part of the law of nations. See *Boson v. Sandford,* 2 *Salk.* 440, 91 *Eng. Rep.* 382 (1691), a maritime case brought by owners of cargo against the owners of a ship for damage done to the cargo while it was under the supervision of the ship's master. The owners of the ship disavowed liability, since they had not personally undertaken to ship the goods, but Lord Holt held that "whoever employs another is answerable for him, and undertakes for his care to all that make use of him." Prior to the English Revolution, this action would probably have been brought in the High Court of Admiralty. By 1691 the triumphant common law courts had adopted Lord Coke's dictum that the jurisdiction of Admiralty is limited to matters that take place on the high seas.
32. G. Edward White states that "it is misleading . . . to speak of separate 'tort' actions, let alone standards of tort liability, before the nineteenth century," and that "the idea of Torts as a separate category of law was not present in the commentaries of . . . Blackstone." He writes, "The crucial inquiry in tort actions prior to the 1870s was not whether a defendant was 'in fault' or had otherwise violated some comprehensive standard of tort liability, but whether something about the circumstances of the plaintiff's injury compelled the defendant to pay the plaintiff damages. Tort liability was no more precise than that." Edward G. White, *Tort Law in America: An Intellectual History* (New York, 1980), p. 14. These statements are correct only in a narrow sense. They fail to take into account the large category of wrongful acts giving rise to civil liability in the late seventeenth and eighteenth centuries. It is true that the separate "action on the case for negligence," as contrasted with the action on the case for negligently causing harm to person or property in any one of a variety of specific ways, emerged only in the eighteenth (not the nineteenth) century. It is true also that Blackstone and others, in writing about civil liability for "trespasses," including "actions on the case," did not develop a general theory that expressly identified liability for harm caused by either negligent or intentional misconduct or by extra-hazardous activity. Nevertheless, those distinctions were made in the context of a general category of noncontractual civil obligations. Blackstone expressly separated obligations arising from contract from obligations arising from delict, which he separated into "public delicts" (crimes) and "private wrongs" (torts). "Personal actions," he wrote, "are such whereby a man claims a debt, or personal duty, or damages in lieu thereof; and likewise whereby a man claims a satisfaction in damages for some injury done

to his person or property. The former are said to be founded in contracts, the latter upon torts or wrongs . . . . Of the former nature are all actions upon debt or promises; of the latter all actions for trespasses, nusances [sic], assaults, defamatory words, and the like." Blackstone, *Commentaries,* 3:117. The latter surely constituted "a separate category of law."

33. T. F. T. Plucknett, *A Concise History of the Common Law,* 5th ed. (Boston, 1956), p. 471, referring to Percy H. Winfield, "The History of Negligence in the Law of Torts," *Law Quarterly Review* 42 (1926), 195. Winfield, in turn, refers to the classification of remedies in Comyns's 1762 *Abridgement of the Laws.*
34. Thus "assumpsit" came to be divided into two forms: "special assumpsit," where there was an express undertaking, and "general assumpsit," where an undertaking could be implied from a preceding debt.
35. See Baker, *English Legal History,* pp. 389–390, 394–395; Holdsworth, *History of English Law,* 3:443; A. W. B. Simpson, "The Place of *Slade's Case* in the History of Contract," *Law Quarterly Review* 74 (1958), 381; John H. Baker, "New Light on *Slade's Case,*" *Cambridge Law Journal* (1971), 51, 213.
36. See *Moses v. Macferlan,* 2 Burr. 1005, 97 *Eng. Rep.* 676 (1760). This was an action brought under the rubric "money had and received." The plaintiff had endorsed promissory notes to the defendant, who had promised that he would not seek payment from the plaintiff but only from the maker of the notes. That promise, however, in a prior proceeding in a small claims court (called "court of conscience"), had been held to be unenforceable, and the plaintiff had been required in that proceeding to honor the indorsements. Lord Mansfield held that the defendant was obliged "by the ties of natural justice" to refund the payment, and that the cause of action was "founded in the equity of the plaintiff's case, as it were upon a contract (*'quasi ex contractu,'* as the Roman law expresses it)." Blackstone cited this decision and quoted from it at length in stating that certain obligations arise from "contracts that are only implied by law [w]hich are such as reason and justice dictate" and that the action for money had and received "lies only for money which *ex aequo et bono* the defendant ought to refund" such as "money paid by mistake, or on a consideration which happens to fail, or through imposition, extortion, or oppression, or where undue advantage is taken of the plaintiff's situation." Blackstone, *Commentaries* 3:162. Mansfield's debt to the civil law of quasi-contract—not the Roman law of Justinian but the Romanist *jus commune* of the seventeenth century—is well brought out in Peter B. H. Birks, "English and Roman Learning in *Moses v. Macferlan,*" *Current Legal Problems* 37 (1984), 1.
37. In 1922 another leading English judge, Lord Scrutton, characterized the "now discarded doctrine of Lord Mansfield" as "that vague jurisprudence which is sometimes attractively styled 'justice as between man and man,'" and as "well-meaning sloppiness of thought." See *Holt v. Markham* (1923) K.B. 504, 513.
38. By a study of the English plea rolls, Thomas Green has shown that from the twelfth through the fifteenth century juries generally convicted only about 20 percent of those indicted for homicide. See Thomas A. Green, "The Jury and the English Law of Homicide, 1200–1600," *Michigan Law Review* 74 (1974), 413. Green concludes (p. 432): "Thus, it appears that during the later Middle Ages jury convictions were largely limited to the most culpable homicides."
39. Giles Dunscombe, in *Trials per Pais* (1682), indicates that even in his time jurors might consult evidence not part of the judicial record: "They may have other Evidence than what is shewed in Court. They are of the Vicinage, the Judge is a Stranger. They may have Evidence from their own personal Knowledge, that the witnesses speak false, which the Judge knows not of may know the witnesses to

be stigmatized and infamous, which may be unknown to the Parties or Court." Quoted in Theodore Waldman, "Origins of the Legal Doctrine of Reasonable Doubt," *Journal of the History of Ideas* 20 (1959), 299, 310. Not until 1705 could the jury be drawn from the county rather than from the immediate vicinity of the place where the controverted facts occurred (p. 308).

40. On the emergence of a new criminal procedure in post-Reformation Germany, see John Langbein, *Prosecuting Crime in the Renaissance: England, Germany, France* (Cambridge, Mass., 1974), pp. 129–209 (comprehensively reviewing the contents of the Carolina, the early sixteenth-century German criminal code, and the circumstances surrounding its promulgation); and Harold J. Berman, "Conscience and Law: The Lutheran Reformation and the Western Legal Tradition," *Journal of Law and Religion* 5 (1987), 188–189 (briefly discussing the relationship of the Carolina to Lutheran thought). For an analysis of the chief elements of Protestant thought on the purposes of criminal law, see John Witte, Jr., and Thomas C. Arthur, "The Three Uses of the Law: A Protestant Source of the Purposes of Criminal Punishment," *Journal of Law and Religion* 10 (1993–94), 433.

41. *The Trial of William Penn and William Mead (Written by themselves),* in *Howell's State Trials,* vol. 6 (1670; reprint, 1816), pp. 951–999.

42. *Bushell's Case, Vaughan Rep.* 135, 124 *Eng. Rep.* 1006 (1670). An annotated version of the opinion of Justice Vaughan is given in *Howell's State Trials,* 6:999–1026. Contrary to the citations in almost all modern treatises, Vaughan and other contemporary reporters spelled "Bushell" with two l's, not one.

43. *Vaughan Rep.,* 147, 124 *Eng. Rep.* at 1012.

44. See the excellent discussion in Thomas A. Green, *Verdict According to Conscience: Perspectives on the English Criminal Trial Jury* (Chicago, 1985), pp. 256–264. On the basis of a study of reports of cases in the Old Bailey, John Langbein has contended that the decision in *Bushell's Case* did not affect "the ordinary criminal trial," as contrasted with trials involving affairs of state ("political trials"), since judges continued to have the power to comment freely on the facts of the case, to make statements prejudicial to the defendant's argument, and even to instruct the jury that it is to return a verdict of guilty. John H. Langbein, "The Criminal Trial before the Lawyers," *University of Chicago Law Review* 45 (1978), 285. Nevertheless, as Langbein acknowledges, the jury could ignore the judge's instructions without penalty (p. 298). After the introduction of counsel for the defendant at the end of the seventeenth century, first in treason trials and, after 1730, also in cases of felonies, counsel could tell the jury that it should decide according to its own conscience and that it, and not the judge, had the final say in deciding all issues in the case. Indeed, it was widely accepted that in criminal cases the jury was the final judge of law as well as of fact.

45. John Hawles, *The Englishman's Right* (London, 1680), p. 1, quoted in Green, *Verdict According to Conscience,* p. 255. Hawles adds: "As juries have ever been vested with such power by law, so to exclude them from, or disseize them of the same, were utterly to defeat the end of their institution."

46. John Hawles, *The Grand Jury Man's Oath and Office Explained* (London, 1680), p. 13, quoted in Green, *Verdict According to Conscience,* p. 259.

47. *Vaughan Rep.* at 141–142, *Eng. Rep.* at 1009.

48. See James Fitzjames Stephen, *A History of the Criminal Law of England,* vol. 1 (London, 1883), pp. 346–350.

49. See Langbein, *Prosecuting Crime,* pp. 21–31.

50. The word "altercation" is used by Thomas Smith, *De Republica Anglorum* (1565),

ed. Mary Dewar (Cambridge, 1982), p. 114. See Stephen, *History of the Criminal Law,* 1:346–349; and Langbein, *Prosecuting Crime,* pp. 29–31.

51. Stephen, *History of the Criminal Law,* 1:358.
52. The word "misdemeanor" came into use in the sixteenth century chiefly to refer to crimes within the jurisdiction of Star Chamber. Prior to that time, minor crimes within the jurisdiction of the common law courts, such as riots, forcible entry, labor offenses, and others, often took the form of indictable trespasses, which combined tort and crime and might be sanctioned by damages to the victim as well as by fines to the Crown and (sometimes) imprisonment. Although the rules forbidding the accused to have counsel or to call witnesses were applicable only to felonies, nevertheless the appearance of counsel in cases of lesser common law crimes was highly unusual. In Star Chamber, by contrast, which had jurisdiction over all non-capital crimes (that is, all crimes other than felonies or treason), and exclusive jurisdiction over the most serious of them (including forgery, perjury, riot, sedition, espionage, maintenance, fraud, libel, and conspiracy), the accused was not only permitted but also required to have counsel. See Stephen, *History of the Criminal Law,* 1:341. It is plausible to suppose that when the common law courts took over the criminal jurisdiction of Star Chamber, they would want to continue Star Chamber's practice of permitting representation by counsel in cases of misdemeanors.
53. Samuel Rezneck, "The Statute of 1696: A Pioneer Measure in the Reform of Judicial Procedure in England," *Journal of Modern History* 2 (1930), 5, 6. Rezneck seems to have been the first historian to recognize that the Treason Trials Act of 1696 was a reflection of the ideology of the Glorious Revolution comparable to the 1689 Bill of Rights and Act of Toleration. In 1980 James R. Phifer wrote: "It is not the least of ironies in English history that an act as important as the Treason Trials Act of 1696 should have received so little scholarly attention. The only historian to give the act more than a few pages is Samuel Rezneck in an article written in 1930." James R. Phifer, "Law, Politics, and Violence: The Treason Trials Act of 1696," *Albion* 12 (1980), 235. More recently the act has been taken more seriously, although its connection with the English Revolution has been largely ignored. See J. M. Beattie, "Scales of Justice: Defense Counsel and the English Criminal Trial in the Eighteenth and Nineteenth Centuries," *Law and History Review* 9 (1991), 221.
54. See Phifer, "Law, Politics, and Violence," p. 255.
55. The Treason Trials Act, 7 William III and Mary II c. 3 (1696). The first draft of the act was introduced in Parliament in 1689 and every year subsequently to 1696. For a history of the prior drafts of the law, see Rezneck, "Statute of 1696," p. 21; and Phifer, "Law, Politics, and Violence," pp. 244–254.
56. See Stephan Landsman, "The Rise of the Contentious Spirit: Adversary Procedure in Eighteenth-Century England," *Cornell Law Review* 75 (1990), 534–539; and Beattie, "Scales of Justice," pp. 224–227 and 230–231. With respect to the right of the accused to see the text of the indictment in advance of trial, see Douglas Hay, "Prosecution and Power: Malicious Prosecution in the English Courts, 1750–1850," in Douglas Hay and Francis Snyder, eds., *Policing and Prosecution in Britain, 1750–1850* (Oxford, 1989), p. 352, n. 31; and William Hawkins, *A Treatise of the Pleas of the Crown,* vol. 2 (New York, 1721), p. 402. It is submitted that these texts show that such a right existed, though it was not absolute. Langbein reads them otherwise. See John Langbein, "The Historical Origins of the Privilege against Self-Incrimination," *Michigan Law Review* 92 (1994), 1047, 1058.

57. See Stephen, *History of the Criminal Law,* 1:334.
58. See Langbein, "Privilege against Self-Incrimination." Landsman correctly states that "by 1800, adversary procedure predominated." See Landsman, "Rise of the Contentious Spirit," p. 502.
59. For the text of the Prisoner's Counsel Act, see 6 & 7 William IV c. 114 (1836).
60. Thus Sir James Mackintosh, who sponsored an earlier version of the Prisoner's Counsel Act, declared that the Treason Trials Act of 1696 produced a "benefit [that] was universally felt as a safeguard for the subject" and that the extension of counsel to felony prosecutions would have the same result. See *Parliamentary Debates,* vol. 4, (London, 1821), p. 1513, quoted in Beattie, "Scales of Justice," p. 252.
61. On the introduction of defense witnesses and other procedural developments in criminal law in the wake of the English Revolution, see Samuel Rezneck, "The Statute of 1696: A Pioneer Measure in the Reform of Judicial Procedure in England," *Journal of Modern History* 2 (1930) 5ff.; and Phifer, "Law, Politics, and Violence." It took time for the reforms of the Treason Trials Act to make themselves felt in ordinary criminal trials. Langbein records, for instance, that into the middle decades of the eighteenth century, defense lacked counsel in most proceedings at the Old Bailey and defense witnesses, where they were available, were generally interrogated by the judge. See John H. Langbein, "The Criminal Trial before the Lawyers," *University of Chicago Law Review* 45 (1978), 263–316.
62. The discussion in the text is supported by Landsman, "Rise of the Contentious Spirit." Langbein, by contrast, stresses the persistence of the non-adversarial "continental" character of the English criminal trial in the eighteenth century, citing especially the active role of the judge in conducting the trial and the limited role of counsel. See Langbein, "Criminal Trial." It is argued here, however, that the shift from a predominantly inquisitorial to a predominantly adversarial mode of criminal trial should be measured not primarily by the extent to which the judge and defense counsel play active or passive roles but rather by the manifestation of what Landsman calls "the contentious spirit" in the right of the accused to refuse to answer questions, the right of the accused's witnesses to testify under oath, the cross-examination of each other's witnesses by the parties, and the division of functions between judge and jury.
63. See Sir Matthew Hale, *Pleas of the Crown: A Methodical Summary* (London, 1982), p. 289 (a facsimile edition of the original work, published in 1678); Blackstone, *Commentaries,* 4:352. In *Pleas of the Crown,* Hale wrote that it is better to acquit five guilty men than to convict one innocent man. In his diary (and perhaps elsewhere), he raised the number from five to ten. Quoted in Harold J. Berman, "The Origins of Historical Jurisprudence: Coke, Selden, Hale," *Yale Law Journal* 103 (1994), n. 147.
64. "In obscuris et in evidentibus praesumitur pro innocentia" (In obscure matters and even in clear matters, there is a presumption in favor of innocence), quoted in Berman, "Origins of Historical Jurisprudence," n. 147. Note that this was an entry in Hale's diary in 1668, while he was sitting on circuit. It may have been a contemporary Latin maxim.
65. The first express judicial application of the general "beyond a reasonable doubt" standard of proof in criminal cases seems to have been in the crown colony of Massachusetts in 1770 in the case of the Boston Massacre. See Anthony A. Morano, "A Reasonable Examination of the Reasonable Doubt Rule," *Boston University Law Review* 55 (1975), 516–519. The first judicial enunciation of the general stan-

dard in the mother country seems to have been in an Irish case in 1798. See John Wilder May, "Some Rules of Evidence: Reasonable Doubt in Civil and Criminal Cases," *American Law Review* 10 (1876), 656–657. The general "preponderance of the evidence" standard of proof in civil cases was first enunciated in the nineteenth century. These broad standards were generalizations of the particular weights to be given to particular types of evidence in particular types of cases, as set forth in the late seventeenth and eighteenth centuries in Gilbert's treatise and in other scholarly writings and in arguments by counsel and in judicial opinions.

66. As indicated earlier, Langbein has attacked the thesis that substantial changes occurred in the English system of criminal procedure in the late seventeenth and early to mid-eighteenth centuries. Based on his study of eighteenth-century criminal trials in the Old Bailey, he has concluded that prior to the 1780s, at the earliest, in ordinary felony trials (as contrasted with "political cases" reported in *State Trials*), there was no effective right to counsel and that consequently the adversary system could not prevail, the jury was dominated by the judge, and the accused was not protected by a requirement of proof beyond a reasonable doubt. See Langbein, "The Privilege against Self-Incrimination." There can be no quarrel with his conclusions concerning the privilege against self-incrimination as he defines it, namely, as the right of an accused not to testify at all: if, without counsel, the accused said nothing, he would have no defense whatever. There is also no basis for doubting the accuracy of Langbein's portrayal of the practice of the Old Bailey. It is a mistake, however, to suppose that because the accused were only infrequently represented by counsel at the Old Bailey, therefore there was no effective right to counsel under English law, when in fact, as Langbein acknowledges, the more well-to-do accused whose felony cases are reported in *State Trials* (not all of which, by any means, were political cases) were represented by counsel quite often. Langbein also does not deny that the trial, both at the Old Bailey and in King's Bench, was often a contest between the prosecutor's witnesses and the accused's witnesses, and to that extent, at least, there was an adversary procedure. Moreover, the fact that at the Old Bailey and elsewhere juries very often brought in verdicts of acquittal, or convictions of lesser offenses than those charged, despite strong judicial directions to the contrary, for which they suffered no reprisals, would seem to justify the conclusion, contrary to Langbein's, that *Bushell's Case* continued to have vitality.

The view presented here that the standard of "satisfied conscience" gave protection to the accused analogous to that of "proof beyond a reasonable doubt" is more difficult to defend. As Langbein emphasizes, the phrase "beyond a reasonable doubt" does not appear in the available legal sources until 1770. Indeed, neither Hale nor Gilbert nor Hawkins nor Blackstone refers to any general standard of proof in criminal or civil cases. Yet it is clear from the non-legal literature that by a "satisfied conscience," which was a term widely used both in law and in moral philosophy, was meant a conscience that has taken into account all the evidence and has weighed in according to standards of probability. It is also clear that both jury practice and the writings of legal scholars and judges reflected a strong aversion to the conviction of accused persons where there were reasonable doubts concerning their guilt. It therefore seems fair to conclude that the seeds, at least, of the "beyond a reasonable doubt" standard were sown in the late seventeenth century.

67. Geoffrey Gilbert, *The Law of Evidence* (New York, 1979) (a facsimile edition of *The Law of Evidence with all the Original References Carefully Compared*, published

in 1754). Sir Geoffrey Gilbert (1674–1726) practiced law first in England and then in Ireland. He was named chief baron of the Irish Exchequer in 1715 but soon thereafter returned to England to serve in the English Exchequer, of which, at his death, he was chief baron. His treatise on the law of evidence was first published twenty-eight years after his death. See Michael MacNair, "Sir Jeffrey Gilbert and His Treatises," *Journal of Legal History* 15 (1994), 252–255 and 258.

68. Gilbert, *Law of Evidence,* p. 1. On Gilbert's relationship to John Locke, who was older, see MacNair, "Sir Jeffrey Gilbert," pp. 255–256. According to MacNair (p. 255), in 1709 Gilbert anonymously prepared and published an essay titled "An Abstract of Locke's Essay Concerning Human Understanding."
69. Gilbert, *Law of Evidence,* p. 3. Cf. *Stillingfleet v. Parker,* 6 Mod. 248, 87 *Eng. Rep.* 995 (1704), which Gilbert cites in support of his formulation of the best evidence rule.
70. See MacNair, "Sir Jeffrey Gilbert," pp. 258–260. Fifteen of Gilbert's treatises were published posthumously and several others remain in manuscript form. Gilbert used Hale's treatise *The Analysis of the Law* as a model, and it is apparent that he had in mind eventually to collect his various treatises in a comprehensive "analysis" of English law as a whole.
71. Hale's *Analysis of the Law* was written in about 1670 and was circulated privately. It was first published in 1713. See Matthew Hale, *The Analysis of the Law* (Chicago, 1971), a facsimile of the 1713 edition. Its original title page does not name Matthew Hale as author, stating only that the work was "Written by a Learned Hand."
72. Hale states (*Analysis of the Law,* p. A3): "Nor shall I confine myself to the Method or Terms of the [Roman] Civil Law nor of others who have given general Schemes or Analysis's of Laws, but shall use that Method . . . that I shall think most conducible to the Thing I aim at."
73. See Matthew Hale, *Pleas of the Crown* (London, 1716).
74. See William Hawkins, *Pleas of the Crown, 1716–1721* (London, 1973), a facsimile edition of Hawkins's two volumes, one originally published in 1716, the other in 1721. The book ran through seven editions in the eighteenth century and one in the nineteenth.
75. Hale, *Analysis of the Law,* p. 6.
76. Ibid. p. 13.
77. Hale's view on the limits to be placed on royal proclamations were developed more fully by Blackstone. See note 78.
78. See William Blackstone, *Analysis of the Laws of England* (1756; reprint, Buffalo, 1997), and idem, *Commentaries.* Both works were based on Blackstone's lectures at Oxford University, commencing in 1753. The *Commentaries* went through eight editions in Blackstone's lifetime, and another fifteen editions up to the middle of the nineteenth century. See David Lieberman, "Blackstone's Science of Legislation," *Journal of British Studies* 27 (1988), 121. In the subsequent extensively revised edition of H. J. Stephen, Blackstone's *Commentaries* continued to be published until after the Second World War. See S. F. C. Milsom, "The Nature of Blackstone's Achievement," *Oxford Journal of Legal Studies* 1 (1981), 1.

For Blackstone's reliance on Hale's *Analysis,* see Alan Watson, "The Structure of Blackstone's *Commentaries,*" *Yale Law Journal* 97 (1988), 799. Blackstone himself stated that "of all the Schemes hitherto made public for digesting the Laws of England, the most natural and scientifical of any, as well as the most comprehensive, appeared to be that of Sir Matthew Hale, in his posthumous *Analysis of the Law,*" and that the "learned Reader" should easily be able to understand at what points he has departed from Hale, while "it may be no unprofitable Employment for the Student to learn by comparing them." See Blackstone, *Analysis,* preface, p. vii.

79. See Blackstone, *Analysis,* p. iv.
80. Michael Lobban argues that Blackstone was attempting to apply to the English common law the deductive logic used by contemporary civilian writers "and thereby create a theoretically coherent view of English law using a Roman structure." Lobban ultimately concludes that Blackstone failed in this attempt because he could not derive English law deductively from logically prior principles of natural law. See Michael Lobban, "Blackstone and the Science of Law," *Historical Journal* 30 (1987), 311, 312, 321, 331. In fact, Blackstone combined natural law principles with the historical method of the English scientific empiricists. His purpose was, indeed, to "create a theoretically coherent view of English law," but not by "using a Roman structure."
81. Bentham's view that Blackstone was a "bigotted or corrupt defender" of English law, who believed that it was "never to be censured . . . [or] found fault with" (see Jeremy Bentham, *The Fragment on Government,* in *A Comment on the Commentaries and a Fragment on Government,* ed. J. H. Burns and H. L. A. Hart [London, 1977], pp. 398–400), is contradicted by many examples from Blackstone's writings. For example, Blackstone criticized in the harshest terms the widespread application of the death penalty, calling it "absurd to apply the same punishment to crimes of different malignity" and endorsing the then radical idea of a descending scale of punishment. See Blackstone, *Commentaries,* 4:17–18. Blackstone also referred to the rule that "the goods of the wife do, instantly upon marriage, become the property and the right of the husband" and various other such rules as "absurd and derogating from the maxims of equity and natural justice." Quoted in Robert William, "Blackstone and the 'Theoretical Perfection' of English Law in the Reign of Charles II," *Historical Journal* 26 (1983), 39, 53. For an excellent analysis and refutation of Bentham's "fundamentally misconceived attack" on Blackstone's *Commentaries,* see Richard A. Posner, "Blackstone and Bentham," *Journal of Law and Economics* 19 (1976), 569, 570, and 571.

    Related to Bentham's attack on Blackstone as a mere apologist for English law is that of Duncan Kennedy, who, from a contemporary "critical" perspective, calls Blackstone "a pivotal figure in the development of the liberal mode of American legal thought," which he defines as one that first postulates a conflict between two "radically opposed imaginary entitles," namely, civil society and the state, and then postulates that this conflict can be overcome by law. Kennedy characterizes the *Commentaries* as "a vast explication of the single notion that the conflict of right with right was illusory, and the same was therefore true of the conflict of right with power." See Duncan Kennedy, "The Structure of Blackstone's Commentaries," *Buffalo Law Review* 28 (1979), 205, 217, 382. It is, of course, true that Blackstone revered the English common law, but he did not hesitate to expose areas of it in which right conflicted with right as well as areas in which right conflicted with power. He was especially critical of excesses of royal power, arguing that the king is "the executive magistrate," whose "constitutions or edicts, which we call proclamations, [should be] binding upon the subject [only] where they do not either contradict the old law, or tend to establish new ones; but only enforce the execution of such laws as are already in being." See Blackstone, *Commentaries,* 1:260–261.

82. Hale and Blackstone did not call their works "Institutes," even though their works

have been characterized as "institutionalist" by Cairns, Watson, Lobban, Lieberman, and others. Coke did, however, call his major work, which could hardly be called Romanist, *The Institutes*—a usage which Cairns and others discount—"because," Coke wrote, "my desire is, they should institute and instruct the studious, and guide him in a ready way to a knowledge of the national laws of England." Quoted in John W. Cairns, "Blackstone, an English Institutionalist: Legal Literature and the Rise of the Nation-State," *Oxford Journal of Legal Studies* 4 (1984), 337. The word is used in a slightly different sense, though not in Luig's sense, in the treatise of Thomas Wood, *An Institute of the Laws of England* (1729; reprint, New York, 1979), which the author stated was to assist students of English law "by supplying them with a Method to help their memories." Wood was a follower of Hale and a precursor of Blackstone.

83. The intensely casuistic and untheoretical nature of the Roman law of Justinian is discussed in Berman, *Law and Revolution,* pp. 135–140, citing, among others, Fritz Schulz, *History of Roman Legal Science* (Oxford, 1953) and Peter Stein, *Regulae Juris: From Juristic Rules to Legal Maxims* (Edinburgh, 1966).

84. See Brian Tierney, "Origins of Natural Rights Language: Text and Contexts, 1150–1250," *History of Political Thought* 10 (1989), 615; idem, "*Ius Dictum a Iure Possidendo:* Law and Rights in *Decretales* 5.40.12," in Diane Wood, ed., *Church and Sovereignty: Essays in Honour of Michael Wilks* (Oxford, 1991), p. 457; idem, "Willey, Ockham, and the Origin of Natural Rights Theories," in John Witte, Jr., and Frank S. Alexander, eds., *The Weightier Matters of the Law: Essays on Law and Religion (A Tribute to Harold Berman)* (Atlanta, 1988), p. 1; Charles J. Reid, Jr., "The Canonistic contribution to the Western Rights Tradition: An Historical Inquiry," *Boston College Law Review* 33 (1991), 37; idem, "Rights in Thirteenth-Century Canon Law: An Historical Investigation," (Ph.D. diss., Cornell University, 1995).

85. Alan Watson argues that Blackstone must have drawn the structure of the *Commentaries,* with its tabular form of presentation, partly from a leading Romanist of the late sixteenth and early seventeenth centuries, Dionysius Gothofredus (1549–1622), and particularly from Gothofredus's massive multivolume edition of the *Corpus Juris Civilis.* See Watson, "Structure of Blackstone's *Commentaries,*" pp. 806–825. It should be observed, however, that although Watson speaks of "the extreme dependence of the structure of Blackstone's *Commentaries* on that of Justinian's *Institutes*" (p. 811), he also notes that Justinian's *Institutes* did not use a tabular form of presentation. The tabular form was one developed first by the jurists of the sixteenth century who presented the *jus commune* in a tabular form based on the topical method introduced first by Philip Melanchthon (see Chapter 3). Also the items listed in Blackstone's table, in contrast to those listed in Gothofredus's table (both of which tables Watson has conveniently presented at pp. 813–825), are classified in terms of rights ("rights of persons" etc.), not law ("law of persons" etc.), and this, again, is in the tradition of the European *jus commune* of the sixteenth and seventeenth centuries rather than of the Roman law of Justinian. Indeed, Blackstone, referring to John Cowell's 1605 *Institutiones Juris Anglicani* (published in an English translation in 1651), wrote of its "endeavour to reduce the Law of England . . . to the Model of [the *Institutions*] of Justinian," that "we cannot be surprized that so forced and unnatural a Contrivance should be lame and defective in its Execution." Blackstone, *Analysis,* p. vi. Nevertheless, Watson is surely right in linking Blackstone's method with that of seventeenth and eighteenth-century European jurists trained in the *jus commune.* As Maitland put it so well, "It was the idea of a law common to all the countries of

Western Europe that enabled Blackstone to achieve the task of stating English law in a rational fashion." F. W. Maitland, "Why the History of English Law Is Not Written," in N. A. L. Fisher, ed., *The Collected Papers of Frederic William Maitland,* vol. 1 (Buffalo, 1911), pp. 484, 489. Blackstone himself was trained in the Roman law and drew frequently on the civilian origins of English legal institutions.

86. Margaret J. Osler, "John Locke and the Changing Ideal of Scientific Knowledge," *Journal of the History of Ideas* 31 (1970), 9.
87. See Barbara J. Shapiro, *Beyond Reasonable Doubt and Probable Cause* (Berkeley, 1991), pp. 1–113.
88. For Locke's distinction between certainty and the highest degree of probability, see his *Essay Concerning Human Understanding,* bk. 4, chap. 16, secs. 6 and 7. "What others called 'moral certainty' was for Locke a species of probability." Shapiro, *Beyond Reasonable Doubt,* p. 8.
89. See Shapiro, *Beyond Reasonable Doubt,* pp. 42–113.
90. See Rose-Mary Sargent, "Scientific Experiment and Legal Expertise: The Way of Experience in Seventeenth-Century England," *Studies in the History and Philosophy of Science* 20 (1989), 19; and Barbara Shapiro, "The Concept of 'Fact': Legal Origins and Cultural Diffusion," *Albion* 26 (1994), 1. See also Peter Dear, "*Totius in verba:* Rhetoric and Authority in the Early Royal Society," *Isis* 76 (1985), 149–151, asserting that in the late decades of the seventeenth century, the authority of the group that has the responsibility of assessing and judging the accuracy and reliability of individual observation came to supplant the authority of leading texts such as Aristotle and Galen. On the role of the Royal Society, see note 100.
91. See Sargent, "Scientific Experiment," p. 38.
92. Ibid., p. 39.
93. See George P. Fletcher, "The Right and the Reasonable," *Harvard Law Review* 98 (1985), 949. On the relationship between "reasonableness" and the characteristically seventeenth-century English concept of "common sense," see Robert Todd Carroll, *The Common-Sense Philosophy of Religion of Bishop Edward Stillingfleet, 1635–1699* (The Hague, 1975), p. 148 (equating "common sense" with "the experience of mankind").
94. Fletcher, "Right and Reasonable," pp. 950–954, 980–982.
95. See Raoul van Caenegem, *Judges, Legislators, and Professors; Chapters in European Legal History* (Cambridge 1987).
96. Otto Kahn-Freund, intro. to Karl Renner, *The Institutions of Private Law and Their Social Functions* (London, 1949), p. 8.
97. There has been no dearth of research on the largely unsuccessful Puritan movement for law reform in the 1640s and 1650s. See, for instance, Nancy L. Matthews, *William Sheppard: Cromwell's Law Reformer* (Cambridge 1984); Donald Veall, *The Popular Movement for Law Reform, 1640–1660* (Oxford, 1970); and Mary Cotterell, "Interregnum Law Reform: The Hale Commission of 1652," *English Historical Review* 83 (1968), 685. Scholarship on legal developments in the later period, however, has been haphazard, except with respect to criminal law. Even in that field, James Stephen's important 1883 work remained more or less isolated for almost a century. Of more recent literature on the subject, the most comprehensive is John Beattie, *Crime and the Courts in England, 1660–1800* (Princeton, 1986). See also Douglas Hay, ed., *Albion's Fatal Tree: Crime and Society in Eighteenth-Century England* (New York, 1975); Peter Linebaugh, *The London Hanged: Crime and Civil Society in the Eighteenth Century* (Cambridge, 1992); Landsman, "Rise of the Contentious Spirit"; John Langbein, "Albion's Fatal Flaws," *Past and Present* 98 (1983),

96; idem, "Shaping the Eighteenth-Century Criminal Trial"; idem, "The Criminal Trial before Lawyers"; and Charles J. Reid, Jr., "Tyburn, Thanatos, and Marxist Historiography: The Case of the London Hanged," *Cornell Law Review* 79 (1994), 1158.

98. See T. F. T. Plucknett, "*Bonham's Case* and Judicial Review," *Harvard Law Review* 40 (1936), 30.

99. In the 1701 Act of Settlement, Parliament declared that royal judges were to serve "during good behavior." See 12, 13 William III c. 2. The purpose of this provision was to prevent the removal of judges for political reasons. The statute had its desired effect. In 1907 John Maxcy Zane wrote, "Since the [Glorious] Revolution there has never been a removal of a judge by the executive power, nor a single known instance of a corrupt decision." See John Maxcy Zane, "The Five Ages of the Bench and Bar of England," in *Select Essays in Anglo-American Legal History*, vol. 1 (Boston, 1907), pp. 625, 709–710.

100. The origins of the Royal Society, perhaps the oldest scientific society in Europe, date from the early 1640s, when—in the midst of civil war—scholars of various disciplines and varying political and religious sympathies gathered on a weekly basis, first at Oxford and then in London, to discuss "the new philosophy." In November 1660 participants in these gatherings agreed to form a "Colledge for the promoting of Physico-Mathematical Experimental Learning," and were granted a royal charter in 1662. Among its famous members during the next decades were the chemist Robert Boyle, the physicist Isaac Newton, the philosopher John Locke, the jurists Matthew Hale and John Vaughan, and the theologians John Wilkins and Gilbert Burnet. Initially, the emphasis of papers and discussions was on scientific concepts and methods that were common to all the various disciples. Eventually, however, with the generally shared repudiation of Cartesian and Leibnizian epistemology and the focus on experimental learning, the natural and humane sciences tended to become more specialized and to break away from each other. General histories of the Royal Society include Marie Boas Hall, *Promoting Experimental Learning: Experiment and the Royal Society, 1660–1727* (Cambridge, 1991), and Martha Bronfenbrenner, *The Role of Scientific Societies in the Seventeenth Century* (Chicago, 1963).

101. See Robert K. Merton, *Science, Technology, and Society in Seventeenth-Century England* (New York, 1970), originally published as an article under the same title in *Osiris* 4 (1938), 360. See I. Bernard Cohen, ed., *Puritanism and the Rise of Modern Science* (New Brunswick, N.J., 1990); M. D. King, "Reason, Tradition, and the Progressiveness of Science," *History and Theory* 10 (1971), 3.

102. See W. M. Spellman, *The Latitudinarians and the Church of England, 1660–1700* (Athens, Ga., 1993) (setting out the philosophical premises of the "middle way" which Anglicanism represented between "Catholic infallibility and the Protestant subjective certainty" (p. 22). Cf. Barbara Shapiro, *John Wilkins: An Intellectual Biography* (Berkeley, 1969). A legal expression of the new epistemology may be seen in Chief Justice Vaughan's assertion, discussed earlier in this chapter, that "the judge and jury might honestly differ in the result from the evidence."

103. See James R. Jacob and Margaret C. Jacob, "The Anglican Origins of Modern Science: The Metaphysical Foundations of the Whig Constitution," *Isis* 71 (1980), 251.

104. See Merton, *Science, Technology, and Society.* Merton does not explore inner connections between the underlying philosophical premises of seventeenth-century scientific developments, on the one hand, and other institutional developments, on the other, but instead is concerned to show that the latter provided a social

context within which the new scientific movements were "legitimated." His theory, he wrote, "does not presuppose that only Puritanism could have served that function." See Benjamin Nelson, "Review Essay" (on Merton's book), *Varieties of Political Expression in Sociology* (Chicago, 1972), pp. 206–207.

105. For the classical statement of this view, see Crawford Brough MacPherson, *The Political Theory of Possessive Individualism: Hobbes to Locke* (Oxford, 1962). The view that earlier Western society was characterized by an unbounded communitarianism is effectively refuted in Colin Morris, *The Discovery of the Individual, 1050–1200* (New York, 1972), and idem, "Individualism in Twelfth-Century Religion: Some Further Reflections," *Journal of Ecclesiastical History* 31 (1980), 1. The literature on twelfth- and thirteenth-century individualism is reviewed in Charles Reid, "Rights in Thirteenth-Century Canon Law" (Ph.D. diss., Cornell University, 1994), p. 3.

10. The Transformation of English Criminal Law

1. The myth of unbroken continuity is preserved in James Fitzjames Stephen's classic three-volume *History of the Criminal Law in England* (London, 1883), as well as in Holdsworth's treatment of criminal law in his *History of English Law* (the several last volumes of which were published some years after his death). More recently, S. F. C. Milsom, writing of the pre–nineteenth-century foundations of English law, distinguishes two formative periods, the first of which he seems to date in the twelfth and thirteenth centuries and the second in the sixteenth century, but of the second period he states that "the system was transformed without anything much being changed. . . . The institutions all remained, as did the rules of law themselves; and both were largely by-passed by mean and untidy expedients." S. F. C. Milsom, *Historical Foundations of the Common Law* (London, 1969), p. 52. Of criminal law in particular Milsom writes: "The miserable history of crime in England can be shortly told. Nothing worth-while was created. There is no achievement to trace. Except in so far as the maintenance of order is in itself admirable, nobody is to be admired before the [nineteenth-century] age of reform" (p. 353). Milsom's evaluation of the history of English criminal law prior to the nineteenth century is the opposite of Stephen's, but his belief in its essentially unchanging character is the same.
2. John Langbein's important work *Prosecuting Crime in the Renaissance: England, Germany, and France* (Cambridge, Mass., 1974) focuses on institutional and procedural changes in the sixteenth century. He and others have followed it with numerous learned articles on particular aspects of English criminal law in the sixteenth and early seventeenth centuries.
3. The standard work is Leon Radzinowicz, *A History of English Criminal Law and Its Administration from 1750*, 5 vols. (London, 1948–1968). Radzinowicz correctly treats the late eighteenth century as a time when Jeremy Bentham and other "Enlightenment" thinkers attacked the traditional English system of criminal law, represented by figures such as William Blackstone and Lord Mansfield, and the nineteenth century as the time when many of the earlier proposals for reform were implemented in practice.
4. This chapter covers the same time period and some of the same terrain that is covered by J. M. Beattie in his important detailed study *Crime and the Courts in England, 1660–1800* (Princeton, 1986), but it presents the subject in a quite different perspective and thereby adds different information. Beattie's concern is primarily with "the way the English courts dealt with crime in a period in which

the foundations of modern forms of judicial administration were laid" (p. 3), and "with the character and social meaning of prosecuted offenses . . . and with the way those accused of them were dealt with by the courts" (p. 4). His sources are drawn chiefly from the quarter sessions and assize records of the county of Surrey (which embraced a portion of London and also some rural territory), but also include evidence from the county of Sussex and the Old Bailey in London. Occasional reference is also made to documents from other parts of the country. Although the book emphasizes that 1660–1800 "was clearly a period in which significant changes were taking place in the criminal law and the system of criminal administration" (p. 4), it is not concerned with how criminal law and administration differed from those of earlier periods or how they were related to the political, socioeconomic, or religious changes which they accompanied. As a result, little or nothing is said about the effect of the abolition of the prerogative courts on the development of the common law of crimes, or about the new role of the King's Bench as *custos morum,* "guardian of morals," a role once reserved to the prerogative courts. Also lacking is a discussion of the effect of the transfer to the common law courts of sophisticated crimes such as forgery and fraud, and the development of a new doctrine of conspiracy. Beattie's neglect of the Puritan background of the English Revolution leads to omission of the fact that prosecution associations, whose activities he describes in detail, had their origin in the religiously motivated Societies for the Reformation of Manners of the late seventeenth century. His failure to take into account theological currents also blinds him to a possible solution to one of the central paradoxes of eighteenth-century English criminal law: the extraordinary expansion of statutory capital crimes and the simultaneous decline in the rate of executions. Finally, by focusing largely on urban records, Beattie fails to give sufficient emphasis to the important role played by the landed gentry in the development of the criminal law and, more particularly, understates the significance of the game laws for the development of English criminal law.

The purpose of this note is not to detract from Beattie's important accomplishment, to which the present study is greatly indebted, but rather to help explain the differences between his purposes and those addressed in this chapter.

Many studies have been made of the agitation for reform of criminal law during the period of Puritan rule from *1640* to *1660.* See especially Donald Veall, *The Popular Movement for Law Reform,* 1640–1660 (Oxford, 1970), pp. 127–166; Nancy L. Matthews, *William Sheppard: Cromwell's Law Reformer* (Cambridge, 1984); Mary Cotterell, "Interregnum Law Reform: The Hale Commission of 1652," *English Historical Review* 83 (1968), 689; Edmund Heward, *Matthew Hale* (London, 1972), pp. 36–47. Only a few of the criminal law reforms advocated in this period were adopted at the time. Many of the proposals of the Hale Commission were adopted after the Glorious Revolution of 1688.

The treatment herein of changes in criminal procedure in the late seventeenth and eighteenth centuries has been filtered from Thomas A. Green's excellent work *Verdict According to Conscience: Perspectives on the English Criminal Trial Jury, 1200–1800* (Chicago, 1985), pp. 105–264.

5. Some of the changes in criminal law in the late seventeenth and eighteenth centuries that served the interests of the landed gentry are treated in Douglas Hay, Peter Linebaugh, and E. P. Thompson, eds., *Albion's Fatal Tree: Crime and Society in Eighteenth-Century England* (London, 1975); Peter Linebaugh, *The London Hanged: Crime and Civil Society in the Eighteenth Century* (Cambridge, 1992); and E. P.

Thompson, *Whigs and Hunters: The Origins of the Black Act* (New York, 1975).

6. For a general discussion of Anglo-Saxon and other Germanic criminal law, see Berman, *Law and Revolution,* pp. 52–61.
7. The Normans also introduced trial by combat into England, with "the battle serv [ing] as the ordeal." T. F. T. Plucknett, *A Concise History of the Common Law,* 5th ed. (Boston, 1956), p. 427.
8. See canon 18, Fourth Lateran Council, in Norman P. Tanner, ed., *Decrees of the Ecumenical Councils,* vol. 1 (London, 1990), p. 244. Cf. John W. Baldwin, "The Intellectual Preparation for the Canon of 1215 against Ordeals," *Speculum* 36 (1961), 613 (reviewing late-twelfth- and early-thirteenth-century canonistic and philosophical debates about ordeals).
9. The Assize of Clarendon (1166) required juries of presentment to present to royal judges those widely reputed to have committed wrongdoing in particular localities. The accused were then subjected to "purgation" (either by ordeal or by oath-helping) to test their guilt or innocence. Much of early grand jury procedure, both in the initial determination of repute and in the reliance on purgation through oath-helping, bore similarities to canon law. See Richard H. Helmholz, "The Early History of the Grand Jury and the Canon Law," *University of Chicago Law Review* 50 (1983), 613; cf. Roger D. Groot, "The Jury of Presentment before 1215," *American Journal of Legal History* 26 (1982), 1. Concerning the size of the grand jury Baker states, "The number of jurors was usually greater than 12, and in later times it was usually 23." John H. Baker, *An Introduction to English Legal History,* 3rd ed. (London, 1990), p. 577 n. 24. The smaller jury of trial was first established for civil cases involving trespass to land and were adapted to criminal cases after the Fourth Lateran Council in 1215 forbade clergy to participate in ordeals.
10. The conviction rate for felonious (capital) homicide in the fourteenth century typically stood at between 10 and 20 percent. Many defendants acquitted of felonious homicide, however, were found guilty of non-felonious accidental killing or killing in self-defense. A verdict of non-felonious homicide resulted in the automatic forfeiture of all of the defendant's goods to the Crown, imposed on the defendant the requirement of obtaining a royal pardon prior to being released from jail, and exposed the defendant to the possibility of civil suit by the victim's relatives. See Green, *Verdict According to Conscience,* p. 59 n. 122, summarizing the research of James B. Given, *Society and Homicide in Thirteenth-Century England* (Stanford, 1977); Barbara Hanawalt, *Crime and Conflict in English Communities, 1300–1348* (Cambridge, Mass., 1979); and Ralph B. Pugh, "Some Reflections of a Medieval Criminologist," *Proceedings of the British Academy* 59 (1973), 83. Cf. Thomas A. Green, "Societal Concepts of Criminal Liability in Mediaeval England," *Speculum* 47 (1972), 669 (arguing that low conviction rates in thirteenth- through fifteenth-century England were the result of social beliefs about homicide that differed considerably from the law "on the books").
11. See Green, *Verdict According to Conscience,* p. 105.
12. In England, after 1170, benefit of clergy protected clerics from secular prosecution (or, if prosecuted and convicted in a secular court, from punishment) for felonies but not for misdemeanors. (In France, for example, the reverse was the case: the clergy could be prosecuted in the secular courts only for serious crimes.) See Berman, *Law and Revolution,* pp. 256–264.
13. See Langbein, *Prosecuting Crime in the Renaissance.*
14. Beginning in the twelfth century, major English cities were empowered by royal

charter to establish courts to hear cases involving a variety of offenses punishable by the imposition of fines. In the thirteenth, fourteenth, and fifteenth centuries, so-called courts of the staple were created in the fourteen English towns that had the most active trade in "staple products" such as wool, leather, and lead. The Statute of the Staple of 1353 formally recognized that the law merchant rather than the English common law governed relations among merchants and their families and households in the staple towns. See Berman, *Law and Revolution,* pp. 347, 380–386; Helen M. Jewell, *English Local Administration in the Middle Ages* (New York, 1972), pp. 133–135.

15. The first Statute of Westminister (1327) referred to "keepers of the peace." These were local persons appointed by the Crown. They were given a role in enforcing the first Statute of Labourers, enacted in 1349 to regulate wages as a result of the labor shortages caused by the Black Death. The Second Statute of Westminster (1361) subsequently transformed the keepers of the peace into "justices of the peace," giving them responsibility "to restrain . . . offenders, rioters, and all other barrators, and to pursue, take, and chastise them according to their trespass or offence; and to cause them to be imprisoned and duly punished according to the laws and customs of the realm, and according to what shall seem best to them to do by their discretions and good deliberations." Quoted in Sir Thomas Skyrme, *History of the Justices of the Peace,* 3 vols. (Chichester, 1991), 1:31. Subsequent statutes in the fourteenth and fifteenth centuries imposed a variety of other duties upon the justices of peace, both in the area of criminal investigation and in the area of the enforcement of economic regulations. See also Charles Beard, *The Office of the Justice of the Peace in England in Its Origin and Development* (New York, 1904). In addition, a considerable portion of the justice's responsibilities were derived from local customs. See J. R. Lander, *English Justices of the Peace, 1461–1509* (Gloucester, 1989), p. 7.
16. On High Commission's criminal jurisdiction, see Roland G. Usher, *The Rise and Fall of the High Commission* (Oxford, 1968). On Admiralty's criminal jurisdiction, see Holdsworth, *History of English Law,* 1:550; on the criminal jurisdiction of the Court of Requests, see 1:413; on Chancery, see 1:457–459 and W. J. Jones, *The Elizabethan Court of Chancery* (Oxford, 1967), pp. 225–235 (discussing the use of contempt and other coercive mechanisms by the sixteenth-century Chancery). Cf. Penry Williams, "The Activity of the Council in the Marches under the Early Stuarts," *Welsh History Review* 1 (1960), 133–160; and R. R. Davies, "The Law of the March," *Welsh History Review* 5 (1970), 1–30. Cf. Thomas Barnes, "Due Process and Slow Process in the Late Elizabethan and Early Stuart Star Chamber," *American Journal of Legal History* 6 (1962), 221.
17. See William Hudson, *A Treatise of the Court of Star Chamber,* written in 1621 though not published until 1792. The 1792 edition has been reprinted with an introduction by Thomas Barnes under the title *A Treatise of the Court of Star Chamber as Taken from Collectanea Juridica* (Birmingham, 1986). See also Cora L. Scofield, *A Study of the Court of Star Chamber* (New York, 1900). Cf. Barnes, "Due Process and Slow Process," and idem, "Star Chamber Mythology," *American Journal of Legal History* 5 (1961), 1.
18. See Barnes, "Due Process and Slow Process," pp. 227–230.
19. John R. Dasent, ed., *Acts of the Privy Council,* 46 vols. (London, 1890–), 1:119 (1543).
20. Ibid., 1:390 (1546).
21. Ibid., 1:249 (1545).
22. Ibid., 11:412 (1579).

23. W. P. Baildon, ed., *John Hawarde: Les reportes del cases in camera stellata, 1593–1609* (April 29, 1596) (privately printed, 1894), p. 39.
24. Ibid., p. 104. The cases cited in this and the preceding notes are drawn from the unpublished collection of cases and materials compiled by John P. Dawson for use by students in his course in Development of Law and Legal Institutions given at Harvard Law School in the 1960s and 1970s.
25. Thomas G. Barnes, "The Making of the English Criminal Law: Star Chamber and the Sophistication of the Criminal Law," *Criminal Law Review* (1977), 316.
26. Edward Coke, *Fourth Institute,* (reprint, Buffalo, 1986), pp. 65–66.
27. See Harold J. Berman, "Medieval English Equity," in *Faith and Order: The Reconciliation of Law and Religion* (Atlanta, 1993), pp. 55–82.
28. Quoted in Holdsworth, *History of English Law,* 1:609.
29. On the ex officio oath, see Mary H. Maguire, "Attack of the Common Lawyers on the Oath Ex Officio as Administered in the Ecclesiastical Courts of England," in Carl Frederick Wittke, ed., *Essays in History and Political Theory: In Honor of Charles Howard McIlwain* (Cambridge, Mass., 1936), pp. 199–229. On the Court of High Commission, see Usher, *Rise and Fall of the High Commission,* pp. 239–249.
30. Holdsworth, *History of English Law,* 1:608.
31. Unlike High Commission, Admiralty, and Requests, the other principal prerogative courts, namely, the Courts of the Marches in Wales and in the North, were not special courts but courts of very wide jurisdiction, with competence to try felonies and to impose capital punishment.
32. The principal procedural changes in the common law of crimes during the sixteenth and early seventeenth centuries came about through the expansion of the role of the justices of the peace in criminal investigations and prosecutions, under the supervision chiefly of Star Chamber. The landed gentry in the countryside, serving as justices of the peace, heard complainants and witnesses, supervised grand jury proceedings leading to indictment, and exercised a limited control over the presentation of evidence by witnesses in both the grand jury and the trial jury proceedings. See Langbein, *Prosecuting Crime in the Renaissance,* pp. 72–73, 79–80 (on supervision by Star Chamber); idem, "The Origins of Public Prosecution at Common Law," *American Journal of Legal History* 17 (1973), 313.
33. After the martyrdom of Becket in 1170, the royal courts lost to the ecclesiastical courts jurisdiction to try "clergy" for felonies. The royal courts later adopted the procedural device of trying persons before inquiring about their clerical status, and only after they were convicted could they plead benefit of clergy and be remitted to the ecclesiastical court. Before so remitting them, the royal court required that they be branded on the thumb to signify that they had now lost the right to plead benefit of clergy in any future secular trial for a felony. In time, the class of "clergy" was extended to anyone who could read (or recite) a particular verse from the Bible. Thus in most trials for felonies, first offenders were, in effect, put on probation. In the late seventeenth century, as Parliament began to increase substantially the number of statutory felonies, it began to identify most of them as "non-clergyable," indicating that the death penalty was to be applied to a first offender, absent a royal pardon. Where benefit of clergy remained applicable, statutes provided that offenders might be sentenced to transportation to overseas colonies.
34. On adultery, see Keith Thomas, "The Puritans and Adultery: The Act of 1650 Reconsidered," in Donald Pennington and Keith Thomas, eds., *Puritans and Revolutionaries: Essays in Seventeenth-Century History Presented to Christopher Hill*

(Oxford, 1978), pp. 257–282. Winfield E. Ohlson, "Adultery: A Review, Part I," *Boston University Law Review* 17 (1937), 350. On the new types of assault, see Holdsworth, *History of English Law,* 8:421–423, 11:535; on forgery, see 11:534; on piracy, see William Blackstone, *Commentaries on the Laws of England,* 4 vols. (London, 1966), 4:71–73; on poaching, see Leon Radzinowicz, "The Waltham Black Act: A Study of the Legislative Attitude toward Crime in the Eighteenth Century," *Cambridge Law Journal* 9 (1947), 56–81; on complicity in larceny, see Holdsworth, *History of English Law,* 11:530–531. The provisions of the Waltham Black Act were preceded in the closing decades of the seventeenth century by a number of more specific statutes addressed to various aspects of poaching. See Holdsworth, *History of English Law,* 6:403.

35. See Holdsworth, *History of English Law,* 11:539–540; 6:404.
36. See Skyrme, *History of the Justices of the Peace,* 1:110–111; 2:69–73. In 1758 the King's Bench held, in Lord Mansfield's words, that it had "no power or claim to review the reasons of the Justices of the Peace, upon which they have formed their judgments." *Rex v. Young and Pitts,* quoted by Skyrme (2:70).
37. *LeRoy versus Sir Charles Sidley,* 1 Sid. 168 (Mich. 15 Charles II B.R.) (translated from Law French by the author).
38. See 4 George II c. 32 and other statutes reviewed in Holdsworth, *History of English Law,* 11:530, 4:71–73.
39. See Radzinowicz, "Waltham Black Act"; cf. Thompson, *Whigs and Hunters.*
40. On the history of the game laws, see Roger Burrow Manning, *Hunters and Poachers: A Social and Cultural History of Unlawful Hunting, 1485–1640* (Oxford, 1993); Chester Kirby, "The English Game Law System," *American Historical Review* 38 (1933), 240–262; Chester Kirby and Ethyn Kirby, "The Stuart Game Prerogative," *English Historical Review* 56 (1931), 239–254. Parliamentary legislation enacted under James I "require[d] freeholders to possess an income of forty pounds a year if they would kill game; persons with life estates must have twice as much; and all others must have four hundred pounds in personal property." Kirby and Kirby, "Stuart Game Prerogative," p. 241.
41. Concerning the Game Act of 1671, P. B. Munsche has observed that it "signalled the transfer of the game prerogative from the king to the landed gentry." See P. B. Munsche, *Gentlemen and Poachers: The English Game Laws, 1671–1831* (Cambridge, 1981), p. 13.
42. Cf. Radzinowicz, *History of English Criminal Law,* 1:57–58.
43. 11 and 12 William III c. 7 (1700).
44. 11 George I c. 9 (1724); 12 George I c. 32 (1725).
45. See Holdsworth, *History of English Law,* 11:533–534.
46. 2 George II c. 25.
47. See Holdsworth, *History of English Law,* 11:489.
48. See Douglas Hay, "Property, Authority, and the Criminal Law," in Hay, Linebaugh, and Thompson, *Albion's Fatal Tree,* pp. 17–18. Hay takes his account of the dramatic increase in capital statutes from Radzinowicz, *History of English Criminal Law,* 1:1–4. Radzinowicz emphasizes that the figures can only be regarded as approximations, in view of the discrepancies in the estimates of the number of statutory capital crimes existing at various dates. Nevertheless, it may be said with some assurance that more than 1,242 people were hanged in London between 1703 and 1772. See Linebaugh, *The London Hanged,* p. 91.
49. 4 George I c. 11, sec. 1. On clergyable and non-clergyable felonies, see note 33. In the period 1718–1769, 15.5 percent of convicted felons were hanged, 69.5 percent were transported to America, and the remainder were given lesser punishments.

See Roger Ekirch, *Bound for America: The Transportation of British Convicts to the Colonies, 1718–1775* (Oxford, 1987), p. 21.

50. See John Langbein, "Albion's Fatal Flaws," *Past and Present* 98 (1983), 96–120. Regarding the victims who brought prosecutions, Langbein has observed: "The victim is usually more propertied than the person who victimized him, although often only slightly. . . . [T]he victims seldom come from the propertied elite. They are typically small shopkeepers, artisans, lodging-house keepers, innkeepers, and so forth." Ibid., p. 106. Cf. Peter King, "Decision-Makers and Decision-Making in the English Criminal Law, 1750–1800," *Historical Journal* 27 (1984), 25–58, esp. pp. 27–28. King acknowledges, however, that "the fact that a broad spectrum of social groups used the law and made discretionary decisions within it does not necessarily invalidate the view that the law was ultimately controlled by a small gentry elite . . . [T]his could, as Hay has suggested, have helped to legitimate it in the eyes of the population as a whole and therefore increased its usefulness to the ruling group" (p. 51). By contrast, Peter Linebaugh has argued that the minimal property requirement for jury service advanced the interests of the landed gentry precisely by placing the responsibility for guilty verdicts in the hands of those who were particularly susceptible to ruling-class domination by their position of relative dependence and vulnerability. See Linebaugh, *The London Hanged,* p. 78. Cf. Peter Linebaugh, "(Marxist) Social History and (Conservative) Legal History: A Reply to Professor Langbein," *New York University Law Review* 60 (1985), 213. But Linebaugh does not reconcile this assertion with the evidence he himself adduces elsewhere in his book establishing that London juries frequently returned verdicts acquitting defendants or reducing the charges against them; see *The London Hanged,* pp. 85–86 (half the women and 40 percent of the men charged with capital offenses in the January 1715 assizes were acquitted). For a critique of Linebaugh's book, see Charles J. Reid, Jr., "Tyburn, *Thanatos,* and Marxist Historiography: The Case of the London Hanged," *Cornell Law Review* 79 (1994), 1158.

51. See Langbein, "Albion's Fatal Flaws," p. 106.

52. John Langbein has stated that the "beyond a reasonable doubt" standard "lacked crisp formulation" until the late eighteenth century. John Langbein, "The Historical Origins of the Privilege against Self-Incrimination at Common Law," *Michigan Law Review* 92 (1994), 1057. Nevertheless, as Barbara Shapiro has shown, by the late seventeenth century, judges were typically instructing juries in language that conveyed the same meaning. Thus juries were instructed to find the defendant guilty only "if your conscience is satisfied" or only "if you believe" the evidence. If they had "any doubt" about the veracity of the evidence, they were instructed to acquit. Shapiro establishes that these and similar formulas were drawn from academic disputes regarding the nature of moral certainty and that accordingly "the term 'beyond a reasonable doubt' was . . . not a replacement for the 'any doubt' test but was added to clarify the notions of moral certainty and satisfied belief." See Barbara Shapiro, *Beyond Reasonable Doubt and Probable Cause: Historical Perspectives on the Anglo-American Law of Evidence* (Berkeley, 1991), p. 21.

To Shapiro's analysis should be added the fact that the concept of moral certainty was first developed in the religious polemics of seventeenth-century England. Henry van Leeuwen has identified one source for this concept in the Anglican response to Roman Catholic claims that certainty was possible only within the fold of the church, since only the pope was qualified to pronounce with certitude on matters of salvation. Beginning with William Chillingworth in the second quarter of the seventeenth century, Anglicans replied to this claim by distinguishing between Scripture, which was inerrantly true, and scriptural interpretation, to which no more than moral certainty could be ascribed. The pope's moral certitude with respect to knowledge of Scripture was said to be no more privileged than anyone else's.

Van Leeuwen summarizes Chillingworth's definition of moral certainty as follows: "[Moral certainty] is the certainty of everyday life about matters of fact and is based on such evidence as for all practical purposes excludes the possibility of error. . . . Moral certainty is described as the certainty a sane, reasonable, thoughtful person has after considering all available evidence as fully and impartially as possible and giving his assent to that side on which the evidence seems strongest." See Henry G. van Leeuwen, *The Problem of Certainty in English Thought, 1630–1690* (The Hague, 1963), p. 23.

53. Hale's remarkable diary was not circulated and was only discovered three centuries after his death. It was edited and published in Maija Jansson, "Matthew Hale on Judges and Judging," *Journal of Legal History* 9 (1988), 201. The portions quoted in the text are at p. 208. Latin phrases used by Hale, and quoted here in translation, are "*tutius probate in mise[re]cordia quam in severitate*" and "*in obscuris et in evidentibus praesumitur pro innocentia.*"

54. The phrase "presumption of innocence" may be traced also to the 1789 French Declaration of Rights of Man and Citizens, which states in Article 9: "Every man being presumed innocent until he has been pronounced guilty, if it is thought indispensable to arrest him all severity that may not be necessary to secure his person ought to be strictly suppressed by law." Thus a person accused of a crime was to be treated as innocent prior to trial. The nineteenth-century Anglo-American doctrine of presumption of innocence, in contrast, was essentially similar to the earlier doctrine, established in the seventeenth and early eighteenth centuries, that the prosecution has the burden of proving the guilt of the accused at trial. The French concern with the rights of the accused prior to trial, arising partly from use of the notorious *lettres de cachet,* was resolved in England and America by the writ of habeas corpus, while the presumption of innocence at trial was maintained in France (as elsewhere in Europe) by the doctrine *in dubio pro reo* ("in doubt, for the accused") and by rules of burden of proof *(onus probandi).* On the historical development of the presumption of innocence in nineteenth-century English law, see C. K. Allen, *Legal Duties and Other Essays in Jurisprudence* (1931; reprint, Aalen, 1977), pp. 253–294.

55. On the influence of Calvinism on Anglican moral theology, see Dudley W. R. Bahlman, *The Moral Revolution of 1688* (New Haven, 1957); cf. Tina Isaacs, "The Anglican Hierarchy and the Reformation of Manners, 1688–1738," *Journal of Ecclesiastical History* 33 (1982), 391.

56. The term "doctrine of maximum severity" was coined by Leon Radzinowicz to describe the proliferation of capital offenses in the eighteenth century; see his *History of English Criminal Law,* 1:231–267. On the relationship of theories of divine justice to capital punishment, see generally Randall McGowen, "The Changing Face of God's Justice: The Debate over Divine and Human Punishment in Eighteenth-Century England," *Criminal Justice History* 9 (1988), 63–98.

57. See Chapter 2 ("Equity").

58. Quoted in Thomas Wood, *English Casuistical Divinity during the Seventeenth Century, with Special Reference to Jeremy Taylor* (London, 1952), p. 138.

59. For the seventeenth-century Anglican bishop John Davenant, the word "mortal" should not be used "to distinguish or discriminate sins, as the Romish Divines are accustomed to do; but to make it evident that the desert of every, even the

least sin, is death according to legal judgment." Quoted in H. R. McAdoo, *The Structure of Caroline Moral Theory* (London, 1949), p. 105. At the same time, Anglican moral theologians stressed that all sins could be forgiven through properly performed repentance, which included four elements: "contrition, confession, amendment of life, and faith" (p. 121). Repentance was itself a product of grace given freely to the believer (pp. 54–55). Cf. C. FitzSimons Allison, *The Rise of Moralism: The Proclamation of the Gospel from Hooker to Baxter* (New York, 1966), pp. 64–65.

60. On this distinction, and the many refinements to which it gave rise, see McAdoo, *Caroline Moral Theory*, pp. 112–119.
61. King, "Decision-Makers," pp. 56–57.
62. Bishop Robert Sanderson, *Ad Populum*, Sermon 4 (from *The Collected Works of Robert Sanderson*, vol. 3), quoted in Wood, *English Casuistical*, pp. 58–59.
63. See Bahlman, *Moral Revolution*, pp. 1–30; cf. Edward Bristow, *Vice and Vigilance: Purity Movements in Britain since 1700* (Dublin, 1977), pp. 11–31.
64. Note that transportation replaced probation for first offenders where the felony was clergyable.
65. See Beattie, *Crime and the Courts in England*, p. 52.
66. See Chapter 12 ("Moral Offenses").
67. In the 1760s and thereafter, landed gentry, frustrated by the refusal of juries to convict persons charged with the capital crimes of poaching game and marauding livestock, formed Associations for the Prosecution of Felons. These consisted essentially of informers paid by gentry to bring prosecutions on their behalf. The difficulty of obtaining jury convictions in such cases persisted, however, and many offenders were prosecuted for misdemeanors in courts of the justices of the peace. It is estimated that there were at least one thousand such Prosecution Associations active in eighteenth-century England, and perhaps as many as four thousand. See sources cited in David Phillips, "Good Men to Associate and Bad Men to Conspire: Associations for the Prosecution of Felons in England, 1760–1860," in V. A. C. Gatrell, Bruce Lenman, and Geoffrey Parker, eds., *Crime and the Law: The Social History of Crime in Western Europe since 1500* (London, 1980), p. 120. See also Adrian Shubert, "Private Initiative in Law Enforcement: Associations for the Prosecution of Felons, 1744–1856," in Victor Bailey, ed., *Policing and Punishment in Nineteenth-Century Britain* (New Brunswick, N.J., 1981), pp. 25–41.
68. On the emergence of the felony-murder rule, see David Lanham, "Felony Murder—Ancient and Modern," *Criminal Law Journal* 7 (1983): 91–97; and J. M. Kaye, "The Early History of Murder and Manslaughter, Part II," *Law Quarterly Review* 83 (1967): 587–601.
69. See Paul H. Robinson, "A Brief History of Distinctions of Criminal Culpability," *Hastings Law Journal* 31 (1980), 815, 838–839; J. F. Quinn and J. M. B. Crawford, *The Christian Foundations of Criminal Responsibility: Historical and Philosophical Analysis of the Common Law* (Lewiston, N.Y., 1991), pp. 306–308.
70. See Green, *Verdict According to Conscience*, pp. 72–85.
71. William Hawkins, *Pleas of the Crown, 1716–1721*, vol 1. (London, 1716), pp. 80–82. See also Graeme Coss, "'God is a Righteous Judge Strong and Patient: and God is Provoked Every Day': A Brief History of the Doctrine of Provocation in England," *Sydney Law Review* 13 (1991), 570–577.
72. See especially Percy Henry Winfield, *The History of Conspiracy and Abuse of Legal Procedure* (Cambridge, 1921). See also James Wallace Bryan, *The Development of the English Law of Conspiracy* (Baltimore, 1909), pp. 9–50; R. S. Wright, *The Law of Criminal Conspiracies and Agreements as Found in the American Cases* (Philadel-

phia, 1887), pp. 5–6; Francis B. Sayre, "Criminal Conspiracy," *Harvard Law Review* 35 (1921–22), 393, 394–398.

73. *The Poulterers' Case,* 9 Coke 55b (1611).
74. *Baggs' Case,* 11 Coke 93b, 98a (1616).
75. *Rex v. Starling,* 1 Sid. 168 and 1 Keb. 650 (1664).
76. In *Rex v. Armstrong, Harrison, et al.,* 1 Vent. 305, 86 *Eng. Rep.* 196 (1677–78), the defendants asserted that the verdict against them—for conspiring to bring false charges against a person—should be stayed because "the bare conspiracy, without executing of it by some overt act, was not subject to an indictment according to the *Poulterers' Case.*" The Court held that "there was as much an overt act as the nature and design of this conspiracy did admit."
77. *Regina v. Bass,* 11 Mod. 55, 88 *Eng. Rep.* 881 (1705). Lord Holt cited, without discussing, the *Poulterers' Case* and *Rex v. Armstrong.*
78. In 1994 the United States Supreme Court cited *Regina v. Bass* in holding that proof of an overt act is not required under a statute punishing conspiracy to violate a narcotics statute. See *United States v. Shabani,* 513 U.S 10, 16 (1994). Writing for a unanimous Court, Justice O'Connor stated: "Shabani reminds us that the law does not punish criminal thoughts and contends that conspiracy without an overt act requirement violates this principle because the offense is predominately mental in composition. The prohibition against criminal conspiracy, however, does not punish mere thought; the criminal agreement itself is the *actus reus* and has been so viewed since Regina v. Bass." Ibid. at 16. The fiction is in the word "overt": an agreement is undoubtedly an act, as contrasted with a purely mental exercise, but the use of the expression "overt act," meaning an open or manifest act, implies something more than a mere agreement. This had been forcefully stated by the Court of Appeals for the Ninth Circuit, in whose jurisdiction the Shabani case was decided, in the following terms: "An overt act which completes the crime of conspiracy to violate federal law is something apart from conspiracy and is an act to effect the object of the conspiracy, and need be neither a criminal act, nor a crime that is the object of the conspiracy, but must accompany or follow the agreement and must be done in furtherance of the object of the agreement." *Marino v. United States,* 91 F. 2d 691, 694–695 (9th Cir., 1937).
79. Quoted in Sayre, "Criminal Conspiracy," p. 402.
80. *Rex v. Journeymen Tailors,* 8 Mod. 10 (1721). The court in this case purported to apply the Statutes of Labourers of 1349 (23 Edward III c. 7 (1349)) and 1351 (25 Edward III c. 1 (1350)), and later courts and writers, both in England and in the United States, erroneously traced the doctrine of conspiracy back to those statutes. In fact, the Statutes of Labourers expressly required not only an unlawful agreement but unlawful acts in pursuance thereof.
81. *Rev v. Edwards,* 8 Mod. 320 (1724).
82. *Jones v. Randall,* 98 *Eng. Rep.* 706, 707 (K.B. 1774).
83. 5 Anne, c. 6, sec. 2 (1706).
84. See Joanna Innes, "Prisons for the Poor: English Bridewells, 1500–1800," in Francis Snyder and Douglas Hay, eds., *Labour, Law, and Crime: An Historical Perspective* (London, 1987), p. 42.
85. See R. B. Pugh, *Imprisonment in Medieval England* (London, 1968), pp. 1–47.
86. See John Witte, Jr., "'Blest be the Ties that Bind': Covenant and Community in Puritan Thought," *Emory Law Journal* 16 (1987), 579, 584. As Witte shows, performance of works was not itself a means to salvation but a sign that one was saved. Only the "covenant of grace" could confer salvation on those who had faith. Yet even those who were not chosen to be saved were to be held to the basic elements of the covenant of works, such as honesty and obedience.

87. Partisans of Max Weber's highly controversial thesis linking the Puritan ethic with the "heroic age" of capitalism will find some support in the linkage presented here between the Puritan emphasis on the covenant of works and certain developments in English criminal law in the seventeenth century, notably the proliferation of statutes imposing severe penalties for crimes adversely affecting the economic interests of the landed gentry and the mercantile class. Neglected, however, in Weber's understanding of Puritanism is an analysis of its theology of covenants and hence of the Puritan emphasis on public spirit, humility, charity, communitarianism, self-sacrifice, and other biblical virtues that do not fit easily with his definition either of Puritan "asceticism" or of the capitalist spirit. See Introduction, Chapter 9, and Chapter 12.
88. See Zachariah Mudge, *Sermons on Different Subjects* (London, 1739), p. 315.
89. Ibid., p. 317.
90. Mercy must be employed "because one punishment must serve for ten thousand crimes, every one of which has yet some thing distinguished, and one law must decide ten thousand cases which have every one their difference." Ibid., p. 315.
91. "If justice . . . be mercy to the injured and innocent part of a community, then certainly a promiscuous pardon of crimes, a general relaxation of punishment, a grace shown undiscriminately to every kind of wickedness, is not so." Ibid., p. 317. Other sermons preached in connection with the enforcement of the criminal law struck similar themes. Thus George Halley, in a sermon preached to condemned prisoners in 1691, emphasized that justice and equity are one, and that they concur in justifying the execution of wicked men, which alone can put a stop to them. See George Halley, *A Sermon Preached at the Castle of York to the Condemned Prisoners* (London, 1691).

Other assize sermons, however, admonished judges to exercise mercy. Thus a sermon preached in 1698 at the assizes at Bury St. Edmund's states: "And here is a caution also for those who have the sword of judicature and authority in their hands: Be wise ye that are judges of the earth, pre-judge not a man wholly by his place, nor yet by his company; though the clamours of the sins of a place in general, be as the clamour and the cry of Sodom, yet *descendite et videte,* look into it nearer, and distinguish of particulars." See William Bedford, *Two Sermons Preached at St. Marie's in Bury St. Edmund's at the Assizes* (London, 1698), p. 13. Similarly, a sermon preached in Edinburgh asserts: "God himselfe reckons justice his *strange work,* a foreign part of his Providence, and which he never works till constrained; and even then with some aversion. . . . The mercy of rulers ought to be a copy of that wondrous compassion God shewed to a destroyed world, and as far as possible an exact transcript of that Grand Exemplar." See James Webster, *A Sermon Preached to the High Church at Edinburgh at the Election of the Magistrates of the City* (Edinburgh, 1694), p. 7. Thanks are due to Gregory Lubkin for his assistance in uncovering and analyzing these sermons.

The reference in James Webster's sermon to God's "strange work" is a quotation from the Lutheran Formula of Concord of 1527, in which the law is characterized as "Christ's strange work," whose three "uses" are to deter recalcitrant people from misconduct by threat of penalties, to make people conscious of their obligations and hence repentant of their sins, and to guide faithful people in the paths of virtuous living. Cf. Paul Tillich, *Love, Power, and Justice: Ontological Analyses and Ethical Application* (London, 1954), p. 49 ("Love, in order to exercise its proper work, namely charity and forgiveness, must provide for a place on which this can be done, through its strange work on judging and punishing"). On the Lutheran doctrine of the uses of the law, see Chapter 2.

11. The Transformation of English Civil and Economic Law

1. Historians of English law have generally treated the history of the English common law of property and contract as an incremental development from the twelfth to the late eighteenth or even nineteenth century, when for the first time, it is said, a modern ensemble of doctrines and principles was derived from analysis of the various evolving common law forms of action. Thus T. F. T. Plucknett tells the story of a gradual unfolding of rules of contract law from the actions of debt and assumpsit, culminating in the synthesis of contract doctrines in Blackstone's treatises and Lord Mansfield's opinions. See T. F. T. Plucknett, *A Concise History of English Law,* 5th ed. (Boston, 1956), pp. 627–656. Property law is treated in a similar fashion by S. F. C. Milsom, who understands its growth as a gradual process, "step by forward step." See S. F. C. Milsom, *Historical Foundations of the English Common Law* (London, 1969), p. 168. Other scholars have recognized the importance of new developments in the seventeenth century. Thus John Baker has noted that in 1651 the word "contract" was first applied "in English law" (by which he means the English law applied in the King's Bench and Court of Common Pleas) to describe "an agreement between two or more concerning something to be done, whereby both parties are bound to each other, or one is bound to the other." See John H. Baker, *An Introduction to English Legal History,* 3rd ed. (London, 1990), p. 361 (quoting Serjeant Sheppard). Baker sees the introduction of the new terminology as important and asserts that "by the end of the seventeenth century the modern distinction between contract and tort was in place" (p. 361). Scholars have also long recognized that the seventeenth century was of decisive importance for the development of modern forms of business associations, especially the joint-stock company, and that important developments also took place in this period in the law of personal property, relating to property in goods and money, including the transformation of the action of trover into an action to try title to chattels and the elaboration of a law of bailments, drawn largely from admiralty law, to protect one who has placed goods into the custody of a carrier or warehouseman. The creation of the new crime of embezzlement may also be mentioned in this connection. What is attempted here is to show the interrelationships of these and other various developments in order to expose the revolutionary character of the transformation of English civil and economic law of which they were a part.
2. See A. W. B. Simpson, *A History of the Land Law,* 2nd ed. (Oxford, 1986), pp. 21–24, 198–199; see also Charles J. Reid, Jr., "The Seventeenth-Century Revolution in the English Land Law," *Cleveland State Law Review* 43 (1995), 221, 241–242.
3. Knight-service in England had its origin in the land which William the Conqueror parceled out to his leading knights, who were expected to provide military service to the Crown in exchange. Wardship, the other relevant incident, consisted of wardship of land and of the body. When a tenant died leaving a minor heir, the lord exercised the heir's rights in the land and received the profits from it until the heir reached majority. Wardship of the body meant that the lord had the right to arrange the heir's marriage, which the heir could refuse only upon payment of a substantial fee. See Reid, "Seventeenth-Century Revolution," pp. 235–236.
4. The Saxon word *socage,* retained after the Norman Conquest, is related to the word *sokemen,* referring initially to a class of free peasants who might owe rent or agricultural services to their manorial lords but not military services. By the thirteenth century, an unfree villein socage had also emerged, which gave villein sokemen, in contrast to other villeins, legal protection against ejection and rent

increases but denied them rights of freeholders. See Paul R. Hyams, *King, Lords, and Peasants in Medieval England: The Common Law of Villeinage in the Twelfth and Thirteenth Centuries* (New York, 1980), pp. 194–195. In this early period, free socage, as contrasted with villein socage, gave those peasants who held it something more than villeinage but something less than the rights of freeholders, such as the right to bring suit in the royal courts. See ibid., pp. 199–200.

5. Thomas More wrote: "Your sheep . . . which are usually so tame and so cheaply fed, begin now, according to report, to be so greedy and wild that they devour human beings themselves and devastate and depopulate fields, houses, and towns. . . . [I]n order that one insatiable glutton and accursed plague of his native land may join field to field and surround many thousand acres with one fence, tenants are evicted. . . . By hook or by crook the poor wretches are compelled to leave their homes—men and women, husbands and wives, orphans and widows, parents with little children and a household not rich but numerous since farming requires many hands. . . . [I]n wandering from place to place, what remains for them but to steal and be hanged—justly, you may say!—or to wander and beg. . . . Thus the unscrupulous greed of a few is ruining the very thing by virtue of what your island was once counted fortunate in the extreme." Thomas More, *Utopia,* vol. 4 of *The Complete Works of St. Thomas More* (New Haven, 1963), pp. 65–71.
6. See I. S. Leadam, *The Domesday of Enclosures 1517–1518* (Nottingham, 1897); Joan Thirsk, *Tudor Enclosures,* 2nd ed. (London, 1989), pp. 214–216; Reid, "Seventeenth-Century Revolution," pp. 254–255. Thirsk stresses the fact that many enclosures were amicable and progressive, being associated with the rationalization of agricultural production.
7. Coke's effort to repeal the anti-enclosure legislation was part of a larger shift in opinion. Sir Walter Raleigh had argued in 1601 that the legislation had restricted English liberty and its repeal would "leave every man free, which is the desire of a true Englishman." The Puritan polemicist Samuel Hartlib raised the question in 1651 whether common fields "do not rather make poor, by causing idleness than maintaine them; and such poor who are trained up rather for the Gallowes or begarry than for the Commonwealth's service." Gabriel Plattes, a disciple of Hartlib, had earlier argued that enclosures were responsible for increasing national wealth and that the poor were thereby benefited by the practice. See sources cited in Reid, "Seventeenth-Century Revolution," pp. 256–259.
8. Ibid., pp. 259–261.
9. In the seventeenth century, leasehold came to be treated as a "chattel real," which meant that it could not descend directly as a fee or a life estate to an heir but could be transferred upon the death of the lessee by instruction to the executor or administrator of his will. See Simpson, *History of the Land Law,* pp. 249–250. These limitations did not diminish the lessee's property rights in the land, and indeed long-term leases came to be widely used in commercial enterprises.
10. The citation continues: "The resettlement which would be created at this point comprised the following steps: (a) S, the life tenant, and the Trustees surrendered their estates to G, the remainderman in tail. This made him a tenant in tail in possession. (b) G suffered a recovery in favor of the family solicitor owner of the fee simple. (c) The family solicitor conveyed to S for life, remainder to G for life, remainder to Trustees for the lives of S and G to preserve contingent remainders, remainders to the first and other sons of G in tail male, remainders to the second and other sons of S in tail male." A. James Casner and W. Barton Leach, *Cases and Text on Property,* 2nd ed. (Boston, 1969), pp. 357–358.

11. Ibid.
12. The strict settlement avoided certain restrictions placed on so-called "perpetuities," defined as grants of land that "perpetuate" ownership for more than twenty-one years beyond the death of any living person named in the grant. The "rule against perpetuities," as it is called, was first enunciated by Lord Nottingham in 1681 in the *Duke of Norfolk's Case* and later elaborated by a succession of eighteenth-century chancellors.
13. Under the statute *Quia Emptores,* 18 Edward I c. 1 (1290), a superior lord could no longer require the tenant seller of a fee simple estate to continue to provide services and payments that attached to the land, but had to exact them from the buyer in the chain of subinfeudation. See Sir Frederick Pollock, *The Land Laws,* 3rd ed. (1896; reprint, Littleton, 1979), pp. 70–71. A slightly earlier statute, *De Donis Conditionalibus,* 13 Edward I c. 1 (1285), placed severe restrictions on the alienability of estates held in fee tail, requiring consent on the part of the tenant in tail before his superior in the chain could alienate the land to another.
14. City land was held chiefly by so-called burgage tenure (*burg* being an Anglo-Saxon word for "city"), which was generally free from all feudal incidents except wardship. Land held by burgage tenure could be alienated freely and could be pledged by mortgage to raise liquid capital.
15. Under Lord Nottingham, who was chancellor for a decade prior to his death in 1682, "the old philosophy of uses . . . gave way to a new philosophy of trusts based upon clearer conceptions of public policy and of the nature and purposes of the law." Austin Wakeman Scott, *The Law of Trusts,* 3rd ed., vol. 1 (Boston, 1967), p. 22. It was then that the common lawyers adapted the two remaining categories of uses—the active use and the use upon a use—to the needs of clients with landed estates. See Percy Bordwell, "The Conversion of the Use to a Legal Interest," *Iowa Law Review* 21 (1935), 1–46; and John L. Barton, "The Statute of Uses and the Trust of Freeholds," *Law Quarterly Review* 82 (1966), 215–225.
16. See Harold Dexter Hazeltine, "The Gage of Land in Mediaeval England," in *Select Essays in Anglo-American Legal History,* vol. 3 (New York, 1909), pp. 646, 647–650. A distinction was made between a "live gage" *(vif gage),* under which the gagee was required to apply profits accruing to the land to the progressive reduction of the debt, and the "dead gage" *(mort gage),* under which the gagee was not so required (hence our word "mortgage").
17. See Berman, *Law and Revolution,* pp. 245–250 and 348–354. Even the best contemporary historians of European contract law have failed to give an adequate account of the decisive influence of the canon law in the modernization of the more formalistic Germanic and Roman law of contracts. The great work of Reinhard Zimmermann, *The Law of Obligations: Roman Foundations of the Civilian Tradition* (Oxford, 1996), touches only occasionally on the influence of the canon law. James R. Gordley, in *The Philosophical Origins of Modern Contract Doctrine* (Oxford, 1991), refers briefly to contrasts between canonist and Roman doctrines in the thirteenth to sixteenth centuries but comes down strongly on the side of Romanist influence. Thus Gordley treats Baldus's express attribution of the concept of *causa* to the canon law as the reading back of a Romanist doctrine (p. 56), neglecting to note that Baldus was both a Romanist and a canonist and that there is nothing in the Roman law of Justinian, but much in the canon law of Huguccio and Hostiensis, to support a general principle of the purpose *(causa)* of the transaction for distinguishing between enforceable and unenforceable promises. Hostiensis, *Summa,* bk. 1, *De pactis,* sec. 1, written in the 1240s, states that "a contract [*pactum*] is the consent of two or more persons, expressed in

words with the intention [*animo*] of binding them to give or do the same [thing], one to the other. . . . And so I say 'with the intention of binding' because if I put forward [something] for the purpose [*causa*] of teaching or for the purpose [*causa*] of telling a joke, that does not bind me." The canonists also often stated the doctrine of *causa* negatively. In a later work a leading canonist declared that "contracts shall be kept . . . so long as they are not against the laws or against public policy [*contra bonos mores*] and not made by fraud." See Richard Helmholz, *Canon Law and the Law of England* (London, 1987), p. 272.

18. A short Latin treatise titled *Lex Mercatoria,* dealing chiefly with procedure, was published in England in about 1280. It is translated in Paul R. Teetor, "England's Earliest Treatise on the Law Merchant," *American Journal of Legal History* 6 (1962), 178–210. The first comprehensive English book on the substantive law merchant seems to have been Gerard Malynes's work of 1622, *Consuetudo, vel Lex Mercatoria,* or *The Ancient Law Merchant.* Malynes explains what he means by "law merchant": "I have entitled the book according to the ancient name of *Lex Mercatoria* . . . because it is customary law approved by the authority of all kingdoms and commonwealths, and not a law established by the sovereignty of any prince." In 1473, it was said by Stillington, Edward IV's chancellor, in *Carrier's Case* (Y. B. Edward IV 9, 64 *Selden Society* 30), that cases involving foreign merchants "shall be determined according to the law of nature, which is called by some the law merchant, which is a universal law throughout the world." See Mary Elizabeth Basile et al., eds., *Lex Mercatoria and Legal Pluralism: A Late-Thirteenth-Century Treatise and Its Afterlife* (Cambridge, Mass., 1998).
19. John H. Baker argues in "The Law Merchant and the Common Law before 1700," *Cambridge Law Journal* 38 (1979), 295–322, that before 1700 the phrase "law merchant" did not refer to a distinct body of substantive law. See also James Steven Rogers, *The Early History of the Law of Bills and Notes: A Study of the Origins of Anglo-American Commercial Law* (Cambridge, 1995), pp. 20–21. Both Baker and Rogers, however, are referring to the fact that fair and town courts, which applied mercantile law to mercantile disputes, also applied the English common law, that is, the law applied by the courts of King's Bench, Common Pleas, and Exchequer Chamber, to other disputes, and their decisions in both types of cases were sometimes reviewed by those courts. In other words, a common law action of debt or covenant or account could be brought in the fair court or town court and would be decided according to the common law; but an action on an executory oral agreement to pay a certain price for delivery of certain goods, for which the common law courts gave no remedy, would be decided by the fair or town court on the basis of a distinct body of substantive mercantile law. The common lawyers—and contemporary historians of English law—often refer to this body of law as "borough law." Hale, however, writing in the latter seventeenth century, states that "the Common Law includes . . . *Lex mercatoria.*" Matthew Hale, *The History of the Common Law of England,* ed. Charles M. Gray (Chicago, 1971), p. 18.
20. See Willard T. Barbour, "The History of Contract in Early English Equity," in Paul Vinogradoff, ed., *Oxford Studies in Social and Legal History* (Oxford, 1909), p. 4.
21. See A. W. B. Simpson, *A History of the Law of Contract: The Rise of the Action of Assumpsit* (Oxford, 1975), pp. 297–302 *(Slade's Case)* and 316–488 (consideration).
22. See Samuel J. Stoljar, *A History of Contract at Common Law* (Canberra, 1975), pp. 147–163; Charles W. Francis, "The Structure of Judicial Administration and the Development of Contract in Seventeenth-Century England," *Columbia Law Review* 83 (1983), 35, 122–125; and Holdsworth, *History of English Law,* 4:64, 72, 75.

23. Simpson, *History of Contract,* p. 446.
24. Aleyn 26, 82 *Eng. Rep.* 897 (1648). This is a more complete report of the case than that given in Style 47, 82 *Eng. Rep.* 519 (1647), which is the one usually reproduced. See David Ibbetson, "Absolute Liability in Contract: The Antecedents of *Paradine v. Jayne,*" in F. D. Rose, ed., *Consensus ad Idem* (London, 1996), p. 1.
25. See Simpson, *History of Contract,* pp. 31–33.
26. Plucknett, *Concise History of the Common Law,* p. 652.
27. See P. S. Atiyah, *The Rise and Fall of Contract* (Oxford, 1979), passim. Atiyah states that the distinction between contract and tort "only slowly evolv[ed] in the seventeenth and eighteenth centuries" (p. 144). Cf. Grant Gilmore, *The Death of Contract* (Columbus, 1974), p. 140 n. 228 ("Until the late nineteenth century the dividing line between 'contract' and 'tort' had never been sharply drawn"). Morton Horwitz, in *The Transformation of American Law,* 1780–1860 (Cambridge, 1977), p. 160, states that "modern contract law is fundamentally a creature of the nineteenth century. . . . Only in the nineteenth century did judges and jurists . . . assert for the first time that the source of the obligation of contract is the convergence of wills of the contracting parties." These widely accepted misconceptions are based, first, on the exclusion from consideration of all branches of English law other than the common law—the exclusion of the English law merchant, of English admiralty law, of the canon law of the English church courts, of English application of international law, and even of many branches of the common law, such as the law of sales; and second, on the failure to see through the formulary procedure that prevailed in the common law until the nineteenth century onto the substantive doctrines that underlay the forms of action and that were debated at the trial stage after the pleadings were settled. The emergence of treatises on contract law in the late eighteenth and nineteenth centuries signaled, to be sure, a new method of systematization of the common law, and the subsequent abolition of the forms of action allowed that method to be refined and expanded. But the notion that the exchange of promises could give rise to contractual obligations did not first emerge, as Atiyah claims (e.g., at p. 139), in the late eighteenth century but existed at least from the time of the thirteenth century canonists—including the English canonists—and prior to its adoption in the common law courts in the late seventeenth century was reflected in the practice not only of English church courts but also of English urban courts, mercantile courts, Admiralty, and Chancery.
28. Rogers, *Early History of the Law of Bills and Notes,* pp. 94ff. and passim.
29. Ibid., p. 103.
30. Max Weber, *The Protestant Ethic and the Spirit of Capitalism,* trans. Talcott Parsons (London, 1992), p. 104.
31. On the act incorporating the Greenland Company, see Samuel Williston, "History of the Law of Business Corporations before 1800," *Harvard Law Review* 2 (1888), 111. On the economic and legal history of the English joint-stock company, see William Robert Scott, *The Constitution and Finance of English, Scottish, and Irish Joint-Stock Companies to 1720,* 3 vols. (1912; reprint, Gloucester, Mass., 1968). See also Frank Evans, "The Evolution of the English Joint-Stock Limited Trading Company," *Columbia Law Review* 8 (1908), 339–361, 461–480. Unfortunately, these works do not discuss, but take for granted, the strong communitarian character of this form of economic and legal enterprise.
32. 5 & 6 William & Mary c. 20 (*1694*).
33. See John Giuseppi, *The Bank of England: A History from Its Foundation in* 1694 (London, 1966), pp. 9–14 (discussing the origins of the bank and the social back-

grounds of its first investors and directors); *Rules, Orders, and By-Laws for the Good Government of the Corporation of the Governor and Company of the Bank of England,* reprinted in *Bank of England: Selected Tracts, 1694–1804* (Farnborough, U.K., 1968), p. 11 (on the weekly meetings of the Court of Directors) and p. 19 (on the biennial meetings of the General Court of shareholders). As in the case of the joint-stock company, so in the case of banking and other forms of crediting, there exists a large economic and legal literature which traces the origins of the modern forms of these institutions to the latter half of the seventeenth century but which takes for granted, without stressing, their strong communitarian character. See, for instance, Frank T. Melton, *Sir Robert Clayton and the Origins of English Deposit Banking, 1658–1685* (Cambridge, 1986); P. G. M. Dickson, *The Financial Revolution in England: A Study in the Development of Public Credit, 1688–1756* (London, 1967); Rogers, *Early History of the Law of Bills and Notes.* 1995).

34. On this development, see Reid, "Seventeenth-Century Revolution," pp. 288–296 and authorities cited there.

35. *Darcy v. Allen,* 72 *Eng. Rep.* 830 (1602), holding that a royal grant of a monopoly of the manufacture of playing cards was not valid. There was no judicial opinion in the case. Coke's report of the case, which he presents as though it were the judicial opinion, may have drawn on the arguments of counsel. See Jacob Corré, "The Argument, Decision, and Reports of *Darcy v. Allen,*" *Emory Law Journal* 45 (1996), 1261–27.

36. See William L. Letwin, "The English Common Law Concerning Monopolies," *University of Chicago Law Review* 21 (1954), 355–385; Donald W. Wagner, "Coke and the Rise of Economic Liberalism," *Economic History Review* 6 (1935), 30ff.; Donald O. Wager, "The Common Law and Free Enterprise: An Early Case of Monopoly." *Economic History Review* 7 (1936), 217ff.; Barbara Malament, "The 'Economic Liberalism' of Sir Edward Coke," *Yale Law Journal* 76 (1967), 1321–58.

37. See Robert Ashton, *The English Civil War: Conservatism and Revolution, 1603–1649* (London, 1989), pp. 84–85, 92: George Unwin, *The Gilds and Companies of London* (New York, 1964), pp. 336–339.

38. For examples of comparable devices to extract money used by rulers of other parts of Europe in the sixteenth and seventeenth centuries, see Carolyn Webber and Aaron Wildavsky, *A History of Taxation and Expenditure in the Western World* (New York, 1986), pp. 262–268. These included the sale of monopolies over activities such as the mining of precious metals, direct and indirect taxes on land and produce, confiscation of property, the exploitation of colonies for crown revenue, and the sale of public offices.

39. See E. E. Rich and C. H. Wilson, eds., *The Cambridge Economic History of Europe,* vol. 5 (Cambridge, 1977), p. 352. Because of the Dutch influence, these innovations were sometimes called "Dutch finance." See Scott B. MacDonald and Albert L. Gastmann, *A History of Credit and Power in the Western World* (New Brunswick, N.J., 2001), pp. 132–133. In fact, however, the English went beyond the Dutch in introducing new methods of finance. See Jan De Vries and Ad van der Woude, *The First Modern Economy: Success, Failure, and Perseverance of the Dutch Economy, 1500–1815* (Cambridge, 1997), pp. 131–132, 141–142, 152, 155.

40. See Edward Chancellor, *The Devil Take the Hindmost: A History of Financial Speculation* (New York, 1999). As early as the 1690s, investors began speculating in stocks in the hope of large profits. Thus the invention of the diving bell, giving rise to the prospect that goods lost at sea might be salvaged, led to the creation of over a dozen companies, some promising returns of 100 percent or better on

investments. Ibid., pp. 36–38. Practices such as selling short and the purchase of options were also the creations of this period. Ibid., p. 39. Although the 1690s "bubble" eventually deflated, the speculative spirit culminated in the notorious South Sea Bubble of 1720, resulting from the overissuance of stock by the South Sea Company, which was formed to exploit recent discoveries in the South Pacific. The directors used proceeds from new subscriptions to pay off previous commitments. Ibid., pp. 66–80. In the wake of this disaster, Parliament outlawed various forms of speculation, such as short sales and trading in options and futures. Ibid., p. 88. See also Peter M. Garber, *Famous First Bubbles: The Fundamentals of Early Manias* (Cambridge, Mass., 2000), pp. 115–120.

41. Prior to the stock bubble of the 1690s, the word "broker" had referred simply to a procurer or pimp. Garber, *Famous First Bubbles,* p. 31.
42. See Chancellor, *Devil Take the Hindmost,* pp. 31–39.
43. Under Queen Elizabeth a series of patents were issued, partly in order to bring to England the innovative technology found elsewhere in Europe. See Christine MacLeod, *Inventing the Industrial Revolution: The English Patent System, 1660–1800* (Cambridge, 1988), pp. 11–13. The Italian city-states, especially Venice, played a particularly important role in the development of patent law. See Pamela O. Long, *Openness, Secrecy, Authorship: Technical Arts and the Culture of Knowledge from Antiquity to the Renaissance* (Baltimore, 2001), pp. 90–95.
44. The terms of the statute are quoted by Adam Mossoff, "Rethinking the Development of Patents: An Intellectual History, 1550–1800." *Hastings Law Journal* 52 (2001), 1255, 1272–73.
45. See Christine MacLeod, "The 1690s Patent Boom: Invention or Stock-Jobbing?" *Economic History Review* 39, 2nd ser. (1986), 549–571.
46. See Richard Rogers Bowker, *Copyright: Its History and Its Law* (Boston, 1912), pp. 25–31. Engraving and prints were given protection by successive acts in 1734 and 1735. Not until the nineteenth century, however, were dramatic performances and designs for manufacturing processes protected, and only then did England begin to bind itself to observe international conventions on the protection of foreign copyright.
47. See Peter L. Bernstein, *Against the Gods: The Remarkable Story of Risk* (New York, 1996), pp. 90ff.
48. Ibid. See also Ralph Straub, *Lloyd's: The Gentlemen at the Coffee-House* (New York, 1938).
49. See Ian Hacking, *The Emergence of Probability: A Philosophical Study of Early Ideas about Probability, Induction, and Statistical Inference* (Cambridge, 1975), pp. 102–110.

12. The Transformation of English Social Law

1. The second Act of Supremacy, enacted upon the accession of Elizabeth I to the throne in 1559, declared her and her successors to be "the only supreme governor of this realm . . . as well in all spiritual or ecclesiastical things or causes as temporal." 1 Elizabeth I c. 1 (1559).
2. The first English prayerbook, drafted principally by Archbishop Thomas Cranmer and adopted by Edward VI in 1549, drew even more on Protestant theology, notably in rejecting the Roman Catholic doctrine of transubstantiation. See Samuel Leuenberger, *Archbishop Cranmer's Immortal Bequest: The Book of Common Prayer of the Church of England: An Evangelical Liturgy* (Grand Rapids, Mich., 1990). There were few major changes in a third Book of Common Prayer adopted

by Queen Elizabeth in 1559, a fourth by James I in 1604, and a fifth and last by Charles II in 1662. Despite some compromises with Calvinist theology, Presbyterian and other dissenting churches were antagonized by the Roman features that remained in the various editions as well as by Anglican ritual practices. See Willian Sydnor, *The Real Prayer Books: 1549 to the Present* (Wilton, Conn., 1979), p. 10.

3. The first English translation of the Bible was written in the fourteenth century by John Wyclif, who relied on the Latin Vulgate as his source. Thereafter an ecclesiastical statute of 1407 declared that to translate any biblical text into English was an act of heresy. In 1526 William Tyndale produced a translation of the Greek New Testament, and in 1530 he published a translation of large parts of the Hebrew Old Testament. By the end of the sixteenth century, other English translations were in existence, and in 1604 King James I appointed a commission of scholars to produce an authorized translation, which appeared in 1611; the King James Bible has remained the official version, required to be read in Anglican churches. See Brooke Foss Westcott, *A General View of the History of the English Bible,* 3rd ed. rev. (New York, 1916).
4. Calvin agreed in principle with Zwingli that everything sensuous—such as music, vestments, ritual gesture, and images—should be eliminated from the service. He came to think, however, that there were benefits to congregational song so long as what was to be sung was restricted exclusively to the Psalms. The first English version of the Psalms in meter was published in 1562. See Richard Arnold, *English Hymns of the Eighteenth Century* (New York, 1991), pp. 4–7. Madeleine Marshall and Janet Todd, in *English Congregational Hymns in the Eighteenth Century* (Lexington, Ky., 1982), p. 12, write that "metrical psalmody was Calvin's gift to England." Eventually the laity grew tired of the "alleged dullness" of the Psalms, and in 1735 John Wesley published a collection of hymns which, with those of Issac Watts and others, "attained an unpredictably high degree of popularity" although the singing of them in what were technically Church of England services remained illegal under parliamentary liturgical legislation until 1859. See Arnold, *English Hymns,* pp. 7–17.
5. Although such preaching was practiced especially by Puritans within the Anglican Church, it was also practiced by some leading non-Puritans. Thus the sixteenth-century archbishop of Canterbury, Hugh Latimer, displayed a preaching style that "champion[ed] . . . a rebirth of feeling" and held out "the promise of justification by faith." See Charles Montgomery Gray, *Hugh Latimer and the Sixteenth Century: An Essay in Interpretation* (Cambridge, Mass., 1950), p. 20.
6. See Chapter 7 ("The Religious Settlement").
7. By statute, responsibility to fill vacant episcopal sees shifted from the Crown to the prime minister in 1714. See Bernard Palmer, *High and Mitred: A Study of Prime Ministers as Bishop-Makers, 1837–1977* (London, 1992), pp. 1–8; cf. Norman Doe, *The Legal Framework of the Church of England: A Critical Study in a Comparative Context* (Oxford, 1996), pp. 163–165.
8. In fact, it took the Glorious Revolution to achieve these Puritan objectives.
9. Christopher Lasch, "The Suppression of Clandestine Marriage in England: The Marriage Act of 1753," *Salmagundi* 26 (1974), 90–91.
10. John Witte writes that "dozens of Anglican and Anglo-Puritan writers, from 1600 onward, expounded this 'commonwealth model' of marriage [whereby it was believed that] 'good members of a family are likely to make good members of church and commonwealth.'" See John Witte, Jr., "The Goods and Goals of Marriage," *Notre Dame Law Review* 76 (2001), 1059, quoting William Gouge, *Of Domesticall Duties: Eight Treatises* (London, 1622), p. 17. See also idem, *From Sacrament to*

Contract: Marriage, Religion, and Law in the Western Tradition (Louisville, Ky., 1997), p. 173.

11. See Richard H. Helmholz, *Roman Canon Law in Reformation England* (Cambridge, 1990), pp. 69–70; and Martin Ingram, *Church Courts, Sex, and Marriage in England, 1570–1640* (Cambridge, 1987), pp. 125–218.
12. See 16 George II c. 33 ("An Act for the better preventing of Clandestine Marriage"). The act required the parties to a marriage to seek a license from their pastor or minister after the publication of banns in their usual place of abode, but also recognized the right of the archbishop of Canterbury and his "proper Officers" to dispense with this requirement in appropriate cases. The act also required the consent of the parents when the parties were under the age of twenty-one. See also Stephen Parker, *Informal Marriage, Cohabitation, and the Law, 1750–1989* (New York, 1990), pp. 29–47; and James A. Brundage, *Law, Sex, and Christian Society in Medieval Europe* (Chicago, 1987), pp. 563–564.
13. On the circumstances under which parliamentary divorces might be granted, see Holdsworth, *History of English Law,* 11:622–623.
14. See 6, 7 William IV c. 85 (1836). Cf. Holdsworth, *History of English Law,* 15:208–209.
15. See Holdsworth, *History of English Law,* 1:619–620.
16. Helmholz, *Roman Canon Law,* pp. 109–114.
17. See Holdsworth, *History of English Law,* 6:404, 11:539.
18. See 6, 7 William III and Mary II c. 11 (1694). To ensure compliance, it was specified that the provisions of the act be read four times a year in church. See Holdsworth, *History of English Law,* 6:404.
19. See 9 William III c. 35 (1697/98).
20. See 12 George II c. 28.
21. See 13 George II c. 19. Cf. 18 George II c. 34 (1746) (establishing weight requirements and other standards to be observed by those entering horses in races).
22. See 10 George II c. 28 (1737) (on the regulation of the theater). Cf. Holdsworth, *History of English Law,* 11:547–549 (analyzing the terms of the statute); cf. Dudley W. R. Bahlman, *The Moral Revolution of* 1688 (New Haven, 1957), pp. 1–30.
23. Bahlman, *Moral Revolution,* p. 31. This account is drawn from pp. 37–38, 40–41, 48–55, 58–59.
24. Bahlman (Ibid., p. 66) concludes that the decline was simply due to loss of "enthusiasm and hope."
25. See Leon Radzinowicz, *A History of English Criminal Law,* vol. 3, *The Reform of the Police* (London, 1956), pp. 144–156.
26. See John H. Langbein, "Shaping the Eighteenth-Century Criminal Trial: A View From the Ryder Source," *University of Chicago Law Review* 50 (1983), 55–67. Sir Robert Peel's Metropolitan Police Act of 1829 founded the first English public police force, popularly called "bobbies" after their founder. Also a director of public prosecutions was appointed "for a limited sphere of series crimes." Ibid., p. 56.
27. The number of endowed grammar schools increased in Elizabeth's reign from 51 to 280 or more, and by 1700 to 400. See James Bowen, *A History of Western Education,* vol. 3 (New York, 1981), pp. 129–130.
28. See S. J. Curtis, *History of Education in Great Britain,* 6th ed. (London, 1965), p. 98. See also Helen M. Jewell, *Education in Early Modern England* (New York, 1988), pp. 25–37.
29. See Lawrence Stone, "The Educational Revolution in England, 1560–1640," *Past and Present* 28 (1965), 41, 77–78.
30. See Samuel Hartlib, *Considerations Tending to the Happy Accomplishment of*

England's Reformation (1627), and John Dury, *The Reformed School* (1649). Both these works are reproduced in Charles Webster, ed., *Samuel Hartlib and the Advancement of Learning* (Cambridge, 1970). See also John Milton, *Tractate of Education,* in Oliver Morey Ainsworth, ed., *Milton on Education* (New Haven, 1928), pp. 51–64. Continental writers in the Reformed tradition who had an impact on English education in the seventeenth century include John Comenius and Hermann Francke. On Comenius, see David Cressy, *Education in Tudor and Start England* (London, 1975), pp. 101–102; on Francke, see Mary G. Jones, *The Charity School Movement: A Study of Eighteenth-Century Puritanism in Action* (Cambridge, 1938), pp. 37–38. See also Irene Parker, *Dissenting Academies in England: Their Rise and Progress and Their Place among the Educational Systems of the Country* (Cambridge, 1914), pp. 1–44.

31. Dury, *The Reformed School,* in Webster, *Samuel Hartlib,* p. 148
32. Ibid., p. 149.
33. Uniformity Act 1662, 1665 Act, Parker 46.
34. The five charter members of the Society for Promotion of Christian Knowledge (SPCK) were prominent members of the Church of England, which was now much more "comprehensive" than before the Revolution.
35. See Jones, *Charity School Movement,* pp. 364–371, for a list of over one thousand charity schools in England returned in the *Account of Charity Schools* for 1724. Jones writes (p. 19): Both [endowed and subscription schools] were charity schools, both aimed at moral improvement of the poor through instruction, both based the education they offered on religious knowledge, both, when they could afford it, gave gratuitous instruction, clothing, and apprentice fees to their pupils, and both the Society for Promotion of Christian Knowledge in England and Wales and the Incorporated Societies in Scotland and Ireland, which coordinated the individual efforts of the charitable into the charity school movement, used the term 'charity school.'"
36. See Craig Rose, "The Origins and Ideals of the SPCK, 1699–1716," in John Walsh, Colin Haydon, and Stephen Taylor, eds., *The Church of England, c. 1689–c. 1833* (Cambridge, 1993), p. 172. Members also gained admission only by recommendation but did not pay annual subscriptions and enjoyed only observer status at meetings.
37. See Jones, *Charity School Movement,* p. 19.
38. See W. O. B. Allen and Edmund McClure, *Two Hundred Years: The History of the Society for Promoting Christian Knowledge, 1698–1898* (New York, 1970), pp. 22–23.
39. Finally an act of Parliament in 1714 exempted elementary schools entirely from the Act of Uniformity. See Parker, *Dissenting Academies,* pp. 48–50.
40. See Jones, *Charity School Movement,* pp. 43–49.
41. See W. K. Lowther Clarke, *A History of the SPCK* (London, 1959), pp. 43–44.
42. See Jones, *Charity School Movement,* p. 73.
43. Clarke, *History of the SPCK,* p. 27.
44. See Jones, *Charity School Movement,* p. 74.
45. Ibid., pp. 106–109.
46. On the role of charity schools in the education of girls, see Jewell, *Education in Early Modern England,* pp. 89–91.
47. Norman Sykes, *Church and State in England in the Eighteenth Century* (New York, 1975), p. 379.
48. See Sidney Webb and Beatrice Webb, *English Local Government: English Poor Law History,* pt. 1, *The Old Poor Law* (London, 1927), p. 397. The first parliamentary

act dealing with the poor as such was the 1531 act "concerning the punishment of beggars and vagabonds," whose preamble referred to "idleness, mother and root of all vices." See 22 Henry VIII c. 12. The act permitted only the aged poor and the infirm to beg, and only in authorized places.

49. See Chapter 6 on sixteenth-century Germany.
50. See 27 Henry VIII c. 25 (1536) (creating the parish office of overseer of the poor); 5 & 6 Edward VI c. 12 (1552) (requiring collectors of alms and assessments to be named in every parish); 14 Elizabeth I c. 5 (1572); (requiring collectors of assessments and overseers of the poor to conduct monthly "views and searches" of the poor); 39 Elizabeth I c. 30 (1598) (requiring churchwardens and four overseers in every parish to put the poor to work and to place pauper children in apprenticeships); and 43 Elizabeth I c. 2 (1602) (reducing to two the number of overseers required in small parishes, but otherwise retaining the provisions of 39 Elizabeth I c. 30). See Katherine L. French, Gary C. Gibbs, and Beat A. Kümin, eds., *The Parish in English Life, 1400–1600* (Manchester, 1997), pp. 74, 77, and n. 15.
51. The Webbs report that in the late seventeenth century there were about three thousand justices of the peace and about nine thousand parishes. A majority of parishes had a population of several hundred or less.
52. See 28 Henry VIII c. 6. The methods of selection, and the bodies to whom the constables, surveyors, and overseers reported, were governed largely by local custom and varied widely. See Webb and Webb, *English Local Government,* pp. 298–299.
53. Ibid., p. 398.
54. Ibid., p. 399. On the justices of the peace, see John P. Dawson, *A History of Lay Judges* (Cambridge, Mass., 1960), pp. 136–145.
55. See Sidney Webb and Beatrice Webb, *English Prisons under Local Government* (London, 1922), pp. 12–13; and Bronislaw Geremek, *Poverty: A History,* trans. Agnieszka Kolakowska (Oxford, 1997), pp. 217–219.
56. On the operation of the Bridewells, see Webb and Webb, *English Prisons,* pp. 12–17.
57. See generally W. K. Jordan, *Philanthropy in England, 1480–1660: A Study of the Changing Pattern of English Social Aspirations* (London, 1959); and W. K. Jordan, *The Charities of London, 1480–1660: The Aspirations and Achievements of the Urban Society* (New York, 1960).
58. The first Act of Settlement was enacted in 1662. See 13 & 14 Charles II c. 12. Other seventeenth-century Settlement Acts include 3 William & Mary c. 11 (1692); and 8 & 9 William III c. 30 (1697). A major reorganization of the law was enacted in 1723. See 9 George I c. 7. It was a basic principle of the Settlement Acts that persons who attempted to leave their local parish to seek work elsewhere were to be returned home.
59. This was a criticism of Sir Dudley North, a leading seventeenth-century exponent of what has come to be known as laissez-faire economics. See Richard Grassby, *The English Gentleman in Trade: The Life and Works of Sir Dudley North* (Oxford, 1994), pp. 247–250. North "strongly encouraged an international mobility of labour" and "blamed the Settlement Acts, which by restricting internal migration and labour mobility, had created artificial differentials in production costs between regions and obstructed the equalization of wage rates." Ibid., p. 247.
60. On the failure of the Bridewells, see Joanna Innes, "Prisons for the Poor: English Bridewells, 1555–1800," in Francis Snyder and Douglas Hay, eds., *Labour, Law, and Crime: An Historical Perspective* (London, 1987), pp. 42–122.
61. See Valerie Pearl, "Puritans and Poor Relief: The London Workhouse, 1649–

1660," in Donald Pennington and Keith Thomas, eds., *Puritans and Revolutionaries: Essays in Seventeenth-Century History Presented to Christopher Hill* (Oxford, 1978), pp. 206, 219.

62. The ordinance of 1647 created the London Corporation of the Poor, which was empowered to organize workhouses and houses of correction and was to be governed by a president, a deputy, a treasurer, and forty assistants elected annually by the Common Council. See Pearl, "Puritans and Poor Relief," pp. 222–223.
63. The 1662 Act of Settlement reincorporated portions of the 1649 act and allowed for the creation of workhouses in London, Westminster, Middlesex, and Surrey. The 1662 act also allowed for the reestablishment of the Corporation of the Poor, although that did not occur until 1698. The reconstituted corporation "resembled the original Corporation in operating as an orphanage which emphasized limited education and training." Ibid., p. 224. Cf. 13 & 14 Charles II c. 12 (the Act of Settlement).
64. See 9 George I c. 7.
65. See Paul Slack, *The English Poor Law, 1531–1782* (Cambridge, 1995), p. 34.
66. *A Discourse Touching Provision for the Poor [1659], written by Sir Matthew Hale, late Lord Chief Justice of the Kings Bench, London: printed by H. Hills, for the John Leigh at Stationers Hall* (London, 1683), p. 25. See chap. 3: "The Remedy propounded: 1. That the Justices of the Peace at the Quarter Sessions do set out and distribute the Parishes in their several Counties into several Divisions, in Each of which there may be a World-House for the common use of the respective Divisions . . . *viz.* One, two, three, four, five or six Parishes to a World-House, according to the greatness or smallness, and accommodation of the several Parishes" (p. 27). "3. That there be yearly Chose by the said Justices a Master for Each Work-House, with a convenient salary out of the said Stock [of the workhouse] or the proceeds thereof to continue for 3 years" (p. 30).
67. See Josiah Child, *A New Discourse of Trade* (London, 1670). Child was a merchant who made his fortune as victualler to the navy under the Commonwealth. He subsequently wrote pamphlets on trade issues and served as governor of the East India Company, where he acted, for a time, as virtually its sole ruler. He is widely considered to be one of England's first economists.
68. Child, *A New Discourse of Trade,* quoted in Webb and Webb, *English Local Government,* p. 103.
69. Ibid. Much of the impetus for reform came from pamphleteers who contrasted conditions in England with the operation of poor relief in Holland and Germany. Richard Haines, a reform advocate, wrote in 1678 that "in Holland . . . they have public workhouses in every city for perpetual confinement in cases requiring the same." Quoted ibid., p. 106.
70. See Timothy Hall Breen, "The Non-existent Controversy: Puritan and Anglican Attitudes on Work and Health," *Church History* 35 (1966), 273–84.
71. See Slack, *English Poor Law,* p. 42, summarizing David Owen, *English Philanthropy: 1660–1960* (Cambridge, 1964).
72. See Slack, *English Poor Law,* p. 43 (citing Owen, *English Philanthropy*).
73. Ibid., p. 44.
74. Cf. Matthew Hale, "A Discourse Touching on Provision for the Poor," in *The Works Moral and Religious of Sir Matthew Hale,* vol. 1 (London, 1805), pp. 515, 516.
75. See Christopher Hill, *Puritanism and Revolution: Studies in the Interpretation of the English Revolution of the Seventeenth Century* (New York, 1964), p. 225.
76. See Geremek, *Poverty: A History,* p. 220.
77. Daniel Defoe wrote in opposition to a bill seeking the further establishment of workhouses: "I think therefore, with submission, to erect Manufactures in every

Town to transpose the Manufactures from the settled places into private Parishes and Corporations, to parcel out our Trade to every Door, it must be ruinous to the Manufacturers themselves, will turn thousands of Families out of their Employments, and take the Bread out of the Mouths of diligent and industrious Families to feed Vagrants, Thieves, and Beggars, who ought rather to be compell'd, by Legal Methods, to seek that Work which it is plain is to be had; and thus this Act will instead of settling and relieving the Poor, encrease their Number, and starve the best of them." See Daniel Defoe, *Giving Alms no Charity* (1704; reprint, Yorkshire, 1972), p. 23.

78. Hale, *Discourse,* 1:7.
79. E. A. Gellner, "French Eighteenth-Century Materialism," in D. J. O'Connor, ed., *A Critical History of Western Philosophy* (New York, 1986), p. 278.
80. See C. John Sommerville, *The Secularization of Early Modern England: From Religious Culture to Religious Faith* (Oxford, 1992), pp. 149,163, 186. Protestantism, he argues further, leads to dissent, which leads to relativism, which leads to Deism, which leads to atheism (pp. 160–162).

Conclusion

1. In the United States, Charles Homer Haskins first developed the proposition that modernity commenced in the twelfth century. He and his protégé Joseph Strayer "set the research agenda of [so-called] medievalists in America from the 1920s to the 1980s." Paul Friedman and Gabrielle M. Spiegel, "Medievalisms Old and New: The Rediscovery of Alterity in North American Medieval Studies," *American Historical Review* 103 (June 1988), 682.

ACKNOWLEDGMENTS

Special acknowledgment is owed to two persons who collaborated in the making of this book—to John Witte, Jr., who as a student at Harvard Law School assisted in the first stage of the research and who, after graduating in 1985, came to work as a full-time research associate in my new post at Emory Law School, where he is now an outstanding scholar and teacher and a valued colleague and close friend; and to Charles J. Reid, Jr., also a distinguished scholar and friend, who worked on the book as research associate for a decade prior to his appointment as Associate Professor of Law at St. Thomas Law School. John Witte's book *Law and Protestantism,* which covers some of the same ground, was published after this book was already in press, and hence I was unable to draw on it. I have, however, drawn on some of his previously published articles and also on some of Charles Reid's published articles.

I am also deeply indebted to Richard Helmholz and James Melton for their helpful comments on portions of the book before it went to press.

My heartfelt thanks go also to Nancy Knaak, my administrative assistant, for her diligence and intelligence in bringing order out of the chaos of reports, correspondence, conferences, travel arrangements, and general paraphernalia that accompanied the making of the book and also for her great skill in producing a legible text out of a seemingly infinite series of rough drafts.

I appreciate also the conscientious and intelligent research assistance of Elizabeth Chappell, who has been a friend and co-worker especially in the later stages of making the book fit for publication.

Gratitude is also due to Emory University both for its generous financial support of the research and for the intellectual and moral support of colleagues in the History Department and in the Law School.

Finally, grateful acknowledgment is due to that unique breed of scholars, the law librarians, both at Harvard and at Emory, for their resourcefulness in providing the necessary research materials. Particular thanks are owed to the guardians of the Harvard Law School Library's special collections, who provided access to rare and precious sixteenth-, seventeenth-, and eighteenth-century legal treatises.

INDEX